EIGHTH EDITION

CONTEMPORARY LOGISTICS

Paul R. Murphy Jr.
John Carroll University

Donald F. Wood
San Francisco State University

PEARSON
Prentice
Hall

Pearson Education International

Editor: Katie Stevens
Editor-in-Chief: Jeff Shelstad
Assistant Editor: Melissa Pellerano
Editorial Assistant: Danielle Serra
Marketing Manager: Michelle O'Brien
Marketing Assistant: Amanda Fisher
Managing Editor (Production): John Roberts
Production Editor: Renata Butera
Production Assistant: Joe DeProspero
Permissions Supervisor: Suzanne Grappi
Manufacturing Buyer: Michelle Klein
Cover Design: Bruce Kenselaar
Cover Illustration/Photo: Digital Vision/Getty Images, Inc.
Composition/Full-Service Project Management: Carlisle Communications
Printer/Binder: RR Donnelly Harrisonburg

Credits and acknowledgments borrowed from other sources and reproduced, with permission, in this textbook appear on appropriate page within the text.

Pearson Education LTD.
Pearson Education Singapore, Pte. Ltd
Pearson Education, Canada, Ltd
Pearson Education–Japan
Pearson Education Australia PTY, Limited

Pearson Education North Asia Ltd
Pearson Educación de Mexico, S.A. de C.V.
Pearson Education Malaysia, Pte. Ltd
Pearson Education, Upper Saddle River, New Jersey

10 9 8 7 6 5 4 3 2 1
ISBN 0-13-122887-0

Contents

Preface

This eighth edition of *Contemporary Logistics* reflects a global landscape vastly different from when the previous edition appeared in 1999. Today's organizations operate in an environment that is influenced by the terrorist attacks on the United States in 2001, threats of war and possible nuclear war, a worldwide economic slowdown, and the ethical meltdowns of multinational companies such as Ahold, Enron and WorldCom. While these and other events have resulted in increased challenges for logistics managers, the logistics discipline still remains fun, exciting, and dynamic, and these characteristics are reflected in our revision.

The reader will find additions, deletions, and modifications of content that reflect reviewer comments, student comments, and the authors' workplace, consulting, and research experiences. One of the most prominent changes in the eighth edition involves a greater discussion of supply chains and supply-chain management. These modifications reflect the growing importance of supply chains in recent years, as well as recognition that logistics is a major component of the supply-chain process. To this end, Chapter 1 has a new title, "Logistics and the Supply Chain," and Chapter 2, "The Supply-Chain Concept," has been substantially revised. Moreover, a new chapter, "Supply Management" (Chapter 11), has been added to reflect upstream supply-chain considerations.

The new edition is also characterized by expanded discussions of information technology. For example, Chapter 3, "Logistics and Information Technology," is new to this edition and reflects information's critical role in contemporary logistics management. Moreover, this edition contains numerous examples of the Internet's growing influence on logistics and supply-chain management, including order management, transportation, and customer service.

We have changed about 20 percent of the end-of-chapter cases in this edition, with a particular focus on increasing their international flavor, as can be seen in Case 8-1, "Aero Marine Logistics." Some figures and tables are also new to this edition. One feature that we continue to provide is cartoons, which highlight the humorous aspects of logistics.

The current edition of *Contemporary Logistics* has been prepared by two coauthors, Paul Murphy and Don Wood. We gratefully acknowledge the substantial contributions that both James C. Johnson and Daniel L. Wardlow made to earlier editions.

It is with profound sadness that the work and passion of Don Wood are acknowledged. Don passed away unexpectedly and late in the production process for the eighth edition. He loved both the logistics discipline and the teaching profession, and each edition of *Contemporary Logistics* has represented his contributions—and his legacy—to both constituencies. Don was a husband, a father, and a grandfather; he was an educator, a scholar, and a friend. He was a kind and thoughtful person who possessed a terrific sense of humor. Don, we'll miss you.

Acknowledgments

We are grateful to the following individuals, whose help and support made possible the writing of this and previous editions: Glen Adams, Standard Oil Company; Fred Altstadt, Four-phase System; Scott A. Ames, Logistics Associates; Folger Athearn, Jr., Athearn & Company; Can Atli; Donald W. Baldra, Schering Corporation; Charles L. Ballard, Hudson Valley Community College; Carl Bankard, York College of Pennsylvania; James H. Barnes, University of Georgia; Tayfun Tugberk Bekiroglu; Warren Blanding, Marketing Publications, Inc.; James F. Briody, Fairchild Camera and Instrument Company; Hank Bulwinkel, Towson State University; Frank Burinsky; W. R. Callister, Del Monte Corporation; Neil D. Chaitin, Challenge Equipment Corporation; W. M. Cheatham, Specialty Brands; Carolyn Coggins; Bill Cunningham, Memphis State University; Bob J. Davis, Western Illinois University; Patricia J. Daugherty, University of Oklahoma; Rick Dawe, Fritz Logistics Institute; George Derugin; Gary Dicer, University of Tennessee; John R. Doggett, *Warehousing Review;* W. R. Donham, Cambridge Plan International; A. J. Faria, University of Windsor; Joseph Garfall; Donald C. Garland, Zellerbach Paper; Navneet Gill; Stanley Groover, Towson State University; Carl Guelzo, Towson State University; Mark Haight, University of Wisconsin Center at Barron County; Jay Hamerslag, Hamerslag Equipment Company; Gerald Hampton; Lowell Hedrick, Phillips Petroleum Company; Weldon G. Helmus, Hewlett-Packard; Lynn Hill, Heublein, Inc.; Stephen G. Hill, Dole Packaged Foods Company; Stanley J. Hille, University of Missouri at Columbia; Donald Horton, American Warehousemen's Association; Rufus C. Jefferson; Creed Jenkins, Consolidated Distribution Services; J. M. Johnson, Johnson & Johnson; J. Richard Jones, Memphis State University; Robert E. Jones, F. E. Warren Air Force Base; Henry M. Karel, Shelby State Community College; R. L. Kemmer, GTE Service Corporation; Bob Kingston, Kaiser Permanente Medical Care Program; David Kupferman; Tibi Lacatus, Sertapak; C. John Langley Jr., University of Tennessee; Art LaPlant, Schlage Lock Company; Joseph R. Larsen, CIBA Pharmaceutical Company; Sean Laughlin; Ron Lennon, Towson State University; Douglas Long; Harry Loomer, University of Wisconsin Center at Barron County; Christopher Low; Irving C. MacDonald; Ernest Y. Maitland, British Columbia Institute of Technology; Don Marsh, United Airlines Maintenance Operations; Darwyn Mass, Rocky Mountain Motor Tariff Bureau; Frank McDonald; Michael McGinnis, University of South Alabama; Chinnubbie McIntosh, Warren Petroleum Company; Jim Meneley, American Honda Motor Company; Henry Metzner, Univeristy of Missouri–Rolla; Edward J. Meyers, Pacific Gas & Electric Company; Donald D. Mickel, Sacramento Army Depot; Lowell S. Miller; Rory K. Miller, California Maritime Academy; Joseph F. Moffatt, University of Southwestern Louisiana; Paul R. Neff, Boeing Company; Donald P. Nelson, National Distribution Agency; David Norton, Nabisco; Thomas Paczkowski, Cayuga Community College; Taeho Park, San Jose

State University; Donald Pefaur, Trammell Crow Distribution Corporation; Ray Perin, Perin Company; Andru M. Peters, Andros, Inc.; Robert R. Piper; Lee Plummer, North Carolina State University; Ira Pollack; Ruby Remley, Cabrini College; Richard L. Rickenbacher, Safeway Stores; Dale S. Rogers, University of Nevada, Reno; Frank R. Scheer, University of Tennessee; Karl Schober; Skip Sherwood, California State University at Fresno; Charles S. Shuken, Metropolitan Warehouse Company; Melvin Silvester; David A. Smith, State University of New York at Buffalo; Jerome V. Smith, Consolidated Freightways; Michael Smith, Christian Brothers University; R. Neil Southern, University of Memphis; F. J. Spellman; Jack M. Starling, North Texas State University; Joseph J. Stefanic, Agrico Chemical Company; Wendell M. Stewart, Kearney Management Consultants; Stephen Stover; T. M. Tipton, USCO Services, Inc.; Teddy N. Toklas, Oakland Naval Supply Center; Lee Totten, Western New England College; Frances Tucker, Syracuse University; Roy Dale Voorhees, Iowa State University; Peter F. Walstad; Bill Walton, Pacific American Warehousing & Trucking Company; Boyd L. Warnick, Utah Technical College; Mary Margaret Weber, Missouri Western State College; Marcus A. Weiss-Madsen; Terry C. Whiteside, Montana State Department of Agriculture; Lynn Williams, Logisticon; Kenneth C. Williamson, James Madison University; Warren Winstead, George Washington University; Doreen Wood; Suzan C. Woods, Logisticon; Jean Woodruff, Western New England College; Ronald S. Yaros; Mark Zborowski; James Ziola, Consolidated Freightways; and Howard Zysman, Morada Distribution, Inc.

At Carlisle Communications, we wish to extend our thanks to Ann Imhof, while at Prentice Hall, we wish to extend our thanks to Renata Butera, Melissa Pellerano, and Katie Stevens.

Paul R. Murphy Jr.
University Heights, Ohio

Donald F. Wood
San Francisco, California

Overview of Logistics

Part 1 sets the stage for this text by introducing the many dimensions of the complex and dynamic subject of logistics and its role within supply chain management. The first three chapters of *Contemporary Logistics* serve as the structural foundation on which the remainder of the text is built.

Chapter 1 discusses logistics concepts and examines the reasons for their recent growth in importance in business firms. It covers the economic impacts of logistics and marketing terms. It also introduces the concept of marketing channels, and tells about the ownership channel, the negotiations channel, the promotions channel, the financing channel, and the logistics channel.

Chapter 2 looks at the supply chain management concept, which links one's suppliers' suppliers and one's customers' customers. Also covered is logistics outsourcing or 3PL (third-party logistics).

Chapter 3 provides an overview of general types of information management systems that are applicable across each business function, and it provides examples of how these general types of information systems are specifically applied in logistics management. The remainder of Chapter 3 covers select opportunities and challenges associated with emerging information technologies.

CHAPTER 1

Logistics and the Supply Chain

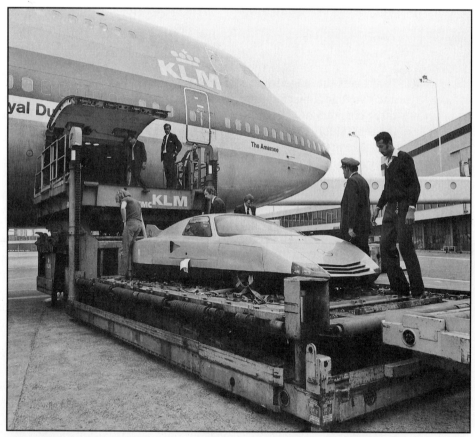

Special logistics staffs handle the movement of items and displays for trade shows and special events. This sleek Mercedes racer is being loaded aboard a KLM Boeing 747. Photo © KLM–Royal Dutch Airlines Photo Archives. Reproduced with permission.

Key Terms

- Channel intermediaries
- Cost trade-offs
- Economic utility
- FIFO
- FOB origin
- FOB destination
- Pricing systems
- Form utility
- Freight absorption
- Landed costs
- LIFO
- Marketing channel
- Phantom freight
- Place utility
- Possession utility
- Reverse logistics
- Supply chain
- Stock-keeping units (SKUs)
- Stockouts
- Systems approach
- Time utility
- Total cost approach

Learning Objectives

- To learn the definition of logistics
- To understand the economic importance of logistics
- To learn of recent events and their influences on logistics practices
- To gain an understanding of logistics practices within a firm
- To learn different pricing policies
- To know about logistics careers

Economic Impacts of Logistics

At this point, you may have limited awareness of, and knowledge about, logistics—the subject matter of this textbook. However, if that is the case, you're really not very different from lots of other people who inhabit this planet, and it might come as a surprise to you that logistics tends to have significant economic impacts. From a macroeconomic perspective, Table 1-1 summarizes U.S. logistics costs in relation to gross domestic product (GDP) for five-year time periods between 1960 and 2000. Note that logistics as a percentage of GDP has declined from approximately 15 percent in 1960 to about 10 percent in 2000 and that annual aggregate logistics costs now exceed $1 trillion. While absolute and relative logistics costs in relation to GDP vary from country to country, logistics is most definitely an important component in a country's economy.

Continuing with a macro perspective, logistics can also play an important role in a nation's economic growth and development. Hannigan and Mangan point out that logistics, particularly improvements in transportation efficiency, played a key role in the explosive growth of Ireland's economy in the mid- and late-1990s (GDP increase of 62 percent in this period). According to Hannigan and Mangan, future growth of Ireland's economy will not be possible without improvements to its

TABLE 1-1 The Cost of the Business Logistics System in Relation to Gross Domestic Product (GDP)

In $ Billion

Year	Inventory Carrying Costs	Transportation Costs	Administrative Costs	Total U.S. Logistics Cost	Logistics As a Percentage of GDP
1960	31	44	3	78	14.7
1965	38	64	4	106	14.7
1970	56	91	6	153	14.7
1975	97	116	9	222	13.5
1980	220	214	17	451	16.1
1985	227	274	20	521	12.4
1990	283	351	25	659	11.4
1995	302	441	30	773	10.4
2000	377	590	39	1,006	10.1

Source: R. Wilson and R. Delaney, Twelth Annual *State of Logistics Report,* 2001.

logistical capabilities.[1] As an example, Ireland is currently upgrading its highway system in order to facilitate the effective and efficient distribution of goods.

Apart from the previous examples of macro-level economic impacts, the economic impacts of logistics can affect individual consumers such as you. These impacts can be illustrated through the concept of **economic utility,** which is the value or usefulness of a product in fulfilling customer needs or wants. The four general types of economic utility are possession, form, time, and place. Logistics clearly contribute to time and place utility.

Possession utility refers to the value or usefulness that comes from a customer being able to take possession of a product. Possession utility can be influenced by the payment terms associated with a product. Credit and debit cards, for example, facilitate possession utility by allowing the customer to purchase products without having to produce cash or a cash equivalent. Likewise, automotive leases allow customers to take possession of a more desirable model than would be possible with conventional automotive loans.

Form utility refers to a product's being in a form that (1) can be used by the customer and (2) is of value to the customer. Although form utility has generally been associated with production and manufacturing, logistics can also contribute to form utility. For example, in order to achieve production economies (i.e., lower cost per unit), a soft-drink company may produce thousands of cases of a certain type of soft drink (e.g., diet cola). You're not likely to purchase diet cola by the thousands of cases (unless you're having a really big social event!) but rather in smaller lot sizes, such as a six- or twelve-

---

[1]K. Hannigan and J. Mangan, "The Role of Logistics and Supply Chain Management in Determining the Competitiveness of a Peripheral Economy," *Irish Marketing Review,* Vol. 14, No. 1, 2001, pp. 35–42.

pack. Through *allocation,* which will be discussed more fully in Chapter 2, logistics can break the thousands of cases of diet cola into the smaller quantities that are desired by customers.

Place utility refers to having products available *where* they are needed by customers; products are moved from points of lesser value to points of greater value. Continuing with the diet cola example, place utility is increased by moving the soda from a point of lesser value (e.g., stored in a warehouse) to a point of greater value (e.g., on a supermarket shelf).

Closely related to place utility is **time utility,** which refers to having products available *when* they are needed by customers. It's important to recognize that different products have different sensitivities to time; three-day late delivery of perishable items likely has more serious consequences than three-day late delivery of non-perishable items.

It's important to recognize that simultaneous achievement of possession, form, place, and time utility goes a long way to facilitating—but not guaranteeing—customer satisfaction. Consider the experience of a student who used an online service to order Valentine's Day flowers for his out-of-state girlfriend. The online service facilitated possession utility by allowing for a secured payment by credit card. A healthy arrangement of the correct bouquet (form utility) arrived at the girlfriend's residence on Valentine's Day (place and time utility). The problem: The greeting card that accompanied the flowers had a wrong name for the girlfriend (but the right name for the boyfriend)!

Logistics: What It Is

Now that you have a better understanding of the economic impacts of logistics, it's important to define what logistics is. Since approximately 1980, tremendous—and rapid—change has occurred in the business logistics field. One consequence of this rapid change is that business logistics has been referred to by a number of different terms, each having slightly different meanings. In recent years, some of the terms used to refer to business logistics have included (but are not limited to) the following:

- Business logistics
- Distribution
- Industrial distribution
- Logistics
- Logistics management
- Materials management
- Physical distribution
- Supply chain management

In essence, each of these terms is associated with managing the flows of goods and information from a point of origin to a point of consumption.

While the aforementioned terms are similar, they aren't the same; from a managerial perspective, this poses a potential problem of comparing apples to oranges as opposed to comparing apples to apples or oranges to oranges. For example, suppose that one organization defines logistics to include two activities—transportation and inventory management—whereas a second organization defines logistics to include three activities—transportation, inventory management, and warehousing. It seems reasonable that the second organization's total cost of logistics would be higher than the first organization's (because the second organization's logistics encompasses more activities). However, it would be a mistake to conclude that, because of the higher total costs, the second organization is less effective or efficient with respect to logistics since the two organizations have different definitions of logistics.

In an effort to avoid potential misunderstanding about the meaning of *logistics,* this book adopts the current definition promulgated by the Council of Logistics Management (CLM), one of the world's most prominent organizations for logistics professionals. According to the CLM, "Logistics is that part of the supply chain process that plans, implements, and controls the efficient, effective forward and reverse flow and storage of goods, services, and related information between the point of origin and the point of consumption in order to meet customers' requirements."[2]

Let's analyze this definition in closer detail. First, logistics is part of the **supply chain** process. We'll talk about the supply chain process and supply-chain management in greater detail in Chapter 2, but the key point for now is that logistics is part of a bigger picture in the sense that the supply chain focuses on coordination among business functions (such as marketing, production, and finance) within and across organizations. The fact that logistics is explicitly recognized as part of the supply chain process means that logistics can impact how well (or how poorly) an individual firm—and its associated supply chain(s)—can achieve goals and objectives.

The CLM definition also indicates that logistics "plans, implements, and controls." Of particular importance is the word *and,* which suggests that logistics should be involved in all three activities—planning, implementing, controlling—and not just one or two. Some suggest, however, that logistics is more involved in the implementation than in the planning of certain logistical policies.[3]

Note that the CLM definition also refers to "efficient and effective forward and reverse flows and storage." Broadly speaking, effectiveness can be thought of as "How well does a company do what they say they're going to do?" For example, if a company promises that all orders will be shipped within 24 hours of receipt, what percentage of orders are actually shipped within 24 hours of receipt? In contrast, efficiency can be thought of as how well (or poorly) company resources are used to achieve what a company promises it can do. For instance, some companies use premium and/or expedited transportation services—which cost more money—to cover for shortcomings in other parts of its logistics system.

---

[2]*www.clm1.org.*

[3]P. R. Murphy, R. F. Poist, and C. D. Braunschwieg, "Role and Relevance of Logistics to Corporate Environmentalism: An Empirical Assessment," *International Journal of Physical Distribution and Logistics Management,* Vol. 25, No. 2, 1995, pp. 5–19; P. R. Murphy and R. F. Poist, "Socially Responsible Logistics: An Exploratory Study," *Transportation Journal,* Vol. 41, No. 4, 2002, pp. 23–35.

With respect to forward and reverse flows and storage, logistics has traditionally focused on forward flows and storage, that is, those directed *toward* the point of consumption. Increasingly, however, the logistics discipline has recognized the importance of reverse flows and storage (*reverse logistics*), that is, those that *originate* at the point of consumption. While the majority of discussion in this book focuses on forward logistics, the relevance and importance of reverse logistics is likely to continue to grow in the future as more companies recognize its tactical and strategic implications.[4] Reverse logistics is also likely to gain additional attention in the future because online purchases tend to have higher return rates than other types of purchases (e.g., in-store, mail-order catalogs).

The CLM definition also indicates that logistics involves the flow and storage of "goods, services, and related information." Indeed, in the contemporary business environment, logistics is as much about the flow and storage of information as it is about the flow and storage of goods. Advances in information technology make it increasingly easy—and less costly—for companies to substitute information for inventory. Consider the U.S. Marine Corps, which is in the midst of a decade-long strategy to improve its logistics. The Marines aim to replace inventory with information so that they "won't have to stockpile tons of supplies—the so-called Iron Mountain—near the battlefield. That's what the armed forces did during the Gulf War, *only to find out they couldn't keep track of what was in containers and didn't even use many of the items.*"[5]

Finally, the CLM definition indicates that the purpose of logistics is "to meet customer requirements." This is important for several reasons, with one being that logistics strategies and activities should be based upon customer wants and needs rather than the wants, needs, and capabilities of other parties. While a customer focus might seem like the proverbial no brainer, one implication of such a focus is that companies actually have to communicate with their customers in order to learn about their needs and wants. It suffices to say that, even today, some companies continue to be hesitant to communicate with their customers.

A second reason for the importance of meeting customer requirements is the notion that since different customers having different logistical needs and wants, a one-size-fits-all logistics approach (*mass logistics*) in which every customer gets the same type and levels of logistics service—will result in some customers being overserved while others are underserved. Rather, companies should consider *tailored logistics* approaches, in which groups of customers with similar logistical needs and wants are provided with logistics service appropriate to these needs and wants.[6]

The principles in this textbook are generally applicable not only to for-profit organizations but also to the workings of governmental and nonprofit entities. For instance, from a governmental perspective, logistics is quite germane to the armed forces, which shouldn't be surprising given that logistics was first associated with the military. Moreover, the terrorist activities of September 11, 2001, provide an excellent example

---

[4]D. S. Rogers and R. Tibben-Lembke, "An Examination of Reverse Logistics Practices," *Journal of Business Logistics,* Vol. 22, No. 2, 2001, pp. 129–148.

[5]F. Keenan, "The Marines Learn New Tactics—from Wal-Mart," *BusinessWeek,* December 24, 2001, p. 74.

[6]J. B. Fuller, J. O'Conor, and R. Rawlinson, "Tailored Logistics: The Next Advantage," *Harvard Business Review,* Vol. 71, No. 3, 1993, pp. 87–98.

of the relevance of logistics to nonprofit organizations. In a relatively short time period, the American Red Cross, with the help of private-sector companies, was able to get relief supplies (e.g., boots, safety goggles, protective clothing) to New York as well as to find warehouses to store these supplies.[7]

The Increased Importance of Logistics

The formal study of business logistics, and predecessor concepts such as traffic management and physical distribution, has existed since the second half of the twentieth century. Quite frankly, from approximately 1950 to 1980, limited appreciation was shown for the importance of the logistics discipline. Since 1980, however, increasing recognition has been given to the importance of logistics, and several key reasons are discussed below.

A Reduction in Economic Regulation

During the 1970s and the 1980s, widespread reductions in economic regulation (commonly referred to as *deregulation*) relaxed government control of carriers' rates and fares, entry and exit, mergers and acquisitions, and more. These controls were particularly onerous in the U.S. transportation industry in the sense that price competition was essentially nonexistent and customers were pretty much forced to accept whatever service the carriers chose to provide. This meant that logistics managers had relatively little control over one of the most important cost components in a logistics system (see Table 1-1).

Reductions in economic regulation in the U.S. airfreight, railroad, and trucking industries allowed individual carriers flexibility in pricing and service. This pricing and service flexibility was important to logistics for several reasons. First, it provided companies with the ability to implement the tailored logistics approach discussed earlier, in the sense that companies could specify different service levels and prices could be adjusted accordingly. Second, the increased pricing flexibility allowed large buyers of transportation services to reduce their transportation costs by leveraging large amounts of freight with a limited number of carriers.

While the preceding discussion has focused on lessened economic regulation in the United States, it appears that deregulation has had similar effects in other countries. For example, lessened economic regulation of transportation has been identified as a primary reason for a reduction in the cost of freight transportation in Ireland.[8]

Recognition by Prominent Non-Logisticians

Professor Stock suggests "that much of the notoriety of present-day logistics . . . came from 'outsiders,' " that is, people with backgrounds and expertise in non-logistics disciplines.[9] For example, one well-known outsider, Michael Porter, developed the concept known as the *value chain*. Significantly, two of the five primary activities in the value

---

[7]J. R. Johnson, "Warehousing Industry Lends a Hand," *Warehousing Management,* Vol. 8, No. 9, 2001, pp. 11–12.

[8]Hannigan and Mangan, 2001.

[9]J. R. Stock, "Marketing Myopia Revisited: Lessons for Logistics," *International Journal of Physical Distribution and Logistics Management,* Vol. 32, No. 1, 2002, pp. 12–21.

chain, inbound logistics and outbound logistics, have a logistics orientation. A significant contribution from Porter and other prominent non-logisticians is their assertion that logistics can be a source of competitive advantage for an organization.

Technological Advances

Prior to the start of every academic year, Beloit College (Wisconsin) releases an annual survey concerning what members of the incoming freshmen class know about the year of their birth. If you were born in the early 1980s or later, you don't remember a world without personal computers. In addition, you probably haven't used (and may have never seen, except in pictures) a self-correcting electric typewriter. We're not trying to take a stroll down memory lane. Rather, our point is that there have been tremendous technological advances—in the course of your lifetime—that have had profound influences for business management, and by extension, for business logistics.

From a logistical perspective, some of the most important technological advances have involved computer hardware and software in the sense that management of logistics involves a tremendous amount of data. The sheer magnitude of these data makes manual analysis a difficult and time-consuming process; technological advances in computer hardware, software, and capacity have allowed logisticians to make faster, more informed, and more accurate decisions with respect to customer service, transportation, inventory management, and other logistics activities. The Internet—virtually unknown and unused until the mid-1990s—has also proven to be a powerful tool for improving logistical effectiveness and efficiency. We discuss logistics technology in greater detail in Chapter 3.

The Growing Power of Retailers

Certain types of retailers, particularly mass merchandisers (such as Wal-Mart) and "category killers" (such as Home Depot), now often wield greater power than the manufacturers that supply them with product. This power shift is relevant since a number of these retailers have explicitly recognized superior logistics as an essential component of their corporate strategies. In some instances, these power retailers bypass traditional channels of distribution; in other instances, power retailers require distribution channels that are designed to meet their particular needs and requirements.

Some power retailers turn (sell) their inventories so quickly that they sell product and collect payment for them *before* their payments to suppliers for the products are due. This forces suppliers to be more efficient in the sense that they should focus on providing those products that will be bought by consumers, as opposed to supplying slower-moving products that may sit on store shelves for long periods of time.

Globalization of Trade

Although countries have traded with each other for thousands of years, globalization's impact is greater today than ever before. Consider that world trade expanded from approximately $200 billion in 1970 to approximately $7.7 trillion in 2000; while world trade in 2001 decreased slightly to approximately $7.5 trillion (due to a global economic slowdown), it is projected to grow by at least 5 percent annually through 2005.[10]

---

[10]"World Economic Outlook," *www.imf.org.*

While many factors, such as rising standards of living and multi-country trade alliances, have contributed to the growth of global trade, it's safe to say that logistics has played a key role, too. Having said this, one should recognize that international logistics is much more challenging and costly than domestic logistics. With respect to challenges, the geographic distances between buyer and seller are often greater (which may translate into longer transit times) and monitoring logistics processes are sometimes complicated by differences in business practices, culture, and language. As for costs, the greater geographic distances tend to result in higher transportation costs, and documentation requirements can be quite costly as well.[11] We present a more detailed discussion of international logistics in Chapter 12.

The Systems and Total Cost Approaches to Logistics

Logistics is a classic example of the systems approach to business problems. From a companywide perspective, the **systems approach** indicates that a company's objectives can be realized by recognizing the mutual interdependence of the major functional areas of the firm, such as marketing, production, finance, and logistics. One implication of the systems approach is that the goals and objectives of the major functional areas should be compatible with the company's goals and objectives. This means that *one logistics system does not fit all companies* since goals and objectives vary from one firm to another.

A second implication is that decisions made by one functional area should consider the potential implications upon other functional areas. For example, implementation of the marketing concept, which focuses on satisfying customer needs and wants, has resulted in a marked increase of the number of **stock-keeping units (SKUs)** or line items of inventory (each different type or package size of a good is a different SKU) offered for sale by many companies. From a logistics perspective, the proliferation of SKUs means (1) more items to identify, (2) more items to store, and (3) more items to track.

Just as the major functional areas of a firm should recognize their interdependence, so too should the various activities that comprise the logistics function (what we'll call *intrafunctional logistics*). The logistics manager should balance each logistics activity to ensure that none is stressed to the point where it becomes detrimental to others.

This can be illustrated by referring to Figure 1-1, which indicates that business logistics is made up of *inbound logistics* (movement and storage of materials into a firm), *materials management* (movement and storage of materials and components within a firm), and *physical distribution* (storage of finished product and movement to the customer). Intrafunctional logistics attempts to coordinate inbound logistics, materials management, and physical distribution in a cost-efficient manner that supports an organization's customer service objectives. Figure 1-2, an advertisement for Cargill Salt, shows how a company can differentiate a commodity product (salt) by stressing a dependable logistics system.

---

[11]D. F. Wood, A. P. Barone, P. R. Murphy, and D. L. Wardlow, *International Logistics,* 2nd edition, New York: AMACOM, 2002.

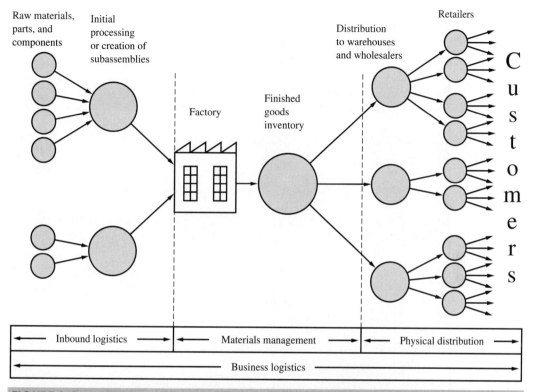

FIGURE 1-1 Control Over the Flow of Inbound and Outbound Movements

In this drawing, the circles represent buildings where inventories are stored, and the lines with arrows represent movement performed by carriers, a stop-and-start process. Current thought deals more with flows, possibly in different volumes and at different speeds, but without the inventory standing still. The supply chain extends to both the left and right of this diagram and includes the suppliers' suppliers and the customers' customers.

Inbound logistics, materials management, and physical distribution can be coordinated in many ways. One way is by using the same truck to deliver materials and component parts and to pick up finished goods. While this may appear to be little more than common sense—and *common sense is one of the keys to being an effective logistics manager*—consider the case of the company that used the same trucking company to deliver materials and parts to one of its production plants as well as to take finished products from the facility. Unfortunately, one truck would arrive early in the morning to deliver the materials and components, and another truck would arrive in the late afternoon to pick up the finished products. How could this happen? Quite simply: The inbound logistics group and the outbound logistics group were unaware that they were using the same trucking company—the two groups never communicated!

Logistics managers use the **total cost approach** to coordinate inbound logistics, materials management, and physical distribution in a cost-efficient manner. This approach is built on the premise that all relevant activities in moving and storing products should be considered as a whole (i.e., their total cost), not individually. Use

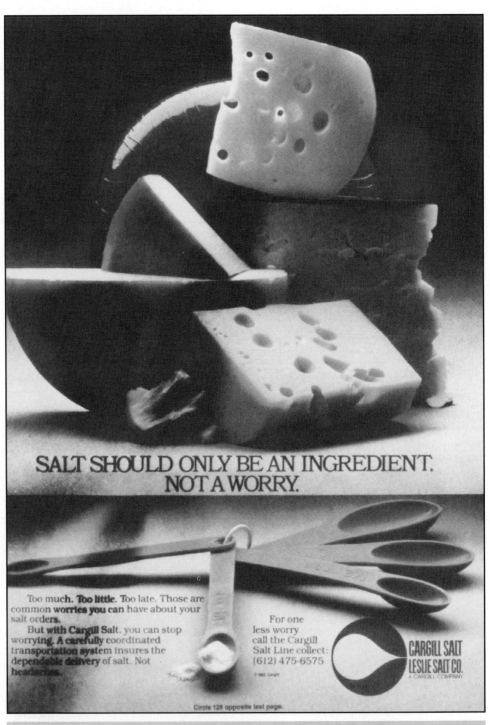

FIGURE 1-2 The Utilization of Logistics Service as a Major Selling Point

Reproduced with permission of Cargill, Incorporated.

of the total cost approach requires an understanding of **cost trade-offs;** in other words, changes to one logistics activity cause some costs to increase and others to decrease.

The key to the total cost approach is that all relevant cost items are considered simultaneously when making a decision. The objective is to find the approach with the lowest total cost that supports an organization's customer service requirements. For example, a decision to use expedited transportation translates into higher transportation costs. At the same time, expedited transportation allows a company to reduce its inventory carrying costs and may also reduce the cost of failing to serve particular customers.[12] Although a company's transportation costs increase when utilizing expedited transportation, the costs of other logistics activities decrease; as a result, the total costs of logistics activities decrease—without negatively impacting customer service.

When employed in the logistics decision-making process, the total cost concept approach forms what is commonly called the *total logistics concept.* This concept is unique not because of the activities performed, but because of the integration of all activities into a unified whole that seeks to minimize distribution costs in a manner that supports an organization's customer service objectives. The total logistics concept can be extended to include a firm's suppliers and customers, such as in supply chain management, which will be covered in Chapter 2.

Logistical Relationships Within the Firm

From a companywide perspective, the system and total cost approaches to logistics require an understanding of logistics and its relationships with other functional areas. With a later chapter devoted specifically to purchasing, our discussion here focuses on logistical relationships with finance, marketing, and production.

Finance

The logistics department regularly interfaces with the finance area, in part because logistical decisions are only as good as the quality of cost data with which they are working. The finance staff, which is concerned with predicting future cash flows, is dependent upon logistics for information concerning the status of finished products that are somewhere between the end of the firm's production line and the purchaser's receiving dock.

The finance staff is often charged with the responsibility of allocating the firm's limited funds to projects desired by the various operating departments. As such, the finance department is often instrumental in approving capital budgeting decisions that affect logistics, such as the acquisition of materials handling equipment (e.g., forklifts) and packaging equipment (e.g., a shrink-wrap machine). In such situations, finance personnel may decide between purchasing or leasing the relevant equipment, assuming they have approved the decision to acquire equipment.

Inventory is another area of interest for finance managers, in part because in financial terms inventory is recorded as an asset; all assets of a firm must be paid for by either short-term (hopefully) or long-term financing. One aspect of concern with

---

[12]P. Bradley, "Speed Curbs Inventory," *Logistics Management,* November 2001, pp. 45–47.

respect to inventory is its valuation; should inventory be valued in terms of **LIFO** (last in, first out) or **FIFO** (first in, first out)? A second concern is that finance often measures inventory in terms of its cost/value in dollars while logistics tends to measure inventory in terms of units.

A third inventory-related concern involves the concept of *inventory float,* which refers to the cash flow associated with holding inventory.[13] In general terms, the inventory costs are for the time period from when one pays a vendor until the time one collects from the customer for the same goods. Unfortunately, there can be a mismatch between inventory turnover (how many times products sell during a time period) and its associated cash flows; suppose, for example, that the inventory turnover is four weeks while the lag between paying vendors and collecting from customers is six weeks.

Marketing

Contemporary marketing places heavy emphasis on customer satisfaction, and logistics strategies can facilitate customer satisfaction through reducing the cost of products, which can translate into lower prices as well as bringing a broader variety of choices closer to where the customer wishes to buy or use the product. Logistics strategies offer a unique way for a company to differentiate itself among competitors, and logistics now offers an important route for many firms to create marketing superiority.

As such, outbound logistics can be a positive (or negative) marketing asset, with key relationships between outbound logistics and the four primary components of the marketing mix. The following discussion about logistics and marketing focuses on the marketing mix, sometimes referred to as the *Four Ps* of marketing (place, price, product, and promotion).

Place Decisions   One important marketing concern is place. Decisions regarding place involve two types of networks: logistics and the marketing channel. Logistics decisions concern the most effective way to move and store the product from where it is produced to where it is sold. Chapter 8 is devoted to the subject of facility location decisions.

An effective logistics system can provide positive support by enabling the firm to attract and utilize what it considers to be the most productive channel and supply chain members. Frequently, the channel members are in a position to pick and choose which manufacturer's products they wish to merchandise. If a manufacturer is not consistently able to provide a certain product at the right time, in the right quantities, and in an undamaged condition, the channel members may end their relationship with the supplier or cease active promotion of the supplier's product.

From a marketing perspective, place decisions may also involve new strategies for reaching new customers. A quite popular strategy in the retailing industry at the turn of the millennium, for example, involves a concept known as *co-branding,* which refers to one location where customers can purchase products from two or more name-brand retailers. YUM! Brands (formerly known as Tricon Global Restaurants), for example, is the parent company of Taco Bell, KFC, and Pizza Hut; you may have eaten at a site where either two or three of these brands are available.

---

[13]J. Cavinato, "What Does Your Inventory Really Cost?" *Distribution,* March 1988, pp. 68–72.

From a marketing perspective, co-branding can (1) offer potential customers convenience (satisfying multiple needs in one place), (2) increase customer spending per transaction, and (3) boost brand awareness.[14] Logistical challenges with co-branding include the costs and timing of product delivery. YUM! has addressed these issues by scheduling one delivery per location, which requires co-loading trailers with products for all three chains (YUM!'s truck trailers carry the Taco Bell, KFC, and Pizza Hut logos).

Price Decisions   It is good business, and common sense, to recognize that a firm cannot be profitable and grow—in fact, it can be doomed—if it does not control its logistics costs. Obviously, the price of a product must cover relevant production, marketing, distribution, and general administrative costs, and firms with serious waste in their logistics systems will be faced with several choices, none of which is particularly attractive. One choice would be to pass on the higher logistics costs to customers, thus increasing product price. A second option would be to keep price the same but reduce product quality or quantity, which might result in customer defections. Alternatively, a firm could absorb the higher costs, which would cause a decrease in product contribution margins.

Transportation cost factors are especially important in determining the method used to quote the firm's selling price. A firm can handle its transportation costs by using one of several pricing methods, the two most common being **FOB origin** and **FOB destination** (delivered) **pricing systems.** An FOB origin price does not include any transportation costs to the purchaser. With this type of pricing, the purchaser is responsible for the selection of the transportation mode(s) and carrier(s) because the buyer assumes the expense of the transportation from a factory or warehouse. This system of pricing is easy for the seller to administer and always yields the same net return from each sale.

Marketers don't necessarily like FOB origin pricing because it is extremely difficult to adopt uniform retail prices on a regional or national basis. Because each purchaser is a different distance from a factory or warehouse, their **landed costs**—the price of the product at the source plus transportation costs to its destination—are different. Since purchasers tend to have a predetermined margin based on total landed costs, the end result is that each purchaser ends up with a different retail price.

In an FOB destination system, the seller quotes the purchaser a price that includes both the price of the product and the transportation cost to the purchaser's receiving dock, and the seller has the prerogative to select the mode(s) and carrier(s) to deliver the product. An average amount of transportation costs is added to the cost of each product, with the idea being that the average transportation cost reflects the cost of shipping the goods to a point that is the average distance from the seller's place of business. Note that with FOB destination, each purchaser ends up with the same landed cost.

Under FOB destination pricing, buyers located relatively close to the seller's point (closer than average) pay more than their share of freight charges, which is called

[14]R. Bauer, "Co-branding: Growing Family or Family Feud?" *Franchising World,* May–June 2002, pp. 22–23.

phantom freight. The opposite situation occurs when the buyer actually pays lower freight charges than the seller incurs in shipping the product, which is known as **freight absorption.** Phantom freight and freight absorption are illustrated in Figure 1-3 for shipments originating in Omaha.

Marketers find FOB destination pricing attractive for several reasons. The first is that it enables a company to expand the geographic area to which its product is sold because distant customers in a region do not pay the full costs of transportation. Second, because each purchaser has the same landed costs, it is much easier for a company to apply a uniform retail price on a regional or national basis. Third, product distribution is managed by the seller who can control the logistics network, making it function in a manner that is most beneficial to the firm's overall objectives.

There are also several drawbacks to FOB destination pricing. As pointed out previously, the seller is responsible for product distribution, which means that it is the seller's responsibility to understand the various distribution activities and the trade-offs among them. This understanding cannot be learned in a short period of time. A second drawback is that this pricing system essentially discriminates based on a company's location; in essence, those firms located closer to the seller subsidize the transportation costs of those firms located further from the seller. Some sellers, to avoid alienating these customers, will allow them to order FOB origin if they so desire.

An important consideration with both FOB origin and destination pricing involves the terms of sale, or when the freight charges are paid. *Freight prepaid* refers to a situation in which the applicable charges are paid at the time a shipment is tendered to a carrier, while *freight collect* refers to charges being paid at the time of shipment delivery.[15] As such, there are three payment options for FOB origin and three for FOB destination:

- *FOB origin, freight collect:* The buyer pays freight charges and owns the goods in transit. This is the most common FOB origin term.
- *FOB origin, freight prepaid:* The seller pays the freight charges, but the buyer owns the goods in transit.
- *FOB origin, freight prepaid and charged back:* The seller pays the freight charges in advance but bills the buyer for them. The buyer owns the goods in transit.
- *FOB destination, freight prepaid:* The seller pays the freight charges and also owns the goods in transit. This is what is generally referred to as *FOB destination pricing.*
- *FOB destination, freight collect:* The buyer pays the freight charges when the goods arrive, and the seller owns the goods while they are in transit.
- *FOB destination, freight prepaid and charged back:* The seller owns the goods in transit, prepays the freight charges, and bills the buyer for the freight charges.

Logistics managers play an important role in product pricing. They are expected to know the costs of providing various levels of customer service and therefore must be consulted to determine the trade-offs between costs and customer service. Because many distribution costs produce per unit savings when larger volumes are handled, the logistics manager can also help formulate the firm's quantity discount pricing policies.

---

[15]J. L. Heskett, N. A. Glaskowsky, and R. M. Ivie, *Business Logistics,* 2nd edition, New York: Ronald Press, 1973.

National Single-Zone Pricing

Every customer in the United States pays $11 per unit.

Multiple-Zone Pricing

There are three zones: The midwestern zone, paying $10.00 per unit, and the East Coast and West Coast zones, paying $11.95 per unit.

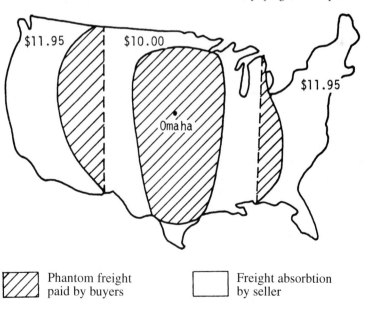

▨	Phantom freight paid by buyers	☐ Freight absorbtion by seller

FIGURE 1-3 Phantom Freight and Freight Absorption

Product Decisions   A number of potential interfaces are possible in terms of product decisions between marketing and logistics. For example, as noted earlier, the marked increase in product offerings—which allows for more customer choice—creates logistical challenges in terms of identification, storage, and tracking.

Another product interface between marketing and logistics involves the amount of particular SKUs to hold. Marketers often prefer to carry higher quantities of particular items, since this reduces the likelihood of **stockouts** (being out of an item at the same time there is demand for it). From a logistics perspective, higher quantities of inventory (1) necessitate additional storage space and (2) increase inventory carrying costs.

Product design, which is often the purview of marketers, can also have important implications for logistical effectiveness and efficiency. For example, long-necked glass beverage containers might be more distinctive than aluminum cans; however, from a logistics perspective, long-necked bottles take up more space and are more likely to be damaged than aluminum cans.

Promotion Decisions   Many promotional decisions require close coordination between marketing and logistics. One important situation concerns the availability of highly advertised products, particularly when a company is running pricing campaigns that lower the price of particular items. Few things are more damaging to a firm's goodwill than being stocked out of items that are heavily promoted in a sales campaign. In addition, in some instances imbalances of product supply and demand can be viewed as *bait and switch tactics*—that is, enticing customers with the promises of a low-priced product, only to find that it is unavailable and that a higher-priced substitute product is readily available.

Once a decision is made to introduce a new product, the logistics staff assumes responsibility for having the product in place on the scheduled release date—not earlier, not later. In certain industries, such as music, motion pictures, and books, the ease of technological piracy has added to the complexity of having a product in place on the scheduled release date. For example, in an effort to lessen potential piracy with the November 2001 U.S. release of the *Harry Potter and the Sorcerer's Stone* motion picture, the distributors divided each print of the film into two separate shipments "so that no single shipment contained the entire version of the film."[16]

Production

Perhaps the most common interface between production and logistics involves the length of production runs. In many cases, the production people favor long production runs of individual products because this allows the relevant fixed costs to be spread over more units, thus resulting in a lower production cost per unit. Long production runs generate large amounts of inventory, and it is often a logistics staff responsibility to store and track the inventory. Another consideration with long production runs is that sometimes excessive inventory for particular products occurs because of limited (or no) demand for them. At a minimum, these products (sometimes referred to as *dead stock*) add to a company's inventory carrying costs and also take up space that could be used to store other products. A situation is known to have occurred in which forklift drivers would periodically move dead stock of about 150 refrigerators from one warehouse area to another, just to ensure that the refrigerators did not sit in the same place for an extended period of time!

---

[16]D. Biederman, "Logistics Wizards Deliver," *Traffic World,* November 26, 2001, p. 8.

Increasing utilization of the *postponement* concept (the delay of value-added activities such as assembly, production, and packaging to the latest possible time[17]) also influences the interface between production and logistics. More specifically, some value-added activities (e.g., case packing, case labeling) that were traditionally performed at a production plant are now performed in warehousing facilities. As a result, warehousing facilities may need to add new types of equipment and be configured differently in order to allow specific value-added activities to take place.[18]

Marketing Channels

Another concept that is useful to studying the marketing relationships between and among firms is to look at marketing channels. The marketing channels concept describes the institutional setting by which goods and services move forward. One takes a broad look at existing transactions and how the markets in which they are carried out were formed. Marketing is a series of processes performed by a coordinated group of firms that facilitate exchange.

> Marketing channels can be viewed as sets of interdependent organizations involved in the process of making a product or service available for use or consumption. From the outset, it should be recognized that not only do marketing channels satisfy demand by supplying goods and services at the right place, quantity, quality, and price, but they also stimulate demand through promotional activities of the units (e.g., retailers, manufacturers' representatives, sales offices, and wholesalers) constituting them. Therefore, the channel should be viewed as an orchestrated network that creates value for the consumer through the generation of form, possession, time, and place utilities.[19]

The principal, traditional actors in the marketing channel are the manufacturer, the wholesaler, and the retailer. Each in turn assumes ownership of the inventory of goods. Each also assumes risks associated with temporary inventory ownership. The channel members in this arrangement, carrying out this task, can also be referred to as the *ownership channel.* The same or related parties also get together in other channel arrangements, and these channels are called the *negotiations channel,* the *financing channel,* the *promotions channel,* and the *logistics channel.* The logistics channel handles the physical flow of product, which is the principal topic of this book. All channels and channel activities can be graphed as networks.

Information is also freely carried up and down, back and forth, and between channels. One of the functions of the channel system is to give each actor sufficient information so that he or she can make a correct, rational decision. Information availability is important to a channel's functioning: Channels will fail if some of the actors feel that necessary information is lacking. Although information flows in both directions,

---

[17]J. J. Coyle, E. J. Bardi, and C. J. Langley, *The Management of Business Logistics: A Supply Chain Perspective,* 7th edition, Southwestern, 2003.

[18]"Taking the Hit-or-Miss Out of Make-to-Order," *Modern Materials Handling,* Mid-May 1999, pp. 14–16.

[19]Louis W. Stern and Adel I. El-Ansary, *Marketing Channels,* 4th edition, Upper Saddle River, NJ: Prentice Hall, 1992, p. 1.

there is some bias in that most channel members are usually more concerned about buyers' needs than sellers' needs. New products, for example, are developed with customers in mind. Selling is carried out more aggressively and is considered more glamorous than procurement. Of course, one channel member's sale is another channel member's purchase.

This coordinated set of firms acting in concert to facilitate exchange has been called a "superorganization."[20] The different firms involved in a channel are interdependent and generally have goals in common, usually that of superior customer service or satisfaction. The companies must work together closely in an atmosphere of trust with free exchange of information for these superorganizations to be successful in today's competitive environment.

According to Professors Stern and El-Ansary, these superorganizations have six defining attributes that describe them:

1. Differentiation of function among the members
2. Interdependency with respect to task performance
3. Communication and criteria for evaluating the communication
4. Structural complexity
5. Cooperation in achieving collective goals
6. Clearly defined superior–subordinate relationship or authority system[21]

When these superorganizations are able to overcome internal barriers and work in a well-orchestrated manner, they often achieve a competitive position in the market that is difficult for competitors to duplicate. Superior supply chain management can create a sustainable differential advantage with a firm's customers.

In late 1994, a problem with a defective computer chip demonstrated the value of the free exchange of information in a supply chain. An individual in a firm designing computers was encountering many troubles. Eventually, an engineer in another company told this individual about a rumored bug in the power management feature of certain Intel 486 chips. This individual then "called Intel for an explanation and was told that in order to learn why one batch [of chips] worked better than the other he and his associates had to sign an agreement not to disclose what they were about to learn."[22] Eventually, the defect became widely known, and Intel suffered considerably from bad publicity. The point is that Intel's initial behavior of withholding information about the product's defect was counter to acceptable channel behavior (as well as consumer interests). Both final consumers and parties such as the individual mentioned, who was trying to design a product that would incorporate the Intel chip, were hurt. Firms that used the Intel chip in their final products also suffered because some consumers blamed them for the poor performance of the final product.

It is safe to assume that over 99 percent of the decisions made within channels are for repeat purchases (also called *rebuys*); hence, many of the transactions are not strictly new but are either exact repeats or repeats with minor modifications from whatever was

---

[20]Louis W. Stern and Adel I. El-Ansary, "Marketing Channels: Strategy, Design, and Management," in James F. Robeson and William C. Copacino (eds.), R. Edwin Howe (assoc. ed.). *The Logistics Handbook*, New York, NY: The Free Press, 1994, p. 137.

[21]Ibid.

[22]*San Francisco Examiner,* January 1, 1995, p. B1.

done yesterday or last week. There is also a stock of goodwill included in many transactions. People prefer doing business with people they like. This is especially true today, when we extol cooperation and partnership rather than adversarial relationships between buyers and sellers. We prefer thinking about rewarding "good" behavior, rather than penalizing "bad." Procter & Gamble, for example, was able to cut its customers' handling costs by $14 million in one year by working with them on a small change in the way in which freight was received at the customer location. Procter & Gamble offered a 10-cent-per-case discount for each time a case was received with the new procedure. While this procedure undoubtedly saved Procter & Gamble more than 10 cents per case, it decided to share in the cost savings with its customers as a reward for cooperation.[23]

Established channels tend to operate with the same channel members over time. Only a few participants are in the action for the first time; when they join a channel, they must establish their credibility and learn that channel's rules of the game. Let us look more closely at how the three traditional parties—the manufacturer, the wholesaler, and the retailer—interact in each of the five mentioned channels.

The ownership channel covers movement of title to the goods. The goods themselves might not be physically present or even exist. If a good is in great demand, one might have to buy it before it is produced, such as a commissioned piece of art or a scarce new consumer product. Sometimes, a product will not be made until there are sufficient financial commitments, which is often the case with new models of airline aircraft. The party owning the good almost always has the right to trade or sell it and bears the risks and costs associated with having it in inventory. Also, while owning the good, one can use it as collateral for a loan, although this may place some restrictions on its use or movement.

The negotiations channel is the one in which buy and sell agreements are reached. This could include transactions face to face or by telephone, e-mail, electronic data interchange, or almost any other form of communication. In many situations, no actual negotiations take place; the price for the product is stated and one either buys at that price or does not. In some trades, auctions are used; in others, highly structured, organized trading takes place, such as markets for some commodities. One part of the negotiations covers how activities in the other channels are to be handled. For example, each buying party will specify the point and time of delivery and the point and time of payment. Even packaging design may be negotiated. (An old Henry Ford story is that suppliers of some parts were directed to ship in wooden crates built of good lumber and to very exacting specifications. It turned out that the empty crates were then partially disassembled and became floorboards in Ford Model Ts.)

Each party to the negotiation assigns a cost to each completed transaction. The cost is for the negotiator's time and any associated expenses, for example, long distance telephone charges or sales commissions. This is of significance to the logistics channel because the size of an order depends in part on the transaction costs. To the extent that the transaction costs can be spread over an order, it is advantageous to order a larger amount because the transaction costs per unit are then less. The buyer might also negotiate to have the order divided into several segments, with one segment being delivered, for example, each week. Options are also employed in which a certain amount of product is purchased

---

[23]Beverly Goldberg, "Building Stronger Supply Chains," *The Journal of Commerce,* April 16, 1997, p. 7A.

and the buyer has the option to repeat the order one or more times within specified limits. In many situations, one combines the transaction costs and the cost of the product. If these combined costs are too high, parties will drop out of the market. They will either seek substitute products or possibly decide to build an item rather than purchase it.

Relevant to the negotiations channel is the issue of power. Parties in the channel possess strengths that vary with their size, their financial assets, their proximity to and knowledge of the final customers, or the popularity of the product handled. A never-ending issue in logistics channels is which party should maintain the inventory, and where. A retailer wants to keep a small reserve stock but also wants the wholesaler to maintain huge reserve stocks and the capability to make almost instantaneous deliveries upon demand. In the previous decade, some powerful retailers have been able to make some extraordinary demands on other channel members due to their ability to control access to the final customers. A few have decided not to deal with wholesalers at all and insist on dealing directly with the manufacturers.

Note that such a strategy, if successful, would allow the retailer to operate with little or no investment in inventory. Such is the power of today's mass merchandisers, with sophisticated information systems and superior knowledge of and access to customers. Manufacturers with power may also develop alternate channels to move some or all of their products. Cambridge Soundworks, for example, sells its stereo system speakers factory direct through catalogs and through a small number of factory-owned retail stores. It is thus able to bypass retail stores and wholesalers.

The financing channel handles payments for goods. More importantly, it handles the company's credit. The multiple participants in the channel have different financial strengths, and often one must help another to keep the entire channel alive. For example, a newly opened retail store may have some of its goods placed on consignment, meaning that the wholesaler, not the store, owns them. The retailer will reimburse the wholesaler only for goods sold; the wholesaler bears nearly all the financial risks. Sometimes, in an effort to develop what it believes is a necessary new product line, a wholesaler will assist the manufacturer by putting up cash in advance along with an order. Alternatively, the wholesaler will place a large, firm order, and the manufacturer can take that order to a bank and use it as a basis for receiving a loan. The logistics channel is often designed so that a payment must be received in order to trigger the release of the order or part of the order. Credit is important to all parties in the channel, who frequently receive or extend it, and credit becomes an integral part of the negotiations. If bills are not paid when due or if credit is overextended, collection becomes a financing channel function.

The promotions channel is concerned with promoting a new or an existing product. This is probably most closely related to the financing channel because monetary allowances are often part of the promotion effort. However, the promotion channel and the logistics channel are linked in several ways. First, there may be special advertising materials, such as coupon books, floor advertising posters, or displays, that must be distributed with the promoted product. Second, some of the cartons or consumer packs may have special labeling, and their placement at retailers must coincide with other promotional efforts. Third, the retailer will be reluctant to take any more of a new product than is necessary, in case the promotion flops. However, if the promotion is successful, the retailer will demand more product, so it is necessary to keep reserve stocks nearby. Fourth, because logistics personnel handle order processing, they have instantaneous records of actual sales, which indicate the initial success of the promotional efforts. Fifth, because some promotions involve price reductions for large orders, the logistics staff must prepare for making large shipments (and then see shipments drop off). Last, the promotion may involve an entirely different product. Most consumers are familiar with "Camel Cash"—the incentive program used by R. J. Reynolds for its Camel cigarettes. Customers collect certificates with each package of cigarettes and then redeem them for gifts. In this situation, the gifts move through an entirely different logistics channel than do the cigarettes.

As mentioned previously, the logistics channel, its components, and its functioning are the main topics of this book. Logistics covers both the movement and the storage of the product, mainly in the direction of the consumer. Sometimes, the reverse move is also of concern. Examples are product recalls and the recycling of products and of packaging.

The most significant contribution that the logistics channel makes to the overall channel process is the *sorting function*. This function involves rearranging the assortment of products as they flow through the channels toward the customer, taking large blocks of single products and rearranging them into quantities, assortments, and varieties that consumers prefer. The sorting function bridges "the discrepancy between the assortment of goods and services generated by the producer and the assortment demanded by the consumer. The discrepancy results from the fact that manufacturers typically produce a large quantity of a limited variety of goods, whereas consumers usually desire only a limited quantity of a wide variety of goods."[24] Nearly a century ago, James H. Ritter said that the jobber "assembles various lines of goods, carries a large and assorted stock, and, by means of travelling salesmen and other agencies, sells these goods to the retailer in small assorted lots, while the retailer supplies the consumer."[25]

The sorting function has four steps, and these are important to understanding the concept of goods flowing through the logistics channel (and the supply chain):

- *Sorting out* is sorting a heterogeneous supply of products into stocks that are homogeneous.
- *Accumulating* is bringing together similar stocks from different sources.
- *Allocating* is breaking a homogeneous supply into smaller lots.
- *Assorting* is building up assortments of goods for resale, usually to retail customers.

These steps take place between the manufacturer and the consumer, which means that they are performed by the wholesaler, the retailer, or specialist intermediaries. It is important here to mention the handling of hazardous materials: They often move through a logistics channel of their own, utilizing specialized carriers and warehouses and sometimes following different routes.

In addition to the major actors or primary participants in a logistics channel, many less well-known actors play minor but essential roles. They are called *facilitators* or **channel intermediaries.**[26] Intermediaries make the entire system function better. They spring up and flourish in areas where communications and other interactions between major parties are not well meshed. In international transactions, for example, translators

---

[24]Stern and El-Ansary, *Marketing Channels*, p. 6.

[25]Cited in Mushtaq, Luqmani et al., "Tracing the Development of Wholesaling Practice and Thought," *Journal of Marketing Channels,* Vol. 2, No. 1, 1991, p. 85. The authors cited Ritter's article in the November 1903 issue of the *Annals of the America Academy of Political Science.*

[26]At one time, they were called middlemen, a word that is rapidly becoming obsolete and is no longer "politically correct."

may be an important intermediary. Intermediaries also function in areas needing orderly routines, such as order processing, and in searching, for example, when customers are looking for products or producers are looking for customers. Intermediaries fill niches, they are very well focused, and they serve as buffers. Usually, they do not take an ownership position in the products or goods being handled.

The five channels discussed previously show where intermediaries function and fit. They are used only when needed, and most channel actors know when to rely on them. For example, a wholesaler has its own warehouse but also rents public warehouse space when needed; the public warehouse is the intermediary. In the ownership channel, the most common intermediary is the bank or finance company, which may assume temporary or partial ownership of goods as part of an ongoing transaction. Often, this is a condition for the extension of credit. Banks routinely loan funds to all parties in a channel, making it possible for goods to be manufactured, marketed, and sold.

In the negotiations channel, we often use the term *broker.* A broker is an intermediary between a buyer and a seller. Commodities are often traded through brokers. When one contracts with a trucker to carry a truckload of freight, one often uses a broker. One reason brokers are used in this situation is that the individual trucker believes that his or her time is more profitably spent driving, rather than being on the phone trying to negotiate for the next load. It is easier for the trucker to let the broker find the load and then give the broker 10 to 15 percent off the top. When one charters ships, two brokers are used, one representing the user, the other representing the vessel owner; shipping is a global market, and both brokers have contacts throughout the world, increasing the likelihood of a successful charter arrangement.

Intermediaries in the financing field are again often banks, who supply the credit necessary for a deal to be finalized. Sometimes, insurance is also a requirement in the agreement, so insurance companies may also serve as intermediaries. Sometimes accountants are called in to verify certain information. For big-ticket items, such as ships or houses, the buyer almost always borrows money to finance part of the purchase. Providers of financing are intermediaries, as are those who bring together buyers, sellers, and sources of credit.

The promotions channel has intermediaries that aid with promotions, such as firms that design, build, and transport product exhibits for display at trade shows. Advertising agencies can handle the preparation and media placement of advertising materials. Shoe manufacturer Nike, for example, uses the Wieden & Kennedy agency in Portland, Oregon, for advertising for many of its shoe lines, but uses Goodby, Silverstein & Partners in San Francisco for its specialty shoe lines (including skateboarding shoes) and for its Niketown retail stores. Firms often use public relations agencies to represent them to the news media. Some companies choose to outsource their personal selling functions by hiring an intermediary to provide them with a contract sales force. These promotion efforts handled by intermediaries must be coordinated with the firm's overall marketing communication activities.

The logistics channel has many intermediaries, and many are mentioned in this book. The most common is the freight forwarder, whose function is to assemble small shipments into larger shipments and then tender them in truckload or railcarload quantities to truck lines or to railroads. In international logistics, intermediaries abound; more than a hundred different types could be listed. One example of specialization is cargo surveyors, who specialize in coffee, devoting their careers to examining and arbitrating damage claims involving shipments of coffee beans.

Activities in the Logistical Channel

In order to successfully apply the systems and total cost approaches to logistics, it is essential to have an understanding of the various logistics activities. Keep in mind that since one logistics system does not fit all companies, the number of activities in a logistics system can vary from company to company. Activities that are considered to be logistics-related include, but are not limited to, the following:

Customer service	Demand forecasting
Facility location decisions	Industrial packaging
Inventory management	Materials handling
Order management	Parts and service support
Production scheduling	Procurement
Returned products	Salvage and scrap disposal
Transportation management	Warehousing management

Customer Service

There can be many definitions of customer service, such as "keeping existing customers happy." Customer service involves making sure that the right person receives the right product at the right place at the right time in the right condition and at the right cost. Customer service is discussed in greater detail in Chapter 4.

Demand Forecasting

Demand forecasting refers to efforts to estimate product demand in a future time period. The growing popularity of the supply chain concept has prompted increasing collaboration among supply chain partners with respect to demand forecasting. Such collaboration can enhance efficiency by reducing overall inventory levels in a supply chain.

Facility Location Decisions

It's often said that the success of a retail store depends on three factors: location, location, location. It can also be said that the success of a particular logistics system is dependent upon the location of the relevant warehousing and production facilities. Facility location decisions are increasingly important as the configuration of logistics systems is altered due to the impacts of multinational trade agreements. Facility location decisions are covered in Chapter 8.

Industrial Packaging

Packaging can have both a marketing (consumer packaging) and logistical (industrial packaging) dimension. Industrial (protective) packaging refers to packaging that prepares a product for storage and transit (e.g., boxes, crates), and industrial packaging has important interfaces with the materials handling and warehousing activities. As such, Chapter 5 discusses industrial packaging in conjunction with materials handling.

Inventory Management

Inventory refers to stocks of goods that are maintained for a variety of purposes, such as for resale to others, as well as to support manufacturing or assembling processes. When managing inventory, logisticians need to simultaneously consider three relevant costs—the cost of carrying (holding) product, the cost of ordering product, and the cost of being out of stock. Chapter 9 provides further discussion concerning inventory management.

Materials Handling

Materials handling refers to the short-distance movement of products within the confines of a facility (e.g., plant, warehouse). Since materials handling tends to add costs (e.g., labor costs, product loss, and product damage) rather than value to logistics systems, managers pursue cost-efficiency objectives such as minimizing the number of handlings and moving the product in a straight line whenever possible. Materials handling considerations are presented in Chapter 5.

Order Management

Order management refers to management of the activities that take place between the time a customer places an order and the time it is received by the customer. As such, order management is a logistics activity with a high degree of visibility to customers; order management is discussed in Chapter 4 (as is customer service).

Parts and Service Support

Parts and service support refers to after-sale support for products in the form of repair parts, regularly scheduled service, emergency service, and so on. These activities can be especially important for distributors of industrial products, and relevant considerations include the number and location of repair part facilities, order management, and transportation.[27] Discussions of parts and service support are in several chapters.

Production Scheduling

Production scheduling refers to determining how much to produce and when to produce it. As noted previously, a key interface between production and logistics involves the quantity to be produced, with increasing tension between make-to-stock (generally involving large production lots) and make-to-order (generally involving small production lots) philosophies. Production scheduling is discussed in several chapters, with particular emphasis in Chapter 11.

Procurement

Procurement refers to the raw materials, component parts, and supplies bought from outside organizations to support a company's operations.[28] Procurement's direct link to outside organizations means that its strategic importance has increased as the supply chain management philosophy has become more popular. Purchasing is discussed in more detail in Chapter 11.

---

[27]L. H. Harrington, "Win Big with Strategic 3PL Relationships," *Transportation & Distribution,* October 1999, pp. 118–126.

[28]D. J. Bowersox, D. J. Closs, and M. B. Cooper, *Supply Chain Logistics Management,* Boston: McGraw-Hill Irwin, 2002.

Returned Products

Products can be returned for various reasons, such as product recalls, product damage, lack of demand, and customer dissatisfaction. The logistical challenges associated with returned products can be complicated by the fact that returned products often move in small quantities and may move outside of forward distribution channels. This topic is examined in Chapter 13.

Salvage and Scrap Disposal

Salvage refers to "equipment that has served its useful life but still has value as a source for parts," while scrap refers to "commodities that are deemed worthless to the user and are only valuable to the extent they can be recycled."[29] Salvage and scrap disposal are among the most prominent reverse logistics activities[30] and are discussed in Chapter 13.

Transportation Management

Transportation can be defined as the actual physical movement of goods or people from one place to another, while transportation management (traffic management) refers to the management of transportation activities by a particular organization. Transportation is often the most costly logistics activity, and can range from 40 percent to 60 percent of a firm's total logistics costs. The transportation system is discussed in Chapter 6, while transportation management is discussed in Chapter 7.

Warehousing Management

Warehousing refers to places where inventory can be stored for a particular period of time. As noted previously, important changes have occurred with respect to warehousing's role in contemporary logistics and supply chain systems. Warehousing is discussed in Chapter 10.

Logistics Careers

The discussions of interfunctional and intrafunctional logistics highlight that the logistics manager has a highly complex and challenging position, in part because the logistician needs to be both a generalist and specialist. As a generalist, the logistician must understand the relationship between logistics and other corporate functions, both within and outside the firm. As a specialist, the logistician must understand the relationships between various logistics activities and must have some technical knowledge of the various activities.

Although the job market for logisticians cooled somewhat during 2001 and 2002 due to a slowing global economy and political uncertainty in the Middle East and the Indian subcontinent, logistics remains the second-largest employment sector in the United States. Logistics-related jobs include, but are not limited to, logistics analyst,

---

[29]Glossary of Public Purchasing and Warehouse Inventory Terms, *fcn.state.fla.us/fcn/centers/purchase/standardmanual/glossary.htm*.

[30]Rogers and Tibben-Lembke, 2001.

consultant, customer service manager, logistics engineer, purchasing manager, transportation manager, and warehouse operations manager.[31] Unlike twenty to thirty years ago, career paths in logistics can lead to the executive suite; indeed, the current CEO of Wal-Mart began his Wal-Mart career in the logistics area. Compensation levels for entry-level positions requiring an undergraduate degree in logistics range from the mid-$30K to the mid-$50K. Moreover, the median compensation for senior-level logisticians was approximately $200,000 in 2001.[32]

Because of the growing importance of logistics, a number of professional organizations are dedicated to advancing the professional knowledge of their members. The rationale for these professional associations is that the state of the art is changing so rapidly that professionals must educate and reeducate themselves on a regular basis. Some of the more prominent professional logistics organizations are summarized in the appendix to this chapter.

SUMMARY

This chapter introduced the topic of logistics, which the CLM defines as "that part of the supply chain process that plans, implements, and controls the efficient, effective forward and reverse flow and storage of goods, services, and related information between the point of origin and the point of consumption in order to meet customers' requirements."

The economic impacts of logistics were discussed along with reasons for the increased importance of logistics since 1980. Systems and total cost approaches to logistics were discussed, as were logistical relationships within a firm, with a particular focus on various interfaces between marketing and logistics. A brief description of a number of logistics activities was presented, and the chapter concluded with a brief look at logistics careers.

QUESTIONS FOR DISCUSSION AND REVIEW

1. Did it surprise you that logistics can be such an important component in a country's economic system? Why or why not?
2. Distinguish between possession, form, time, and place utility.
3. How does logistics contribute to time and place utility?
4. How can a particular logistics system be effective but not efficient?
5. Does the fact that information can be substituted for inventory decrease or increase the difficulty of logistics management? Support your response.
6. Explain the significance of the fact that the purpose of logistics is to meet customer requirements.
7. Explain how an understanding of logistics management could be relevant to your favorite charitable organization.
8. Discuss three reasons for why logistics has become more important since 1980.
9. Which reason for the increased importance of logistics do you believe is most important? Why?
10. What are some practical implications of the idea that one logistics system does not fit all companies?
11. Distinguish between inbound logistics, materials management, and physical distribution.

---

[31]*www.clm1.org.*

[32]B. LaLonde and J. Ginter, "2001 Career Patterns in Logistics," *Council of Logistics Management Annual Conference,* 2001.

12. What is the systems approach to problem solving? How is this concept applicable to logistics management?
13. Explain what is meant by the total cost approach to logistics.
14. Define what is meant by a cost trade-off. Do you believe that this concept is workable? Why or why not?
15. What are several areas in which finance and logistics might interface?
16. Briefly discuss each of the four basic aspects of the marketing mix and how each interfaces with the logistics function. In your opinion, which component of the marketing mix represents the most important interface with logistics? Why?
17. Why do marketers tend to prefer FOB destination pricing rather than FOB origin pricing?
18. What are several ways in which logistics and production might interface?
19. Discuss five activities that might be part of a company's logistics department.
20. Logistics managers must be both generalists and specialists. Why is this true? Does this help to explain why there tends to be an imbalance in the supply of, and demand for, logistics managers?

Suggested Readings

Bowersox, Donald J., Patricia J. Daugherty, Cornelia L. Dröge, and Richard Germain. *World Class Logistics: The Challenge of Managing Continuous Change.* Oak Brook, IL: Council of Logistics Management, 1995.

Bowersox, Donald J., David J. Closs, and Theodore P. Stank. "Ten Mega-trends That Will Revolutionize Supply Chain Logistics." *Journal of Business Logistics,* Vol. 21, No. 2, 2000, pp. 1–16.

Gammelgaard, Britta, and Paul D. Larson. "Logistics Skills and Competencies for Supply Chain Management." *Journal of Business Logistics,* Vol. 22, No. 2, 2001, pp. 27–50.

Knemeyer, A. Michael, and Paul R. Murphy. "Logistics Internships: Employer and Student Perspectives." *International Journal of Physical Distribution & Logistics Management,* Vol. 32, No. 2, 2002, pp. 135–152.

Lewis, Ira. "Logistics and Electronic Commerce: An Interorganizational Systems Perspective." *Transportation Journal,* Vol. 40, No. 4, 2000, pp. 5–13.

Lowe, David, *Dictionary of Transport and Logistics.* London: Kogon Page, 2002.

Lynagh, Peter M., Paul R. Murphy, and Richard F. Poist. "Career-Related Perspectives of Women in Logistics: A Comparative Analysis." *Transportation Journal,* Vol. 36, No. 1, 1996, pp. 35–42.

Mollenkopf, Diane, Antony Gibson, and Lucie Ozanne. "The Integration of Marketing and Logistics Functions: An Examination of New Zealand Firms." *Journal of Business Logistics,* Vol. 21, No. 2, 2000, pp. 89–112.

Stock, James R. "Marketing Myopia Revisited: Lessons for Logistics." *International Journal of Physical Distribution & Logistics Management,* Vol. 32, No. 1, 2002, pp. 12–21.

C A S E S

Case 1-1   Sudsy Soap, Inc.

Frank Johnson was outbound logistics manager for Sudsy Soap, Inc. He had held the job for the past 5 years and had just about every distribution function well under control. His task was made easier because shipping patterns and volumes were unchanging routines. The firm's management boasted that it had a steady share in "a stable market," although a few stockholders grumbled that Sudsy Soap had a declining share in a growing market.

The Sudsy Soap plant was in Akron, Ohio. It routinely produced 100,000 48-ounce cartons of powdered dish soap each week. Each carton measured about half a cubic foot, and each working day, 15 to 20 railcar loads were loaded and shipped to various food chain warehouses and to a few large grocery brokers. Johnson worked with the marketing staff to establish prices, so nearly all soap was purchased in railcar-load lots. Shipments less than a full carload did not occur very often.

Buyers relied on dependable deliveries, and the average length of time it took for a carton of soap to leave the Sudsy production line and reach a retailer's shelf was 19 days. The best time was 6 days (to chains distributing in Ohio), and the longest time was 43 days (to retailers in Alaska and Hawaii).

Sudsy Soap's CEO was worried about the stockholders' criticism regarding Sudsy's lack of growth, so he hired a new sales manager, E. Gerard Beever (nicknamed "Eager" since his college days at a Big Ten university). Beever had a 1-year contract and knew he must produce. He needed a gimmick.

At his university fraternity reunion he ran into one of his old fraternity roommates, who was now sales manager for an imported line of kitchen dishes manufactured in China and distributed by a firm headquartered in Hong Kong. The product quality was good, but competition was intense. It was difficult to get even a toehold in the kitchen dinnerware market. Beever and his contact shared a common plight: They were responsible for increasing market shares for products with very little differentiation from competitors' products. They both wished they could help each other, but they could not. The reunion ended and each went home.

The next week, Beever was surprised to receive an e-mail message from his old roommate:

We propose a tie-in promotion between Sudsy Soap and our dishes. We will supply at no cost to you 100,000 each 12-inch dinner plates, 7-inch pie plates, 9-inch bread and butter plates, coffee cups, and saucers. Each week you must have a different piece in each package, starting with dinner plates in week 1, pie plates in week 2, and so on through the end of week 5. Recommend this be done weeks of October 3, October 10, October 17, October 24, and October 31 of this year. Timing important because national advertising linked to new television show we are sponsoring. We will give buyers of five packages of Sudsy Soap, purchased 5 weeks in a row, one free place setting of our dishes. Enough of your customers will want to complete table settings that they will buy more place settings from our retailers. Timing crucial. Advise immediately.

Beever was pleased to receive the offer but realized a lot of questions had to be answered before he could recommend that the offer be accepted. He forwarded the message to Johnson with an added note:

Note attached message offering tie-in with dishes. Dishes are of good quality. What addi-tional information do we need from dish distribu-tor, and what additional information do you need before we know whether to recommend accep-tance? Advise ASAP. Thanks.

QUESTIONS

1. Assume that you are Frank Johnson's assis-tant and he asks you to look into various scheduling problems that might occur. List and discuss them.
2. What packaging problems, if any, might there be?
3. Many firms selling consumer goods are concerned with problems of product liabil-ity. Does the dish offer present any such problems? If so, what are they? Can they be accommodated?
4. Should the exterior of the Sudsy Soap package be altered to show what dish it contains? If so, who should pay for the extra costs?
5. Assume that you are another one of Johnson's assistants and your principal responsibility is managing the inventories of all the firm's inputs, finished products, packages, and outbound inventories. What additional work will the dish proposal cause for you?
6. You are Beever. Your staff has voiced many objections to the dish tie-in proposal, but you believe that much of the problem is your staff's reluctance to try anything inno-vative. Draft a message to the dish com-pany that, although not accepting their pro-posal, attempts to clarify points that may be subject to misinterpretation and also takes into account some of your staff's legitimate concerns.

Case 1-2   KiddieLand and the Super Gym

KiddieLand is a retailer of toys located in the Midwest. Corporate headquarters is in Chicago, and its 70 stores are located in Minnesota, Wisconsin, Michigan, Illinois, Indiana, Ohio, Iowa, and Kentucky. One distri-bution center is located in Columbus (for Kentucky, Indiana, Michigan, and Ohio) and one in Chicago (for Illinois, Iowa, Minnesota, and Wisconsin).

KiddieLand markets a full range of toys, elec-tronic games, computers, and play sets. Emphasis is on a full line of brand-name products together with selected items sold under the KiddieLand brand. KiddieLand's primary competitors include various regional discount chains. The keys to KiddieLand's success have been a comprehensive product line, aggressive pricing, and self-service.

Donald Hurst is KiddieLand's logistics manager. He is responsible for managing both distribution centers, for traffic management, and for inventory control. Don's primary mission is to make sure all stores are in stock at all times without maintaining excessive levels of inventory.

One morning in late January, while Don was reviewing the new year's merchandising plan, he discovered that starting in March, KiddieLand would begin promoting the Super Gym Outdoor Children's Exercise Center. Don was particularly interested that the new set would sell for $715. In addition, the Super Gym is packaged in three boxes weighing a total of 450 pounds. "Holy cow!" thought Don, "the largest set we have sold to date retails for $159 and weighs only 125 pounds."

"There must be some mistake," thought Don as he walked down the hall to the office of Olga Olsen, KiddieLand's buyer for play sets. Olga was new on her job and was unusually stressed because both of her assistant buyers had just resigned to seek employment on the West Coast.

As soon as Olga saw Don, she exclaimed, "Don, my friend, I have been meaning to talk to you." Don knew right then that his worst fears were confirmed.

The next morning Don and Olga met with Randy Smith, Don's traffic manager; A. J. Toth, general manager for KiddieLand's eight Chicago stores; and Sharon Rabiega, Don's assistant for distribution services. Because the previous year had been unusually profitable, everyone was in a good mood because this year's bonus was 50 percent larger than last year's.

Nevertheless, A. J. got to the point: "You mean to tell me that we expect somebody to stuff a spouse, three kids, a dog, and 450 pounds of Super Gym in a small sedan and not have a conniption?"

Randy chimed in, "Besides, we can't drop ship Super Gyms from the manufacturer to the consumer's address because Super Gym ships only in quantities of 10 or more."

Olga was now worried. "We can't back out of the Super Gym now," she moaned. "I have already committed KiddieLand for 400 sets, and the spring–summer play set promotion went to press last week. Besides, I am depending on the Super Gym to make my gross margin figures."

"What about SUVs?" asked Toth. "They make up half the vehicles in our parking lots. Will the three packages fit inside them?"

By now the scope of the problem had become apparent to everyone at the meeting. At 3 P.M. Don summarized the alternatives discussed:

1. Purchase a two-wheeled trailer for each store.
2. Find a local trucking company that can haul the Super Gym from the KiddieLand store to the customer.
3. Stock the Super Gym at the two distribution centers and have the truck that makes delivery runs to the retail stores also make home deliveries.
4. Charge for delivery if the customer cannot get the Super Gym home.
5. Negotiate with the Super Gym manufacturer to ship directly to the customer.

When the meeting adjourned, everyone agreed to meet the following Monday to discuss the alternatives. On Thursday morning a record-breaking blizzard hit Chicago; everyone went home early. KiddieLand headquarters was closed on Friday because of the blizzard. By Wednesday, the same group met again.

Don started the meeting. "Okay," Don began, "let's review our options. Sharon, what did you find out about buying trailers for each store?"

"Well," Sharon began, "the best deal I can find is $1,800 per trailer for 70 trailers, plus $250 per store for an adequate selection of bumper hitches, and an additional $50 per year per store for licensing and insurance. Unfortunately, bumpers on the newest autos cannot accommodate trailer hitches."

"Oh, no," moaned Olga, "we only expect to sell 5.7 sets per store. That means $368 per Super Gym for delivery," she continued as she punched her calculator, "and $147 in lost gross margin!"

Next, Randy Smith summarized the second option. "So far we can get delivery within 25 miles of most of our stores for $38.21 per set. Actually," Randy continued, "$38.21 is for delivery 25 miles from the store. The rate would be a little less for under 25 miles and about $1.50 per mile beyond 25 miles."

A. J. Toth chimed in, "According to our marketing research, 85 percent of our customers drive less than 25 minutes to the store, so a flat fee of $40 for delivery would probably be okay."

Randy continued, "Most delivery companies we talked to will deliver twice weekly but not daily."

Sharon continued, "The motor carrier that handles shipments from our distribution centers is a consolidator. He said that squeezing an 18-wheeler into some subdivision wouldn't make

sense. Every time they try, they knock down a couple of mailboxes and leave truck tracks in some homeowner's lawn."

Olga added, "I talked to Super Gym about shipping direct to the customer's address, and they said forget it. Whenever they have tried that," Olga continued, "the customer gets two of one box and none of another."

"Well, Olga," Don interrupted, "can we charge the customer for delivery?"

Olga thought a minute. "Well, we have never done that before, but then we have never sold a 450-pound item before. It sounds like," Olga continued, "our choice is to either absorb $40 per set or charge the customer for delivery."

"That means $16,000 for delivery," she added.

"One more thing," Don said. "If we charge for shipping, we must include that in the copy for the spring–summer brochure."

Olga smiled. "We can make a minor insert in the copy if we decide to charge for delivery. However," she continued, "any changes will have to be made to the page proofs—and page proofs are due back to the printer next Monday."

QUESTIONS

1. List and discuss the advantages and disadvantages of purchasing a two-wheeled trailer for each store to use for delivering Super Gyms.
2. List and discuss the advantages and disadvantages of having local trucking companies deliver the Super Gym from the retail stores to the customers.
3. List and discuss the advantages and disadvantages of stocking Super Gyms at the distribution centers, and then having the truck that makes deliveries from the distribution center to the retail stores also make deliveries of Super Gyms to individual customers.
4. List and discuss the advantages and disadvantages of charging customers for home delivery if they are unable to carry home the Super Gym.
5. Which alternative would you prefer? Why?
6. Draft a brief statement (catalog copy) to be inserted in the firm's spring–summer brochure that clearly explains to potential customers the policy you recommended in question 5.
7. In the first meeting, A. J. asked about SUVs, but there was no further mention of them. How would you follow up on his query?

A p p e n d i x

Logistics Professional Organizations

APICS—The Educational Society for Resource Management *(www.apics.org)*

In recent years, APICS has expanded from its initial focus on production and inventory control to encompass integrated resource management. It offers two certification programs: Certified in Integrated Resource Management (CIRM) and Certified in Production and Inventory Management (CPIM).

American Society of Transportation and Logistics (AST&L) *(www.nitl.org; www.astl.org)*

AST&L was founded by industry leaders "to ensure a high level of professionalism and promote continuing education in the field of transportation and logistics." It offers a certification program: Certified in Transportation and Logistics (CTL). As of early 2002, AST&L became a subsidiary of the National Industrial Transportation League.

Association for Transportation Law, Logistics and Policy *(www.uprada.com/atllp)*

The Association for Transportation Law, Logistics and Policy is the "Nation's oldest and largest professional organization of lawyers, economists and others specializing in the field of transportation law and policy."

Canadian Association of Supply Chain and Logistics Management (SCL) *(www.infochain.org)*

The SCL is for business professionals in Canada who are interested in improving their logistics and distribution management skills.

Council of Logistics Management (CLM) *(www.clm1.org)*

The CLM is a nonprofit professional organization for people interested in logistics management. It is one of the world's largest professional logistics associations, with approximately 14,000 members.

Delta Nu Alpha (DNA) *(www.deltanualpha.org)*

DNA is an "international organization of professional men and women in all areas and at all levels of transportation and logistics." Its primary focus is on education.

International Society of Logistics *(www.sole.org)*

The International Society of Logistics, formerly the Society of Logistics Engineers, is an "international professional society composed of individuals organized to enhance the art and science of logistics technology, education and management." It has one certification program: Certified Professional Logistician (CPL).

Warehousing Education and Research Council (WERC) *(www.werc.org)*

WERC is a "professional association for those in warehousing and distribution."

CHAPTER

The Supply-Chain Concept

Enhance productivity with spring-loaded latches on doors and walls for fast set-up, knock-down, and interior access.

- <u>First</u> with drop doors in the walls for quick, easy product access.

- <u>First</u> with a long side wall door to deliver secure, rigid stacking.

- <u>First</u> with solid, one-piece base for handling any load up to 2,000 lbs.

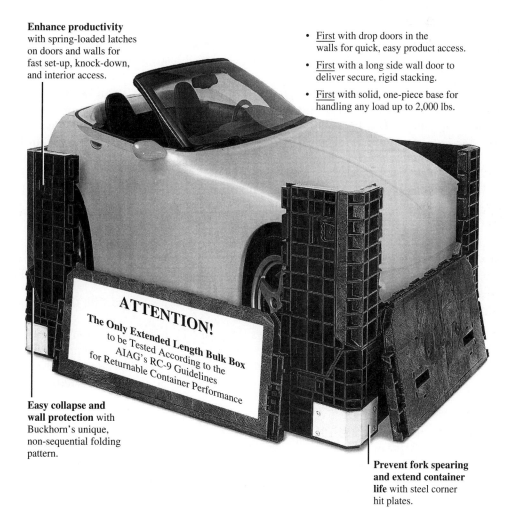

ATTENTION!
The Only Extended Length Bulk Box to be Tested According to the AIAG's RC-9 Guidelines for Returnable Container Performance

Easy collapse and wall protection with Buckhorn's unique, non-sequential folding pattern.

Prevent fork spearing and extend container life with steel corner hit plates.

Key Terms

- Bullwhip effect
- Contract logistics
- Coopetition
- Customer power
- Fourth-party logistics (4PL)
- JIT II
- Lead logistics provider (LLP)
- Logistics outsourcing
- Partnerships

- Relational exchanges
- SCOR model
- Strategic alliances
- Supply chain
- Supply-chain councils
- Supply-chain management
- Third-party arrangements
- Third-party logistics
- Transactional exchanges

Learning Objectives

- To learn about supply-chains and their management
- To understand differences between transactional and relational exchanges
- To realize the importance of leveraging technology
- To appreciate barriers to supply-chain management

A dominant logistics philosophy throughout the 1980s and into the early 1990s involved the integration of logistics with other functions in an organization in an effort to achieve the enterprise's overall success.[1] The early to mid-1990s witnessed a growing recognition that there could be value in coordinating the various business functions not only within organizations but *across* organizations as well—what can be referred to as a **supply-chain management (SCM)** philosophy. According to Professor Mentzer and colleagues, "the supply-chain concept originated in the logistics literature, and logistics has continued to have a significant impact on the SCM concept."[2]

Since the early to mid 1990s there has been a growing body of literature focusing on supply chains and supply-chain management, and this literature has resulted in a number of definitions for both concepts. As was the case when defining logistics, it's important that we have a common understanding of what is meant by **supply chain** and **supply-chain management.**

A **supply chain** "encompasses all activities associated with the flow and transformation of goods from the raw material stage (extraction), through to the end user, as well as the associated information flows."[3] Figure 2-1 presents illustrations of several types of supply chains, and it's important to note several key points. First, supply chains are not a new concept in that organizations traditionally have been dependent upon suppliers and organizations traditionally have served customers. For example, Procter & Gamble (P&G), a

---

[1]Richard F. Poist, "Evolution of Conceptual Approaches to Designing Business Logistics Systems," *Transportation Journal,* Vol. 25, No. 1, 1986, pp. 55–64.

[2]John T. Mentzer et al., "Defining Supply Chain Management," *Journal of Business Logistics,* Vol. 22, No. 2, 2001, pp. 1–25.

[3]Robert B. Handfield and Ernest L. Nichols, Jr., *Introduction to Supply Chain Management,* Upper Saddle River, NJ: Prentice Hall, 1999.

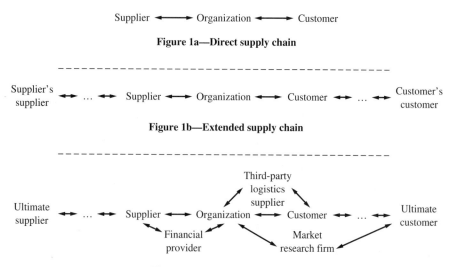

FIGURE 2-1 Different Supply-Chain Configurations

Source: John T. Mentzer et al., "Defining Supply Chain Management," *Journal of Business Logistics,*
Vol. 22, No. 2, 2001, pp. 1–25.

prominent multinational company that produces consumer products, needed raw materials to make soap, as well as customers for the soap, when it was founded in 1837; today, P&G still needs raw materials to make soap—as well as customers for the soap.

Figure 2-1 also points out that some supply chains can be much more complex (in terms of the number of participating parties) than others, and coordinating complex supply chains is likely to be more difficult than doing so for less complex supply chains. Moreover, complex supply chains may include "specialist" companies, such as third-party logistics providers, to facilitate coordination among various supply-chain parties. Note also that customers are an integral component in supply chains, regardless of their complexity.

Supply-chain management can be defined as "the systemic, strategic coordination of the traditional business functions and the tactics across these business functions within a particular company and across businesses in the supply chain, for the purposes of improving the long-term performance of the individual companies and the supply chain as a whole."[4] Importantly, while nearly any organization can be part of a supply chain(s), SCM "requires overt management efforts by the organizations within the supply chain."[5]

Successful supply-chain management requires companies to adopt an enterprise-to-enterprise point of view, which can cause organizations to accept practices and adopt behaviors that haven't traditionally been associated with buyer–seller interactions (as will be seen in the following section). Moreover, successful supply-chain

---

[4]John T. Mentzer et al., 2001.

[5]Ibid.

management requires companies to apply the *systems approach* across all organizations in the supply chain. When applied to supply chains, the systems approach suggests that companies must recognize the interdependencies of major functional areas within, across, and between firms. In turn, the goals and objectives of individual supply-chain participants should be compatible with the goals and objectives of other participants in the supply chain. For example, a company that is committed to a high level of customer service might be out of place in a supply chain comprised of companies whose primary value proposition involves cost containment.

One widely used model of supply-chain management, the **SCOR (Supply-Chain Operations Reference) Model,** currently identifies five key processes—*Plan, Source, Make, Deliver, Return*—associated with supply-chain management (see Figure 2-2). Earlier versions of the SCOR model did not include the return process; as a result, the current model explicitly recognizes that returns should be considered in the design (and management) of supply chains.

Moreover, closer analysis of the five key processes, and their definitions, indicates the important role of logistics in supply-chain management. It can be argued that logistics has some involvement in both sourcing and making; for example, with respect to making, recall the discussion in Chapter 1 about the concept of postponement resulting in value-added activities being performed in warehousing facilities. Alternatively, logistics can be heavily involved in delivering and returning; the definition of delivery specifically mentions the key logistics components of order management, transportation management, and distribution management.

The food and beverage industry provides an excellent real-world example of the importance of logistics to supply-chain management. Interviews with key executives

FIGURE 2-2 Five Processes in the Supply-Chain Operations Reference (SCOR) Model

SCOR Process	Definitions
Plan	Processes that balance aggregate demand and supply to develop a course of action which best meets sourcing, production, and delivery requirements
Source	Processes that procure goods and services to meet planned or actual demand
Make	Processes that transform product to a finished state to meet planned or actual demand
Deliver	Processes that provide finished goods and services to meet planned or actual demand, typically including order management, transportation management, and distribution management
Return	Processes associated with returning or receiving returned products for any reason. These processes extend into post-delivery customer support

Source: SCOR Model, Version 5.0, Pittsburgh: Supply-Chain Council, Inc.

from North American and European food and beverage organizations suggested that supply-chain management is the single most important strategy for ensuring success in an industry that is experiencing tremendous competitive pressures. According to these executives, the most pressing technological investments for facilitating supply-chain superiority involve software associated with the logistical activity of order fulfillment.[6]

Conventional wisdom suggests that company-versus-company competition will be superseded in the twenty-first century by supply-chain-versus-supply-chain competition. While this may occur in a few situations (e.g., companies having sole-sourcing relationships), such competition may not be practical in many instances because of common or overlapping suppliers or the lack of a central control point, among other reasons.[7]

Rather, a more realistic perspective is that individual members of a supply chain will compete based on the relevant capabilities of their supply network, with a particular emphasis on immediately adjacent suppliers or customers. For instance, Bose Corporation (a manufacturer of stereo equipment) developed a supplier integration program known as **JIT II.** Under JIT II, various suppliers have in-plant offices at Bose that allow them to personally interact with other suppliers and Bose personnel on a daily basis. The suppliers' employees stationed at Bose have the authority to place purchasing orders from Bose for their employer's goods (rather than having the purchasing orders placed by Bose employees).[8]

While much of the discussion so far has focused on domestic supply chains, one should recognize that supply chains are becoming increasingly global in nature. Reasons for the increased globalization of supply chains include lower-priced materials and labor, the global perspective of companies in a supply chain, and the development of global competition, among others.[9] While supply-chain integration can be complex and difficult in a domestic setting, the complexity and difficulty are even greater in global supply chains due to cultural, economic, technological, political, spatial, and logistical differences.

Key Attributes of Supply-Chain Management

A number of key attributes are associated with supply-chain management, including customer power; a long-term orientation; leveraging technology; enhanced communication across organizations; inventory control; and interactivity, interfunctional, and interorganizational coordination. Although each of these is discussed in the following paragraphs as discrete entities, interdependencies exist among them. For example,

---

[6]McHugh Software and Tompkins Associates, *Food and Beverage Industry Report,* 2001.

[7]James B. Rice and Richard M. Hoppe, "Supply Chain vs. Supply Chain," *Supply Chain Management Review,* Vol. 5, No. 5, 2001, pp. 46–52.

[8]Ibid.

[9]Pedro Reyes, Mahesh S. Raisinghani, and Manoj Singh, "Global Supply Chain Management in the Telecommunications Industry: The Role of Information Technology in Integration of Supply Chain Entities," *Journal of Global Information Technology Management,* Vol. 5, No. 2, 2002, pp. 48–67.

advances in technology could facilitate enhanced communication across organizations, while a long-term orientation could facilitate interorganizational coordination.

Customer Power

Supply chains recognize the power of consumers and view customers as assets. In recent years, a clear shift of power has moved away from the manufacturer and toward **customer power.** Today's customers "are demanding that companies recognize them as individuals and conduct business on their terms."[10] For example, today's customers are relatively unconcerned with a retailer's trade class distinction (e.g., department store, specialty store) and more concerned with retailers' honesty, trust, and respect. Two of the most successful retailers in the contemporary environment are Wal-Mart and Target—both recognized as having superior supply chains.[11]

The increasing power of customers has important implications for the design and management of supply chains. Because customer needs and wants change relatively quickly, supply chains should be fast and agile, rather than slow and inflexible. *Fast* encompasses a speed/time component, while *agile* focuses on an organization's ability to respond to changes in demand with respect to volume and variety.[12]

Failure to be fast and agile can result in decreased market share, reduced profitability, lower stock price, and/or dissatisfied customers for supply-chain participants. This is well illustrated in the 2002 bankruptcy and reorganization of Kmart, a prominent discount retailer. Although Kmart's bankruptcy was caused by myriad factors, its supply-chain problems included a failure to react to shifts in customer demand, as well as an inability to record replenishment stock in a timely fashion—in other words, a supply-chain that was neither fast nor agile. Moreover, some supply-chain members have been affected by Kmart's bankruptcy in the form of lowered revenues and depressed stock prices.[13]

Long-term Orientation

Note that the definition for supply-chain management indicates that supply chains exist to improve "the long-term performance of the individual companies and the supply chain as a whole." This emphasis on long-term performance suggests that supply chains should employ a long-term as opposed to a short-term orientation with the various participants—suppliers, customers, intermediaries, and facilitators.

Importantly, a long-term orientation tends to be predicated on **relational exchanges** while a short-term orientation tends to be predicated on **transactional exchanges.** In order for relational exchanges to be effective, a transactional "What's in it for me?" philosophy needs to be replaced by a relational "What's in it for us?" philosophy. Relational exchanges tend to be characterized by a far different set of attributes than are transactional exchanges, including—but not limited to—trust, commitment, dependence, investment, and shared benefits.[14]

---

[10]"The Retail Landscape: Redefining," *Chain Store Age,* May 2002, pp. 3A–15A.

[11]Ken Cottrill, "Blue Light Blues," *Traffic World,* January 28, 2002, pp. 11–12.

[12]Martin Christopher, "The Agile Supply Chain," *Industrial Marketing Management,* Vol. 29, No. 1, 2000, pp. 37–44.

[13]Liz Simpson, "Not So Special Kmart," *Supply Management,* Vol. 7, No. 7, 2002, pp. 22–25.

[14]Robert M. Morgan and Shelby D. Hunt, "The Commitment–Trust Theory of Organizational Commitment," *Journal of Marketing,* Vol. 58, No. 3, 1994, pp. 20–38.

At a minimum, relational exchange may result in individual supply-chain participants having to rethink (and rework) their approaches to other supply-chain participants. Commitment, for example, suggests that supply-chain participants recognize the importance of maintaining the relationship that has been established, as opposed to regularly changing participants in order to take advantage of short-term bargains. Moreover, relational exchanges—and by extension, supply-chain management—cannot be successful without information sharing among various participants. However, this is much more easily said than accomplished, in part because the long-standing business bromide "Information is power" can make supply parties somewhat hesitant to share information, lest they jeopardize their competitive advantages.

Partnerships, which can be loosely described as positive, long-term relationships between supply-chain participants, are part and parcel of a relational exchange. A key decision with partnerships involves the degree to which it will be formalized. Some partnerships can be as informal as a handshake agreement between the relevant parties, while some partnerships involve ownership of multiple supply-chain participants by one company. Alternatively, partnerships can be formalized by some type of contractual agreement among the various participants. As a general rule, formal partnership agreements are more likely than informal partnerships to result in improved long-term performance.

Leveraging Technology

It is argued that technology has been at the center of changes taking place that affect the supply chain, and that two key factors—computing power and the Internet—have sparked much of this change.[15] With respect to the former, supply chains can be complex entities consisting of multiple organizations, processes, and requirements. As such, attempts at mathematical modeling of supply chains in an effort to maximize shareholder wealth or minimize costs were (1) not very practical prior to the advent of computers and (2) took a great deal of time even after computers were introduced. However, the introduction and continued development of the computer chip now allows for fast, low-cost mathematical solutions to complex supply-chain issues.

Business futurists Joseph Pine and James Gilmore have referred to the Internet as "the greatest force of commodization known to man, for both goods and services."[16] With respect to supply chains, the Internet can facilitate efficiency and effectiveness by providing opportunities for supply chains to simultaneously improve customer service and reduce their logistics costs.[17]

It's important to recognize that the Internet has important implications for both the business-to-consumer links as well as for business-to-business links within supply chains. (These implications are more fully discussed in later chapters.) For now, it suffices to say that the Internet can allow one supply-chain party to have virtually instantaneous visibility to the same data as other parties in the supply chain. Such instantaneous visibility offers the opportunity for supply chains to become more proactive and

---

[15]Barbara Rosenbaum, "The Technology-Enabled Supply Chain Network," *Industrial Management,* Vol. 43, No. 6, 2001, pp. 6–10.

[16]B. Joseph Pine and James H. Gilmore, *The Experience Economy,* Boston: Harvard Business School Press, 1999.

[17]George Gecowets and Michael J. Bauer, "The e-ffect of the Internet on Supply Chain & Logistics," *World Trade,* Vol. 13, No. 9, 2000, pp. 71–80.

less reactive, which can translate into lower inventories and improved profitability throughout the supply chain.[18]

Enhanced Communication Across Organizations

Because supply chains depend on huge quantities of real-time information, it is essential that this information can be seamlessly transmitted across organizations. For example, retail point-of-sale information can be transmitted directly to suppliers and translated into orders for replenishment product. Alternately, vendors may allow customers to query vendor inventory records to determine what products are in stock and where the stocks are located. The enhanced communication across organizations is dependent upon both technological capabilities as well as a willingness to share information (part of a long-term orientation). Figure 2-3 shows a handheld computer with radio-frequency connections used to communicate some real-time inventory information regarding the truck and its contents.

Inventory Control

Another attribute of supply-chain management involves various activities that can be lumped under the inventory-control rubric. For example, supply-chain management attempts to achieve a smoother and better-controlled flow of inventory with fewer expensive inventory "lumps" along the way. In this situation, the focus is on reducing the so-called **bullwhip effect,** which is characterized by variability in demand orders among supply-chain participants—the end result of which is inventory *lumps.*[19] In short, one aspect of inventory control in supply-chain management is to move from stops and starts to continuous flow.

A second aspect of inventory control in supply-chain management involves a reduction in the amount of inventory in the supply chain, or what one scholar has termed a **JAZ (just about zero)** approach.[20] There are a number of ways to reduce inventory, such as smaller, more frequent orders; the use of premium transportation; demand-pull, as opposed to supply-push, replenishment; and the elimination and/or consolidation of slower-moving product, among others. Importantly, the supply-chain disruptions caused by the aftermath of the September 11, 2001, terrorist attacks (e.g., delayed shipments and the consequent manufacturing shutdowns) have caused some supply chains to reassess their emphasis on inventory reduction.

Interactivity, Interfunctional, and Interorganizational Coordination

Until the past 20 or so years, managers tended to be concerned with optimizing the performance of their particular activities (e.g., inventory management, warehousing, transportation management), particular functions (e.g., production, marketing, logistics), or particular organizations. By contrast, supply-chain management requires managers to subordinate their particular activities, functions, or organizations in order to optimize the performance of the supply chain.

---

[18]Rosenbaum, 2001.

[19]Hau L. Lee, V. Padmanabhan, and Seungin Whang, "The Bullwhip Effect in Supply Chains," *Sloan Management Review,* Vol. 38, No. 3, 1997, pp. 93–102.

[20]Richard W. Oliver, "The End of Inventory?" *The Journal of Business Strategy,* Vol. 20, No. 1, 1999, pp. 8–11.

FIGURE 2-3   Information Supplied By the Truck Driver Is Recorded and Then Transmitted By the Small Computer

Source: Photo courtesy of the Telxon Corporation.

The interconnected nature of supply chains suggests that optimal performance will be elusive without coordination of activities, functions, and processes. Additionally, there's little question that interorganizational coordination is more challenging and difficult than either interfunctional or interactivity coordination. Because the remainder of this book discusses interactivity and interfunctional coordination in greater detail, we'll look here at several methods of interorganizational coordination.

Supply-chain councils, which represent one method of supply-chain coordination, are made up of supply-chain participants, including representative (or the most important) customers. These councils meet periodically to evaluate supply-chain performance and to offer suggestions for potential improvements, such as cost reduction and the elimination of non–value-added processes and activities.[21]

---

[21]Handfield and Nichols, 1999.

A second way to facilitate interorganizational coordination involves literally placing personnel from one supply-chain participant into the facility of another supply-chain participant. This allows face-to-face communication between the organizations and can result in quicker solutions to problems that may arise. As an example, Procter & Gamble, headquartered in Cincinnati, Ohio, has a number of its employees stationed at the Bentonville, Arkansas, headquarters of Wal-Mart, one of P&G's major customers.

Interorganizational coordination can also be increased by acceptance of **co-opetition,** a concept that recognizes that while companies can be competitors in some situations, they can work together in other situations. For example, General Motors, Ford, and DaimlerChrysler, long-standing competitors in the automobile industry, are also equity partners in Covisint, an online trading exchange. Covisint, which handles purchasing for production and nonproduction materials in the automobile industry, was established with the express purpose of removing waste from the automotive supply chain.

Barriers to Supply-Chain Management

While supply-chain management may sound attractive from a conceptual perspective, a number of barriers block its effective implementation, and these are discussed in the following paragraphs.

Regulatory and Political Considerations

Several decades ago, many of the supply-chain arrangements in use today would have been considered illegal under certain regulatory statutes. In the United States, for example, cross-business coordination was fostered by the passage of the National Cooperative Research and Development Act of 1984. Long-term commitments, which are one of the bedrocks of supply-chain management, may stifle competition to the extent that they make it more difficult for others to enter particular markets. While the overall global climate for business has shifted toward allowing more cooperation among firms, it still would be wise to have sound legal advice before entering into future supply-chain arrangements.

Political considerations such as war and governmental stability can also act as a barrier to supply-chain management. With respect to war, the early years of the twenty-first century have witnessed increased tensions in the Middle East, as well as between Pakistan and India (both with nuclear weapon capabilities). These political uncertainties might cause some organizations to shy away from joining or developing supply chains that rely on companies located in warring countries. Governmental stability is also a key consideration, because supply-chain management is so dependent on interorganizational coordination. Governmental policies that either discourage such coordination or discourage doing business with certain countries would obviously have a negative impact on supply-chain efficiency.

Lack of Top Management Commitment

Top management commitment is regularly cited as an important component when individual companies attempt to initiate and implement new initiatives, programs, and products. For example, as pointed out in Chapter 1, the topic of reverse logistics has become increasingly important in recent years, and its importance should continue to increase in the future. Recent research suggests that the relevant reverse logistics goals are more likely to be achieved when there is a high degree of management commitment to them.[22]

Because of supply-chain management's interorganizational focus, top management commitment is absolutely essential if supply-chain efforts are to have any chance of success. Unfortunately, top management is sometimes hesitant to fully commit to supply-chain management because it is uncomfortable with (or does not understand) one or more of its underpinnings. For example, some companies may be uncomfortable with the concept of customer power in supply chains. Alternatively, other companies may be hesitant to enter into long-term relationships because such relationships might be perceived as limiting their operational flexibility.

Reluctance to Share, or Use, Relevant Data

As pointed out previously, the business bromide "Information is power" can make information (data) sharing somewhat problematic, particularly with data that companies might regard as proprietary. However, a reluctance to share data likely decreases the overall effectiveness and efficiency of supply chains because other members may be making decisions based on erroneous data and/or assumptions.

Furthermore, advances in computer hardware and software now permit copious amounts of data to be processed and analyzed relatively quickly. To this end, *data mining,* a technique that looks for patterns and relationships in relevant data, allows companies to lend order and meaning to their data. As an example, frequent shopper cards, such as those offered by grocery chains, offer the opportunity to develop highly detailed profiles of individual customers. Some companies, however, are reluctant to fully utilize the information that comes from this data; they believe that the highly detailed data that can be provided by frequent shopper cards—what was purchased, when it was purchased, where it was purchased, how it was purchased—potentially violate the customer's right to privacy.

Incompatible Information Systems

One barrier to interorganizational coordination in the past was incompatible computer hardware. It's more likely today, by contrast, that software compatibility is the more pressing issue, particularly with the growing popularity of enterprise resource planning (ERP) systems. Although ERP systems offer tremendous potential for increasing organizational effectiveness and efficiency, the installation of ERP systems can cost hundreds of millions of dollars and take several years to complete.

While ERP systems may be strong in terms of financial and billing applications, most tend to be relatively weak when it comes to logistics and supply-chain requirements. In order to achieve these requirements, other software packages have to be integrated with the chosen ERP system—and these integrations don't always proceed smoothly. One well-known example involved the attempt by Hershey Foods integrate

---

[22]Patricia J. Daugherty, Chad W. Autry, and Alexander E. Ellinger, "Reverse Logistics: The Relationship Between Resource Commitment and Program Performance," *Journal of Business Logistics,* Vol. 21, No. 1, 2000, pp. 107–123.

an ERP system with two other specialized software packages. The growing pains of this integration included unfilled candy orders for Halloween and Christmas, longer delivery times, increased inventory levels, and upset customers.[23]

Incompatible Corporate Cultures

Because supply-chain management emphasizes a long-term orientation and partnerships between various participants, it is important that participants be comfortable with the companies that they will be working with. In a broad sense, corporate culture refers to "how we do things around here" and reflects an organization's vision, values, and strategic plans.

The myriad manifestations of a company's culture include, but are not limited to, office décor, company brochures, company rituals, and dress codes. All manifestations of corporate culture may provide important clues about the ability of companies to work together. For instance, one of the more notable supply-chain failures in recent years involved the dissolution of the relationship between Office Max and Ryder Integrated Logistics. While a number of reasons explain why this relationship didn't succeed, the two companies had quite different dress codes. Indeed, a Ryder manager has stated it was clear from the first face-to-face meeting that the companies were going to have difficulty working together—in large part because of their vastly different dress codes!

Supply-Chain Management and Integration

An individual firm can be involved in multiple supply chains at the same time, and it's important to recognize that expectations and required knowledge can vary across supply chains. For example, food manufacturers may sell to grocery chains, institutional buyers, specialty firms (which might position the food items as gifts), and industrial users (which might use the product as an ingredient in another product that they manufacture). It seems reasonable that the packaging expectations of specialty firms might be more demanding than those of industrial users.

Supply chains are integrated by having various parties enter into and carry out long-term mutually beneficial agreements. These agreements are known by several names, to include **partnerships, strategic alliances, third-party arrangements,** and **contract logistics.** Whatever they are called, these agreements should be designed to reward all participants when cooperative ventures are successful, and they should also provide incentives for all parties to work toward success. In a similar fashion, the participants should share the consequences when cooperative ventures are less successful than desired.

When an organization enters into a long-term agreement with a source or customer, the organization must keep in mind how this arrangement could affect the rest of the supply chain. Ideally, all participants in the supply chain will meet at one time and work out whatever agreements are necessary to ensure that the entire supply chain functions in the most desirable manner.

In order to integrate a particular supply chain, the various organizations must recognize the shortcomings of the present system and examine channel arrangements as

---

[23]Craig Stedman, "Failed ERP Gamble Haunts Hershey," *Computerworld,* November 1, 1999, pp. 1–2.

they currently exist and as they might be. All of this is done within the framework of the organization's overall strategy, as well as any logistics strategies necessary to support the goals and objectives of the firm's top management.

Broadly speaking, organizations can pursue three primary methods when attempting to integrate their supply chains. One method is through *vertical integration,* where one organization owns multiple participants in the supply chain; indeed, the Ford Motor Company of the 1920s owned forests and steel mills and exercised tight control over its dealers. The most common examples of vertical integration today are some lines of paint and automotive tires. It's important to recognize that there may be regulatory limitations (often in the form of state laws) as to the degree of vertical integration that will be permitted in particular industries.

A second possible method of supply-chain coordination involves the use of *formal contracts* among various participants. One of the more popular uses of contracts is through franchising, which attempts to combine the benefits of tight integration of some functions along with the ability to be very flexible while performing other functions. From a supply-chain perspective, a franchiser may exert contractual influence over what products are purchased by a franchisee, acceptable vendors (suppliers) of these products, and the distribution of the product to the franchisee. For example, distribution for many McDonald's franchisees in the United States (e.g., food, beverage, and store supplies) is provided by the Martin-Brower Company.

A third method of supply-chain coordination involves *informal agreements* among the various organizations to pursue common goals and objectives, with control being exerted by the largest organization in the supply chain. While this method offers supply-chain participants flexibility in the sense that organizations can exit unprofitable and/or unproductive arrangements quickly and with relative ease, organizations should be aware of potential shortcomings. For one, the controlling organization may be so powerful that the supply chain becomes more like a dictatorship than a partnership. Moreover, the same flexibility that allows for exiting unprofitable or unproductive arrangements also allows parties the ability to switch supply chains when presented with what appears to be a better deal.

Third-Party Logistics

In Figure 2-1, we see that the ultimate supply chain contains several types of organizations (e.g., financial provider, third-party logistics supplier, market research firm) that exist to facilitate coordination among various supply-chain participants. Because this is a logistics textbook, the most relevant facilitator for our purposes is the third-party logistics supplier, so it is especially relevant to examine its impact on logistics and supply chains.

Third-party logistics, also called **logistics outsourcing,** or **contract logistics,** continues to be one of the most misunderstood terms in logistics and supply-chain management. As is the case with supply-chain management, there is no commonly accepted definition of third-party logistics (3PL). The general idea behind third-party logistics is that one company (say, a manufacturer) allows a specialist company to provide it with one or more logistics functions (e.g., warehousing, outbound transportation). Some well-known 3PL providers include DanzasAEI, Exel Logistics, Menlo Logistics, Penske Logistics, and C. H. Robinson Logistics, among others.

What we'll call *contemporary* third-party logistics began to emerge in the second half of the 1980s. Its importance in logistics and supply-chain management prompted annual expenditures for contemporary third-party logistics services in the United States of $10 billion in the early 1990s. In the early years of the twenty-first century, annual U.S. 3PL expenditures are approaching $70 billion—which is only about 10 percent of the potential U.S. market for 3PL services.[24] In addition, it has been estimated that by 2005 U.S. 3PL users may be spending about one-third of their total logistics budgets, up from 20 percent in 2000, for 3PL services.[25]

While third-party logistics is not a new idea, several factors distinguish contemporary 3PL from previous incarnations. First, there tend to be formal contracts between providers and users that are at least one year (typically three to five years) in duration. Contemporary 3PL also tends to be characterized by a relational (as opposed to a transactional) focus, a focus on mutual benefits, and the availability of customized (as opposed to standardized) offerings.[26] Thus, a contemporary 3PL provider views its customer as a party with whom it is going to have a long-term, as opposed to short-term, relationship. In addition, 3PL providers and users actively seek out policies and practices, such as cost reduction, that can benefit both parties. Finally, the nature and scope of customized offerings can be specified in the relevant contract, and they often require both parties to make specific investments in order to fulfill the relationship.

All 3PL customers can demand a number of different activities, with some of the most common involving inbound and outbound transportation, carrier negotiation and contracting, and freight consolidation.[27] Because the services demanded by 3PL customers can vary widely in both nature and scope, it's not possible to discuss a typical 3PL relationship. However, the two actual relationships presented below provide a sense of what they might encompass.

Penske Logistics manages the outbound distribution network for the finished appliances of Whirlpool Corporation. Penske's responsibilities involve all relevant activities within Whirlpool's regional and local distribution centers, including warehousing, materials handling, and transportation from the distribution centers to the next party in the supply chain.[28] Exel Logistics developed an interesting relationship with the Harley Owners Group (HOG) concerning the August 2003 celebration of Harley-Davidson's 100th anniversary in Milwaukee, Wisconsin. To allow European members to attend this event, Exel and HOG put together a special package that allowed HOG members to have their motorcycles collected, transported to an airport/port, packaged, and shipped to the United States via either air or water transportation.[29]

---

[24]Helen Atkinson, "Year of the 3PLs," *JoC Week,* February 18, 2002, pp. 12–14.

[25]Toby B. Gooley, "Growth Spurt," *Logistics Management and Distribution Report,* November 2000, pp. 77–84.

[26]J. M. Africk and C. S. Calkins, "Does Asset Ownership Mean Better Service?" *Transportation and Distribution,* Vol. 35, No. 5, 1994, pp. 49–61.

[27]A. Michael Knemeyer, Thomas M. Corsi, and Paul R. Murphy, "Logistics Outsourcing Relationships: Customer Perspectives," *Journal of Business Logistics,* Vol. 24, No. 1, 2003, pp. 77–109.

[28]www.penskelogistics.com

[29]www.exel.com

A variety of different activities also can be performed by third-party logistics providers, with some of the most common including development of distribution systems, electronic data interchange capability, and freight consolidation.[30] Moreover, some 3PL providers have begun to offer so-called *supplemental* services—such as final product assembly, product installation, and product repair, among others—which are beyond their traditional offerings. As noted in Chapter 1, these supplemental 3PL services can blur traditional distinctions among supply-chain participants (e.g., product assembly has generally been performed by the manufacturing group). Importantly, however, this blurring of distinctions may actually facilitate supply-chain integration, in that there is less emphasis on functional issues and more emphasis on cross-functional processes.[31]

One measure of the pervasiveness of third-party logistics in supply-chain management can be seen in the evolution of **fourth-party logistics (4PL),** or the **lead logistics provider (LLP)** concept. Because 4PL/LLP is still in its infancy, there is some disagreement as to an exact definition. However, a number of experts currently suggest that a 4PL/LLP should be viewed as a general contractor whose primary purpose is to ensure that various 3PLs are working toward the relevant supply-chain goals and objectives.[32]

At the present time, the 4PL/LLP concept appears best suited for large companies with global supply chains, such as General Motors and Hewlett-Packard. In fact, General Motors is actively engaged in 4PL/LLP through Vector SCM, a joint venture between itself and CNF, Inc. Vector SCM is charged with managing and integrating all of GM's logistics service providers, currently some 2,000 strong. Vector SCM is also charged with reducing GM's $6 billion annual logistics bill, as well as reducing order cycle time from approximately 85 days to the 15-to 20-day range.[33]

Supply-Chain Software

It has been pointed out on several occasions that the interorganizational coordination of activities, functions, and processes is a daunting task. A large part of the challenge of interorganizational coordination involves the tremendous amount of data to be transmitted across, and available to, supply-chain participants. To this end, supply-chain software packages have been developed to address the data and informational needs of supply-chain participants. Some of the more prominent supply-chain software companies include EXE Technologies, i2 Technologies, Manhattan Associates, Manugistics, and SAP.

Such a tremendous proliferation of supply-chain software packages has occurred during the past 10 to 15 years that "determining which specific systems and applications can provide a specific supply chain with the greatest benefit is not at all clear."[34]

---

[30]Paul R. Murphy and Richard F. Poist, "Third-Party Logistics: Some User Versus Provider Perspectives," *Journal of Business Logistics,* Vol. 21, No. 1, 2000, pp. 121–133.

[31]Remko I. van Hoek, "The Contribution of Performance Measurement to the Expansion of Third-Party Logistics Alliances in the Supply Chain," *International Journal of Operations & Production Management,* Vol. 21, No. 1/2, 2001, pp. 15–29.

[32]William Armbruster, "4PL," *JoC Week,* June 24–30, 2002, pp. 11–13.

[33]David Hanson, "GM Hatches Plan to Cut 70 Days from OC Time," *Purchasing,* July 5, 2001, p. 61.

[34]Handfield and Nichols, 1999.

Moreover, because many of these software packages are developed for general application, users may need to modify the packages to address their specific needs and processes, which adds to the costs of purchasing the software.

With so many different types of supply-chain software, it's not possible to provide a comprehensive discussion here about them. As a general rule, the supply-chain software packages look to coordinate and integrate functions, processes, and/or systems across multiple supply-chain participants. Thus, some software packages focus on specific functional areas such as transportation, warehousing, or inventory management. Other software packages focus on specific supply-chain processes, such as customer relationship management (CRM) or collaborative planning, forecasting, and replenishment (CPFR). Still other packages attempt to simultaneously optimize supply-chain processes across organizations.

Estimates of the annual potential savings from supply-chain software—just in the United States—range from approximately $200 billion to $450 billion.[35] While the potential monetary savings from supply-chain software are certainly attractive, the costs of various packages can be quite expensive, ranging from tens of thousands of dollars to millions of dollars, not including installation expenses.

SUMMARY

This chapter focused on the supply-chain concept and began by defining supply chain and supply-chain management. Supply chains consist of a number of different parties and include the end customer; supply-chain management requires companies to adopt an enterprise-to-enterprise point of view.

The chapter also discussed key attributes of supply-chain management, such as customer power, a long-term orientation, and leveraging technology. Various barriers to supply-chain management, such as lack of top management commitment and reluctance to share, or use, relevant data, were also presented. We also looked at integration in supply-chain management with a particular emphasis on third-party logistics and supply-chain software.

QUESTIONS FOR DISCUSSION AND REVIEW

1. Discuss the differences between supply chain and supply chain management.
2. Using the SCOR model as a reference, explain the role of logistics in supply-chain management.
3. Do you believe that competition in the twenty-first century will involve supply chain versus supply chain? Why or why not?
4. What are four key attributes of supply-chain management?
5. Why do contemporary supply chains need to be fast and agile?
6. What is the difference between relational and transactional exchanges? Which is more relevant for supply-chain management? Why?
7. This chapter suggests that technology has been at the center of changes taking place that affect the supply chain. Do you agree or disagree? Why?
8. Discuss the impact of the Internet on supply-chain management.
9. Discuss some of the ways that inventory can be reduced in the supply chain.

---

[35]"Supply Chain Software Can Offer Great Savings, Says AMR," *Unigram X*, 12/01/2000, p.N.PAG.

10. What are supply-chain councils, and how do they operate?
11. What is meant by coopetition? How is it relevant to supply-chain management?
12. How might regulatory and political conditions act as barriers to supply-chain management?
13. Some companies are hesitant to use frequent shopper cards because the data provided could violate the customer's privacy. Do you agree or disagree? Why?
14. Why are compatible information systems important for effective and efficient supply-chain management?
15. Do you think corporate cultures are relevant for supply-chain management? Why or why not?
16. Discuss the three primary methods that organizations can use to integrate their supply chains.
17. Discuss the factors that distinguish contemporary third-party logistics from earlier types of third-party logistics.
18. Name some of the *supplemental* services that are currently offered by third-party logistics companies. How can these supplemental services facilitate supply-chain management?
19. Do you agree or disagree with the sentiment that fourth-party logistics companies (lead logistics providers) merely add unnecessary cost and few service improvements to supply chains? Why?
20. Discuss the various types of supply-chain software.

SUGGESTED READINGS

Bolumole, Yemisi A., "The Supply Chain Role of Third-Party Logistics Providers." *International Journal of Logistics Management,* Vol. 12, No. 2, 2001, pp. 87–102.

Bowersox, Donald J., David J. Closs, and Theodore P. Stank, "Ten Mega Trends That Will Revolutionize Supply Chain Logistics." *Journal of Business Logistics,* Vol. 21, No. 2, 2000, pp. 1–16.

Brewer, Peter C., and Thomas W. Speh, "Using the Balanced Scorecard to Measure Supply Chain Performance." *Journal of Business Logistics,* Vol. 21, No. 1, 2000, pp. 75–93.

Chapman, Sharon, Lawrence P. Ettkin, Marilyn M. Helms, and Ed Czupryna, "Do Small Businesses Need Supply Chain Management?" *IIE Solutions,* Vol. 32, No. 8, 2000, pp 31–35.

Cooper, Martha C., Douglas M. Lambert, and Janus D. Pagh, "Supply Chain Management: More Than a New Name for Logistics." *International Journal of Logistics Management,* Vol. 8, No. 1, 1997, pp. 1–14.

Farris, M. Theodore, and Paul D. Hutchinson, "Cash-to-Cash: The New Supply Chain Management Metric." *International Journal of Physical Distribution & Logistics Management,* Vol. 32, No. 4, 2002, pp. 288–298.

Lummus, Rhonda R., Dennis W. Krumwiede, and Robert J. Vokurka, "The Relationship of Logistics to Supply Chain Management: Developing a Common Industry Definition." *Industrial Management & Data Systems,* Vol. 101, No. 8, 2001, pp. 426–431.

McAfee, R. Bruce, Myron Glassman, and Earl D. Honeycutt, "The Effects of Culture and Human Resource Management Policies on Supply Chain Management Strategy." *Journal of Business Logistics,* Vol. 23, No. 1, 2002, pp. 1–18.

Mentzer, John T., W. DeWitt, J. S. Keebler, S. Min, N. W. Nix, C. D. Smith, and Z. G. Zacharia, "Defining Supply Chain Management." *Journal of Business Logistics,* Vol. 22, No. 1, 2001, pp. 1–26.

Tan, Keah C., Steven B. Lyman, and Joel D. Wisner, "Supply Chain Management: A Strategic Perspective." *International Journal of Operations and Production Management,* Vol. 22, No. 6, 2002, pp. 614–631.

CASES

Case 2-1 Johnson Toy Company

Located in Biloxi, Mississippi, the Johnson Toy Company is celebrating its seventy-fifth year of business. Amy Johnson, who is president, and Lori Johnson, who is vice president, are sisters and are the third generation of their family to be involved in the toy business. The firm manufactures and sells toys throughout the United States. The toy business is very seasonal, with the majority of sales occurring before Christmas. A smaller peak occurs in the late spring–early summer period, when sales of outdoor items are good.

The firm relies on several basic designs of toys—which have low profit margins but are steady sellers—and on new designs of unconventional toys whose introduction is always risky but promises high profits if the item becomes popular. The firm advertises regularly on Saturday morning television shows for children.

Late last year, just before Christmas, the Johnson Toy Company introduced Jungle Jim the Jogger doll, modeled after a popular television show. Sales skyrocketed, and every retailer's stock of Jungle Jim the Jogger dolls was sold out in mid-December; the Johnson Company could have sold several million more units if they had been available before Christmas. Based on the sales success of this doll, Amy and Lori made commitments to manufacture 10 million Jungle Jim the Jogger dolls this year and to introduce a wide line of accessory items, which they hoped every doll owner would also want to have. Production was well underway, and many retailers were happy to accept dolls in January and February because they were still a fast-selling item, even though the toy business itself was sluggish during these months.

Unfortunately, in the aftermath of a Valentine's Day party in Hollywood, the televi-

sion actor who portrayed Jungle Jim the Jogger became involved in a widely publicized sexual misadventure, the details of which shocked and disgusted many readers and TV viewers, and we would be embarrassed to describe them. Ratings of the television series plummeted, and within a month it had been dropped from the air. On March 1, the Johnson Company had canceled further production of the Jungle Jim the Jogger dolls, although it had to pay penalties to some of its suppliers because of the cancellation. The company had little choice because it was obvious that sales had stopped.

On April 1, a gloomy group assembled in the Johnson Company conference room. Besides Amy and Lori, those present included Carolyn Coggins, the firm's sales manager; Cheryl Guridi, the logistics manager; Greg Sullivan, the controller; and Kevin Vidal, the plant engineer. Coggins had just reported that she believed there were between 1.5 million and 2 million Jungle Jim the Jogger dolls in retail stores, and Sullivan had indicated there were 2,567,112 complete units in various public warehouses in Biloxi. Vidal said that he was still trying to count all the unassembled component parts, adding that one problem was that they were still being received from suppliers, despite the cancellation.

Amy said, "Let's wait a few weeks to get a complete count of all the dolls and all the unassembled component parts. Lori, I'm naming you to work with Carolyn and Kevin to develop recommendations as to how we can recycle the Jungle Jim item into something we can sell. Given the numbers involved, I'm willing to turn out some innocuous doll and sell it for a little more than the cost of recycling because we can't take a complete loss on all these damned Jungle Jim dolls! Greg says we have nearly 2.6 million of them to play with, so let's think of something."

"Your 2.6 million figure may be low," said Coggins. "Don't forget that there may be nearly 2 million in the hands of the dealers and that they will return them."

"Return them?" questioned Amy. "They're not defective. That's the only reason we accept returns. The retailers made a poor choice. It's the same as if they ordered sleds and then had a winter with no snow. We are no more responsible for Jungle Jim's sex life than they are!"

Cheryl Guridi spoke up: "You may be underestimating the problem, Amy. One of our policies is to accept the dealer's word as to what is defective, and right now there are a lot of dealers out there claiming defects in the Jungle Jim dolls. One reason that Kevin can't get an accurate count is that returned dolls are showing up on our receiving dock and getting mixed up with our in-stock inventory."

"How can that happen?" asked Amy, angrily. "We're not paying the freight, also, are we?"

"So far, no," responded Guridi. "The retailers are paying the freight just to get rid of them."

"We've received several bills in which the retailer has deducted the costs of the Jungle Jim dolls and of the freight for shipping them back from what he owes us," said Sullivan. "That was one item I wanted to raise while we were together."

"We can't allow that!" exclaimed Amy.

"Don't be so sure," responded Sullivan. "The account in question has paid every bill he's owed us on time for 40 years. Do you want *me* to tell him we won't reimburse him?"

"This is worse than I imagined," said Amy. "Just what are our return policies, Lori?"

"Well, until today, I thought we had only two," said Lori. "One for our small accounts involves having our salespeople inspect the merchandise when they make a sales call. They can pick it up and give the retailer credit off the next order."

"Sometimes they pick up more than defective merchandise," added Coggins. "Often,

they'll take the slow movers out of the retailer's hands. We have to do that as a sales tool."

"That's not quite right," interjected Vidal. "Sometimes, the returned items are just plain shopworn—scratched, dented, and damaged. That makes it hard for us because we have to inspect every item and decide whether it can be put back into stock. When we think a particular salesperson is accepting too many shopworn items, we tell Carolyn, although it's not clear to me that the message reaches the salespeople in the field."

"I wish I had an easy solution," said Coggins. "We used to let our salespeople give credit for defects and then destroy everything out in the field. Unfortunately, some abused the system and resold the toys to discount stores. At least now we can see everything we're buying back. I agree we are stuck with some shopworn items, but our salespeople are out there to sell, and nothing would ruin a big sale quicker than for our salespeople to start arguing with the retailer, on an item-by-item basis, as to whether something being returned happens to be shopworn."

"Is there a limit to what a salesperson is permitted to allow a retailer to return?" asked Amy.

"Well, not until now," responded Coggins. "But with this Jungle Jim snafu we can expect the issue to occur. In fact, I have several phone queries on my desk concerning this. I thought I'd wait until after this meeting to return them."

"Well, I think we'd better establish limits—right now," said Amy.

"Be careful," said Lori. "When I was out with the salespeople last year, I gathered the impression that some were able to write bigger orders by implying that we'd take the unsold merchandise back, if need be. If we assume that risk, the retailer is willing to take more of our merchandise."

"Are there no limits to this policy?" asked Amy.

"Informal ones," was Coggins's response. "It depends on the salesperson and the account. I don't think there is much abuse, although there is some."

"How do the goods get back to us under these circumstances?" asked Amy.

"The salespeople either keep them and shuffle them about to other customers, or—if it's a real loser—they ask us what to do," replied Coggins.

"Greg," said Amy, "do our records reflect these returns and transfers?"

"Oh, fairly well," was his response. "We lose track of individual items and quantities, but if the salesperson is honest—and I think ours are—we can follow the dollar amount of the return to the salesperson's inventory, to another retailer, or back here to us. We do not have good controls on the actual items that are allowed for returns. Kevin and I have difficulty in reconciling the value of returned items that wind up back here. Carolyn's records say they're okay for resale, and Kevin says they're too badly damaged."

"I insist on the reconciliation before we allow the goods back into our working inventory," said Guridi. "That way I know exactly what I have here, ready to ship."

"You know, I'm finding out more information about inventories and returns than I thought existed," said Amy.

"Too many trips to Paris, dearest," said Lori, and the others all suppressed smiles.

Amy decided to ignore Lori's remark, and she looked at Guridi and asked, "Are you satisfied with your control over inventories, Cheryl?"

"I have no problem with the ones here in Biloxi," was Guridi's response, "but I have an awful time with the inventories of return items that salespeople carry about with them, waiting to place them with another retailer. I'm not always certain they're getting us top dollar, and each salesperson knows only his or her own territory. When Carolyn and I are trying to monitor the sales of some new item, we never know whether it's bombing in some areas and riding around in salespeople's cars as they try to sell it again."

"Have you now described our returns policy, such as it is?" asked Amy, looking at everybody in the room.

"No," was the response murmured by all. Sullivan spoke: "For large accounts we deduct a straight 2 percent off wholesale selling price to cover defectives, and then we never want to hear about the defectives from these accounts at all."

"That sounds like a better policy," said Amy. "How well is it working?"

"Up until Jungle Jim jogged where he shouldn't, it worked fine. Now a number of large accounts are pleading 'special circumstances' or threatening to sue if we don't take back the dolls."

"They have no grounds for suit," declared Amy.

"You're right," said Coggins, "but several of their buyers are refusing to see our sales staff until the matter is resolved. I just heard about this yesterday and meant to bring it up in today's meeting. I consider this very serious."

"Damn it!" shouted Amy, pounding the table with her fist. "I hope that damned jogger dies of jungle rot! We're going to lose money this year, and now you're all telling me how the return policy works, or doesn't work, as the case may be! Why can't we just have a policy of all sales being final and telling retailers that if there is an honest defect they should send the goods back here to us in good old Biloxi?"

"Most of the small accounts know nothing about shipping," responded Vidal. "They don't know how to pack, they don't know how to prepare shipping documents, and they can't choose the right carriers. You ought to see the hodgepodge of shipments we receive from them. In more cases than not, they pay more in shipping charges than the products are worth to us. I'd rather see them destroyed in the field."

Sullivan spoke up. "I'd object to that. We would need some pretty tight controls to make certain the goods were actually destroyed. What if they are truly defective, but improperly disposed of, then fall into the hands of children who play with them and the defect causes an injury? Our name may still be on the product, and the child's parents will no doubt claim the item was purchased from one of our retailers. Will we be liable? Why can't we have everything come back here? We have enough volume of some returned items that we could think in terms of recycling parts."

Vidal responded, "Recycling is a theoretical solution to such a problem, but only in rare instances will it pay. In most instances the volume is too small and the cost of taking toys apart is usually very high. However, the Jungle Jim product involves such a large volume that it is prudent and reasonable to think up another product that utilizes many of the parts. It would even pay to modify some machines for disassembling the Jungle Jim doll."

"As I listen to this discussion," said Lori, "one fact becomes obvious: We will never have very good knowledge about volume or patterns of returns until it's too late. That's their very nature."

Guridi asked, "Could we have field representatives who do nothing but deal with this problem? The retailers would be told to hang onto the defectives until our claims reps arrive."

Coggins replied, "That would be expensive, because most retailers have little storage space for anything and would expect our claims rep to be there PDQ. Besides, it might undermine our selling efforts if retailers could no longer use returns to negotiate with as they talked about new orders."

"That may be," interjected Amy, "but we cannot continue having each salesperson tailoring a return policy for each retailer. That's why we're in such a mess with the jogger doll. We have to get our return policy established, made more uniform, and enforced. We cannot go through another fiasco like Jungle Jim the Jogger for a long time. We're going to lose money this year, no matter what, and I have already told Kevin that there will be virtually no money available for retooling for next year's new products."

QUESTIONS

1. From the standpoint of an individual concerned with accounting controls, discuss and evaluate Johnson Toy Company's present policies for handling returned items.
2. Answer question 1, but from the standpoint of an individual interested in marketing.
3. Propose a policy for handling returns that should be adopted by the Johnson Toy Company. Be certain to list circumstances under which exceptions would be allowed. Should it apply to the Jungle Jim dolls?
4. Should this policy, if adopted, be printed and distributed to all of the retailers who handle Johnson Toy Company products? Why or why not? If it should not be distributed to them, who should receive copies?
5. Assume that it is decided to prepare a statement on returns to be distributed to all retailers and that it should be less than a single double-spaced page. Prepare such a statement.
6. On the basis of the policy in your answer to question 3, develop instructions for the Johnson Toy Company distribution and accounting departments with respect to their roles and procedures in the handling of returns.
7. Assume that you are Cheryl Guridi, the firm's logistics manager. Do you think that the returns policy favored by the logistics manager would differ from what would be best for the firm? Why or why not?
8. Until the policy you recommend in your answer to question 3 takes effect, how would you handle the immediate problem of retailers wanting to return unsold Jungle Jim the Jogger dolls?

Case 2-2   Wyomo Grocery Buyers' Cooperative

Located in Billings, Montana, the Wyomo Grocery Buyers' Cooperative served the dry grocery and produce needs of about 150 area food stores from Great Falls to Butte in the northwest and from Casper to Cheyenne in the southeast. All dry groceries were shipped out of a 20,000-square-foot warehouse in Billings, built by the co-op in 1968. Produce was handled out of the Billings warehouse and small, rented warehouses in Cheyenne and Great Falls. At these warehouses, the co-op bagged some bulk products, such as potatoes, onions, and oranges, into 5-, 10-, and 20-pound bags carrying the co-op label. The warehouses also stocked items used by the stores, such as butcher paper, cash-register tape, plastic produce bags, and various sizes of brown bags.

The co-op had its own fleet of 15 tractors and 19 trailers that operated out of Billings, as well as 6 straight trucks with refrigerated bodies, with 2 each working out of Billings, Cheyenne, and Great Falls. Dry grocery deliveries were made once or twice a week, and produce deliveries were handled separately and were made two or three times a week, depending on each store's volume. Both dry grocery and produce trucks traveled approximately the same routes each week, and goods for both large and small stores were carried aboard the same truck. Stores were responsible for placing orders with the co-op, although a co-op representative would call on a weekly basis, and one of her or his functions was to help some store operators complete their order forms.

The co-op was owned by member grocery stores and run by a board of directors elected by the member stores. The directors hired the general manager, Peter Bright. Directors were elected with member stores having at least one vote. Stores with larger sales volumes got more votes, although their additional votes were not proportional to their additional sales. (This was because several years ago smaller stores realized they could lose their power, so they capped the additional votes a larger store could be given.)

Goods were being sold to members on the basis of cost to the co-op plus 23 percent to cover warehousing and transportation from the warehouses to the members' retail stores. Each year the co-op's revenues exceeded costs by a small margin; 20 percent of this excess was returned to the members in direct proportion to their purchases from the co-op, and the remainder was considered capital and reinvested in the co-op. The co-op's level of business was not growing. Its members were losing sales to chain food stores and chain discount department stores, which were moving into the region.

A continual problem facing the board of directors was the political split between small and large stores belonging to the co-op. Small grocery stores stocked only 1,000 to 2,000 different items or lines of merchandise (stock-keeping units or SKUs) carried by the co-op, whereas larger members needed to carry 6,000 to 8,000 SKUs to compete with the chains. The latter group of co-op members consisted of the more aggressive merchants, most of whom felt that the co-op should forget about its small members and instead help them battle the chains. From time to time they threatened to form their own co-op.

At issue was a long-standing controversy that was debated at every quarterly meeting of the co-op's directors. Indeed, it had been a problem since the 1950s, when tissue manufacturers started manufacturing toilet paper and facial tissues in colors in addition to white. Later they introduced floral patterns for facial tissue and, more recently, started packaging in a variety of designer dispenser boxes. The tissue manufacturers did this to capture more shelf space in retailers' stores. For example, if only white tissue were sold, it could be displayed on a shelf and occupy only 12 inches of shelf space (measured along the front). If white, pink, yellow, blue, and green tissue were all to be displayed, each would require its own 12 inches of shelf space, so a total of 60 inches of shelf space would be needed. The same held for toilet paper (and many other products).

From the co-op's standpoint, five colors of tissue multiplied the warehouse workload because each color of tissue was handled as a separate product or SKU. Each required a line on order forms, each required its own slot in warehouses, and each had to be picked separately. However, total volume of tissue handled remained the same. The volume that was once white was now merely spread over five colors. From the co-op's warehousing standpoint, the only result had been to raise handling costs as a percentage of sales volume.

The co-op's small-store members, which continued to carry only white tissue and toilet paper, thought that it was unfair for the co-op to raise its handling charges because some of its large-store members now wanted to carry five colors of tissue. Large-store members retorted that they had to carry this variety if they were to compete successfully with the chains.

The main warehouse, built in 1968, had now reached its capacity. Actually, it was over capacity. It was built and engineered to carry 7,000 to 7,500 SKUs, but it was now carrying just over 8,000. Some items were doubled up in slots or left in aisles or at one of the receiving docks, but these practices were causing operational difficulties and driving up costs.

At the directors' quarterly meeting, a proposal was made to raise the co-op's charges to its members from 23 percent to 27 percent to generate more funds for capital investment.

Money was needed for a new 32,000-square-foot warehouse in Billings that could handle up to 10,500 SKUs.

At the meeting, Seth Hardy, a long-time director who operated a small store at Absarokee, Montana, and who generally spoke for the small-store members said, "Our warehouse now handles over 8,000 different items. We're told that we need a new one, costing God-knows-what so we can handle 10,000 to 11,000 different items. It's the tissue issue all over again. The manufacturers want to make the same thing in 10 colors and want 10 times the shelf space and 10 separate bins in our warehouse!"

"Big stores see things differently," said Peter Bright, the co-op's general manager. "Manufacturers are so anxious to get shelf space for new products that they'll even bribe a store owner to give them space on a shelf. They call it a 'stocking allowance.'"

"That hasn't happened to me," retorted Hardy. "Is it because my store is too small or that I look too honest?"

"Probably both," was Bright's reply.

"How's the bribe paid?" asked Chris Jones, a director who owned a large store.

"I'm not sure that I should know the answer to that," said Bright, "but I've been told that if they're dealing with the store owner they offer several free cases of other items in their product line that the store is already carrying. If they're dealing with a salaried manager, they may slip him or her some cash, or so I've been told."

"Maybe we can get them to bribe us to stock their goods in our warehouse," commented Jones.

Hardy gave Jones an angry look and then snapped, "We're straying from the topic. Our business as a co-op is not increasing. Therefore, I make the following motion: Resolved, that to keep the number of different items our warehouse handles limited to 8,000, all Wyomo buyers be limited to a certain number of SKUs, with the total assigned to all buyers totaling 8,000. If a buyer wants to add a SKU, he or she will have to drop another."

QUESTIONS

1. Co-op members presently pay for goods "on the basis of cost to the co-op plus 23 percent to cover warehousing and transportation from the warehouses to the members' retail stores." Is this a fair way to cover warehousing costs? Can you think of a better way? If so, describe it.

2. Answer the problem posed in question 1 with respect to transportation costs.

3. Toward the end of the case, Bright describes how some manufacturers pay bribes in order to get shelf space in retail stores. Should retailers accept such bribes? Why or why not?

4. The case says, "Stores were responsible for placing orders with the co-op, although a co-op representative would call on a weekly basis, and one of her or his functions was to help some store operators complete their order forms." Is this a function that the co-op should be performing? Why or why not?

5. The case mentions that some of the larger stores that belonged to the co-op sometimes threatened to form their own co-op. Assume that you are hired by some of them to study the feasibility of such a move. List the various topics that you would include in your study.

6. How would you vote on Hardy's motion? Why?

7. Would it make a difference whether you represented a large or small store? Why?

8. Are there other strategies that the co-op might pursue to overcome this problem? If so, describe.

3

Logistics and Information Technology

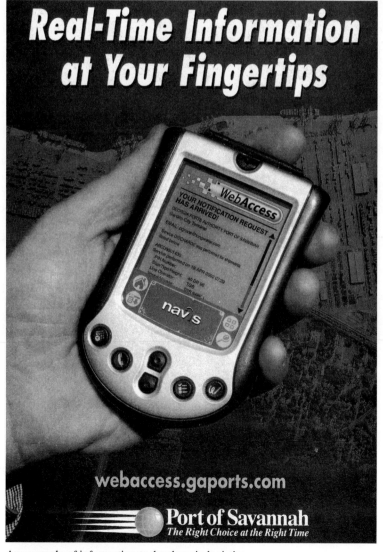

An example of information technology in logistics

Key Terms

- Application service providers (ASP)
- Artificial intelligence (AI)
- Automatic identification technologies
- Data mining
- Decision support system (DSS)
- E-fulfillment
- Electronic data interchange (EDI)

- Enterprise resource planning (ERP) system
- Logistics exchanges
- Logistics information system (LIS)
- Office automation system
- Simulation
- Transaction processing system (TPS)

Objectives

- To appreciate the importance of effective and efficient utilization of information for logistics management
- To learn about general types of information systems and their logistical applications
- To understand the impact of electronic commerce on channel design
- To understand key differences between the logistics of e-fulfillment and the logistics of traditional fulfillment

There have been many changes in the logistics discipline since the first edition of this book was published in the mid-1970s. The first edition, for example, primarily focused on physical distribution management and the corresponding definition emphasized the *movement and storage of goods.* The current edition of this book, by contrast, is focused on logistics and its role in supply-chain management. Moreover, the corresponding definition of logistics (see Chapter 1) mentions the *flows and storage of goods, services, and related information.*

The effective and efficient utilization of information can be quite beneficial to logistics and supply-chain management. According to Professor Rutner and colleagues, four of the more prominent benefits include the following:

- Greater knowledge and visibility across the supply chain, which makes it possible to replace inventory with information
- Greater awareness of customer demand via point-of sale data, which can help improve planning and reduce variability in the supply chain
- Better coordination of manufacturing, marketing, and distribution through enterprise resource planning (ERP) tools
- More streamlined order processing and reduced lead-times enabled by coordinated logistics information systems[1]

In short, the effective and efficient use of information allows organizations to simultaneously reduce their costs and improve customer satisfaction. For example, the ability

---

[1]Stephen M. Rutner, Brian J. Gibson, Kate L. Vitasek, and Craig G. Gustin, "Is Technology Filling the Information Gap?" *Supply Chain Management Review,* March/April 2001, pp. 58–63.

to replace inventory with information reduces costs and improves customer satisfaction in the sense that organizations are more capable of stocking the inventory that is closer to what their customers will demand.

Before proceeding further, it's important to distinguish between *data* and *information*. Professors Zikmund and d'Amico note that "data are simply facts—recorded measures of certain phenomena—whereas information is a body of facts in a format suitable for decision making."[2] Advances in technological hardware and software now allow contemporary logisticians access to abundant amounts of data in relatively short periods of time. Contemporary logisticians and supply-chain managers must determine which data are relevant for their purposes, must organize and analyze this data, and then must act on it—and do so in as short a time period as possible.

The first part of this chapter will provide an overview of general types of information management systems that are applicable across each business function. In addition, examples of how these general types of information systems might be specifically applied in logistics management are provided. The remainder of the chapter focuses on select opportunities and challenges that are associated with new technologies such as electronic commerce.

General Types of Information Management Systems

Professor Steven Alter has identified six different types of information systems that are applicable to every business function.[3] These six categories, summarized in Figure 3-1, form the basis of the discussion in this section.

Office Automation System

Office automation systems provide effective ways to process personal and organizational business data, to perform calculations, and to create documents.[4] Included in office automation systems are general software packages—word processing, spreadsheet, presentation, and database management applications—that most students probably learned in an introductory computer class.

The most relevant general software package for logisticians is the spreadsheet. Whereas early spreadsheet programs for personal computers were little more than speedy calculators, today's spreadsheets have a multitude of capabilities that allow managers to solve a variety of business problems relatively quickly and inexpensively.

Indeed, logistics spreadsheet applications into the early 1990s tended to reflect the rather limited capabilities of the existing software packages. For example, representative topics included economic order quantity (EOQ) calculations, warehouse sizing, transportation modal and carrier decisions, production planning, and center of gravity location decisions, among others.[5] As we moved through the 1990s, increased spread-

---

[2]William G. Zikmund and Michael d'Amico, *Marketing,* 7th edition, Cincinnati, OH: Southwestern, 2001, p. 125.

[3]The framework in this section is adapted from S. Alter, *Information Systems,* 4th edition, Upper Saddle River, NJ: Prentice Hall, 2002.

[4]Steven Alter, *Information Systems,* 4th edition, Upper Saddle River, NJ: Prentice Hall, 2002, p. 191.

[5]John E. Tyworth and William L. Grenoble, "Spreadsheet Modeling in Logistics: Advancing Today's Educational Tools," *Journal of Business Logistics,* Vol. 12, No. 1, 1991, pp. 1–25.

System type	Logistics examples
Office automation system: provides effective ways to process personal and organizational business data, to perform calculations, and to create documents	Spreadsheet applications to calculate optimal order quantities, facility location, transport cost minimization, among others
Communication system: helps people work together by interacting and sharing information in many different forms	Virtual meetings via computer technology Voice-based order picking
Transaction processing system (TPS): collects and stores information about transactions; controls some aspects of transactions	Electronic data interchange Automatic identification technologies such as bar codes Point-of-sale systems
Management information system (MIS) and executive information system (EIS): converts TPS data into information for monitoring performance and managing an organization; provides executives information in a readily accessible format	Logistics information system
Decision support system (DSS): helps people make decisions by providing information, models, or analysis tools	Simulation Application-specific software such as warehouse management systems Data mining
Enterprise system: creates and maintains consistent data processing methods and an integrated database across multiple business functions	Logistics modules of enterprise resource planning systems

FIGURE 3-1 General Types of Information Management Systems

Source: Taken from Steven Alter, *Information Systems,* 4th edition, Upper Saddle River, NJ: Prentice Hall, 2002, p. 191.

sheet capabilities allowed organizations to analyze issues that had traditionally been solved by specially designed computer programs. In this vein, the classic issue of transportation cost minimization—transporting products from multiple sources to multiple destinations, at a minimum transportation cost—could be analyzed using spreadsheet software.[6] More recently, spreadsheets have been used to determine the optimal number of warehouse locations for key customers of a regional chemical distributor.[7]

---

[6]Brian J. Parker and David J. Caine, "Minimizing Transportation Costs: An Efficient and Effective Approach for the Spreadsheet User," *Transport Logistics,* Vol. 1, No. 2, 1997, pp. 129–137.

[7]Charles A. Watts, "Using a Personal Computer to Solve a Warehouse Location/Consolidation Problem," *Production and Inventory Management Journal,* Vol. 41, No. 4, 2000, pp. 23–28.

Communication System

Communication systems help various stakeholders—employees, suppliers, customers—work together by interacting and sharing information in many different forms.[8] From a logistical perspective, the importance of well-defined and well-executed communication systems was highlighted by the events of September 11, 2001, especially for companies that use or provide airfreight services. Because of the total shutdown of the U.S. aviation system for several days following the terrorist attacks, many air shipments were diverted onto trucks, thus delaying many shipment deliveries. As such, airfreight providers such as FedEx worked feverishly to inform customers when their shipments would be arriving.[9]

Many advances in telecommunication technology—such as fax machines, electronic mail, cellular phones, among others—have occurred in the not-too-distant past. As recently as the 1990s, some of these technologies were considered workplace "luxuries." Today, by contrast, many of these technologies are essential for enabling the contemporary logistician to perform his or her job.

For example, companies with global logistics operations are now using technology to assist with *virtual meetings* in which employees located around the world can simultaneously "attend" a particular meeting. One manager can lead the meeting with information transmitted to all attendees via computer, and each attendee has the opportunity to contribute individual insights through online feedback.[10]

Moreover, the effectiveness and efficiency of logistics communications continues to be enhanced with evolutions in telecommunication technology. For instance, an emerging technology as this book is being prepared involves the ability for managers to access e-mail through cell phones. However, in the not-too-distant future, it may be possible to conduct video conferencing through cell phones, thus reducing "the maze of communication difficulties that confront any global logistics operation."[11]

Voice-based order picking represents another example of how an organizational communication system can improve logistical effectiveness and efficiency. Early voice-based picking systems were characterized by high adoption costs, poor voice quality, and systems that were easily disrupted by other noises. Contemporary voice-based systems, by contrast, are less costly, more powerful, have better voice quality, and are less cumbersome for workers to use. Companies that have adopted newer-generation voice-based technology have reported productivity increases in terms of lower employee turnover and higher pick accuracy.[12]

Transaction Processing System (TPS)

A **transaction processing system** collects and stores information about transactions and may also control some aspects of transactions. The primary objective of a TPS is the efficient processing of transactions, and to this end, organizations can choose to do

---

[8]Alter, 2002, Chapter 5.

[9]Kristen S. Krause, "FedEx's 9–11 Response," *Traffic World,* September 9, 2002, pp. 12–13.

[10]"Technology Boosts Communication Options for Global Logistics Operations," *Transportation & Distribution,* June 2001, pp. 6–7.

[11]Ibid.

[12]Andrew Kaplan, "Putting Your Warehouse on Speaking Terms," *Food Logistics,* March 15, 2002, pp. 48–49.

batch or real-time processing.[13] With batch processing, data are collected and stored for processing at a later time, with the later time perhaps being based on schedule (e.g., process every 6 hours) or volume (e.g., process once 25 transactions have accumulated) considerations. Real-time processing, not surprisingly, means that transactions are processed as they are received. Although batch processing might be somewhat out of step with the contemporary emphasis on speed and time reduction, it can be quite effective when real-time processing is not necessary. Moreover, in comparison with real-time systems, batch processing tends to be less costly and easier for employees to learn.

A prominent example of a logistics-related TPS is **electronic data interchange (EDI),** the computer-to-computer transmission of business data in a structured format. Since EDI provides for the seamless transmission of data across companies (assuming technological compatibility), it can facilitate the integration of, and coordination between, supply-chain participants. Thus, firms with strong EDI links to both suppliers and customers have a substantial advantage over supply-chain arrangements without good EDI implementations. Common uses of EDI include invoicing, purchase orders, pricing, advanced shipment notices, electronic funds transfer, and bill payment.

EDI has a number of benefits, including reductions in document preparation and processing time, inventory carrying costs, personnel costs, information float, shipping errors, returned goods, lead times, order cycle times, and ordering costs. In addition, EDI may lead to increases in cash flow, billing accuracy, productivity, and customer satisfaction. Potential drawbacks to EDI include a lack of awareness of its benefits, high setup costs, lack of standard formats, and incompatibility of computer hardware and software.

These drawbacks, and the dramatic rise of the Internet, have resulted in speculation that EDI is an obsolete technology and unlikely to be relevant to logistics and supply-chain management in the future. In reality, many supply-chain professionals argue that EDI will continue to play a key role in logistics and supply-chain management, in part because it reduces costs associated with inventory, order management, and transportation.[14] Moreover, the Internet may actually be a complement to, rather than substitute for, EDI, in that current users indicate their future EDI transactions are likely to involve a combination of the more traditional value-added networks and the Internet—as opposed to solely using the Internet for EDI transactions.[15]

Widespread global usage of EDI in the foreseeable future may be limited by several factors. First, approximately two-thirds of the world's population lacks access to telephones; as a result, EDI will be used primarily in developed countries. Moreover, EDI standards are not uniform across countries, and the situation has been complicated in recent years with the growth of the Internet and XML (extensible markup language). Importantly, however, the two most prominent global EDI standards—ANSI and EDIFACT—have agreed to work with the Electronic Business XML initiative "to establish a set of core components for global business-process integration."[16]

---

[13]Alter, 2002, Chapter 5.

[14]Amy Zuckerman, "EDI: Not Dead Yet," *Purchasing,* September 16, 1999, pp. 26–27.

[15]"E-Commerce Study: EDI Still Popular Among Distributors," *Purchasing,* February 2, 2001, pp. 96–98.

[16]Michael Meehan, "EDI, EBXML Groups Agree to Cooperate," *Computerworld,* July 2, 2001, pp. 1–2.

Automatic identification technologies, another type of logistics-related TPS, include optical character recognition (which can read letters, words, and numbers), machine vision (which can scan, inspect, and interpret what it views), voice-data entry (which can record and interpret a human voice), radio-frequency identification (which is used where there is no line of sight between scanner and label), and magnetic strips.

Nevertheless, bar code scanners currently remain the most popular automatic identification system in use. They work to integrate suppliers and customers along the supply chain because all parties read the same labels; in addition, the transfer of goods between parties can be recorded by simple electronic means. Traditionally, laser scanners have been used to read bar codes. The scanners record inventory data and may be directly attached to a computer that uses the data to adjust inventory records and track product movement.

Numerous advances have been made in recent years in bar code technology. For example, the traditional 12-digit universal product code (UPC), while well suited to products in packaged units (e.g., box of cereal, DVD player), is somewhat lacking with respect to products that are sold by weight (e.g., hamburger, fish, deli items). Because these products typically need more detail than can be provided by the 12-digit UPC, modified bar code symbology, in the form of Reduced Space Symbology (RSS), has been developed. The RSS allows for more data to be included on the bar code.[17] The different advances in bar code technology often require a generation of bar code readers beyond the laser scanner. So-called "smart cameras" are an especially popular choice in the early years of the twenty-first century because of their ability to read traditional as well as two-dimensional bar codes—something that cannot be done by laser scanners.[18]

Automatic identification systems are an essential component in point-of-sale (POS) systems. Operationally, POS systems involve scanning UPC labels, either by passing the product over an optical scanner or recording it with a handheld scanner. The UPC is read and recorded into a database that supplies information such as the product's price, applicable taxes, whether food stamps can be used, and so on. The specific price of each product and its description are also flashed on a monitor screen positioned near the counter. When all the products have been recorded, the customer receives verification that lists the products purchased, the price of each article, and the total bill.

Ultimately, the idea behind POS systems is to provide data to guide and enhance managerial decision making, as illustrated by the variety of ways that POS data can be used in the restaurant industry. One restaurant with multiple dining areas, for example, uses POS data to identify potential no-shows by analyzing customers who have reserved tables in the same evening for two (or more) of the dining areas. Another restaurant implemented a POS system that resulted in a substantial improvement in order fulfillment; the POS system virtually eliminated the largest cause of mistakes: handwritten orders.[19]

---

[17]"The Incredible Shrinking Barcode," *Chain Store Age,* July 2001, p. 62.

[18]Susan Snyder, "Smart Cameras—The Future of Bar Code Scanners?" *Frontline Solutions,* November 2001, pp. 67, 75.

[19]Margaret Sheridan, "Touch Control," *Restaurants & Institutions,* October 15, 2000, pp. 94–97.

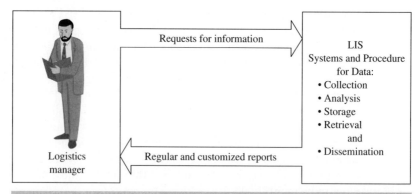

FIGURE 3-2 Structure and Function of a Logistics Information System

Source: Adapted from Michael Etzel, Bruce Walker, and William Stanton, *Marketing,* 12th edition (New York, NY: McGraw-Hill Irwin, 2001), p. 182.

Management Information System (MIS) and Executive Information System (EIS)

These systems convert TPS data into information for monitoring performance and managing an organization, with the objective of providing managers and executives with the information they really need.[20] To this end, a **logistics information system** (LIS) can be defined as "The people, equipment, and procedures to gather, sort, analyze, evaluate, and distribute needed, timely, and accurate information to logistics decision makers."[21]

As shown in Figure 3-2, an LIS begins with a logistics manager requesting information and ends with the manager receiving regular and customized reports. In order for logistics managers to receive *needed* information, it's important that they be fairly specific when submitting requests. For example, if a logistics manager wants information about a specific warehouse or distribution center, then she or he needs to request information on, say, "the Chicago warehouse" rather than information on "corporate warehouses."

Timely information would appear to be incumbent upon the effectiveness and efficiency of a company's particular LIS, and timely information can encompass several dimensions. On the one hand, *timely* can refer to the up-to-date status of information, which can be influenced by a company's collection and analysis procedures. Information collection should emphasize both internal and external sources; unfortunately, internal sources of logistics information are not always as plentiful as desired. Indeed, research into the business value attributable to logistics discovered that "logistics measurement is happening much less frequently than one might imagine."[22] External sources focus on information from outside the company and includes infor-

---

[20]Alter, 2002, Chapter 5.

[21]Adapted from a definition of marketing information system provided by Gary Armstrong and Philip Kotler in *Marketing: An Introduction,* 5th edition, Upper Saddle River, NJ: Prentice Hall, 2000, Chapter 4.

[22]James S. Keebler, Karl B. Manrodt, David A. Durtsche, and D. Michael Ledyard, *Keeping Score: Measuring the Business Value of Logistics in the Supply Chain,* Oak Brook, IL: Council of Logistics Management, 1999, Chapter 2.

mation about customers, competitors, and suppliers, along with information about economic, technological, political, legal, and sociocultural environments.

With respect to information analyses, the POS systems described in the previous section are excellent for collecting data—but the data also must be analyzed to be of any value to managers. Consider the following quote from a restaurant consultant: "When restaurants come to us with financial problems, the first thing I ask to see is the data. When they show me a year's worth of numbers, *many times no one has really looked at it* (authors' emphasis)."[23] The following section on decision support systems provides more about information analyses.

Timely also can refer to how quickly managers receive the information requested; this is impacted by each company's retrieval and dissemination procedures. A manager's ability to quickly receive information can be impacted by computer hardware and software, and faster and more powerful microchips have helped to reduce retrieval and dissemination times. In a similar vein, timely dissemination of information has been facilitated by advances in personal digital assistants and cell phones. Alternatively, retrieval and dissemination can be slowed by hardware and software glitches, including power outages, system crashes, and computer viruses.

Accurate information may also reflect the effectiveness and efficiency of a company's logistics information system. As such, an LIS must be concerned with the nature and quality of the relevant data; for instance, while the Internet can provide access to tremendous amounts of external information at a very low cost, the validity of some Internet information is suspect. Keep in mind the *GIGO*—garbage in/garbage out—principle: Information that is erroneous, misrepresented, and/or unclear will likely result in poor decisions by logisticians.

Decision Support Systems (DSS)

Decision support systems help managers make decisions by providing information, models, or analysis tools,[24] and they can be widely applied and used by logisticians. Several of the more prominent logistics-related DSS techniques are discussed in the following paragraphs.

Simulation involves a computer model that is a series of mathematical relationships, often expressed as a series of linear equations. Simulation reliability is achieved by making the model as akin to the real world as possible. Such factors as transport mode availability, transportation costs, location of vendors, warehouse locations, customer locations, customer service requirements, and plant locations must all be accurately reflected in the model.

The primary advantage of simulation is that it enables the firm to test the feasibility of proposed changes at relatively little expense. In addition, it prevents firms from experiencing the public embarrassment of making a major change in their logistics system that might result in a deterioration of customer service levels or an increase in total operating expense.

---

[23]Sheridan, 2000.

[24]Alter, 2002, Chapter 5.

Many logistics system simulation models exist, and they differ according to mathematical approach, computer capacity needed, and amount of data input. Many of the programs have as their initial focus the improvement of customer service. A second focus is to integrate inbound and outbound logistics functions. Although simulation can be a powerful analytic tool, a poorly constructed simulation involving bad data or inaccurate assumptions about the relationships among variables can deliver suboptimal or unworkable solutions to logistics problems. Insights gleaned from simulation experts provide a list of what not to do:

1. Performing a simulation without a clear definition of the objectives
2. Believing that the model itself can compensate for poor data collection
3. Lacking an understanding of statistical processes
4. Failing to do order profiling
5. Ignoring the effects of randomness
6. Incorporating randomness inappropriately
7. Failing to consider down time
8. Making illogical assumptions
9. Failing to question the results
10. Failing to recognize that simulation is a study tool[25]

Simulation is an important tool and is discussed also in Chapter 14. As Figure 3-3 illustrates, very little business behavior cannot be simulated.

Artificial intelligence (AI) "is a branch of computer science that studies the computational requirements for tasks such as perception, reasoning, and learning, and develops systems to perform those tasks."[26] AI is a highly sophisticated use of the computer in which it can be programmed to "think" as a trained, skilled human would in specific situations, and AI encompasses a number of different areas such as expert systems, fuzzy logic, and neural networks. Anyone who is familiar with computers knows computers can be programmed to respond to different questions, often by asking more definitive questions. In theory, one needs to know the questions to ask, when and how to ask them, and also the various relationships among all possible answers—a difficult but not impossible task.

Seminal AI research in logistics involved the development of AI systems for managing certain parts inventories of the United States Air Force.[27] This research utilized eight human experts to develop and critique a long list of decision rules that a computer model had to follow to answer questions regarding inventory stocking levels. The magnitude of the task is illustrated by the fact that the final expert system that was devised contained nearly 450 separate decisions rules. One of the more popular recent applications of AI in logistics is focused on select issues with highway traffic, to include predicting urban traffic flows and managing traffic congestion.

---

[25]Karen A. Field, "Data Quality Can Make or Break a Simulation," *Modern Materials Handling,* January 1997, p. 57.

[26]David B. Leake, "Artificial Intelligence," in *Van Nostrand Scientific Encyclopedia,* 9th edition, New York: Wiley, 2002.

[27]Mary K. Allen, *The Development of an Artificial Intelligence System for Inventory Management Using Multiple Experts,* Oak Brook, IL: The Council of Logistics Management, 1986.

"It can't actually think, but when it makes a mistake,
it can put the blame on some other computer."

FIGURE 3-3 Computers Can Simulate Many Forms of Business Behavior

Source: Reproduced by permission of the artist and the Masters Agency.

A third type of DSS is what can be broadly labeled as *application-specific software,* which has been developed to help managers deal with specific logistics functions or activities. This software can focus on either planning or operational (execution) capabilities and includes, but is not limited to, supply-chain management (SCM) software, transportation management systems (TMS), and warehouse management systems (WMS).[28]

Although growth in the global economy has been slow in the early part of the twenty-first century, rapid growth (in excess of 10 percent per annum) has occurred in the usage of application-specific software in logistics, particularly among those packages with an operational (execution) emphasis.[29] Some of the more prominent vendors of application-specific software include i2 Technologies, SAP, Manugistics, and Manhattan Associates.

---

[28]Sunil Chopra and Peter Meindl, *Supply Chain Management: Strategy, Planning, and Operation,* Upper Saddle River, NJ: Prentice Hall, 2001, Chapter 12.

[29]Diane Trommer, "Supply Chain Software Grows Up," *EBN,* September 2002, pp. 22–24.

Data mining, which can be defined as "the application of mathematical tools to large bodies of data in order to extract correlations and rules,"[30] is a DSS technique that has grown in popularity in recent years. Data mining utilizes sophisticated quantitative techniques to find "hidden" patterns in large volumes of data; hopefully, these patterns will allow managers to improve their decision making abilities. Although data mining has been characterized as a "fishing expedition" of sorts—in the sense of applying sophisticated quantitative techniques merely to find relationships, whether meaningful or not—data mining, in reality, should follow a well-defined methodology.[31]

Data mining has experienced widespread applications in terms of customer satisfaction and customer relationship management. In this vein, logistical benefits from data mining can arise when supply and demand data are analyzed together, rather than separately. Analysis of a grocery chain's frequent shopper programs, for example, might reveal that several slower-selling items are consistently purchased by high-spending households. Rather than eliminating these slow-moving items, stores might continue to stock limited quantities of them in deference to the high-spending households.[32]

Enterprise System

Enterprise systems, the final general type of information management system to be discussed, create and maintain consistent data processing methods and an integrated database across multiple business functions.[33] The most prominent example of enterprise systems are probably **enterprise resource planning (ERP)** systems, with Baan, J. D. Edwards, Oracle, PeopleSoft, and SAP considered as the leading providers of these systems. The attractiveness of ERP systems comes from their potential for lower costs as well as increased productivity and customer satisfaction.[34]

Although contemporary ERP systems encompass a firmwide perspective, their origins can be traced back to logistics and manufacturing in the form of inventory control and materials requirement planning programs.[35] Unlike these earlier programs, today's ERP systems (conceptually, at least) provide an opportunity for all functional areas within a firm to access and analyze a common database—which might not have been previously possible because certain data was proprietary to a particular functional area.

Theoretically, the goal of ERP systems is enterprisewide coordination of relevant business processes. However, this is a task of monumental proportions, so most contemporary ERP systems focus on achieving three objectives: integrating financial data, standardizing manufacturing processes, and standardizing human resource data.[36]

---

[30]Sam Joseph and Daniel Scuka, "AI," *Japan Inc.,* November 2001, pp. 20–28.

[31]Michael S. Garver, "Try New Data-Mining Techniques," *Marketing News,* September 16, 2002, pp. 31–33.

[32]Eddy Goldberg, "Consumer Knowledge Creates Better Trading Relationships," *Food Logistics,* September 15, 2000, pp. 52–54.

[33]Alter, 2002, Chapter 5.

[34]Lori MacVittie, "Buckle Up: Implementing an ERP Takes Time and Patience," *Network Computing,* Vol. 12, No. 6, pp. 97–100.

[35]Kuldeep Kumar and Jos van Hillegersberg, "ERP Experiences and Evolution," *Communications of the ACM,* Vol. 43, No. 4, 2000, pp. 23–26.

[36]MacVittie, "Buckle Up."

These three objectives tend to reflect the specific competencies of important ERP providers; for example, PeopleSoft's historical expertise (perhaps not surprisingly, given its name) has been in human resource management issues.

One of the most frequently mentioned shortcomings of ERP systems involves the costs of installation. It's common knowledge that ERP software is relatively expensive; for many years, ERP systems were only affordable to high-revenue organizations (e.g., Fortune 500). However, the software is only one part of ERP implementation costs. For example, the vast amounts of data necessary for ERP systems may necessitate new or upgraded computer hardware. Other hidden or frequently overlooked costs of ERP implementation include employee training, data conversion (converting existing data into a usable and consistent format), and integrating and testing a new system.[37]

A second shortcoming is that implementation of ERP systems can be a very time-consuming process. Indeed, many of the hidden costs of ERP implementation mentioned in the previous paragraph are the result of hidden time associated with ERP implementation. For instance, employee training, data conversion, and integrating and testing the new system all require time beyond the installation of the ERP software itself. A general rule of thumb is that actual time to implement ERP systems may range from two to four times longer than the time period specified by the ERP vendor.

The preceding discussion on costs and time suggests that some ERP implementations may not go as smoothly as planned. Moreover, glitches in ERP implementation often have led to multiple logistical problems. For example, one industrial supplier's botched ERP implementation resulted in its having to use manual documentation for customer shipments for several months after installation. To compound matters, this company was unable to bill its customers—and thus collect revenues—for approximately a four-month period. In a similar fashion, ERP implementation at a large chemical company resulted in over twice as much inventory and poorer on-time delivery performance when compared to pre-ERP times—and the company continues to struggle to achieve pre-ERP inventory and delivery performance.[38]

The logistical capabilities of today's ERP systems might be characterized as uneven. Because the core competencies of key ERP providers have tended to be in areas outside of logistics (such as PeopleSoft's human resource focus), some early ERP programs did not offer logistics modules. While logistics modules are now available with some of the more prominent ERP programs (such as SAP R/3), these modules may not always be installed when individual companies adopt a particular ERP system.

Some organizations choose to address the logistical deficiencies of ERP systems by linking or attaching specialized logistics software such as WMS and/or TMS to the chosen ERP system. This is not always a smooth and seamless process; it can require large amounts of computer code and can be both costly and time-consuming.

---

[37]John Leitch, "The Cost of Cutting Costs," *Contract Journal,* March 6, 2002, pp. 8–9.

[38]Charlie Rooney and Chuck Bangert, "Avoiding the Pitfalls in ERP Implementation," *Adhesives Age,* Vol. 43, No. 12, 2000, p. 64.

Electronic Commerce and Logistics

Electronic commerce has been defined as "any form of economic activity that can be conducted via electronic connections."[39] Although electronic connections can include phone and telegraph lines, electronic communications are most commonly associated with computer-to-computer connections, such as EDI and the Internet. This section focuses on electronic connections via the Internet, in part because of suggestions that the Internet will "become the only medium for electronic transactions within the next decade."[40] Certainly the Internet can influence logistical strategies and tactics with respect to both business-to-consumer (B2C) and business-to-business (B2B) transactions.

The Internet has had profound impacts upon individual logistics functions as well as upon channel design. With respect to the former, the Internet offers the potential for both cost reduction and service improvement across and within logistics functions. Research by Professor Lancioni and colleagues found transportation and order management to be the two logistics functions with the highest amount of Internet usage. Within transportation, the Internet can be used to monitor the on-time performance of carriers and to monitor claims; the Internet's use within order management includes customer order placement and providing customer price quotes.[41] These are just a few of the ways in which the Internet can be used for transportation and order management. Numerous examples also demonstrate how the Internet can be utilized in other logistics functions.

As for channel design, the Internet allows companies to offer an alternate distribution channel to already existing channels. In some cases, this alternate channel is direct (i.e., no intermediaries between the producer and final customer) in nature because the final customer orders directly from the producer rather than through an intermediary. The logistical challenges of direct channels can be quite different from those of indirect channels; for example, individual customers are likely to order in much smaller quantities than are intermediaries. These smaller quantities require different packaging, materials handling, and transportation capabilities than do larger quantities.

Logistical intermediaries. While the Internet is thought to result in channel disintermediation—that is, the removal of intermediaries between producer and consumer—it has spawned several new types of logistical intermediaries. These intermediaries are particularly prevalent in B2B transactions. Two of the more prominent examples are **logistics exchanges** and **application service providers.**

At the present time, there does not appear to be a consensus definition of what is meant by a *logistics exchange.* However, there is general agreement that logistics exchanges are online portals offering services in at least one of four categories: (1) enhancing procurement services through posting and sharing general information;

---

[39]R. T. Wigand, "Electronic Commerce: Definition, Theory, and Context," *The Information Society,* Vol. 13, No. 1, 1997, pp. 1–16.

[40]Werner Delfmann, Sascha Albers, and Martin Gehring, "The Impact of Electronic Commerce on Logistics Service Providers," *International Journal of Physical Distribution & Logistics Management,* Vol. 32, No. 3, 2002, pp. 203–222.

[41]Richard A. Lancioni, Michael F. Smith, and Terence A. Oliva, "The Role of the Internet in Supply Chain Management," *Industrial Marketing Management,* Vol. 29, January 2000, pp. 45–56.

(2) matching shippers and carriers; (3) executing relevant transactions; and (4) helping companies transact with their partners.[42] National Transportation Exchange (NTE) is often credited as being the first online logistics exchange; it started in the mid-1990s as an auction site where shippers could find carriers for their freight.[43] Other logistics exchanges, to name just a few, include Celarix, Logistics.com, and Nistevo.

Even though there is general agreement that the long-term future for logistics exchanges is bright, there has been a noticeable contraction in their ranks during the early years of the twenty-first century. This contraction among logistics exchanges, which is expected to continue, takes several forms. For example, some logistics exchanges ceased operations due to lack of customers, lack of sufficient funding, or poorly thought out value propositions. A second method of contraction involves merger or acquisition; for example, in late 2002 Manhattan Associates announced its intentions to acquire Logistics.com.

As is the case with logistics exchanges, the relative newness of application service providers (ASP) has yet to generate a consensus definition of the concept. In this text, an ASP refers to "a company that offers individuals or enterprises access over the Internet to applications and related services that would otherwise have to be located in their own personal or enterprise computers."[44] ASPs allow individuals or enterprises to rent or lease particular software applications for a particular period of time, thus avoiding capital expenditures for purchasing computer hardware, software, and other necessities. A number of logistics exchanges offer their services through applications service providers.

ASPs offer numerous advantages to potential customers. As pointed out in the previous paragraph, customers avoid capital investment, which should speed up their return on investment. In addition, many of the service agreements specify that ASPs provide software applications, Web servers, and around-the-clock customer support. Importantly, software upgrades are the ASP's responsibility, meaning that customers should have access to the latest software at a relatively low cost.[45]

Although ASPs appear to be quite attractive, particularly from a financial perspective, they have potential drawbacks. For example, because the Internet is the primary transaction medium, sensitive or proprietary data might not be as secure as would be the case with other mediums. Another potential problem is that response time may be slower if there is heavy Internet volume. Moreover, because of the growing number of ASPs, it is important for customers to use those ASPs that will best serve their needs.[46]

E-Fulfillment

The growth of electronic commerce has spawned a number of associated concepts, with one of the most important for our purposes being **e-fulfillment.** Like many other concepts related to electronic commerce, a myriad of definitions are currently in use

---

[42]Amanda Loudin, "Online Traffic Jam," *Food Logistics,* April 15, 2001, pp. 34–36.

[43]James Aaron Cooke, "A Virtual Transformation," *Logistics Management & Distribution,* March 2001, pp. 81–83.

[44]"Application Service Providers: Are They Ready for You?" *Nation's Restaurant News,* May 21, 2001, pp. 12–13.

[45]James Rogers and Jack Smith, "Advantages and Challenges of Implementing ASPs," *Plant Engineering,* October 2001, pp. 61–63.

[46]*Nation's Restaurant News,* May 21, 2001.

for *e-fulfillment*. Recent capstone logistics classes taught by one of this text's authors have come up with nearly 25 distinct definitions, ranging from "providing customers with a high level of service to satisfy their needs" to "coordinated inbound and outbound logistics functions that facilitate the management and delivery of customer orders placed online." The latter definition guides this text's discussion of e-fulfillment.

The importance of e-fulfillment was highlighted, in rather unfortunate fashion, by some egregious retailer failures during the 1999 holiday season. A number of online retailers proved that, while they were quite good at stimulating demand and receiving orders for certain products, they were far less adept at delivering the orders in a timely fashion. Orders that were supposed to be delivered before Hanukkah or Christmas arrived weeks or months late—if they arrived at all. The promises made versus actual performance disconnect of some online companies during that season was so pronounced that several ending up paying fines to the U.S. Federal Trade Commission.

A postmortem of the 1999 holiday season indicated two primary problems. First, a number of "pure" dot-com companies (i.e., those without alternate distribution channels) had limited knowledge of logistics and quickly became overwhelmed with having to satisfy customer demands once orders were received. Second, some of the "hybrid" companies (i.e., those with multiple retailing channels) had difficulties adapting their logistics systems to fit the nuances of online commerce. These companies were attempting to apply one-size-fits-all logistics strategies and tactics (or, mass logistics) to a situation that requires different types of logistics strategies and tactics.

One key decision concerns how e-fulfillment activities and practices will be integrated with the activities and practices of traditional fulfillment. Should an organization modify existing operating procedures? Should it expand existing facilities to incorporate e-fulfillment areas? Should it design and build a facility solely dedicated to e-fulfillment? Should it use an external e-fulfillment specialist? Should it require suppliers to ship orders directly to customers?[47] As noted previously, there's no single right or wrong answer, but it's important for an organization to carefully weigh the advantages and disadvantages of each alternative.

The logistics of both e-fulfillment and traditional fulfillment contain similarities. For example, many logistical functions and activities—such as transportation, warehousing, materials handling, and order management—occur in both e-fulfillment and traditional fulfillment. Likewise, both may use the same type of equipment and materials, such as bar coding and warehouse management systems.

Alternatively, powerful differences exist between e-fulfillment and traditional fulfillment with respect to the execution of logistics functions and activities. For example, the orders associated with e-fulfillment tend to be more plentiful and in much smaller quantities than those associated with traditional fulfillment. As such, e-fulfillment requires an order management system capable of handling high volumes of orders, and it's also essential that the information management system be capable of correctly transmitting each order so that it can be filled in a timely fashion.

Some experts believe that two of the primary logistical impacts of e-fulfillment involve order picking and packaging. Because of smaller order quantities, e-fulfillment

---

[47]Norman Saenz, Jr., "Picking the Best Practices for E-fulfillment," *IIE Solutions,* Vol. 33, No. 3, 2001, pp. 37–40.

is characterized by open-case, rather than full-case, picking; open-case picking is facilitated by materials handling equipment, such as totes and push carts. Moreover, open-case picking necessitates that products be slotted (placed) in locations that facilitate picking effectiveness and efficiency. Not surprisingly, e-fulfillment's smaller order quantities have important packaging implications as well, in the sense that companies need containers—small cartons, envelopes, bags—that are well suited to holding small quantities of product.[48]

Two other key logistical considerations for e-fulfillment involve transportation and returned orders. The smaller order quantities occasioned by e-commerce tend to favor transport companies with extensive delivery networks and expertise in parcel shipments. This, in turn, suggests that outbound shipments tend to be picked up at a loading dock by small-capacity vehicles, such as delivery vans.

While returned orders are an issue in all types of retailing, the return rates associated with e-commerce tend to be much higher than with other types of retailing; one estimate suggests 10 percent return rates for traditional forms of retailing, compared to approximately 30 percent for online purchases.[49] Because many of these returns are from individual customers, not businesses or organizations, companies engaged in e-commerce should attempt to make the return process as painless as possible, in part because many individual customers have limited, if any, knowledge about reverse logistics. As such, when online customers receive their orders, they might also receive information on how to return the order, return labeling, and a return container, such as an envelope or bag.

SUMMARY

This chapter discussed key issues of logistics and information technology. Six general types of information management systems were examined, with a particular emphasis on relevant logistical applications. Topics discussed include EDI, automatic identification technologies, artificial intelligence, data mining, and enterprise resource planning systems, among others.

The Internet and its impact on logistics management were discussed, as were logistical intermediaries, such as logistics exchanges, that have been spawned by the adoption of Internet technology. The chapter concluded with a discussion of the logistical challenges of e-fulfillment.

QUESTIONS FOR DISCUSSION AND REVIEW

1. In what ways can information be helpful in logistics and supply-chain management?
2. Name the six general types of information management systems, and give one logistics application for each one that you've named.
3. Do you view the spreadsheet as the most relevant general software package for logisticians? Why or why not?
4. How did communication systems facilitate logistics management in the immediate aftermath of the September 11, 2001, terrorist attacks?

---

[48]Saenz, 2001.
[49]Ibid.

5. What advances in telecommunications technology do you view as being most beneficial to logistics management? Why?
6. Discuss the benefits and drawbacks of EDI.
7. Do you believe that EDI is a viable technology for contemporary logistics management? Support your answer.
8. Discuss the relationship between automatic identification technologies and point-of-sale systems.
9. Discuss the importance of timely information to a logistics information system.
10. Discuss the importance of accurate information to a logistics information system.
11. The chapter listed 10 logistics simulation what not to do's. Which two do you think are most important? Why?
12. What kind of uses does artificial intelligence have for logistics?
13. What is data mining? How might it be used in logistics?
14. Discuss advantages and disadvantages of enterprise resource planning systems.
15. Go to the Web site of one of the ERP vendors mentioned in this chapter and learn about the package's logistical capabilities. Are you surprised by your findings? Why or why not?
16. Refer back to the logistical activities listed in Chapter 1; pick two that you're interested in and research how they have been influenced by the Internet. Are you surprised by your findings? Why or why not?
17. Do you think that logistics exchanges will exist in 2010? Support your answer.
18. Discuss the advantages and disadvantages of application service providers.
19. How is e-fulfillment similar to, and different from, traditional fulfillment?
20. Discuss some of the logistical implications of e-fulfillment with respect to order picking and packaging.

SUGGESTED READINGS

Angeles, Rebecca and Ravi Nath, "Partner Congruence in Electronic Data Interchange (EDI)-Enabled Relationships." *Journal of Business Logistics,* Vol. 22, No. 2, 2001, pp. 109–127.

Auramo, Jaana, Anna Aminoff, and Mikko Punakivi, "Research Agenda for E-Business Logistics Based on Professional Opinions." *International Journal of Physical Distribution & Logistics Management,* Vol. 32, No. 7, 2002, pp. 513–531.

Ayers, James B., "Supply Chain Information Systems: Putting the Process First." *Information Strategy: The Executive's Journal,* Spring 2000, pp. 11–17.

Green, Forrest B., "Managing the Unmanageable: Integrating the Supply Chain with New Developments in Software." *Supply Chain Management: An International Journal,* Vol. 6, No. 5, 2001, pp. 208–211.

Hill, Craig A., and Gary D. Scudder, "The Use of Electronic Data Interchange for Supply Chain Coordination in the Food Industry." *Journal of Operations Management,* Vol. 20, 2002, pp. 375–387.

Lancioni, Richard A., Michael F. Smith, and Terence A. Oliva, "The Role of the Internet in Supply Chain Management." *Industrial Marketing Management,* Vol. 29, 2000, pp. 45–56.

Larson, Paul D., and Jack D. Kulchitsky, "The Use and Impact of Communication Media in Purchasing and Supply Management." *Journal of Supply Chain Management: A Global Review of Purchasing & Supply,* Vol. 36, No. 3, 2000, pp. 29–39.

Lewis, Ira, "Logistics and Electronic Commerce: An Interorganizational Perspective." *Transportation Journal,* Vol. 40, No. 4, 2001, pp. 5–13.

Parker, Brain J., and David J. Caine, "Minimizing Transportation Costs: An Efficient and Effective Approach for the Spreadsheet User." *Transport Logistics,* Vol. 1, No. 2, 1997, pp. 129–137.

Rutner, Stephen M., Brian J. Gibson, Kate L. Vitasek, and Craig M. Gustin, "Is Technology Filling the Information Gap?" *Supply Chain Management Review,* Vol. 5, No. 2, 2001, pp. 58–64.

Sanders, Nada R., and Robert Premus, "IT Applications in Supply Chain Organizations: A Link Between Competitive Priorities and Organizational Benefits." *Journal of Business Logistics,* Vol. 23, No. 1, 2002, pp. 65–83.

Sedlak, Patrick S., "The Second Wave of E-Fulfillment." *Supply Chain Management Review,* Vol. 5, No. 3, 2001, pp. 82–88.

Van Hoek, Remko, "E-supply Chains—Virtually Non-Existing." *Supply Chain Management,* Vol. 6, No. 1, 2001, pp. 21–28.

Williams, Lisa R., Terry L. Esper, and John Ozment, "The Electronic Supply Chain: Its Impact on the Current and Future Structure of Strategic Alliances, Partnerships, and Logistics Leadership." *International Journal of Physical Distribution & Logistics Management,* Vol. 32, No. 8, 2002, pp. 703–719.

CASES

Case 3-1 Sports Car Care

Tayfun Bekiroglu, living in Santa Barbara, is a dot-com millionaire with a car collection consisting of 20 vintage sports cars. He wants to show five of these cars at the Pebble Beach Concours d'Elegance. Recently he realized that five of his cars needed both repair and repainting, although some needed total repainting while others needed only some touch-up work. He had his own shop with two bays, one for repairs and one for painting. Painting and repainting would occur after the repairs.

Tayfun wants to have his cars repaired and repainted within 30 working days. Each of the cars' repair and repaint times are indicated in Exhibit 3-A.

Use a Gantt chart and the following approach to answer the case questions. Information about Gantt Charts can be found on the Internet, as well as in operations management textbooks. Use this approach to figure out the order of the cars that

are going to be taken in for repairing and repainting. The cars needing the least amount of repair time should be taken first, whereas the cars with the least amount of paint/repaint time should be taken last. Once you find the car with the least amount of repair time, you put that car in first place and set the order for the remaining cars. The same applies to the car with the least amount of repaint time. You find the car with the least amount of repaint time, put it in last place, and deal with the remaining cars.

Therefore, you start from the beginning and from the end of the order and finish the order in the middle. At the middle, you may need to do some slight reshuffling. The next step is to draw the Gantt chart (Exhibit 3-B) according to the order you determined. Then, according to the Gantt chart that you draw, you should be able to determine the total time that is going to be consumed in the body shop.

EXHIBIT 3-A

Cars	Repair (days)	Paint (days)
(P) Porsche 911 Carrera 2	5	2
(F) Ferrari Testarossa	1	6
(A) Audi S8	9	7
(L) Lamborghini Diablo	3	8
(B) Bentley Continental GT	10	4

EXHIBIT 3-B

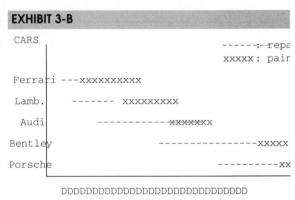

QUESTIONS

1. If Tayfun had a sixth car to repair/repaint, could he fit it inside the 30 working days limit? If so how long could the repairs and paint/repaint take?

2. Somewhat to his embarrassment, Tayfun suddenly learned that only cars built in the United States were to be shown at Pebble Beach. Luckily, he had some in his stable, though they also would need some repairs and painting/repainting. Following are the five U.S.-built cars with their required times for repair and paint/repaint.

Cars	Repair (days)	Paint (days)
(Q) Qvale	4	3
(F) Ford Shelby	2	7
(O) Olds Toronado	8	6
(C) Corvette	1	7
(D) Dodge Viper	9	5

Determine the order of the U.S. cars that are going to be taken into repair and repaint.

3. Draw a Gantt chart of the given work processes.

4. Calculate the total least amount of processing time for the work processes.

5. If Tayfun had a sixth U.S. car to repair/repaint, could he fit it inside the 30 working days limit? If so how long could the repairs and paint/repaint take?

Case 3-2   Just-in-Time in Kalamazoo

Jim Ballenger was president of a medium-size firm that manufactured mini motor homes in Kalamazoo, Michigan. The firm had expanded from a local Midwest market to a national one, including Southern California and New England. As markets had expanded, so too had sources of supply for the company, with major suppliers located in Southern California, the

Pacific Northwest, and Michigan. The decision to found the company in Michigan had been made for two reasons: Jim's former associates in the auto industry were there, and the largest single component of the mini—the truck or van chassis upon which the rest of the vehicle is built—was purchased from one of the U.S. light-truck makers.

Like others in the field, Jim's company actually manufactured very few of its components. Virtually the entire product was assembled from components purchased from outside vendors. There was, however, a well-defined order in which the components could most efficiently be installed in the vehicle. Recently, it had become clear to Jim that transportation and inventory costs were a relatively large portion of his component parts expenses and that they might be ripe for a substantial reduction. He had been hearing about just-in-time (JIT) systems. According to some notes he had taken at a professional meeting, the JIT production system was developed by the Toyota Motor Company more than 45 years ago. It involves an approach to inventory that, in turn, forces a complementary approach to production, quality control, supplier relations, and distributor relationships. The major tenets of JIT can be summarized as follows:

1. Inventory in itself is wasteful and should be minimized.
2. Minimum replenishment quantity is maintained for both manufactured and purchased parts.
3. Minimum inventory of semifinished goods should be maintained—in this case, partially completed motor homes.
4. Deliveries of inputs should be frequent and small.
5. The time needed to set up production lines should be reduced to the absolute minimum.
6. Suppliers should be treated as part of the production team. This means that the vendor makes every effort to provide outstanding service and quality and that there is usually a much longer-lasting relationship with a smaller number of suppliers than is common in the United States.
7. The objective of the production system is zero defects.
8. The finished product should be delivered on a very short lead time.

To the U.S. inventory planner, vice president of logistics, and production planner, an operation run on the preceding principles raised a number of disturbing prospects. Jim Ballenger was very aware of the costs that might arise if a JIT production system were to be established. From the materials management standpoint, the idea of deliberately planning many small shipments rather than a few large ones appeared to ensure higher freight bills, especially from more distant suppliers, for which freight rates would make the most difference.

With regard to competition among suppliers, Jim often had the opportunity, in the volatile mini-motor-home market, to buy out parts and component supplies from manufacturers that were going out of business. Those components could be obtained at a substantial savings, with the requirement that inventory in the particular parts be temporarily increased or that purchases from existing vendors be temporarily curtailed. Perhaps the greatest question raised by JIT, however, had to do with the probability of much more erratic production as a result of tight supplies of components. Both with suppliers' products and with his own, Jim operated with the (generally tacit) assumption that there would be some defective components purchased and that there would likely be something wrong with his product when it first came off the assembly line. For this reason, the Kalamazoo minis were extensively tested (Their advertising said, "We hope you'll never do what we do to your Kalamazoo mini."), as were the components prior to installation. To the extent that only a few of a particular type of component were on hand, the interruption in the production schedule would be that much greater. It might entail expensive rush orders for replacement components or equally expensive downtime for the entire plant.

Jim was also concerned about his relationship with his suppliers, as compared, say, to a large auto manufacturer. In the mini-motor-home business, generally the manufacturers are small and the component makers are large. In this situation, it was somewhat more difficult to see the idea of the supplier as a part of the production team, in the sense that the supplier would be expected to make a special effort in either quality control or delivery flexibility on behalf of one of its almost miniscule accounts.

Despite these concerns, Jim was painfully aware that he was using a public warehouse near his plant that usually contained between $500,000 and $1,000,000 in inventory, on which he paid more than 1.5 percent per month for the borrowed funds used to buy it, as well as expenses relating to the use of the warehouse itself. In addition, his firm was now producing so many different models (one with a bath, one with a shower only) and using so many different appliances (various types of radio, three varieties of refrigerator, and so forth) that the costs of a safety stock for each component were going up every day.

As an aid to making his decision on whether to try a JIT orientation at his plant, Jim's executive assistant, Kathy Williams, drew up a table that summarized the anticipated impacts of a JIT system (see Exhibit 3-C). The figures are based on random samples of inventory items. The major component of any mini motor home—the chassis—would always be purchased on a one-at-a-time basis from Ford, Chevrolet, Dodge, or International. With rare exception, it would always be available on demand. It would be delivered through the local dealer. If the

dealer did not have one in stock, one could easily be obtained from another area dealership.

Exhibit 3-C is a representative 10 percent sample of Ballenger's components inventory. It covers weekly use of each item, the current lot size purchased, and so on. Before figuring the total costs under the present and JIT systems, several additional facts must be noted. First, Ballenger's inventory carrying costs are assumed to be 20 percent per year on the average investment in inventory on hand, including its acquisition and transportation costs.

Second, under the current system, the number of units of each type of component kept in stock is calculated as follows: For those items purchased from vendors more than 500 miles away, a safety stock representing four weeks of use is maintained. For items from vendors between 100 and 500 miles away, a safety stock representing two weeks of use is maintained. For items from closer sources, a safety stock representing one week of use is maintained. In addition to safety stocks, the average inventory of any item is the current lot size purchased, divided by 2.

If you are familiar with Excel or other spreadsheet software, you might try using it here, although it is not necessary.

EXHIBIT 3-C 10 Percent Random Sample of Component Inventory.

	Current system					Using JIT		
Item	*Distance from vendor (in miles)*	*Average number of units used each week*	*Current lot size purchased*	*Unit cost*	*Average freight cost per unit*	*JIT lot size*	*Unit cost*	*Average freight cost per unit (surface)*
Gas range	1,145	10	200	$100	$20	10	$105	$22
Toilet	606	10	240	80	18	10	100	18
Pump	26	56	125	16	3	7	15	4
Refrigerator (large)	22	6	120	110	20	6	113	25
Refrigerator (small)	22	7	15	95	15	1	85	15
Foam cushion	490	675	1,500	8	2	75	7	3
DVD Player (type D)	1,800	9	24	136	11	3	130	26
Dome lights	3	824	1,720	2	0	36	4	0
Awning brackets	48	540	1,200	4	1	60	5	1
Insect screens	159	570	1,240	7	1	50	7	2

Note: The plant operates 52 weeks per year and produces 10 mini motor homes per week.

QUESTIONS

1. What is the total annual cost of maintaining the components inventory under the present system?

2. What would be the total annual cost of maintaining the components inventory under the JIT system (assuming no safety stocks)?

3. Should Ballenger take into account any other costs or benefits from the JIT system? If so, what are they?

4. If the JIT system is adopted, are there safety stocks of any item that should be maintained? If so, which ones and how much?

5. If the JIT system is adopted, what changes, if any, should occur in the relationships between Ballenger's firm and his suppliers of components? Discuss.

6. Assume that Ballenger has switched to the JIT system and that he receives a surprise phone call from a competitor who is going out of business. The competitor wants to sell Ballenger 7,000 dome lights of the type listed in Exhibit 3-C. Should Ballenger buy them? If so, at what price?

7. Carrying costs are 20 percent. Is there a level of carrying costs at which both Ballenger's present system and a JIT system have similar costs? If so, what is it?

Elements of Logistics Systems

Part II presents a detailed examination of many elements of logistics systems. It is written with an emphasis on outbound movements. Chapter 4 looks at the order management and customer service systems. Order management deals with incoming orders, and customer service deals with keeping one's existing customers happy. Protective packaging and materials handling are covered in Chapter 5; both are related to a product's physical movement.

Two chapters are devoted to transportation: Chapter 6 covers the domestic transportation system that is available to shippers, and Chapter 7 covers the nitty-gritty aspects of industrial transportation management.

The topic of Chapter 8 is selecting the site for one's production or distribution center. Inventory management, possibly the key to successful logistics management, is handled in Chapter 9. Inventories are kept in warehouses and distribution centers, which is the subject of Chapter 10. Chapter 11 looks at the purchasing/supply fulfillment function.

Chapter 12, the last chapter in this section, deals with international logistics, although certain other aspects of international logistics are touched upon in other chapters. International logistics management is a rapidly growing field.

4

Order Management and Customer Service

Some shipments and some customers require extra attention. This aircraft fuselage, being loaded aboard an Atlantic Container Line Ro/Ro vessel, was being shipped by Boeing to the Paris Air Show. *Source:* Atlantic Container Line.

Key Terms

- Customer service
- Efficient Consumer Response (ECR)
- Load planning
- Order cycle
- Order delivery
- Order entry
- Order handling

- Order management
- Order picking and assembly
- Order processing
- Order transmittal
- Quick Response (QR)
- Replenishment cycle

Learning Objectives

- To understand how a firm processes incoming orders
- To understand the importance of customer service to a firm's marketing activities
- To relate the role of logistics in the customer service area
- To examine why customer service standards should be specific and measurable
- To describe how a customer service program is established and maintained

This chapter deals with two closely related logistics activities: order management and customer service. Order management is obviously an early step in the logistics channel. The order, possibly transferred from the negotiations channel, must be handled. In a supply chain, today's order may be just one of many repeat orders executed under an agreement negotiated a long time ago.

Customer service is loosely defined as keeping existing customers happy. With that definition, one might think that it belongs at the tail end of the logistics process. That is not quite so because customer service begins for some products before the sale is made. A simple example might be a printing order for which a customer service representative is assigned to work with a buyer to ensure that the text, artwork, and layout of the job are satisfactory before the actual printing is begun. Also, in many fields, quality customer service results in repeat orders that require very little sales effort. Customer service is the catalyst for reorders along the supply chain. Clearly, the principles of customer service can be practiced throughout the entire logistics channel described in this and following chapters.

Order Management

Order management has several definitions, which differ only in the degree of precision with which they are applied. In general terms, the phrase means how a firm handles incoming orders; more specifically, order management is the activities that take place in the period between the time a firm receives an order and the time a warehouse is notified to ship the goods to fill that order.

Order cycle is a related phrase, also with several meanings, depending on one's perspective. From the seller's standpoint, it is the time from when an order is received from a customer to when the goods arrive at the customer's receiving dock. From the buyer's standpoint, the order cycle is from when the order is sent out to when the goods are received. (This is also known as the **replenishment cycle** for goods needed on a regular basis.) The shorter and more consistent the order cycle is, the less inventory is needed by one's customers.

There is also a link between order management and sales forecasting. A firm does not simply wait for orders to arrive in order to learn what's happening. Forecasts are made of sales and of the inventories that must be stocked so that the firm can fill orders in a satisfactory manner.

Individuals involved with the order management part of business agree that the order cycle is getting shorter. The order is handled more expeditiously when it is received, is physically processed and picked with considerable assistance from computerized systems, and delivered by a carrier observing a highly disciplined schedule. During the entire process, the customer also has the ability to *track* the order, that is, to determine its status or geographic location.

Today, the word *quality* is frequently used in conjunction with logistics systems and is usually associated with customer service. It is assumed that delivery systems are subject to the same types of quality management techniques as those associated with conventional assembly lines. Firms also benchmark their logistics performance against that of other firms.

Many firms analyze their customer service standards in terms of five aspects, or stages, of the **order cycle:** order planning, order transmittal, order processing, order picking and assembly, and order delivery.

Order Planning

To even out workloads, some firms develop plans that space orders more evenly. A major problem area in achieving an efficient **order handling** system (either centralized or decentralized) is bunching, which results when a high percentage of customers make their orders at the same time. Such an overload on the order handling system causes delays in handling. The results, of course, are that the entire order cycle time is increased and the firm's customer service is lowered. The key to reducing bunching problems is to control when customers place their orders. If customers' ordering schedules can be influenced, a firm can balance them out and thereby minimize the peaks and valleys in the order handling workload.

Three techniques are commonly used to control customer ordering patterns. The first is the use of field, or outside, salespeople, who take orders when they call on customers. Many customers prefer the ease of ordering directly from salespeople with extensive knowledge of product lines. Thus, when customers know that a firm's representative arrives the first Monday of every month, they usually hold their orders for that salesperson.

The second procedure involves the use of phone salespeople (or inside salespeople). A firm's representative calls the customer at one or more given times during the month and takes the customer's order. This method is especially attractive because it is easy.

The third technique is to offer a substantial price discount to customers who place their orders on certain dates, such as every fourth Monday. Avon Products, whose representatives make door-to-door sales, uses this method. Each representative has a specific day to submit the order every two weeks. By selecting the day of the week an order is submitted, Avon is able to balance the workload in its branches and consolidate orders into truckload quantities.

Order Transmittal

Order transmittal is the series of events that occur between the time a customer places or sends an order and the time the seller receives the order. In recent years, this aspect of the order cycle has received increasing attention for two reasons. First, firms that calculate the order transmittal time to be between 2 and 5 days via the U.S. Postal Service feel that this is unreasonably long. Second, mail service has unpredictable variations making it difficult to provide consistency in fulfilling orders on time. (The buyer assumes that the seller receives the order almost immediately after it is mailed.)

To correct these deficiencies in order transmittal, many companies arrange for their salespeople and customers to order directly by phone or some other electronic method. Some firms that receive orders have a caller ID program keyed to the incoming phone number, which gives the person receiving the order a record of other recent orders from the same phone number. Another use of telephones is FAX transmission of orders. Figure 4-1 is a mail-in order form used by a firm that sells equipment to the tow-truck industry. The form may be mailed or faxed or the customer may phone in the order or use the vendor's Web site.

Another method of order transmittal that is becoming more common utilizes scanners and bar codes. One wholesale company supplying drugstores that uses this method provides each of its retail customers with an electronic ordering machine that is slightly larger than a handheld calculator. The store employee walks through the store at a regular time and notices which products are low on inventory. He or she then passes a pencil-like scanner, which is attached to the ordering device, across a label affixed to the shelf. After all the products with low inventory have been scanned, the employee places the order by dialing the supplier's phone number and then places the phone in a device (known as an acoustic coupler) that sends information from the ordering machine. Orders are shipped to the drugstore the following day. Radio is also used to transmit orders. In some cities, Coca-Cola distributors use salespeople to get retailers' orders, which are then radioed in via handheld radio units.

Some of the largest chain stores have their ordering systems linked to their point-of-sale registers. For some products, each retail sale sets in motion an order for a replacement. More often, a running total of the sales, is kept and when a specified level or number is reached, a reorder is transmitted.

By far the biggest development in order transmittal has been the Internet. Sellers have their catalogs on their Web sites, and buyers can order via the Web. This method is quick and accurate. Several grocery chains have Internet-shopping options for customers who can select from thousands of items, charge their purchases, and either pick them up at the store or have them delivered (usually for an additional fee). Figure 4-2 shows the online order form for the Online Gift Shop of the Museum of Fine Arts in Boston.

Sears has over 6,000 suppliers and was linked electronically to only about 10 percent of them. Sears determined that it wished to be connected electronically to all its suppliers. Sears relied on a third party to integrate this link in its supply chain and to assist its suppliers to develop electronic connections. It first sent a letter to all suppliers indicating that it wanted to develop the electronic connections. The integrator determined that "1,200 suppliers could connect via an existing system; 600 suppliers needed

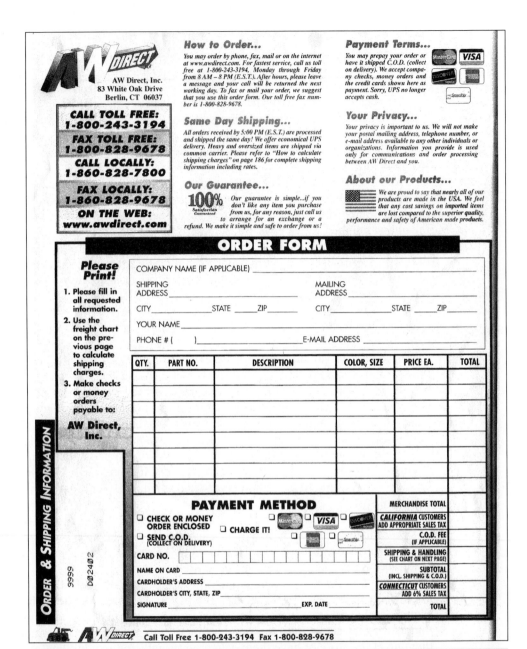

FIGURE 4-1 Mail-in Order Form Used by AW Direct

Source: AW Direct, Inc.

OnlineMuseumShop

For FedEx shipments, your order must be submitted by 11 a.m. ET for next-day delivery.

If ordered items are to be shipped FedEx and one of these items is on backorder, the backordered item(s) will be sent seperately at an additional FedEx shipping charge. Please check to see if your order contains items on backorder.

FedEx shipping cannot be applied to Canada or oversea addresses.

Questions about an item? Call our customer service department 8 a.m. to 5 p.m. ET at 1-800-227-5597.

If you are submitting a message for your gift, please limit it to 60 characters in length. Thank you.

1. Review your order from Museum of Fine Arts, Boston - Online Gift Shop

Item	Options	Unit Price	Quantity	Subtotal
Wallets	MFA Signature Gift Presentation?: No Description: Edward Hopper Notecard Wallet	13.95	1	13.95
	Subtotal for Museum of Fine Arts, Boston - Online Gift Shop			13.95

Shipping and tax may be added to your order. For terms, see the Info page.

2. Enter the Coupon Code
If you have a coupon that can be redeemed from Museum of Fine Arts, Boston - Online Gift Shop, please enter the offer code in the box below.

Coupon Code: [＿＿＿＿＿＿＿＿＿＿＿＿＿＿＿＿＿] (optional)

3. Choose the shipping address

First Name: [＿＿＿＿＿＿＿] Last Name: [＿＿＿＿＿＿＿]
Address: [＿＿＿＿＿＿＿＿＿＿＿＿＿＿＿＿]

City: [＿＿＿＿＿＿＿] State: [＿＿＿＿＿＿＿]
Zip: [＿＿＿＿＿＿＿] Phone: [＿＿＿＿＿＿＿]
Country: [US United States ▾]

4. Specify gift options for your order
Include this message with my gift:

5. Choose shipping options for Museum of Fine Arts, Boston - Online Gift Shop

[Standard Shipping ▾]

[Cancel] [Continue]

FIGURE 4-2 Order Form Used by the Online Gift Shop of the Museum of Fine Arts, Boston

Source: Museum of Fine Arts, Boston Catalog.

direct application-to-application capabilities; 2,800 selected documents in the Web browser; about 900 suppliers chose a fax to electronic conversion; and 100 suppliers opted for mail-to-electronic conversion."[1]

Order Processing

Order processing typically includes such activities as the following:

1. The order information is checked for completeness and accuracy.
2. A credit check is made by the credit department.[2]
3. The order is "entered" into the system so it may be filled (this step is known as **order entry**).
4. The marketing department credits the salesperson with the sale.
5. The accounting department records the transaction.
6. The inventory department locates the warehouse closest to the customer, advises it to pick the shipment, and updates the firm's master inventory controls. (If the firm builds to order, the production department is instructed to build the item. An extreme example is the supplier of dash board "cockpits" for 2002 Jeep Libertys, who is given 204 minutes to build and deliver one of a certain color and trim to the Chrysler assembly line, 9 miles away.[3])
7. The transportation department arranges for the shipment's transportation from the shipping dock to the buyer.

The various activities associated with order processing are shown in Figure 4-3. Along the bottom, one could show days or hours. Incoming orders are divided into two categories. Electronic data interchange links with established buyers bypass the routine steps that might be applicable to first-time buyers. Web site order forms are designed in a way that minimizes errors and omissions, i.e., they may not move forward if there is no zip code or if sales tax is not included in the total cost calculations. The order triage function segments the orders into different customers' specific needs. Some might want only 100 percent complete orders; some might want shipments in truckload quantities only; others might want custom labeling or bar coding. There may also be some emergency orders for, say, repair parts.

Working within the supply-chain concept, buyers will specify when they want the goods, often within as narrow an opening as a one-hour—or less—delivery window (time span within which an order must arrive). In these situations, the seller must look at the right side of the chart first and take into account the time that the goods will be

---

[1]Larry R. Smeltzer, "Integration Means Everybody—Big and Small," *Supply Chain Management Review,* September/October, 2001, p. 40.

[2]For most computerized order management systems today, a customer credit unit is built into records; the computer either approves credit for the order or sets it aside for a person to decide. Charge cards can also be verified instantaneously.

[3]*Supply Chain Management, Automotive Supplement,* July/August 2002, p. 6. The "cockpit" consists of the dashboard, front seats, consoles, and related electronic components. There are 200 different color and trim combinations available, and 900 units are shipped every day. Hence 900 orders are processed daily, although not all steps have to be performed for each order. The term *Quick Response Manufacturing* (QRM) is coming into use, and it means manufacturing with little or zero lead times.

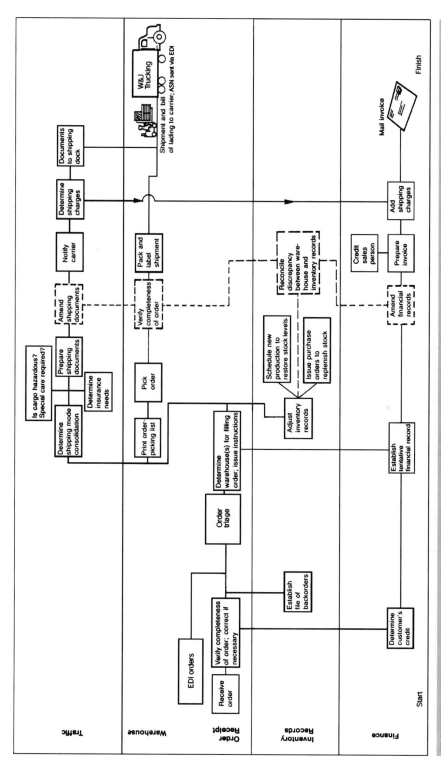

FIGURE 4-3 Flowchart of Order Handling (Order Processing) System

in transit. Adding these two times, the seller would know when to place the order into the queue of orders being handled so that it leaves at the needed time.

As the goods leave, an advance shipping notice (ASN) is sent to consignees via EDI. Consignees then think of these goods as incoming inventory rather than as goods on order. Figure 4-3 also shows us that the goods are being sold free on board (FOB) source, because the transportation costs must be determined before the final bill is prepared so that they may be added to the invoice. At the very end of the process, the invoice is sent via mail or EDI to the customer.

Nearly all major firms have computerized their order handling systems. Order forms, whether printed or in computer format, are designed so that the use of computers by both the customer and the vendor is facilitated. The billing of customers is increasingly done through computerized and electronic networks.

One additional situation that every firm must contend with is a stockout. In most cases, the best procedure is to notify the customer of the situation as soon as possible. This can be done immediately if the seller's inventory system is computerized and the customer is ordering via EDI or a phone call-in system or on a Web site. If the order has been mailed, the customer should be contacted via phone, fax, mail, or e-mail. In any case, the customer should be notified when the order will be shipped and given the option of accepting similar products currently in stock.

Figure 4-4 is a simplified chart showing how an export order might be handled. In this case, the order arrives in the form of a letter of credit, which is a bank document guaranteeing payment after all conditions are met (usually meaning that the product is delivered to the buyer in good order). If the seller cannot meet the specified conditions, the seller moves to have the letter of credit amended, which must be agreed to by the buyer. An international freight forwarder is retained both to prepare shipping documents and to make arrangements with the ocean carrier. (Note in this example that the forwarder consolidates this exporter's cargo with cargo of other clients.) A number of documents must be assembled, and some are delivered to the port of export. If some are late, they are flown to meet the cargo at the port of import. Once the shipment arrives in good order, the bank is notified and the seller paid.

Order Picking and Assembly

The next stage of order management is **order picking and assembly.** It starts with producing a document telling a specific warehouse to assemble a given order for a customer. An actual order picking list, indicating which items are to be assembled, is given to a warehouse employee. The order picking and assembly function includes all activities from the time the warehouse receives an order to ship items until goods are loaded aboard an outbound carrier.

The trend is for the order pickers' activities to be scheduled by computer. At the L. L. Bean distribution center in Freeport, Maine, each order picker is given a computer printout that specifies which products to pick, where to find them, and in what sequence the products should be gathered for each order. This system has provided impressive results. During the peak of Bean's shipping season, the firm's 60 order pickers select from 13,000 products in a 50,000-square-foot picking area and can process over 33,000 orders per day.

A further refinement in the use of computers in the order picking process is reported by the E. J. Brach Company, a large manufacturer of candy. Each order picker

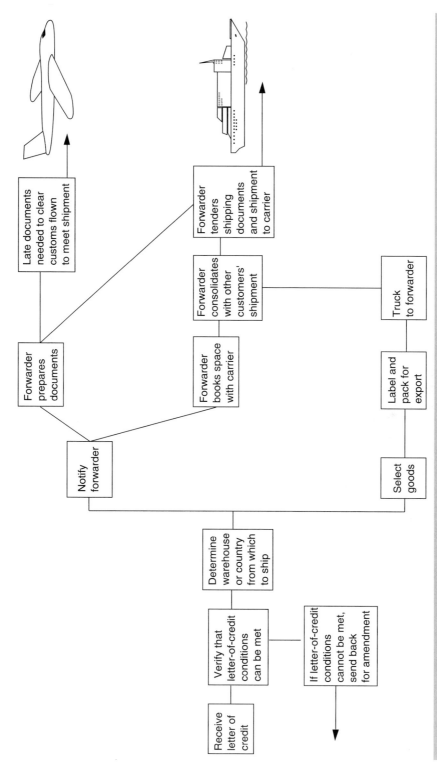

FIGURE 4-4 Processing or Handling of an Export Order (Terms of Sale Are Not Specified. They Would Indicate Point to Which Exporter Is Involved.)

carries a handheld computer that functions as an order picking terminal. It tells the picker what to pick, the quantity to pick, and the location of the product. When each product has been picked, the employee presses the button labeled "Task Done." The warehouse computer then shows the employee his or her next assignment on the handheld terminal. The phrase *paperless warehouse* is used to describe warehouse operations in which computers have replaced the use of paper documents.

After orders have been picked, the assembled orders are checked to ensure that they were accurately picked. If there is a stockout on a particular item, the information is sent back to the order handling department so that original documents can be adjusted. A packing list is enclosed with each outgoing order, indicating what items were picked and the initials of the individuals who prepared the order for shipment. The consignee will check the packing list on receipt of the order and verify that all items are present.

Order Delivery

The final phase of the order cycle is **order delivery,** the time from when a carrier picks up the shipment until it is delivered to the customer's receiving dock. Professors R. W. Haessler and F. B. Talbot once suggested that **load planning** (i.e., the arrangement of goods within the trailer or container) could be considered as a customer service element.[4]

Carriers establish their own service standards, and shippers using them have to incorporate the carrier's estimated delivery times into calculations of the entire length of the order cycle. Chapters 6 and 7 examine the various transportation alternatives available for order delivery. In some situations, carriers guarantee a delivery schedule; some will pay a penalty payment to the shipper if the delivery is later than a specified time.

Some customers will pick up their orders. Grocery chains that have large fleets of trucks making deliveries from company distribution centers to retail stores may schedule some of their returning trucks to pick up goods at wholesalers to carry back to their distribution centers. An example of what can happen at the retail level follows:

> "On Sears.com, customers who select in-store pickup for an item enter their zip code, which triggers a preliminary check of store inventories in a customer's area. The customer selects a local Sears store that has the item in stock and then submits a credit card, transmitting the Web order to a handheld wireless terminal at the local store carted around by a Sears employee, who locates the desired item and reserves it for the customer.... Picking up an item is swifter than a normal visit to Sears. Customers head straight for the merchandise-pickup area of the store and punch their phone number into a computer kiosk, which notifies a Sears employee to bring the item to a counter. Once the clerk takes an impression of the customer's credit card to verify his or her identity, the customer can head home with the purchase."[5]

---

[4]Robert W. Haessler and F. Brian Talbot, "Improving Customer Service Through Load Planning," *Journal of Business Logistics,* Vol. 12, No. 2, 1991, pp. 115–127.

[5]*Wall Street Journal,* July 15, 2002, p. R11.

Importance of the Order Cycle

When the five stages of the order cycle—order planning, order transmittal, order processing, order picking and assembly, and order delivery—are carefully run and skillfully coordinated, impressive gains in performance can be realized. The firm is then able to use the disciplined order cycle as a potent marketing and sales tool. This was written as though product were always available. Sometimes this is not so. "To encourage satisfying delivery performance, it is advisable to involve production scheduling in the preparation of delivery promises."[6]

An efficient order cycle can also be a valuable internal tool. Many of the same steps occur for intrafirm transactions, and some steps, such as credit verification, can be eliminated or modified. Intrafirm movements can also be conducted at very high service levels.

Efficient consumer response (ECR) is a faster order cycle that can, at the risk of oversimplification, be considered the near equivalent of JIT adapted to consumer products. Related to ECR is **quick response** (QR), which involves manufacturers' and retailers' implementing computerized automatic product identification technologies to perform routine business transactions, with the emphasis on product movement. Efficient consumer response includes QR and focuses on purchasing, distribution, and product promotion.

An industry study of ECR users estimated that ECR practices result in savings of 10.8 percent of consumer prices. These savings were from four different areas:

1. More efficient store assortments and better use of store space (1.5 percent), better utilization of retail space because of less space devoted to inventory, and increased inventory turns.
2. More efficient replenishment (4.1 percent), flow-through logistics (i.e., inventories moved continuously, rather than stopping and starting; automated rather than manual ordering).
3. More efficient promotion (4.3 percent), less warehousing costs for "forward buy" inventories. Previously, price-cutting deals would result in large lumps moving through the system every so often, followed by a drop-off in activity.
4. More efficient product development (0.9 percent), fewer unsuccessful product introductions, better value products.[7]

Both ECR and QR are widely used in the grocery industry and by other mass merchandisers. Usually, point-of-sale data are used to trigger replenishment. Both ECR and QR represent a change in wholesaling and promotion channel behavior. Previously, price-cutting deals were offered and the retailer would buy a large block of stock at a lower price and then sell the product at a reduced retail price. Sometimes, a retailer would delay placing an order or would reorder in very small amounts because it was waiting for the next deal to be announced. ECR and QR, instead, are keyed to a more orderly, regular flow of product and to smaller inventories.

---

[6]Harold J. Ogden and Ronald E. Turner, "Customer Satisfaction with Delivery Scheduling," *Journal of Marketing Theory and Practice,* Spring 1996, p. 87.

[7]*Modern Materials Handling,* December 1994, p. 13.

Similar replenishment systems exist in the service industries. Following is a partial description of a continuous replenishment planning (CRP) system used by Kendall Healthcare Products Company for supplying hospitals:

> The inventory on hand balances and open customer orders are transmitted . . . for updating into Kendall's item balance record for each location and item. The sales tracings of what Kendall products were sold the day before . . . to the hospital are used for daily forecast consumption and transmitted. Once the CRP order is created by Kendall and sent to the distribution center for picking, purchase order confirmation is sent to create a purchase order receiver plus provide visibility to customer service of what will be delivered on the next truck. The following day after the order has been shipped from the Kendall distribution center the Advance Shipment Notification provides the transportation information. When the order is received a receipt is sent to confirm quantities and to relieve the in-transit inventory.[8]

Customer Service

Customers are important! Today, many businesses claim that they are "customer-driven." **Customer service** is the collection of activities performed in a way that keeps customers happy and creates in the customer's mind the perception of an organization that is easy to do business with. It is an excellent competitive weapon and has a special advantage over price competition. If a firm cuts its selling price, its competitors can initiate a matching price reduction immediately and eliminate the first company's comparative advantage. Customer service improvements take longer to establish, and they are much more difficult for competitors to imitate. Elements of customer service occur in three phases: Some occur before the transaction, others are involved as part of the transaction, and still others occur after the transaction has been completed.

Special supplier–user relationships develop over a period of time and help integrate relationships within logistics channels. "Customer service is a process for providing significant value-added benefits to the supply chain in a cost-effective way."[9] In this context, *value-added* means some extra services supplied. One example is to provide bar-code labels on cartons, which make it easier for all parties in the logistics chain to handle and tally the cartons. Another example is to arrange a carton (or a pallet or truck) in the same sequence that the user wishes to use or unload it. Other examples of value-added services are shrink-wrapping; inserting documents into cartons; blending products; adding graphics for export goods; adding price tags; and assembling kits (say, taking a tennis racket from one source, tennis balls from another source, and placing them in a single package for retail sale).

---

[8]Fred R. Ricker and Peter Sturtevant, "Continuous Replenishment Planning (CRP): The Driving Force in the Healthcare Industry," *Annual Conference Proceedings of the Council of Logistics Management,* 1993, p. 529. The phrase "relieve the intransit inventory" means that a separate inventory record exists for goods in transit.

[9]Bernard J. LaLonde, Martha C. Cooper, and Thomas G. Noordewier, *Customer Service: A Management Perspective,* Oak Brook, IL: Council of Logistics Management, 1988, p. 5.

Sharing information is always important. A Cap Gemini Ernst & Young survey of over 2,000 manufacturers dealing with collaboration along the supply chain (which they called the "value chain") indicated that the logistics activity that benefited most from increased exchange of information was customer service. "Respondents stated that the top reward from sharing information was the tangible benefit of improved customer service."[10]

Supply-chain thinking is strengthening the links between vendors and their customers. Supply chain integration with the overseas manufacturers required the supplier to make expensive investments in foreign assembly operations fed from the main component manufacturing site in the United States. These operations brought increased product customization, shorter delivery lead times, and easier communications with the customers' purchasing, technical, and logistics personnel—critical in a business culture based on personal relationships. The supplier also sought to bring complementary capabilities into the relationship and did so by providing technical information and advice backed up by substantial industry-leading research relating to the manufacture of key sub-systems. Furthermore, the supplier invested in customized marketing programs to demonstrate how using its product and subsequent product releases, in comparison to using the competition's, would enable the customer to reduce manufacturing costs (e.g., increase yields and throughput speeds) and improve the performance of the finished product (e.g., lighter, less power-consuming, more durable).[11]

Because this chapter deals with reaching the customer, it is necessary to place the costs of customer service activities in focus as a cost of doing business. According to logistics consultant Herbert W. Davis, "Warehousing, transportation, order management/customer service, distribution administration, and inventory are an integral part of selling the product and servicing the customer."[12] Davis has been keeping track of these costs, by industry, for some years. In 1997, for example, the cost elements expressed in dollars per hundred pounds of product were transportation of finished goods, $13.24; warehousing, $10.79; customer service/order management, $4.07; distribution administration, $2.53; and inventory-carrying cost (at 18 percent), $18.13—a total of $47.48.[13] Looking at the year 2001, the cost elements expressed in dollars per hundred pounds of product were transportation of finished goods, $19.18; warehousing, $11.38; customer service/order management, $3.70; distribution administration, $2.40; and inventory carrying cost $23.62—a total of $60.28.[14] Note that customer

---

[10]Cap Gemini Ernst & Young, *High Performance Value Chains,* Philadelphia: Ernst & Young, 2000, p. 11.

[11]*Logistics,* a newsletter published by Mercer Management Consulting, Chicago, Spring 1996, p. 19.

[12]Herbert W. Davis, "Physical Distribution Costs: Performance in Selected Industries, 1987," *Council of Logistics Management, Fall 1987 Annual Conference Proceedings,* Vol. 1, Oak Brook, IL: CLM, 1987, p. 372.

[13]Herbert W. Davis and William H. Drumm, "Physical Distribution Cost and Service, 1997," *Council of Logistics Management, Annual Conference Proceedings, 1997,* Oak Brook, IL: CLM, 1997, p. 72 The cost elements expressed as percentages of sales were transportation of finished goods, 4.08 percent; warehousing, 2.40 percent; customer service/order management, 0.55 percent; distribution administration, 0.36 percent; and inventory-carrying cost, 1.81 percent—a total of 9.02 percent.

[14]www.hwd.com, July 17, 2002. The cost elements expressed as percentages of sales in 2001 were transportation of finished goods, 4.36 percent; warehousing, 1.80 percent; customer service/order management, 0.55 percent; distribution administration, 0.36 percent; and inventory-carrying cost, 2.07 percent—a total of 9.14 percent.

service/order management is a small, and shrinking, part of the pie. One reason for this has been the increased use of computer systems and computer networks to perform the work.

Establishing Specific Objectives

Some companies distinguish goals from objectives when establishing customer service standards. Goals tend to be broad, generalized statements regarding the overall results that the firm is attempting to achieve. Objectives, the means by which the goals are achieved, have certain minimum requirements. Usually, a company determines a minimum set of requirements needed to meet an objective and then attempts to improve on it. The E. I. DuPont de Nemours & Company's goals and objectives adopted some time ago illustrate this difference:

> Our Primary Goal is to provide a level of service equal to or better than major competition in select area markets of opportunity, and in other areas, improvements requiring little or no physical system change.

> Our Secondary Goal (in support of the primary goal) [is to have]: adequate stock available at all times to satisfy customer requirements promptly; dependable shipments and delivery service of products within the established objectives or the date specified by the customer; and prompt notification to customer upon any deviation from standard terms.[15]

Objectives are more specific than goals. One example of an objective is to reduce the number or rate of errors in shipment from, say, 3 per 1,000 shipments to 2 per 1,000 shipments. Objectives should be specific, measurable, achievable, and consistent with the firm's goals. Although many measures can be used to achieve specific objectives, the following four areas deserve special attention:

1. The total elapsed time from when the customer places an order until the customer receives the order.
2. The percentage of customer orders that can be filled immediately and completely from stock located in the warehouse.
3. The total elapsed time from receipt of the order until the shipment is tendered to the transport mode for delivery to the customer.
4. The percentage of customer orders that are picked and sent correctly.

As an example of a more specific objective, L. L. Bean, Inc., used

> several measures to assess customer convenience in dealing with the company via telephone, including: the percentage of customer calls connected with an agent (or recorded message) within 20 seconds and the percentage of abandoned calls. The established objective for the former measure is to respond to between 85 and 90 percent of all calls within 20 seconds. From the customer's point of view, this corresponds to a response in no more than three rings. The target abandoned-call-rate is less than two percent.[16]

---

[15]T. R. Elsman, "Export Customer Service," *Annual Proceedings of the National Council of Physical Distribution Management,* Chicago: National Council of Physical Distribution Management 1972, p. 172.

[16]LaLonde, Cooper, and Noordewier, *Customer Service: A Management Perspective,* p. 119.

Unfortunately, some firms' statements of customer service goals are couched in platitudes lacking specific objectives specifying how the goals are to be achieved. This is a serious problem because if the customer service objectives or standards are not stated in specific terms, they may be ignored or be too vague to provide any real guidance to operating personnel. In addition, the logistics department may become the scapegoat for the marketing department. If a new product flops, the marketing department might argue that the new product introduction failed because customer service standards were too low. Without specific guidelines, the customer service staff lacks a base to prove that acceptable levels of customer service were maintained.

In some firms, the standards are very specific, such as "97 percent of all orders filled completely and accurately, and shipped within 24 hours of receipt." Then management and employee bonuses are tied to achieving such goals.

Because customer service is a competitive tool, one must also determine what one's competitors are doing. Caterpillar, Inc., periodically tests itself and its major competitors (both original equipment manufacturers and firms that build only replacement parts). The testing method employed by Caterpillar is straightforward. It selects specific machine or engine models to be tested and selects normal repair situations. It selects repair parts that would be needed and uses an outside party to purchase the parts at both Caterpillar and competing dealers to determine how long it takes for them to be available.

Herbert W. Davis has tallied the performance of many firms' logistics functions and reports this finding each year. In 2001, the total order cycle time was 7 days. In 1991, it had been 8 days. For the years between, it had ranged between 6 days and 9 days. Another measure is product availability, meaning percentage of goods available to ship when needed. In 2001, 87 percent of orders could be filled immediately; the comparable percentage for 1991 was 83. In 2001, 93 percent of the cases required were available; in 1991, the percentage was 95.[17]

Returned Products

One important post-transactional customer service activity is the handling of returned materials or merchandise. Like recycling, one of the effects of returns is to set up new flows of products. "Returns require a different infrastructure from outbound shipments."[18] (A specialized type of return movement, the product recall, is discussed in Chapter 13.)

"The numbers associated with returns are daunting. Across all retail operations, more than 100 million parcel packages a year are returned at a cost of more than $150 billion, according to the Center for Logistics Management at the University of Nevada, Reno."[19] Goods and materials are returned for a variety of reasons. Sometimes, the shipper makes an error when filling an order. Sometimes, the goods are damaged in transit and the carrier responsible for the damage wants the shipper to determine the costs of repairs. Sometimes, the customer makes an error in ordering, such as writing down the incorrect part number. In this day of sophisticated electronics, some

---

[17]www.hwd.com, July 17, 2002.

[18]*MH Solutions,* March 2001, p. 14.

[19]"Why Are Returns So Tough?" *Modern Materials Handling,* October 2001, p. 45.

customers just cannot get whatever they bought to work. "Experts say that even in a good year, as many as ten percent of computers sold will be returned to stores by disgruntled customers."[20] These are relatively straightforward reasons for which merchandise might be returned.

The most difficult part of maintaining good relationships within channels is the return of defective goods. Defects discovered by the customer immediately after unpacking a shipment are usually easy to handle, but sometimes defects are not discovered until later, as when a retail customer attempts to return a purchased good, often after heavy use, claiming it is defective. A merchant may have over-ordered an item that is not selling well and then decides to examine the materials again and again until he or she discovers defects and then has a reason for returning the entire lot.

As part of a customer service policy, companies should establish procedures for handling, inspecting, and allowing claims on returned materials. A hypothetical example of such a policy in the sporting goods field follows:

> Returns of merchandise for credit or exchange will not be accepted under any conditions unless a return authorization form obtained from and signed by John Doe Company is enclosed with the items. A minimum 10 percent restocking charge will be made on all returned merchandise unless it is for reasons caused by the John Doe Company. Cost for work or repairs necessary to put returned merchandise into new, saleable condition will be made in addition to the 10 percent restocking charge. Include the invoice number and the price of the merchandise returned. Returns must be shipped prepaid and insured. If a return is made because of John Doe Company's error, carrier fees will be credited. Returns will be credited at your wholesale or current wholesale cost, whichever is lower. Claims must be made within three weeks of invoice date.

Another reason for returned goods is related to spare parts. The customer may know that something is wrong with the clutch, for example, and order a new, complete clutch assembly. After disassembling the defective clutch mechanism, the customer discovers that only a small bolt is needed and then wants to return all the other parts for credit.

Logistics personnel dealing with customer service can expect to confront problems arising from claims and must be able to develop procedures for handling them. Retailers making claims against manufacturers are often caught between a customer who has returned the good, claiming it is defective and wanting his or her money back, and the manufacturer claiming that nothing is—or was—wrong with the good in question. Time is also an issue: The customer may think that the distributor is making the decision when, in reality, the distributor has referred the entire matter to the manufacturer who may be located somewhere else.

It is usually best to settle claims quickly since the customer or retailer will be unhappy while awaiting settlement.[21] Persons who ordered over the Internet expect almost instantaneous delivery and cannot accept the fact that returns are not handled expeditiously. Delays in handling a return can lose a customer very quickly. Firms keep records of claimants and take into account the number and nature of complaints already filed by the same party.

---

[20]*Time,* January 5, 1995, p. 61.

[21]"Why Are Returns So Tough?" p. 45.

Returned goods must be examined by the manufacturer to determine whether they can be placed back in the finished goods inventory or require some cleaning or additional repairs. Other alternatives are to dispose of them as seconds, to donate them to a charity, or to disassemble them, saving the usable parts. In some instances, they are destroyed. (If they are not removed from the market, they may compete with the manufacturer's products.) Tallies should also be kept of reported defects; in some instances, the product—or package—might be in need of redesign.

In some retail operations, it is necessary to haul away the product that the newly sold item replaces. Common examples are mattresses and refrigerators. The traded-in items usually have no positive value, but the practice is necessary to making the sale.

Grocery reclamation centers located in major cities deal with damaged grocery products, as well as products not sold prior to their expiration date. Retail stores often use empty banana boxes to accumulate these goods, which are then sent to reclamation centers. At the reclamation centers, the conventional checkout scanner is used to record the products received, item by item, and to note both the store from which they came and their manufacturer. The goods can then be

- Repackaged for resale
- Donated to charities that feed the homeless
- Resold to small retailers that handle and resell damaged goods
- Sold to pet food industries for use as filler (e.g., some cereals and pasta)
- Hauled to a landfill site if they have no value
- Recycled (e.g., packaging and containers).

Manufacturers often have their own policies for how they want their goods handled in the reclamation centers. For example, many do not want the goods resold to retailers that handle damaged goods because of the possibility that they (the manufacturers) are still liable for defective products. The centers are expected to hold products for a certain number of days in case the manufacturer wishes to conduct an audit. Some manufacturers argue that retailers use the system for disposing of merchandise that they over-ordered. The customer service element of reclamation centers is that the grocery manufacturers support a system that allows retailers to dispose of damaged or overage items and then receive credit for them.

The Role of Logistics in Establishing Customer Service Levels

Because customer service standards can significantly affect a firm's overall sales success, establishing goals and objectives is an important senior management decision. Distribution is closely related to customer service, so the outbound logistics department plays an important role in the establishment of customer service goals and objectives.

Adviser to Marketing

Generally, the marketing department is very influential in establishing customer service standards. As part of marketing, the outbound logistics operation serves a particularly important advisory function. Marketing executives are occasionally guilty of equating sales maximization and profit maximization. Some marketing practitioners still believe that the most important objective of a firm is to increase sales. The result is that the customer service goals and objectives are set at unreasonably high levels that ignore the costs incurred to achieve them.

The outbound logistics department must then act as marketing's conscience by asking "Are you aware that the goals and objectives you want established are going to cost _____? Relatively small increases in the overall level of customer service objectives can substantially increase the costs of maintaining the increased level of customer service. This shows the need to consistently keep the costs of the firm's customer service goals and objectives in mind. The logistics staff can outline the alternative means of delivering products to customers and calculate the cost for different levels of service: the size of inventories, the number of shipping points, the order-processing requirements, warehousing, and transportation. It can do all this, but it should not set actual customer service standards. That is management's job, with sales and marketing helping to determine the levels of customer service that the competitive situation requires—and that pricing policies and profit objectives will allow.

Establishing a Customer Service Program

A central element in the establishment of customer service goals and objectives is determining the customer's viewpoint. This means asking customers what they feel is important about service.

The first aspect involves asking questions about additional elements of service. What services would the customer like to receive that are presently not available? For example, could the method of order transmittal be improved? If yes, how? Would it be helpful to have order shipment notification? If yes, why?

The second aspect of customer service involves determining which aspects of service are most important to the customer. Is the present speed of the order or replenishing cycle acceptable? If not, why? A key question for those who indicate that some aspect of the current customer service level is unsatisfactory is "Are you willing to pay more to receive a higher level of service?" Actually, many customer variables are involved. Depending on definitions, some of these variables might be considered other parts of the marketing mix.

The third aspect, which is very important, is how the customer evaluates the service levels of competing vendors. Some customers' procurement staffs will release this information.

The nature of the product also affects the level of the customer service that should be offered. Substitutability is one aspect. It refers to the number of products from which a firm's customers can choose to meet their needs. If a firm has a near monopoly on an important product, a high level of customer service is not required because a customer that needs the product will buy it under any reasonable customer service standard. However, if many products can basically perform the same task, then customer service standards become important from a competitive marketing point of view. One should also observe where the product is in its product life cycle. A product just being introduced needs a different kind of service support than one that is in a mature or declining market stage. Professor J. Cavinato commented about the decline stage:

> Purchasing and distribution strategies in the decline stage stress cash management. Inventory control—and the entire materials management—is more crucial than ever. Inventory is viewed as a poor second to cash. Accountants push

materials and distribution to evaluate inventories for obsolescence write-offs. Capital expenditures are rarely considered. Cannibalization and substitute uses of warehouse space are more fruitful.[22]

Establishing minimum acceptable order sizes is an increasing problem because many customers, driven by JIT philosophies, want to order small quantities at more frequent intervals. There are diminishing (and eventually negative) contributions to profits made by orders of decreasing size. In any particular marketing situation, detailed analysis is needed regarding both why small orders are placed and the possible reactions of existing customers to a new policy that requires either a large minimum order size or a surcharge on small orders to offset losses.

When customer service information has been thoroughly analyzed, it is possible to put customer service goals and objectives in writing. It has been said that talk is cheap and actions dear. In other words, grandiose statements regarding a firm's level of customer service represent little more than rhetoric unless the customer service standards are actually implemented. To accomplish the latter, a systematic program of measurement and control is required.

Economic considerations involve the cost of different levels of customer service. Do we have sufficiently detailed and accurate costs for each activity? Eastman Kodak once provided the same level of customer service for all products, but it then realized that its users' needs varied by degrees. The director of customer operations support noted the following:

> For example, a photo finisher, if he runs out of paper, he has to send his people home. If a retailer runs out of film for amateur photographers, it's not as crucial. Of course we don't want him running out of film, but it's not as crucial as sending people home.[23]

This is a form of tailored logistics wherein the firm segments the market in terms of its logistical needs. Current literature suggests that the practices of customer service will soon be described as "relationship management." This would include not only activities mentioned to this point but also a determined effort to contribute to each customer's success. Related to this, cultivating each customer's needs would allow the seller to understand the actual level of customer service needed to ensure that specific customer's success. Note that this "is in direct contrast to the principles of mass marketing and is certainly cost prohibitive to all but the most narrowly defined market niche firms."[24]

Using the Internet

Customer service is one function of logistics that has benefited greatly from the Internet. The cost of customer contact has dropped dramatically. One estimate of cost per customer contact was $10 in person; $7.50 for a telephone call; and only 18 cents for a

---

[22]Joseph Cavinato, "Product Life Cycle: Logistics Rides the Roller Coaster," *Distribution,* September 1987, pp. 12–20.

[23]"Customer Service: How Much Is Enough?" *Distribution,* May 1988, p. 33.

[24]Donald Bowersox, David Closs, and Theodore Stank, "Ten Mega-Trends That Will Revolutionize Supply Chain Logistics," *Journal of Business Logistics,* Vol. 21, No. 2, 2000, p. 3.

contact via the Internet.[25] Owner's manuals can be placed on Web sites for users to read or download. They can be much more extensive than a firm might care to print and distribute with each individual product. They can also include some interactive processes that might help the consumer self-diagnose problems with his or her purchase. Dell Computers receives over 100,000 customer product support queries weekly. E-mail addresses or connections are also offered on some customer service Web sites.

Firms can also publish their customer service policies on their Web sites. One outlined its complaint procedure this way: "When a complaint is received, it is automatically logged, a complaint file is created and a reference number allocated to it via the system. The Complaint Services Manager receives, monitors and distributes the complaints to the relevant Client Manager. The Client Manager decides on the best way forward, and verbal contact is made to the complainant within the same working day. The Customer Service Manager will monitor each complaint file, on a 24-hour basis, to ensure all of e-clear's Customer Service Standards are met and a satisfactory outcome has been achieved within the set time scale."[26] An adjoining page provided a form that the unhappy customer could use to describe the nature or his or her complaint that would be submitted as e-mail.

Use of the Internet for customer service applications is increasing rapidly. System security is an issue, in part because customers are afraid their personal data will be distributed to others. Unscrupulous people are also developing ways to defraud companies via their customer service Web sites.

Measuring and Controlling Customer Service

The ability to measure is the ability to control, and effective control is what management is all about. The value of any corporate objective or goal depends to a large extent on the tools used to measure it. A firm's customer service program must be written and monitored.

A problem encountered when measuring actual customer service standards is determining what factors to measure. Many firms choose those aspects of customer service that are the easiest to measure, rather than those that may be the most important from the customer's point of view. For example, instead of measuring the complete order or replenishment cycle, some firms may only measure order handling and order picking times because these elements are readily available to them. The problem is, of course, that measurement of these aspects tells nothing about the quality of other parts of the order cycle, such as order transmittal and delivery, which are more difficult to measure and consequently most susceptible to problems.

How can a firm most effectively measure those aspects of customer service that the customer values? One technique is the *performance model*. It is based on a questionnaire designed to determine the percentage of times the firm accomplishes specific goals and objectives. This can be done on a sampling basis. Sometimes, it can be accomplished by enclosing a return postcard with each product for the buyer to fill out and mail in. Figure 4-5 is a form used by a firm located in northern Spain for its customers

[25]*ISOURCE Business,* February 2001, p. 22.

[26]www.eclear.co.uk/complaint.htm, July 3, 2002.

⊘ temper

CONTROL DEL TIEMPO DE TRANSPORTE

*Estimado cliente: estamos intentado reducir al mínimo el tiempo de transporte de nuestro almacén al suyo. Le agradeceríamos mucho si nos indica el día y la hora aproximada en que recibió este material y **nos pasa este documento por fax.***

Albarán nº

RECIBIDO EL DIA /   /   **HORA APROXIMADA** :

COMENTARIOS

Número de fax GRATUITO: 900 121 875

¡ MUCHAS GRACIAS POR SU AYUDA !

FIGURE 4-5 Form Used By a Spanish Firm for Surveying the Time Element of Delivery Service. The customer is asked to provide the invoice number, note the date that the order was received, and fax it (toll-free) to the shipper.

Source: SFT Group.

to report when goods were delivered. Figure 4-6 shows another form used for measuring various elements of customer service.

Another way of measuring performance is to audit credit memos, the documents that must be issued to correct errors in shipping and billing. Comparing them with the volume of error-free activity gives a measure of relative activity accuracy in performance. This system is not foolproof, however, because customers who receive more than they are billed for may not call that type of error to the shipper's attention. The same might be true if the goods received are not those requested but are of similar or greater value.

Meeting Customer Demands

Discussion thus far has focused on the measurement of customer service goals and objectives; also important is control. *Control* is the process of taking corrective action when measurements indicate that the goals and objectives of customer service are not being achieved. Measurement by itself is merely wasted time and effort if no action is taken based on the feedback received. The actions taken after deficiencies have been identified make for a strong and effective customer service program.

CALIDAD DEL SERVICIO DE ALMACÉN

Estimado cliente,

Con objeto de seguir mejorando nuestro servicio, le rogamos conteste a este breve cuestionario y nos lo envíe a nuestro **fax GRATUITO 900 121 875**, *o por correo, a la atención de la Srta. Rosa Pereda, si desea asegurar la confidencialidad (en algunos envíos por fax consta el nombre de la empresa).*

- ¿ Hay equivocaciones en las cantidades de los materiales que les suministramos ?

Muchas veces	☐
A menudo	☐
Algunas veces	☐
Casi nunca	☐
Nunca lo tuvimos	☐

OBSERVACIONES Y CONSEJOS:

_____
_____

- ¿ Hay equivocaciones en las referencias de los materiales (servir un tipo por otro)?

Muchas veces	☐
A menudo	☐
Algunas veces	☐
Casi nunca	☐
Nunca lo tuvimos	☐

OBSERVACIONES Y CONSEJOS:

_____
_____

- El embalaje, ¿ es el correcto y los materiales llegan bien o no es correcto y los productos llegan dañados ?

Mal muchas veces	☐
Mal a veces	☐
Normal	☐
Bueno (mejor que la media)	☐
Muy bueno	☐

OBSERVACIONES Y CONSEJOS:

_____
_____

- El paquete exteriormente y el albarán interior, ¿ recogen toda la información que Vd. necesita ?

Información mala	☐
Información normal	☐
Información buena	☐

OBSERVACIONES Y CONSEJOS:

_____
_____

FIGURE 4-6 Form Used By a Firm Located in Northern Spain to Query Customers About Several Service Elements. Question 1 asks about mistakes in quantities shipped. Question 2 asks whether correct goods were shipped. Question 3 asks about the adequacy of packaging, and question 4 is about labeling. The completed form can be returned by toll-free fax.

Source: SFT Group.

Firms are demanding higher levels of customer service for various reasons. First, reliable service enables a firm to maintain a lower level of inventory, especially of safety stocks. The lower average level of inventory produces lower inventory holding costs. Second, the increased use of vendor quality-control programs necessitates higher levels of customer service. In recent years, many firms, especially retailers and wholesalers, have become more inventory conscious. This emphasis has resulted in computer-assisted analysis to identify vendors who consistently give either good or bad levels of service. In the past, with manual systems, repeated and serious customer service errors occurred before a vendor's activities were singled out for corrective action. Today, these factors are automatically programmed into computers, and companies are able to closely monitor the quality of service they receive from each vendor.

Third, in an increasingly automated and computerized world, the relationships between customers and vendors often become dehumanized. This situation is both frustrating and often inefficient from the customer's viewpoint. The firm that can offer a high level of customer service, especially on a personal basis, finds that it has a powerful sales advantage in the marketplace.

Should the seller charge buyers for any, some, or all of the customer services provided? Computer software providers have to decide early whether to provide toll-free telephone numbers for their customers to use when they call for assistance. A newsletter of a trade group of truck body manufacturers asked member firms whether—and what—they specifically charged a customer for delivering a completed new truck with installed body. Answers fell into three categories, with about one-third of the respondents falling into each category. One-third did charge; one-third did not charge within a given radius; and one-third built the costs into their original price quotes.

Generally, respondents indicated they just want to recover their expenses, so the markup on freight is not a profit center. "We charge $1.25 per mile to deliver vehicles to customers," said Mike Poppe of Williams Acquisition Corporation of Indianapolis. "This can sometimes be used by sales as a bargaining tool. We use designated trained drivers who can give instruction upon delivery of the unit."[27]

Overall Customer Service Policy

Customer service is composed of many elements, as seen in the preceding discussion. A checklist of internal and external customer service policies or other literature can also be helpful. For example, Campbell Soup Company has published its C3 program—Campbell's Customer Care—in a lavish 12- by 14-inch color brochure filled with many photographs of Campbell memorabilia. The program and booklet, addressed to Campbell's wholesalers and retailers, covers topics mentioned earlier in this chapter as well as in others. For instance, in its discussion of ordering, the booklet mentions the company's use of delivery windows, order tracking, EDI links with customers, end-aisle display shippers (product cartons that can be used to display featured products in retail stores), and order cycle times. Another part of the brochure deals solely with issues involving the use of pallets. Campbell noted that it was switching from a 44- by 48-inch

---

[27]"Members Speak Out on Charging Freight to the Customer," *TENews,* October 1997, p. 7.

pallet to a 40-by-48-inch pallet, the size recommended by the Grocery Manufacturers Association (GMA). In addition, case sizes were reduced to less than 50 pounds, with one exception, meeting another GMA goal to reduce the weights that workers must lift. Return of damaged or distressed merchandise was also discussed. Ongoing performance was monitored in this way:

> Each month, Campbell gathers and reviews data from every one of our plants concerning customer service. This includes statistics on warehouse load/unload times, on-time pickup/delivery performance, order and case fill, shipping errors, damage levels, [and] backhaul delivery schedules. Additional input comes from regularly scheduled focus meetings and operating reviews with our customers.[28]

Also discussed in the brochure were programs that apply statistical quality performance measures to carriers that Campbell uses, consultation services regarding the warehousing of Campbell products, use of scannable bar codes on cases (they were already being used on individual consumer packages and cans), Campbell's toll-free telephone numbers for handling retail customers' complaints, and working with retailers on product promotions.

Note mention of the toll-free phone numbers for customers to call. They are often called "consumer hot lines" and are used by customers to call for a variety of information and sometimes to voice complaints. (At a Council of Logistics Management's annual meeting, in a discussion following a presentation, the distribution manager of one of the nation's largest firms said that each week the subjects of the consumer hotline calls to his firm were tallied and classified and that he frequently used this information to start his weekly staff meeting.)

SUMMARY

Order management deals with the handling of orders. Customer service is defined as the collection of activities that includes order management and keeping the customer happy. Customer service helps integrate the seller's logistical activities, because they must pull together to help the customer.

Also discussed were the order cycle and order management. The customer views the order cycle as the period of time from when the order is placed until it is received; the seller has a shorter view: from the time the order is received until the goods are shipped. Today, many orders are placed through computerized and electronic networks.

Customer service standards are important yardsticks of performance. Often, they are told to customers (who may even collect reimbursement if the standards are not met). Customer service standards are an important competitive tool and take time to develop and maintain.

Policies for returned products were discussed, as well as the role of the logistics staff in helping establish customer service goals. Also discussed were the measurement and control of customer service.

---

[28]*Campbell's Customer Care,* Camden, NJ: Campbell Soup Company, 1991, p. 9.

QUESTIONS FOR DISCUSSION AND REVIEW

1. Discuss why customer service is an important aspect of outbound logistics management.
2. Who in the firm should establish the customer service goals and objectives? Which departments should assist in arriving at this decision? Why?
3. Define in general terms customer service goals and customer service objectives. Give a specific example of each.
4. What are the most commonly used specific objectives for customer service programs?
5. Does the consumer buy a product, or does the consumer buy a product that is bundled with accompanying services? Discuss.
6. Define and describe the order cycle. Why is it considered an important aspect of customer service?
7. Discuss fully the basic parts that combine to form the order cycle.
8. Which part of the order cycle do you believe is the most important? Why?
9. Discuss the customer service aspects of returned products.
10. What are three basic types of information that should be ascertained prior to designing a customer service program?
11. The text indicates that the role of the logistics staff is to act as an adviser to the marketing department regarding customer service standards. Explain the rationale for this statement.
12. Assume that you are asked to establish a firm's customer service goals and objectives. What information should you collect, and how would you gather it?
13. Discuss the importance of measurement and control in achieving an effective customer service program.
14. A potential weakness in the measurement of customer service standards is that the wrong elements may be measured. Discuss why this could happen.
15. It has been argued that customers are demanding higher levels of customer service from their vendors. Why is this happening? Should customers be charged for the customer service elements they receive?
16. How costly are various elements of customer service? Discuss.
17. Should all customers receive the same levels of service?
18. What procedures should firms employ to handle returned merchandise?
19. How important is the customer service offered by one's competitors? Why?
20. Have you ever stopped doing business with a firm because of poor customer service? If so, describe the circumstances.

SUGGESTED READINGS

Allen, Mary K, Robert L. Cook, M. Bixby Cooper, Omar Keith Helferich, and George D. Wagenheim. "Enhancing the Customer Service Edge with Knowledge Base Transfer." In *Annual Proceedings of the Council of Logistics Management, 1991,* Vol. 1. Oak Brook, IL: Council of Logistics Management, 1991, pp. 71–98.

Bowersox, Donald J., David J. Closs, and Theodore P. Stank. "Ten Mega-Trends That Will Revolutionize Supply Chain Logistics." *Journal of Business Logistics,* Vol. 21, No. 2, 2000, pp. 1–16.

Chopra, Sunil, and Peter Meindl. *Supply Chain Management,* Second Edition (Upper Saddle River, NJ: Prentice Hall, 2004).

Christopher, Martin. "The Agile Supply Chain—Competing in Volatile Markets." *Industrial Marketing Management,* Vol. 29, 2000, pp. 37–44.

Foster, Jerry R., Sandra Strasser, and Alicia Thompson. "The Effect of Written Customer Service Policies on Customer Service Implementation by Carriers and Shippers." *Transportation Journal,* Vol. 31, No. 3, 1992, pp. 4–10.

Gilmore, James H., and B. Joseph Pine II. "The Four Faces of Mass Customization." *Harvard Business Review,* January–February 1997, pp. 91–101.

Harrington, Thomas C., Douglas Lambert, and Martin Christopher. "A Methodology for Measuring Vendor Performance." *Journal of*

Business Logistics, Vol. 12, No. 1, 1991, pp. 83–104.

Innis, Daniel, and Bernard J. LaLonde. "Modeling the Effects of Customer Service Performance on Purchase Intentions in the Channel." *Journal of Marketing Theory and Practice,* Vol. 2, No. 2, 1994, pp. 45–69.

Lawrence, F. Barry, Daniel F. Jennings, and Brian E. Reynolds. *EDistribution* (Mason, OH: Thomson/Southwestern, 2003).

McLaughlin, Curtis P., and James A. Fitzsimmons "Strategies for Globalizing Service Operations." *International Journal of Service Industry Management,* Vol. 7, No. 4, 1996, pp. 43–57.

Murphy, Paul R., and Richard F. Poist. "The Logistics–Marketing Interface: Techniques for Enhancing Cooperation." *Transportation Journal,* Vol. 32, No. 2, 1992, pp. 14–23.

O'Brien, David, and Gerald McNerney. "Supply Chain Application Investments Pay Off." *Supply Chain Management Review,* Vol. 6, No. 3, 2002, pp. 17–19.

Ogden, Harold J., and Ronald E. Turner, "Customer Satisfaction with Delivery Scheduling." *Journal of Marketing Theory and Practice,* Vol. 4, No. 2, 1996, pp. 79–88.

O'Neil, Brian F., and Jon L. Iveson. "An Operational Procedure for Prioritizing Customer Service Elements." *Journal of Business Logistics,* Vol. 12, No. 2, 1991, pp. 157–191.

Scannell, Thomas V., Shawnee K. Vickery, and Cornelia L. Dröge. "Upstream Supply Chain Management and Competitive Performance in the Automotive Supply Industry." *Journal of Business Logistics,* Vol. 21, No. 1, 2000, pp. 23–46.

Stank, Theodore P., Margaret A. Emmelhainz, and Patrica Daugherty. "The Impact of Information on Supplier Performance." *Journal of Marketing Theory and Practice,* Vol. 4, No. 4, 1996, pp. 94–105.

Weber, Mary Margaret, "A Framework of Analyzing Sources of Variance in the Supplier–Buyer Relationship: Determining the Contribution of Buyer Planning and Supplier Performance to Total Variance." *Journal of Marketing Theory and Practice,* Vol. 4, No. 2, 1996, pp. 61–71.

Case 4-1   Cheezy Wheezy

Starting as a small retail store in New Glarus, Wisconsin, the Cheezy Wheezy firm had slowly grown into a chain of nine retail shops located in southern Wisconsin and northern Illinois. In recent years, nearly all of its competitors had begun issuing catalogs, widely distributed in late October, advertising gift packages of cheeses, jams, jellies, and other fancy food items. Henry Wilson, son of the firm's founder, had convinced his father that Cheezy Wheezy should also issue a catalog.

It was then March, and the last snows were melting. Henry Wilson had called his third staff meeting in as many weeks to discuss the catalog project. Present were Henry (whose title was vice president); Susan Moore, the sales manager; Jeff Bell, the inventory manager; and Robert Walker, the traffic manager. Also present was Robert Caldwell, from a Milwaukee-based ad agency that was handling many aspects of the catalog project.

Moore and Caldwell had just finished describing the catalog's tentative design and the allocation of catalog pages to various product lines. Caldwell then said, "We are to the point where we must design the order form, which will be stapled inside the center pages. It will be a single 8½-by-11-inch sheet. The customer will remove it from the catalog, complete it, fold it into the envelope shape, lick the gummed lines, and mail it in. The order form will be on one side of the sheet. On the other will be the instructions for folding and Cheezy Wheezy's mailing address in New Glarus; the remainder of the space will be ads for some impulse items. Right now we're thinking of a Santa Claus–shaped figure molded out of cheese."

"Enough of that," said Wilson, "this group isn't here to discuss Santa dolls. We're here to design the order form. We may also have to talk a little about selling terms. Susan?"

Responding to her cue, Moore said, "Our biggest problem is how to handle the transportation and shipping costs. We've studied all of our competitors' catalogs. Some absorb the costs into the product's price, some charge by weight of the order, some charge by money value of order, and some ship COD."

"How important are shipping costs, Susan?" asked Bell.

"Plenty," was her response. "They run $2 to $3 for a 1- or 2-pound package. If you take a pound of cheese that we sell in our retail stores for $2, here are our costs if it goes by catalog: cost of goods, $1; order management, 50 cents; overhead, including inventory carrying costs, 50 cents; packaging for shipment, 50 cents; and transportation costs to any point in the United States ranging between $1.75 and $3.20. If, however, we're dealing with bigger shipments, the relative costs vary."

"I'm not following you," said Wilson.

"It's like this," responded Moore. "The wholesale cost of cheese to us is the same per pound, no matter how much is sold. Order-processing costs are approximately the same for each order we'll be receiving by mail. Overhead and inventory carrying costs are always present but may be allocated in a variety of ways. Packaging costs are also about the same per order. They go up only a few cents as we move to larger cartons. Transportation costs are hard to describe because of their tapers. Right now our whole catalog project is bogged down with the problem of transportation cost tapers."

"Tapers?" said Wilson, turning to Walker. "You've never told me about tapers before. It sounds like some kind of animal."

"That's tapir, t-a-p-i-r," said Walker. "We're talking about tapers, t-a-p-e-r-s."

"Oh," said Wilson. "What are they?"

"When one ships small packages of cheese," said Walker, "rates are based on two factors, the weight being shipped and the distance. As weight or distance increases or both—the rates go up but not as quickly. This is called the *tapering principle.* To ship 2 pounds of cheese from New Glarus to St. Louis costs $2.40; 3 pounds cost $3.30; 5 pounds cost $4.60; and so on. One hundred pounds—no, 50 pounds is a better example because some of the parcel services we'll be using won't take 100 pounds—50 pounds would cost $21. There's also a distance taper. The 2-pound shipment that costs $2.40 to St. Louis is $3.40 to Denver and $4.15 to Los Angeles."

"Can't we use the average transportation costs?" asked Bell. "That's what we do with inventory carrying costs."

"Won't work," said Caldwell. "You'll be overpriced for small, short-distance shipments and will lose sales. For heavy long shipments, you'll be underpriced and will make so many sales that you might soon go belly up."

Wilson shuddered and inquired, "Does that mean we charge by weight and by distance?"

Moore answered, "It's not that easy. In the cheese business, people buy by the pound, but shipping weights—which include packaging—are actually more. A customer who orders 3 pounds of cheese is in fact receiving 3 pounds of cheese plus 6 ounces of packaging materials. I wish we could sell a pound of cheese that consisted of 14 ounces of cheese and 2 ounces of packing material, but that would be illegal at worst, and of questionable ethics, at best."

"We have the same problems with distance," added Walker. "We're trying to sell in 50 states, but who knows how far they are from New Glarus? We could have tables and maps in the catalog, but they take up valuable selling space. Also, if it looks too complex, we may just turn off some potential customers before they complete their orders."

"Some of our clients have another problem," added Caldwell, "and that is split orders. The customer will want 10 pounds of cheese, but it will be five 2-pound packages sent to five different locations. That has an impact on both packaging and transportation costs."

"So, what do we do?" asked Wilson.

QUESTIONS

1. Assume that Cheezy Wheezy goes into the catalog order business. What policy should it adopt for handling stockouts—that is, what should the company do when it receives mail orders that it cannot completely fill because one or more of the desired items are out of stock?

2. Some mail customers will complain that the items Cheezy Wheezy shipped never arrived. What policy should Cheezy Wheezy adopt to deal with this?

3. Should the order form, which will be stapled into the center of the catalog and will be addressed to Cheezy Wheezy, be of the postage-paid type, which means that

Cheezy Wheezy will pay the first-class postage rate plus a few cents on each envelope delivered to it, or should the customer be expected to add a first-class stamp to the order before he or she mails it? Discuss.

4. Cheezy Wheezy's headquarters are in New Glarus, but the company also operates in southern Wisconsin and northern Illinois. Is New Glarus the best address to use for receiving mail orders for cheese? Might there be advantages, perhaps, in having the mail addressed to a more major city—say, Madison, Milwaukee, or Chicago? Discuss.

5. From the facts that have been presented in the case, how would you handle the matter of charging for the *packaging* costs of each shipment? Why?

6. How would you handle the matter of charging for the *transportation* costs of each shipment? Why?

7. Taking your answers to questions 5 and 6, write out in either text or tabular form the explanation of shipping charges that your catalog customers will read. (*Note:* As used here, *shipping* includes both packaging and transportation.)

8. On a single 8½-by-11-inch sheet of paper, design a catalog order form for use by Cheezy Wheezy.

9. Contemplate a simple Web site for Cheezy Wheezy to sell its products within the United States. How, if at all, would the order form used in its Web site differ from an order form printed and mailed as part of a catalog? Would any sales or shipping policies be changed? Discuss.

Case 4-2   Handy Andy, Inc.

Handy Andy, Inc., produced garbage/trash compactors at a factory in St. Louis, Missouri, and sold them throughout the United States. Nearly all sales were in large urban areas where trash-collection costs were high.

The basic unit was about 3 feet high, 2 feet deep, and 1½ feet wide. A deluxe model had the same dimensions but contained more features. Because most of the sales represented units to be placed in existing kitchens, a wide variety of colors and trims were manufactured, providing an exterior that would match almost any kitchen decor. The standard model came in five colors with three different trims for a total of 15 different combinations. The deluxe model came in eight colors and four different trims for a total of 32 different combinations. Retail prices were set by the dealer, with prices for the standard model ranging between $310 and $350 and for the deluxe model between $390 and $450. Sales in an area were usually slow until trash collectors, faced with rising landfill costs, raised their rates per can of refuse picked up.

Because of the sporadic sales patterns and the wide number of colors and trims available, retailers usually stocked only a display unit or two. They had available an expensively printed brochure that included paint chips so buyers could select the color and finish they wanted. When the retailer completed the sale, he or she would take the order and promise delivery and installation within a given number of days. In each major city, there was one major Handy Andy dealer (factory distributor). Each dealer maintained a complete stock of all styles and trims of the Handy Andy compactors. (Handy Andy, Inc., insisted that these factory distributors stock at least five units each of the 47 different styles available.) The general agreement between the factory distributors and Handy Andy was that the factory distributor would deliver and install the compactor within 5 days after the distributor who had made the sale informed the factory distributor. For the delivery and installation, the factory distributor received 9 percent of the unit's wholesale price, half paid by distributor who had made the sale and half paid by Handy Andy as a credit against future orders.

José Ortega worked in Handy Andy's distribution department in the St. Louis headquarters. He currently was working on a project to determine whether the compactor's warranty should be extended from 1 year to 2 years. The units were well built, and there had been almost no warranty work requested in the first year of each model's life. Because Handy Andy would have no records of work performed after the 1-year period had expired, Ortega was randomly contacting buyers, using long-distance phones. Their names and phone numbers came from postcards they had mailed in to register the warranty at time of purchase (see Exhibit 4-A). The phrase at the bottom of the card referring to Handy Andy's records was to keep the buyer from waiting for a problem to occur and then mailing in the card. Whether this statement was necessary was unknown because so few defects had been reported. Ortega was in the process of contacting 500 purchasers who had owned the compactors for between 1 year and 4 years (when they had first been introduced) to determine whether the compactors had required repairs and, if so, the extent and cost of the repairs. In talking to purchasers, Ortega was impressed by the fact that there were remarkably few complaints involving the durability of the compactors.

Another type of complaint did arise, however, one that Ortega had difficulty understanding until he heard many buyers, usually from the same few cities, tell an almost identical story. It appeared that in these cities the factory distributor would contact individuals who had purchased Handy Andy compactors from other, smaller dealers and would attempt to have them cancel the original order. The factory distributor told the buyer that the model originally requested was out of stock but that a better model could be supplied for the same price. The factory distributors also indicated that the buyers would receive better service if they bought from them because, they claimed, they provided service for all Handy Andy models sold in their area. In addition, the factory distributors in these few cities indicated that they, not Handy Andy, Inc., stood behind the 1-year warranty.

Ortega realized that he was uncovering a larger problem than he had been assigned to explore. He chatted briefly with his supervisor, who told him to revise the format of his interview to include a few more questions concerning the installation. She also told him to begin calling individuals who had owned compactors for less than a year. Ortega did this, and the only new information he uncovered was that the factory distributors in almost all cities did a better job of installing compactors that they had sold than they did those sold by smaller dealers. The delivery was faster (in terms of elapsed time since sale), more time was spent explaining to the customer how the compactor worked, and phone calls were made to the customer 3 days and 10 days after installation to make certain that the customer had no additional questions concerning the compactor's operation. When a compactor that had been sold by a smaller dealer was delivered, it was frequently left in the middle of the kitchen with scarcely a word exchanged between the customer and the installation personnel.

Ortega had another meeting scheduled with his supervisor. As he entered her office, he was surprised to see Handy Andy's vice president of marketing also sitting in the office. Ortega's supervisor asked him to tell the vice president the results of his interviews.

The marketing vice president asked Ortega, "Do you think this pattern exists in all markets?"

"No," was Ortega's reply. "I'd say it was a problem in Jacksonville, Baltimore, Cleveland, Louisville, Denver, and San Diego. It may be a problem in Dallas and New Orleans. My sample wasn't very well structured in a metropolitan market sense; you will recall that it was a nationwide sample that was trying to look at repairs."

MAIL WITHIN FIVE DAYS OF INSTALLATION!

Serial Number _____
(8-digit number under the switch)
Purchased from:
Dealer's name_____

City_____

Date of purchase_____/_____/200_____
                       MONTH   DAY
Your
name_____

Address_____

City_____State_____ZIP_____

This card requires no postage. Just fill out and drop in any mailbox. Your warranty is good for one year from the date of purchase, as determined by our records. Contact your dealer first if you have questions.

HANDY ANDY, INC.
St. Louis, MO 63129

EXHIBIT 4-A Return Postcard

QUESTIONS

1. Is this a customer service problem? Why or why not?
2. Marketing channels are the arrangement of intermediaries (wholesalers, retailers, and the like) that the firm uses to achieve its marketing objectives. Is the problem discussed in Handy Andy's marketing channels? Why or why not?
3. Logistics channels handle the physical flow of goods or services. Is the problem discussed in Handy Andy's logistics channel? Why or why not?

4. It appears that the factory distributors are exploiting the smaller dealers. Yet from what we can tell, Handy Andy in St. Louis has heard no complaints from the smaller dealers. Why wouldn't they complain?

5. What should Handy Andy's marketing vice president do? Why?

6. Redesign the warranty postcard, staying within the same dimensions, and include questions or statements that will make it easier for Handy Andy headquarters to detect whether installation practices of the type discussed in this case occur.

7. In the case is the statement "The factory distributors in these few cities indicated that they, not Handy Andy, Inc., stood behind the 1-year warranty." Is this a problem for Handy Andy? Why or why not?

8. Assume that the situation described in question 7 is a problem. How should the firm deal with it?

5

Protective Packaging and Materials Handling

This shipment required extra attention. These container cranes, built in Shanghai, were being delivered to the Port of Oakland. The Golden Gate Bridge is in the background. The time selected for passing under the bridge was at low tide, and vehicular traffic on the bridge was halted briefly to reduce the weight pushing down on the deck of the bridge.

Photo courtesy Port of Oakland. ©Robert Campbell, 2002.

Key Terms

- Building-blocks concept
- Bulk materials
- Compliance labeling
- Ergonomics
- Materials handling
- Package testing

- Pallets
- Recycled content
- Slip sheet
- Unitization
- Unit loads

Learning Objectives

- To know how product features affect packaging and materials handling
- To identify the functions performed by protective packaging
- To analyze the utilization of unit loads in materials handling
- To appreciate how the environmental protection movement has affected packaging and package choice
- To learn materials handling principles

This chapter deals with the physical handling of products. Packaged goods are handled by the package. Bulk materials are free flowing or loose rather than in packaged form and are handled by pumps, shovels, or conveyor devices. Each product has unique physical properties that, along with the accepted volumes or quantities in which it is traded or moved, determine how and when the product is packaged. The distinction is not absolute, because a good may move in bulk form from the manufacturer to a wholesaler who packages it for retail distribution.

Packaging and materials handling are closely related to several topics currently considered on the cutting edge of logistics thinking and operations. Materials requirements planning (MRP) is concerned with obtaining more efficient management over the flow of all materials and products in a firm's production system. Robotics, although still used mainly in manufacturing, is being increasingly used in a number of functions related to the handling of both packaged and bulk materials. Packaging is also closely tied to choice of transportation mode, and varying packaging costs are one part of the equation as the shipper looks for a solution of lower total cost. Choice of packaging is related to many recycling issues. Supply-chain thinking results in use of packaging and labels that can be used throughout the entire chain.

Product Characteristics

Each product has unique physical properties. Density of **bulk materials** varies. The ability to withstand exposure to the elements is another quality: Coal piles can be exposed to the rain; salt piles cannot. Some products can be exposed to freezing weather; others cannot. Substances exist in three forms—solid, liquid, or gas—and the form that they happen to be in is a function of temperature.

The physical characteristics of some goods change while they are moving in the logistics channel. Even a dry product such as pet food or potato chips settles in bags as it moves through a system. Fresh fruits and vegetables are the best-known examples. Even after they are picked, they continue to give off gases and moisture and to generate heat—a process known as *respiration.* Fruits and vegetables are harvested before they are ripe so that they will reach the retail stores as they ripen. Ripening processes can be delayed through the use of lower temperatures or application of gases.

Products such as fresh produce, meats, fish, and baker's yeast are referred to as *perishables.* They require special packaging, loading, storage, and monitoring as they are moved promptly from source to customer. The growth in popularity of washed, cut lettuce being sold in plastic bags is an example of how packaging can benefit several members of the supply chain. The lettuce grower benefits because smaller, misshaped heads can be used, not merely the eye-pleasing, "perfect" heads. Both the retailer and the customer benefit because the shelf life is much longer for bagged lettuce than for head lettuce.[1]

Some years ago, an experiment was conducted to determine whether Colorado and California carnations should be picked and shipped as buds rather than as full flowers. The buds had better transport characteristics because they were less voluminous (more could be loaded into a carton), and they weighed less because the stem with the bud contained less water than the stem with the full flower. An advantage at the receiving end of the shipment was that the buds had a longer shelf life because ripening could be delayed by keeping the buds at a low temperature. The disadvantages were at the receiver's end, because ripening the carnations required temperature-controlled space and some labor to trim and place the stems into buckets of ripening solutions.

Producers of fresh fruits were also interested in developing systems to slow ripening. Consider this item:

> The two ships that called at Wilmington over the last week are the first of six climate-controlled vessels the Chilean company is building in Japan. They represent a major step forward in controlled-atmosphere technology, which has been evolving for about 15 years.
>
> The technology seals a ship's cargo holds and rapidly reduces the oxygen level from a normal of about 20 percent to three percent, halting the ripening process. Precise instruments in the control room constantly monitor oxygen level.
>
> [The owners] expect that the demand for certain crops will increase. Chilean winter blueberries, which now must travel by air and often sell for $3.99 per half-pint, can go by ship now—and sell for 59 cents a half-pint.[2]

In addition to physical characteristics, products possess chemical characteristics that affect the manner in which they should be handled. Certain pairs of products are incompatible. For example, commodities that are sensitive to ethylene, such as

---

[1]*Vancouver Sun* August 21, 2002, p. D5. There is a much higher markup on the bagged lettuce and, according to the article, "Dole and Fresh Express officials won't say how profitable the bagged salad business is or how much they spend on marketing. But competitors and government officials say they profit enough to aggressively market their lines, giving away cases of free produce to stores and paying slotting fees to supermarkets to help their salad get the best real estate in the produce aisle. These fees can range from CAN$10,000 to a small retailer, according to one USAD report, to CAN$10 million to get into one of the . . . largest chains."

[2]*The Journal of Commerce,* February 16, 1994, p. 1B.

mangoes, bananas, and broccoli, should never be held for more than a few hours in the same area as those products that emit ethylene, such as apples, avocados, and cantaloupes.

Tropical fish are carried in plastic bags with enough water to cover them, but no more than necessary, to keep weight down. The area in the bag above water is filled with oxygen. Sometimes, tranquilizers are added to water to keep fish calm. The bag is sealed and placed in a plastic foam cooler, similar to a picnic cooler, which is then placed inside a cardboard box. Fish must be transported within 36 hours, although the time can be extended if oxygen is added to the bags.[3]

The various properties of goods must also be made known to consumers to help them to make the correct buying decision and care for the product properly. Figure 5-1 is a portion of a fabric care label that goes on Levi's jeans sold in Japan. Figure 5-2 is used for marking lumber. The (a) position is for the trademark of the accrediting agent, such as the National Hardwood Lumber Association or the Pacific Lumber Inspection Bureau; (b) identifies the specific mill; (c) indicates whether lumber is heat-treated; and (d) is for the country of origin, necessary if the lumber is exported. During 2002, there was interest in having an additional symbol that indicated wood used for packing was free of insects. Nations in various parts of the world were concerned that untreated wood and wood materials used in packing carried a wide variety of unwanted insects.

FIGURE 5-1 Portion of Fabric Care Label for Levis Jeans Sold in Japan

From left to right the pictures say, Wash at 40° centigrade, use no chlorine bleach, iron at the medium temperature setting; the jeans can be dry cleaned. The text below the label gives the fabric content the nation of origin, and the name Levi Strauss.
Source: Courtesy of Levi Strauss Japan K.K.

---

[3]In any event, be thankful that you aren't a tropical fish.

US$^{(d)}$ - 001$^{(b)}$ Trademarked $^{(a)}$
Agency
HTC/NHTNC Logo
$_{(c)}$

FIGURE 5-2 Lumber Markings

Source: American Lumber Standard Committee, Inc.

Hazardous Cargo

Under certain conditions, almost any material can possess hazardous qualities. Flour dust can explode, and grain in elevators can self-ignite and burn. Special care is needed to handle these and many other substances. Governmental regulations address the movements of hazardous materials and are often classified into seven categories: explosives, compressed gases, flammable liquids, oxidizers, poisons, radioactive materials, and corrosive materials.

The specific requirements differ for each hazardous commodity, but all of them involve labeling, packaging and repackaging, placing warnings on shipping documents, and notifying carriers in advance. A common requirement on transferring flammable materials is that the vehicle and the receiving or discharging device both be electrically grounded. Care must be taken to properly clean tanks, pumps, hoses, and cleaning apparatus to avoid contamination of the next cargo that is handled. Legislation passed after the Exxon *Valdez* oil spill requires petroleum carriers and tank farms to have in place extensive response plans for dealing with possible spills. As part of their response plan, these companies make extensive commitments to have available equipment and trained personnel to deal with spills. Many belong to industry cooperatives, meaning that they expect to help, and be helped by, each other. Some large cleanup contractors can also be relied upon to help.

All levels of government issue numerous regulations, with differences between domestic and international moves. Effective on October 1, 1994, the United States adopted for domestic use the global hazardous materials packaging and labeling regulations developed through the United Nations. However, these regulations are not used in all nations. At the local level, sometimes prohibitions apply to the use of certain tunnels or bridges during specified hours by trucks carrying explosives or other dangerous cargo. In Laredo, Texas, the U.S. Customs Service forced trucks carrying hazardous materials away from a route that went through downtown to an international bridge 18 miles west of town. "On November 11 [1996] all hazardous materials cargo was made to cross the Columbia—Solidarity International Bridge west of Laredo. Local Customs brokers, freight forwarders and short-haul truckers have fiercely resisted any mandates to use the Columbia Bridge, which connects to the Mexican state of Nuevo Leon, while Laredo connects to the state of Tamaulipas. The change disrupts cozy business relations that add numerous costs to cross-border trade."[4]

Shipping documents must also indicate whether the cargo is of hazardous nature, and sometimes additional documentation is required. Packages, containers, trailers, and railcars carrying hazardous materials must carry distinct signs, or placards, identifying the hazard.

---

[4]*The Journal of Commerce,* January 10, 1997, p. 3A.

Environmental Protection

Public concern for environmental protection has had an impact on packaging and materials handling practices. Many materials used in packaging can be recycled. Use of disposable packing materials is often viewed as wasteful, and it is increasingly expensive as costs increase for dumping in landfill sites.

Dust and vapors produced during bulk-cargo transfer operations are also being scrutinized more closely by public agencies. Coal dust can be blown for several miles from a large coal pile. In port areas, bulk materials that were once stored outside are now in enclosed structures. For products still left outside, elaborate vacuum systems are used to capture the dust created by handling, and ditches around the facility capture rainwater runoff so that it can be run through filters. Some states require handlers of petroleum products, including retail gasoline stations, to install vapor recovery systems. For liquids with vapor-escape problems, the transfer processes are redesigned so that tanks and other receptacles are loaded from the bottom rather than the top.

The environmental protection movement has had a profound impact on the packaging industry on a worldwide basis. Receiving considerable publicity are the German requirements for recycling. Retail stores are required to accept from customers all packaging of the retail product. (If you bought a new TV, you could take it home in its carton, unpack it, and then take all the packaging materials back to the retailer's shop for the retailer to worry about.) In a similar manner, retailers could return to wholesalers whatever additional packaging had been used for the move from the wholesaler to the retailer. Likewise, the wholesaler could return the transportation-related packaging and packing materials to the manufacturer. Rumors are that in some areas the law is not working as intended; the scrap material is collected and then sent for disposal in neighboring nations that have yet to enact or enforce sufficient restrictions. Nonetheless, the law is indicative of the direction in which the world is moving. One problem facing those trying to choose packaging materials is that each nation's (and, for that matter, each state's) regulations differ regarding which packaging is acceptable.

One reason that regulations differ is that different areas view environmental problems differently and enact regulations that address the issues of current concern to them. Many regulations in the United States are aimed at reducing the amount of material that ends up in landfills. Landfills are, of course, only part of the problem. One study that attempted to look at a wider range of environmental issues dealt with soft-drink containers. Containers studied were four sizes of plastic PET (polyethylene terephthalate) containers, aluminum cans, and four sizes of glass containers, including one that was refillable. It was assumed that 20 percent of the plastic containers, 50 percent of the aluminum cans, and 10 percent of the glass containers (except for the refillable bottles, which were used eight times), were recycled. Environmental impacts measured were energy needed to produce the container and three forms of waste associated with the containers' disposal: air (atmospheric), waterborne, and solid (landfill). The reusable glass bottle required the least energy, the aluminum can contributed the least to solid waste by volume, and the plastic containers scored best in atmospheric wastes and in solid waste by weight.[5] The findings were very dependent on the assumed rates of recycling of the container types. Purchasers may also show a preference for products packed in recycled materials, and recycling has an impact on choice of materials used in packaging.

Firms can adopt environmentally friendly packaging strategies that follow one of four routes, although portions of the routes may be combined. The first is to reduce the amount of packing materials used. This is easier said than done because carriers responsible for the goods while in transit insist that packaging be adequate. Chapter 6 describes carriers' rate-making procedures, including classifying freight, and notes that the packaging is often specified precisely.

At this early point, the shipper could follow a second strategy by using packaging materials that are more environmentally friendly. Unfortunately, little consensus is evident as to what those specific materials might be. A consumer with a fireplace or wood-burning stove would view scrap wooden packing material in a different manner than would a consumer without one (although fireplace fires are themselves suspected of being environmentally unfriendly). The shipper could use packaging that is made of recycled material, although again there are disagreements as to how packaging with **recycled content** can be labeled.

> When making a claim of recycled content in anything, state laws require full disclosure. That is, you must use a full sentence and explain what the percentage of post-consumer content is in the package. For example, you cannot say "recycled" but you can say "This box contains 35 percent post-consumer recycled fibers; 60 percent total recovered fibers." Since there are no agreed-upon definitions of recycled paper, ask your paper supplier how they define "post-consumer" content.[6]

A third strategy is to use reusable containers. Refillable glass beverage bottles are the best example. This cannot be done for all products, because problems arise when goods in reused containers are contaminated by traces of whatever product had been carried earlier. It was necessary for the U.S. Food and Drug Administration (FDA) to issue an order restricting the reuse of containers to avoid food contamination. Dressed poultry often carries salmonella organisms (which are killed in cooking), and the organisms survive in the wooden crates and spread to vegetables if they are transported later in the same crate. This strategy works best in closed-loop systems, in which carriers are in place to haul empty containers back to their place of origin. The best example of this is in the auto industry, where parts suppliers send parts packed in reusable containers and the same trucks delivering parts haul the empty containers back to the suppliers for another load. For completed new autos, Greenbriar Companies uses a folding auto rack that, after loading, is placed into intermodal containers, which protect the new autos. For the return trip, the racks unfold, and all are placed in one container, leaving the rest available for hauling other freight.

---

[5]*Comparative Energy and Environmental Impacts for Soft Drink Delivery Systems,* prepared for the National Association for Plastic Container Recovery by Franklin Associates, Prairie Village, Kansas, 1989.

[6]*Transportation and Distribution,* October 1994, p. 50. Another area where labeling is imprecise is use of the word "organic."

Just-in-time production strategies result in shorter inventory replenishment cycles which reduces the number of containers to be managed. Secondly, JIT systems utilize fewer suppliers "which improves the ability to control empty containers."[7]

Some Michigan State University researchers studied returnable reusable packaging, and one of their conclusions dealt with tracking the container (i.e., knowing its location at any time):

> Container tracking was one of the least considered, and most problematic, factors. But it is an important factor in reducing the number of containers in the cycle. The one firm [studied] that did re-engineer their information system to track containers . . . found that they dramatically reduced the number needed, from two weeks down to three days' supply.[8]

The fourth strategy is to retain or support services that collect used packaging and recycle it. The economies of scale principle works here; if sufficient amounts of similar waste materials are collected, it is easier to process them for reuse. However, in mid-2002, New York City's mayor announced that the city would stop collecting glass and plastic containers for recycling because of costs, though sanitation workers would continue to collect newspaper and metals.[9]

Some package recovery firms specialize in handling used containers that carry pharmaceutical products. When the container of a product is first shipped to the customer, the container also has a prepaid shipping label addressed to the package recovery firm. At the package recovery firm, the used containers are inspected and either returned to the manufacturer for reuse or sent to a recycler. Other firms specialize in pallet recovery/recycling.

Note that both the third and fourth strategies add a returned packaging loop to the supply chain.

Packaging Scrap Disposal

Firms that receive larger quantities of packaged goods must make provision for reusing or scrapping the waste materials. Several recycling methods were just mentioned that should reduce, if not nearly eliminate, the accumulation of used packaging to be dealt with. It is still sometimes necessary to collect and reduce used packaging so that it can be disposed of. Today, that often means reducing it to a state in which it can be sold to a recycler for either a positive or a negative price, with a negative price meaning one still pays the recycler to haul the material away. Depending on the prices that the recycler may receive from its buyers, it may either sell the scrap or haul it to a landfill site. From a supply-chain standpoint, ending up in a landfill must represent the end of the line. If the materials are recycled, they are fed back into a loop or into somebody else's supply chain.

---

[7]Diana Twede, "Logistics Issues in Returnable Packaging," *Proceedings of the 29ᵗʰ Annual Transportation and Logistics Educators Conference,* September 24, 2000, p. 199.

[8]Wendee V. Rosenau, Diana Twede, Michael Mazzeo, and S. Paul Singh, "Returnable/Reusable Logistical Packaging: A Capital Budgeting Investment Decision Framework," *Journal of Business Logistics,* Vol. 17, No. 2, 1996, p. 159.

[9]www.cnn.com/US, June 30, 2002.

FIGURE 5-3 A Pallet Shredder Designed to Reduce the Cubic Volume of Wooden Pallets and Crating So That They Cost Less to Transport

Source: Courtesy of Blower Application Company, Inc.

Figure 5-3 shows a pallet shredder used to reduce wooden **pallets** and crating to pieces of wood averaging 50 square inches in plane area. This reduces the cubic volume of the scrap by about 75 percent, making it easier to ship and to process.

Metric System

More and more products are being packaged and sold in metric units. New packages are in metric units, and the nonmetric equivalents are printed in smaller type. Although the entire change may take several decades, many of the steps necessary to implement the adoption of the new system must be taken in the next few years.

One U.S. industry that has converted to metric containers is the wine- and liquor-producing industry, which has introduced new sizes of bottles. The conversion was successful, in spite of the fact that the industry is subjected to more than its share of regulation because its product is heavily taxed and many of the taxes were drawn up to be applicable to containers of other sizes.

U.S. exporters are coming under increasing pressure to market their products overseas in metric units. Some importing nations levy fines against products that are not sold in metric measurements.

Packaging

Packaging can be thought of in terms of the **building-blocks concept:** The smallest units are the retail, or consumer, packages or cartons on the shelves of stores. These are packed into boxes of 1 to 2 cubic feet, which are light enough in weight to be carried by a stock clerk. This discussion of the building-blocks concept emphasizes rectangular containers, though it can be applied to other shapes as well.

The building-blocks hierarchy is important to remember because each of the different building blocks is inside another, and their total effect must be to protect the product. They function in a complementary sense. When the consumer-size package—those one sees on the shelves of stores—is very solid, the larger packaging elements require less-sturdy packaging materials because the smaller packages are themselves sturdy. At the other extreme are light bulbs, with a retail packing of single-face corrugated fiberboard that may protect them from breakage but contributes nothing to the internal strength of the larger container.

Promotional Functions of Boxes

Although boxes are thought to be primarily protective, they may also contain features with a sales orientation. Some products are sold in either a consumer-size pack or a larger box or case. Some merchants build displays using box or case lots of goods to create the impression they have made an extra-large purchase of a certain item, presumably at a lower price per unit that is being passed on to the consumer. In this instance, it would be appropriate to display some advertising on the outside of the box. Some boxes are designed so that they do not have to be unpacked by the stock clerk for stocking on shelves. Instead, the stock clerk cuts away the top two-thirds of the box and places the bottom one-third, with its contents still in place, on the shelf. Figure 5-4 illustrates a display box that has been packed as we see it at the factory. The retailer needs only to remove the front and add the header card at the top.

The promotional and protective functions of packaging sometimes conflict. Although from a retailing standpoint it may be desirable to have an attractive promotional message on the outside of each box, when these boxes are in a warehouse the same message might make it easier for a thief to determine quickly which boxes contain the most valuable items. Using code numbers alone on the outside of the box slows down the thief.

Sometimes the marketing staff wants a package with a large surface so that large artwork can be used. An extreme example is from the music industry, where record jackets for 12-inch records have much more space for artwork than do tape or CD cases. Mass merchandising usually means very little sales help on the floor, so for many products customers can examine only the printing and pictures on closed cartons before making their choices.

Figure 5-5 illustrates another issue involving sales and protective packaging. The razor-blade container, shown at the bottom, is quite small. Because razor blades are

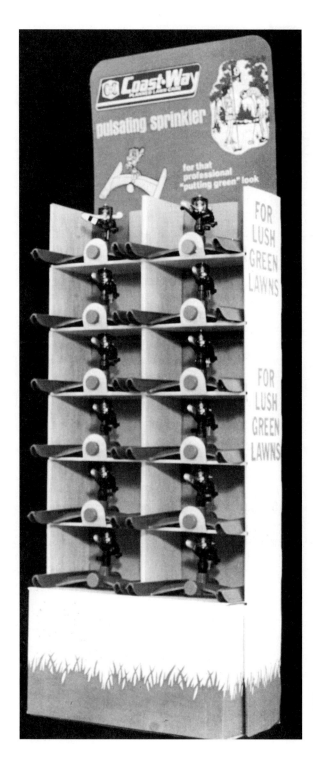

FIGURE 5-4 Shipping and Display Carton

Source: Courtesy of Stone Container Corporation.

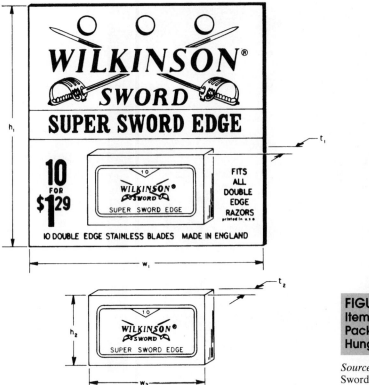

FIGURE 5-5 Impact on Item's Cube Due to Packing It So It Can Be Hung on Rack

Source: Courtesy of Wilkinson Sword Limited, a subsidiary of Warner-Lambert Company.

often displayed next to chain-store checkout stands, from a marketing standpoint it is useful to display them on a rack. However, to reduce the problem of shoplifting, it is necessary to mount the blades on a stiff card that is larger than most people's pockets. The net effect of these two steps is to increase the cube, or volume, of each razor-blade package by over 700 percent. Other small products, such as camera film, batteries, and compact discs, must also be placed in large packages to reduce shoplifting. Airlines want packages that they handle to be at least 1 cubic foot in size. One reason is that this is large enough to be difficult to conceal on one's person, making theft and pilferage more difficult.

Protective Functions of Packaging

A protective package should perform the following functions:

1. Enclose the materials, both to protect them and protect other items from them. Figure 5-6 shows a toy race car and controls packaged inside a form made of expanded polystyrene.
2. Restrain them from undesired movements within the container when the container is in transit.

FIGURE 5-6 Two Race Cars Packaged in a Form Made of Expanded Polystyrene

Source: Alliance of Foam Package Recyclers

3. Separate the contents to prevent undesired contact, such as through the use of corrugated fiberboard partitions used in the shipment of glassware. (A unique example of separating a package's contents is a package used for expensive water faucets. The plumber pulls at the horizontal tab, which is between the top and bottom of the box. This removes the top, outer half, giving the plumber access to all the fittings necessary to install the faucets, which is the most time-consuming of the plumber's tasks. The bottom part of the package holds the expensive faucets themselves, which are used last in the installation process. Because the plumber will not remove them until they are needed, they are less likely to be lost, scratched, or dirtied.)

4. Cushion the contents from outside vibrations and shocks.

5. Support the weight of identical containers that will be stacked above it as part of the building-blocks concept. This could mean, in some situations, stacks in a warehouse that are up to 20 feet high.

6. Position the contents to provide maximum protection for them. If one were packaging combined sets of wastebaskets and lamp shades, the package would be designed so that the lamp shades were protected by the wastebaskets.

7. Provide for fairly uniform weight distribution within the package, because most equipment for the automatic handling of packages is designed for packages

whose weight is evenly distributed. Also, individuals handling packages manually assume that the weight inside is evenly distributed.

8. Provide enough exterior surface area that identification and shipping labels can be applied along with specific instructions such as "This Side Up" or "Keep Refrigerated." Today, this would also mean providing a uniform location for the application of bar codes. Handling symbols, such as a picture of an umbrella meaning "Keep Dry," might also be used.

9. Be tamperproof to the extent that evidence of tampering can be noticed (mainly at the retail level of packaging for some foods and drugs).

10. Be safe in the sense that the package itself (both in conjunction with the product carried and after it has been unpacked) presents no hazards to consumers or to others.

Figure 5-7 is a checklist prepared by the Fibre Box Association, indicating the range of considerations that go into package choice. Firms that sell packaging material are helpful sources of information to potential users. Often, they provide technical advice.

Carriers' tariffs and classifications influence (if not control) the type of packaging and packing methods that must be used. In freight classification documents, the type of packaging is specified. The commodity is listed, followed by a comma and then by a phrase—such as "in machine-pressed bales," "in barrels," "in bales compressed in more than 18 lb. per square foot," "folded flat, in packages," "celluloid covered, in boxes," "SU" (set up), or "KD" (knocked down—or disassembled and packed so that it occupies two-thirds or less of the volume it would occupy in its set-up state). The carriers established these different classifications for two main reasons. First, packaging specifications determined by product density encourage shippers to tender loads in densities that make best use of the equipment's weight and volume capabilities. For example, bicycles are broken down so their cartons take up less of the cube. Figure 5-8 is a device used to measure the length, width, height, weight, and density of packages.[10] IKEA, the Swedish-based home furnishings chain, designs many of its products so that they can be shipped in a dense form. Such products are often displayed unassembled in retail stores, and customers realize that they can take them home easily in their autos.

Specifications that deal with protective packaging reduce the likelihood of damage to products while they are being carried; this, in turn, reduces the amount of loss and damage claims placed against the carrier. Figure 5-9 shows the type of label that motor carriers and railroads require on fiber boxes used for shipping freight. It's called the "box maker's certificate" (BMC) and is the fiber box manufacturer's assurance to the motor carriers and railroads that the boxes will be sturdy enough to meet their handling specifications. Note that a number of measures are used. For example, the size limit shown, 75 inches, means that the material should not be used in a package where the total length, width, and height, when added together, exceed 75 inches. "Size limit is important because, as package size increases, typically, the overall contribution to strength decreases."[11]

---

[10]"Cubing Is Hardly Square," *Modern Materials Handling,* July 2001, pp. 73–75.

[11]*Parcel Shipping & Distribution,* September 2000, p. 33.

checklist for box users

The corrugated box contains and protects your product, but it can also serve many functions which aid in packing, storage, distribution, marketing and sales. This checklist is a guide to the information you'll want to supply to your box maker. He can then offer suggestions and recommendations to utilize every value-added advantage that corrugated can offer.

YOUR PRODUCT

	yes	no
1. Have you given your box maker a description of your product and its use, the exact dimensions, weight and physical characteristics?	☐	☐
2. Is the product likely to settle or shift?	☐	☐
3. Is it perishable, fragile, or hazardous in any way?	☐	☐
4. Will it need extra protection against vibration, impact, moisture, air, heat or cold?	☐	☐
5. Will it be shipped fully assembled?	☐	☐
6. Will more than one unit be packed in a box?	☐	☐
7. Will accessories, parts or literature be included with the product?	☐	☐
8. Have you provided your box maker with a complete sample of your product as it will be packed?	☐	☐

YOUR PACKING OPERATION

	yes	no
1. Is your box inventory adequately geared to re-order lead time?	☐	☐
2. Is your box inventory arranged to efficiently feed your packing lines?	☐	☐
3. Is your inventory of boxes properly stored?		
4. Will you be setting up the boxes on automatic equipment? (If so, what type? Size? Method of closure?)	☐	☐
5. Will your product be packed automatically? (If so, with what type of equipment?)	☐	☐
6. If more than one unit or part goes into each box, have you determined the sequence?	☐	☐
7. Will inner packing—shells, liners, pads, partitions—be inserted by hand?	☐	☐
8. Is your closure system—tape, stiches, glue—compatible with the box, packing line speed, customer needs and recycling considerations?	☐	☐
9. Will the box be imprinted or labeled?	☐	☐
10. Will a master pack be used for a multiple of boxes to maintain cleanliness or appearance?	☐	☐

YOUR STORAGE

	yes	no
1. Have you determined the gross weight of the filled box?	☐	☐
2. Does the product itself help support weight in stacking?	☐	☐
3. Will the bottom box have to support the full weight in warehouse stacking?	☐	☐
4. Will boxes be handled by lift trucks which use clamps, finger lifts or special attachments?	☐	☐
5. Will filled boxes be palletized? (The size of pallet and pallet pattern may justify a change in box design or dimensions, if only to reduce or eliminate overhang.)	☐	☐
6. Would a change in box style or size make more efficient use of warehouse space?	☐	☐
7. Will filled boxes be subject to unusual conditions during storage—high humidity, extreme temperatures, etc.?	☐	☐
8. Is the product likely to be stored outdoors at any time during its distribution?	☐	☐
9. Would color coding simplify identification of various packed products?	☐	☐

YOUR SHIPPING

	yes	no
1. Have you reviewed the appropriate rules of the transportation service you intend to use (rail, truck, air, parcel post, etc.)?	☐	☐
2. Is your container authorized for shipment of your product?	☐	☐
3. If the package is not authorized, have you requested appropriate test shipment authorization from the carrier?	☐	☐
4. Does your product require any special caution or warning label or legend for shipment?	☐	☐
5. Have you determined the actual inside dimensions of the transportation vehicle so that you can establish how your filled boxes will be stacked or braced?	☐	☐

YOUR CUSTOMER

	yes	no
1. Does your customer have any special receiving, storage or handling requirements that will affect box design?	☐	☐
2. Will the box be used as part of a mass display?	☐	☐
3. Is the box intended as a display-shipper?	☐	☐
4. Will it contain a separate product display?	☐	☐
5. Will it be used as a carry-home package, requiring a carrying device?	☐	☐
6. Does it need an easy-opening feature?	☐	☐
7. Can surface design, symbols or colors relate to promotional materials or to other products of the same corporate family?	☐	☐
8. Should instructions or opening precautions be printed on the box?	☐	☐
9. Can the box be made to better sell your product?	☐	☐

FIGURE 5-7 Checklist for Box Users

Source: Copyright permission granted from the Fibre Box Association.

131

FIGURE 5-8 Device for Calculating Package Cube and Density

Source: Cubiscan 100 by Quantronix.

Carrier specifications are precise. Following is an excerpt from an item that was considered by the motor carriers' National Classification Committee:

> Subject 24: Proposes to amend Package 1254, which is authorized for the shipment of dishwashers as named in item 119540, by adding the following options for the base and the corner posts: the specifications for the base would include the following wording: "Expanded polystyrene foam base pad having a minimum density of 1.6 pcf, providing a thickness at bottom of ⅝-inch and ⅞-inch at sides, with sides extended upward a minimum of 2⅞ inches"; and the specifications for corner posts would include the following option: "a ¾-inch clearance must be maintained between article and inside wall of container by mandrel-formed tubular L-shaped solid fibre corner posts."[12]

---

[12] *Transport Topics,* February 24, 1992, p. 25.

FIGURE 5-9 Boxmaker's Guarantee

Source: Courtesy of the American Trucking Association.

It is difficult to know exactly how much carrier tariffs and classifications control shippers' packaging. Responsibility for damage in transit is one issue subject to carrier–shipper contract negotiation; if the carrier remains liable, the carrier specifies the level of packaging protection to be used. If the shipper assumes responsibility, the shipper may choose the type of packaging to use. Carrier deregulation has allowed corrugated packaging manufacturers and their customers to innovate with performance outside of the traditional carrier packaging rules. As specific contract rates are negotiated between individual carriers and shippers, packaging requirements may, of course, be one element of negotiation. (However, when a group of West Coast traffic managers participating in a panel at San Francisco State University were asked whether packaging requirements were an element in their negotiations with carriers, they answered "no." They said that in the negotiations the carriers desired to limit their own liability for loss and damage claims so much that the shippers were subsequently reluctant to cut back on their packaging because the risk for damage in transit had been passed to them.)

Airlines, express delivery companies, and the U.S. Postal Service also have packaging requirements, although they are somewhat less detailed than those used by rail and motor common carriers. Export packing is discussed briefly in Chapter 12. The International Air Transport Association regulates packaging of air shipments. Fewer requirements apply to ocean shipments. However, exporters nearly always buy additional insurance coverage for their export shipments, and the type of packing influences the insurance rates.

Package Testing

When new products or new packaging techniques are about to be introduced, it is sometimes advisable to have the packages pretested. Various packaging material

FIGURE 5-10 Results of Compression Test

Source: Courtesy of Sertapak Group.

manufacturers and trade organizations provide free **package testing.** Independent testing laboratories can also be used. The packages are subject to tests that attempt to duplicate all the expected various shipping hazards: vibrations, dropping, horizontal impacts, compression (having too much weight loaded on top), overexposure to extreme temperatures or moisture, and rough handling. Figure 5-10 shows the side of a corrugated container that failed a compression test. Figure 5-11 shows more detailed testing of several types of paperboard to determine their resistance to heat and to crushing. They are pictured inside an oven.

To properly design a protective package system, the engineer requires three important kinds of information: the severity of the distribution environment, the fragility of the product to be protected, and the performance characteristics of various cushion materials.

Sometimes, specialized tests are devised. The following describes tests conducted on a new type of pallet:

FIGURE 5-11 Testing Paperboard for Strength

Source: Courtesy of Sertapak Group.

After bearing a 2,400-pound load for 48 hours and being checked for deformation, the pallet was again loaded with a 2,400-pound load and run through a series of tests.

Twenty times picked up and set back down on the four-by-fours in a rough and careless manner. Four times picked up off the supporting beams with one fork under the center of the pallet only and lifted to a height of 4 feet, then rapidly lowered and raised.

This attempt was to crack the pallet in the center. Ten times raised 6 inches by a fork that had a fast fork drop rate, and then very rapidly dropped back on its supporting beams.

We then tried to mutilate the loaded pallet by

1. Twisting the forks within the pallet-fork openings; that is, backing up at an angle before disengaging the forks from the pallet. We were able to put a slight tear near the corner of one fork opening.
2. Roughly, we pushed the pallet to different positions while flat on the floor with one fork. This was done in the attempt to split the outside corners.[13]

Figure 5-12 shows a "shake table" used to produce a rotary motion vibration. As pictured, it is testing a metal rack shown inside the cage.

---

[13]Anonymous source.

FIGURE 5-12 Testing a Metal Rack on a "Shake Table"

Source: Courtesy of Sertapak Group.

In addition to the testing of new products or new packages, shippers should keep detailed records on all loss and damage claims. Statistical tests can be applied to the data to determine whether the damage pattern is randomly distributed. If it is not, efforts are made toward providing additional protection for areas in the package that are overly vulnerable. Carriers also have provisions that allow shippers to follow special rules while testing new packaging materials. UPS customers ship sample parcels to various UPS district offices, and UPS employees at those sites then report back with comments about how well the packaging withstood the UPS trip.

Related to package testing is actual monitoring of the environment the package must pass through. This is done by enclosing recording devices within cartons of the product that are shipped. The measuring devices may be very simple, such as hospital-like thermometers that record only temperature extremes and springs that are set to snap only if a specified number of g's (a measure of force) is exceeded. Kaiser Aluminum, which was troubled with problems of water-stain damage, devised the small sticker with the happy face shown in Figure 5-13. Above the happy face's smile are two eyes, but one of the eyes is printed in a special ink that dissolves when it comes into contact with moisture. If the receiver of the shipment notices that the eye is distorted, he or she can assume that the shipment has been exposed to moisture and

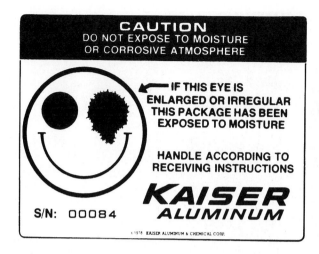

FIGURE 5-13 Kaiser Aluminum's Moisture-Alert Label

When the product is shipped, both eyes are normal; that is, they look like the eye on the left. The figure shows how the label looks after the product is exposed to moisture. The receiver is to record the conditions of the label in the shipping document.

should be inspected for damage. More sophisticated devices record over time a series of variables, such as temperature, humidity, and acceleration force and duration (in several directions). Acceleration force and duration are usually recorded along three different axes, making it possible to calculate the precise direction from which the force originated.

Sophisticated monitors are expensive, but they may be necessary to solve a problem of recurrent in-transit damage. Less complicated devices are used to record temperatures and may or may not be used as the basis for a damage claim against a carrier. They may be used aboard a shipper's own equipment to ensure quality control. A frozen food distributor wants to be certain that its product has not thawed and been refrozen in transit. Large shipments of apples are accompanied by a mechanical temperature recorder, which provides the receiver with a greater workable knowledge of each load, such as information on temperature variation that may affect the speed at which the receiver should handle and merchandise the apples.

Labeling

Once the material being packaged is placed into the box and the cover is closed, the contents are hidden. At this point, it becomes necessary to label the box. Whether words or code numbers are used depends on the nature of the product and its vulnerability to pilferage. Retroflective labels that can be read by optical scanners may also be applied. Batch numbers are frequently assigned to food and drug products, so they may be more easily traced in case of a product recall. Figure 5-14 shows a small sampling of labels that can be purchased for individual placement on cartons or pallets.

Many regulations govern the labeling of consumer-size packages, including the labeling of weight, specific contents, and instructions for use. Today, many of these must also be placed outside the larger cartons as well, because some retail outlets sell in carton lots and the buyer does not see the consumer package until he or she reaches home.

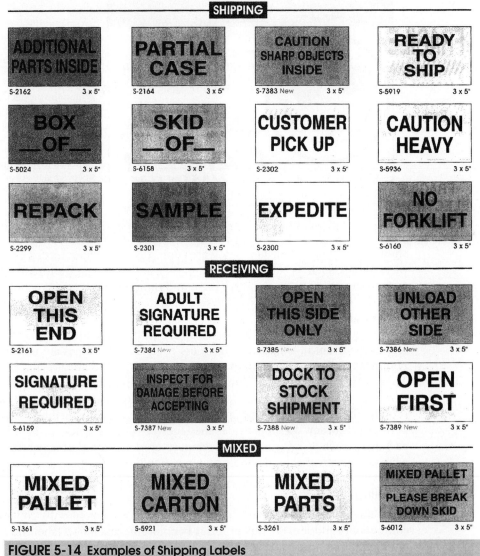

FIGURE 5-14 Examples of Shipping Labels

Source: Uline.

Labeling can also be used to enable a parcel to pass through customs and other inspection points as it travels in international commerce. Following are the markings on a box of flowering bulbs distributed by Eddie Bauer:

OPEN IMMEDIATELY UPON ARRIVAL

GARDEN BULBS GROWN IN THE NETHERLANDS

Pre-cleared in the Netherlands by the U.S.D.A.

This is to certify that the plant material in this consignment was grown in the Netherlands; that it was inspected by me or under my direction both during the growing season and at the time it was packed and was found and believed by me to be free of injurious insects and plant diseases; that it is free from all sand, soil, or earth; that the packing material used is of the type approved under the provisions of Nursery Stock Plant and Seed Quarantine no. 37, and that the plant material was grown on land which, on the basis of an inspection made in the preceding spring, was free of the golden nematode (*Heterrodera rostochiensis Wol.*).

(signed) De Bruin
Director of the Plant Protection Service of the Netherlands

Packaging is usually done at the end of the assembly line. Package labeling also occurs there because using this location avoids accumulating an inventory of preprinted packages. This is also a key point for control because this is where there is an exact measure of what comes off the assembly line. As the packaged goods are moved from the end of the assembly line, they become stocks of finished goods and become the responsibility of the firm's outbound logistics system. Near the point where product packaging occurs, it is necessary to maintain a complete inventory of all the packages, packing materials, and labels that will be used. Today, with laser printers, it is possible to print labels as needed, for example, 24 labels in French. This has lessened the requirement for inventorying printed labels.

The discussion in the last few paragraphs, and for much of this chapter, emphasizes the outward movements of finished goods. For sophisticated materials management systems, it is also necessary to label inbound parts and components so that their location can be continually monitored throughout the supply chain. The worldwide auto industry is about to adopt a single standard for labeling components. Another example is the Pennsylvania Liquor Control Board (PLCB), a state agency that buys and distributes liquor throughout the state. On its Web site is a notice specifying that "the following information be on all cases of products received in any of our warehouses: UPC [Universal Product code] (barcode and readable); the PLCB/State item number; a brief description of the product (including name, size and vintage or proof); the Shipping Container Code (SCC)— barcode and readable—must appear on two adjacent sides"[14] The term **compliance labeling** is used to describe responding to a buyer's demands for specific labeling that facilitates movement of the item through the supply chain.

Bar codes are widely used, and they are read by scanners, or sensors. (Figure 5-15 shows simple handheld bar-code label applicators, and Figure 5-16 shows a bar-code laser scanner.) Scanners often do more than signal the presence of a container or part. They also give the computer as much information as it needs about that part to maintain accurate production and inventory records and to determine the routing of that part from one workstation to another. Leading firms are moving away from the one-dimensional bar code to a code with two dimensions, which can hold considerably more information in a small space.

---

[14]www.lcb.state.pa.us/abi_labeling_requirements.asp, July 10, 2002.

FIGURE 5-15 Two Handheld Bar-Code Applicators

Source: Courtesy of SATO PROMO Touch Hand Applicators.

Not all labels are visible to the naked eye. Some are tiny chips that are embedded into the product and can be read using various electronic devices. Information contained in the chips can be updated as they move through the supply chain. They are sometimes called *smart labels* or RFID labels (radio frequency identification). Some firms places them on reusable pallets. As their price drops, their use will increase, and they are expected to eventually take the place of printed bar codes. In 2002, Wal-Mart was testing them in conjunction with some of its major suppliers.[15] Widespread adoption of RFID labels should allow companies to cut costs, waste, and theft.[16]

Unit Loads in Materials Handling

As mentioned earlier in this chapter, the packaging of materials is based on the building-blocks concept: putting products in containers that will provide efficient yet manageable units. This section discusses unit loads, an extension of the building-blocks concept to very large quantities. The basic unit in unit loading is the pallet or skid. Unit loading involves the securing of one or more boxes to a pallet or skid so that the boxes can be handled by mechanical means, such as a forklift. The boxes or other containers secured to a pallet are known as a **unit load.** The term **unitization** is used to describe

---

[15]*WERCsheet,* April 2002, p. 7.

[16]Nic Fildes, "Tag That Stores Detailed Data May Cut Costs, Waste, and Theft," *Wall Street Journal,* March 19, 2003, p. B4A.

FIGURE 5-16 A Handheld Laser Scanner Scanning Labels on a Pallet Load of Product Sitting in a Warehouse Rack

Source: Courtesy of PSC Inc.

this kind of handling. Figure 5-17 shows a computer printout of 28 possible ways to arrange 12-by-8- by-6-inch cartons on a 40-by-48-inch pallet.

More often than not, the unit load is placed on a wooden pallet. Although somewhat lowly in status, wooden pallets receive considerable attention both in trade journals and at trade meetings. The degree of attention is usually correlated to the price of lumber, and pallets are no longer thought of as free. Shippers are requiring consignees to return the same number of pallets or billing them separately for unreturned pallets. Wooden pallets are popular; a survey of U.S. firms showed that 86 percent of pallets they used were made of wood.[17]

One disadvantage of the conventional pallet is its height (approximately 6 inches). A pallet may occupy as much space as a layer of cases of canned soft drinks. When goods are loaded aboard pallets into railcars, trailers, or containers, the space occupied by the pallet is unproductive. The alternative is to place a sheet of flexible heavy plastic or fiberboard material, known as a **slip sheet,** under the unit load in place of the pallet and then use either straps or shrink wrap to attach the unit load to the slip sheet. The disadvantage is that handling time is increased because the forklift operator must

---

[17]*Modern Materials Handling,* June 2002, p. 29.

```
                    PALLET PATTERN CONFIGURATIONS
  PALLET     PATTERN      TOTAL      NO. OF     TOTAL      TOTAL      SPACE
  NUMBER      TYPE      ON COURSE   COURSES   ON PALLET   WEIGHT   UTILIZED
    1       Unitblock      18          9         162        972      90 %
    2       Unitblock      20          9         180       1080     100 %
    3       Multiblock     20          9         180       1080     100 %
    4       Multiblock     18          9         162        972      90 %
    5       Multiblock     18          9         162        972      90 %
    6       Multiblock     19          9         171       1026      95 %
    7       Multiblock     17          9         153        918      85 %
    8       Pinwheel       18          9         162        972      90 %
    9       Pinwheel       18          9         162        972      90 %
   10       Pinwheel       18          9         162        972      90 %
   11       Pinwheel       20          9         180       1080     100 %
   12       Irregular      18          9         162        972      90 %
   13       Irregular      17          9         153        918      85 %
   14       Irregular      19          9         171       1026      95 %
   15       Irregular      19          9         171       1026      95 %
   16       Irregular      20          9         180       1080     100 %
                    12 more patterns to see

< KEY RETURN=SELECT;SPACE=DOWN;BACKSPACE=UP;B=BACK SCREEN;N=NEXT SCREEN


                    PALLET PATTERN CONFIGURATIONS
  PALLET     PATTERN      TOTAL      NO. OF     TOTAL      TOTAL      SPACE
  NUMBER      TYPE      ON COURSE   COURSES   ON PALLET   WEIGHT   UTILIZED
   17       Irregular      19          9         171       1026      95 %
   18       Irregular      19          9         171       1026      95 %
   19       Irregular      18          9         162        972      90 %
   20       Irregular      19          9         171       1026      95 %
   21       Irregular      20          9         180       1080     100 %
   22       Irregular      19          9         171       1026      95 %
   23       Irregular      19          9         171       1026      95 %
   24       Irregular      17          9         153        918      85 %
   25       Irregular      19          9         171       1026      95 %
   26       Irregular      18          9         162        972      90 %
   27       Irregular      18          9         162        972      90 %
   28       Irregular      17          9         153        918      85 %
              THESE ARE ALL POSSIBLE PALLET SOLUTIONS

< KEY RETURN=SELECT;SPACE=DOWN;BACKSPACE=UP;B=BACK SCREEN;N=NEXT SCREEN
```

FIGURE 5-17 Computer Printout Showing Alternative Ways to Arrange Cartons on Pallets

Source: Courtesy of Professional Micro Systems, Milwaukee, WI.

use the equipment much more carefully to avoid damaging the product. Many firms have mechanical pallet loaders at the ends of their assembly lines that automatically load, build, and strap a pallet. Figure 5-18 shows how a related device is programmed to drape a hood over a loaded pallet to provide additional protection for the load.

Even though the wooden pallet occupies space in a vehicle, its construction and physical properties provide a favorable cushioning effect. However, the quality of individual pallets varies widely. The grocery industry once attempted to establish a pallet interchange pool that was to have minimum standards of quality, but it lost interest because some members believed that slip sheets would replace pallets in unit loading. There is considerable disagreement concerning the relative merits of slip sheets and wooden pallets. However, both involve unit loads and unitization. The disagreement is over the best way to handle them.

In place of the pallet pool, Chep USA, a private firm, performs almost the same function by renting out pallets. Chep USA works mainly in the grocery industry. Most

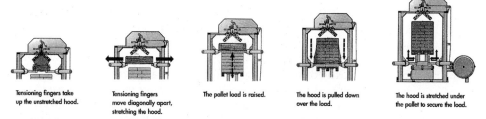

FIGURE 5-18 Device for Dropping Hoods Over Palletized Loads

This is not quite the same as shrink-wrapping, where heat would be applied later to make the covering taut.

Source: Courtesy of Mollers North America, Grand Rapids, MI.

of its deliveries of empty pallets go to food processors and manufacturers. Later, it takes back the empty pallets from retail stores. The pallets are inspected, repaired or replaced if necessary, and fed back to manufacturers. Dole, for example, has adopted Chep USA's plastic pallet pooling system. Pallet receivers are responsible for the pallets and must call to have them picked up. From a supply-chain perspective, this is a loop that operates alongside the main product chain.

The grocery industry is currently considering plastic pallets made from recycled plastic containers. The plastic pallet has no nails that might protrude to injure handlers, damage cargo, or scratch floors in retail stores. The problem is getting a sturdy plastic pallet that will weigh under 50 pounds (reflecting a goal in the industry to have everything that is manually handled under 50 pounds in weight). Plastic pallets are finding markets in closed-loop systems, that is, where the same pallets sent out always come back. Metal pallets are expensive and are used only in closed-loop systems, the largest user being the airfreight industry.

The unit load offers several advantages. It gives some additional protection to the cargo because the cartons are secured to the pallet by straps, shrink-wrapping, or some other bonding device. This provides a sturdier building block. Pilferage is discouraged because it is difficult to remove a single package or its contents. Also, a pallet can be stacked in such a manner that the cartons containing the more valuable or more fragile items are on the inside of the unit load. The major advantage of the unit load is that it enables mechanical devices to be substituted for hand labor. Many machines have been devised that can quickly build up or tear down a pallet load of materials. Robots can be used when more sophisticated integrated movements are needed for loading or unloading pallets. An example of robot-assisted palletizing and de-palletizing exists in the printing industry, in which bundles of printed pages must be stacked in a specified order.

The unit load does have its limitations, however. It represents a larger quantity of an item than a single box—often 30 to 50 times as much. Therefore, it is of limited value to shippers or consignees who deal in small quantities. Some shippers recognize this and have a price break at both the pallet-load quantity and the pallet-layer quantity. Thus, a canner ships in pallet loads to a distributor, which sells to retailers that may buy only in pallet layers or loads. All of the distributor's items are in boxes that can be arranged on the conventional 48-by-40-inch pallet (although the number of boxes that would cover one layer varies). Nonetheless, the distributor's price break is at the pallet-layer quantity, so the retailer might decide to order one layer (which might be 12 boxes or cases) of canned peaches, two layers (which might be 15 cases each) of catsup, and so on. The distributor would load each layer separately, yet the goods would leave its warehouse as a full pallet, or unit load. The distributor would have given an even lower price if the retailer had purchased a full pallet load of a single item because in that instance the distributor would have completely avoided manual handling of the product; it would merely have shipped one of the full pallet loads it had received from the canner.

A *rainbow pallet load* consists of different products, say, flavors of soft drinks, each stacked in a different column. Discount retailers and wholesale buying clubs order products this way. The distributor must build the pallet load by hand. After being delivered to the store, the pallet is taken to the retail area. The shrink-wrap is removed, and consumers can choose their flavor of drink, picking it off the stack.

The military also uses pallet-size boxes having the 40-by-48-inch base:

> Of all the materials handling equipment used by U.S. forces in the Persian Gulf in the early 1990s, a simple wooden box turned out to be one of the most versatile items around. One version of the box, constructed of 1/4-inch-thick plywood and patented hardware and measuring 48 inches long by 40 inches wide by 27.5 inches high, was used to handle and move everything from foodstuffs to ammunition. Designed to be shipped and stored in a knocked-down format (at a 5:1 ratio), the easy-to-assemble box can be assembled with a rubber mallet and a screwdriver in just 10 minutes.[18]

Lift trucks are the common workhorse used around warehouses to move pallets. They come in many designs. Figure 5-19 shows a lift truck used for picking stock in warehouses; in this model, the operator rides with the load rather than at ground level. This truck is also battery-powered, which is common for lift trucks used inside buildings. Batteries are recharged at night.

The discussion in this chapter thus far emphasizes the building of loads from small blocks into large blocks. However, the reverse is also true; that is, the large units or blocks must be broken down into their smaller component blocks, with the very smallest unit being the single item that the retail customer carries home. Figure 5-20 illustrates by showing a high-rise warehouse four tiers high. At the right, a lift truck places full unit loads into a gravity-flow rack system. As they are used, the pallets move to the left, where order pickers break down the unit loads into single boxes. This also results in a FIFO inventory retrieval system, i.e., the first item in is also the first item out.

Intermodal Containers

For surface cargo, the next-size block beyond the unit load is the intermodal container, which is usually 8 feet wide, 8 or more feet high, and 20, 28, 35, 40, or more feet long. Containers are widely used in U.S. foreign trade and domestic trade, although contain-

---

[18]*Modern Materials Handling,* July 4, 1991, p. 61.

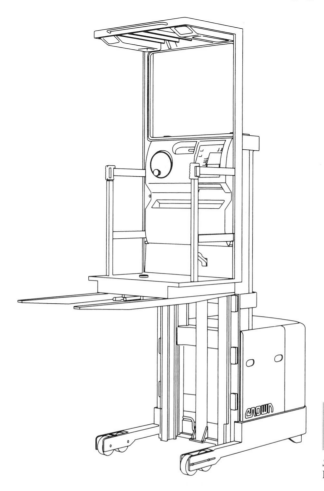

FIGURE 5-19 A Battery Powered Lift Truck Used for Stock Picking

Source: Courtesy of Crown Equipment Corporation.

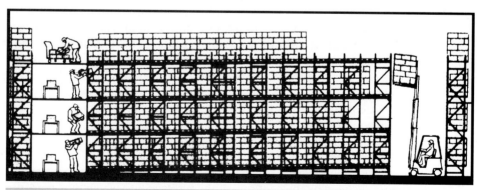

FIGURE 5-20 A Warehouse Where Unit Loads Are Broken Down into Boxes

Source: Courtesy of the Interlake Corporation.

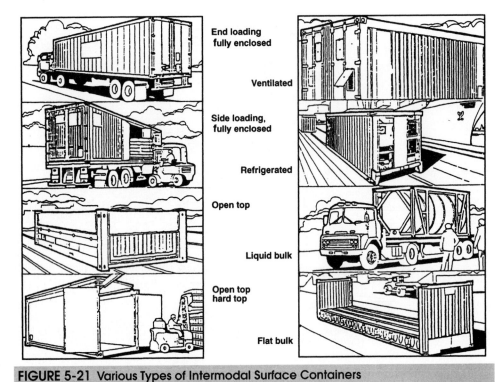

FIGURE 5-21 Various Types of Intermodal Surface Containers

Source: Ports of the World, 14th edition, CIGNA Property & Casualty Companies.

ers used domestically are usually 102 inches wide. Because they are interchangeable among rail, truck, and water carriers, containers can be used in intermodal applications and can provide the advantages offered by each of several modes. Both ocean carriers and railroads have developed methods of handling two or more containers at one time, thereby reducing the number of individual lifting and storage moves.

Most containers are dry-cargo boxes. Some are insulated and come with temperature-controlling devices; others contain one large tank; still others are flatbed. Containers are also specially designed for the transport of livestock and automobiles: With one device, as many as six autos are rolled into a rack that a special loader mechanically inserts into a container for transport. The racks are collapsible and can fit six to a container when they are knocked down. Figure 5-21 shows several different intermodal containers.

Some airlines use 8-by-8-by-20-foot containers constructed of lightweight metals, which are interchanged between air and motor carriers. Only the largest jumbo jets carry containers of this size. Most other aircraft containers have somewhat irregular shapes, dictated by the contours of the fuselage into which they must fit.

Manufacturing operations often receive components from their suppliers loaded on custom-made reusable racks, which are then returned for reloading. The

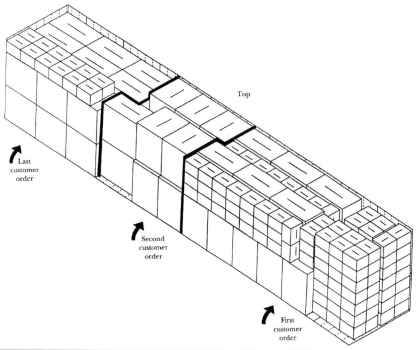

FIGURE 5-22 Computer-Generated Load Plan

Source: Courtesy of TOPS Engineering Corp.

racks are designed with certain pallet-like characteristics because they are handled with mechanized equipment and, ideally, maximize use of the vehicle's cubic carrying capacity.

Equipment Loading

The next step in the building-blocks process is to stow the unit-load pallets into a waiting truck trailer, railcar, or container van. Figure 5-22 shows a computer printout from load-planning software; it suggests how to load a container with different sizes of cartons and tells where the loads for several customers should be loaded. The software recognizes, for example, that some cartons cannot be laid on their sides or cannot have other cartons placed on top of them. The software also takes into account the load's center of gravity and the allowable weights on axles. When planning for refrigerated loads, the software will also take into account the need for air spaces.

Slight clearances must be maintained between pallets to allow for the loading and unloading processes. Bracing or inflatable dunnage bags are used to fill narrow empty spaces. When inflated, they fill the void space and function as both a cushion and a brace. Figure 5-23 shows inflated dunnage bags. A problem involved with any

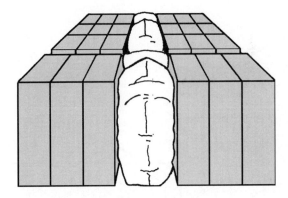

FIGURE 5-23 Inflated Dunnage Bags between Pallets

Source: Courtesy of Sea-Land Service Inc.

bracing or cushioning device is that the load is subjected to forces from all directions. Figure 5-24 shows five of the forces to which a surface sea load may be subjected. Sea loads are subjected to more forces than the ones illustrated in the figure because a vessel in rolling seas can encounter almost any pattern of forces. Even when cargoes are properly braced, the various forces can still cause damage: Continued vibrations may loosen screws on machinery or cause the contents of some bags or packages to settle, changing the type of support they give to the materials packed above them.

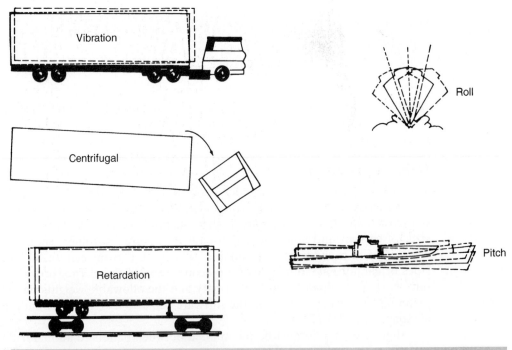

FIGURE 5-24 Various Forces to Which Cargo is Subjected

Source: Courtesy of Sea-Land Service Inc.

For products that present this problem, special preloading vibrators are used to cause the load to settle immediately.

Stroh's had difficulties shipping beer in intermodal containers. The product was heavy and a loaded container *weighed out,* meaning that a full container was too heavy to be legally carried on the highway. The container could not just be loaded in the front because that would disturb its front-to-rear balance. Some *space braces* were devised to fill the empty spaces. The braces were formed from cardboard, and they hung between the beverage loads.[19]

Some goods are so heavy that they utilize the railcar's, trailer's, or container's weight capacity without filling its cubic capacity. These loads, such as heavy machinery, must be carefully braced, and the weight must be distributed as evenly as possible. In highway trailers, for example, it is dangerous to have one side loaded more heavily than the other. In addition, the load should be distributed evenly over the axles.

Finally, the building-blocks concept includes the container or vehicle load, although carriers offer rate incentives for multiple-container, -trailer, or -railcar shipments. Indeed, most carrier–shipper contracts today involve movements in those quantities. Interestingly, CSX Transportation offered special grain rates in 15-car lots, in part because that number of cars is equal to one barge load.

Figure 5-25 summarizes the building-blocks concept insofar as it relates to building up a load. The concept does, of course, also work in reverse, going back down to the consumer-size pack.

Materials Handling

Materials flow through the supply chain. How they are handled physically is the subject of **materials handling.** Mechanical devices are often used for all or parts of this movement.

Nearly all products that are packaged—often in consumer-size boxes, bottles, or cans—are handled by the building-block concept of packaging that has been described previously. The other way that products, especially large quantities of products, are handled is in *bulk.* Bulk materials are loose rather than in packaged form and are handled by pumps, shovel devices, conveyor belts (Figure 5-26) or the mere force of gravity. The decision must be made as to where in the supply chain the bulk materials should be placed into smaller containers for further sale or shipment. Sometimes, bagged and bulk quantities of the same material are part of the same shipment. In vessels, bagged rice is placed on top of bulk rice to provide load stability.

Bulk cargoes have various handling characteristics. One is *density.* The Great Lakes steamer *Richard J. Reiss* uses only two-thirds of its cubic capacity when carrying iron ore, yet the 15,800 tons of ore lower the vessel to its maximum allowable draft of 24 feet, 8 inches. When loaded with coal, the vessel cubes out; that is, the cubic capacity is filled and the vessel is lowered to only 20 feet, 6 inches. Grain loads are even lighter; the *Richard J. Reiss* draft with grain is slightly less than 20 feet.[20] Port facilities for

---

[19]*The Journal of Commerce,* August 26, 1996, p. 5B.

[20]Correspondence from the Reiss Steamship Company to the authors.

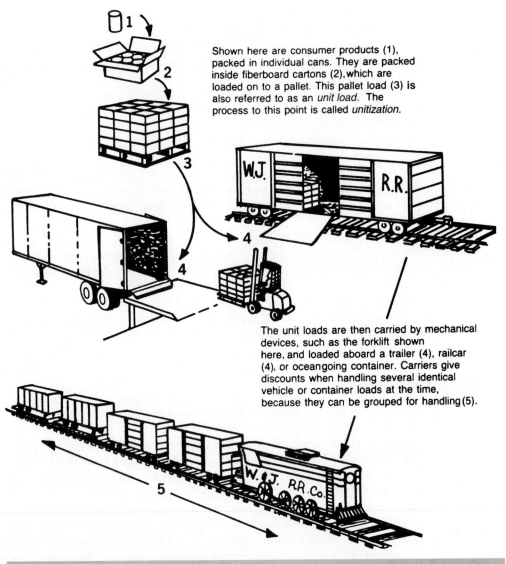

Shown here are consumer products (1), packed in individual cans. They are packed inside fiberboard cartons (2), which are loaded on to a pallet. This pallet load (3) is also referred to as an *unit load*. The process to this point is called *unitization*.

The unit loads are then carried by mechanical devices, such as the forklift shown here, and loaded aboard a trailer (4), railcar (4), or oceangoing container. Carriers give discounts when handling several identical vehicle or container loads at the time, because they can be grouped for handling (5).

FIGURE 5-25 The Building-Blocks Concept of Packaging: A Summary

handling three different bulk materials—coal, iron ore, and grain—are illustrated in Chapter 6.

A material's *angle of repose* is the size of angle that would be formed by the side of a conical stack of that material. The greater the angle, the higher the pile of materials that can be placed on a specific land area. Anthracite coal has an angle of repose of approximately 27 degrees, whereas for iron ore the angle is 35 degrees. This means more cubic yards of ore can be stockpiled on a given site and that the ore can be carried on a slightly steeper, narrower conveyor belt.

FIGURE 5-26 Imported Raw Sugar Moving Along and Up a Convey or Belt in Galveston

Source: Courtesy of the Port of Galveston.

Bulk liquids also have unique handling characteristics. Resistance to flow is measured as viscosity, which can be lowered by increasing the temperature of a liquid. Molasses, cooking oils, and many petroleum products are heated before an attempt is made to pump them.

Gases have unique handling properties, although most of them are handled within completely enclosed pipeline systems. An exception is liquefied natural gas, or LNG, which is cooled and compressed into liquid form that is $\frac{1}{630}$ of its volume in gaseous state. In its liquefied, highly pressurized state, it is transported by oceangoing vessels in special tanks.

The handling process itself may change the characteristics (or quality) of the product. Rice grains cannot fall far without being broken. This influences the design of loading and unloading facilities so that the grains of rice never drop more than a few feet at any one time. When sugar is handled, a dust is formed because of abrasion between sugar crystals. This dust is also sugar, but it is in much finer form and has different sensitivities to moisture. The dust must be separated from the rest of the sugar, or the quality of the final bakery product in which the sugar is used will be affected.

An ideal equipment configuration for one bulk cargo may not be able to handle another. Another consideration is the size of particle of the cargo in question; costs are involved in pulverizing to a uniform size so it can be handled by pneumatic or slurry devices.

Materials Handling Principles

Materials handling is a branch of engineering and deals with the short-distance movement of the material between two or more points. As a supply chain is linked together, one of the concerns of those involved with logistics is the physical transfer of the product from one party to another: How will it be handled? In what form will it be? In what quantities? What kind of equipment is needed to handle or to store it? Materials handling processes generally receive little public attention. An exception to this was the new luggage-handling system at the Denver Airport, which was initially so defective that it delayed the airport's opening by many months.

The College–Industry Council on Materials Handling Education has developed and refined a list of 24 materials handling principles. Most materials handling systems are designed and tested through rigorous engineering analysis. The principles are more important when laying out the intended design or when troubleshooting to learn why a system is not performing well. The principles are as follow:

1. The *orientation principle* requires that one look at the entire system first to learn how and why it operates. One would also look at relationships to other systems and to physical limitations.
2. What is the system expected to do? The *requirements principle* focuses on answering that question.
3. All storage and handling operations must be coordinated, and that is known as the *integrated system principle*.
4. The *standardization principle* means just that. It is important in the selection of packaging to be used. Other things being equal, it is advantageous to standardize on as small a number of packages or wraps as possible.
5. The *just-in-time principle* holds that products are not moved until needed.
6. The *unit-load principle* conflicts with the just-in-time principle in that it emphasizes the importance of handling materials in large blocks, such as the unit loads mentioned earlier in this chapter.
7. Systems should be set up so that loads move for the shortest distances; this is the *minimum travel principle*.

8. The *space utilization principle* requires one to make good use of space. Some materials handling equipment is designed to fit into otherwise underutilized space.

9. **Ergonomics** involves an understanding of how the human body functions as it performs physical tasks. The *ergonomic principle* is used to justify manufacturing and materials handling systems that protect workers from performing difficult and repetitive functions—such as bending or lifting—that ultimately result in injuries or disability.

10. The *energy principle* aims at reducing energy consumption by the materials handling activities.

11. The *ecology principle* calls on us to devise systems that are environmentally friendly, with an example being the choice of materials to use in packaging. (Figure 5-27).

12. Using machines, where justified, to replace human effort is called the *mechanization principle.*

13. The *automation principle* involves the development of equipment that is preprogrammed or self-controlled. Some machines can be programmed to make simple decisions given certain conditions. Some equipment today can respond to radio signals or even voice commands.

14. The *flexibility principle* is important for systems in which there are changes from time to time in the tasks that the system is expected to perform.

15. The *simplification principle* means what it says: Avoid overly complicated systems.

16. The *gravity principle* is easy to understand; one should rely on gravity to move materials wherever possible. Many figures in this book showing materials being handled involve the use of gravity to accomplish part of the task. Note, for example, the warehouse shown in Figure 5-20.

17. The *safety principle* emphasizes the importance of having equipment that is safe to operate and to be near.

18. The *computerization principle* recognizes the widespread use of computers to operate both individual pieces of equipment and massive supply chains spread across several continents. Computers allow better, faster use of information. Material flows are integrated with information flows.

19. The *systems flow principle* calls for an orderly and logical flow of materials.

20. The *layout principle* requires that the system be laid out in a manner that takes all these listed principles into account.

21. The *cost principle* recognizes that all materials handling alternatives have associated costs and that these costs must be carefully considered as the system is devised. Investment proposals must be presented to top management for approval.

22. Once in operation, a system must be maintained. This is recognized by the *maintenance principle,* which includes taking various maintenance alternatives into account.

23. Many existing systems include equipment that has been in service for some time. The *obsolescence principle* recognizes that this equipment must be phased out, taking into account its usefulness, as well as tax and accounting considerations.

FIGURE 5-27 Knowing Which Packaging to Choose Is a Problem for Many Enterprises

Source: Courtesy of Phil Frank. Copyright © 1991 by the *San Francisco Chronicle.* Reprinted by permission.

FIGURE 5-28 Airplane Refueling, Circa the 1920's

Source: Lufthansa Airlines.

24. The *team solution principle* means that materials handling challenges are sufficiently large and complex that often teams of people are needed to devise the best system.[21]

Various materials handling principles are applied to each situation. Two figures illustrate the difference in scale. Figure 5-28 is from the 1920s and shows a relatively unsophisticated device for refueling Lufthansa airplanes. By way of contrast, Figure 5-29 shows a massive piece of railroad equipment designed to handle taconite pellets and limestone. The entire unit consists of a transfer car plus 15 hopper cars stretching a total of 1,013 feet along railroad tracks, plus the length of the locomotive needed to move it. It is used for winter movements of ore pellets in Cleveland, which have been stockpiled at other Cleveland docks by Great Lakes vessels during the open navigation season. This is a short-haul movement, but because it occurs during the winter, persons loading the cars must break up large frozen chunks of pellets that would clog the system. A conveyor belt runs the length of the 16 cars

---

[21]See "The 24 Principles of Material Handling," prepared by the College–Industry Council on Materials Handling Education and appearing in *Material Handling Engineering Directory Issue, 1993–1994,* pp. A13–A18.

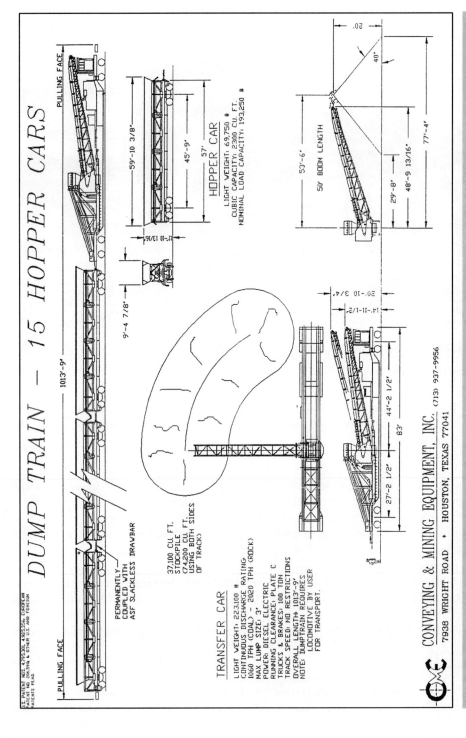

FIGURE 5-29 A Dump Train Consisting of 15 Hopper Cars That Feed to a Transfer Car

The cars are permanently coupled and a conveyor belt runs the entire length of the train, feeding material from left to right to the transfer car, which has a 50-foot boom that can be elevated to 20 feet and can reach both sides of the car. This allows it to place materials in stacks 20 feet high on either side of the train. The device can unload 1,060 tons of coal per hour and 2,020 tons per hour of rock.

Source: Courtesy of David C. Curtis, Manager Traffic & Marketing, LTV Steel Railroads.

and is controlled and operated hydraulically. A special heater was installed to keep the hydraulic fluid from congealing.[22]

Materials Handling in the Supply Chain

Products are designed so that they can move throughout the entire supply chain. Auto frames, for example, are built so that they can be packed together compactly on their journey to the assembly line. They may also come with brackets that are useful on the assembly line but have no particular value once the auto is assembled. Much of this discussion of packaging has dealt with a system that built loads up into truckload quantities. Chapter 10 describes how these large loads of individual products are received at a warehouse, broken down, and assembled and shipped out in entirely different arrays as desired by the next party along the chain.

Bar codes, two-dimension codes, and radio-frequency identification code systems are designed so that they can be used along the entire supply chain. This facilitates integration of the supply chain.

Sometimes, the product does not change but technology and relative labor costs do. An example is garments that now are often shipped hanging in containers. They move from the production line to the container to the truck or vessel to the warehouse to the retailer, always on a hanger. Because they are always on hangers, they can be placed on display at the retailer's without requiring ironing.

SUMMARY

As this chapter demonstrates, many considerations must be taken into account as one chooses protective packaging. Much depends on the physical characteristics of the specific product. Some products are hazardous to either the environment or to persons handling them, and they require special packaging and attention. Common carriers often specify the packaging that must be used. Concerns about recycling and environmental protection also impact the choice of packaging materials.

Packages have a sales function as well, and a sturdy package contributes to a product's solid image. In recent years, retail packages have been provided with protective seals, which make it easier to detect tampering.

Retail packages are placed into cartons, which are loaded onto pallets to form unit loads. Then, the unit loads are loaded by forklifts into intermodal containers, truck trailers, or railcars. Palletization and unitization both refer to the utilization of pallet loads as a form of building block.

All materials have their unique handling and storage characteristics. A list of materials handling principles provides guidance for system design.

QUESTIONS FOR DISCUSSION AND REVIEW

1. What is the difference between the selling and protective functions of packaging? How are the two functions related? Explain.
2. Describe the function of conventional pallets. What are their advantages? Disadvantages?

---

[22]CSX Transportation's entry in the *Modern Railroads* Golden Freight Car Competition, 1990, unpublished.

3. Discuss the specific protective functions that a protective package must accomplish. Does every package have to accomplish every function? Discuss.

4. Discuss some of the packaging requirements associated with hazardous cargo.

5. What environmentally friendly packaging strategies might a firm adopt?

6. Discuss the role of labeling in logistics management.

7. What are some advantages and disadvantages of plastic pallets?

8. Discuss intermodal surface containers.

9. What is unit loading?

10. What is noteworthy about the German requirements for recycling?

11. What information is needed to design a protective package properly?

12. How does supply-chain integration affect packaging? Discuss.

13. What is the building-blocks concept? How is it applied to the handling of packaged goods?

14. Discuss the relationship between the level of protective packaging used relative to the packaging requirement of common carriers. How has carrier deregulation affected shippers' packaging? Discuss.

15. Give some examples of package testing.

16. Describe some of the devices that are used to monitor conditions during the journey that a shipment makes.

17. What are materials handling principles? What function do they serve?

18. Describe a materials handling situation with which you are familiar, and point out those materials handling principles that you think are applicable.

19. Is materials handling an issue within a firm, or is it a supply-chain issue? Discuss.

20. Give some examples of package recycling efforts with which you have been involved.

SUGGESTED READINGS

Agbegha, Gerald Y., Ronald H. Ballou, and Kamlesch Mathur. "Optimizing Auto-Carrier Loading." *Transportation Science,* Vol. 32, No. 2, 1998, pp. 174–188.

Bookbinder, James H., and Dominique Gervais. "Material-Handling Equipment Selection Via an Expert System." *Journal of Business Logistics,* Vol. 13, No. 1, 1992, pp. 149–172.

Chopra, Sunil, and Peter Meindl. *Supply Chain Management,* 2nd ed. Upper Saddle River, NJ: Prentice Hall, 2004.

CIGNA. Ports of the World—A Guide to Cargo Loss Control, 15th ed. Philadelphia: CIGNA, 1992.

Freese, Thomas L., *Logistics Needs of Non-Traditional Retail.* Chagrin Falls, OH; Freese & Associates, 1999, pp. 1–5.

Haessler, Robert W., and F. Brian Talbot. "Improving Customer Service Through Load Planning." In *Annual Conference Proceedings of the Council of Logistics Management,* Vol. 2, Oak Brook, IL: Council of Logistics Management, 1990, pp. 251–256.

Hildebrandt, Glenn. "Case Study: Installation of Inbound Returnable Containers at the John Deere Horicon Works." In *Council of Logistics Management Annual Conference Proceedings, 1993.* Oak Brook, IL: Council of Logistics Management, 1993, pp. 289–292.

Krupp, James. "Pack to Order: An Antidote for Brand Multiplicity." *Production and Inventory Management Journal,* Vol. 40, No. 2, 1999, pp. 16–20.

Pennsylvania Liquor Control Board, Pennsylvania Liquor Control Board Labeling Requirements (revised January 2002), www.lcb.state.pa.us/abi_labeling_requirements.asp, July 10, 2002.

"The Process of Logistical Packaging Innovation." *Journal of Business Logistics,* Vol. 13, No. 1, 1992, pp. 69–94.

Twede, Diana. "Logistics Issue in Returnable Packaging." *Proceedings of the 29th Annual Transportation and Logistics Educators Conference,* September 24, 2000, pp. 197–215.

U.S. Department of Agriculture, Official Inspection and Weighing Services, www.usda.gov/gipsa/programsfgis/services.htm, June 13, 2002.

C A S E

Case 5-1   Let There Be Light Lamp Shade Company

Started in Madison, Wisconsin, after the student unrest of the 1960s had died down, the Let There Be Light Lamp Shade Company served an upscale local market for many years. It designed and built custom lamp shades and lamp globes. In the mid-1980s, some architects who had once studied under Frank Lloyd Wright in nearby Spring Green were commissioned to design several large public buildings in Asia. A total of 5,400 identical lights were to be installed, and the Let There Be Light Lamp Shade Company wished to bid on the work. Terms of sale would include delivery to the foreign port where the buyer would take possession.

Transportation costs would be a hurdle. In the initial design, the shades were cylinders that were 11 inches high and 11 inches in diameter and were packed into boxes that were 12 by 12 by 12 inches. (We refer to these shades as style A.) The packages cost 60 cents each and weighed 1 pound each. The shades cost $4 each to manufacture. They weighed 9 pounds each and 10 pounds packaged.

They would be shipped to the Port of Oakland. The land rate to Oakland was $1,000 per 40-foot container, without regard to weight, although the weight of the load could not exceed 44,000 pounds per loaded container because of highway weight restrictions. The interior dimensions of the intermodal container were 8 feet wide by 8.5 feet high by 40 feet long.

Ocean rates from Oakland to the overseas port were $22 per ton (2,000 pounds), except that the ocean conference used a measurement

ton that indicated that for bulky loads every 40 cubic feet would equal 1 ton for rate-making purposes. (That is, a shipment weighing, say, 130 pounds and occupying 80 cubic feet would cost as though it weighed 4,000 pounds.) Insurance costs were 2 percent of the value of the shipment ready to be loaded aboard ship in Oakland. (This is calculated as all of the company's costs up to this point.)

Because of the large size of the order, Let There Be Light Lamp Shade Company realized that it could custom design a shade that, rather than being a cylinder, would be shaped like a cone. The advantage to that was that the shades could be nested. Some padding would be required between the shades, but the nested shades would also help protect each other. However, cutting out material for conical shapes results in waste, so production costs would be higher. Two alternative cone-shaped designs were proposed (referred to as styles B and C).

Style B cost $5 per shade to manufacture and could be shipped nested in packages of six. The package dimensions were 12 by 12 by 48 inches, and when holding six shades, a package weighed 62 pounds. Each package cost $2, and this included padding between the shades.

Style C cost $6 per shade to make and could be shipped nested in packages of 10. The package dimensions were 12 by 12 by 50 inches, and when holding 10 shades, a package weighed 101 pounds. Each package cost $3, including padding between the individual shades.

QUESTIONS

1. How many style A shades can be loaded into an intermodal container?
2. How many style B shades can be loaded into an intermodal container?
3. How many style C shades can be loaded into an intermodal container?
4. What are the total costs of delivering the style A shades to the port of importation?
5. What are the total costs of delivering the style B shades to the port of importation?
6. What are the total costs of delivering the style C shades to the port of importation?
7. Which style would you recommend? Why?

The Domestic Transportation System

The equipment available for shipping products has changed. The top photograph shows a tank car from 1865, built by placing two wooden tubs on a flat car. The bottom photograph shows a tank car as it is used today. The sign in the center of the car includes a toll-free telephone number for product emergencies.
Photos courtesy of Union Tank Car Company.

Key Terms

- Broker
- Bulk cargo
- Consignee
- Freight classification
- Freight forwarder
- Intermodal transportation
- LTL
- Nodes
- Parcels

- Parcel carriers
- Private transportation
- Project cargo
- Routing guides
- Shippers' cooperatives
- Terminal
- TL (truckload) rate
- Ton-mile

Learning Objectives

- To relate the mode of transport to the user's shipping volume
- To understand the use of routing guides
- To realize the role of freight forwarders and other intermediaries
- To understand the difference between LTL and TL motor carriers
- To appreciate the use of terminals as transfer points for bulk materials
- To appreciate trade-offs when using vehicles with self-loading/unloading equipment
- To learn about project cargo
- To learn the basics of freight rate determination

Transportation is the movement of goods and people between two points. While many other logistics activities are site specific, transportation is not. At one time, logistics systems were thought of as inventory storage points (**nodes**) connected to others by transport carriers (links). Goods in transit between two nodes were almost in a state of limbo. Their removal from the shipping point would be recorded by subtracting them from that facility's records. When they arrived at their destinations, they would be unloaded and added to the facilities' inventories. Today, much closer tabs are kept on inventories in motion, and carriers are so well disciplined that goods in transit can always be counted on to arrive when needed. (Well, almost always.)

This chapter looks at the nation's domestic transportation system, starting with service available to the shippers of small amounts and moving to shippers that think in terms of trainloads or bargeloads. It assumes that readers have some knowledge of parcels and smaller freight shipments, and it spends more time on carriers that handle large movements of bulk materials. Chapter 12 covers international transport.

Transportation encompasses five different types, or modes: truck, rail, air, water, and pipeline. Between 75 and 80 percent of the domestic expenditures for freight transportation go to some form of trucking, which is one reason why that mode is emphasized in this chapter. **Intermodal transportation** occurs when two modes or more work closely together on a regular basis, utilizing the advantages of each. For purposes of this chapter, intermodal transportation refers to carriage when utilizing a container or other device that can be transferred from the vehicle of one mode to the vehicle of another (sometimes the same) mode without the contents of the device being reloaded or disturbed.[1]

Transportation is pivotal to the successful operation of any supply chain since it carries the goods, literally, as they move along the chain.

1. Transportation costs are directly affected by the location of the firm's plants, warehouses, vendors, and customers.
2. Inventory requirements are influenced by the mode of transport used. High-speed, high-priced transportation systems require smaller amounts of inventories near customer locations.
3. The transport mode selected determines the packaging required, and carrier classification rules dictate package choice.
4. The type of carrier used dictates a manufacturing plant's materials handling equipment, such as loading and unloading equipment and the design of the receiving and shipping docks.
5. An order-management methodology that encourages maximum consolidation of shipments between common points enables a company to give larger shipments to its carriers and take advantage of volume discounts.
6. Customer service goals influence the type and quality of carrier and carrier service selected by the seller.

We generally know when to use mail, fax, phone, or e-mail, after some trial and error. If we know that we will make certain shipments in the future, we may call around or surf the Web to determine prices and services available, or the other party to our transaction may advise or instruct us. **Routing guides** (sometimes called shipping guides), used by almost all shippers, contain instructions for choice of mode and carrier for every shipment. In the shipping room of many firms, the routing guide often was in a three-ring binder, and if one had a 42-pound shipment that had to reach Atlanta in four days, the guide would tell the lowest-cost dependable method to use.

Today, many of these guides are computerized, and the decision regarding how to ship is determined at the time of order processing, with the appropriate shipping documents and labels produced by computer. For example, at the shipping dock of a computer-manufacturing plant in California's Silicon Valley, three trailers were being loaded as packaged computers and accessories came off the end of the packing line. Above each trailer was a banner (supplied by the carrier) saying "FedEx" (Federal Express), "UPS" (United Parcel Service), or a specific nationwide motor carrier. Each of the three carriers offered a different class of service, and the manufacturer's own computerized system was programmed to make the carrier selection. Routing guides are also sometimes supplied to vendors (or placed on the purchaser's Web site), with specific instructions as to how incoming goods must be routed.

As previously stated, nodes, are points to and from which shipments are made. They are an integral part of the transportation and logistics system. They represent points where one achieves access to or exit from a transport system, and they are

---

[1]This definition comes from Barton Jennings and Mary Collins Holcomb, "Beyond Containerization: The Broader Concept of Intermodalism," *Transportation Journal,* Spring 1996. Intermodal shipments frequently travel under a single bill of lading.

FIGURE 6-1 Switching Milk Cans from a Farmer's Buggy to a Truck on a Rural Road in North Carolina, 1929

Source: Photo courtesy of U.S. Department of Agriculture.

where cargoes are exchanged between modes, carriers or vehicles. Figure 6-1 shows a simple node, circa 1930. Many nodes are known as *terminals.* Here, the word *terminal* has two meanings: a transfer point or the end of a move. Often, inventories are kept at terminals to provide a cushion to accommodate the different patterns of inbound and outbound flow. The bulk terminals described later in this chapter, and the warehouses, described in Chapter 10, all hold inventories.

As supply-chain managers attempt to integrate all facets of their systems, they often find it desirable to have the capability of tracking all shipments so that they always can determine their geographic locations. Hence, their own equipment or that provided by carriers is now frequently equipped with some tracking-type device. Global tracking devices can be located by satellite. Dispatchers handling local delivery and collection fleets can use them to determine which truck should be assigned to make a pickup that has just been phoned in. A few carriers offer mapping software so customers can visualize where, geographically, the shipments or vehicles are.

Parcel carriers have labels on each parcel and, at various stages in each parcel's journey, its label is scanned and that information is saved in case the shipper or consignee asks about its most recent recorded location. When some parcel companies deliver parcels, that fact is recorded on a handheld device the delivery person is carrying, and that information is transmitted almost immediately to the parcel carrier's main computers.

Hence, a carrier today is expected not only to move materials but also to tell the customers where they are in the geographic pipeline. The shipment's location in the pipeline has become a piece of information that supply-chain managers now expect to have.

Small-Volume Shippers

The smallest of businesses are probably operated out of people's homes. Mail and parcel post can reach any address in the United States and virtually any address elsewhere in the world (with varying degrees of reliability). One can purchase supplies on a delivered basis, and the seller has to arrange for transportation. One can also sell FOB (free on board), in which case customers will pick up their purchases. One's own auto or light truck can be used for local carriage of goods. In some cities, taxis can be used to deliver packages; local delivery services will pick up and deliver packages within certain geographic areas. This section describes packages weighing up to 150 pounds, those that are often referred to as **parcels;** firms that specialize in their carriage are called **parcel carriers.**

In recent years, a number of franchisers of shipping/packaging outlets have located in store fronts and shopping centers, office buildings, office parks, and industrial parks. Walk-in customers bring in materials to be packaged and sent via mail, UPS, or other forms of transport. Such outlets often have fax machines, photocopiers, and mailboxes and sell packaging materials and some office supplies. They give the occasional shipper access to all forms of carriage, and they relieve the shipper of the need to inventory packaging supplies. They charge the carrier's rate plus an additional percentage, and they arrange for insurance. These franchises offer an entry into most services that the occasional shipper of small packages needs. They will also represent their customers if some problem with a carrier occurs at some later stage. They also have access to the online computer services that carriers offer to enable shippers to trace shipments or query their status.

As one's volume of shipments increases, one studies the various services available for handling small movements of product. Parcel Post is a service of the U.S. Postal Service that has definite size and weight limitations (approximately 70 pounds). Charges are based on weight and distance and are relatively low. In most cases, a parcel must be carried to the post office, but it will be delivered to the receiver. The Postal Service also offers various levels of mail and parcel service and parcel pickup.

The best-known parcel carrier is United Parcel Service (UPS), which now operates in 200 countries and financially dwarfs any other transportation company in the United States. The firm has over 345,000 employees, 157,000 trucks, and 600 planes.

Worldwide, it delivers 3 billion packages and documents annually.[2] This company has experienced growth because it has earned a reputation for very reliable service. UPS rates include both pickup and delivery. It offers a range of services via several modes of transport, and users of its air service can purchase next-day, second-day, or third-day deliveries. UPS also provides computer software to assist with documentation and to allow the customer access, via a modem, to those segments of the UPS computer system that the customer uses to track the status of his or her shipment. UPS's dominant role in the country's transportation system was evident during its employee strike in 1997. Some firms that were completely dependent on UPS had to shut down as the strike took its toll. A similar strike was barely averted in 2002.

UPS has been one of the major beneficiaries of the e-commerce boom and helps many companies handle their order fulfillment and packing needs, as well as managing returns. They also help to provide the logistics content of their customers' Web sites. UPS feels that many B2B (business to business) firms lack the infrastructure to successfully develop business on the Internet in a manner that generates an ample and continuous flow of outbound goods and inbound funds.

FedEx runs on a similar concept, relying on a huge fleet of planes to carry parcels to and from several major hubs each night. Its specialty is overnight delivery. In most major markets, at least a half dozen companies offer overnight delivery of small packages. Both UPS and FedEx offer service to many foreign countries and, as a part of this service, also handle the many documentation needs associated with export and import transactions. Recently FedEx entered into an alliance with the U.S. Postal Service, part of which involves FedEx providing a large portion of the Postal Service's domestic air transportation.

Passenger carriers also carry small packages, which usually have to be delivered to and picked up from the carrier's terminal. Bus package service is offered by intercity bus companies. The maximum weight per package is from 100 to 150 pounds. The packages travel in special compartments on the intercity buses. The service is fast and reliable, and packages delivered 30 minutes before a bus's departure will be aboard that bus. There is no pickup or delivery service. Some airlines offer next-flight-out service and accept parcels at the passenger ticketing and check-in gates at the airport's terminal.

LTL Shippers

As one starts dealing with larger shipments, the next step in the progression is referred to as less-than-truckload, or **LTL,** traffic. Shipments in this category range from about 150 to 10,000 pounds. They are often too big to be handled manually, yet they do not fill a truck. Trucks that carry LTL freight have space for and plan to carry shipments of many other customers simultaneously.

The majority of the nation's large trucking firms are LTL carriers. Since deregulation, a handful have developed high-quality, nationwide service for less-than-truckload amounts. Leaders are Yellow Freight, Roadway Express, and ABF Freight System,

---

[2]*iSource Business,* February 2001, p. 100.

which serve nationwide. (Some LTL carriers are regional). All operate in virtually the same manner. They have numerous terminals spread throughout the nation. From each **terminal,** small trucks go out to customers, delivering and picking up shipments. These shipments are then taken to the terminal, where they are loaded aboard line-haul trucks, which are driven to a terminal near the freight's destination (sometimes this line-haul move occurs with a container or trailer riding on a railcar). The goods are unloaded from the line-haul carrier, move through the terminal, and are loaded aboard a small truck for local delivery.

Consignees are receivers of freight. Some consignees consolidate their inbound freight by specifying that all shipments made to them be routed via a specific LTL or parcel carrier. In that carrier's local terminal, all shipments to be delivered to the specified consignee are loaded on one truck. There is therefore only one delivery each day of several packages, rather than numerous deliveries, each at a different time by a different carrier with a single package.

Shipments of this size also move by air. They can be tendered directly to the airline at an airport, or they can be given to a freight forwarder for consolidation. Most air freight is carried on passenger-airline aircraft. A small number of airlines carry freight exclusively. The following product groups represent the largest users of air freight:

- Wearing apparel
- Electronic or electrical equipment and parts
- Printed matter
- Machinery and parts
- Cut flowers and nursery stock
- Auto parts and accessories
- Tapes, televisions, radios, and recorders
- Fruits and vegetables
- Metal products
- Photographic equipment, parts, and film.

As this list illustrates, products that are air freighted tend to be high in value and are often of a perishable nature or otherwise require urgent delivery. Airfreight rates discourage bulky cargo and use a practice called *dimensionalizing* to obtain more revenue from cargo that has a high volume-to-weight ratio.

Air freight moves in air cargo containers. Air cargo containers have varying shapes, designed to take into account each plane's interior contours. Each airline uses only containers that fit into its own aircraft. Some air cargo containers are interchangeable among different models of aircraft. For example, in its booklet describing containers that can be used aboard its aircraft, KLM, the Royal Dutch Airlines, lists about 20 different sizes of containers and pallets. The largest container is 8 by 8 by 20 feet. Thought it looks like the rail/truck/water container, its tare (empty) weight is much less, and it is engineered to higher standards because it is designed to be an integral part of a loaded aircraft. Such containers are used on the main decks of wide-bodied aircraft. The next-smaller KLM container is half that size, 8 by 8 by 10 feet, and is also designed for the main deck on wide-body planes. Some containers are igloo-shaped for main-deck placement on smaller all-cargo jets, and lower-deck containers have one bottom corner tapered to fit inside the plane.

Freight Forwarders, 3 PLs and Other Consolidators

Freight forwarders are not modes, but from the shipper's viewpoint they are analogous to other carriers. The two types of domestic freight forwarders—surface and air—can best be thought of as consolidators of freight.

Freight forwarders operate as agents. Both surface and air carriers give volume discounts to customers shipping large quantities of freight at one time. For example, the motor carrier rate from city A to city B might be $5 per 100 pounds for shipments under 20,000 pounds. This is called an *LTL rate*. The **TL (truckload) rate** might be $2 per 100 pounds when shipments of 20,000 pounds or more are tendered. The freight forwarder exists by offering a service to shippers that must use LTL rates because they do not generate enough volume to use TL rates. Without the freight forwarder, the small shipper has to use the $5 LTL rate. The freight forwarder, however, offers the same transportation service for a rate between the LTL and TL rate—say, $4. This is possible because the freight forwarder consolidates all the small shipments it has and gives them to the carrier (a trucker in this case) and hence qualifies for the $2 TL rate. The freight forwarder typically offers pickup and delivery service but does not perform the line-haul service. This is done by motor carriers or railroads. Forwarders also function as transportation departments for small firms, performing other transportation-management functions.

Some forwarders specialize in certain cargoes. A common example is in the garment industry, in which many small garment firms send large numbers of a few garments each to retail shops in most large cities. The garment forwarders use special containers in which the garments are on hangers and thus ready for display on arrival. Another specialized forwarder relocates house pets. The firm handles health inspection prior to shipment, arranges for cages and quarantines (if required), books flights, and handles all documentation.

Rock-It Cargo, in Los Angeles, specializes in carrying cargo for rock groups:

> In one of its most ambitious tasks, Rock-It Cargo is helping the Rolling Stones send their equipment to concert sites. . . . Each of the six stages being moved around the world for the group's "Voodoo Lounge" tour fills 16 40-foot cargo containers. In addition, the Rolling Stones travel with 500,000 pounds of musical, video, and lighting equipment.[3]

The air forwarding industry works with the air carriers. The forwarders consolidate shipments and tender them in containers that are ready for aircraft loading. This results in significant ground-handling time savings for the airlines. Therefore, airlines encourage forwarder traffic because it results in an agreeable division of labor: The forwarders provide the retailing function and deal with each individual shipper and consignee, and the airline concentrates on wholesaling, moving the forwarders' loaded containers among major cities. From the forwarder's standpoint, in the air freight industry, the forwarder–carrier partnership should be based on the following elements:

1. Honoring of space commitments made by forwarder
2. Fixed, competitive rates

---

[3]*The Journal of Commerce,* December 19, 1994, p. 3.

3. Honored rebates, based on forwarder performance
4. As little bulk as possible, tender whole containers
5. Airline guarantees lift
6. Improved on-time delivery by airlines
7. Preferred access to capacity during peak periods
8. No competition at the retail level.[4]

The following excerpt from a routing guide differentiated nicely as to when to use an air freight forwarder and when to deal directly with an airline:

> Harcourt Brace & Company utilizes air freight forwarders whose responsibilities (from door to door) [are] generally a requirement of our business, whereas an airline's primary concern is to move freight between airports with secondary emphasis on pickup and delivery. Both offer immediate tracing service.
>
> For the most part, our air freight shipments can run anywhere from five pounds to three hundred pounds. Depending upon destination plus service requirements, it would be well to utilize the airline itself for the movement of shipments in excess of three hundred pounds in order to effect cost savings and accomplish our intent.[5]

Shippers' cooperatives perform basically the same function as surface and air freight forwarders, except they do not operate as profit-making organizations. All profits achieved through their consolidation programs are returned to members. This type of consolidation program has been well received by shippers.

Third-party logistics (3PL) services are active providers of transportation. Some own bricks-and-mortar structures, trucks, and trailers. They try to find clients with complementary carriage needs so that they can increase equipment utilization. Many of these third-party providers were spin-offs from carriers or from management consulting firms. Some were spun off from large manufacturing firms whose top management decided that logistics industrial transportation management was not on the list of core competencies that they wished to maintain. Some third-party providers have no equipment other than computers, and one writer referred to them as "infomediaries."[6] Some infomediaries become gigantic storehouses of information that their clients can access. Or they may take the client's information and be able to analyze with more powerful programs than the client would be likely to have in-house. Lastly, they operate some Internet-based auctions where loads are matched and unused capacity is filled.

The term *broker* is used frequently in transportation. A *broker* is a facilitator who brings together a buyer and seller. Some brokers handle LTL shipments. They consolidate shipments and then turn them over to truckers, forwarders, or shippers' associations.

---

[4]Klaus Geissler, "The True Role of the International Freight Forwarder," *CNS Focus,* Vol. 11, No. 4, Winter 1996, p. 19.

[5]*Harcourt Brace & Company Logistics Services Procedures Manual,* Orlando, FL: Harcourt Brace, 1994, pp. 16–17.

[6]Amelia Regan, "Transforming the Freight Industry," *Access,* Spring 2002, p. 28.

Parcels and less-than-truckload shipments comprise the type of transportation the vast majority of U.S. firms use. The ubiquitous brown UPS truck and other delivery trucks are likely familiar to all readers. It is for parcels and LTL shipments that carriers use published rates, similar in format to those described toward the end of this chapter. These rates are based on three factors: the size of the shipment, the distance traveled, and the product's handling characteristics.

When switching from less-than-truckload to truckload shipping, one may feel uncertain when to take the step. Each shipper must define under what circumstances he or she should save up a sufficient amount of freight to qualify as a truckload. This occurs not only between a truckload and less than a truckload; similar situations occur in rates for intermodal containers and for blocs of railcars. Assume that the LTL rate for widgets is 30 cents per pound, the TL rate is 20 cents per pound, and 40,000 pounds of widgets fill a truck. At a particular point, the shipper would do better to claim to be shipping enough to qualify for the 20 cents per pound, even though the load is less than 40,000 pounds. Consider, for example, the trucker who expects a full load and revenues of $8,000 (40,000 × 20 cents). If the shipper has ⅔ of the 40,000 pounds, or 26,667 pounds., he could use either the TL or LTL rate. If he has a quantity between 26,667 and 40,000 pounds, he should claim to be shipping 40,000 pounds and pay the rate for 40,000 pounds.

Interestingly, this paid-for but unused weight must be shown on the trucker's bill of lading because when the trucker is halted at a weigh scale, he or she must produce documents that show how much weight the truck is carrying, and this should be about what the truck weighs on the scale (less tare weight of truck and fuel). In trucking, this unused—but paid-for—weight is called *deficit weight, phantom weight,* or *dead weight.* This practice was also used in railroading when railroads carried less than carload (LCL)[7] traffic and the railroad term was "shipping wind." This concept is important because the practice influences the size of shipments moving among nodes.

Truckload and Carload Shippers

When one's individual (or consolidated) shipments reach weights of, say, 20,000 to 30,000 pounds, one can start thinking of truckload (TL) or surface container-load shipments. The exact weight depends on the product, and it is close to the amount that would physically fill a truck trailer. For glassware, this might be 18,000 pounds; for canned goods, it might be 40,000 pounds. If one's shipments are larger, railcars are viable, although carload weights tend to be heavier. The shipper can also use intermodal surface containers. These containers used in domestic trades are usually 102 inches wide, 8½ feet high, and 40 feet long.[8] The shipper probably handles these shipments like truck shipments; the trucker, however, may turn the container over to a railroad for a portion of the move.

---

[7]*LCL* used to mean "less-than-railcar load." Today, it is more likely to mean "less-than-intermodal container load."

[8]Intermodal surface containers used for international moves are 96 inches wide and range in length from 20 to 55 feet.

Truckload shipments cost less per pound than LTL shipments for three reasons:

1. The shipper loads and the consignee unloads the trailer.
2. The load goes directly from shipper to consignee without passing through termi-nals.
3. Paperwork, billing, and control costs are no more for a truckload than they would be for a 10-pound LTL shipment.

The same logic explains why container loads and railcar loads cost less per pound than LCL shipments. Also, at this size of shipment, the rate for each haul may be nego-tiable. The price is a function of supply and demand for transportation. For example, when the demand is high for trucks to carry fresh agricultural product eastward from California, the rate per truckload is often six times as high as it is for trucks heading from the Midwest to California.

Not all truckload or other vehicle-load contracts are calculated on a one-shot, or single-trip, basis. They may be negotiated to cover a span of time—say, two truckloads a week for one year. Additional services might be negotiated as part of the contract, such as a split delivery, in which the truck carries a full load but delivers portions of that full load to several addresses.

Truckload freight haulers specialize in truckload lots, using either their own equip-ment or contracting with owner-operators. The largest firm in this category is Schneider National Van Carriers, and nearly the same size is J. B. Hunt Transport. Other firms are smaller. Firms in this sector of the industry tend to be less well-known because they advertise less often and do not need to maintain a nationwide presence. Truck firms in this category make use of owner–operators to perform much of their hauling. Many have long-term relationships profitable to both.

Shippers may consider utilizing specialized trucks or railcars to handle the move-ment of these larger quantities. Sometimes, the shipper provides them; sometimes, the carrier does. When the shipper provides and operates its own equipment, it is known as **private transportation.** Dedicated equipment is carrier owned but assigned to serve specific customers for indefinite periods. The following list provides examples of the variety of specialized truck bodies:

A-frame glass-carrying	Cargo van	Farm
Acid tank	Cattle rack	Feed
Air compressor	Cement mixer	Fertilizer spreading
Armored car	Cleaner and dryer	Florist
Asphalt tank	Coal	Food product
Bakery	Concessionaire	Frozen food
Beer	Concrete	Fuel oil
Beverage	Contractor	Furniture
Bookmobile	Delivery	Garbage
Brick-loading/unloading	Department store	Gas cylinder
Bulk cement	Dry freight	Gasoline transport
Canopy	Dump	Grain

Grocers'	Logging	Platform
High-lift	Lumber	Produce
Horse van	Meat packer	Public utility service
Ice-control spreader	Milk delivery	Refrigerator
Ice cream	Oil field equipment	Road-building
Insulated	Open-top	Self-unloading
Laundry	Pallet-loading	Telephone installation
Limestone spreader	Parcel delivery	Tree trimmer
Livestock	Pickup	Wrecker[9]

Some of these vehicles are used for purposes other than transporting goods, but the list demonstrates that in some trades one often uses and owns a truck to carry products and sometimes workers. Some railcars and barges are specialized, although not with as many variations as trucks.

Shippers utilizing conventional railroad service need to have a railroad siding on their property and must also make certain that the consignee is able to receive shipments by rail. Railroads specialize in transporting raw materials and unprocessed products in carload quantities. During the first seven months of 2002, railroads carried just over 10 million carloads of freight. Four million tons of this were coal, and other major movements were chemicals, grain, and sand and gravel.[10] At one time, almost all businesses of any size had rail sidings, but today that is no longer true. At one time, railroads typically shipped general merchandise in boxcars, and because this portion of their business is in a long-term decline, the industry finds itself with excess general-purpose boxcars. The industry is buying container and piggyback-trailer handling equipment and is increasingly dependent upon trucks to provide intermodal connections.

Large Bulk Shippers

Bulk cargo travels in loose rather than in packaged form and is handled by pumps, scoops, conveyor belts, or the force of gravity. Shippers must decide where in the distribution system the bulk cargo should be placed into smaller containers for sale or shipment to the next party in the supply chain.

Bulk cargo has various handling characteristics. An ideal equipment configuration for one bulk cargo may not be able to handle another. Another consideration is the costs involved in pulverizing cargo particles to a uniform size so they can be handled by pneumatic or slurry devices.

Materials shipped in bulk move by truckload, rail carload, or vessel-size lots or via pipeline. Lot sizes differ. A truckload may be 20 to 30 tons, a rail carload runs from 40 to 80 tons, a barge holds about 1,000 tons, a Great Lakes vessel holds 25,000 to 50,000 tons, and the largest of ocean vessels can carry 500,000 tons.

---

[9]Donald F. Wood, *Commercial Trucks* (Osceola, WI: Motorbooks International, 1993), pp. 205–206.

[10]*Traffic World*, August 19, 2002, p. 35. During the same period, the U.S. railroads carried 1.5 million trailers and 4 million containers of intermodal traffic.

Truckload Hauls

Trucking of bulk materials involves either for-hire or private trucks, with specialized bodies if necessary. For-hire trucks are retained for a specific haul or for a span of time or for a task (say, to move tomatoes from fields to a cannery). Brokers are often used by shippers to find and contract with independent truckers; the broker takes a certain percentage off the top of the rate. Many truckload transactions are now handled on Web sites.

Railroads

Rail rates and contracts encourage multiple-car shipments because the railroad can switch and haul a number of cars as easily as one. The largest of rail hauls are handled on unit trains. This is a train of permanently connected cars that carries only one product nonstop from origin to destination. It can be thought of as a conveyor belt. Once the product is delivered, the train returns empty to its origin and makes another nonstop run. Unit trains benefit both the railroads and their customers: The trains achieve a very high percentage of car utilization and usually provide less expensive and more dependable service. Currently, over 90 percent of all coal movement is by unit trains.

Water Carriers

Freight moves by water on the Great Lakes and on inland waterways, or barge, systems. Waterborne commerce also moves via oceangoing vessels between the mainland states (Lower 48) and Alaska, Hawaii, and Puerto Rico. One of the largest domestic movements is oil from Alaska, which moves on large tankers from Valdez to Panama. The tankers are nearly 1,000 feet long, carry 1.5 million barrels, and are too large to transit the Panama Canal. At Panama, the oil is unloaded at a tank farm and pumped via pipeline across the isthmus to a tank farm on the Atlantic. There, it is reloaded aboard smaller tankers and taken to U.S. Gulf of Mexico and East Coast ports.

European nations are also served by an extensive network of barge routes that fan out from their major ports. In Asia, deep-draft navigation is used extensively to connect islands with the mainland and with major ports.

Domestic U.S. water carriers have specialized in transporting bulk products at very low prices at slow average speeds (6 miles per hour). Petroleum and related products account for 36 percent of total barge commerce. Coal is second, with 28 percent. Other products that move extensively in the inland waterway system are grain and grain products, industrial chemicals, iron and steel products, forestry products, cement, sulfur, fertilizers, paper products, sand and gravel, and limestone. In most cases, these products are tendered to the carriers in barge-load lots. There are also barge-oriented freight forwarders offering services on the inland waterways system. Their main sales tool is to offer a smaller minimum tender requirement to shippers. One forwarder bases its rates on shipments as small as 100 tons, whereas common carrier barges serving the same area require minimum shipments of 800 tons.

A problem faced by inland waterway carriers operating in the northern states and on the Great Lakes is ice closing their systems and preventing year-round operation. Because of this, customers must stockpile inventories in the fall to last through the winter months.

Pipelines

Crude oil and product are two types of oil pipelines. Two types of crude oil lines transport petroleum from wells to refineries, with approximately 150,000 miles of crude oil pipelines in the United States. Somewhat more than half of the crude oil line mileage is in the form of *gathering lines,* which are 6 inches or smaller in diameter and are frequently laid on the ground. These lines start at each well and carry the product to concentration points. Trunk lines are larger-diameter pipelines that carry crude oil from gathering-line concentration points to the oil refineries. Their diameter varies from 3 to 48 inches; 8- to 10-inch pipe is the most common size. A large pipeline's capacity is also impressive. The 48-inch Trans-Alaska pipeline, which is 789 miles long, has a discharge capacity of two million barrels per day.

The other type of petroleum pipeline is a *product pipeline* and carries products such as gasoline or aviation fuel to tank farms located nearer to customers. The products are stored at the tank farms and then delivered to customers by truck or by rail.

Slurry systems grind the solid material to a certain particle size, mix it with water to form a fluid muddy substance, pump that substance through a pipeline, and then decant the water and remove it, leaving the solid material. Railcars can also carry slurry. For example, kaolin (a clay used in papermaking) is mined and separated from the accompanying sand by a water process. The sand-free clay is then subjected to a number of mechanical processes that reduce its moisture content to about 35 percent. The result is a substance that has the viscosity of heavy cream, which is about the consistency desired by the papermaking plants, so it is shipped in this form, despite the fact that, by weight, a substantial percentage of what is shipped is water. In this instance, the economics are such that it is less costly to transport the water than it is to remove it near the quarry and add it after shipment at the paper mill.

A large coal slurry line in operation today is the Black Mesa pipeline, which transports pulverized coal in an 18-inch pipe 273 miles from strip mines in northern Arizona to an electric-generating station on the Colorado River near Davis Dam, Nevada. The slurry line was constructed because unit-train operation was not feasible over the terrain involved. The 50 percent water, 50 percent coal mixture moves at 4 miles per hour and makes the trip in 3 days. The speed of the movement must be carefully maintained because excessive speed makes the coal powder act like sandpaper on the inside of the pipe, and insufficient speed causes the coal powder to fall out of suspension and build up on the bottom of the pipe. When the slurry solution reaches its destination, centrifuges spin out the water. The coal is then fed into the furnaces.

Pipelines also carry water, sewage, and natural gas. Pneumatic pipelines operate over very short distances and carry dry materials such as flour and cement.

Dry Bulk-Handling Systems

Systems for handling dry bulk materials are often large and custom engineered to fit specific needs. Figures 6-2, 6-3, and 6-4 provide an idea of the scale at which these facilities are designed and constructed and give an indication of the equipment used to load and unload vehicles. Figure 6-2 is a cross-sectional view of a coal car unloading facility. The cars carrying coal are joined in a unit train, whose cars are permanently coupled. However, this coupling is unique because it allows each car to swivel and be turned upside down while remaining coupled. The train comes to a stop with the first coal car

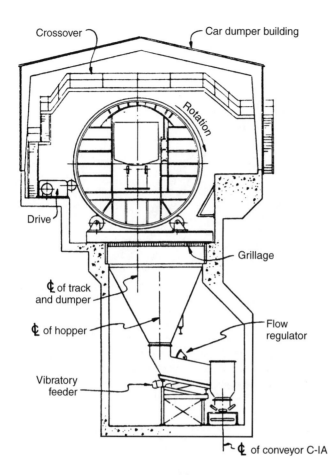

Crossover

Car dumper building

Rotation

Drive

Grillage

₵ of track
and dumper

₵ of hopper

Flow
regulator

Vibratory
feeder

₵ of conveyor C-IA

FIGURE 6-2 Cross-Section of a Coal Car-Dumping Building in St. Louis, Missouri

Source: Courtesy of McNally Wellman (a Svedala Group Company).

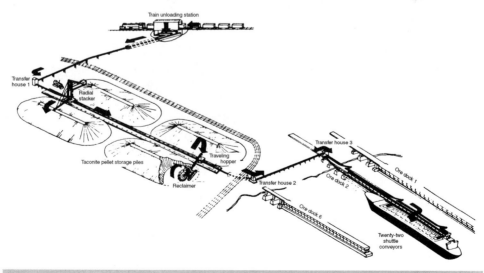

Train unloading station

Transfer
house 1

Radial
stacker

Transfer house 3

Ore dock 1

Taconite pellet storage piles

Traveling
hopper

Ore dock 2

Reclaimer

Transfer house 2

Ore dock 6

Twenty-two
shuttle
conveyors

FIGURE 6-3 Taconite Storage and Loading Facility at Two Harbors, Minnesota

Source: Duluth, Missabe, and Iron Range Railway Company.

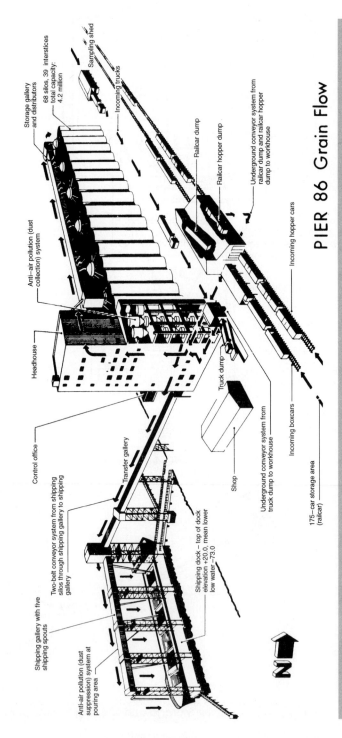

FIGURE 6-4 Export Grain Elevator at the Port of Seattle

Source: Courtesy of Port of Seattle.

in exact position within the rotating drum. Grips extend from the drum to secure the car, and it is rolled over, nearly 180 degrees, to dump the coal. It is rolled back and released, and the train moves ahead until the next car is in position. It takes 90 seconds to unload each car, which can hold 100 tons of coal. The unit train consists of 110 cars.

A taconite loading facility is shown in Figure 6-3. It is located at Two Harbors, Minnesota, on the western end of Lake Superior. Taconite is partially processed iron ore in pellet form. The site in question can store two million tons of taconite (about 20,000 rail carloads). The ore is received by unit train at the unloading station shown at the top of the figure (which is similar to the facility shown in Figure 6-2). The ore pellets are then moved out to the storage piles, where they are held until loaded aboard a vessel via conveyor belts. One reason such a large storage area is needed is the difference in receiving and shipping seasons. Taconite is received year-round but is shipped only during an 8-month season because most of the Great Lakes are closed to navigation during the winter.

Figure 6-4 illustrates another bulk cargo handling facility: a large grain elevator located at the Port of Seattle. The facility receives grain both by rail and by truck. Note the references to dust collection and dust suppression systems. Also note that incoming trucks have their grain sampled. The grain is graded to determine its price. (Shipments received by rail have already been graded at the initial inland elevator where they were handled, whereas most truck shipments received here are direct from the farm.)

Vehicle and Vessel Equipment Choice

Bulk cargo movements are unique in that they almost always utilize a vehicle's entire capacity. A bulk cargo shipper thinks in terms of truckloads, barge loads, railcar loads, or shiploads. Various types of equipment are used to transport and transfer bulk materials. One must think of the entire segment of the supply chain through which the cargo will pass. One equipment innovation that has replaced carriage and handling of bagged dry cargo is the use of pneumatic systems for the rapid loading and unloading of dry-cargo truck trailers, railcars, and barges. Approximately a hundred flowable commodities, such as cement, chemicals, and grains, are now carried in this type of equipment.

Choice of equipment is also influenced by the investment the shipper and consignee want to make. Great Lakes coal docks using self-unloaders do not have to invest in vessel-unloading facilities—the vessel owner has made the investment in the conveyor and discharge system. Great Lakes vessel rates for carrying coal on self-unloaders are about 10 percent higher than for vessels that the consignee must unload. The consignee can pay that higher rate or invest in its own shore-based unloading equipment.

Another consideration with respect to bulk cargo handling deals with equipment ownership. The several handling facilities discussed in this chapter involve massive investments in fixed facilities and specialized vehicles. From a logistics management standpoint, bulk cargoes require unique, often custom-built handling facilities, and there is always uncertainty as to who should provide them—the buyer, the seller, or a third party.

A marketing problem may be that a specialized unloading device will pay for itself only if a specified number of customers install a new type of receiving equipment. What kinds of financial incentives should the seller offer so that customers will install the new receiving equipment? What types of long-term commitments must each party make to the other to ensure a necessary return from the required investment? An example of this situation comes from the food industry, where liquid-egg distributors supply the contents of shelled eggs or egg-based concentrates to food processors, commercial bakeries, and institutional food service industries. Because eggs in the shell have unfavorable transportation characteristics, a truck carrying the eggs' contents after they are shelled can carry about twice as much weight in the same space as a truck carrying eggs in conventional cartons. The supplier must invest in an egg-breaking machine located near the egg farms, as well as in trucks with refrigerated tank trailers that can pump out their own contents. Sanitation is important and must be maintained. The customers' investments are in one or more tanks to receive the yolks, the egg whites, or a mixture of both. Even without knowing the quantities or the costs involved, it is clear that quite a few calculations would have to be made and numerous alternatives considered.

Some liquid cargoes are heated so that they will flow more easily. Sometimes, the heating equipment is at the shipping point; sometimes the heavily insulated truck, railcar, or barge also carries its own heating system to maintain a high temperature. A common example is trucks that haul liquid asphalt at over 400 degrees Fahrenheit directly to construction sites. Careful calculations must be made of the time and distance of the haul and the outdoor temperatures to determine the temperature to which the cargo should be heated.

Project Cargo

Recurring shipments usually lend themselves to logistics analysis that results in either lower-cost shipments or a more efficient method of handling the shipment, or both. In some industries, however, each movement is so unique and so difficult that a specialized engineering–logistics study is needed to determine how the move should be accomplished. This would be considered **project cargo:** a one-time unique movement of substantial volume. Following is an example from Canada.

> An old oil refinery is now on its way from the west coast of Canada for use in a new refinery complex in the Middle East. In January the Sharjah Oil Refining Co. bought old oil refinery equipment at Shellburn Terminal in Burnaby, near Vancouver. All summer a team of dismantlers, logistics experts, truckers, and dockworkers have been hard at work, taking the old Shell Canada refinery apart, step by step.
>
> A single ship was chartered to carry most of the dismantled refinery with 52 filled containers and more than 500 other pieces of cargo, the longest of which was a 100-foot tower.[11]

One of the most spectacular project moves occurred when two specially designed Japanese barges were used to tow two halves of a wood-pulp processing plant, built in Japan, to a site in Brazil's Amazon River basin. Two barges were built in the Japanese

---

[11]*The Journal of Commerce,* September 19, 1997, p. 1B.

yard, and then the pulp plant was built on top of one and the accompanying power plant was built on top of the other. Very careful attention was paid to determining how the weight of the pulp and power plants would be distributed on their respective barges. The plants were then towed by tugs to their final destination on the Jari River in Brazil, which had been partially enclosed by a dike. Inside the diked area, wooden pilings had been driven into the river bottom. When the two barges arrived, they were towed inside the diked area and moored next to the pilings. The dike was then extended to enclose the area completely, and water was pumped in to raise the barges. The barges were floated directly above the piles and the water was drained, so the barges holding the two plants were then resting on top of the piles. Windows were cut in the sides of the barges, and the barges became the lower floors of the pulp and power plants. It was estimated that construction costs were reduced by 20 percent and that two years were saved by having the plant built in Japan and towed to Brazil rather than having it constructed at the Brazilian site.

Another example of a project cargo occurred in 1991 when the Bechtel Group, a U.S. engineering firm, organized and orchestrated the movement of 200,000 tons of cargo to fight the oil-well fires in Kuwait after the Persian Gulf War. Over 8,000 pieces of construction equipment were involved, including bulldozers, cranes, computers, and ambulances.

Oversized Moves

Sometimes, a product, such as a machine, is assembled at a factory to make sure that it functions and then disassembled for shipment because it is too large for any carrier to deliver whole. Rather, it is delivered in pieces and reassembled at on-site. Clearly, there can be savings if the amount of disassembly and reassembly involved can be reduced. Therefore, studies have to be made of shipping routes and procedures that will accommodate shipments with unusual dimensions.

High-weight trucks are sometimes used. Heavy dollies, with their additional axles, are placed under the load so that less weight is exerted on each axle. When passing over a bridge of limited capacity, the dollies must be spaced sufficiently apart that no more than the allowable weight is on the bridge at any one time. Once the bridge is crossed, the load is stopped, and the dollies are placed closer together again to make it easier to negotiate curves. Special permits and escort vehicles are required, and police sometimes keep other traffic off the road. Highway engineers along the route determine the maximum allowable load. If bituminous pavement is involved, the move may be restricted to cooler times of the year or day since the cooler pavement is less likely to be permanently marked by the tires of the dollies. Equipment such as this can carry loads of 500 tons or more, if enough dollies are used.

Weight is only one limitation of special moves; height restrictions, such as electric wires (which can be moved) or tunnels (which cannot), are another. Modular housing (prebuilt structures that are transported to homesites) is not especially heavy, but it tends to be large. Access to the interstate highway system is of absolute necessity. In addition, siding needs for outbound shipment from modular housing plants are vastly different than for ordinary industrial sites. When going by rail, the modules will travel on long cars and in trainload lots. Minimum curvatures of about 400 feet and accessible siding lengths of about 250 feet are needed.

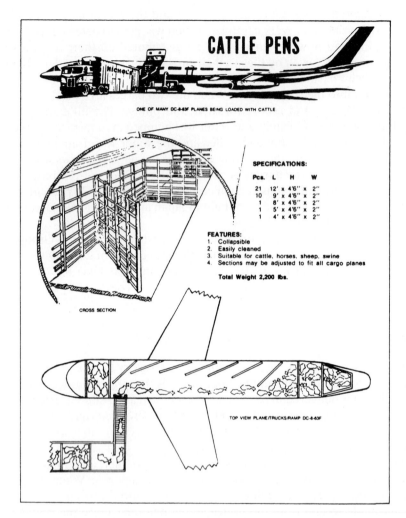

CATTLE PENS

ONE OF MANY DC-8-63F PLANES BEING LOADED WITH CATTLE

SPECIFICATIONS:

Pcs.	L	H	W
21	12' x	4'6" x	2"
10	9' x	4'6" x	2"
1	8' x	4'6" x	2"
1	5' x	4'6" x	2"
1	4' x	4'6" x	2"

FEATURES:
1. Collapsible
2. Easily cleaned
3. Suitable for cattle, horses, sheep, swine
4. Sections may be adjusted to fit all cargo planes

Total Weight 2,200 lbs.

CROSS SECTION

TOP VIEW PLANE/TRUCKS/RAMP DC-8-63F

FIGURE 6-5 Sometimes Small Transportation Firms Specialize

This is one firm's special DC-8, outfitted for carrying cattle. The grille along the side is to protect the plane from the animals' hoofs, and the right-angle gates keep the weight of the herd distributed the length of the plane. *Source:* Courtesy Alex Nichols Agency, Long Island, New York.

Curvature of the road or steepness of grade imposes still other limitations. The move must be carefully analyzed by individuals who are familiar with both the transportation complexities and the equipment being moved. Allowable highway widths have been increased from 96 to 102 inches, making it possible for truck trailers and buses to be built wider. Other products shipped on highways can also now be built wider, an example being trailered boats. Some railroad tunnels are being raised, mainly to accommodate double-stack container trains. Other high cargo will also benefit.

It is also possible to charter (or rent) an entire aircraft to handle specific shipments. Figure 6-5 shows a special body built inside a DC-8 for carrying cattle. Cattle are shipped overseas by air because the trip is less difficult for them than movement by sea. Sometimes, small aircraft are chartered to deliver repair parts to combines that are stranded in grain fields or in other emergency situations. The Boeing 747 can carry about one hundred tons (see Figure 6-6). A former Soviet military transport is even larger. Chartered aircraft are expensive, compared with other modes of transport.

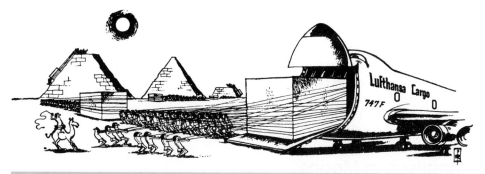

FIGURE 6-6 Air Freight Capabilities

Source: Courtesy of Lufthansa Cargo.

Hazardous Materials

Hazardous materials have the potential of endangering the carrier's equipment, other products, people, and the environment. Although they can go on any mode of transport, they are subject to many restrictions. They usually move in very special dedicated or shipper-owned equipment. Railroads seem to haul more than their share of hazardous materials. This is because of their equipment, their routes, and their relatively low incidence of accidents. In addition, "railroads are common carriers. As common carriers, railroads have a duty to carry all commodities, even if they are dangerous, unless the federal government has relieved them of the duty to carry a particular commodity."[12]

Both state and federal regulations cover the movement of hazardous materials. For example, in late 1994 the National Park Service banned commercial vehicles carrying hazardous materials from using the 22 miles of U.S. Highway 191 that pass through Yellowstone National Park.[13] Employee training programs, special packaging, and markings are often required. Diamond placards can be seen on the sides of trucks, railcars, and containers carrying hazardous materials.

Owners and carriers of hazardous materials have many special responsibilities. The Oil Pollution Act of 1990 (OPA) requires owners of tank vessels and facilities to prepare a plan for responding to a worst-case discharge of oil or a hazardous substance. For onshore facilities, the requirements apply to those sites that, because of their location, could be expected to harm the environment by discharge in navigable waters or along shorelines. Nearly all modes of transport were involved, as were several government agencies. The most stringent regulations deal with tank vessels, of any size, operating within 200 miles of the United States. Approximately 1,500 oil response plans covering more than 6,000 vessels have been submitted to the Coast Guard. A spill response plan contains six requirements:

1. It must be consistent with other existing plans.

---

[12]Michael F. McBride, "Railroads May Not Refuse to Carry Dangerous Commodities," *Journal of Transportation Law, Logistics and Policy,* Vol. 69, No. 4, 2002, p. 391.

[13]*Transport Topics,* September 26, 1994, p. 22.

2. It must designate persons with full authority to act in spill situations; and that person is expected to notify the appropriate federal agency promptly whenever a spill occurs.

3. It must identify and ensure by contract the private parties who will supply personnel and equipment to deal with minimizing the spill and its effects.

4. It must describe training and testing of personnel.

5. It must be updated from time to time.

6. It must be resubmitted to approval of each significant change.[14]

Comparison of Modes

Every logistics manager must decide which transportation mix will best meet the company's objectives. Earlier editions of this book compared modes in terms of speed, dependability, rates, fuel efficiency, and so on, and also reported the results of surveys as to which service features appealed most to transportation managers making the choice of modes. Such comparisons are less relevant today for three reasons.

The first is intermodalism, which has already been discussed. An intermodal carrier can combine the various service and cost aspects of several modes in order to offer the mix desired by the shipper.

Second, negotiated contracts between carriers and shippers are now widely used. Through negotiations, the shipper can express exactly what it does or does not want and can expect to see this reflected in the final bottom-line price it must pay.

Third, carriers are no longer constrained with respect to the variety of services they may offer. About a decade after deregulation began, Professor J. R. Stock noted the following:

> Before deregulation, the purchase of transportation was a fairly straightforward corporate decision because of regulated pricing and service controls. After deregulation some carriers not wishing to become a part of an undifferentiated market with only price as a competitive variable developed strategies to distinguish themselves from others.[15]

Stock further described how some carrier firms provide services allowing shippers access to carrier computers to track freight, give shippers monthly analyses of their flows of freight, manage shippers' inventories, and provide warehousing. These additional services help the carrier form strategic alliances with its customers.

Some broad comparisons serve to emphasize the modal differences. Using fairly current national transportation data, one can compare, in rough terms, the intercity revenues and ton-miles carried by each mode to get an idea as to the relative costs per ton-mile. (A **ton-mile** is one ton of freight carried 1 mile.) Pipeline costs are about 1.3 cents per ton-mile, with water being a close second, at 1.7 cents per ton-mile. Rail costs are about twice as high, at 2.9 cents per ton-mile. Truck costs are over 10 times higher, or 36 cents per ton-

[14]Pamela Garvie and Susan B. Geiger, "Spill Response Planning—All Modes of Transportation Feel the Impact of the Oil Pollution Act of 1990," *Transportation Practitioners Journal,* Vol. 61, No. 3, Spring 1994, p. 299. See also Robert Thomas Hoffman II and Donald F. Wood, "Impacts of U.S. Environmental Controls Upon Ocean Tankers," *Journal of Transportation Management,* Vol. 8, No. 1, 1997, pp. 35–42.

[15]James R. Stock, "The Maturing of Transportation: An Expanded Role for Freight Carriers," *Journal of Business Logistics,* Vol. 9, No. 2, 1988, pp. 15–16.

mile, and air freight is 89 cents per ton-mile. Carriers in most modes offer a variety of service levels and charge differently for each. One researcher, looking at intermodal rates, noted, "Because the rail portion of these intermodal moves typically involves operating relatively light trains at relatively high speeds, railroad rates are relatively high compared to the rates for moving bulk commodities such as grain or coal. Intermodal rates are likely to range between 8-10 cents per ton-mile, while the rates for the movement of dry-bulk commodities typically range between 1-3 cents per ton-mile."[16]

Differences in speed are obvious, with air being the fastest and water or pipeline being the slowest. One reason that water transport is slow is that many navigation routes are circuitous. For short hauls, truck is faster than rail. For longer hauls, truck and rail are more evenly matched, although the truck must have more than one driver. A railroad that wants the speed advantage in a certain market can obtain it by assigning high priority to specific trains.

On-time delivery is often used as a criterion. Pipelines, air express services, and some truckers have the best records. Weather affects all modes except pipelines, although water transportation in the North shuts down completely during winter months. A bad snowstorm can bring air, truck, and rail traffic to a halt. Flooding is another disaster that can interfere with transport operations. During the floods on the Mississippi River in 1993, impacts were significant. Portions of the Mississippi, Missouri, and Illinois Rivers totaling 1,600 miles were closed to barge navigation for lengths of time ranging from 10 to 45 days. At least one lock on the Mississippi was closed for a duration of 52 days, thereby blocking use of the entire river. Grain exports from New Orleans declined during this period because of the drop in barge deliveries. About 3,800 miles of rail line were shut down, and over 1,000 trains were rerouted, with delays of up to 5 days for some freight cars. There were many highway closures, especially in Missouri, and long detours became common. Finally, 34 small airports were closed. In this disaster, barges were interrupted the most, then rail, and then truck.[17]

Transportation Regulation and Deregulation

For many years, most of the nation's transportation service was subject to economic regulation, meaning that the services offered and rates charged were subject to approval by a government agency. This applied to both interstate and intrastate movements. Carriers were allowed to operate as monopolists or oligopolists and in return assumed the common carrier obligation. The common carrier has four specific obligations: to serve, to deliver, to charge reasonable rates, and to avoid discrimination.

Beginning in the late 1970s, various sectors of the transportation industry were deregulated. In 1995, the federal government eliminated state economic regulation of motor carriers; this ban removed regulations that about 40 states were still enforcing. Some carriers are still subject to economic regulation. They include the following:

- Railroads, especially rail service to captive shippers, that is, those that have no viable alternative means of transport (the most common example being mines and coal-burning electricity-generating plants)

---

[16]Nick J. Rahall, *Transportation and the Potential for Intermodal Efficiency Enhancements in Western West Virginia* (Huntington, WV: Marshall University, 2000), p. 33.

[17]*Transportation Statistics, Annual Report 1994* (Washington, DC: U.S. Department of Transportation, 1994), pp. 90–98.

- Household goods movers
- Many petroleum pipelines
- Many natural gas pipelines
- Some inland waterway traffic
- Some water transport and some joint motor–water transport between the mainland and Hawaii, Puerto Rico, and Alaska

The common carrier obligation, dating to English common law, is the foundation of all carrier regulation, as well as the old-time traffic manager's view of the transport world. Professors Nelson and Wood of San Francisco State University surveyed a group of transportation managers; one of their survey questions asked, "In your opinion, what is the status of the 'common carrier obligation'? Do you still rely on it?" Twelve respondents claimed they did not understand the question, and 13 answered "yes," with one commenting, "You betcha! As railroads continue to diminish in number the common carrier obligation will be all the more important." Thirty-six indicated that they did not rely on the common carrier obligation, but within this group 15 said that the reason was that all their shipments move under contract. One of these indicated that he or she used the obligation as a starting point for negotiations.[18]

Today's transportation manager must be able to operate in both the deregulated and regulated transportation environments. Numerous regulations at all levels of governments address vehicle operations, dimensions, and the safety of operators and the general public. The existing structure of the nation's transportation industry was heavily influenced by regulation and by deregulation. Many of its problems are blamed on either regulation, deregulation, or both.

Transportation Rates

Transportation rates are complex, and the structures employed date to the time of regulation, when rate bureaus (committees of carriers) would establish rates subject to the approval of some state or federal regulatory agency. The rate structure deals with three factors:

1. Relationships between *different products,* in terms of their handling characteristics, for example, the difference between carrying 2,000 pounds of ballpoint pens and 2,000 pounds of live chickens.
2. Relationships between shipments of *different weights,* for example, shipments of 1 pound each, 100 pounds each, or 100,000 pounds each.
3. Relationships between *different distances* the products are carried, for example, from Boston to Albany or from Atlanta to Spokane. ("In the latest twist in the package-delivery wars, FedEx revealed plans . . . to adopt a once-shunned distance-based pricing format for all domestic shipments. For FedEx customers, the move means that rates are based on weight, size and, most importantly, distance. . . . [A] UPS spokesman said the move by FedEx mirrored UPS's action in '96.

---

[18]Donald F. Wood and Richard S. Nelson, "Industrial Transportation Management: What's New?" *Transportation Journal,* Winter 1999, p. 29.

Been there, done that. If what I am hearing about FedEx is correct, they followed our lead."[19])

Rate making has to define all three relations in numeric form and then has to devise methods of tying those numbers into a rate of so many cents per hundredweight (cwt) for a specific haul. The three relationships mentioned previously are of continual importance to the logistics manager because if they can be altered, the total transportation charges will be lowered.

With respect to handling characteristics, density is especially important. Wastebaskets that are perfect cylinders cost more to ship than wastebaskets that have a tapered shape and can be packed with one partially inside the other (nesting). Freight consolidation means assembling many small shipments so that one large shipment can be tendered to the carrier. Distances are also significant: It almost always costs more to ship a product for a longer distance.

Whereas most rates today are negotiated between carriers and shippers, the rate structures and the common carrier obligation are both referred to in the negotiation process. Often, they are points of departure from which negotiations begin. An understanding of traditional freight rate determination is still necessary. The reason is that carriers, as they compete, often quote prices in terms of percentage discounts from existing or published rates.

One widely used classification tariff is the National Motor Freight Classification *(NMFC),* which has 23 separate ratings, or classes, from 500 to 35.[20] The higher the rating, the greater the relative charge for transporting the commodity. A multitude of factors are involved in determining a product's specific class or rating. Four factors are the primary inputs used to determine a **freight classification;** probably the most expensive is density of the product (how heavy it is in relationship to its size). Following are classification numbers for swimming pool skimmers, in boxes or in crates: With a density in pounds per cubic foot of

Less than 1	400
1 but less than 2	300
2 but less than 4	250
4 but less than 6	150
6 but less than 8	125
8 but less than 10	100
10 but less than 12	92.5
12 but less than 15	85
15 or greater	70[21]

---

[19]*The Journal of Commerce,* January 23, 1997, pp. 1A, 8B.

[20]In mid-2002, the list of motor carriers that used the NMFC was 36 pages long and ranged from nation-wide truckers to local delivery companies. See www.nmfta.org/Products2.htm, June 27, 2002.

[21]*National Classification Committee Disposition Bulletin 1270,* May 10, 2002. The classification number is important; it is one of three multiplied together that yields the total transportation charges. If a manufacturer of swimming pool skimmers could increase its packaged product's density from 3 to 7 pounds per cubic foot, its annual transportation bill would be cut in half.

The other three factors are *stowability* (how easy it is to pack into a load); *ease or difficulty of handling;* and *liability to damage and theft.* The last factor is also related to the value of the product. Motor carrier classification numbers are established by the National Motor Freight Traffic Association, a group representing trucking firms. Classification numbers are very important since they are code words that describe cargo in a manner that carriers and shippers understand, and some of the load-matching systems of the Web require that the shipper provide its product's classification number. Classification descriptions also specify the packaging that must be used and that carriers require. For example, the Web site for a forwarder serving Alaska says, "Packaging requirements for Alaska shipping are the same as required in the National Motor Freight Classification Directory."[22]

Figure 6-7 shows a page of the National Motor Freight Classification. Note the detail. *NOI* stands for "not otherwise indexed by number," i.e., one cannot find a definition that fits more closely. Packages are referred to by number; they are described in great detail in the classification document.

Once the commodity rating, or class, is determined, it is necessary to establish the rate bases number from the applicable tariff. This number is based on the approximate distance between the cities of origin and destination. Computers make these calculation utilizing the zip codes of the shipment's origin and destination. With the commodity rating and the rate bases number, the specific rate per hundred pounds can be located in another tariff. Finally, to establish the specific cost of moving commodity A between city B and city C, one must use the following formula:

Weight (in hundred-pound units) × rate (per hundred pounds) = charge

Additional, or accessorial, charges are sometimes associated with a freight system. Figures 6-8 and 6-9 show some that may be used by Yellow Freight. They also are probably subject to negotiation. The same carrier also offers several levels of service, and each level of service has a higher charge for the same shipment. Yellow Freight has an Exact Express service, Definite Delivery service, and Standard Ground service. FedEx offers three levels of overnight service: FedEx First Overnight, FedEx Priority Overnight, and FedEx Standard Overnight, plus some that take longer.

By now, most shippers and carriers have computerized many aspects of their freight-moving activities. Buyers, sellers, and carriers regularly exchange data via electronic means, including electronic data interchange (EDI) and e-mail. Most transportation rates are now on carrier Web sites, and the shipper must know how to access them. These are all for LTL shipments. Most work about the same way: One enters in the origin and destination zip codes, the weight and classification of each shipment, any supplemental services needed, and whatever discount the carrier has awarded the shipper. There are bidding or auction sites for truckload shipments, as well as for shipments on other modes.

Some carriers have their rates on a mainframe computer and allow access via the Internet system, feeling that potential shippers can access rates via that route. Therefore, some shippers may have to surf the Internet to find the best rates. For some carriers, rates are not fixed, in the sense that they are trying to fill space every day.

---

[22]www.pafak.com/aboutpaf.htm, July 15, 2002.

ITEM	ARTICLES	CLASS
	GLASS: subject to item 86500	
86700	**Glass,** flat, see Note, item 86736, NOI:	
86720	Bent, NOI, in boxes or crates:	
Sub 1	220 united inches or less; when in shipments weighing less than 30,000 pounds, see Note, item 86512 .	85
Sub 2	Exceeding 220 united inches but not exceeding 15 feet in length nor 9 feet in breadth; when in shipments weighing less than 24,000 pounds, see Note, item 86512.	100
Sub 3	Exceeding 15 feet in length or 9 feet in breadth; when in shipments weighing less than 24,000 pounds, see Note, item 86512	250
86730	Not bent, see Note, item 86731, in boxes, crates or Packages 195, 198, 235, 785, 2008, 2025, 2147, 2149, 2160, 2239, 2245, 2281 or 2497; when in shipments weighing less than 40,000 pounds, see Note, item 86512:	
Sub 1	220 united inches or less, see Note, item 86737	65
Sub 2	Exceeding 220 united inches but not exceeding 15 feet in length nor 9 feet in breadth	100
Sub 3	Exceeding 15 feet in length or 9 feet in breadth.	200
86731	NOTE—Flat glass, not bent, may also be cut to size, edges beveled or ground, or holes cut or drilled.	
86736	NOTE—The term 'flat' applies to glass known as sheet, plate, polished prism, rolled, window or float glass, whether or not polished, laminated, colored, opalescent, opaque, chipped, decorated, wired, etched, figured, acid dipped, ground, sandblasted, metalized (sprayed with atomized metal while glass is hot) or tempered, but not when silvered for mirrors, nor flashed, nor framed or leaded (set in or framed by lead or other metal).	
86737	NOTE—Provisions will also apply on shipments weighing 40,000 pounds or more when glass is shipped on its flat surface in wooden boxes on pallets.	
86750	**Glass,** leaded, see Note, item 86752; when in shipments weighing less than 24,000 pounds, see Note, item 86512:	
Sub 1	With landscape, pictorial or religious designs, packed in boxes	200
Sub 2	With curved, angled or straight line patterns, or with designs other than landscape, pictorial or religious, in boxes	100
86752	NOTE—The term 'leaded glass' means glass either colored or clear, set in lead or in other metal.	
86770	**Glass,** microscopical slide or cover, see Note, item 86771, in boxes; when in shipments weighing less than 36,000 pounds, see Note, item 86512.	70
86771	NOTE—Does not apply on microscope slides or slide cover glasses. Applies only on the glass from which these articles are manufactured.	
86830	**Glass,** rolled, overlaid with aluminum strips with metal terminals attached, in boxes or crates; when in shipments weighing less than 30,000 pounds, see Note, item 86512.	77.5
86840	**Glass,** rolled, overlaid with aluminum strips, NOI, in boxes or crates; when in shipments weighing less than 36,000 pounds, see Note, item 86512	70
86900	**Glass,** silvered for mirrors, not framed, nor backed nor equipped with hangers or fastening devices:	
Sub 1	Shock (window glass, silvered), in boxes, see Note, item 86902; when in shipments weighing less than 30,000 pounds, see Note, item 86512.	85
Sub 2	Other than shock glass, in packages shown:	
Sub 3	Bent; when in shipments weighing less than 24,000 pounds, see Note, item 86512:	
Sub 4	Not exceeding 15 feet in length nor 9 feet in breadth, in boxes	100
Sub 5	Exceeding 15 feet in length or 9 feet in breadth, in boxes	250
Sub 6	Not bent, see Package 785:	
Sub 7	120 united inches or less, in boxes, crates or Packages 198 or 235; when in shipments weighing less than 30,000 pounds, see Note, item 86512	70
Sub 8	Exceeding 120 united inches but not exceeding 15 feet in length or 9 feet in breadth, in boxes or crates; when in shipments weighing less than 40,000 pounds, see Note, item 86512	100
Sub 9	Exceeding 15 feet in length or 9 feet in breadth, in boxes or crates; when in shipments weighing less than 40,000 pounds, see Note, item 86512	200
86902	NOTE—Glass, silvered for mirrors, which has been framed or backed, or equipped with hangers or fastening devices, is subject to the classes for mirrors, NOI.	
86940	**Glass,** window, other than plate, with metal edging other than sash or frames, in boxes; when in shipments weighing less than 30,000 pounds, see Note, item 86512.	77.5
86960	**Glazing Units,** glass, not in sash, see Note, item 86966, in boxes, crates or Packages 2149 or 2281; when in shipments weighing less than 30,000 pounds, see Note, item 86512.	70
86966	NOTE—Applies on units consisting of sheets of glass separated by air or vacuum, sealed at all edges with same or other materials.	
87100	**Glass Factory Flattening Stones, Floats, Gathering Rings or Pot Rings or Glasshouse Pots,** clay; in boxes, crates, drums or on skids; or loose when weighing each 2,500 pounds or more packed in packing material and securely braced	85
87500	**GLASSWARE GROUP:** Articles consist of Glassware or Glass Articles, see Note, item 87512, as described in items subject to this grouping.	
87512	NOTE—All articles of glassware which are plated, mounted or trimmed with gold or silver will be subject to the provisions provided for glassware, gold or silver deposit, gold or silver mounted or gold or silver trimmed.	
87520	**Ampoules (Ampuls),** in boxes, drums or Package 2362	100
87540	**Aquariums or Terrariums,** capacity over ½ gallon, see Note, item 87552, in boxes, crates or drums:	
Sub 1	Each in individual fibre box, two or more smaller sizes nested within one larger.	85
Sub 2	NOI.	150
87550	**Aquariums or Terrariums,** NOI, capacity ½ gallon or less, see Note, item 87552, in boxes, crates or drums .	100
87552	NOTE—Applies only on aquariums or terrariums constructed with metal or plastic frames.	
87560	**Aquariums or Terrariums,** glass, with plastic frames, disassembled into panels, in boxes	70
87570	**Ballotini (Decorative Glass Globules),** in boxes.	85
87590	**Balls,** lightning rod, in boxes or drums.	85

FIGURE 6-7 Page from National Motor Freight Classification

Source: Reprinted from the National Motor Freight Classification © ATA 2002

```
ÉÉÉÉÉÉÉÉÉÉÉÉÉÉÉÉÉÉÉÉÉÉÉÉÉÉÉÉÉÉÉÉÉÉÉÉÉÉÉÉÉÉÉÉÉÉ
èèèèèèèèèèèèèèèèèèèèèèèèèèèèèèèèèèèèèèèèèèèèèè£Ü
¤ ACCESSORIAL CHARGES                        ¤Ü
¤ááááááááááááááááááááááááááááááááááááááááááá¤Ü
¤     COD Fee                                 ¤Ü
¤        Change COD                           ¤Ü
¤        Inside delivery                      ¤Ü
¤        Marking or tagging                   ¤Ü
¤        Notify before delivery               ¤Ü
¤        Redelivery                           ¤Ü
¤        Residential delivery                 ¤Ü
¤        Sorting and segregating              ¤Ü
¤        Storage                              ¤Ü
¤        Miscellaneous Charge                 ¤Ü
¤                                             ¤Ü
¤                                             ¤Ü
¤                                             ¤Ü
¤                                             ¤Ü
¤ááááááááááááááááááááááááááááááááááááááááááá¤Ü
¤                                             ¤Ü
¤ Repeat function on/off, press "R".          ¤Ü
àèèèèèèèèèèèèèèèèèèèèèèèèèèèèèèèèèèèèèèèèèèèèè¥
Select/deselect accessorial by positioning arrow then press space bar.
 F1   Explanation of Accessorial Charges                    F10   Finished
```

FIGURE 6-8 List of Accessorial Charges

Source: Courtesy of Yellow Freight System.

```
                    Explanation of Accessorial Charges

COD Fees:   COD <=700    40.00        Change COD: 23.00
            COD <=800    46.00        Notify before delivery: 22.00
            COD <=900    51.50        Residential delivery: 33.00
            COD <=1000   57.50
            COD > 1000   COD * 0.05750
            Maximum :    1000.00      Storage: 1.10 per CWT * days
                                        Daily Minimum: 6.00
Marking:    Pieces * 1.00              Shipment Minimum: 31.00
            Minimum: 17.00
                                      Single Shipment (Weight < 500):
Sorting and segregating:                  17.40 or 10.50 depending on zip
     Pieces  *  0.35 or
     0.60 per CWT                     Redelivery:   3.30 per CWT
                                          Minimum:   25.00
                                          Maximum: 435.00

                                      Inside delivery:   4.00 per CWT
                                                Minimum:   50.00
                                                Maximum:  500.00

Press ENTER to continue
```

FIGURE 6-9 Amounts Charged for Accessorial Services on Yellow Freights ZIP Disk System

Source: Courtesy of Yellow Freight System.

Hence, if considerable uncommitted space exists on tomorrow's plane, railcar, or barge, the rate for tomorrow may be reduced in an attempt to fill the space. On several Web sites, a shipper may list its cargo and where it should be shipped and wait for rate quotations. The Internet is also used for booking and tracking cargo. It is also possible to use the same computer software to generate the various shipping documents needed by the carrier. In addition, other documents or information useful to the transportation manager and to the supply-chain manager can be generated at the same time.

SUMMARY

Transportation is the links portion of the links and nodes that make up the logistics operation. Transportation is pivotal to the success of any logistics or supply-chain operation. The shippers of small quantities rely on the post office or parcel carriers such as UPS or FedEx. The next step is to ship by an LTL motor carrier that picks up goods and takes them to a local terminal, where they are loaded aboard a line-haul truck to a terminal near the consignee. A small truck then makes deliveries from the terminal. In terms of numbers of shippers, the vast majority use only parcel or LTL services.

The next step, in terms of shipment size, is to ship in truckload, railcar-load, or barge-load volumes or to use a pipeline. The rates are negotiable, and service considerations are part of the negotiations. Carriers encourage multiple truckloads, multiple railcar loads, and so on. Specialized equipment is also used with these volumes of traffic. Specialized terminals are also custom designed for handling each different type of bulk commodity.

Parcel and LTL shippers pay rates established in carrier tariffs. To prepare a tariff, the carriers need three different types of information before they know the exact rate for a specific shipment. The information needed is length of haul, size of shipment, and the cargo's handling characteristics. Cargo handling characteristics are usually incorporated into a product's classification number. This number is influenced by the product's density. This, in turn, is taken into account when the product is designed and when packaging is selected.

Today, many tariffs appear on the Internet and one can calculate rates using a computer.

QUESTIONS FOR DISCUSSION AND REVIEW

1. What are terminals? What functions do they serve?
2. Why is transportation important to a firm's supply-chain operations?
3. What are routing guides? How are they used?
4. With some guidance from your instructor, contact your local post office and offices of UPS, FedEx, some motor carriers, airlines, and so on to learn of the services they offer and the rates they charge for typical domestic shipments.
5. What is LTL traffic? How is it handled by the LTL carriers?
6. List some products that frequently move by air freight. Why do you think that air freight was selected as the mode to use?
7. What are freight forwarders? How do they function? What services do they perform?
8. What is a shippers' cooperative?
9. How do truck TL operations differ from truck LTL operations?
10. What is bulk cargo?
11. What is a unit train? How does it function?
12. What types of product move by barge? In what ways would they differ from typical products carried by air?
13. What are pipeline slurry systems? How do they function?
14. Discuss some of the issues associated with specialized unloading devices for bulk cargoes.
15. What is project cargo?
16. Compare the five modes of transport—air, motor, pipeline, rail, and water—by at least three different criteria that you think are important.

17. Assume that the LTL rate for widgets is 50 cents per pound, the TL rate is 30 cents per pound, and 40,000 pounds of widgets fill a truck. At what weight would the shipper be indifferent to paying the TL or LTL rate?
18. What is product classification as used by carriers?
19. Why do railroads seem to haul so many hazardous shipments?
20. How would a shipper use a computer to access the transportation rates for different carriers?

SUGGESTED READINGS

Bigras, Yeon and Jacques Roy. "The Use of New Information Technologies: The Case of the Quebec Trucking Industry." *Journal of the Transportation Research Forum,* Vol. 39, No. 3, 2000, pp. 157–168.

Bombe, Anita, and B. Starr McMullen. "Measuring the Non-Pecuniary Costs of Triple Trailer Operation in Oregon." *Journal of the Transportation Research Forum,* Vol. 36, No. 1, 1996, pp. 19–28.

Hage, Jarod. "The Effects of Yield Management on Rail Shippers." *Proceedings of the 35th Annual Meeting of the Transportation Research Forum,* 1997, pp. 87–108.

Holcomb, Mary Collins, and Karl B. Manrodt. "The Shippers' Perspective: Transportation and Logistics Trends and Issues." *The Transportation Journal,* Vol. 40, No. 1, Fall 2000, pp 15–25.

Jennings, Barton, and Mary Collins Holcomb. "Beyond Containerization: The Broader Concept of Intermodalism." *Transportation Journal,* Vol. 35, No. 4, 1996, pp. 5–13.

Kidd, Willis V. "Redefining Grain Railroad Service in the New Millennium." www.agecon.ksu.edu/ abiere/agec632/kidd.pdf, June 13, 2002.

Kling, James A., and David Sirgey. "Motor Carrier Quality Programs, Measurement and Performance." *Proceedings of the 35th Annual Meeting of the Transportation Research Forum,* 1997, pp. 269–278.

Lee, Chungwon, Christopher Oswald, Randy Machemehl, Mark Euritt, and Rob Harrison. "A Survey Approach for the Acceptability of Highway Tolling and Congestion Pricing in Texas." *Journal of the Transportation Research Forum,* Vol. 36, No. 1, 1996, pp. 43–58.

McBride, Michael F. "Railroads May Not Refuse to Carry Dangerous Commodities." *Journal of Transportation Law, Logistics and Policy,* Vol. 69, No. 4, 2002, pp. 391–397.

Muller, Gerhardt. *Intermodal Freight Transportation,* 3rd ed. Westport, CT: Eno Foundation, 1995.

Pautsch, Gregory, Bruce Babcock, and C. Philip Baumel. "Estimating the Value of Guaranteed Rail Service." *Journal of the Transportation Research Forum,* Vol. 36, No. 1, 1996, pp. 59–73.

Prater, Marvin, and Michael Babcock. "Determinants of Profitability of Grain Dependent Short Line Railroads." *Proceedings of the 35th Annual Meeting of the Transportation Research Forum,* 1997, pp. 536–567.

Rahall, Nick J. *Transportation and the Potential for Intermodal Efficiency Enhancements in Western West Virginia.* Huntington, WV: Marshall University, 2000.

Spraggins, H. Barry. "The Potential for International Intermodal Movement of Goods from Alberta to the U.S. and Mexico." *Proceedings of the 35th Annual Meeting of the Transportation Research Forum,* 1997, pp. 279–310.

Stephenson, Frederick J., and Richard J. Fox. "Driver Retention Solutions: Strategies for For-Hire Truckload (TL) Drivers." *Transportation Journal,* Vol. 35, No. 4, 1996, pp. 12–25.

Taylor, John C., and George C. Jackson. "Conflict, Power, and Evolution in the Intermodal Transportation Industry's Channel of Distribution." *Transportation Journal,* Vol. 39, No. 3, 2000, pp. 5–17.

Wisner, Joel D., and Ira A. Lewis. "Quality Improvement Programs in the Motor Carrier Industry." *Transportation Journal,* Vol. 35, No. 3, 1996, pp. 31–48.

Wood, Donald F., and James C. Johnson. *Contemporary Transportation,* 5th ed. Upper Saddle River, NJ: Prentice Hall, 1996.

Wood, Donald F, and Richard S. Nelson. "Industrial Transportation Management: What's New?" *Transportation Journal,* Vol. 39, No. 2, 1999 pp. 26–30.

C A S E

Case 6-1   Boone Shoe Company

This case shows how a carrier's transportation charges were determined using printed tariff documents, in the pre-computer era. It begins with an example and then turns into a problem with questions.

Assume that an archaeology museum wants to move 30,000 pounds of bones from Sioux Falls, South Dakota, to Hannibal, Missouri. It wants to use railroads because this shipment is in no particular hurry. To establish the rating (class), it is necessary first to find the commodity in the Uniform Freight Classification (UFC) index. Exhibit 6-A contains the page from the index that contains human bones. Note that the letters *noibn* follow "human bones." The letters stand for "not otherwise indexed by name." We are referred to item number 13350. Exhibit 6-B is the page in the UFC that contains item number 13350. This tariff also specifies how the human bones are to be packaged for presentation to the carrier. (This is important for all products: The classification dictates how products must be packaged.) On the right-hand edge of Exhibit 6-B are the appropriate ratings, or classes. The first rating of 200 is the less-than-carload (LCL) rating. (*LCL* stands for "less-than-carload" and dates to the time when railroads carried small shipments of mixed freight weighing, say, a few hundred or thousand pounds each.) Then, Exhibit 6-B states that if 20,000 or more pounds are tendered to the carrier, the carload (CL) rating is 100. Because this shipment involves 30,000 pounds, the CL rating of 100 will be used. The next requirement is to determine the rate bases number. Exhibit 6-C illustrates a typical tariff page containing this information. The appropriate rate bases number between Sioux Falls, South Dakota, and Hannibal, Missouri, is 448. Finally, it is necessary to establish the specific rate per hundred pounds. Exhibit 6-D contains a tariff page that uses the rating (class) and rate bases number to determine the rate, which is $3.07 in this example. The total charge can now be determined using this formula:

Rate (per hundred pounds) TIMES weight (in hundred-pound units) = charge
or $3.07 × 300 = $921

"Red" Boone founded the Boone Shoe Company in St. Joseph, Missouri, during the 1930s. Red started to make moccasins for friends who had always admired the ones he had made for himself. Over time, the reputation of Boone shoes spread, and Red expanded his product line and hired additional employees. The real growth of the company took place during World War II. In 1942, almost as a joke, Red submitted a bid to the War Department to produce 100,000 pairs of combat boots. Much to his surprise, the contract was accepted, probably because Red noted in the bid that a sufficient noncombat labor force (females and retirees) to produce boots existed in the area.

The main production input, leather, was easily obtained at the nearby Kansas City stockyards. After the war, the Boone company expanded its production of civilian shoes and related products and also continued to supply the military with all types of leather footwear. Red Boone's son, Barry, was in charge of all marketing and distribution activities.

Larry Gitman functioned as the firm's warehouse, purchasing, and traffic manager.

UNIFORM FREIGHT CLASSIFICATION 7

INDEX TO ARTICLES

STCC No.	Article	Item	STCC No.	Article	Item
	Hulls,Concluded:			Huskers,Concluded:	
20 914 45	Cottonseed, mixed with meal	37130		Corn, and fodder shredders, combined, ot hand, SU	3370,14050
20 914 25	Cottonseed, not ground	31250,131270	35 225 23		
20 939 46	Fleaseed (psyllium)	33800,80090	34 236 79	Corn, hand (husking gloves)	36260
34 412 15	Launch, steel	11690	35 225 60	Corn, noibn, ot hand, KD	3360,14050
37 329 12	Launch, wooden, in the white, KD.	11490	35 225 59	Corn, noibn, ot hand, SU, on wheels	3360,14050
37 329 13	Launch, wooden, in the white, SU.	11490	35 227 30	Green corn.	62530
20 939 55	Nut, noibn.	86140		Husking gloves, corn (corn huskers)	36260
20 418 30	Oat.	47110	34 236 80	Husking pins.	36500
20 999 28	Peanut, crushed or ground	37530	01 199 30	Husks, corn (shucks)	37350
20 939 20	Peanut, not crushed nor ground.	37540	33 219 16	Husks, or sections	29520
20 939 46	Psyllium seed (fleaseed)	33800,80090	28 311 51	Hydrants.	δ
20 449 15	Rice, ground and rice bran, feed.	37580	01 915 13	Hydrastis canadensis (golden seal) roots, ground or powdered	33590,33800
20 449 20	Rice, ground, feed	37590		Hydrastis canadensis (golden seal) roots, not ground nor powdered.	33620,33800
20 449 25	Rice, unground (rice chaff), feed.	37600	35 329 10	Hydraulic accumulators, mining, ore milling or smelting.	63480
09 131 55	Shrimp	δ	32 411 15	Hydraulic cement.	21680,177130
20 923 16	Soybean, ground	37640	35 999 16	Hydraulic cylinders, ot rotary, steel	60780
20 923 17	Soybean, not ground	37640	35 691 45	Hydraulic rams.	161240,64890
20 939 56	Sunflower seed	83440	35 329 10	Hydraulic rotary swivels, oil, water or gas well.	72070
20 939 22	Tung nut	52790	29 912 10	Hydraulic system fluid, ot, petroleum.	14690
20 939 64	Velvet bean, ground	95550		Hydraulic wheel presses	166800
20 939 66	Velvet bean, not ground	95560	34 434 38	Hydro-pneumatic tanks, copper, cylindrical closed at both ends.	89040
28 311 21	Human blood, liquid, frozen or chilled.	11355	34 434 40	Hydro-pneumatic tanks, silicon bronze, cylindrical, closed at both ends.	89050
39 998 21	Human bones, noibn.	13350	34 434 42	Hydro-pneumatic tanks, steel, 14 gauge or thicker, cylindrical, closed at both ends.	89060
39 994 10	Human hair	48320	38 213 15	Hydrobarometers	32990
39 994 20	Human hair goods, noibn.	48390	28 139 92	Hydrocarbon gas, noibn	45630
39 994 15	Human hair samples, mounted on cardboard	48360	35 599 78	Hydrocarbon recovery systems.	δ
40 291 47	Human hair waste, not stumps nor combed hair	95490	28 194 50	Hydrochloric (muraitic) acid	2340,33800
	Humidifiers:		28 194 34	Hydrocyanic acid.	2260
41 111 10	Air and blowers or fans combined, mounted on freight automobile.	73400	28 194 42	Hydrofluoric and sulphuric acid, mixed.	2280,33800
35 857 20	Air and blowers or fans combined, noibn,	130740,58510	28 194 38	Hydrofluoric acid	2270,33800
35 857 45	Air bakers', cast iron.	58610,158720	40 251 65	Hydrofluoric acid waste, aqueous.	δ
37 142 12	Coolers and filters, air, automobile, non-electric	8125	28 194 46	Hydrofluosilicic acid	2290,33800
34 336 49	Hot air house heating furnace, automatic	12700	28 139 20	Hydrogen bromide, anhydrous, liquefied.	45410
34 299 30	Humidors, ot display.	52800	28 139 22	Hydrogen chloride, anhydrous, liquefied.	45420
14 917 15	Humus.	27320	28 199 31	Hydrogen dioxide.	24020,33800
33 992 50	Hungarian nails, noibn, brass, bronze or copper.	149771,50810	28 134 60	Hydrogen gas.	45640
33 152 25	Hungarian nails, noibn, steel, with ot steel or zinc heads	149781,50820	28 199 31	Hydrogen peroxide	24020,33800
33 152 30	Hungarian nails, noibn, steel, with steel heads	149781,50830	28 139 46	Hydrogen sulphide	45650
33 152 35	Hungarian nails, noibn, steel, with zinc heads	149781,50840	20 469 10	Hydrol (corn, sorghum grain or wheat sugar final molasses).	37360
	Hurdles, track, steel with wooden cross bars, noibn.	7580	38 219 14	Hydrometers	33000
	Hurdles, track steel with wooden cross bars, uprights folded to base, or SU nstd, in nests of five or more.	7580	28 186 20	Hydroxy acetic acid	2300,33800
22 995 73	Hurds, hemp or ramie.	52810	40 251 62	Hydroxy aldehydes, waste, containing not less than 40% water.	96090
35 225 29	Huskers and pickers combined, corn.	3390,14050	28 612 20	Hypernic extracts, dry	35860
35 225 61	Huskers and shellers, combined, corn, ot hand.	3380,14050	28 612 21	Hypernic extracts, liquid or paste.	35870
	Huskers:		40 291 57	Hypo-mud, photo silver	95720
35 225 24	Corn and fodder shredders, combined, ot hand, KD	3370,14050			

EXHIBIT 6-A Index Page from Freight Classification

After 2 years as a management trainee with a large motor carrier, Larry had accepted the position at Boone Shoe Company. Because of the firm's steady annual growth rate of 15 percent, Barry Boone had authorized Larry to hire an assistant.

Steve Knapp, just out of high school, was working part-time from 1:00 to 6:00 P.M. and also attending the local community college. Steve had progressed so rapidly that Larry felt comfortable taking a 3-week vacation, his first extended vacation in some years.

During Larry's vacation, Steve assumed Larry's responsibilities. As Steve sat in his office, the intercom buzzed and Barry asked Steve to pick up line 3 and take part in the conversation. The call was from Tom Cook, Boone's salesman for Minnesota and Wisconsin. Tom stated, "I'm

UNIFORM FREIGHT CLASSIFICATION 7   13250-13470

Item	ARTICLES	Less Carload Ratings	Carload Minimum (Pounds)	Carload Ratings
	BOILERS, FURNACES, RADIATORS, STOVES, RELATED ARTICLES OR PARTS NAMED (Subject to Item 11960)—Concluded:			
	Group No. 1			
13250	Coal hods (scuttles) or vases, steel; cookers or steamers, stock feed, noibn; furnaces, house heating, hot air, with or without equipment of air conditioning apparatus or thermostats; griddles, kettles, pots, skillets or spiders, sheet steel; holloware, cast iron, as described in Item 49880; house heating furnace casing parts; sugar or syrup evaporator kettles, iron; stove or range cabinets, closets or high shelves, steel; stove or range ovens; stove or range parts, iron or steel, other than castings; stove pipe drums or drum ovens; stove pipe or elbows, sheet iron, steel or tin plate, side seams closed; stove pipe thimbles, plate or sheet iron or steel or tin plate, side seams closed; stove or range reservoirs or reservoir attachments; tee joints and draft regulators combined, stove pipe.			
	Group No. 2			
13260	Air registers, noibn, including air louvres, iron or steel; andirons, iron; ash scrapers; heating furnace pipe or elbows, sheet iron, steel or tin plate; house heating furnace castings, iron; burners, gas, for coal, oil or wood stoves, see Note 58, Item 13271; oil burning outfits for brooders or coal or wood stoves; pans, baking, dripping or frying, sheet steel; fire pokers, iron; sad irons, with or without stands, other than self-heating; stove boards, iron or metal clad wood or fibreboard; stove cover lifters, iron; stove or range castings, iron; stove pipe, sheet iron, steel or tin plate, side seams not closed, nested; dampers, noibn, iron; stove pipe thimbles, cast iron or plate or sheet iron or tin plate, side seams not closed, nested; stove shovels, sheet steel; water heaters, noibn			
13261	Note 52.—Weight of articles in Group 2, Item 13260, must not exceed 50% of weight upon which charges are assessed.			
13265	Mixed CL of two or more of the following articles, viz.: Stoves or ranges, iron or steel; dampers, noibn, iron; electric logs, see Note 54, Item 13266; fireplace grates or grate baskets, with or without heating units; fireplace grate parts, noibn; gas logs; heaters, gas, with or without clay radiants; andirons (fire dogs); fenders or fireplace guards or screens, brass, see Note 54, Item 13266; fenders or fireplace guards or screens, iron or steel, plain or brass coated or plated, or with brass trimming; fireplace sets (shovels and tongs), with or without hearth brushes, holders or pokers, brass or brass and iron combined, see Note 54, Item 13266; fireplace sets (shovels and tongs), with or without hearth brushes, holders or pokers, iron; lighters, fire, brass or iron, see Note 54, Item 13266; or wood holders or racks, fireplace, see Note 54, Item 13266	......	24,000R	45
13266	Note 54.—Aggregate weight of articles subject to this note must not exceed 50% of weight upon which charges are assessed.			
13267	Note 56.—Section 2 of Rule 34 is not applicable.			
13270	Superheaters, other than locomotive:			
	SU, loose or in packages	70	24,000R	40
	KD, or superheater parts, KD, loose or in packages	65	24,000R	40
13271	Note 58.—Ratings apply only on burners for converting coal, oil or wood stoves into gas stoves.			
13272	Note 60.—Weight of articles subject to this note shall not exceed 10% of weight upon which charges are assessed.			
13280	Tanks, oil stove, sheet steel, 26 gauge or thicker, capacity not exceeding 5 gallons, in boxes or crates	110	16,000R	60
13281	Note 66.—Ratings also apply on stoves or ranges designed for separate permanent installation of oven and surface cooking units.			
13282	Note 68.—CL ratings will include iron or steel garbage or offal incinerators, not exceeding 25% of the weight upon which freight charges are assessed.			
13295	Bolster rolls for beds, couches or lounges, fibreboard with plywood ends and reinforcing ribs, upholstered, in Package 9F	150	10,000R	100
13300	Bolster rolls for beds, couches or lounges, noibn, in boxes or crates	200	10,000R	100
13310	Bone, charred filtering (animal charcoal), other than spent, in bags or barrels	70	36,000	35
13320	Bone, charred filtering (animal charcoal), spent, in bags	50	40,000	20
13330	Bone, charred filtering, synthetic, in bags or barrels	70	36,000	35
13340	Bone ash, in bags or boxes	55	36,000	30
13350	Bones, human, noibn, prepaid, in barrels or boxes	200	20,000R	100
13360	Bones, noibn, ground or not ground, LCL, in bags or barrels, or in barrels with cloth tops; CL, loose or in packages	50	40,000	22½
13370	Book ends, moulded wood or plaster, in boxes	85	24,000R	55
13380	Book stacks, library, consisting of iron brackets, floor framing, stairs, railings, standards, and shelves, in packages; also CL, loose	70	36,000	40
13390	Boot or shoe arch supports or arch support insoles, in boxes	100	20,000R	70
13400	Boot or shoe forms or trees, in barrels or boxes	85	20,000R	55
13410	BOOTS, SHOES, OR BOOT OR SHOE FINDINGS:			
13420	Boot or shoe findings, noibn, in bales, barrels or boxes, or in barrels with cloth tops	100	16,000R	70
13430	Boots or shoes, noibn, see Note 1, item 13431, in boxes; in trunks in crates; in salesmen's sample trunks, locked; in Packages 277 or 1197; also in straight CL in Packages 1126	100	24,000R	70
13431	Note 1.—Ratings also apply on Huaraches (Mexican leather sandals) in bamboo baskets or hampers, tops securely closed.			
13440	Boots or shoes, old, used, leather, having value other than for reclamation of raw materials, prepaid, see Note 2, Item 13441, in packages; also CL, loose	85	36,000	50
13441	Note 2.—Old used shoes rebuilt or repaired, will be rated as shoes, noibn.			
13450	Boots or shoes, plastic, rubber or rubber and canvas, felt or wool combined, in bales or boxes	100	15,000R	70
13460	Boots or shoes, wooden or leather with wooden soles, in packages	92½	24,000R	65
13470	Box toe boards, in packages; also CL, loose	70	36,000	35

EXHIBIT 6-B Page Showing Classification of Articles

calling from the buying office of Lawson Department Stores in Green Bay. Although they're currently overstocked in shoes, they are interested in buying a sizable quantity of our Light Stride arch-support insoles. They plan on giving them away with their shoes in order to stimulate shoe sales. They want to buy FOB destination. I need to know in the next few minutes the cost of sending 17,000 pounds of the arch supports from St. Joseph to Green Bay."

APPLICATION OF RATE BASES

BETWEEN (See Item 100) / **AND** (See Item 100)

RATE BASES APPLICABLE

AND (See Item 100)	Greeley Centre, Neb.	Green Bay, Wis.	Greenbush, Minn.	Grenville, S.D.	Grinnell, Iowa	Grover, Colo.	Hallock, Minn.	Hannaford, N.D.	Hannibal, Mo.	Harvard, Ill.	Hawarden, Iowa	Hartun, Colo.	Hays, Kan.	Hazen, N.D.	Herington, Kan.	Hermansville, Mich.	Hermosa, S.D.	Herrick, S.D.	Hettinger, N.D.	Hibbing, Minn.
Rugby . . . . . . N.D.	716	716	233	340	680	944	202	128	855	768	465	914	939	306	824	687	609	714	461	372
Rulo . . . . . . Neb.	240	619	712	627	237	546	718	621	251	477	244	438	318	699	179	715	619	347	669	636
Russell . . . . . . Kan.	335	844	919	834	479	474	925	828	457	606	451	482	27	906	121	941	695	506	875	868
St. Cloud . . . . . . Minn.	489	350	262	223	317	828	287	241	495	401	250	737	712	433	596	367	558	487	461	193
St. Francis . . . . . . Kan.	309	918	935	850	568	502	941	844	620	809	467	363	363	922	332	985	646	487	892	884
St. Ignace . . . . . . Mich.	937	256	681	735	619	1277	713	722	659	392	713	1186	1098	914	959	166	1064	935	966	477
St. James . . . . . . Minn.	358	380	430	345	220	697	436	363	408	388	133	607	581	488	465	414	498	356	457	314
St. Joseph . . . . . . Mo.	281	579	737	652	213	587	743	646	207	437	269	479	293	724	154	676	657	383	694	614
St. Louis . . . . . . Mo.	583	458	854	812	305	890	880	833	⊕	⊕	545	783	561	983	414	553	940	668	952	719
Sabetha . . . . . . Kan.	223	640	740	655	273	524	747	649	267	498	272	414	277	727	155	736	604	349	697	666
Sabula . . . . . . Iowa	492	246	639	597	146	832	665	618	⊕	⊕	364	741	625	792	486	343	756	572	762	504
Sac City . . . . . . Iowa	250	464	545	460	143	589	552	472	317	362	115	499	462	561	347	540	510	302	530	442
Salem . . . . . . S.D.	330	539	456	359	313	670	442	304	488	512	76	579	553	383	438	572	340	328	352	437
Salina . . . . . . Kan.	258	767	842	757	402	526	848	751	380	619	374	405	104	829	44	864	618	429	798	791
Salisbury . . . . . . Mo.	412	515	778	734	201	720	804	757	91	362	383	612	393	838	253	611	771	497	808	649
Sanborn . . . . . . Minn.	376	407	396	311	238	715	402	329	427	415	151	625	599	454	483	430	470	374	423	325
Sanish . . . . . . N.D.	793	817	368	428	768	962	336	247	942	871	543	933	1016	227	901	815	628	791	447	506
Sargent . . . . . . Neb.	102	750	766	681	408	475	773	675	530	641	298	389	406	754	308	816	538	314	723	716
Sauk Centre . . . . . . Minn.	517	392	234	181	359	857	254	199	537	443	279	766	740	391	625	409	546	515	419	228
Sault Ste Marie . . . . . . Mich.	955	273	685	739	664	1294	717	726	708	452	730	1203	1144	918	1004	184	1082	953	984	481
Sawyer . . . . . . Kan.	405	872	987	903	522	656	994	897	480	719	520	552	210	975	158	968	765	576	944	923
Schley . . . . . . Minn.	648	427	146	276	476	988	178	258	654	518	409	897	871	450	756	399	670	646	522	82
Scott City . . . . . . Kan.	461	959	1044	959	594	437	1051	953	572	811	576	486	244	1032	228	1055	726	632	1001	993
Scottsbluff . . . . . . Neb.	365	980	897	804	638	175	883	746	729	871	529	145	565	765	467	1046	222	544	735	946
Sedalia . . . . . . Colo.	490	1105	1095	1001	762	130	1081	943	832	996	554	180	361	963	505	1171	420	669	932	1071
Sedalia . . . . . . Mo.	413	568	831	787	254	709	857	792	144	415	415	603	371	870	224	664	794	529	840	702
Seney . . . . . . Mich.	891	210	605	660	601	1231	637	646	644	388	667	1140	1080	838	941	120	1012	889	906	401
Severy . . . . . . Kan.	375	757	920	835	410	643	926	829	364	605	452	522	231	907	114	854	735	521	877	811
Sharon Springs . . . . . . Kan.	355	965	982	897	608	317	988	891	623	851	514	366	140	969	287	1031	606	534	938	931
Shawano . . . . . . Wis.	690	38	553	544	403	1030	585	570	447	190	498	939	882	956	743	107	860	721	763	351
Shawnee . . . . . . Wyo.	479	1023	864	771	731	165	850	677	843	948	539	259	612	732	581	1056	190	575	702	940
Sheboygan . . . . . . Wis.	700	63	613	604	356	1040	645	631	397	129	522	949	835	817	696	159	905	745	822	411
Sheldon . . . . . . Ill.	653	275	802	760	304	986	828	781	⊕	⊕	533	881	717	962	578	372	925	738	931	601
Sheldon . . . . . . Iowa	267	471	464	379	216	607	471	392	395	415	43	516	490	480	375	505	429	265	449	404
Shenandoah . . . . . . Iowa	218	571	657	572	189	547	663	566	268	429	189	441	383	644	243	556	577	303	614	562
Sheridan Lake . . . . . . Colo.	536	1034	1120	1035	669	361	1126	1029	647	886	652	411	319	1107	303	1131	651	707	1077	1069
Sidney . . . . . . Neb.	328	943	908	815	601	102	894	757	691	834	492	73	504	776	429	1009	233	507	746	909
Simpson (Johnson Co.) . . . . . . Ill.	733	552	995	953	446	1040	1021	974	⊕	⊕	686	933	711	1123	564	649	1081	818	1093	835
Sioux City . . . . . . Iowa	211	527	512	427	236	550	518	421	398	453	44	459	434	499	318	561	444	209	468	461
Sioux Falls . . . . . . S.D.	299	499	437	340	273	639	444	337	448	473	46	548	522	422	407	533	380	297	392	397
Bisseton . . . . . . S.D.	537	503	318	193	439	831	304	230	627	552	284	786	760	385	645	521	496	535	354	370
Smithboro . . . . . . Ill.	625	432	858	816	309	932	884	837	⊕	⊕	549	825	604	987	464	528	944	710	956	711
South Beloit . . . . . . Ill.	588	150	634	592	242	928	660	613	⊕	⊕	433	837	721	805	581	247	819	653	802	434
Sparta . . . . . . Ill.	637	490	908	866	359	944	934	887	⊕	⊕	599	837	607	1036	460	587	994	722	1006	769
Spencer . . . . . . Iowa	303	443	500	415	180	643	507	428	359	379	79	552	527	516	411	486	465	302	486	386
Spooner . . . . . . Wis.	570	253	353	379	473	909	385	394	510	328	345	818	786	586	659	247	697	568	599	149
Springfield . . . . . . Ill.	580	369	794	752	261	894	820	773	⊕	⊕	501	786	584	938	445	486	895	665	908	642
Stafford . . . . . . Kan.	360	841	942	858	479	568	949	852	449	688	475	507	165	930	113	937	720	531	899	880
Stanley . . . . . . N.D.	795	804	348	419	759	1023	317	214	934	856	544	993	1018	315	903	799	688	793	535	488
Stapleton . . . . . . Neb.	212	827	843	759	485	423	850	753	575	718	376	385	411	831	313	893	519	391	800	973
Sterling . . . . . . Colo.	343	958	948	855	616	106	934	796	707	849	507	33	460	816	443	1024	273	522	785	924
Stiles Jct. . . . . . . Wis.	722	28	576	575	419	1061	607	602	463	207	530	971	899	788	759	75	892	753	794	371
Stockton . . . . . . Kan.	271	838	867	782	481	539	874	776	399	418	217	854	157	914	604	442	824	817		
Strasburg . . . . . . Colo.	477	1086	1003	1015	730	144	1094	957	779	973	635	194	299	977	443	1153	434	656	946	1053
Stratton . . . . . . Neb.	256	866	883	798	516	275	889	792	586	757	415	202	329	870	298	932	442	435	839	832
Streator . . . . . . Ill.	583	297	732	690	231	916	758	711	⊕	⊕	460	811	648	888	505	370	852	668	858	556
Streeter . . . . . . N.D.	582	630	304	241	547	810	290	134	721	687	332	780	805	257	690	648	475	580	327	411
Studley . . . . . . Kan.	303	923	956	871	558	388	963	865	536	775	488	398	157	944	200	1006	677	409	913	906
Sturgeon Bay . . . . . . Wis.	762	58	630	621	449	1102	662	648	492	238	570	1011	928	834	788	154	934	793	839	428
Sublette . . . . . . Kan.	479	971	1062	977	606	473	1069	971	580	819	564	523	261	1049	240	1067	763	650	1019	1007

⊕ For rates refer to I. F. A. Tariff No. I-1002, I. C. C. No. 757, R. G. Raasch, Agent.

EXHIBIT 6-C Tariff Page Showing Point-to-Point Rate Bases

CLASS RATES IN CENTS PER 100 POUNDS

RATE BASIS NUMBERS	| CLASSES																						
	400	300	250	200	175	150	125	110	100	97½	95	92½	90	87½	85	82½	80	77½	75	73½	72½	70	67½	65
5	328	246	205	164	144	123	103	90	82	80	78	76	74	72	70	68	66	64	62	60	59	57	55	54
10	356	267	223	178	156	134	111	98	89	87	85	82	80	78	76	73	71	69	67	65	65	62	60	59
15	384	288	240	192	168	144	120	106	96	94	91	89	86	84	82	79	77	74	72	71	70	67	65	63
20	408	306	255	204	179	153	128	112	102	99	97	94	92	89	87	84	82	79	77	75	74	71	69	67
25	420	315	263	210	184	158	131	116	105	102	100	97	95	92	89	87	84	81	79	77	76	74	71	69
30	448	336	280	224	196	168	140	123	112	109	106	104	101	98	95	92	90	87	84	82	81	78	76	74
35	460	345	288	230	201	173	144	127	115	112	109	106	104	101	98	95	92	89	86	85	83	81	78	76
40	480	360	300	240	210	180	150	132	120	117	114	111	108	105	102	99	96	93	90	88	87	84	81	79
45	492	369	308	246	215	185	154	135	123	120	117	114	111	108	105	101	98	95	92	90	89	86	83	81
50	504	378	315	252	221	189	158	139	126	123	120	117	113	110	107	104	101	98	95	93	91	88	85	83
55	524	393	328	262	229	197	164	144	131	128	124	121	118	115	111	108	105	102	98	96	95	92	88	86
60	536	402	335	268	235	201	168	147	134	131	127	124	121	117	114	111	107	104	101	98	97	94	90	88
65	556	417	348	278	243	209	174	153	139	136	132	129	125	122	118	115	111	108	104	102	101	97	94	92
70	564	423	353	282	247	212	176	155	141	137	134	130	127	123	120	116	113	109	106	104	102	99	95	93
75	572	429	358	286	250	215	179	157	143	139	136	132	129	125	122	118	114	111	107	105	104	100	97	94
80	588	441	368	294	257	221	184	162	147	143	140	136	132	129	125	121	118	114	110	108	107	103	99	97
85	600	450	375	300	263	225	188	165	150	146	143	139	135	131	128	124	120	116	113	110	109	105	101	99
90	616	462	385	308	270	231	193	169	154	150	146	142	139	135	131	127	123	119	116	113	112	108	104	102
95	624	468	390	312	273	234	195	172	156	152	148	144	140	137	133	129	125	121	117	115	113	109	105	103
100	636	477	398	318	278	239	199	175	159	155	151	147	143	139	135	131	127	123	119	117	115	111	107	105
110	656	492	410	328	287	246	205	180	164	160	156	152	148	144	139	135	131	127	123	121	119	115	111	108
120	676	507	423	338	296	254	211	186	169	165	161	156	152	148	144	139	135	131	127	124	123	118	114	112
130	700	525	438	350	306	263	219	193	175	171	166	162	158	153	149	144	140	136	131	129	127	123	118	116
140	720	540	450	360	315	270	225	198	180	176	171	167	162	158	153	149	144	140	135	132	131	126	122	119
150	740	555	463	370	324	278	231	204	185	180	176	171	167	162	157	153	148	143	139	136	134	130	125	122
160	756	567	473	378	331	284	236	208	189	184	180	175	170	165	161	156	151	146	142	139	137	132	128	125
170	784	588	490	392	343	294	245	216	196	191	186	181	176	172	167	162	157	152	147	144	142	137	132	129
180	796	597	498	398	348	299	249	219	199	194	189	184	179	174	169	164	159	154	149	146	144	139	134	131
190	812	609	508	406	355	305	254	223	203	198	193	188	183	178	173	167	162	157	152	149	147	142	137	134
200	828	621	518	414	362	311	259	228	207	202	197	191	186	181	176	171	166	160	155	152	150	145	140	137
210	852	639	533	426	373	320	266	234	213	208	202	197	192	186	181	176	170	165	160	157	154	149	144	141
220	868	651	543	434	380	326	271	239	217	212	206	201	195	190	184	179	174	168	163	159	157	152	146	143
230	884	663	553	442	387	332	276	243	221	215	210	204	199	193	188	182	177	171	166	162	160	155	149	146
240	900	675	563	450	394	338	281	248	225	219	214	208	203	197	191	186	180	174	169	165	163	158	152	149
260	940	705	588	470	411	353	294	259	235	229	223	217	212	206	200	194	188	182	176	173	170	165	159	155
280	964	723	603	482	422	362	301	265	241	235	229	223	217	211	205	199	193	187	181	177	175	169	163	159
300	996	747	623	498	436	374	311	274	249	243	237	230	224	218	212	205	199	193	187	183	181	174	168	164
320	1032	774	645	516	452	387	323	284	258	252	245	239	232	226	219	213	206	200	194	190	187	181	174	170
340	1060	795	663	530	464	398	331	292	265	258	252	245	239	232	225	219	212	205	199	195	192	186	179	175
360	1092	819	683	546	478	410	341	300	273	266	259	253	246	239	232	225	218	212	205	201	198	191	184	180
380	1116	837	698	558	488	419	349	307	279	272	265	258	251	244	237	230	223	216	209	205	202	195	188	184
400	1148	861	718	574	502	431	359	316	287	280	273	265	258	251	244	237	230	222	215	211	208	201	194	189
420	1180	885	738	590	516	443	369	325	295	288	280	273	266	258	251	243	236	229	221	217	214	207	199	195
440	1204	903	753	602	527	452	376	331	301	293	286	278	271	263	256	248	241	233	226	222	219	211	203	199
460	1228	921	768	614	537	461	384	338	307	299	292	284	276	269	261	253	246	238	230	226	223	215	207	203
480	1260	945	788	630	551	473	394	347	315	307	299	291	284	276	268	260	252	244	236	232	228	221	213	208
500	1288	966	805	644	564	483	403	354	322	314	306	298	290	282	274	266	258	250	242	237	233	225	217	213
520	1308	981	818	654	572	491	409	360	327	319	311	302	294	286	278	270	262	253	245	240	237	229	221	216
540	1344	1008	840	672	588	504	420	370	336	328	319	311	302	294	286	277	269	260	252	247	244	235	227	222
560	1368	1026	855	684	599	513	428	376	342	333	325	316	308	299	291	282	274	265	257	251	248	239	231	226
580	1396	1047	873	698	611	524	438	384	349	340	332	323	314	305	297	288	279	270	262	257	253	244	236	230
600	1420	1065	888	710	621	533	444	391	355	346	337	328	320	311	302	293	284	275	266	261	257	249	240	234
620	1448	1086	905	724	634	543	453	398	362	353	344	335	326	317	308	299	290	281	272	266	262	253	244	239
640	1476	1107	923	738	646	554	461	406	369	360	351	341	332	323	314	304	295	286	277	271	268	258	249	244
660	1508	1131	943	754	660	566	471	415	377	368	358	349	339	330	320	311	302	292	283	277	273	264	254	249
680	1532	1149	958	766	670	575	479	421	383	373	364	354	345	335	326	316	306	297	287	282	278	268	259	253
700	1560	1170	975	780	683	585	488	429	390	380	371	361	351	341	332	322	312	302	293	287	283	273	263	257
720	1592	1194	995	796	697	597	498	438	398	388	378	368	358	348	338	328	318	308	299	293	289	279	269	263
740	1616	1212	1010	808	707	606	505	444	404	394	384	374	364	354	343	333	323	313	303	297	293	283	273	267
760	1640	1230	1025	820	718	615	513	451	410	400	390	379	369	359	348	338	328	318	307	301	297	287	277	271
780	1672	1254	1045	836	732	627	523	460	418	408	397	387	376	366	355	345	334	324	314	307	303	293	282	276
800	1700	1275	1063	850	744	638	531	468	425	414	404	393	383	372	361	351	340	329	319	312	308	298	287	281
825	1724	1293	1078	862	754	647	539	474	433	420	409	399	388	377	366	356	345	334	323	317	312	302	291	284
850	1756	1317	1098	878	768	659	549	483	439	428	417	406	395	384	373	362	351	340	329	323	318	307	296	290
875	1784	1338	1115	892	781	669	558	491	445	433	424	413	401	390	379	368	357	346	335	328	323	312	301	294
900	1812	1359	1133	906	793	680	566	498	453	442	430	419	408	396	385	374	362	351	340	333	328	317	306	299
925	1840	1380	1150	920	805	690	575	506	460	449	437	426	414	403	391	380	368	357	345	338	334	322	311	304

EXHIBIT 6-D Tariff Page Showing Application of Rate Bases to Charges

In this table interpolation is not used. Instead, if you cannot find the exact number in the left hand column use the next higher printed value.

Steve asked, "Will they accept a rail shipment?

Tom replied, "The buyer said he expected the shipment to come via rail."

Barry came on the line and asked, "Steve, can you look up this info for Tom?"

Steve said, "No problem. I'll call you back with the answer in 15 minutes or less."

QUESTIONS

1. Assume there are no commodity or exception rates in effect for this shipment. Using Exhibits 6-B, 6-C, and 6-D, calculate the applicable charge.

2. Steve remembered that he had heard Larry speak of shipping "wind." This involved paying the CL minimum weight in order to receive the CL rate, even if the shipment actually weighed less than the carload minimum weight. Should this technique be used for the shipment? Why or why not?

3. The buyer will pay upon receipt of the shipment, which is valued at $21,000 plus any transportation charges. Boone Shoe Company borrows money from the bank regularly on an open line of credit and is currently paying interest on its debt at the rate of 15 percent per year. If rail LCL service is used, delivery time to Green Bay will be about 10 days. If rail CL service is used, delivery time will be 6 days. What is the additional advantage to Boone Shoe Company if it chooses to use CL service?

4. (This is a continuation of question 3.) Boone Shoe Company also owns several large trucks, although Steve is uncertain whether they are available for immediate use. He knows that they could make the delivery to Green Bay in 2 days. He checks the highway distance from St. Joseph to Green Bay and finds that it is 588 miles. Larry had once told Steve that it cost the company 85 cents per mile to operate its highway trucks. Do you think that a truck should be used if it is available? Why?

5. (This is a continuation of questions 2 and 3.) Another alternative is to make the shipment by rail from Boone's St. Louis warehouse. Rail delivery time will be 4 days. What price should Tom Cook be told to quote to Lawson's?

6. Boone Shoe Company often sells large quantities—from 10,000 up to 30,000 pounds—of arch-support insoles on an FOB-delivered basis. After referring to Exhibit 6-B, do you think there is a minimum weight (in this 10,000- to 30,000-pound range) that customers should be encouraged to order? If so, what is it?

CHAPTER

Industrial Transportation Management

A train carrying intermodal containers in the Pacific Northwest. Each bloc consists of five joined, articulated cars, each carrying two containers.
Source: Don Wilson, Port of Seattle.

Key Terms

- Bill of lading
- Demurrage and detention
- Diversion
- Expediting
- Hazardous material
- Loss and damage
- Private transportation

- Rate and service negotiations
- Rate determination
- Reconsignment
- Reparations
- Shipment consolidation
- Tracing
- Transit privileges

Learning Objectives

- To examine the background of the transportation management function
- To discuss the functions of transportation management
- To identify the role negotiations play in the transportation management function
- To examine the new options available for private carriage
- To understand the purpose of freight consolidation

Moving freight used to be an uncomplicated job down on the loading dock for men with strong backs and little education. Transport concerns at the boardroom centered on company products arriving undamaged and at their destination within a reasonable time period. Who wanted to go down to the cold, drafty factory floor or to the traffic manager's cramped and linoleum-floored office right off the assembly line when the important corporate decisions were made in the warm, carpeted offices of the sales, marketing, and financial divisions? Increasingly, however, many senior executives are responding to the famous aphorism of the German military historian Von Clausewitz, who wrote "War is too important to be left to the generals." Today, shipping simply has become too important to be left only to those in charge of the shipping department.[1]

Today more than ever before, senior management is concerned about transportation management because transportation represents a major expense item. In general terms, freight transportation accounts for 6 percent of gross domestic product. Today, riding on the crest of enthusiasm for the supply-chain concept, the corporate transportation manager is considered an important member of the management team. The continual restructuring of carriers has sparked top management's interest in transportation issues. We should, however, note that transportation activities represent one topical area of logistics that is often farmed out to third-party logistics providers.

It is difficult to generalize about how deregulation has changed the transportation manager's responsibilities. Many of the pre-deregulation rules remain in effect; what we read or hear about are negotiations concerning departures from these established rules. A simple example is claims for loss and damage; the carrier was and still is responsible unless, in the course of negotiations, the shipper relieves the carrier of part or all of its obligation.

A study by Nelson and Wood asked transportation managers how they allocated their time. Following is a weighted distribution of how respondent transportation man-

---

[1]*The Journal of Commerce,* August 18, 1998, p 6A.

agers devote their time by function. The hours that all respondents spent on each task were totaled, and a percentage of the total was assigned to each task. Following is the percentage time distribution:

rate and service negotiations, 20
rate analysis and determination, 14
carrier selection, 13
documentation, 7
expediting and tracing freight, 7
human resource management functions, 6
carrier assignment, 5
routing, 5
freight claim settlement and prevention, 4
freight consolidation, 4
demurrage and detention, 2
hazmat shipments, 2
billing and auditing, 1[2]

Respondents were asked how they divided their time among customers, vendors, and so forth. Following are the answers:

- customers, 13 percent;
- vendors, 17 percent;
- superiors, 11 percent;
- peers within company, 18 percent
- subordinates, 28 percent
- third-party providers, 10 percent
- others, 3 percent

They were also asked to divide their time according to whether it was devoted to outbound, inbound, or interplant shipments. Median percentages were outbound, 68; inbound, 22; and interplant shipments, 10. The firms in the sample made a median of 12,250 inbound shipments, 36,000 outbound shipments, and 2,650 interplant shipments.

The following sections of this chapter discuss the primary duties of today's transportation department. First, though, it should be pointed out that transportation managers are also involved with many other operations of the firm. They assist marketing by quoting freight rates for salespeople, suggesting quantity discounts that can be based on transportation savings, and selecting carriers and routes for reliable delivery of products. Figure 7-1 is a page from a catalog issued by a firm that sells supplies to the tow-truck industry. It shows shipping rates for various size shipments, using several modes of transport. The firm happens to have warehouses on each coast, so its charges to mid-America are higher. Transportation managers help manufacturing by advising on packaging and materials handling and making certain that an adequate supply of transportation is available when it is needed. Transportation managers aid the outbound shipping process by providing simplified shipping or routing guides, drawing up

---

[2]Transit privileges and appearing before regulatory agencies each accounted for less than 1 percent. Donald F. Wood and Richard S. Nelson, "Industrial Transportation Management: What's New?" *Transportation Journal,* Vol. 39 No. 2, 1999, pp 26–30.

SHIPPING CHARGES – HOW TO CALCULATE

1. Most products in our catalog can be shipped via parcel service (usually UPS). Only those items too large or heavy for UPS are shipped by truck and are noted with a truck symbol.

   Also, if the combined weight of your order exceeds 150 pounds, it may then be more economical to ship by truck.

2. Add the weights of each item in your order and check the appropriate parcel or truck weight category.

3. Determine your shipping zone (where your order is to be shipped) from our map and follow down this column to the weight category which corresponds to your order.

4. Orders shipped C.O.D. (collect on delivery) must add a carrier imposed C.O.D. fee. The fees are:
   Parcel Service ....$7.95   Truck....$15.00   UPS Air Service....$7.95

UPS requires a shipping surcharge on hazardous items such as fire extinguishers and flares. Please add $20.00 to ground shipping. If you would prefer air delivery, please add $30.00 to your shipping charges.

SHIPPING ZONE CHART

UPS
2ND DAY AIR®
2 DAY DELIVERY
AS LOW AS $8.50

ANYWHERE IN THE U.S.A.
(including Alaska, Hawaii and Puerto Rico)

TOTAL WEIGHT (lbs)	CONTIGUOUS STATES	AK/HI/PR
0-5	$9.50	$14.50
6-10	$14.75	$20.25
11-15	$20.25	$29.75
16-20	$25.75	$36.25
21-25	$31.00	$42.75

C.O.D. ORDERS ADD AN ADDITIONAL $7.95.

CALL FOR RATES ON WEIGHTS OVER 25 LBS. UPS NEXT DAY DELIVERY AIR SERVICE IS ALSO AVAILABLE.

ORDERING & SHIPPING INFORMATION

AW SHIPPING CHARGES BY ZONE

TOTAL WEIGHT (lbs)	A	B	C
0-5	$5.00	$5.75	$6.25
6-10	$5.50	$6.75	$7.50
11-15	$6.50	$7.75	$9.50
16-20	$7.25	$9.50	$12.00
21-25	$9.00	$11.25	$14.25
26-30	$10.25	$12.50	$16.50
31-40	$12.00	$15.50	$19.50
41-50	$13.75	$19.50	$24.00
51-60	$15.50	$22.75	$28.00
61-70	$16.50	$24.75	$33.50
71-90	$24.75	$32.00	$39.75
91-120	$32.50	$41.25	$52.25
121-150	$44.25	$53.00	$66.00

UPS GROUND SERVICE*

*Not available to Alaska, Hawaii & Puerto Rico – Please use air service

C.O.D. ORDERS ADD AN ADDITIONAL $7.95

	A	B	C
Up to 300	$60.00	$75.00	$85.00
301-500	$80.00	$90.00	$100.00
over 500	$115.00	$130.00	$150.00

TRUCK**

C.O.D. ORDERS ADD AN ADDITIONAL $15.00

** The truck symbol at the end of a price chart indicates that product must be shipped via truck due to its size or weight.

FIGURE 7-1 Page From a Catalog by AW Direct Showing Shipping Charges

Source: AW Direct Inc.

transportation documents, and encouraging shipment consolidations. Finally, they help purchasing by advising about methods to control the costs and quality of inbound deliveries and by tracing and expediting lost or delayed shipments of important inputs.

Many firms now rely on mission statements to provide guidance for the firms and all their component parts. The Nelson–Wood survey asked transportation managers for copies of their mission statements. Following are examples of two that they received:

> To secure the transportation necessary to deliver the service requirements of the corporation at the lowest cost; and to provide technical support to the corporation on matters related to the movement of materials, supplies, and finished goods.

> The goal of the transportation department is to ensure that all material arrives at the factory or customer at the proper time, and in good condition. It is our responsibility to achieve and maximize internal and external customer satisfaction through efficient and effective routings, carrier and information management, and prompt handling of emergency requests. The department will strive for total customer satisfaction, while focusing on improvements in operations that lead to a better service at a lower total cost to the company.

> Given overall objectives such as these, the transportation manager finds him- or herself responsible for many crucial details in the supply-chain process.

Rate Determination and Negotiation Activities

Chapter 6 dealt with published carrier rates. From the transportation department's standpoint, rate-associated duties can be divided into four categories. The categories are interrelated because they may all involve rates for the same shipment, and whichever category results in the lowest rate is the one used. The categories are (1) published rate determination; (2) working with carrier classification bureaus to publish new, usually lower classifications (available to all shippers with identical products); (3) negotiating with a specific carrier for a contract rate to carry most of the shipper's business; and (4) appearing before a regulatory board in those few instances in which they still have jurisdiction.

Rate Determination

Rate determination is very important to every transportation manager. At one time, all rates appeared in printed tariffs and one had to thumb through several tariffs to find the lowest rate. Although the carrier has a legal obligation to determine the correct rate, there may be more than one correct rate and the shipper, of course, wants the lowest one. Figure 7-2 is a page from a Port of Houston tariff. Updated versions of that tariff now appear on the Port's Web site.

Some carriers have Web sites that potential shippers can use to inquire about rates. ABF Freight System's site asks for the following information for LTL shipments:

- Origin and destination by city or zip code
- Will shipper load?
- Will consignee unload?

SECTION FIVE: Sixtieth Revised Page No. 87

ITEM NO. 65   <u>LOADING, UNLOADING AND WHARFAGE CHARGES</u>
(CONT'D.)   ALL HANDLING charges are in cents per 100 pounds and apply
                     to all shipments at actual weight, except as otherwise noted.
                     ALL WHARFAGE charges are in cents per ton of 2,000 pounds and
                     apply to all shipments at actual weight, except as otherwise noted.

COMMODITY	Loading or Unloading Except as Noted	WHARFAGE Export/Import, Intercoastal, Coastwise, and Intracoastal	ARTICLE NUMBER
Vehicles, Machinery (Self Propelled) Automobiles, Trucks, Trailers, Utility Vehicles, Military Ordinance Vehicles, Agricultural Machinery, (Tractors, Combines, etc.)			
Driven On/Off Land Carrier Equipment......	51	(I) 429	867A
Lift on or Lift Off Carrier Equipment.....	122	(I) 429	867B
Knock Down, Parts........................	99	(I) 310	867C
Exception 1 (Driven On/Off Carrier Equipment) Minimun Charge: $ 37.80 Maximum Charge: $162.00			
Exception (Wharfage Only) 1: Agricultural Machinery		(I) 220	867D
Exception (Wharfage Only) 2: Used Grading or Road Making Machinery being returned to the United States		(I) 220	867E
Note: Outfits consisting of vehicles modified or equipped with attachments, apparatus, or implements will be rated as above.			
A service charge of $35.00 each applies to vehicles, imported or to be exported, when necessary to drain or add fuel or water or disconnect or connect battery cables.			

Issued: November 24, 1993   Effective: January 1, 1994

FIGURE 7-2 Page from a Port of Houston Tariff Showing Some Loading, Unloading, and Wharfage Charges

Source: Courtesy of Port of Houston Authority.

- Dimensions of load (or cube)
- Number of units (packages/pallets, etc.) to be handled
- Weight
- National Motor Freight Classification number
- Description of material to be moved

Additional services that the shipper might want include sorting and segregating, COD, inside delivery or pickup, residential delivery or pickup, and arrival notification.[3] Other Web sites exist can be used for air freight and international surface container movements. Numerous Web sites also exist for matching shippers of truckload quantities with providers of truckload service. Some appear to take the form of an auction. (Some sites are not open to the public but are used within the trucking industry to better allocate equipment.)

Freight Classification

As presented in Chapter 6, freight classification values relate to the handling characteristics of freight and are one of the factors determining freight charges. Such classifications are taken as given in contract negotiations between shippers and carriers. Rate classification bureaus are made up of carrier representatives and enjoy immunity from antitrust prosecution. Transportation managers appear before the bureaus in attempts to have the classification of specific commodities or movements lowered. Shippers must also combat the carriers' attempts to increase classification numbers. A typical issue was the classification of flashlights:

> Flashlights in boxes, without batteries are designated less-than-truckload class 100 or truckload class 55 with a minimum weight of 20,000 lbs. Flashlights with their normal complement of batteries are considered LTL class 70 or truckload class 45 with a minimum weight of 24,000 lbs.[4]

Because the classification committee felt that flashlights without batteries were too light in the sense that a truck filled with them would cube out (i.e., be full but still have unused weight capacity), they proposed classifications of 150 LTL (less-than-truckload) and 100 TL (truckload), increases of 50 and 82 percent, respectively. The classification committee conducted surveys showing that the density of the flashlights shipped without batteries was 6.9 pounds per cubic foot. Shippers countered with their surveys, showing densities ranging from 10.5 to 11.3 pounds per cubic foot.

Figure 7-3 shows an excerpt from the National Motor Freight Classification Committee's hearing docket concerning a proposal to adopt new classifications for spark plugs. The present classification is described first in the figure, and then the proposal is shown. Note that changing density appears to be an important factor. Figure 7-4 shows an applicant's completed worksheet for submission to the classification committee.

For goods moving in foreign trade, some tariffs today list commodities by the harmonized number covering the commodity in the Harmonized Tariff Schedule of the

[3]www.abfs.com/tools/ltlquotes, June 27, 2002.

[4]*The Journal of Commerce,* February 3, 1994, p. 2B.

PROPOSED

PRESENT CLASSIFICATION: (Show specific NMFC item number and description under which commodity is now being classified.)

ITEM NO.	DESCRIPTION	LTL	TL	MW

PRESENT

ITEM NO.	DESCRIPTION	LTL	TL	MW
177080	Spark Plugs, NOI, in boxes:			
Sub 1	Card mounted, blister packed or skin packed	100	55	24
Sub 2	Other than card mounted, blister packed or skin packed	85	45	30

PROPOSED AMENDMENTS: (Show description, classes and MW exactly as you propose them to be established in the Classification.)

ITEM NO.	DESCRIPTION	LTL	TL	MW

PROPOSED

ITEM NO.	DESCRIPTION	LTL	TL	MW
177080	Spark Plugs, NOI, in boxes:			
Sub 1	Card mounted, blister packed or skin packed	100	55	24
Sub 2	Other than card mounted, blister packed or skin packed :			
>Sub 3	Density less than 30 pounds per cubic foot; or actual value exceeding $6.00 per pound; or where no density or value is shown at time of shipment	85	45	30
>Sub 4	Density in pounds per cubic foot of 30 or greater, and actual value not exceeding $6.00 per pound, see Note, item NEW	70	37.5	36
NEW	NOTE -- Shipper must certify on shipping orders and bills of lading at time of shipment that density is 30 pounds or greater per cubic foot and that the actual value per pound does not exceed $6.00.			

JUSTIFICATION: Due to the density, value per pound and ease of handling of the involved commodities, the proposed changes are warranted.

_____

_____

_____

If you have any questions regarding the proper execution of these forms or require technical assistance please contact our staff at (703) 838-1869.

FIGURE 7-3 Motor Carrier Classification Docket Proposal for Changing the Classification of Spark Plugs

Source: Permission to reproduce this material has been granted by the National Motor Freight Traffic Association, Inc.

United States (or "TSUSA"). This is the number shown on export declarations and used by shippers and is a number that most shippers know or know how to get. Typically, the first four to six digits of the nine digit harmonized number is used.

Rate and Service Negotiations

Selecting the mode and then the specific carrier within that mode are other fundamental activities of the transportation department. However, the decision regarding which transport mode or modes to use may not be exclusively determined by the transportation manager. In many corporations the decision to use more expensive forms of transport (such as air freight) is made by senior management. Indeed, initial decisions to

TRANSPORTATION CHARACTERISTICS

I. **DENSITY:** (Please base your calculations on the exterior dimensions and the shipping weight of the commodity as packaged for shipment.)

Model	Description of Package	Length	Width	Height	Weight	Density*
Spark	packaged individually,	38"	38"	42"	1280 #	36.5
plugs	then packaged into cartons					
(boxed)	of 10, then packaged into					
	cartons of 100. Shipped					
	in master cartons on skids.					

*To determine the density (pounds per cubic foot), multiply the three dimensions of the article as packed for shipment. If the result is in cubic inches, divide by 1728 to convert to cubic feet. Then divide the weight by the cubic feet. To determine the cubic feet of space occupied by a drum, pail, or other cylindrical container, square the greatest diameter and multiply that result by the height or length. If the package is of irregular shape, use the greatest dimensions, including all projections.

II. **LIABILITY**

1) Claim value per package (Please match the models with those reported under **DENSITY**)

Model	Description of Package	Weight	Dollar Amount	Value Per Pound
Spark	packaged individually,	1280 #	$7200	$5.63
plugs	then packaged into cartons			
(boxed)	of 10, then packaged into			
	cartons of 100. Shipped			
	in master cartons on skids.			

2) Does the commodity require temperature control?   NO

3) Is the commodity subject to U.S. Department of Transportation Regulations governing hazardous materials?
   Yes ___ No XX If yes, what HMT commodity description and label are required?

   _____

4) Does commodity have protruding edges?   NO

5) Is commodity liquid NO dry NO paste NO

FIGURE 7-4 Worksheet for Motor Carrier Classification Docket Proposal for Changing the Classification of Spark Plugs *(Continued)*

Source: Permission to reproduce this material has been granted by the National Motor Freight Traffic Association, Inc.

II. **LIABILITY - continued**

  6) Claims Experience (Motor Common Carrier Shipments):

    a) Number of claims (one year period) __NONE_____

    b) Dollar amount of claims _____ Amount Paid _____

    c) Total number of shipments made (one year period) _____

    d) Total amount of freight paid (one year period) _____

    e) Claims filed by shipper _____ receiver (consignee) _____

    f) If the information is available, please indicate the percentage of claims for:

      loss _____ damage _____

III. **HANDLING:**

  1) Is freight palletized? Yes __XX__ No ____ If yes, are pallets unitized? Yes __XX__ No ___

  2) Does the commodity require more than one person to load or unload? Yes ____ No __XX__

  3) Does the product as packaged for shipment require the use of mechanical handling equipment?

    Yes __XX__ No _____ If yes, what type? pallet jack or forklift

  4) Does the commodity require special handling in loading or unloading? Yes ____ No __XX__

    If yes, please explain what care and attention is necessary.

    _____

  5) Are there other instructions or precautionary markings on the shipping packages or shipping documents?

    Yes ____ No __XX__ If yes, please state what they are:

    _____

IV. **STOWABILITY**

  1) Form of shipment: SU __XX__ KD ____ KD Flat ____ Folded ____ Folded Flat ____

    Nested _____ Nested Solid _____ (See Definitions Below)

  2) Is commodity capable of being tiered for shipment? Yes __XX__ No ___

    If yes, how high? ____two_____

  3) If the shipping package is other than square, rectangular or cylindrical, please attach a diagram or photo

  4) Does commodity have any projections or extensions which are not enclosed by the package?

    NO

    _____

  5) If commodity is wheeled, does the article rest on its wheels during shipment? Yes ___ No __XX__

DEFINITIONS OF SHIPPING FORMS

These definitions are derived from Item (Rule) 110, Sections 12 and 13, of the National Motor Freight Classification and are the applicable ones for classification purposes:

"**Set Up (SU)**" means the article is in its assembled condition or is disassembled, folded or telescoped but not meeting the definitions of "Knocked Down," "Knocked Down Flat," "Folded " or "Folded Flat."

"**Knocked Down (KD)**" means that the article is taken apart, folded or telescoped in such a manner as to reduce its bulk at least 33 1/3 percent from its normal shipping cubage when set up or assembled.

"**Knocked Down Flat (KD Flat)**" means that the article is taken apart, folded or telescoped in such a manner as to reduce its bulk at least 66 2/3 percent from its normal shipping cubage when set up or assembled.

"**Folded**" means that the article is folded in such a manner as to reduce its bulk at least 33 1/3 percent from its normal shipping cubage when not folded.

"**Folded Flat**" means that the article is folded in such a manner as to reduce its bulk at least 66 2/3 percent from its normal shipping cubage when not folded.

"**Nested**" means that three or more different sizes of the article are placed each smaller within the next larger or that three or more of the same article are placed one within the other so that each upper article does not project above the next lower article by more than one-third of its height.

"**Nested Solid**" means that three or more of the same article are placed one within or upon the other so that the outer side surfaces of the one above are in contact with the inner surfaces of the one below and so that each upper article does not project above the next lower article by more than 1/4 inch.

FIGURE 7-4 (Continued)

locate facilities may have been based on modal choice. The traditional site for a warehouse was often the point where it was most cost-effective to have shipments go in by rail and out by truck.

When contract carrier **rate and service negotiations** are being considered, both rates and service are brought to the table for negotiation. Rail contracts were of questionable legality until 1980, when they were authorized by the Staggers Rail Act.

Following are summaries of some of the service elements of agreements negotiated between two railroads and a firm in the grocery business:

- In an agreement with a railroad involving the carriage of grocery products from Northlake, Illinois, to eight consignees in the St. Louis area, the shipper agreed to pay the railroad an additional amount (ranging from $117 to $159 per car) when the car was delivered on a precise, previously scheduled, day.
- In an agreement with another railroad for shipments of grocery products moving in trailers aboard flatcars from Houston to Chicago, the shipper agreed to ship a minimum of six million pounds per year. The shipper further agreed to pay an additional $75 per trailer when 90 percent or more of the trailers completed the rail movement within 96 hours. The railroad agreed to furnish sufficient trailers to meet the six million pounds per year volume requirement.

These contract provisions illustrate the various aspects of service that are important to the shipper and that may be subject to negotiation. They also indicate that shippers are willing to pay for improved quality of railroad service. Once a contract is entered into, the burden of meeting the shipper's obligations and monitoring the carrier's performance rests on the shipper's transportation manager.

The Nelson–Wood survey asked transportation managers, "Do you impose service standards on carriers who serve you?" Nearly all answered "yes." A following question asked, "If 'yes,' how are they monitored and enforced?" Many respondents indicated that some form of electronic data interchange (EDI) was used.

> "Monthly reports."
> "Quarterly with annual monetary penalties."
> "Exception reports."
> "Carrier self-reports."
> "Deductions taken for late arrival or no arrival, credit given if delays are at our plant."
> "Customer complaints."
> "Satellite tracking."
> "We expect 98 percent on-time deliveries; if not, carrier put on 2-to 6-week probationary period."

Just-in-time (JIT) practices have both reduced transit times and improved the performance of "on-time" deliveries. The transportation manager once waited for specific railroad cars to arrive within a range of 2 or 3 days. Today's motor carrier is much more disciplined. Respondents in the Nelson–Wood survey reported the average opening of their delivery "windows" to have a median value of only 4 hours. The average window was nearly 11 hours, but this was heavily influenced by one respondent in the forest products industry with a 5-day window who commented, "We require railroads to deliver on a certain day plus or minus 24 hours. They never do."

Since carrier deregulation, many articles and checklists have been prepared to help both sides in the shipper–carrier negotiation process. One such list included the following items of importance:

- Contract duration
- Contract termination
- Renegotiation and reopening of contract

- Transportation service level
- Carrier insurance
- Lead times
- Waiver of terms
- Detention time
- Articles and commodities covered
- How loss and damage claims are handled
- Schedule of rates and charges
- Estimated transportation volume
- Billing procedures
- Carrier equipment and drivers
- Carrier notification requirements
- Confidential contract
- Arbitration
- Audit rights
- Pallet loading
- Proof of delivery
- Adjustments to rates
- Basis for charges

A survey of large shippers, conducted by the Logistics Institute at Georgia Tech found that the top criteria for selecting carriers were as follows, in descending order:

- On-time delivery
- Cost
- Safety
- Tracking/communications
- Reliability
- Reputation
- Claims
- Service range
- Carrier's financial stability
- Quality of operating personnel
- Backhauling capability
- Equipment availability[5]

Following is an example of a food processor contracting for air freight. The firm spent huge sums on surface transportation for its products. Its use of air freight, often for carrying promotional products, was difficult to tally. After some investigation, the firm determined that it was spending between $2 million and $4 million per year on air freight. It then decided to contract with two air carriers—one for correspondence, another for freight—to handle this entire business. After consultation with the firm's regional offices, the following specifications for air freight carriers were drawn up:

1. Service available 24 hours per day, 365 days per year
2. Carrier service and service representatives at cities where the firm had offices

---

[5]*Inbound Logistics,* December 2001, p. 10.

3. Deferred service option (i.e., lower rates for less urgent shipments—second-, third-, and fourth-morning delivery)
4. Door-to-door rates
5. Nondimensional rates (some of the firm's advertising was oversized)
6. Loss and damage liability of $9.07 per pound
7. Temperature-controlled cargo space
8. Tracing services
9. Proof-of-delivery service
10. Computer-reporting process
11. EDI capability
12. End-of-month reports concerning the firm's traffic patterns.

The requirements were mailed out along with a volume history of the firm's air shipments, a questionnaire intended to determine the carrier's strength and weakness, and a request for rate proposals. After receiving responses, the firm invited seven carriers to make presentations, and two—an air-express company and a forwarder—were selected. The final issues were service first and price second.

As previously noted, one important change in logistics thinking has been to encourage long-term relationships with suppliers and customers. Contracting with carriers is one way of doing this, although the contracts may be for more than the carriage of products. An example was the 5-year agreement between a railroad and the Ford Motor Company for an auto distribution facility at Meridian, Mississippi. The railroad assumed the responsibility of distributing Ford, Lincoln, and Mercury products from assembly plants directly to dealers in Mississippi, Florida, Alabama, and Louisiana. The railroad built the facility, which sits on a 17-acre site. The railroad also contracted with an auto-haulaway trucking firm to handle movements from Meridian to the dealers; however, Ford deals only with the railroad. Two computer programs are used in the operation. One monitors damage to new autos and links it to the haulaway driver. The other program gives the haulaway carrier shipment information early so the truck movements to dealers can be planned. The railroad also has a contractor who unloads the railcars and prestages the autos in position for each truck trailer. The unloading contractor has a Ford-originated printout before the vehicles arrive at Meridian. He knows immediately where to place the vehicle upon arrival.

Under deregulation, carriers lost much of their immunity from antitrust laws. As a result, negotiators should take some *antitrust considerations* into account before negotiations begin.

Another agreement with carriers that the transportation department also must negotiate and administer is an *average weight agreement*. This involves agreements as to weights of various items shipped repetitively, so that each individual shipment does not have to be weighed.

Rate Regulatory Bodies

In a few instances, transportation rates are still subject to the approval of a regulatory body. In that situation, the transportation manager follows the quasi-judicial hearings and participates to represent his or her company's interests. For example, in instances in which rail users are dependent on a single railroad for service, they are referred to as "captive shippers" and are still subject to protection by the Surface Transportation Board, which has replaced the ICC. In a case settled in 1994, the ICC adopted the "stand-alone cost constraint" in which the ICC estimated the cost of an efficiently designed and operated hypothetical stand-alone railroad with which to compare the rates charged to the captive coal customer. (As mergers reduce the number of railroads, more and more shippers will find themselves in the *captive* category.)

In the situations just described, the issues may seem esoteric, but that was often the nature of rate regulation. The point to realize here is that in these situations the transportation manager is expected to proceed in a lawyer-like manner. In the Nelson–Wood survey, only nine respondents indicated that they had participated in hearings since January 1, 1995 (when intrastate motor carriers were deregulated). Bodies they appeared before included the U.S. Department of Commerce Foreign Trade Zone Board, a Department of Transportation (DOT) committee working on hazardous material (hazmat) regulations, and a House of Representatives subcommittee hearing.

Private Transportation

In the field of domestic logistics, the term **private transportation** is used when firms own and operate their own trucks, railcars, barges, ships, and airplanes. Weyerhauser Corporation has a subsidiary that runs seven ships. These ships carry mainly Weyerhauser cargo but also carry other cargo during slow periods.

Transportation managers who are frustrated with inconsistent service on some shipments are sometimes forced into private trucking. Most firms also run a few small trucks and vans for use around plants or for trips to and from the post office and airport (usually the transportation manager's responsibility).

In 2002, Wal-Mart operated the largest private truck fleet in the United States, consisting of 7,767 tractors and 26,117 trailers. Seventeen other firms operated fleets consisting of at least 1,000 tractors, including Tyson Foods, Interstate Bakeries, Georgia-Pacific, Albertson's, Frito-Lay, Kroger, Winn-Dixie, Safeway, Halliburton, International Paper, and ExxonMobil.[6] Most fleets had many more trailers than tractors because trailers were dropped off and left to be loaded or unloaded.

The growth of private trucking is related to a number of factors. The most important single factor is the improved level of customer service that private trucking makes feasible. Another advantage of private trucking is the advertising of products by way of the billboards that appear on the trucks. This factor can be especially important when the vehicles are attractively designed and have courteous drivers, creating a positive impression on the thousands of potential customers who see the vehicles each day. When the transportation manager uses both private carriage and contract carriage, he or she has a good working knowledge of the costs of running trucks and is in a better position to evaluate the merits of carrier rate proposals. Petroleum companies like to have deliveries to filling stations made in tank trucks carrying their brand name, rather than having the station's tanks filled from an unmarked truck.

---

[6]*Transport Topics,* July 22, 2002, pp. 22–23.

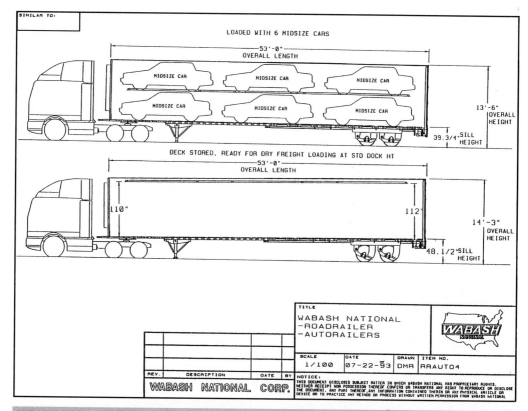

FIGURE 7-5 RoadRailer Trailer Designed to Carry Autos in One Direction and General Freight Return. Note Rail Wheels on Rear; Rig Can Operate On Highway or On Rails

Source: Courtesy of RoadRailer Division, Wabash National Corp.

For many companies, private trucking also offers the advantage of being less expensive than motor common carriers. This is typically the case when the private trucking operation is able to achieve full loads in both directions. Figure 7-5 shows a trailer designed to carry new autos in one direction and general freight in the other. Many private fleet managers use the services of a broker to ensure a backhaul load of other products.

Also available to private fleet managers is the option of establishing an in-house brokerage service. The private fleet manager can now, acting as a broker, solicit additional business for the firm's for-hire trucking service. The firm can also generate business for other for-hire carriers and be paid by them, usually between 5 percent and 10 percent of the transportation charges.

With the development of third-party logistics, private fleets are being formed in conjunction with warehousing and distribution services. A Missouri trucking firm and a Texas warehousing and logistics company formed Quality Express of Arlington, Texas, to distribute Whirlpool appliances. The trucks carry the Whirlpool logo and the new firm's drivers "not only take the goods to the retailer [but also] call ahead. The trucking company put cellular phones in the cabs and ramps or liftgates on the vehicle."[7]

The decision to enter into a private trucking operation should be carefully researched and analyzed well in advance. One factor commonly ignored in the cost calculations of private trucking is the requirement that the operation be managed by a professional. All too often, transportation managers assume that, along with their many other responsibilities, they will also supervise the private trucking operation. Later, when it is discovered that all but the smallest fleets each require a full-time manager (to supervise vehicle scheduling, maintenance, labor relations, and so on), the firm is faced with a large, unanticipated expense.

Private fleets are also subject to safety regulations. In the 1990s, the federal DOT's Office of Motor Carrier Safety (OMC) closed down the fleet operated by the transportation division of a New Jersey food distributor for flagrant safety violations. According to the OMC, the carrier failed to conduct annual vehicle inspections, test its drivers for drugs, keep hours-of-service records and daily vehicle inspection reports, and maintain minimum insurance.

Documentation

The transportation department is responsible for completing all of the documents needed to transport the firm's products. Today, many carriers provide software that enables the shipper to use computers to generate all of the commonly used documents. Shippers also have their own order processing software, which is capable of generating transportation documents.

The most important single transportation document is the bill of lading which is the basic operating document in the industry. The **bill of lading** functions as a delivery receipt when products are tendered to carriers. On receipt of the freight, the carrier signs the bill of lading and gives the original to the shipper. The signed original of the bill of lading is the shipper's legal proof that the carrier received the freight.

The bill of lading is a binding contract, specifying the duties and obligations of both carrier and shipper. The bill of lading contract for surface carriers is basically standardized by law and greatly simplifies the transportation manager's job because it specifies exactly the duties of the shipper and carrier.

There are two types of bills of lading: the straight bill of lading and the order bill of lading. On a *straight bill of lading,* which is printed on white paper, the name of the consignee is stated in the appropriate place and the carrier is under a strict legal obligation to deliver the freight to the named consignee and to no one else. Ownership of the goods is neither stated nor implied. On the *order bill of lading,* which is printed on yellow paper, the name of the consignee is not specified. For example, assume that a lumber company in Seattle has loaded a boxcar of plywood that it has not yet sold. It would use an order bill and tender the shipment to the Burlington Northern Railroad, which would start the car moving toward Chicago. Once a buyer for the plywood is found, the shipper would send the original copy of the order bill by mail to a bank near

---

[7] *Transport Topics,* February 10, 1992, p. 11.

the buyer and would also tell the buyer which bank had possession of the order bill. The buyer would go to the bank and pay for the plywood, and the bank would give the original copy to the buyer. The buyer would take it to the railroad, and the railroad would deliver the carload of plywood. (Order bills are used in one other situation—that involving slow payers—because they guarantee that the customer must pay for the products prior to receipt.)

An additional classification of bills is the specific form: long, short, and preprinted. The *long-form bill of lading,* which may be either an order or straight bill, contains the standard information on the face of the bill (see Figure 7-6), and on the reverse side it contains the entire contract between carrier and shipper. The reverse side is printed in extremely small print. Because of the difficulty of reading the long-form contract and the printing costs of including the contract on all bills, in 1949 the railroads and motor carriers adopted the short-form bill of lading. The short form has the following statement on its face: "Every service to be performed hereunder shall be subject to all the terms and conditions of the Uniform Domestic Straight Bill of Lading."

Another kind of bill of lading—which may be long, short, order, or straight—is preprinted. In theory, the bill of lading is prepared and issued by the carrier. In fact, however, most shippers buy their bills and then have them preprinted with a list of the products they regularly ship. Figure 7-7 illustrates a *preprinted short-form bill of lading.* Shippers go to the expense of buying and printing their own bills because, in practice, they frequently prepare them prior to calling the carrier. The preparation is part of their computerized order management procedures. The preprinted bill can be prepared more rapidly and with less chance of error. The shipper can insert the correct classification rather than letting the carrier determine it.

A few shippers are adopting their own bills of lading, which carriers may be reluctant to accept because the carriers may be subject to new liabilities specified in the documents. Carriers are advised to supply drivers with stickers to place on the bills of lading indicating that their signature means only that they have picked up the freight.

Another basic document that the transportation manager must be familiar with is the *freight bill,* an invoice, submitted by the carrier, requesting to be paid. Often, the transportation manager must approve each freight bill before it is paid. An issue involving freight bills that received considerable attention in the 1990s was referred to as *off-bill discounting.* In this situation, the carrier would send the freight bill to the shipper, who would add the charges on the bill to the costs of goods on the invoice sent to the buyer. Unknown to the buyer of the goods, the shipper would receive a rebate for a portion of the transportation charges shown on the freight bill.

Freight Payment and Audit Services

Carriers must be paid within a specific numbers of working days. Shipper–carrier contracts also specify how quickly bills must be paid. In an attempt to meet these time limits conveniently, many transportation managers participate in bill-paying services. These services were originally known as *bank payment plans,* because banks were the first to offer the service. Now, a variety of other firms, in addition to banks, offer these automated *freight bill-paying services.* Once the transportation manager initiates the

UNIFORM FREIGHT CLASSIFICATION 7

(Uniform Domestic Straight Bill of Lading, adopted by Carriers in Official and Western Classification
territories, March 15, 1922, as amended August 1, 1930, and June 15, 1941.)

UNIFORM STRAIGHT BILL OF LADING

Original—Not Negotiable

(To be Printed on "White" Paper)

Shipper's No.........
Agent's No...........

Company

RECEIVED, subject to the classifications and tariffs in effect on the date of the issue of this Bill of Lading,

at..., 19...

from..

the property described below, in apparent good order, except as noted (contents and condition of contents of packages unknown), marked, consigned, and destined as
indicated below, which said company (the word company being understood throughout this contract as meaning any person or corporation in possession of the property
under the contract) agrees to carry to its usual place of delivery at said destination, if on its own road or its own water line, otherwise to deliver to another carrier on
the route to said destination. It is mutually agreed, as to each carrier of all or any of said property over all or any portion of said route to destination, and as to each
party at any time interested in all or any of said property, that every service to be performed hereunder shall be subject to all the conditions not prohibited by law,
whether printed or written, herein contained, including the conditions on back hereof, which are hereby agreed to by the shipper and accepted for himself and his
assigns.

(Mail or street address of consignee—For purposes of notification only.)

Consigned to..

Destination...State of.......................County of.................

Route...

Delivering Carrier..Car Initial....................Car No.................

No. Pack-ages	Description of Articles, Special Marks, and Exceptions	*Weight (Subject to Correction)	Class or Rate	Check Column	Subject to Section 7 of conditions, if this ship-ment is to be delivered to the consignee without recourse on the consign-or, the consignor shall sign the following state-ment: The carrier shall not make delivery of this shipment without pay-ment of freight and all other lawful charges.
....					
....					
....					(Signature of consignor.)
....					
....					If charges are to be pre-paid, write or stamp here, "To be Prepaid."
....					
....					....
....					Received $............ to apply in prepayment of the charges on the property described hereon.
....					
....					Agent or Cashier.
....					Per........................ (The signature here acknowl-edges only the amount prepaid.)

*If the shipment moves between two ports by a carrier by water, the law requires that the bill of lading shall state whether it is
"carrier's or shipper's weight."

Note.—Where the rate is dependent on value, shippers are required to state specifically in
writing the agreed or declared value of the property.
The agreed or declared value of the property is hereby specifically stated by the shipper to be not
exceeding

....per.

Charges advanced:

$....................

....Shipper.   ....Agent.

Per...............................   Per...............................

Permanent postoffice address of shipper...

FIGURE 7-6 A Long-Form Bill of Lading

program with the payment service, the carriers submit their freight bills directly to the service. The payment service treats the freight bills as checks drawn on the shipper's freight account and then pays the carriers. The Department of Defense (DOD) uses a private bank's payment services to pay out over one billion dollars annually for moving military cargos. Fund transfers to carriers are made electronically. In 2001, DOD pay-

FIGURE 7-7 A Preprinted Short-Form Bill of Lading

ments went to 430 trucking firms, 25 barge operators, 20 pipelines, 20 railroads, and 15 ocean carriers.[8]

An effort also should be made to correlate invoices for goods with freight bills for carrying the goods.

The payment service provides summaries of traffic activity that are useful to shippers when planning future freight consolidation. Computerized programs are also used to detect duplicate billings. Payment services also offer bill-auditing service; that is, they ensure that the proper rate was charged. Some prepayment services have the tariffs their clients use loaded into their computer databases and pre-audit bills prior to paying them it.

---

[8]*American Shipper,* June 2002, p. 4.

ATLAS TRAFFIC CONSULTANTS CORP.
FREIGHT AUDITING SERVICE
18-42 COLLEGE POINT BLVD., FLUSHING, N. Y. 11356 · (212) 461-0555

CARRIER CODE	CARRIER'S O/C NO.	CLAIM DATE	ATLAS CLAIM NUMBER
XYZR		1/07/93	0454799W

CLIENT NAME NO. 3096200 — XYZ CHEMICAL CO. *

SWL

TARIFF AUTHORITY
TARIFF NO. 3355F ITEM 4455H
CLASS'N. ITEM SUB
CLASS

CARRIER:
ABC RAILROAD CO.
1 PACIFIC PLAZA
LOS ANGELES, CA 94110
OVERCHARGE CLAIM DEPARTMENT

SUP 358-CINN INTERMEDIATE TO ANDERSON
IND - ROUTE 130260 NO 138170 AS
AUTHORIZED IN NOTE 2

ENCLOSURES:
1 ☐ FREIGHT BILL
☐ B/L
☐ SUPPORTING STATEMENT

F.B. NO.	DATE	ORIGIN / DESTINATION / DESCRIPTION AS SHOWN BY YOUR BILL	AS CHARGED WEIGHT	AS CHARGED RATE	AS CHARGED CHARGES	AS SUGGESTED WEIGHT	AS SUGGESTED RATE	AS SUGGESTED CHARGES
868569	5/16/92	ELDON TX CINN OH T/C ISOCYANATE	190000	486	9,234.00	165150	312	5,152.68
			TOTALS *	* *	9234.00			5152.68

OUR AUDIT INDICATES ERROR IN CHARGES AS STATED. KINDLY ARRANGE FOR PROMPT SETTLEMENT PAYABLE TO OUR CLIENT NAMED ABOVE, MAILING VOUCHER AND CORRESPONDENCE TO **ATLAS TRAFFIC CONSULTANTS CORP.**

*DUE OUR CLIENT $ 4081.3

ATLAS TRAFFIC CONSULTANTS CORP. HEREBY AGREES TO PROTECT THE CARRIER WITH WHOM THIS CLAIM IS FILED BY REASON OF SETTLEMENT WITHOUT SURRENDER OF THE ORIGINAL PAID FREIGHT BILL AND WE UNEQUIVOCALLY GUARANTEE REIMBURSEMENT.

J B Silverman
President

* PLEASE AMEND IF IN ERROR ADD 6% INTEREST.

CARRIER COPY

FIGURE 7-8 An Overcharge Claim Form

Source: Courtesy of Atlas Traffic Consultants Corporation, Flushing, NY.

Some shippers also audit their own freight bills. If this work is conducted by employees of the company, it is known as an *internal audit.* The *external audit* is performed by an independent third party; some freight-bill auditors also offer freight payment services. Both types of audit are designed to detect current errors that result in overcharges and to correct these errors in the future. Figure 7-8 is an example of a form letter used by a freight-bill auditor to request that a common carrier reimburse the auditor (on behalf of the auditor's client) for the carrier's overcharges.

A 1994 trade journal article indicated that external audit companies were finding that their clients were being overcharged an average of between 4 and 5 percent.[9] The usual arrangement is to split 50–50 the amount recovered between the audit service and its client. Since freight bill auditing is seldom an area where large firms care to maintain core competence, freight bill auditing and payment functions are frequently farmed out. A survey in 2001 indicated that 52 percent of large U.S. manufacturers

[9]*Transportation and Distribution,* March 1994, p. 53.

relied on outside freight payment services.[10] In mid-2002, several freight payment services declared bankruptcy, with money owed to both clients and carriers. This was unfortunate, but it may encourage firms using third-party logistics providers to supervise them more closely.

Routing

The top sections of Figures 7-6 and 7-7 show a line entitled "route." Shippers have the right to select the carriers along the route to their shipment's destination. For domestic shipments today, this is almost a non-issue because LTL motor carriers have nationwide authority and rail mergers have resulted in many geographic areas being served by a single railroad only.

The Nelson–Wood survey asked transportation managers, "Do you generally 'route' shipments (i.e., specify the route) or do you just tender the shipments to a carrier?" The answers were about evenly split, and some were accompanied by comments of interest.

"Route rail, tender truck shipments to a single carrier."
"Route rail and intermodal, tender to truck."
"We use a software package that rates and routes and recommends carrier."
"Route for consolidation purposes or to find backhaul loads for carriers."
"Routes needed for hazmats."
"Route international, domestic tendered to packaged freight carrier."
"We set up carriers on specific routes with backup availability. For LTL we have designated a single carrier nationwide and penalize suppliers who use other carriers."
"Route via zip codes and weight break parameters."

With respect to hazardous material movements, local restrictions on highway movements and warehouse storage of certain hazardous materials often place severe limitations on routes the hazardous goods can move. Even some cargoes are incompatible or at least disliked by carriers (see Figure 7-9). Urban traffic congestion is costly to trucks; in addition, truck movements and parking are sometimes restricted to permit more auto traffic to be handled.

Computers are widely used for routing today. Figure 7-10 shows some computer-generated truck routes for the St. Louis area.

Firms sometimes issue routing guides as part of their purchase orders and expect vendors to follow instructions. If they do not, the vendors become liable for penalties. General Dynamics Corporation has its inbound traffic routing guide on a Web site. Shipments up to 70 pounds are to go by UPS ground. Shipments between 70 and 10,000 pounds are to go on truck lines listed as "preferred carriers" on an attached list. For shipments over 10,000 pounds, the vendor is instructed to contact the traffic administrator at General Dynamics. Similar rules apply to shipments by air, although the General Dynamics purchase order must specify use of air.[11]

---

[10]*Modern Materials Handling,* December 2001, p. 15.

[11]www.nasco.com/suppliers/tr route.html, July 10, 2002.

"IT'S CARRYING A LOAD OF FERTILIZER."

FIGURE 7-9 Undesirable Cargo

Source: Reproduced by permission of *Jet Cargo News*.

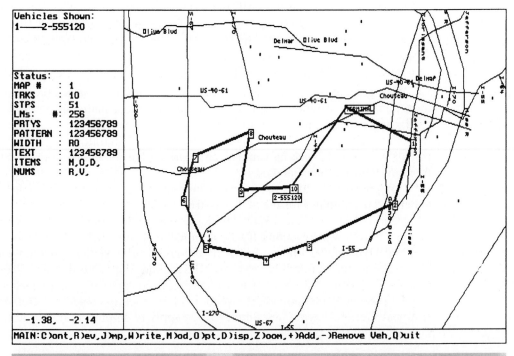

FIGURE 7-10 Computer-Generated Route Map for Trucks, St.Louis

The transportation manager must also plan for contingencies and have alternative routes and, sometimes, carriers as occurred with the UPS strike in 1997. In the early 1990s, when water levels in the Mississippi River system were too low, grain shippers had to switch from barge to rail for many of their downbound shipments. In 1993, the Mississippi was too high, and grain shippers sent exports out on the Great Lakes–St. Lawrence River route. As a long-term strategy, the transportation manager sometimes gives a small amount of regular business to different modes or carriers for insurance purposes, such as would be needed in the situations just mentioned.

One allowable exception to the common carrier's service obligation is an embargo. This usually happens when excessive congestion is found at a destination or when delivery is impeded because of storm-related damage to the carrier's right-of-way or terminals. In late September 2002, when West Coast ports were closed because of a labor dispute, inland railroads placed an embargo on export shipments headed to West Coast ports.

Diversion and Reconsignment

Diversion occurs when the shipper notifies the carrier, prior to the shipment's arrival in the destination city, of a change in destination. **Reconsignment** is similar, but it occurs after the shipment has arrived in the destination city. These services are commonly used in conjunction with order bills of lading. They are also used by shippers of perishables that start their loads in the direction of the market and sell them while they are en route. The tariff of Matson Navigation covering westbound container freight from the mainland to Hawaii devoted an entire page to "Reconsignment, Diversion, or Redelivery." Matson charged $7.85 for amending the bill of lading, and then its charges varied according to (1) whether the destination port in Hawaii was changed, (2) whether it was necessary to rehandle the container, and (3) whether the shipment had already left the port.[12]

Tracing and Expediting

Tracing is the attempt to locate lost or late shipments. When the transportation department determines that a shipment has not arrived at its destination on time, it may contact the carrier to whom it tendered the shipment and ask the carrier to trace the shipment. This is a no-cost service offered by most carriers. Tracing should be requested only when a shipment is unreasonably late. Many airlines and large trucking companies, as well as almost all railroads, have computer systems that monitor the progress of freight movements throughout their systems. This enables almost instantaneous tracing by the carriers. As carriers become more computerized, they can better keep track of equipment and shipments. Many computer programs allow shippers to access portions of their systems. Drivers for some parcel delivery companies carry the equipment that enables them to record and report the instant each parcel is delivered.

---

[12]*Westbound Container Tariff No. 14F, effective January 14, 1994* (San Francisco: Matson Navigation Company, 1994), p. 46.

Expediting is another no-cost service of some carriers. It involves notifying the carrier as far in advance as possible of the need to expedite or rapidly move a shipment through the carrier's system. The carrier makes every effort to ensure that the shipment is delivered to its destination with maximum speed. The carrier must have sufficient lead time to alert its employees regarding the shipment to be expedited. For the railroads, this involves alerting the yardmaster at each relevant classification yard so that the expedited car can be singled out when it arrives and immediately switched to the proper outbound train. Motor carriers generally notify the operations manager of each freight terminal that the product will be flowing through; in this way, the operations manager can ensure that the product will be quickly placed on the next outbound vehicle. (A specific responsibility sometimes assigned to a shift supervisor in a motor carrier terminal is to see that each piece of expedited freight is removed from the inbound truck and placed on the next outgoing truck.)

A general observation today would be that both tracing and expediting are less likely to be used. This is because shippers can use carriers who can pinpoint the location of shipments whenever necessary, and carriers do a much better job of performing on-time deliveries.

Loss and Damage

Cargo **loss and damage** has been the bane of the transportation industry since day one. Transportation manager respondents in the Nelson–Wood survey reported that loss and damage involved an average of 1.1 percent of all shipments; the value of this loss and damage equaled an average of 2.7 percent of the shipments' value.

Filing claims against carriers is a routine matter. Many carriers post instruction on their Web sites for claims filing. One site carried these instructions: "Claims must be in writing; the claim must be supported by the original freight bill, the original bill of lading, and the original invoice for the goods being shipped; filing of claims should take place as soon as possible after the occurrence, and must be filed within nine months of the delivery date to meet the bill of lading contract requirements."[13]

If a carrier and shipper are not able to resolve a dispute over a loss and damage claim, the dispute is handled by the court system. There are time limitations within which the claim must be filed. Note that there are administrative costs in handling freight claims that are absorbed by the shipper or consignee.

> One of the most difficult and challenging aspects of claim work is the determination of the exact dollar amount of the damage. The law states that the common carrier is responsible for the full actual loss sustained by the shipper or consignee. How can this figure be determined? A common rule of thumb is the following: The basic thought underlying the federal statutes which define the liability and prescribe the measure of damages in cases of this kind is that the owner shall be made whole by receiving the proper money equivalent for what has actually [been] lost; or, in other words to restore [the owner] to the position he would have occupied, had the carrier performed its contract.[14]

---

[13]www.bullocks-express.com/claims.htm, August 13. 2002.
[14]*Atlantic Coast Line Ry. Co.* v. *Roe*, 118 So. 155.

A key factor in determining the value of the full actual loss is the word *earned.* Assume that a retailer owned the products shipped via a common carrier and that they were damaged beyond repair. The question arises, "Should the retailer recover the wholesale price or the retail price?" If the products destroyed were going into a general inventory replacement stock, the retailer would recover the wholesale price plus freight costs (if they had been paid) because the retail price has not been earned. Assume, instead, that a product is ordered especially for a customer. When the product arrives, it is damaged and the retailer's customer states that he or she will wait no longer and cancels the order. In this situation, the retailer is entitled to the retail price because the profit would have been earned if the carrier had properly performed its service.

Another difficult area for shippers and carriers alike involves *concealed loss or damage.* If a shipment arrives in damaged condition and the damage is detected before the consignee accepts the goods, the issue is not whether the carrier is liable but the dollar amount of the claim that the carrier must pay. However, concealed loss and damage cases are more difficult to handle because the exterior package does not appear to be damaged or tampered with. At a later date, the consignee opens the package and finds that the product is damaged or missing. As can be appreciated, carriers are reluctant to pay concealed loss and damage claims for two reasons. If the package came through the shipment with no exterior damage, then there is a strong possibility that the product was improperly protected on the inside. If this is the case, the carrier is exempted from liability because improper packaging is the fault of the shipper. Second, the possibility exists that the consignee's employees broke or stole the products.

Since deregulation, the volume of claims activity has dropped because, during the negotiation process, the shipper may agree to hold the carrier less liable for claims in return for lower transportation charges. In addition, the transportation deregulation acts have reduced carrier liability. The Staggers Act permits railroads to establish released value rates (wherein the shipper agrees that a commodity is worth no more than so many dollars per hundred pounds in case a claim is filed, in return for a lower rate).

Related to this is the ability of railroads to have deductibles in damage claims (wherein the shipper assumes responsibility for the first so many dollars of a claim in return for a lower rate). Last, the "Staggers Act expressly permits rail carriers to negotiate contracts that specify all terms of the shipping transportation, including those related to liability."[15] The 1980 Motor Carrier Act made changes in motor carrier liability requirements; however, by no means were the requirements eliminated.

The Nelson–Wood survey asked transportation managers: "How do you process freight loss and damage claims?" Some answers follow:

"Does not pay to file since LTL carriers have low liability limits."
"Pay customer and file with carrier."
"Filed by EDI based on product's retail value."
"A third-party logistics provider handles our claims."

---

[15]Paul Stephen Dempsey and William Thoms, *Law and Economic Regulation in Transportation* (New York: Quorum Books, 1986), p. 263.

"As provided in contract with carrier."

"Notify carrier, await their inspection, determine salvage and disposition, file claim."

"By contract, insurance deductible shared with carrier."

"We carry blanket cargo and warehousing insurance. We file against insurance broker, who files against carrier."

"Claims packages are put together by the tracing group who give customer credit. The claim is forwarded to the traffic group who enters the claim into a software package which forwards it to the carrier."

Transportation managers and carriers also work together to reduce freight claims, because any reduction benefits them both. Figure 7-11 shows a map produced by CSX Transportation through use of earth satellites. The CSX railcar carried a solar-powered radio that was activated when the rail ride became unusually rough so that its location could be recorded. At the bottom, we can see that the events occurred at different times during the trip and that the shock measurement is shown along three dimensions.

Several shipper and carrier organizations formed the Transportation Arbitration Board (TAB). Shippers and carriers may use this as a means of settling claim disputes. When a claimant and shipper (or consignee) agree to submit their case to TAB, they both pay a fee. The claimant prepares the claim file, including a written statement explaining why it is believed that the claim should be paid. This is sent to the carrier, which adds its file and contentions to the claim file. The claim file is then returned to the claimant, who has a final opportunity to offer a rebuttal brief, with a copy of the rebuttal going to the carrier. The claimant then sends the entire file to TAB, where a decision is made.

A supply-chain policy issue that the shipper must address with respect to claims deals with salvage rights to the damaged goods. Ordinarily, the carrier, or the carrier's insurer, takes possession of the damaged goods after paying the freight claim. However, there are some disadvantages for the shipper. First, to the extent that the damaged goods are salvaged to the point they can be sold, they will compete in the marketplace with the shipper's own product. Second, if a consumer buys a salvaged product that turns out for some reason to be defective, the consumer will hold responsible the original manufacturer of the product, including legally.

Transit Privileges

Transit privileges, offered by some carriers, allow cargo to be stopped en route between its initial origin and final destination and to be unloaded, stored, or processed and then reloaded for shipment to its final destination. Although the products move from A to B and, later, from B to C, the total charges are for only A to C. Because of tapering rates, one long shipment is less costly to the carrier than two shorter trips equal in distance to the long trip. (Tapering transportation costs, or rates, expressed in terms of cents per mile, increase as distance increases, but at a slower rate because the carrier's terminal costs are spread over a larger number of miles.)

In-transit operations often imply that the goods are stored for awhile. This is a common practice in seasonal situations (i.e., for products harvested once a year but consumed over a 12-month period, or vice versa). Since the rail industry has moved to

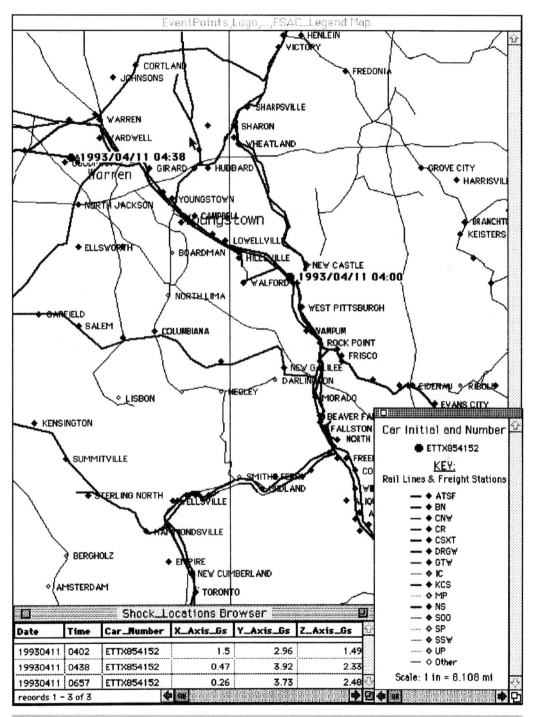

FIGURE 7-11 Map Showing Incidence of Rough Rail Rides

Source: Courtesy of CSX Transportation, Inc., Jacksonville, FL.

223

contract rate making, many transit privileges have been eliminated. They do continue to be used in the household-goods moving and storage industry.

Related to formal in-transit storage arrangements are the less formal ones that take advantage of slow railroad service by using the railroad as a temporary warehouse. A question on the Nelson–Wood survey said, "Just-in-time does not apply to all markets. Does your firm ever pick slower carriers or a longer route to receive advantages of storage-in-transit?" One third of the respondents answered "yes," accompanied with comments such as the following:

> "When merchandise is not hot, we generally route shipments intermodal."
> "We use boxcars and low-priority intermodal."
> "We ship by rail to get longer transit time."
> "We shift from truck to rail to slow delivery."
> "Domestically, we'll often instruct our inbound motor carrier to slow things down; internationally, I do this with carrier routings with my freight forwarder."

Very little has been written about storage-in-transit in recent years, yet we can report that the practice is alive and well.

Reparations

Reparations can occur in the remaining regulated segments of the transportation industry. **Reparations** are payments made to a shipper by a carrier that has charged illegally high rates in the past. The traffic manager must be assertive to protect the interests of his or her company, even if it involves alienating carriers. Hence, if a regulatory body finds that past rates were illegal, the shipper must then attempt to collect the difference between what was charged and what the regulatory body determined should have been charged. An example from 2001 was when the Surface Transportation Board decided a case entitled *Wisconsin Power and Light Company v. Union Pacific Railroad,* concluding that the carrier possessed market dominance, had a rate that was "unreasonably high," and owed reparations to Wisconsin Power and Light.[16]

Reparations are also collected in some instances in which carriers do not live up to the terms of their contracts with shippers. In late 1997, the Union Pacific Railroad was encountering many operating difficulties in the Los Angeles area, resulting in lost and delayed shipments. "The service breakdown has prompted some shippers to launch court action for reparations due to missed deliveries and delays."[17]

Demurrage and Detention

Demurrage is a penalty payment made by the shipper or consignee to a railroad for keeping a railcar beyond the time when it should be released back to the carrier. Demurrage is also collected by inland water carriers if their barges are kept by the shipper or consignee for a longer period than allowed. Pipelines are involved with

---

[16]Surface Transportation Board Decision, docket number 42051, decided September 12, 2001.

[17]*The Journal of Commerce,* October 17, 1997, p. 14A.

demurrage if oil stored in tanks at destination is not removed within specified time limits. **Detention** is basically the same concept as demurrage except that it usually refers to the trucking industry. Users of containers owned by the airlines are subject to similar charges. The carriers' concern is that their equipment will be used as temporary warehouses by either shippers or consignees.

For many transportation managers, handling demurrage and detention are important responsibilities. The rail demurrage tariffs typically state that demurrage payments will start after the expiration of the applicable free time. For example, the tariff of South Orient Railroad, which operates in Texas and connects with the Mexican railroad system, says, "Free time for each car will be 36 hours," and the charge is "$50.00 per car day or fraction thereof."[18]

Many transportation managers who are large users of railcars find it advantageous to enter into averaging agreements with the railroads. In an averaging agreement, an accounting system of debits and credits is established. A credit is received every time the shipper or consignee releases a railcar 1 day early, and a debit is recorded each time a car is surrendered to a carrier 1 day late.

Since deregulation, carriers are able to modify some of their detention and demurrage policies. The policies can be negotiated with shippers.

Transportation of Hazardous Materials

A **hazardous material** is defined in the Hazardous Materials Transportation Act of 1974 as "a substance or material in a quantity and form which may pose an unreasonable risk to health and safety or property when transported in commerce." Hazardous materials are very common and include some everyday household items.

The potential danger involved in the transportation of hazardous materials has been recognized for some time; the federal government began regulating its transport in 1838. The amount of hazardous materials being produced in the United States has increased rapidly, especially in recent years. The 1838 law (the Act to Provide for the Better Security of the Lives of Passengers on Board Vessels Propelled in Whole or in Part by Steam) specified proper packaging, marking, and stowing requirements for such products as camphene, naphtha, benzene, coal oil, petroleum, oil of vitriol, and nitric acid. In 1866, Congress passed a law stating that the newly discovered superexplosive nitroglycerin could not be transported in a vehicle or boat that was carrying passengers.

Federal regulations deal with the movement, storage, and packaging of hazardous materials. Since 1866, hundreds of changes have been made to federal statutes dealing with the transportation of hazardous materials. Today, one is required to know, track, and record the location of all hazardous materials that one owns or controls or that are being generated. Originating shippers' documents must include a phone number that will be answered 24 hours a day. The transportation manager, as well as many other managers in a firm's logistics operation, are concerned with hazardous materials. In addition, U.S. regulations have been modified to resemble more closely those issued by the United Nations regarding international movements of dangerous goods.

---

[18]The railroad's entire demurrage rules totaled one full page.

States have their own hazardous materials transportation regulations. Several assess special fees or taxes on shippers of hazardous matter and use the funds to help support local hazardous-spill response teams.

Transportation managers working for firms that handle hazardous materials have several important responsibilities. While the hazardous materials are under the managers' control, they must see that the materials are moved safely. Federal requirements prescribe the training of personnel to handle the materials, the packaging of the product, the marking and labeling of the packages, the placarding of the vehicles that transport the materials, and the information required on shipping documents. Sometimes, only certain routes may be used to move the cargo. The color, symbols, and numbers of the diamond-shaped placards seen on truck trailers, containers, and railcars identify the hazardous properties of the products being carried. Fire and rescue personnel arriving at the scene of an accident involving a hazardous materials carrier can take information from the placard and phone (via an 800 number) Chemtrec, the Washington-based office of the Chemical Manufacturers Association, for immediate advice.

Firms that manufacture or sell hazardous materials use Web sites to instruct customers and dealers how to handle their transport. One example is an Ohio firm that used six pages for instructions, including U.S. regulations and regulations covering both ground and air shipments. Discussed were documentation, use of "dangerous goods declaration," labeling, mixing of products, packaging, marking, and listing of a 24-hour hot line to give advice in case of spills.[19] Figure 7-12 shows a container designed specifically for carrying drums of hazardous materials; should one rupture, it would drain into a sump.

Hazardous wastes are a related topic, for they are a subset of hazardous materials.

An example of the confusion that can arise [between hazardous waste and hazardous materials] was related by the manager of a trucking terminal. A gallon container of a liquid material considered hazardous was accidentally punctured by the fork of a lift truck. His employees were trained in handling this sort of incident and reacted quickly, using sawdust to absorb the mildly hazardous common household liquid. The sawdust absorbent was placed into a plastic container along with the damaged gallon pail. When it came time to dispose of the sawdust, they discovered that they had created hazardous waste from what had been only hazardous material. Disposal problems took a quantum leap from that point.[20]

Consolidating Small Shipments

The small shipments problem represents one of the most bewildering situations faced by the transportation manager. Small shipments are usually defined as those that weigh more than 150 pounds and less than 500 pounds. Shipments under those weights

---

[19]"Distributor Shipping Guide Domestic Ground and Air Transportation," available on Web site of Loctite, www.loctite.com, January 2000.

[20]*Material Handling Engineering*, February 1992, pp. 55–56.

FIGURE 7-12 Specialized Container with Sump to Capture Hazardous Waste Leaks from Barrels

Source: Safety Storage, Inc.

can be handled relatively expeditiously and inexpensively by either the postal system or UPS.

The nature of transportation costs is that it costs less on a per-pound basis to ship a larger quantity. This is because certain costs (fixed, administrative, or terminal) are the same per shipment. When the shipment is larger, such costs can be allocated over a larger weight. The transportation manager is therefore often trying to consolidate large numbers of small shipments into small numbers of large shipments. Some **shipment consolidation** activities are shown in Figure 7-13.

Virtually all forms of shipment consolidation involve the aggregation of customer orders across time or place or both. Aggregation across time occurs when the shipper holds orders or delays purchases to consolidate shipments.

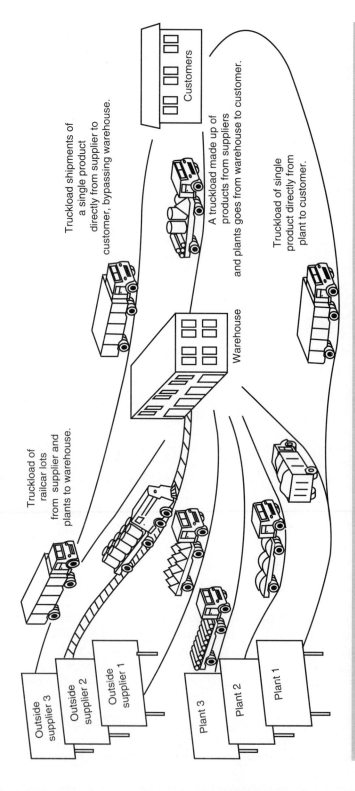

Outside supplier 3

Outside supplier 2

Outside supplier 1

Plant 3

Plant 2

Plant 1

Truckload of railcar lots from supplier and plants to warehouse.

Warehouse

Truckload shipments of a single product directly from supplier to customer, bypassing warehouse.

A truckload made up of products from suppliers and plants goes from warehouse to customer.

Truckload of single product directly from plant to customer.

Customers

FIGURE 7-13 The Transportation Manager Consolidates Shipments Whenever He or She Can

Rather than ship each order immediately, the shipping plan might schedule the release of shipments every second, third, or fourth day. Aggregation across place involves the consolidation of shipments to different destinations within the same general area.[21]

Related to consolidation analysis is an understanding of the *postponement principle,* which is the deliberate delay in shipping, labeling, or otherwise committing inventory. One of the reasons for this is to be able to consolidate shipments. Also, once inventory is committed, it no longer is available for filling other orders, even though its carrying costs continue. Professors Walter Zinn and Donald J. Bowersox have analyzed the use of the postponement principle. They believe there are five types of postponement. Four of these deal with form: labeling, packaging, assembly, and manufacturing. The fifth type is time.[22]

Smaller shipments are problems for shippers for two reasons. First, truckers are reluctant to accept certain small shipments because of their physical characteristics. These products are often called *balloon traffic* because they are light in weight. Typical products in this category are toys, stuffed animals, and furniture. Second, motor carriers are reluctant to accept small shipments based on the low volume of shipments tendered by the shipper, because carriers often believe that they lose money on low-volume customers.

The transportation manager must be innovative to compensate for the high cost and poor service given to small shipments. Among numerous solutions, several approaches appear to be most readily used. One involves the use of interfirm consolidation or *shipper cooperatives.* A second type of solution involves *intrafirm consolidation.* In the latter case, the transportation manager seeks ways to consolidate shipments within his or her own firm. This typically involves a systematic study of the firm's past shipments in order to locate consolidation possibilities. The result of this analysis is the use of either make-bulk or break-bulk distribution centers. Products move rapidly through these facilities.

A consolidation, or make-bulk, center is illustrated in Figure 7-14. Here, a U.S. chain store importing consumer goods from various Asian countries establishes a consolidation point in Hong Kong. All the Asian vendors are instructed to ship their products to the Hong Kong consolidator, which loads them into containers and ships the full containers to the United States.

Figure 7-15 illustrates a break-bulk operation. It shows a three-compartment recycling container of the type seen frequently. It is used as an early step in the recycling process. Each of us is asked to take the metal, plastic, and glass containers from our trash and place them into the recycling container's three compartments. We do the original sorting, and the containers are emptied into trucks that also have three compartments to keep the glass, plastic, and metal separate. In this situation, the individuals who separate the containers in our trash perform a break-bulk function. The trucks that unload the

---

[21]John E. Tyworth, Joseph L. Cavinato, and C. John Langley Jr., *Traffic Management: Planning, Operations, and Control* (Reading, MA: Addison-Wesley, 1987), p. 265. See also Randolph W. Hall, "Consolidation Strategy: Inventory, Vehicles, and Terminals," *Journal of Business Logistics,* September 1987, pp. 57–73.

[22]Walter Zinn and Donald J. Bowersox, "Planning Physical Distribution with the Principle of Postponement," *Journal of Business Logistics,* September 1988, pp. 117–135.

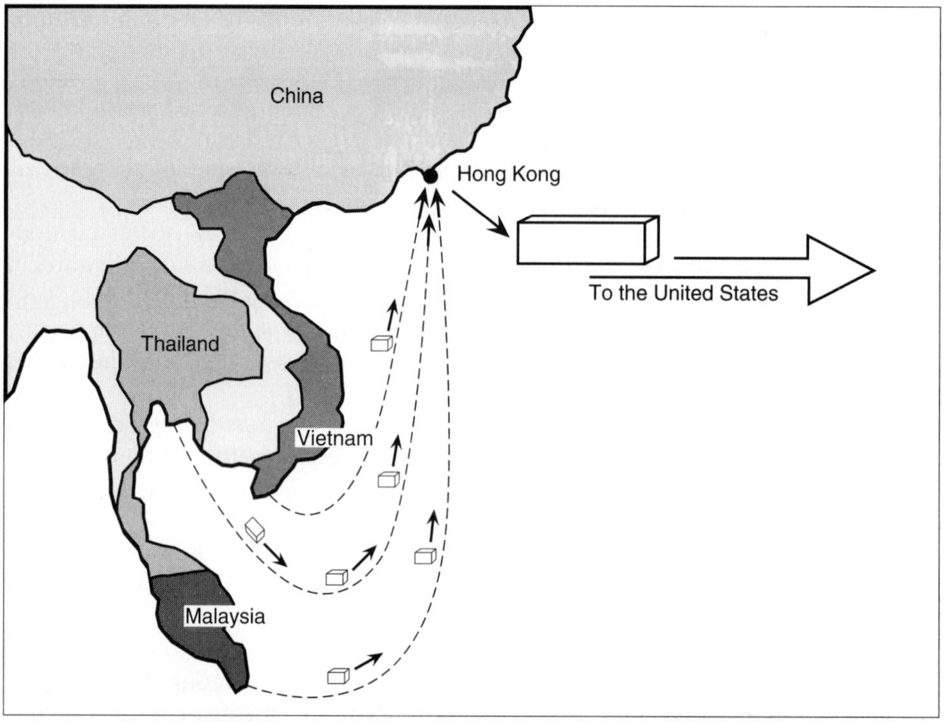

FIGURE 7-14 Using a consolidation point in Hong Kong for goods bound for the United States. United States, chain stores buying in Southeast Asia have goods shipped to a consolidator in Hong Kong who sends full containers to the United States.

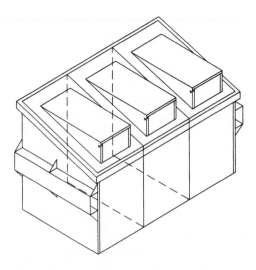

FIGURE 7-15 A Three-Compartment Recycling Container

Source: Courtesy of Consolidated Fabricators Corp., Vernon, CA.

recycling container into their own larger compartments are performing a make-bulk function as they add the segregated contents of more and more recycling containers.

Shippers study the rate structures of UPS and other parcel delivery firms to determine at which point it is least expensive to tender the shipments to the parcel carrier. L. L. Bean uses UPS to make deliveries, but often it finds it cheaper to send a trailer or container load to the West Coast and tender it there to UPS for local deliveries.

Computer programs that make consolidations easier to achieve are now available. Figure 7-16 shows a computer printout of a route and schedule for grocery deliveries. The printout shows only the results of the consolidation analysis. According to the software firm, the routing logic considers store time commitments, order sizes, equipment constraints, and road speeds and distances. There is also an order-splitting and consolidation feature that can be set to deal with greater-than-truckload splits, making it easier to prevent overflows and less-than-truckload splits and thus achieve better equipment utilization.

Achieving Transportation Quality

In both this and the previous chapter, considerable mention has been made of efforts of carriers and shippers to improve the quality of service in the transport sector. Transportation performance can be measured and usually improved upon. By almost all measures of quality, carriers are doing better now than 5 to 10 years ago. The customers are insisting on it and are monitoring their performance using hourly rather than daily measures.

SUMMARY

This chapter covered transportation management: the purchasing or use of transportation services. Since carrier deregulation, a firm's transportation manager has had to become more agile in dealing with carriers. The transportation manager has many specific duties. One duty is determining the correct lowest published rate or negotiating with carriers for an even lower rate. In negotiating for a contract, the shipper must also recognize the carrier's needs, some of which are monetary. Other carrier needs are to fill empty backhauls or otherwise improve equipment utilization.

The transportation manager is responsible for correctly preparing many of the documents associated with the shipment, including the bill of lading. Computers assist in these and many other transportation management operations. Other transportation management responsibilities include handling loss and damage claims, attempting to receive reparations in situations of carrier overcharges, minimizing demurrage and detention charges from failure to return carrier equipment promptly, and tracing lost or delayed shipments. The shipment of hazardous materials requires additional care. An ongoing responsibility of the transportation manager is to consolidate traffic because carrier rates per pound are always less for larger shipments.

QUESTIONS FOR DISCUSSION AND REVIEW

1. In recent years, senior corporate management has stressed the importance of the transportation management function. Discuss briefly the factors responsible for this trend.
2. What duties take most of a transportation manager's time?

CAPITOL FOOD SERVICE
Route Data Summary Report
Route Group: Dc1

Page: 1

Route: 002   Class: 1   Type: L   Driver: DriverID   Tractor: TractorID   Trailer: TrailerID

Stop Number	Location Identifier	Arrival	Departure	Time Zone	Drive Time	Off-Duty Time	Wait Time	Service Time	Drive Distance	Weight	Volume	Pieces	Pallets
D1	DC	05/31/1998 03:44	03:59	EST				0:15		29,088.00	1,850.00	249.00	0.00
01	100015	05/31/1998 04:53	05:18	EST	0:54			0:25	11.90	760.00	180.00	24.00	0.00
02	100013	05/31/1998 05:22	05:41	EST	0:04			0:19	0.80	5,863.00	346.00	44.00	0.00
03	500155	05/31/1998 05:53	06:10	EST	0:12			0:17	3.10	6,432.00	365.00	49.00	0.00
04	200033	05/31/1998 06:36	07:06	EST	0:26			0:30	4.90	4,827.00	270.00	33.00	0.00
05	500149	05/31/1998 07:07	07:39	EST	0:01			0:32	0.40	3,916.00	231.00	37.00	0.00
06	200032	05/31/1998 07:53	08:10	EST	0:14			0:17	2.70	3,874.00	256.00	32.00	0.00
07	300043	05/31/1998 08:29	09:03	EST	0:19			0:34	8.50	834.00	94.00	12.00	0.00
08	100011	05/31/1998 09:52	10:06	EST	0:12	0:19	0:18	0:14	14.00	2,592.00	108.00	18.00	0.00
09	DC	05/31/1998 10:28	10:43	EST	0:22			0:15	12.00				
					2:44	0:19	0:18	3:08	58.30	29,088.00	1,850.00	249.00	0.00

FIGURE 7-16 Computer Printout Showing Route and Schedule for Grocery Deliveries

Source: Reprinted with the permission of STSC, Inc., 2115 E. Jefferson St., Rockville, MD 20852.

3. Discuss how transportation managers are involved with other operations of the firm.
4. What are four rate-associated duties of transportation departments?
5. Why should a transportation manager be concerned with freight rate determination if the carrier is willing to tell him or her the correct rate? Discuss fully.
6. What are average weight agreements? Why are they used?
7. Private trucking has been experiencing growth during recent years. Discuss the factors responsible for this growth.
8. The bill of lading is the most important single document in transportation. Discuss some of the basic functions it performs.
9. Distinguish between the straight bill of lading and the order bill of lading.
10. Discuss the basic types of freight bill auditing. Why is this procedure necessary in the first place?
11. Distinguish between diversion and reconsignment.
12. Why are tracing and expediting less likely to be used today?
13. What is the basic rule of thumb regarding the determination of the full actual loss sustained by the shipper or consignee in a loss or damage claim situation?
14. Discuss the basic issues, conflicts, and problems involved in concealed loss and damage claims.
15. What is a transit privilege?
16. What are reparations? How does a shipper collect reparations?
17. Discuss the basic idea of demurrage and detention and how averaging agreements can be helpful in this area.
18. What are some of the important responsibilities of transportation managers with respect to handling hazardous materials?
19. What is freight consolidation? Why is it performed?
20. Which aspect of industrial traffic management do you believe is most challenging? Why?

Suggested Readings

Augello, William J., and George Carl Pezold. *Freight Claims in Plain English,* 3rd ed. Huntington, NY: Transportation Claims and Prevention Council, 1995.

Bigras, Yeon and Jacques Roy. "The Use of New Information Technologies: The Case of the Quebec Trucking Industry." *Journal of the Transportation Research Forum,* Vol. 39, No. 3, 2000, pp. 157–168.

Brown, Terence, and Janet Greenlee. "Private Trucking Since Deregulation." *Private Carrier,* September 1996, pp. 16–21, 32.

Chopra, Sunil, and Peter Meindl. *Supply Chain Management,* 2nd ed. Upper Saddle River, NJ: Prentice Hall, 2004.

Christopher, Martin. "The Agile Supply Chain— Competing in Volatile Markets." *Industrial Marketing Management,* Vol. 29, 2000, pp. 37–44.

Gibson, Brian J., Harry L. Sink, and Ray A. Mundy. "Shipper–Carrier Relationships and Carrier Selection Criteria." *Logistics & Transportation Review,* Vol. 29, No. 4, 1993, pp. 371–382.

Holcomb, Mary Collins and Karl B. Manrodt. "The Shippers' Perspective: Transportation and Logistics Trends and Issues." *Transportation Journal,* Vol. 40, No. 1, 2000, pp 15–25.

LaLonde, Bernard, James M. Masters, Arnold B. Maltz, and Lisa R. Williams. *The Evolution, Status, and Future of the Corporate Transportation Function.* Columbus: Ohio State University, 1991.

Lawrence, F. Barry, Daniel F. Jennings, and Brian E. Reynolds. *EDistribution.* Mason, OH: Thomson/Southwestern, 2003.

McBride, Michael F. "Railroads May Not Refuse to Carry Dangerous Commodities." *Journal of Transportation Law, Logistics and Policy,* Vol. 69, No. 4, 2002, pp. 391–397.

MacDonald, James M. "Transactions Costs and the Governance of Coal Supply and Transportation

Agreements." *Journal of the Transportation Research Forum,* Vol. 34, No. 1 1994, pp. 63–74.

Maltz, Arnold. "Private Fleet Use: A Transaction Cost Model." *Transportation Journal,* Vol. 32, No. 3 1993, pp. 46–53.

Murphy, David J., and Martin T. Farris. "Time-Based Strategy and Carrier Selection." *Journal of Business Logistics,* Vol. 14, No. 2, 1993, pp. 25–40.

Murphy, Paul R., and Richard F. Poist. "Third-Party Logistics: Some User Versus Provider Perspectives." *Journal of Business Logistics,* Vol.21, No. 1, 2000, pp. 121–133.

Ogden, Harold J., and Ronald E. Turner. "Customer Satisfaction with Delivery Scheduling." *Journal of Marketing Theory and Practice,* Vol. 4, No. 2, 1996, pp. 79–88.

Pautsch, Gregory, Bruce Babcock, and C. Philip Baumel. "Estimating the Value of Guaranteed Rail Service." *Journal of the Transportation Research Forum,* Vol. 36, No, 1, 1996, pp. 59–73.

Pilarski, Kim, and M. Ted Nelson. "Impacts of the 1990 Clean Air Act Amendments on Coal Transportation in the U.S.: An Initial Inquiry." *Waterways and Transportation Review,* Vol. 2, No. 1, 1994, pp. 35–47.

Wood, Donald F., and Richard S. Nelson. "Industrial Transportation Management: What's New?" *Transportation Journal,* Vol. 39, No. 2, 1999, pp 26–30.

C A S E S

Case 7-1 Chippy Potato Chip Company

Located in Reno, Nevada, since 1947, the Chippy Potato Chip Company manufactured potato chips and distributed them within a 100-mile radius of Reno. It used its own trucks for delivery in the Reno, Carson City, and Lake Tahoe area and common carrier trucking for all other outgoing shipments. All of its motor carrier shipments were on an LTL basis. The applicable motor carrier freight rating, or classification, for LTL potato chips was 200. This classification was high, although potato chips are often given as textbook examples of bulky freight that will cause a truck to cube out. Even after much of the motor carrier industry was deregulated, Chippy had difficulty finding contract truckers interested in negotiating specific contract rates. This was because potato chips—as a result of their bulk—were not a desirable cargo from the truckers' point of view.

The potato chips were packed in bags containing 8 ounces of chips. Twenty-four 8-ounce bags were packed in cartons that were 12 inches by 12 inches by 36 inches. The packed carton weighed 14 pounds. The 8-ounce bags of chips

wholesaled FOB plant for 40 cents each and retailed at 59 cents.

Recently the Chippy firm acquired rights to produce a new type of chip, made from powdered potatoes yielding chips of identical shape that could be packed in tubular containers. A 5-ounce paper tube of chips would wholesale (FOB plant) at 40 cents and retail for 59 cents. The new chips were much less bulky: Twenty-four 5-ounce containers could be packed in a carton measuring 1 cubic foot. The filled carton weighed 10 pounds. (The difference between the weight of chips and that of cartons is due to packaging materials. The carrier is paid on the basis of carton weight.)

Chippy management believed that since the new chips were less bulky, the LTL classification of 200 was too high. Management decided to ask the motor carrier classification bureau for a new, lower classification. (Motor carrier rates for a movement are the classification multiplied by a distance factor. If the classification were lowered, the rate would be lowered proportionally for all shipments.)

QUESTIONS

1. If you worked for Chippy, what new classification would you ask for? Give your reasons.
2. Classifications are based on both cost and value of service. From the carrier's standpoint, how has cost of service changed?
3. Given the existing LTL classification of 200, how has value of service to the customer changed?

4. The new tubular containers are much sturdier. If you worked for Chippy, how—if at all—would you argue that this factor influences classification?
5. You work for the motor carrier classification bureau and notice that the relationship between the weight of potato chips and the weight of packaging have changed. How, if

at all, should this influence changes in the product's classification?

6. One of Chippy's own trucks, used for local deliveries, has two axles, an enclosed body measuring (inside) 7 feet by 8 feet by 20 feet, and limited by law to carrying a load of no more than 8,000 pounds. Because the truck is not supposed to be overloaded, what combinations, expressed in terms of cartons of both new- and old-style chips can it legally carry? (*Hint:* Use a piece of graph paper.)

Case 7-2   Nürnberg Augsburg Maschinenwerke (N.A.M.)

The Nürnberg Augsburg Maschinenwerke, one of Germany's most successful manufacturing companies, enjoys a long tradition. It dates from 1748, when the St. Antony Iron Mill opened in Oberhausen (located in the heart of the Ruhrgebiet industrial region) during the beginning years of German industrialization. The owners soon founded additional iron and coal mills, then established the firm as Gute Hoffungshuette (GHH). Shortly following, in Augsburg and Nürnberg, several companies joined together to form Nürnberg Augsburg Maschinenwerke (N.A.M.). These two firms, GHH and N.A.M., would ultimately merge in the early twentieth century. In the interim, N.A.M. had distinguished itself through the work of Rudolf Diesel, who invented his famous engine and then brought it to N.A.M. late in the nineteenth century. The Diesel engine competed with the internal combustion engine in early automotive design and today powers heavy trucks, turbines, railroad engines, and ships. Based on this success, N.A.M. swiftly expanded manufacturing operations and distribution across the globe, only to have its foreign operations compromised by international politics on two occasions. First, N.A.M. lost most of its foreign property in the wake of World War I, a setback that, among other adjustments, encouraged its merger with GHH in 1920. Second, N.A.M. lost all of its foreign property again after World War II and had to rebuild and restructure much of its domestic operation as well. In 1955, the company opened a truck unit in Munich, which would later become the new company headquarters.

By 2003 the company had reclaimed its preeminence as a global player in heavy truck and bus design, engineering and manufacturing, as well as in print technology, rocket, and energy science. It had reestablished both its plants and sales offices across the globe. It is one of the largest diesel engine makers in the world. Karl Huber was the N.A.M. regional vice president of sales for South America. He supervised a team of local sales representatives in the countries of that continent, plus a small group of people in the Munich headquarters.

On August 15, Huber received an e-mail from Leopold Escabar in Caracas, who had just returned from an important meeting with local authorities in charge of redesigning the local public transportation systems for the Brazilian cities of São Paulo and Rio de Janeiro. Escabar had attended the meeting along with salespeople from competing truck and bus companies. Escabar gave Huber some good news and some bad news. Escabar had been told N.A.M. was favored to receive an order for 224 N.A.M. class #4-G two-section articulated buses (or "accordion" buses, as Escabar liked to call them), with the possibility of securing a contract for an additional 568 buses. To win the business, however, N.A.M. would have to meet cost and timing guarantees.

The customers first required that N.A.M. must match or beat the total price per unit, including shipping, that N.A.M. had received for a shipment of 233 buses to the transit district of Buenos Aires, 6 months earlier. That price was (Eurodollar) 124,500 per bus. Huber had built in a small extra profit margin on the Buenos Aires deal, so he felt confident that to meet their pricing demand he could shave profit a little, if necessary, in this case.

The second guarantee, however, was more worrisome: The Brazilian authorities were feeling political heat because they were badly behind schedule implementing their transportation plan and needed proof to show to the public that their new programs were underway. So they had made this offer to N.A.M. on strict condition that the company could ensure delivery of the first 25 buses to Santos, the port that serves São Paulo, by November 15 (only 3 months away). If N.A.M. delivered this initial 90-day order on time, the company would receive a contract for the remaining 199 vehicles to be delivered in full within the following 15 months. The follow-on order for 568 more vehicles was, essentially, contingent on meeting terms of the initial contract to the letter, with regard to the 224 buses. All buses were to be delivered to Santos, a principal Brazilian port.

Huber whistled softly to himself as he read Escabar's e-mail. This would be a major order. In a single stroke, it could move him ahead of his regional sales targets for several quarters to come. Huber immediately sent back an e-mail, instructing Escabar to tentatively accept the offer, assuring the local authorities that they'd have their 25 buses in 90 days and the rest within 18 months. N.A.M. would formally agree to the proposal within 5 working days. Then he scratched his head and tried to figure out how. Huber had 4 days before the next managing

director's meeting, at which time he would present the project and, with the vice president for production, propose a plan to accomplish it. Huber lunged for the phone and, scarcely glancing at the number pad, his fingers automatically dialed 4823.

Dieter Berndsen, the production V.P., listened as his old friend Huber described the opportunity, jotting down notes as he went. He explained to Huber that the factory in Munich was already producing to its limits and the two other German facilities were also facing a backlog of orders through the fourth quarter. So Berndsen offered two immediate possibilities. First, he considered wait listing a 40-bus order from the Thai military at the Munich plant. He said he was reluctant to do this, however, because the Thais had ordered several product modifications and the Munich line had already set up to handle them. Second, Berndsen suggested sending the new Brazil order to N.A.M.'s Prague facility. Prague was the smallest of all the European plants and had the oldest, slowest assembly lines, but they were just finishing up manufacture of an order of #4-G's and, due to a recent order cancellation, would now be working at only 70 percent capacity through year-end. Within 8 weeks, figured Berndsen, Prague could easily handle the order for Brazil's first 25 buses.

Huber eagerly agreed as Berndsen decided to recommend Prague for this assignment. The problem was that this facility could not produce fast enough to fulfill more than 20 percent of the rest of the contract (for the 224 buses), which meant that he would have to coordinate production and delivery on the rest of this order from other plants. Sighing audibly over the phone line, Berndsen said, "Thanks a lot for the new headache, Hubie. Let me mull this one over for a bit before I call you back. But don't worry, we'll make your deadline—and you will make your bonus. Just remember to cut me in for a piece."

Huber chuckled, thanked him, and hung up.

Berndsen decided to split the full order (224 buses) among the factories in Prague and the much larger plant in Munich. To finalize both scheduling and pricing, he now needed to estimate the time it would take to fulfill the order, as well as the cost of transportation. He was inclined to use the Deutsche Bundesbahn to transport the buses by train to the North Sea port of Bremerhaven, but he wasn't sure that this was the best solution for each of the plants involved.

Berndsen's immediate problem was the first shipment of buses, which would be ready to leave Prague on October 15. Berndsen asked Marcus Weiss, his supply-chain analyst, to create a work sheet that would show all costs and times required to get the buses from the Prague factory to the port of Bremerhaven, and he also asked Weiss to identify viable alternatives. (Europe possesses an extensive network of rivers and channels that connect together its network of commercial waterways. Barges represent alternatives to the road and railroad. The European Green movement continually asked shippers to use the water routes and, occasionally, would attempt to publicly embarrass shippers who used trucks rather than water.) Consequently, the Prague plant sometimes transported buses on barges via the Elbe,

north to Hamburg. The German plants occasionally shipped north to Bremerhaven or Hamburg, via a network of industrial waterways, or westward, over the River Rhein, to the port of Rotterdam in the Netherlands. (See Exhibit 7-A.)

Following is some of the information Weiss assembled for Berndsen:

- By train, the geographic distances between plants and ports were as follows: Prague to Hamburg 490K, Prague to Rotterdam 640K
- N.A.M. would need 3 days to get the buses from the factories in Prague to the port of Bremerhaven or Hamburg by train and 4 or 5 days to reach Rotterdam. The advantage of Rotterdam comes, however, in the shipping time from there to Santos, which saves a day versus Bremerhaven or Hamburg, and ocean shipping charges are 5 percent less.
- The Czech railway could transport the load to the border with Germany, where the Deutsche Bundesbahn would take over the flatcars, which carry two buses each. The

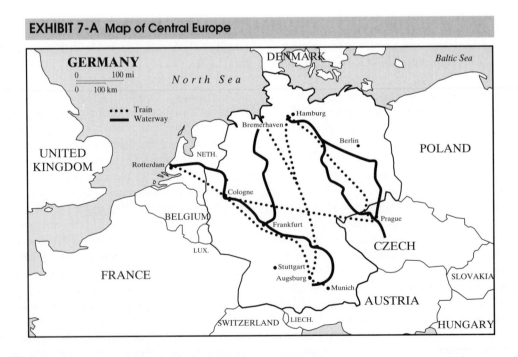

EXHIBIT 7-A Map of Central Europe

Bundesbahn quotes a price of €1,643 per flatcar from Prague to Hamburg, which includes the service by its Czech partner. If rail were used from Prague to Rotterdam, the cost per flatcar would be €1,943. In either port, it costs another €45 per bus to have it unloaded and driven to alongside the vessel. The vessel line can load and pack 20 buses per day charging €25 per bus and up to 30 buses with overtime charges. The overtime charges would amount to an additional €15 per bus (for buses 21, 22, and so on). All charges per bus included detaching the two halves.

- Using the waterways instead of trains to reach the Hamburg port from Prague would decrease the transportation cost by €48 per bus. Waterway transportation would increase the transport time necessary by 3 days to Hamburg.
- For transoceanic shipping on any of these routes, N.A.M. works with Hapag-Lloyd AG. Hapag-Lloyd is able to offer a cheap

and flexible commodity cost, through its alliance with NYK, P&O Nedlloyd, MISC, and OOCL, for the ocean transport of the buses. One vessel could carry up to 125 buses as deck cargo, but they would have to be disassembled at their accordion junctions and then reassembled again at their destination.

- The cost per bus (in shipments of 20 buses or more) from Bremerhaven or Hamburg to Santos is quoted at €6,000, and the trip requires 18 days. Hapag-Lloyd indicates that deck space is available for the initial shipment of 25 buses on vessels departing Hamburg on October 24, October 27, October 31, and November 3. Hapag-Lloyd also has space on vessels leaving from Rotterdam to Santos on October 23, October 28, and November 2.
- Handling (unloading) in Santos is estimated to cost another €94 per bus, and this includes reattaching the two halves.
- The interest for N.A.M.'s line of credit is 10 percent.

QUESTIONS

1. Assume that you are Weiss. How many viable alternatives do you have to consider regarding the initial shipment of 25 buses?
2. Which of the routing alternatives would you recommend to meet the initial 90-day deadline for the 25-bus shipment? Train or waterway? To which port(s)? What would it cost?
3. What additional information would be helpful for answering question 2?
4. How important, in fact, are the transport costs for the initial shipment of 25 buses?
5. What kinds of customer service support must be provided for this initial shipment of 25 buses? Who is responsible?
6. The Brazilian buyer wants the buses delivered at Santos. Weiss looks up the International Chamber of Commerce's year 2000 Incoterms and finds two categories of "delivered" at a receiving port:

- *DES (Delivered Ex Ship).* In this type of transaction, the seller must pay all the costs and bear all the risk of transport up to the foreign port of unloading but not including the cost or risk of unloading the cargo from the ship.
- *DEQ (Delivered Ex Quay).* This is the same as DES, except that the terms provide for the seller to pay the costs of unloading the cargo from the vessel and the cost of import clearance.

How should he choose? Why?

7. Would you make the same routing recommendation for the second, larger (199 buses) component of the order, after the initial 90-day deadline is met? Why or why not?
8. How important, if at all, is it for N.A.M. to ship via water in order to show its support of the Green movements desires?

8

Distribution Center, Warehouse, and Plant Location

When large tonnages of raw materials are involved, a site that is adjacent to water transport routes is often used. This site is in Chicago, and stockpiles of materials, conveyor equipment, and a self-unloading Great Lakes vessel are all visible.

Photo courtesy of KCBX Terminals Co., Chicago, IL.

Key Terms

- Center-of-gravity approach
- Empowerment zone
- Facility location
- Facility relocation
- Free trade zone
- Grid system
- Maquiladoras
- National competitive strategy
- Pure materials
- Right-to-work laws
- Sweatshops
- Tax-free bonds
- Weight-gaining products
- Weight-losing products

Learning Objectives

- To examine the screening or focusing concept of plant/warehouse location
- To describe the major factors that influence location decisions
- To explain the general process of determining the optimum number of facilities
- To explain systems to determine the location that minimizes transportation costs
- To examine a site's specialized location characteristics
- To learn about free trade zones

Facility location is a logistics/supply-chain activity that has evolved from a tactical decision to one of tremendous strategic importance in numerous organizations. In particular, this chapter discusses **facility location** in terms of siting distribution centers, warehouses, and production facilities in ways that accommodate the movement of inventories to customers. In retailing, it is often said that the three factors necessary for success are "location, location, and location." The location of warehousing facilities to serve retail outlets is also important in terms of cost savings and the ability to efficiently manage the production and flow of materials along the supply chain. This chapter also discusses locational issues regarding production facilities and will examine general and specialized influences on facility location, describe several elementary techniques for choosing general locations, and conclude with an examination of facility relocation and facility closing.

The major factors influencing locational decisions are markets and resource availability; most facilities are located near one or the other. Labor and transport services are two other key factors in facility location. Labor is of special significance because it can be considered as both a market (in the sense of demand for products) and a resource (in terms of human resources to staff a particular facility). The transportation system makes other resource factors mobile and allows a firm to combine factors of production that originate great distances apart.

Advances in technology and communications have had considerable influence on locational decisions in recent years. Consider the experience of Westflex Pipe Manufacturing, which has corporate headquarters in California. Because 40 percent of its sales are to customers located east of the Rocky Mountains, Westflex decided to add a production facility in closer proximity to these customers. How did Westflex choose the location of this facility? It used the Internet to gather relevant data that narrowed the choice to a few locations, and Westflex ultimately located the new production plant in Nebraska. The Internet allowed Westflex to collect the data inexpensively and relatively quickly.[1]

Facility location has traditionally relied on a cost/value tradeoff, in the sense that firms were looking for the most value at the least cost. Since the late 1980s, however, a third dimension has been added to facility location, namely, time considerations. As a result, facility location decisions increasingly seek to balance cost, value, and time considerations; firms are seeking the most value at the least cost in the least elapsed amount of time.[2]

The location decision process involves several layers of screening or focus, with each step becoming a more detailed analysis of smaller areas or sites. The initial focus is on the region, the delineation of which can vary depending upon whether a company has a multinational or domestic focus. Thus, a multinational company might initially focus on a region of the world, such as Western Europe, the Pacific Rim, or North America. By contrast, a domestic focus might target a state (province/territory) or group of states (provinces/territories).

The next focus is more precise; it usually involves a selection of the area(s) in which the facility will be located, as illustrated in Figure 8-1 from a brochure describing

FIGURE 8-1
Advertisement Showing a Site's Location as an Advantage in Reaching British and Continental European Markets

Source: Warrington and Runcorn Development Corporation, England.

---

[1]Lance Yoder, "How the Internet Impacts the Site Selection Process," *Expansion Management,* Vol. 16, No. 9, 2000, p. 10.

[2]George Stalk Jr. and Thomas M. Hout, *Competing Against Time* (New York: Free Press, 1990).

a site in the Manchester-Liverpool area of England. Once this has been determined, a detailed examination of various locations within the selected area is appropriate. Figure 8-2 shows a map of a specific site along the Little Calumet River, between Chicago, Illinois, and Hammond, Indiana.

This detailed examination should include a physical inspection of the location as well as a thorough analysis of relevant zoning and regulatory considerations. Failure to do so can result in costly—and potentially embarrassing—mistakes, as illustrated by the unfortunate experience of a major supermarket chain. The company picked a site for a new grocery store, received the appropriate construction permits, built the store, hired relevant personnel, and stocked the store with products. Several days before the store's grand opening, the parent company was threatened with legal action by a competing supermarket that had a store located across the street from the new store because the relevant zoning laws prohibited any new grocery store from being built within a 1-mile radius of the existing grocery store. As a result, the company had to cancel its grand opening, close the brand-new store, transfer the products to other stores, and lay off many of the newly hired personnel.[3]

Determining the Number of Facilities

An early, albeit overlooked, step in the facility location decision should involve determining the total number of facilities that a firm should operate. That is, rather than asking the question "Where should we locate a new facility?" organizations should be thinking about the optimal number of facilities in their system. While an additional facility may indeed be required, the general trend in recent years has been for companies to reduce the number of facilities in their distribution networks.

Few firms start business on one day and have a need for large-scale production and distribution the next day. Rather, distribution and production facilities tend to be added one at a time, as needed. The need for additional distribution and production facilities often arises when an organization's service performance from existing facilities drops below "acceptable" levels. Retailers, for example, might add a distribution center when some of its stores can no longer consistently be supplied within 3 days from existing facilities.

Most analytical procedures for determining the number of facilities are computerized because of the vast number of permutations involved, as well as the complementary relationships between current facilities in a distribution network. Analyzing, for example, whether an organization with 250 stores and five distribution centers should add or remove one distribution center is challenging enough in and of itself. By factoring in that each distribution center is designed to serve a specific number of retail locations—and serve as a backup to one or more of the other distribution centers—the decision becomes even more complex. Furthermore, conducting sensitivity analysis on varying levels of customer service could result in an entirely different series of ideal facility locations, depending upon the level of customer service.

---

[3]Example drawn from one author's personal experience.

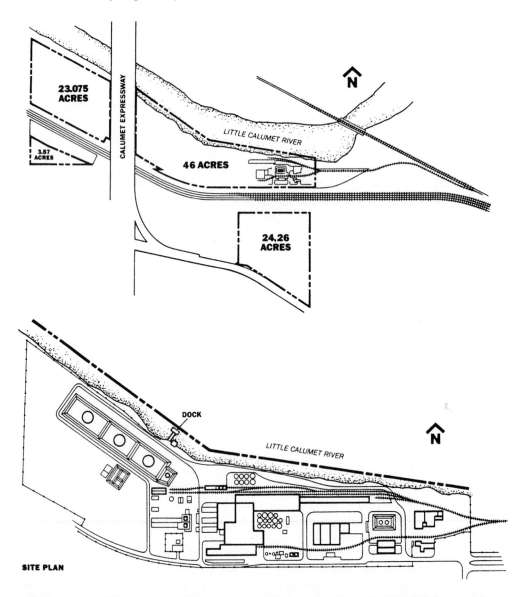

FIGURE 8-2 Location Map and Site Plan for an Available Industrial Site on the Little Calumet River

Source: Courtesy of Donald F. Schroud of Hiffman Shaffer Anderson, Inc.

Fortunately, a number of software packages exist to help organizations determine both the number and location of facilities in their logistics networks. Chicago Consulting, for example, annually develops a list entitled the "10 Best Warehouse Networks" for serving the U.S. population. While this list is limited in the sense that it only looks at one component in location (how long it takes to get from a particular city—or cities—to the majority of the U.S. population), the network is valuable in showing how altering the number of facilities affects transit time to the U.S. population. With respect to the 2002 data, for example, going from two to five warehouses allows a company to save about a half day in lead time to the U.S. population. By contrast, moving from five to ten warehouses saves a bit less than a quarter day in lead time.[4]

General Factors Influencing Facility Location

Tangible products are the combination of raw materials, component parts, and labor—with the mixture varying from product to product—made for sale in various markets. Thus, raw materials, component parts, labor, and markets all influence where to locate a manufacturing, processing, or assembly facility. Warehouses, distribution centers, and cross-docking facilities exist to facilitate the distribution of products. Their locations are influenced by the locations of plants whose products they handle and the markets they serve.

The discussion that follows covers the location of manufacturing, processing, assembly, and distribution facilities along the supply chain. The relative importance of each factor varies with the type of facility, the product being handled, its volume, and the geographic locations being considered. Although much of the discussion deals with single facilities, the decision process often involves a combination of facilities, in which case one must take into account the relationships among them.

Natural Resources

The materials used to make a product must be extracted directly from the ground or sea (as in the case of mining or fishing) or indirectly (as in the case of farm products). In some instances, these resources may be located great distances from the point where the materials or their products will be consumed. For materials that lose no weight in processing, known as **pure materials,** the processing point can be anywhere near the raw material source and the market.

However, if the materials must be processed at some point between where they are gathered and where they are needed, their weight-losing or weight-gaining characteristics become important for facility location. If the materials lose considerable weight in processing, known as **weight-losing products,** then the processing point should be near the point where they are mined or harvested, largely to avoid the payment of unnecessary transportation charges. If the raw materials gain weight in processing, known as **weight-gaining products,** then the processing point should be close to the market. Sugar derived from sugar beets provides an example of a weight-losing product (a yield of roughly 1 pound of sugar from 6 pounds of sugar beets), while bottled soft drinks are an example of a weight-gaining product.

In addition to its use for bottling, water (of one type or another) is a requirement for the location of many facilities. For some industrial processes, water is used for cooling, and in some climates it is possible to use naturally flowing water for air conditioning during warm months. Some processing operations require water both for cleaning purposes and as a medium for carrying away waste. Water is also necessary for fire protection, and the fire insurance premiums charged depend upon the availability of some type of water supply.

---

[4]Kristin S. Krause, "The Best in Warehousing," *Traffic World,* April 15, 2002, p. 15.

Historically, the relationship between natural resources and facility location revolved around how the natural resources would be incorporated into products making their way toward consumers. Over the past quarter century, however, discussion of natural resources and facility location has increasingly factored in environmental considerations of one type or another. One set of considerations involves the various types of pollution, namely, air, noise, and water. Another environmental consideration involves the conservation of natural resources—and not necessarily the natural resources used in production processes. For example, a U.S.-based electronics association has urged its members to boycott tantalum (a metallic element) that originates in the Congo because the tantalum is being mined from a nature and wildlife preserve.[5]

Moreover, developing nations often face an interesting dilemma with respect to facility location—especially manufacturing plants—and environmental considerations. By limiting the number and scope of environmental regulations associated with manufacturing facilities, developing countries can speed their economic growth and thus help raise their standards of living. Doing so, however, greatly increases the likelihood of damaging, perhaps irreversibly, a country's natural resources, not to mention potential health-related problems for its citizens.[6]

Regarding real estate, distribution and production facilities may require large parcels of land in order to facilitate effective and efficient operations. An example of land requirements for a particular type of facility is a 250,000-square-foot distribution center that could require at least 50 acres of land. In general, real estate tends to be more plentiful and less costly in more rural locations—locations that might not have adequate transportation or labor resources. Some companies, particularly those needing large-capacity facilities, view the availability and costs of real estate as important a locational determinant as transportation and labor considerations.[7]

Population Characteristics—Market for Goods

Population can be viewed as both a market for goods and a potential source of labor. The following addresses population as it relates to a market for goods; the next section focuses on population as a source of labor.

Planners for consumer products pay extremely close attention to various attributes of current and potential consumers. Not only are changes in population size of interest to planners, but so are changes in the characteristics of the population—particularly as those characteristics influence purchasing habits. With respect to population size, one reason that China and India are potentially attractive to consumer products marketers is that the two countries account for approximately one-third of the world's population. As for population characteristics, longer life spans can increase the demand for health-related products such as prescription medications.

In an effort to learn more about population size and characteristics, many countries conduct a detailed study, or census, typically once every 10 years or so. Although

---

[5]George Leopold, "Boycott Is Urged on Tantalum from Congo," *Electronic Engineering Times,* April 23, 2001, p. 42.

[6]"Call for Alternatives to Rigid Eco Regulations," *Bahrain Tribune,* October 30, 2001, no pages listed.

[7]William Atkinson, "DC Siting—What Makes the Most Sense?" *Logistics Management & Distribution Report,* May 2002, pp. S63–S66.

census methodologies and the type of information collected often vary across countries, the resulting data can provide valuable insights for distribution planners in terms of where populations are growing and at what rates. For instance, while the 2000 United States Census showed approximately a 13 percent population increase from 1990 to 2000, the population growth was far from uniform across the 50 states. Indeed, the five states with the highest growth rates Nevada (66 percent), Arizona (40 percent), Colorado (31 percent), Utah (30 percent), and Idaho (29 percent) are all located in the western United States.[8]

Population Characteristics—Labor

Labor is a primary concern in selecting a site for manufacturing, processing, assembly, and distribution. Organizations can be concerned with a number of labor-related characteristics: the size of the available workforce; the unemployment rate of the workforce; the age profile of the workforce; its skills and education; the prevailing wage rates; and the extent to which the workforce is, or might be, unionized. These and other labor characteristics should be viewed as interrelated rather than distinct attributes. For example, there may be a positive relationship between the age of the workforce and the prevailing wage rates (i.e., higher wage rates may be associated with an older workforce). Alternatively, there may be an inverse relationship between unemployment and wages (i.e., higher unemployment rates may be associated with lower relative wage rates).

Labor wage rates appear to be a key locational determinant as supply chains become more global in nature. For example, hourly compensation data (including benefits) among manufacturing firms in 2000 indicate average compensation of $19.86 in the United States, $22 in Japan, and $22.29 in Germany. By contrast, hourly compensation rates in Taiwan were $5.98, while they were $2.46 in Mexico.[9]

Thus, in relative terms, a company could have approximately similar compensation costs by hiring eight Mexican workers or one U.S. worker. This wage differential at least partly explains the popularity of the **maquiladora** assembly plants located just south of the U.S.–Mexican border. These plants, which began in the mid-1960s, provided much needed jobs to Mexican workers and allowed for low-cost, duty-free production so long as all the goods were exported from Mexico. In recent years, however, maquiladoras have been struggling, in part because some companies have established production plants in even lower-wage countries such as China and Guatemala.[10]

Companies interested in locating in countries with low-cost labor should recognize that there are sometimes limits to the number of supervisory personnel that can be brought in from other countries. The host country's government may also insist that its own nationals be trained for and employed in most supervisory posts. In addition, countries with low-cost labor often have a multitude of **sweatshops,** or places in which workers are employed for long hours at low wages and under unhealthy conditions. Sweatshops are most frequently associated with the apparel industry, and if you're wearing clothing or a cap with your college's logo, it may have been manufactured in a sweatshop somewhere in the world.

---

[8]www.census.gov.

[9]www.bls.gov.

[10]Geri Smith, "The Decline of the Maquiladora," *Business Week,* April 29, 2002, p. 59.

A workforce's union status is also a key locational determinant for some organizations. From management's perspective, unions tend to result in increased labor costs, due to higher wages, and less flexibility in terms of job assignments, which often forces companies to hire additional workers. As a result, some organizations prefer geographic areas where unions are not strong; in the United States, for example, some states have **right-to-work laws,** which mean that an individual cannot be compelled to join a union as a condition of employment. Indeed, since the mid-1990s, four non-U.S. automakers have constructed production plants in Alabama, in large part because Alabama is a right-to-work state.[11] However, the mere presence of a union doesn't necessarily mean that the union is strong, as illustrated by the case of an apparel sweatshop in Shanghai, China; while 70 percent of the workers belonged to the factory's union, the union was run by the factory's management![12]

Declining union membership (as measured by the percentage of workers who belong to unions) in industrialized nations such as the United States and Australia has resulted in efforts to unionize workers in "nontraditional" areas such as government agencies and service organizations. Such unionization efforts may cause new types of supply-chain disruptions and add new considerations to facility location decisions. For example, toll takers on the Ohio Turnpike are now represented by the Teamsters Union. If these toll takers decide to strike turnpike management, Teamster truck drivers would honor the strike by refusing to drive the Ohio Turnpike. Alternate routes would need to be found for the freight, a situation that would likely increase transit times and shipment costs.

Racial, ethnic, and cultural considerations may also be important population characteristics. Many organizations, particularly those with a national or international presence, have workforces comprised of different races, ethnicities, and cultures. There may be a hesitancy to establish facilities in areas that are not racially, ethnically, or culturally diverse, since it may be difficult to transfer workers to such locations. Moreover, an emerging issue involves managing so-called *expatriate* workers, or those employees who are sent to other countries for extended periods of time. Expatriate assignments can be costly, ranging up to $1 million per assignment, and turnover rates currently run between 20 percent and 40 percent. What makes the expatriate situation relevant to the current discussion is that the turnover tends to be caused by socialization, rather than technical (i.e., employee knowledge and skills) factors. As such, organizations must ensure that the expatriates (and their families, if relevant) are comfortable with the social and cultural factors of the country where they will be employed.[13]

Taxes and Subsidies

Although labor considerations are important for location decisions, taxes can also be important, particularly with respect to warehousing facilities. Warehousing facilities,

---

[11]Jay Reeves, "Deep South Emerges as Automotive Powerhouse: Hyundai Adds to Alabama's Growing List of Auto Plants," *Ottawa Citizen,* April 3, 2002, p. D1.

[12]Dara O'Rourke, "Sweatshops 101," *Dollars & Sense,* September/October 2001, pp. 14–18.

[13]Sarah B. Lueke and Daniel J. Svyantek, "Organizational Socialization in the Host Country: The Missing Link in Reducing Expatriate Turnover," *International Journal of Organizational Analysis,* Vol. 8, No. 4, 2000, pp. 380–400.

and the inventories they contain, are often viewed as a prime source of tax revenues by the relevant taxing organizations. From a community's standpoint, warehousing facilities are desirable operations to attract because they add to the tax base while requiring relatively little in the way of municipal services.

Tax policies differ by location, and organizations should enlist the expertise of knowledgeable parties to determine the actual tax requirements of a particular site. Even when areas have what appear to be identical taxes, there may be significant differences in the manner in which assessments are made or in which collections are enforced. Some localities are so anxious to attract new business that they either formally or informally agree to go easy on the new operation for its first several years. No list of taxes is complete; a partial list includes sales taxes, real estate taxes, corporate income taxes, corporate franchising taxes, fuel taxes, unemployment compensation taxes, social security taxes, and severance taxes (for the removal of natural resources).

Of particular interest to logisticians and supply-chain managers is the *inventory tax,* analogous to personal property taxes paid by individuals. As a general rule, the inventory tax is based on the value of inventory that is being held on the assessment date(s). Not surprisingly, many logistics managers attempt to have their inventories as low as possible on the assessment date(s), and businesses may offer sales to reduce their inventory prior to the assessment date.

Although many U.S. states have inventory taxes, there may be exemptions for items of political and/or economic importance. For example, Wisconsin, a state noted for its production of cheese, exempts natural cheese that's being aged in storage; likewise, Virginia, a state noted for tobacco production, exempts tobacco that is in the possession of its producer. Other inventory exemptions deal more explicitly with distribution activities or functions. Some states exempt goods that are stored in public warehouses; some states exempt goods passing through the state on a storage-in-transit bill of lading.

As if business taxes are not difficult enough to understand, they represent only one side of the coin; the other side is to know the value of services being received in exchange for the taxes. Unfortunately, a general rule of thumb is that the services received represent only about 50 percent of the taxes paid. This imbalance may cause businesses to invest more money to receive the required level of service. For example, inadequate police services might cause a warehousing facility to hire its own security force.

To further complicate matters, governments may offer subsidies and/or incentive packages as an inducement for firms to locate in a particular area. For example, some localities subsidize new business by issuing **tax-free bonds** to prepare plant sites and construct buildings. Although this can be very attractive for enticing new businesses, this arrangement often places a burden on existing taxpayers. With respect to incentive packages, in 2002 the state of Alabama approved nearly $120 million of incentives, including $75 million for assembly-line training, to convince Hyundai to locate its first U.S. automobile plant near the city of Montgomery.[14]

---

[14]Jay Reeves, April 3, 2002.

Furthermore, the U.S. Department of Housing and Urban Development created **empowerment zones** in several cities beginning in the mid-1990s. The purpose of these zones is to encourage business development—through various tax credits—in economically depressed portions of cities. For example, between 1994 and 2000, the empowerment zone for Detroit, Michigan, is estimated to have attracted approximately $6 billion in investment money and generated approximately 15,000 jobs.[15]

On the international level, nations subsidize or otherwise promote or protect many types of commerce. The term **national competitive strategy** is employed in reference to a nation's attempts to adopt policies that will strengthen its economic position vis-à-vis the rest of the world.

Transportation Considerations

Transportation considerations, in the form of transportation *availability* and *costs,* also play an important role in facility location. Transportation availability refers to the number of transportation modes (*intermodal competition*) as well as the number of carriers within each mode (*intramodal competition*) that could serve a proposed facility. The evaluation of transportation availability is likely to depend on the type of facility that is being looked at. For instance, a manufacturing plant might need both rail service (in order to bring in raw materials) and truck service (to carry the finished goods), while a distribution center might need just truck service. Figure 8-3 illustrates a warehousing firm's available truck links to points in the Midwest and Northeast.

As a general rule, the existence of competition, whether intermodal, intramodal, or both, tends to have both cost and service benefits for potential users. Limited competition generally leads to higher transportation costs and means that users have to accept whatever service they receive. Moreover, transportation considerations are a key aspect of facility location decisions because transportation often represents such a large portion of total logistics costs. Thus, a poor location can significantly increase transportation costs as well as negatively impact customer service.

Geographically central facility locations are often the result of transportation costs and service considerations. With respect to transportation costs, centralized facilities tend to minimize the total transit distances, which likely results in minimum transportation costs. Centralized facilities can also maximize a facility's service area, as shown in Figure 8-4, which illustrates truck distances from the state of Oklahoma. Note how many states are located within 1,000 miles (generally two-day service by truck) of Oklahoma.

Customer Considerations

Customer considerations, particularly as they affect customer service, play a key role in where consumer goods companies tend to locate their distribution facilities. In fact, the popular press is replete with stories involving distribution facilities being located in a

---

[15]John Reosti, "Hitting the Streets by Forsaking Branches," *Small Business Banker,* July 2001, pp. 13–14. The term *enterprise zones* is also used.

**Modern warehousing and distribution facilities
in Hazleton, Wilkes-Barre and Scranton, PA**
- Single story complexes-two million sq. ft./26-35 ft. high
- Finest material handling equipment
- State of the art theft, fire & sanitation control
- EDI communication
- In house, sophisticated state of the art data processing facilities

Full service logistics solution specialist
- Nationwide transportation services
- Inland port of entry/U.S. customs bonded
- Conrail, CP-D&H sidings
- Proven management experience

Distribution support services
- Value added services
- Third party public and contract services
- Shrinkwrapping, bundle pack, pick pack, repack
- Light assembly
- Commercial records storage
- Bar code scanning product reclamation/reverse logistics

Call Stanley Gutkowski (717) 654-2403 FAX (717) 654-4206
Valley Distributing and Storage Co., One Passan Drive, Wilkes-Barre, PA 18702

FIGURE 8-3 Ad Emphasizing a Warehouse's Centralized Location

Source: Courtesy of Valley Distributing and Storage Co. Reprinted with permission.

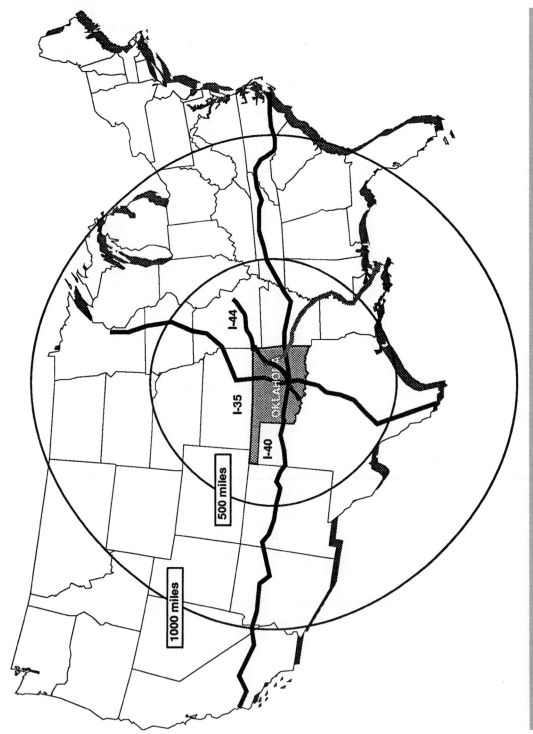

FIGURE 8-4 Truck Distances from Oklahoma

Source: Oklahoma Department of Commerce.

particular area so that companies can better serve their current and potential customers. What might not be as well-known is that customer considerations can also play a key role in the location of manufacturing plants. A recent study by the Manufacturer's Alliance revealed that the top two factors—by far—in plant location decisions were labor and proximity to customers.[16]

Customer considerations may be relevant in business-to-business (industrial) situations as well. One example involves so-called *supplier parks,* a concept that developed around automakers and their suppliers in Europe. In general, supplier parks "force their main component makers to locate in specially created industrial complexes adjacent to assembly plants."[17] Supplier parks, if well managed, offer the opportunity for increased efficiency and lower costs.

Trade Patterns

Firms producing consumer goods follow changes in population in order to better orient their distribution systems, and there are shifts in the markets for industrial goods as well. General sources of data regarding *commodity flows* can be studied, much like population figures, to determine changes occurring in the movement of raw materials and semi-processed goods. The availability and quality of such data often vary from country to country, and it may be difficult to compare data across countries because of different methodologies used to collect the data.

With respect to commodity flows, logisticians are especially interested in (1) how much is being produced and (2) where it is being shipped. If a firm is concerned with a distribution system for its industrial products, this information would tell how the market is functioning and, in many instances, how to identify both the manufacturers and their major customers. At this point, the researcher would understand the existing situation and would try to find a lower-cost production-distribution arrangement. Should the firm join the existing patterns of trade (which is easier to do in an expanding market) or should it produce at a point where no manufacturers of similar products are located?

The development and implementation of multicountry trade agreements have generated profound impacts on trade patterns. For example, the United States, Canada, and Mexico are part of the North American Free Trade Agreement (NAFTA). While Canada has long been the United State's largest trading partner, since NAFTA's passage, Mexico has become the United State's second-largest trading partner. From a logistics perspective, this has increased the north–south movement of product, and the Interstate 35 corridor (which runs north–south between Mexico and Canada) has become a hotbed for distribution activity. Oklahoma City, Oklahoma, and Dallas, Texas, are two locations along Interstate 35 that have seen a dramatic increase in the construction of distribution facilities in recent years.

Trade patterns have also been influenced among those countries that are members of the European Union (EU). The virtual elimination of trade barriers among EU member countries has allowed companies to move from having distribution facilities in many countries toward having one or two facilities. Because of their relatively central

---

[16]John S. McClenahen and Jill Jusko, "Labor Drives Location Decisions," *Industry Week,* August 13, 2001, pp. 12–13.

[17]Rhoda Miel, "European Cost-Cutting Concepts Cross Atlantic," *Automotive News,* January 14, 2002, pp. 18–19.

location and strong transportation infrastructures,[18] the so-called "Benelux" countries (Belgium, the Netherlands, Luxembourg) have become a favored location for distribution facilities to serve EU countries.

Quality of Life Considerations

An increasingly important locational factor is what can broadly be called *quality-of-life considerations*. While it may be difficult to develop a standardized list of quality-of-life factors, their intent is to incorporate nonbusiness factors into the business decision of where to locate a plant or distribution facility. For instance, *Expansion Management* magazine has developed a Quality of Life Quotient™ that measures approximately 50 different quality-of-life factors that compare the attractiveness of various U.S. metropolitan areas. The factors include cultural attractions such as a ballet and an orchestra, an area's cost of living, crime rates, and educational opportunities, among others.[19]

Quality-of-life considerations can be especially important when companies are thinking of facility locations in nondomestic countries. For example, despite temperatures that can reach 120 degrees for six months of the year, Dubai is viewed as a premier city in the Persian Gulf region—at least for prospective employers from Western Europe and North America. From a quality-of-life perspective, Dubai has a number of excellent hotels, a world-class airport, plentiful and affordable housing, low taxes and crime rates, shopping malls, and outstanding schools.[20]

Locating in Other Countries

Besides the considerations discussed previously, many other factors are to be considered if a firm is looking for a plant, office, or distribution site outside of its home country. Many of these considerations are governmental in nature and deal with the relevant legal system, political stability, bureaucratic red tape, corruption, protectionism, nationalism, privatization, and expropriation (confiscation), as well as treaties and trade agreements.

Social unrest and crime are concerns in many parts of the world and increase the risks associated with conducting business. Some of the world's more dangerous places, in terms of crime, include Washington, DC; Mexico City, Mexico; Sao Paolo, Brazil; and Moscow, Russia. In terms of social unrest, Israel, Pakistan, and India are areas of concern.

Other differences to be noted include culture, customs, holidays, language and language diversity, level of education, and religion. Currency fluctuations and devaluations can result in frequent cost changes for expatriate workers. Tax laws in the host country, and the ability to repatriate profits limit one's ability to use profits that operations in the host country might generate.

On an international scale, some workforces are considered mobile (migrants) and will move from one nation to another in search of work. Because of poor economic conditions in their home countries, migrant workers are quite willing to do menial jobs for very low pay. These workers travel from country to country, following jobs and

---

[18]Karen Thuermer, "IKEA Opens Massive Distribution Center Near Lyon," *Expansion Management,* January 2002, pp. 46–47.

[19]Bill King and Les Gramkow, "The Best Places to Live and Work," *Expansion Management,* May 2001, pp. 57–60.

[20]"Dubai Gets Hot," *Export Today's Global Business,* August 2000, p. 20.

sending part of their earnings back home. As this book is being revised, a political backlash against migrant workers appears to be developing, in that anti-migration politicians have won elected office in several European countries.

Specialized Location Characteristics

The preceding discussion focused on some of the more common general considerations in selecting the site of a manufacturing, distributing, or assembling facility. This section deals with more specialized, or site-specific, considerations that should be taken into account in the facility location decision. Most of these considerations are invisible boundaries that can be of great significance in the location decision.

Land may be zoned, which means that there are limits on how the land can be used. For example, a warehouse might be allowed only in areas set aside for wholesale or other specified commercial operations. Restrictions on manufacturing sites may be even more severe, especially if the operation might be viewed as an undesirable neighbor because of the fumes, noise, dust, smoke, or congestion it may create. Distribution facilities are often considered to be more desirable because the primary complaints tend to involve only traffic volume and congestion caused by the trucks that serve the facilities. If a community is attempting to encourage, or discourage, business activity, zoning classifications can be changed, although the process may be time-consuming.

Union locals have areas of jurisdiction, and a firm's labor relations manager may have distinct preferences with which locals he/she is willing to deal. Even though an individual union may ratify national labor agreements, local supplemental agreements often reflect the unique characteristics of a particular area. The different supplemental agreements provide companies with differing levels of managerial flexibility (or inflexibility).

Once a precise site is under consideration, many other issues should be dealt with before beginning construction or operations. For example, a title search may be needed to make sure that a particular parcel of land can be sold and that there are no liens against it. Engineers should examine the site to ensure that it has proper drainage and to ascertain the load-bearing characteristics of the soil.

Environmental regulations may require that due diligence be carried out with respect to who previously owned a prospective site and how it was used. For example, *brownfields,* "properties for which use and redevelopment is complicated by past use,"[21] sometimes contain hazardous waste materials, while in other cases the soil and water have been contaminated by previous users.

Another specialized location characteristic involves the weather, which, at a minimum, can affect transportation operations. Indeed, while it is well-known that Federal Express's first air hub was in Memphis, Tennessee, because of Memphis's central geographic location in the United States, it is less well-known that the Memphis airport has very few weather-related disruptions during the year.

Free Trade Zones

A highly specialized site in which to locate is a **free trade zone,** also known as *foreign trade zones* and *special economic zones.* Free trade zones have become extremely popular in recent years, with over 600 such zones worldwide, about 250 of which are

---

[21]www.brownfieldcentral.com.

located in the United States. Nondomestic merchandise may be stored, exhibited, processed, or used in manufacturing operations without being subjected to duties and quotas until the goods or their products enter the customs territory of the zone country. Free trade zones are often located at, or near, water ports, although they can also be located at, or near, airports. *Free trade subzones* refer to specific locations—such as an individual company—where goods can be stored, exhibited, processed, or manufactured on a duty-free basis. For example, General Motors has a number of free trade subzones located throughout the United States.[22]

Finding the Lowest-Cost Location

Many products are a combination of several material inputs and labor. Traditional site location theory can be used to show that one or several locations will minimize transportation costs. Figure 8-5 shows a laboratory-like piece of equipment that could be used to find the lowest-cost location, in terms of transportation, for assembling a product consisting of inputs from two sources and a market in a third area.

While most solutions to locational problems currently involve computer analysis, such analysis may not be needed if the relevant parameters are not too complex. Thus, grid systems can be used to determine an optimal location (defined as the lowest cost) for one additional facility.

Grid Systems

Grid systems are important to locational analysis because they allow one to analyze spatial relationships with relatively simple mathematical tools. **Grid systems** are checkerboard patterns that are placed on a map, as in Figure 8-6, and the grid is numbered in two directions: horizontal and vertical. Recall from geometry that the length of the hypotenuse of a right triangle is the square root of the sum of the squared values of the right triangle's two legs. Grid systems are placed so that they coincide with north–south and east–west lines on a map (although minor distortion is caused by the fact that east–west lines are parallel while north–south lines converge at both poles).

A **center-of-gravity approach** can be used for locating a single facility so that the distance to existing facilities is minimized. Figure 8-6 shows a grid system placed over a map of five existing retail stores. At issue is where a warehousing facility to serve these stores should be located. Assuming that each store receives the same volume and that straight-line distances are used, the best (lowest-cost) location for a warehousing facility to serve the five stores is determined by taking the average north–south coordinates and the average east–west coordinates of the retail stores.

In Figure 8-6, the grid system has its lower left (southwest) corner labeled as point zero, zero (0,0). The vertical (north–south) axis shows distances north of point 0,0. The horizontal (east–west) axis shows distances to the east. In this example, the average distance north is (3 + 1 + 3 + 2 + 3) or 12. This figure is divided by the number of stores (5), resulting in a north location of $\frac{12}{5}$ or 2.4 miles. The average distance east is (1 + 2 + 3 + 4 + 6) or 16; 16 divided by 5 equals 3.2 miles. Thus, the best (lowest-cost) location is one with coordinates 2.4 miles north and 3.2 miles east of point zero.

---

[22]See www.foreign-trade-zone.com.

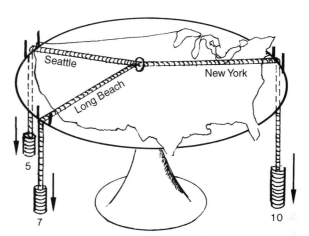

Seattle

New York

Long Beach

5

7

10

This is a simplified demonstration showing the various "pulls" which exist to determine the industrial location which minimizes the total ton miles of transportation used to transport both inputs and output. This method can be used for situations where there are "pulls" in three directions—either two sources of supply and one market, or one source of supply and two separate markets.

Assume we have two inputs, one produced in Long Beach and one produced in Seattle. The two inputs are combined to make a product which is sold in New York City. Assume further that to produce ten tons of the product consumed in New York, we must combine seven tons of the product which comes from Long Beach with five tons of the product which comes from Seattle. Assume finally that a transportation system is available anywhere and that the transport costs per ton mile are the same for either input or for the final product.

We take a circular table, placing a map of the U.S. on it and pairs of pegs on the table edge in the vicinity of Long Beach, Seattle, and New York as they are on the tabletop map. The pairs of pegs are so that a piece of string can pass between them.

We knot together three pieces of string, with all of them ending in one knot. To one of the pieces of string, which we pass through the pegs near Seattle on our map, we attach five identical metal washers (each one representing one ton). We attach seven washers to a second piece of string and pass it through the pegs in the vicinity of Long Beach on our tabletop map. To the third piece of string we attach ten washers and place it through the pegs in the vicinity of New York.

Then we take the knot and gently lift it to a point above the center of the table, with the washers on all three strings pulling down. We then drop the knot and it comes to rest at the spot on the map which represents the point in the U.S. where the manufacturing operation (for combining these two inputs into the single product) should locate. No other point will require less transportation effort—measured in ton-miles of freight moved.

(If transportation costs, or rates, differ on a per ton mile for each of the commodities or products involved, this can be taken into account by having the number of washers "weighted" to take into account the varying rates as well as the differences in weight being shippped. If for example in the situation described above carriers charged twice as much per ton mile to carry the finished product as they charged for carrying inputs, one would attach 20 washers (2 × 10) on the string reaching toward New York.)

Adapted from: Alfred Weber, *Theory of the Location of Industries,* translated by Carl J. Friedrich (Chicago: Univ. of Chicago Press, 1929).

FIGURE 8-5 Example of Transportation Forces Dictating Plant Location

Adapted from: Alfred Weber, *Theory of the Location of Industries,* translated by Carl J. Friedrich (Chicago: Univ. of Chicago Press, 1929).

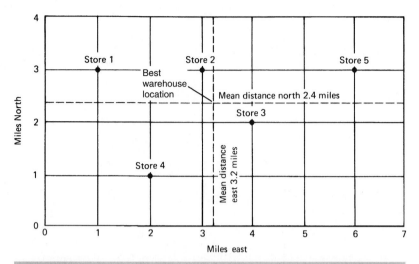

FIGURE 8-6 Center-of-Gravity Location for a Warehouse Serving Five Retail Stores

Because it's not likely that each store will place equal demands on a prospective warehousing facility, the center-of-gravity approach can be easily modified to take volume into account—the *weighted center-of-gravity approach.* The idea behind the weighted center-of-gravity approach is that a prospective warehousing facility will be located closer to the existing sites with the greatest current demand.

To illustrate the weighted center-of-gravity approach, consider the preceding five-store example, but modify the assumption that each store receives the same volume. Assume that store 1 receives 3 tons of shipments per month; store 2 receives 5 tons; store 3 receives 4 tons; store 4 receives 2 tons; and store 5 receives 6 tons. To calculate the north weighted center-of-gravity location, each north coordinate is multiplied by the corresponding volume and these values are summed; this total is then divided by the sum of the monthly volume. This procedure is repeated to calculate the east weighted center-of-gravity location.

The new data (see Table 8-1) indicate that the monthly volume for the five locations is 20 tons (3 + 5 + 4 + 2 + 6) and that the weighted center-of-gravity location is 2.6 miles north and 3.7 miles east. Thus, the weighted approach locates a warehousing facility slightly more north and more east than what was determined in the basic center-of-gravity approach (2.4 miles north; 3.2 miles east).

The two approaches just described are relatively simple and straightforward and the calculations can be done relatively quickly to provide approximate locations of centralized facilities, at least in a transportation sense. Because neither the center-of-gravity nor the weighted center-of-gravity approach is very sophisticated, adjustments may have to be made to take into account real-world considerations such as taxes, wage rates in particular locations, volume discounts, the cost and quality of transport services, and the fact that transport rates taper with increased distances. These considerations increase the complexity, as well as the time, to do the necessary calculations and partially explain why some companies have turned to specialized software packages to help them with facility location decisions.

TABLE 8-1 Weighted Center-of-Gravity Example

Store	North location	East location	Monthly volume (tons)	North × volume	East × volume
1	3	1	3	(3 × 3) = 9	(1 × 3) = 3
2	3	3	5	(3 × 5) = 15	(3 × 5) = 15
3	2	4	4	(2 × 4) = 8	(4 × 4) = 16
4	1	2	2	(1 × 2) = 2	(2 × 2) = 4
5	3	6	6	(3 × 6) = 18	(6 × 6) = 36
Total			20	52	74
Weighted average				2.6	3.7

Locating Inside Another Firm's Existing Channels

It is also possible to attempt to locate within another firm's existing channel structure. As pointed out in Chapter 1, a popular contemporary retail strategy involves *co-branding,* which refers to companies collaborating at one location where customers can purchase products from two or more name-brand companies. For example, the Starbucks Coffee Company has outlets located in select upscale department stores and lodging chains.

Dreyer's Ice Cream and Starbucks have a partnership for making several brands of coffee-flavored ice cream. Starbucks was able to utilize the Dreyer's direct-delivery-to-store system involving established transport routes and frozen-food carrying capability. Dreyer's also already had shelf space. It would have been prohibitively expensive for Starbucks to duplicate such a frozen-food distribution network.

It is generally believed that location within another firm's channel is feasible, assuming that the products involved are complementary. Many shopping malls, for example, have food courts that cater to the hungry and thirsty shopper—and increasingly, the food courts are populated by name-brand companies such as McDonald's, Pizza Hut, and Subway. Location within another firm's channels can be an excellent way of entering nondomestic markets. For example, when Starbucks initially expanded into Japan, it formed a joint venture with a Japanese restauranteur.

Facility Relocation and Facility Closing

Two specialized cases conclude this discussion of location choice, one involving facility relocation and the other involving facility closing. They are distinguished as follows: **facility relocation** is associated with business growth, while facility closing is associated with business contraction. More specifically, facility relocation occurs when a firm decides that it can no longer continue operations in its present facility and must move operations to another facility in order to better serve suppliers and/or customers. **Facility closing,** by contrast, occurs when a company decides to discontinue operations at a current site because the operations may no longer be needed or can be absorbed by other facilities. When the dot-com bubble burst in 2001, many firms in California's Silicon Valley went out of business.

A common reason for facility relocation involves a lack of room for expansion at a current site, often because of a substantial increase in business. In the United States, this has involved the relocation of industrial plants and warehousing facilities from aging and congested central cities to more attractive sites in suburban locations. Land costs and congestion in the central cities often make expansion difficult (or impossible), and transportation companies generally prefer the suburban sites because there is less traffic congestion to disrupt pickups and deliveries.

In theory, the relocation decision involves a comparison of the advantages and disadvantages of a new site to the advantages and disadvantages of an existing location. While this inevitably involves quantitative comparisons, companies should also consider the potential consequences of relocation on their human resources—consequences that may not be easily quantified.

Employers should keep current employees informed of planned relocations and how such relocations might affect them. Relocation information from other sources could lead to confusion, anger, and lower morale and could easily affect the productivity of the existing facility at a time when hiring replacements is likely to be very difficult. It's also important for employers to be cognizant of relevant legislation at the federal and state levels. For example, U.S. federal legislation in the form of the Worker Adjustment and Retraining Notification (WARN) Act mandates that employers give 60 days notice about plant closings and mass layoffs. Many individual states have additional requirements concerning large-scale employee layoffs.

In addition, while a company should develop policies for hiring workers at a relocated facility, these policies may be influenced to some extent by the union status of current employees. How many current employees will be offered positions at the new facility? Will the company use years of service, employee productivity, or other factors to decide who gets offered positions at the new facility? What percentage, if any, of relocation expenses will be paid by the employer? Will older employees be offered incentives to retire rather than relocate? Will employees who decide not to relocate be offered severance benefits?

Companies should also recognize that, no matter how well planned beforehand, a relocation from one facility to another is rarely trouble-free; at a minimum, relocation glitches can add to logistics costs and detract from customer service. For example, transferring equipment, furniture, and supplies from an old facility to a new one may take longer than expected. Also a newly constructed plant or warehousing facility is likely to have flaws or shortcomings that are only discovered after occupancy.

Facility closings can occur for various reasons, such as eliminating redundant capacity in mergers and acquisitions, improving supply-chain efficiency, poor planning, or an insufficient volume of business. An orderly process for facility location and relocation is essential, as is an orderly process for facility closings. Companies should seek answers to a number of different questions before proceeding with facility closings: Why should a facility be closed? What are the costs of closing a facility? What are the benefits of closing a facility? Are there alternate uses or customers for the facility? What will happen to the furniture and equipment in the facility?

While facility closings are largely a business-oriented decision, substantial obstacles can be part of closing individual facilities. Union contracts, for example, may prohibit (or limit) certain facilities from being closed. The human impact of facility closings should be considered as well; individuals are not only losing their jobs and pay, but some individuals may suffer a loss of self-esteem as well. Unpleasant as that may be, employees should be kept informed by their employers throughout the closing process.

Poorly handled facility closings often result in tremendous amounts of unwanted negative publicity for a company, as illustrated during the bankruptcy of LTV Steel in the early twenty-first century. Unfortunately, many LTV workers first learned about key pieces of information from various media, including television and the Internet, before being notified by the company.[23]

SUMMARY

This chapter discussed several issues associated with the location of warehousing, manufacturing, and assembly facilities. General factors in facility location were looked at, including population and trade patterns. Population characteristics are a double-edged sword in facility location in the sense that population serves both as a market for goods as well as a source of labor. Changing trade patterns, spurred in part by multicountry trade alliances, have had a profound influence with respect to the location of distribution facilities.

This chapter also discussed specialized location characteristics, with a particular emphasis on free trade zones. It presented several examples of how grid systems can be useful for determining the lowest-cost location for a facility. The chapter concluded with a look at facility relocation and facility closing. Companies should be cognizant of the human dimension associated with both relocation and closing.

QUESTIONS FOR DISCUSSION AND REVIEW

1. How can advances in technology and communication influence the facility location decision?
2. Discuss the factors that influence the number of facilities that a firm chooses to operate.
3. Briefly describe the general factors influencing facility location.
4. How does a raw material's status as pure, weight-losing, or weight-gaining influence the facility location decision?
5. Discuss how environmental considerations might influence the facility location decision.
6. Discuss how population can be viewed as both a market for goods and a source of labor.
7. How might the factors considered important for locating a manufacturing facility differ from the factors considered important for locating a distribution facility?
8. Discuss the advantages and disadvantages to locating manufacturing, assembly, and/or distribution facilities in countries with relatively low wages.
9. What are right-to-work laws? How do they influence locational decisions?
10. What is an expatriate worker? What challenges do they face?
11. Do you think inventories should be taxed? Why or why not?
12. What are empowerment zones? What is their relevance to locational decisions?
13. What mode of transportation do you think is the most important to firms when evaluating new sites? Why?
14. What are supplier parks? Give some examples.
15. Discuss how multicountry trade agreements have influenced the location of production and/or distribution facilities.
16. What quality-of-life considerations do you think are the most important for locational decisions? Why?
17. Beyond the general factors discussed in this chapter, what additional considerations are important when a firm is thinking of locating a facility (facilities) in other countries?

---

[23]Jennifer Scott Cimperman and Sandra Livingston, "Stumbling LTV Losing Support, Critics Say; Poor Handling of Crisis Has Angered Public, Union and Politicians," *The Plain Dealer,* April 15, 2001, pg. 1A +.

18. What is a free trade zone? What functions might be performed in it?
19. Discuss advantages and disadvantages to grid systems, such as the center-of-gravity and weighted center-of-gravity approaches.
20. Distinguish between facility relocation and facility closing. How should companies deal with their human resources (workers) in both situations?

SUGGESTED READINGS

Arntzen, Bruce C., Daniel W. Mulgrew, and Garry J. Sjolander. "Redesigning 3M's Worldwide Product Supply Chains." *Supply Chain Management Review,* Winter 1998, pp. 16–27.

Garretson, Sara P. "Successful Site Selection: A Case Study." *IIE Solutions,* Vol. 32, No. 4, 2000, pp. 33–37.

Ietto-Gillies, Grazia. "What Role for Multinationals in the New Theories of International Trade and Location?" *International Review of Applied Economics,* Vol. 14, No. 4, 2000, pp. 413–426.

"Meet the Gurus of Site Selection," *Corporate Location,* March/April 2001, pp. 16–20.

Morphy, Erika. "Sweatshops in the Supply Chain," *Export Today's Global Business,* Vol. 16, No. 10, 2000, pp. 22–29.

Schlegel, Gregory L. "Supply Chain Optimization: A Practitioner's Perspective." *Supply Chain Management Review,* Winter 1999, pp. 50–57.

Vlachopoulou, Maro, George Silleos, and Vassiliki Manthou. "Geographic Information Systems in Warehouse Site Selection Decisions." *International Journal of Production Economics,* Vol. 71, No. 3, 2001, pp. 205–212.

Watts, Charles A. "Using a Personal Computer to Solve a Warehouse Location/Consolidation Problem." *Production & Inventory Management Journal,* Vol. 41, No. 4, 2000, pp. 23–28.

C A S E S

Case 8-1   Aero Marine Logistics

Aero Marine Logistics (AML) was incorporated as a Private Limited Company in South Delhi in the year 1996. The promoters of AML are two professionals who had gathered 15 years of experience working for Tata Steel (one of the biggest and oldest companies in India) in the field of shipping, customs clearance, forwarding, and transportation. Over the last 5 years, AML has been successful in building an infrastructure and pool of experienced personnel to handle the entire gamut of logistics. In fact, it was one of the first companies to offer door-to-door delivery. It considers itself the specialists in customized solutions and services—a concept that is still unheard of in the transportation industry in the rural belts of northern India. AML handles the entire package of logistics for all its customers. Some of the services they offer include the following:

- *Import consolidation.* AML has a well-spread network of offices and trade connections in the United States, Europe, the Far East, and the Middle East to render import consolidation by both air and sea to any part of India. It promises a personalized prompt service with value for cost.
- *Door-to-door services.* AML is fully equipped to deliver door to door, which includes cargo pickup from the supplier's warehouse, warehousing prior to customs clearance, complete customs clearance of exports from overseas, and freight booking with airlines/shipping lines to receive cargo in India. It also undertakes local customs clearance and transportation to deliver to the door of the customer.
- *Exports.* AML has expertise in handling exports of various kinds of cargo by ocean

and by air freight. It ensures the timely movement of cargo at the most competitive rates. It takes care of both the complete export documentation formalities and the physical movement of cargo.
- *Consultancy on customs and logistics.* AML is well equipped with professionals to guide customers regarding various modes of transportation and to help customers to optimize utilization of space and save on freight. It acts as liaison with different authorities like the RBI (Reserve Bank of India), Port Authority of India, India Civil Aviation Regulatory Body, TEXPROCIL (The Cotton Textiles Export Promotion Council of India), DGFT (Directorate General of Foreign Trade), etc., on behalf of clients for various permissions and quotas related to import and export of cargo. This could perhaps be classified as its most valuable service, which it hopes will build up its brand image. The red tape, bureaucracy, lack of work ethic and corruption preclude anyone lacking either clout or established relationship channels (with *babus* or permanent government employees notorious for their apathy toward fulfilling job duties and with a penchant for bribe taking) to do business in India.

To enable it to offer these services, AML has partnered with various associates all over the globe to render forwarding services to all its customers. It has covered warehouse space of 1,000 square meters and has the ability to arrange for additional space. It has its own two 407 Tata trucks for pickup and delivery of small consignments. It has dedicated a fleet of five low-bed trailers for pickup and delivery of containers. All the field personnel have been provided with two-wheelers for faster conveyance between various points of work.

AML has grown rapidly and recently established an online presence whereby clients can place orders online and check the status of their cargo. So far the increase in sales from the online presence has not been much. Most of AML's clients are spread out in rural areas and, except for customers in Delhi, most do not have access to the Internet.

Today AML is handling an average of 200-plus TEUs (20-foot container equivalents) of imports and exports every month between Delhi and Mumbai (Bombay), which is the nearest big port (a distance of 1,407 kilometers). (See Exhibit 8-A.) Luckily, most containers are used for traffic in both directions; moving empties is

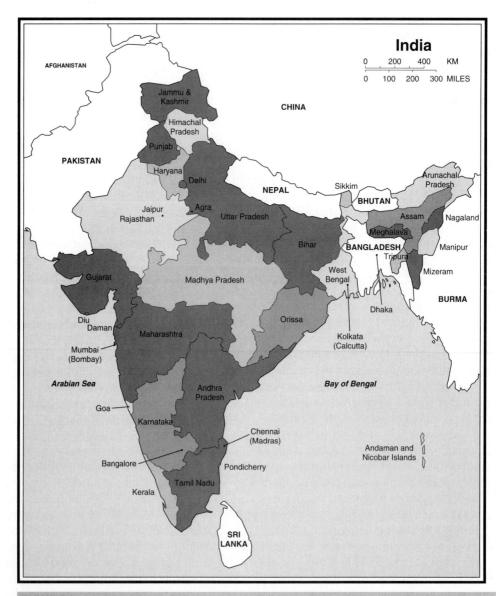

EXHIBIT 8-A Map of India

unproductive. Main items for export are bathroom fittings and spares, machine spares and agricultural equipment, machine spares and chemicals, scientific equipment, medical equipment spares and chemicals, food processing machinery, furniture and kitchen equipment, and interiors. Main items for import are automobile engines and spares, cotton yarn, food products, electronics, televisions and components, rice, stone for stone crafting, etc.

Recently, one of the AML partners, Mr. S. Singh, was approached by the chairman of Freshfoods, Mr. R. Maan, with a promise of a huge potential volume (150,000 kilograms per month) for importing frozen mushrooms from Europe if AML would build up its Indian infrastructure to handle such volumes. Freshfoods is the biggest regional exporter/importer of food products in North India. It was founded 20 years ago by a collective of farmers wanting to find markets for their surplus produce of exotic and non-native foods (like avocados, strawberries, etc.) that did not have much local demand except for five-star hotels catering to mostly foreign tourists. The shift in eating habits in recent years had prompted Mr. Maan to promote mushrooms as a daily food item in a major way. To keep the price of imported mushrooms comparable with locally grown food items, huge quantities would have to be transacted to make use of economies of scale.

Mr. Singh realized that the first order from Mr. Maan was an experiment and that further orders would depend on whether the product caught on or not. AML needed to bet on a huge surge in demand for frozen mushrooms in the region if it wanted to be part of this new trend from the very beginning. Singh's partner—Mr. Kumar—is wary of investing heavily on the basis of this one order. After some bargaining, Mr. Mann agreed that Freshfoods would ship approximately 150,000 kilograms of mushrooms per month, for 12 months, and will pay $.20US per kilogram of mushrooms.

If AML decided to handle this product, it would need to add some equipment to its flatbed trailers to provide power to the refrigeration units on the containers. This is a one-time cost of 9 lakhs (one lakh = $2,222US). With temperatures soaring to 50 degrees Celsius (and the hot wind called *loo*—notorious for deaths associated with heat waves), for most of the long hot summer the energy costs of meeting special conditions could be prohibitive. AML expects them to total about 3 lakhs on an annual basis.

Mr. Singh then made inquiries to his rail carrier about the costs of leasing refrigerated containers. He was disappointed to learn that leasing was almost impossible. The container leasing companies wanted exorbitant rates because there was no backhaul traffic requiring refrigerated equipment and because some areas in North India were too isolated if they needed to send a worker to service malfunctioning equipment. The container leasing company did, however, offer to sell used refrigerated 20-foot containers for 7 lakhs apiece and would agree to service them for one year at an additional cost of 1 lakh per container. The used containers could be expected to last another 5 years. In a meeting involving Mr. Singh, Mr. Maan, and Mr. Veejay, a carrier representative, it was decided that ten 20-foot containers would be sufficient to handle the projected volume of mushrooms. Each container would make one round-trip each month. The cost of ocean freight expense from Amsterdam to Mumbai is $1700US for a single 20-foot container. The cost of land transportation per single 20-foot container from Mumbai to Delhi is $300US. Return costs for empty containers from Delhi to Mumba to Amsterdam are half as much, although about 10 percent of the time another cargo can be found that will cover the costs of return transport.

As the meeting broke up, Mr. Veejay said that the mushrooms were not a very dense cargo and that Mr. Singh could be using 40-foot refrigerated containers, which held twice as much as a 20-foot container, though handling costs were less than twice as much. The cost of ocean freight from Amsterdam to Mumbai is $2600US for a single 40-foot container. The cost of transportation per single 40-foot container from Mumbai to Delhi is $500US. Return costs from Delhi to Mumbai to Amsterdam are half as much, although about ten percent of the time another cargo can be found that will cover the costs of return transport. Mr. Veejay felt that the 40-foot containers would need to be purchased. Five would be needed, with each making one round-trip per month.

Containers were only available new, and the cost would be 15 lakhs apiece. Maintenance anywhere was guaranteed for the first year, and the containers had an estimated life of 10 years.

QUESTIONS

1. What would the first-year costs be to AML if it purchased the ten used 20-foot containers? How long would it take to recoup the investment, assuming that the mushroom traffic continued?

2. What would the first-year costs be to AML if it purchased five new 40-foot containers? How long would it take to recoup the investment, assuming that the mushroom traffic continued?

3. Is one of the alternatives in questions 1 and 2 riskier? Why?

4. Mr. Singh has read about the supply-chain concept that attempts to identify and link all the participants from suppliers' suppliers to customers' customers. Who are all the participants in the supply chain, a part of which has been discussed in the case?

5. Logistics partnerships involve sharing costs and risks. What are *all* the costs and risks that this venture entails? How might they be shared?

6. With some help from your instructor, divide into groups representing most or all of the supply-chain members identified in question 4 and negotiate an agreement or agreements that share the costs, risks, and possible profits and losses from the venture being considered.

Case 8-2 Alberta Highway Department, Region VI

The Alberta Highway Department, Region VI, is headquartered in an area west of Lethbridge, Calgary, and Red Deer. One of its most important responsibilities, in the public's mind, is to keep open Canadian Route 1, which travels across all of Canada. At the very west of Region VI are the Rocky Mountains, and in a 6-mile stretch between Lake Louise and the British Columbia border, the highway climbs from 3,000 to 6,000 feet. The climb in this stretch is uniform, the road's elevation increases 500 feet each mile as it moves to the west (see Exhibit 8-B).

A highway maintenance station is near Lake Louise, 1 mile to the east of the 6-mile section. At this station are based several heavy-duty dump trucks that in the winter are mounted with snowplows in the front and sand-spreading devices in the rear.

Sanding is used after frost or freezing rains and in the spring when melting snows refreeze at night. The higher elevations require more sanding because they are subject to more freezing temperatures. For more than 10 years, since the highway was opened, records have been kept for the amount of maintenance required by each mile of highway. In terms of sanding, the average number of days per year that each mile requires sanding are as follows:

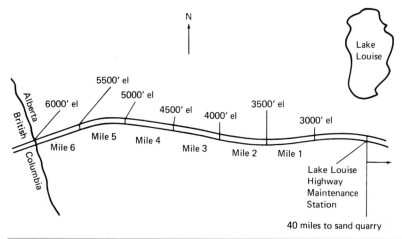

EXHIBIT 8-B Canadian Route I

Mile 1   3000'–3500' elevation 40 days
Mile 2   3500'–4000' elevation 48 days
Mile 3   4000'–4500' elevation 53 days
Mile 4   4500'–5000' elevation 58 days
Mile 5   5000'–5500' elevation 65 days
Mile 6   5500'–6000' elevation 70 days

The dump trucks can carry 10 tons of sand, which is enough to spread over 1 mile of highway in both the eastbound and westbound lanes. Spreading sand is a slow process because, under slippery conditions, highway traffic moves slowly. Several trucks are required because when sanding is needed, it is needed quickly.

At the Lake Louise maintenance station are large silos for holding the salt-treated sand. At present, the silos can hold nearly 6,000 tons of sand, some of which is used for lower stretches of highway. During the summer months, the silos are filled by special trailer dump trucks that carry the sand up from a quarry near Bow Valley, 40 miles to the east of the Lake Louise maintenance station. The silo is designed so that it can be split into two. Split segments of the silo can hold different capacities or equal capacities of sand. However, their total capacity is 6,000 tons.

Through a departmental program for encouraging employee suggestions, a proposal had been received from a sander truck driver

that a portion of the Lake Louise sand silos be moved west toward the higher elevations, where more frequent sandings are needed.

The highway was constructed so that at 1-mile distances (in this case, at elevations of 3,000, 3,500, 4,000, 5,000, 5,500, and 6,000 feet) it is possible for maintenance trucks to turn around. The shoulders are also wide enough at these points so that the silos can be placed alongside. The silo relocation can be performed during summer months using regular maintenance crews and equipment, with no additional costs.

The principal reason for splitting and relocating a portion of the silos is to place sand closer to where it is needed and to reduce the travel time of maintenance trucks to and from the silos. The work crews are paid a constant rate for a fixed number of hours; if they are not sanding, they are performing other tasks. Hence, the only relevant costs are those of truck operation.

The facts and assumptions to be used in the analysis follow:

1. Costs of trucking sand from the quarry to the Lake Louise silos or to the relocated silos are 3 cents per ton-mile for the length of the full haul in one direction. (Empty backhaul costs are taken into account by these calculations.)

2. Some sand silo capacity must be kept at the Lake Louise maintenance station.

3. Spreader dump trucks are more costly to operate for carrying sand between silos and to where it is needed. The cost is 10 cents per ton-mile (which also takes empty backhauls into account).

4. No costs are assigned for spreader trucks to reach silos initially. The reason for this is that they are randomly located on the highway at the time the decision is made to spread sand. Truck crews are then dispatched by radio.

5. If a new silo is located, it must be at one of the turnaround sites between each of the miles.

6. If a new silo is located an even number of miles from the Lake Louise station, a mid-point will be established halfway between the two silos and sanders will load at the silo nearest the mile of road needing sand.

7. If a new silo is located an odd number of miles from the Lake Louise maintenance station, a determination must be made as to which silo will provide sand for the middle one. (This is because maintenance trucks cannot turn at the middle of mile sections.)

8. No costs are assigned to operating the spreaders within a mile on either side of the silo. This is because they start spreading sand immediately upon leaving the silo. However, for sanding a stretch that is, say, between 2 and 3 miles from the silo, the cost of reaching the area would be $2 (10 tons × 10 cents × 2 miles).

QUESTIONS

1. Should one portion of sand silos at the Lake Louise maintenance station be relocated to a point to the west at a higher elevation? If yes, where should it be relocated, how much capacity should it have, and what are the projected annual savings in truck operating costs? Show your work.

2. Assume that it is discovered that it would be impossible to split the silo into sections. However, it would be feasible to move the entire silo to a site farther up the slope. The section of highway from the Lake Louise maintenance station stretching west 1 mile to where it reaches the 3,000-foot elevation point must be sanded for 30 days per year. All points east of the Lake Louise maintenance station can be serviced from other points. Should the entire silo be moved to another point? If so, to where? What will the savings be? Show your work.

3. Ignore all statements made in question 2 and assume, instead, that the silo can be divided into three sections: one remaining at Lake Louise and the other two located somewhere along the 6-mile stretch. If two sections are to be located within the 6-mile section, where should they be placed? What will the savings be over the present system? Show your work.

4. This case was written some time ago, when fuel costs were very low. Assume now that the spreader dump truck costs 35 cents per ton-mile to operate (compared to 10 cents) and that the trailer dump truck used to move sand from the quarry costs 20 cents per ton-mile to operate (up from 3 cents). Answer question 1 again, but this time take into account the new truck operating costs.

5. Answer question 2 again but using the new trucking costs outlined in question 4.

6. Answer question 3 again, taking into account the new trucking costs outlined in question 4.

CHAPTER

9

Inventory Management

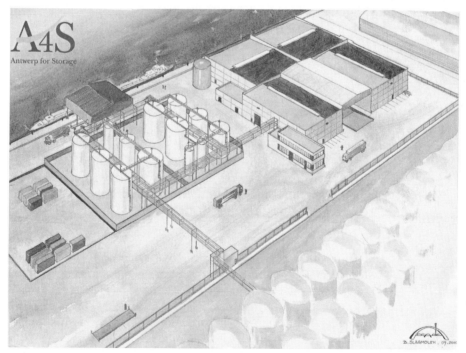

This facility, located in the Port of Antwerp, is designed for the storage and handling of hazardous materials. The facility serves deep-sea ships, barges, rail, and trucks. Some of the value-added services the operator offers are bagging, drumming, container stacking; filtration, heating, and sampling. Each tank is served by a separate, dedicated route of pumps and piping. The facility is operated as a 50/50 joint venture between a terminal company and a chemicals distributor.
Source: A4S N. V. (Antwerp for Storage).

Key Terms

- ABC analysis
- Economic order quantity (EOQ)
- Fixed order interval system
- Fixed order quantity system
- Handling costs
- Insurance costs
- Inventory carrying (holding) costs
- Inventory shrinkage
- Marginal analysis

- Obsolescence
- Opportunity cost
- Reorder point (ROP)
- Safety stocks
- Stockouts
- Storage costs
- Taxes
- Vendor-managed inventory (VMI)

Learning Objectives

- To determine the costs of holding inventory
- To identify the costs associated with a stockout
- To understand the EOQ concept
- To differentiate the various inventory flow patterns
- To appreciate the role of scanners in inventory control

Inventories are stocks of goods and materials that are maintained for many purposes, the most common being to satisfy normal demand patterns. In production and selling processes, inventories serve as cushions to accommodate the fact that items arrive in one pattern and are used in another pattern. For example, if you eat one egg a day and buy eggs by the dozen, every 12 days you would buy a new container of eggs, and the inventory of eggs remaining in your refrigerator declines at the rate of one egg per day. Figure 9-1 shows a bulk handling operation where a bin is between a vessel being discharged and a truck being loaded.

Inventory management is a key component of supply-chain management, in part because inventory decisions are often a starting point, or driver, for other business activities such as warehousing, transportation, and materials handling. Moreover, different organizational functions can have different inventory management objectives. Marketing, for example, tends to want to ensure that sufficient inventory is available for customer demand in order to avoid potential stockout situations—which translates into higher inventory levels. Alternatively, the finance group generally seeks to minimize the costs associated with holding inventory, which translates into lower inventory levels. As if managing these seemingly conflicting objectives within one organization isn't challenging enough, supply chains are made up of multiple organizations—each of which may have its own distinct inventory management philosophy. Indeed, each link in the supply chain would prefer having other links maintain the inventory.

One of the most prominent concerns about inventory is its cost, which is presented in greater detail later in this chapter. It is important to note here that because inventory costs money, increases in inventory are not always desirable. For example, a firm may manufacture much more than it can reasonably sell, or a firm may manufacture products so that its warehousing facilities look full.

It is also important to recognize that inventory carries its greatest cost after value has been added through manufacturing and processing; finished goods inventories are,

FIGURE 9-1 Coal Is Being Unloaded at Longview, Washington

Coal from the ship is dumped into the bin, where it is fed by a conveyor belt to the waiting trucks. The inventory of coal in the bin act as a cushion between the differing rates of loading and unloading.
Source: Port of Longview, Washington.

therefore, much more expensive to hold than raw materials or work in progress. Carrying costs for inventories can be significant, and the return on investment to a firm for its funds tied up in inventory should be as high as the return it can obtain from other, equally risky uses of the same funds.

The focus on inventory costs has intensified in recent years because of concern with inventory turnover, or the number of times that inventory is sold in a 1-year period. Inventory turnover can be calculated by dividing the cost of goods sold for a particular period by the average inventory for that period. For example, if the cost of goods sold annually is $200,000 and average inventory on hand is $50,000, inventory turnover equals 4.

While there is no optimal inventory turnover ratio, inventory turnover figures can provide important insights about an organization's competitiveness and efficiency. Thus, a particular organization can compare its turnover figures to those of direct competitors and/or other organizations with "desirable" turnover ratios. With respect to efficiency, low turnover indicates that a company is taking longer to sell its inventory, perhaps because of product obsolescence or pricing problems.[1] By contrast, high turnover may signal a low level of inventories, which can increase the chance of product stockouts. The fact that stockouts can be quite costly to an organization is explored later in this chapter.

It's easy to say that organizations should strive for a proper balance of inventory; actually achieving it can be quite difficult because of the trade-offs that are involved. On the one hand, low inventory turnover results in high inventory carrying costs and low (or no) stockout costs. On the other hand, higher inventory turnover results in low inventory carrying costs and some (high) stockout costs.

This chapter begins with a look at various classifications of inventory and a discussion of inventory-related costs, followed by discussion of when to order and how much to order. This chapter also looks at several contemporary approaches to managing inventory. It concludes with a discussion of special concerns related to inventory management.

Inventory Classifications

It's important to know the key classifications of inventory because the classification influences the way that inventory is managed. While inventory generally exists to service demand, in some situations inventory is carried to stimulate demand, also known as *psychic stock*. This type of inventory is associated with retail stores, and the general idea is that customer purchases are stimulated by inventory that they can see.[2] This concept helps to explain, in part, why some retailers stock huge amounts of certain merchandise.

Inventory that services demand is most frequently classified as cycle (base) stock, safety (buffer) stock, pipeline (in-transit) stock, or speculative stock. Each type is explained in the following paragraphs.

Cycle, or base, stock refers to inventory that is needed to satisfy normal demand during the course of an order cycle. With respect to the egg example at the beginning of this chapter, one dozen (12) eggs represents the cycle stock—we use one egg per day and we buy eggs every 12 days.

Safety, or buffer, stock refers to inventory that is held in addition to cycle stock to guard against uncertainty in demand and/or lead time. For example, uncertainty in demand could come from the fact that you occasionally decide to make a three-egg omelet as opposed to eating one egg per day. As an example of lead-time uncertainty, you may sometimes buy eggs every 14 days, rather than every 12 days. In both cases, a few extra eggs would ensure that you won't run out of eggs.

[1] " 'Turns' for the Better—Inventory Turns Impact Profits and Stock Prices," *Dow Theory Forecasts,* Vol. 58, No. 4, 2002, pp. 1, 4.

[2] Paul D. Larson and Robert A. DeMaris, "Psychic Stock: An Independent Variable Category of Inventory," *International Journal of Physical Distribution & Logistics Management,* Vol. 20, No. 7, 1990, pp. 27–37.

Pipeline, or in-transit, stock is inventory that is en route between various nodes (i.e., fixed facilities such as a plant, warehouse, store) in a logistics system. Pipeline inventory is represented here by eggs that are in transit between a chicken farm and, say, a food wholesaler's distribution center or between the retail store and your kitchen.

Speculative stock refers to inventory that is held for several reasons, including seasonal demand, projected price increases, and potential shortages of product. For example, the fact that eggs are associated with Easter (e.g., Easter egg rolls, colored eggs) tends to cause an increase in demand for them prior to the Easter holiday.

Inventory-Related Costs

Inventory Carrying Costs

As noted, a prominent concern involves the costs associated with holding inventory, which are referred to as **inventory carrying (holding) costs.** In general, inventory carrying costs are expressed in percentage terms, and this percentage is multiplied by the inventory's value. The resulting number represents the dollar value associated with holding the particular inventory. So, if the value of a particular item is $100 and the inventory carrying costs are 18 percent, the relevant annual inventory expense is $18.

Not surprisingly, an increase or decrease in the carrying cost percentage will affect the relevant inventory expense. Generally speaking, companies prefer to carry lower inventory as the carrying cost percentage increases, in part because there is greater risk (e.g., obsolescence) to holding the inventory. As a result, the determination of a carrying cost percentage should be quite important for many companies. Surprisingly, however, the calculation of a carrying cost percentage can be quite unstructured; some organizations, for instance, simply pick a percentage figure for carrying costs.[3] In fact, a commonly used estimate today for inventory carrying costs is 25 percent—a figure that dates from the mid-1950s.[4]

Inventory carrying costs consist of a number of different factors or categories, and the importance of these factors can vary from product to product. For example, perishable items such as dairy products, meat, and poultry are often sold with expiration dates, causing them to have little or no value after a certain date. By contrast, a box of lead pencils loses its value much more slowly through time. These two examples illustrate the **obsolescence** category of inventory carrying costs and refer to the fact that products lose value through time. Note that some products lose their value much more quickly than do others.

Inventory shrinkage is another component of inventory carrying cost and refers to the fact that more items are recorded entering than leaving warehousing facilities. Shrinkage is generally caused by damage, loss, or theft, and while shrinkage costs can be reduced, such efforts often generate other costs. For example, while better packaging may reduce damage, loss, or theft costs, better packaging likely translates into increased packaging costs.

---

[3]"Inventory Carrying Costs: Is There a 'Right' Way to Calculate Them?" *Ioma's Report on Managing Logistics,* February 2002, pp. 6, 7, 10.

[4]See L.P. Alford and John R. Bangs (eds.), *Production Handbook,* New York: Ronald, 1955.

Another component of inventory carrying costs, **storage costs,** refers to those costs associated with occupying space in a plant, storeroom, or warehousing facility. Some products have very specialized storage requirements; ice cream, for example, must be stored at a temperature below −20 degrees Fahrenheit. **Handling costs** involve the costs of employing staff to receive, store, retrieve, and move inventory. There may also be inventory **insurance costs,** which insure inventory against fire, flood, theft, and other perils. Insurance costs are not uniform across products; diamonds, for example, are more costly to insure than shampoo.

Taxes represent yet another component of inventory carrying costs, and they are calculated on the basis of the inventory on hand on a particular date; considerable effort is made to have that day's inventory be as low as possible. Some states (such as Nevada) have become popular locations for distribution facilities due to their low, or nonexistent, inventory taxes as well as their proximity to large markets in nearby inventory-taxing states. Furthermore, **interest charges** take into account the money that is required to maintain the investment in inventory. In the United States, the prime rate of interest has traditionally provided a convenient starting point when estimating the interest charges associated with maintaining inventory.

Some inventory items have other types of carrying costs because of their specialized nature. Pets and livestock, for example, must be watered and fed. Tropical fish must be fed and have oxygen added to the water in which they are kept. Another cost, although it is generally excluded from carrying cost, is **opportunity cost**—the cost of taking a position in the wrong materials. This can be an issue for those companies that engage in speculative inventory. Opportunity costs are also incurred by firms that hold too much inventory in reserve for customer demand.

Stockout Costs

If avoiding an oversupply were the only problem associated with inventories, the solution would be relatively simple: Store fewer items. However, not having enough items can be as bad as, and sometimes worse than, having too many items. Such costs can accrue during **stockouts,** when customers demand items that aren't immediately available.

Although calculation of stockout costs can be difficult and inexact, it is important for organizations to do so because such knowledge can be beneficial when determining how much inventory to hold, while remembering that a trade-off must be balanced between inventory carrying costs and stockout costs. Estimating the costs or penalty for a stockout involves an understanding of customer reaction to a company being out of stock when a customer wants to buy an item.

Consider the following customer responses to a particular stockout situation. How should they be evaluated?

1. The customer says, "I'll be back," and this proves to be so.
2. The customer says, "Call me when it's in."
3. The customer buys a substitute product that yields a higher profit for the seller.
4. The customer buys a substitute product that yields a lower profit for the seller.
5. The customer places an order for the item that is out of stock (a *back order*) and asks to have the item delivered when it arrives.
6. The customer goes to a competitor only for this purchase.
7. The customer goes to a competitor for this and all future purchases.

TABLE 9-1 Determination of the Average Cost of a Stockout

Alternative	Loss	Probability	Average Cost
1. Brand-loyal customer	$ 00.00	.10	$ 00.00
2. Switches and comes back	37.00	.65	24.05
3. Lost customer	1,200.00	.25	300.00
Average cost of a stockout		1.00	$324.05

These are hypothetical figures for illustration.

Clearly, each of these situations has a different cost to the company experiencing a stockout. For example, the loss in situation 1 is negligible because the sale is only slightly delayed. The outcome from situation 2 is more problematic in that the company doesn't know whether the customer will, in fact, return. Situation 7 is clearly the most damaging, because the customer has been lost for good, and it's necessary to know the cost of developing a new customer to replace the lost customer. A commonly used guideline is that it costs five times as much to get a new customer as it does to retain an existing one.

To illustrate the calculation of stockout costs, assume for simplicity's sake that customer responses to a stockout can be placed into three categories: *delayed sale* (brand loyalty), *lost sale* (switches and comes back), and *lost customer.* Assume further that, over time, of 300 customers who experienced a stockout, 10 percent delayed the sale, 65 percent switched and came back, while the remaining 25 percent were lost for good (see Table 9-1).

The probability of each event taking place can be used to determine the average cost of a stockout. More specifically, as illustrated in Table 9-1, each probability is multiplied by the respective loss to yield an average cost per event. These average costs are then summed, and the result is the average cost per stockout. A delayed sale is virtually costless because the customer is brand loyal and will purchase the product when it becomes available. The lost sale alternative results in a loss of the profit that would have been made on the customer's purchase. In the lost customer situation, the customer buys a competitor's product and decides to make all future purchases from that competitor; the relevant cost involved is that of developing a new customer.

Although the example presented in Table 9-1 is quite simplified, several important points bear highlighting. As a general rule, the higher the average cost of a stockout, the better it is for the company to hold some amount of inventory (**safety stock**) to protect against stockouts. Second, the higher the probability of a delayed sale, the lower the average stockout costs—and the lower the inventory that needs to be held by a company. Table 9-1 provides strong evidence for the importance of a company's developing brand-loyal customers.

Trade-Offs Exist Between Carrying and Stockout Costs

As mentioned, higher levels of inventory can lessen the occurrence of stockouts. **Marginal analysis,** which focuses on the trade-off between carrying and stockout costs, allows a company to determine an optimum level of safety stocks. Marginal analysis helps define the point at which the costs of holding additional safety stock are equal to the savings in stockout costs avoided.

TABLE 9-2 Determination of Safety Stock Level

Number of Units of Safety Stock	Total Value of Safety Stock ($480 per Unit)	25% Annual Carrying Cost	Carrying Cost of Incremental Safety Stock	Number of Additional Orders Filled	Additional Stockout Costs Avoided
10	$ 4,800	$1,200	$1,200	20	$6,481.00
20	9,600	2,400	1,200	16	5,184.80
30	14,400	3,600	1,200	12	3,888.60
40	19,200	4,800	1,200	8	2,592.40
50	24,000	6,000	1,200	6	1,944.30
60	28,800	7,200	1,200	4	1,296.20
70	33,600	8,400	1,200	3	972.15

An example of marginal analysis is presented in Table 9-2. In this example, we assume that inventory can only be ordered in multiples of 10 and that each unit of inventory is valued at $480 with carrying costs of 25 percent. As a result, the incremental carrying costs of moving from 0 units of safety stock to 10 units of safety stock are (10 × $480) × .25, or $1,200. Likewise, the incremental carrying costs of moving from 10 to 20 units of safety stock are $1,200.

This example also assumes that the various levels of safety stock prevent a certain number of stockouts. For example, holding 10 units of safety stock for an entire year allows the firm to prevent 20 stockouts; moving from 10 units to 20 units of safety stock allows 16 additional orders to be filled. Using the average cost of a stockout ($324.05) from Table 9-1, a safety stock of 10 units allows the firm to prevent 20 stockouts, which saves the firm $6,481 ($324.05 × 20). The savings of $6,481 is much greater than the additional carrying costs of $1,200, so the firm wants to hold at least 10 units of safety stock. Twenty units of safety stock result in $1,200 of additional carrying costs, while the additional stockout costs avoided are $5,184.80 (16 × $324.05).

According to the data in Table 9-2, the optimum quantity of safety stock is 60 units. At this point, the cost of 10 additional units of inventory is $1,200, while $1,296.20 is saved in stockout costs. If the safety stocks are increased from 60 to 70 units, the additional carrying costs are again $1,200, while the savings are only $972.15. Therefore, the firm is best served by planning about three stockouts to occur each year.

When to Order

A key issue with respect to inventory management involves when product should be ordered; one could order a fixed amount of inventory (**fixed order quantity system**) or orders can be placed at fixed time intervals (**fixed order interval system**). In a fixed order quantity system, the time interval may fluctuate while the order size stays constant; for example, a store might always order 200 cases of soft drinks. Its first order might be placed on January 3, a second order placed on January 6 (3-day interval), with a third order placed on January 11 (5-day interval). By contrast, in a fixed order interval system, the time interval is constant while the order size may fluctuate. For example, a man goes grocery shopping with his wife every Sunday. While the time interval for shopping is constant at seven days, the shopping list (inventory requirements) differs from week to week.

There needs to be a reorder (trigger) point, i.e., the level of inventory at which a replenishment order is placed, in order for there to be an efficient fixed order quantity system. Reorder points (ROP) are relatively easy to calculate, particularly under conditions of certainty; a **reorder point** is equal to the average daily demand (DD) in units times the length of the replenishment cycle (RC):

$$ROP = DD \times RC$$

Suppose, for example, that average daily demand is 40 units and the replenishment cycle is 4 days. The reorder point in this example is 40×4, or 160 units; in other words, when the inventory level reaches 160 units, a reorder is placed.

The reorder point under conditions of uncertainty can be calculated in a similar manner; the only modification involves including a safety stock (SS) factor:

$$ROP = (DD \times RC) + SS$$

The fact that a fixed order quantity system works best when there is a predetermined reorder point indicates that this system requires relatively frequent, if not constant, monitoring of inventory levels. Under a fixed order quantity system, if sales start to increase, the reorder point will be reached more quickly and a new order will automatically be placed. In most fixed order interval systems, by contrast, inventory levels are monitored much less frequently—often just before the scheduled order time. The infrequency of inventory monitoring makes the fixed interval system much more susceptible to stockout situations, and one is more likely to see higher levels of safety stock in a fixed interval system. It's entirely possible that a company could have some of its inventory under a fixed order quantity system, while other inventory uses a fixed order interval system.

How Much to Reorder

Economic Order Quantity

A long-standing issue in inventory management concerns how much inventory should be ordered at a particular time. The typical inventory order size problem, referred to as the **economic order quantity (EOQ),** deals with calculating the proper order size with respect to two costs: the costs of carrying the inventory and the costs of ordering the inventory.

If there were no inventory carrying costs, customers would hold an immense inventory and avoid the vagaries of reordering. Alternatively, if there were no costs to ordering, one would continually place orders and maintain virtually no inventory at all, aside from safety stocks. There are, however, costs of carrying inventory and costs of ordering inventory. Inventory carrying costs are in direct proportion to

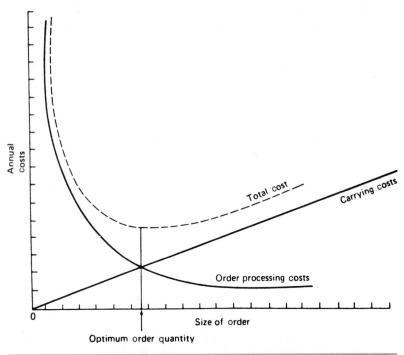

FIGURE 9-2 Determining EOQ by Use of a Graph

order size; that is, the larger the order, the greater the inventory carrying costs. Ordering costs, by contrast, tend to decline with the size of the order, but not in a linear relationship. The nature of carrying costs and ordering costs are presented in Figure 9-2.

Although some view the EOQ as an outdated technique, others suggest that "most organizations will find it (EOQ) beneficial in at least some aspect of their operation."[5] This is due to the fact that the EOQ determines the point at which the sum of carrying costs and ordering costs is minimized, or the point at which carrying costs equal ordering costs (see Figure 9-2). Assuming that carrying costs and ordering costs are accurate, the EOQ "is absolutely the most cost-effective quantity to order based on current operational costs."[6]

Mathematically, the EOQ can be calculated in two ways; one presents the answer in dollars, the other in units. In terms of dollars, suppose that $1,000 of a particular item is used each year, the order costs are $25 per order submitted, and inventory carrying costs are 20 percent. The EOQ can be calculated using this formula:

$$EOQ = \sqrt{2AB / C}$$

---

[5]Dave Piasecki, "Optimizing Economic Order Quantity," *IIE Solutions,* Vol. 33, No. 1, 2002, pp. 30–33, 39.
[6]Ibid.

Where

EOQ = the most economic order size, in dollars

A = annual usage, in dollars

B = administrative costs per order of placing the order

C = carrying costs of the inventory (expressed as an annual percentage of the inventory dollar value)

Thus:

$$EOQ = \sqrt{2 \times 1000 \times 25 \, / \, .20} = \sqrt{250,000} = \$500 \text{ order size}$$

Alternatively, the EOQ can be calculated in terms of the number of units that should be ordered. Using the same information as in the previous example, and assuming that the product has a cost of $5 per unit, the relevant formula is:

$$EOQ = \sqrt{2DB \, / \, IC}$$

Where

EOQ = the most economic order size, in units

D = annual demand, in units (200 units; $1,000 value of inventory/$5 value per unit)

B = administrative costs per order of placing the order

C = carrying costs of the inventory (expressed as an annual percentage of the inventory's dollar value)

I = dollar value of the inventory, per unit

Thus:

$$EOQ = \sqrt{2 \times 200 \times 25 \, / \, .20 \times 5} = \sqrt{10,000 \, / \, 1} = 100 \text{ units}$$

While we've calculated EOQs, how do we know that the answers are correct? Since the EOQ is the point where carrying costs = ordering costs, we need to calculate both of these costs (see Table 9-3). Ordering cost can be calculated by multiplying the number of orders per year times the ordering cost per order. For example, since an order size of $1,000 means that we're ordering once a year, the ordering cost would be 1 × $25, or $25.

Because of the assumption of even outward flow of goods, inventory carrying costs are applied to one-half of the order size, a figure that represents the average inventory. Average inventory is multiplied by the carrying costs of the inventory (expressed as a percentage of the dollar value). Thus, when ordering once per year, the order size of $1,000 is divided by 2, yielding $500. This, in turn, is multiplied by .20, resulting in a carrying cost of $100. The $25 ordering cost and $100 carrying cost are not equal, thus indicating that we haven't found the EOQ.

TABLE 9-3 EOQ Cost Calculations

Number of orders per year	Order size ($)	Ordering cost ($)	Carrying cost ($)	Total cost (sum of ordering and carrying cost) ($)
1	1,000	25	100	125
2	500	50	50	100
3	333	75	33	108
4	250	100	25	125
5	200	125	20	145

Recall that we calculated $500 (100 units) to be the EOQ. As shown in Table 9-3, a $500 order size means that we'll be ordering twice per year; the corresponding ordering costs are $50. Average inventory for a $500 order size is $250, meaning that our carrying costs are $50. Thus, we've proven that at an order size of $500, our ordering costs and carrying costs are equal. Table 9-3 presents the total cost calculations for several other order sizes. Note that ordering costs = carrying costs at the EOQ and that the total cost is minimized as well.

Several caveats bear mention. First, EOQs, once calculated, may not be the same as the lot sizes in which a product is commonly bought and sold. Second, the simple EOQ formulation does not take into account the special discounts given to encourage larger orders or increased volumes of business. Third, there is an implicit assumption of demand certainty, that is, demand is continuous and constant over time. The inclusion of one, or more, of these caveats will alter EOQ calculations.

Inventory Flows

The figures from the fixed order quantity (e.g., EOQ) and the safety stock calculations can be used to develop an inventory flow diagram, which graphically depicts the demand for, and replenishment of, inventory. Figure 9-3 presents an illustration of inventory flow, based on the following assumptions: an EOQ of 120 units; safety stock of 60 units; average demand of 30 units per day; and a replenishment or order cycle of 2 days. Further, the beginning inventory is equal to the safety stock plus the EOQ (60 + 120 = 180). Recall from earlier in this chapter that the reorder point can be calculated as (daily demand × replenishment cycle) + (safety stock), or (30 × 2) + (60) = 120 units.

As shown in Figure 9-3, 180 units of inventory are available for sale at the beginning of day 1 (point A). The daily demand of 30 means that 150 units are available for sale at the beginning of day 2, and 120 units are available at the beginning of day 3. Since 120 units represent the reorder point (point B), an order is placed at the beginning of day 3. Because safety stock is not to be used under normal circumstances, reordering at 120 units means that 60 units (safety stock) will be on hand 2 days later

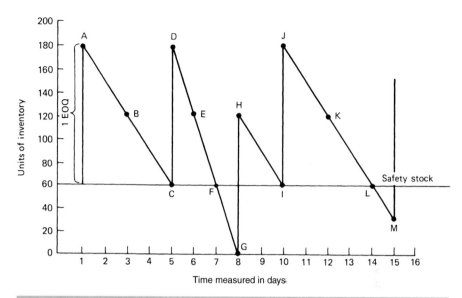

FIGURE 9-3 Inventory Flow Diagram

when the EOQ arrives. The EOQ of 120 units arrives at point C, and then total inventory increases to 180 units at point D.

The rate of sales doubles to 60 beginning on day 5, the reorder point is hit at 120 units at the beginning of day 6 (point E), and another order is placed. Demand continues at 60 units on day 6, meaning that the regular inventory is exhausted, and at point F the safety stock is starting to be used. Demand is also 60 on day 7, leaving us with no inventory (point G) at the end of day 7. The EOQ arrives before opening on day 8, boosting the inventory to 120 units (point H), which is also the reorder point. Beginning on day 8, the demand settles back to 30 units per day.

Continuing with Figure 9-3, from point H inventory is depleted 30 units on day 8 and 30 more on day 9, leaving the inventory at 60 (point I). The inventory ordered on day 8 arrives prior to opening on day 10, meaning that we have 180 units in stock at the beginning of day 10 (point J). Thirty units are demanded on days 10 and 11; inventory is thus 120 units (point K), and another reorder is placed at the beginning of day 12. Demand is 30 units on days 12 and 13, and inventory has reached 60 units (point L). However, because of a transportation delay, the replenishment cycle is 3 days instead of 2, and instead of arriving at the beginning of day 14, it arrives at the beginning of day 15. Day 14's demand of 30 units will be satisfied from safety stock (point M), and the EOQ arrives shortly thereafter.

The inventory flow example presented in Figure 9-3 illustrates that safety stock can prevent against two problem areas: an increased rate of demand and a longer-than-normal replenishment. This example also illustrates that when a fixed order quantity system such as an EOQ is used, the time between orders may vary. As long as demand was normal at 30 units and the replenishment cycle took 2 days, the time between orders was 4 days. However, when sales doubled to 60 units per day, the time between orders fell to 2 days.

As noted earlier in this chapter, one requirement for the utilization of a fixed order quantity system is that the level of inventory must constantly be monitored; when the reorder point is hit, the fixed order quantity is ordered. With continuing advances in computer hardware and software, many firms have the capability to constantly monitor their inventory and hence have the option of using a fixed order quantity system such as the EOQ. A reorder point for each item can be established electronically so it can indicate when the stock has been depleted to the point where a new order should be placed. Increasingly, these orders can be transmitted electronically.

Contemporary Approaches to Managing Inventory

What has been described represents elementary thinking about inventory management. While such thinking continues to be relevant, additional approaches have evolved. Several of the more prominent approaches are presented in this section.

ABC Analysis

ABC analysis of inventory, which can be applied in several different ways, recognizes that inventories are not of equal value to a firm and that, as a result, all inventory should not be managed in the same way. An individual firm may stock hundreds or thousands of items, and it is a real challenge to determine the relative importance of each item. One commonly used rule of thumb (the *80/20 rule*) is that 80 percent of a company's sales come from 20 percent of its products (conversely, 20 percent of sales come from 80 percent of products). From a managerial perspective, this indicates that the primary focus should be on the 20 percent of products that generate the 80 percent of sales. For example, it might not be in a company's best interests to store very slow-moving inventories in all its warehousing facilities; doing so increases inventory carrying costs and likely reduces its inventory turnover ratio.

Measures that can be used to determine ABC status include sales volume in dollars, sales volume in units, the fastest-selling items, item profitability, or item importance. For instance, with respect to item importance, one consideration with repair parts inventory would be how critical a part might be to customers. Likewise, a firm supplying medicine to hospitals might need to stock certain items because they are critically important. Thus, in terms of item importance, ABC might be operationalized as follows: A items could be the ones with the highest criticality; B items could be those with moderate criticality; C items could have low criticality. Similar approaches could be applied to other measures of ABC status.

One issue with ABC analysis involves a determination of what percentage of items should be classified as A, B, and C, respectively. While no right or wrong answers characterize this issue, it's important to recognize that either too high or too low a percentage of A items may reduce the potential efficiencies to be gained from the classification technique.

A second issue with ABC analysis involves how it can be used by managers. One use, as suggested above, is that ABC analysis can determine stocking patterns in warehousing facilities. For example, one company achieved a 25 percent space reduction in its logistics network by locating safety stock at only one warehousing facility.[7] In addition, as pointed out earlier in this chapter, ABC analysis could be used to determine how frequently inventory gets monitored. Thus, A items might be checked daily (or, increasingly, hourly), B items weekly, and C items monthly.

Before proceeding further, it should be noted that some companies are adding a fourth classification, D, to ABC analysis. *D* stands for either "dogs" or dead inventory or inventory for which there is no remaining demand. Note that such inventory serves to increase inventory carrying costs, as well as to reduce inventory turnover. Dead inventory is discussed in more detail later in this chapter.

Just-in-Time (JIT) Approach

One of the most popular contemporary approaches to managing inventories is the just-in-time (JIT) philosophy. Many believe that JIT originated with Japanese manufacturers, but the concept actually started in the United States in the 1920s with Henry Ford's integrated production and assembly plants. Japanese manufacturers, in particular Toyota Motor Company, refined the JIT approach to the point where it gave it distinct advantages over its competitors.

Although the events of September 11, 2001, have caused some firms to reassess their usage of and commitment to JIT (because of supply-chain disruptions), most U.S. manufacturers continue to have at least some materials supplied to them on a JIT basis.[8] While the just-in-time approach is generally associated with inventory management because of its focus on minimizing inventory, the consequences of JIT actually go far beyond inventory management.

From an inventory perspective, the JIT approach seeks to minimize inventory by reducing (if not eliminating) safety stock, as well as by having the required amount of materials arrive at the production location at the exact time that they are needed. The JIT approach views inventory as waste, whereas the so-called JIC (just-in-case) approach requires additional levels of inventory just-in-case something unexpected occurs.

The JIT approach has a number of important implications for supply-chain efficiency. One implication is that suppliers must deliver high-quality materials to the production line; because of JIT's emphasis on low (no) safety stock, defective materials result in a production line shutdown. Improved product quality from suppliers can be facilitated by looking at suppliers as partners, as opposed to adversaries, in the production process. Chapter 2 noted that relational exchanges are one of the cornerstones of supply-chain management.

This chapter has explored the trade-off between ordering costs and carrying costs: As ordering costs go up, carrying costs go down, and vice versa. When using JIT, since it emphasizes minimal inventory levels, customers tend to place smaller, more frequent orders. As such, it is imperative that suppliers' order systems be capable of handling an

---

[7]Mary Aichlmayr, "The Quick, the Dead, and the Slow Movers," *Transportation & Distribution,* February 2002, pp. 38–42.

[8]John S. McClenahen and Jill Jusko, "JIT Inventory Systems Hold Appeal," *Industry Week,* May 7, 2001, p. 11.

increased number of orders in an error-free fashion. In addition, because the transit-time reliability tends to decrease with distance, suppliers need to be located relatively close to their customers. The supplier park concept that was discussed in Chapter 8 is an excellent example of this.

The combination of smaller, more frequent shipments and close supplier location suggests that trucking is an important mode of transportation in the JIT approach. As such, production and distribution facilities should be designed to support truck shipments—that is, there should be truck docks to facilitate product loading and unloading. While this may appear to be the proverbial no brainer, consider the case of a U.S. manufacturer that designed a state-of-the-art distribution facility to be served by rail, only to switch to a JIT approach, thus making the new facility totally worthless. In fact, some companies involved in JIT have designed their production facilities so that trucks can drive inside them, thus bringing the product that much closer to the actual production point. Figure 9-4 shows a truck trailer that opens on its side for rapid discharge of parts for JIT inventory management.

Other inventory minimization (lean inventory) philosophies include *Efficient Consumer Response (ECR),* which is associated with the grocery and beverage industries, and *Quick Response (QR),* which is associated with the apparel industry. Where JIT tends to encompass movement of materials and component parts from supplier to producer, lean inventory philosophies such as ECR and QR tend to focus on product movement from manufacturer to retailer. Just as collaboration among supply-chain participants is key to successful JIT initiatives, collaboration among supply-chain participants is also essential for ECR and QR to be successful.[9]

Vendor-Managed Inventory (VMI)

In traditional inventory management, the size and timing of replenishment orders are the responsibility of the party using the inventory, such as a distributor or retailer. Under **vendor-managed inventory (VMI),** by contrast, the size and timing of replenishment orders are the responsibility of the manufacturer. Operationally, VMI allows manufacturers to have access to a distributor's or retailer's sales and inventory data, and this access is accomplished electronically by EDI and/or the Internet. While VMI is often associated with consumer products, it also has been applied to industrial products such as fasteners (e.g., bolts, screws), as well as to heating and cooling systems.

VMI represents a huge philosophical shift for some organizations in the sense that they are allowing another party to have control over their inventories. This is a situation that necessitates tremendous trust on the part of distributors and retailers because of the potential for unscrupulous manufacturers to abuse the system by pushing unneeded inventories onto downstream parties.

VMI's benefits for distributors and retailers tend to involve a reduced number of stockouts and higher inventory turns, while manufacturer benefits include improved demand forecasting because of earlier access to data. One potential drawback to VMI is inadequate data sharing between the relevant parties, in part because of trust and

---

[9]Karl Edmunds, "ECR: Ready for Action," *Beverage World,* March 15, 2001, pp. 76–78.

FIGURE 9-4 Trailer That Opens on the Side and Is Used for Rapid Discharge of Parts

It was designed for use by carriers serving manufacturers with just-in-time inventory management systems.

Source: Photo courtesy Fruehauf Corporation.

control concerns. Another drawback is infrequent stock replenishment by the manufacturer, a situation that can cause stockouts of certain fast-moving products.[10]

Inventory Tracking

Advances in technology are making it easier (and less costly) to keep track of inventory, which can translate into marked improvements in supply-chain efficiency. While

---

[10]Mary Aichlmayr, "DC Mart: Who Manages Inventory in a Value Chain?" *Transportation & Distribution,* October 2000, pp. 60–64.

the ubiquitous bar code is perhaps the most familiar tracking technology, *radio-frequency identification (RFID) chips* are growing in popularity. Unlike bar codes, RFID chips are able to transmit data through packaging, which offers the ability to monitor inventory without opening sealed boxes. The most prominent drawback to RFID chips at present is their cost, currently slightly less than $1 per chip. The chips likely need to cost around $.25 each to spur widespread adoption.[11]

Inventory Management: Special Concerns

Generalizations concerning inventory management are often hard to make. Each commodity has its own handling characteristics, and the framework through which each product is marketed may vary as well. What follows, then, is a discussion of different factors that might affect the management of inventories.

Defining Stock-Keeping Units (SKUs)

Organizations should classify their materials as stock-keeping units (SKUs) or line items. Each SKU represents a type of individual item or product for which separate records are maintained. In addition to designating each product and product variation or size as an SKU, the inventory manager must designate the quantity—or minimum lot size—with which the inventory records will deal. As a result, the definition of *SKU* may vary depending on a party's position in the supply chain. Let's assume, for example, that we're concerned with managing 12-ounce cans of XYZ Company's regular-flavored tomato sauce. A retailer typically keeps records in terms of individual items or case lots (with a case holding 12, 24, or some other number of individual items). As such, an SKU for a retailer might be the number of 12-ounce cans of XYZ's regular-flavored tomato sauce.

The warehouse that supplies the retail store may deal only with case lots or pallet loads of product; pallet loads might contain between 24 and 50 cases, depending on the product. An SKU for the warehouse might be the number of 24-can cases of XYZ's 12-ounce cans of regular tomato sauce. In turn, the distributor that sells to warehouses may deal with only pallet loads or vehicle loads, and it may accept orders only for pallet loads or vehicle loads of product. The distributor might view an SKU as the number of 42-case pallets containing 24-can cases of XYZ's 12-ounce cans of regular tomato sauce.

Dead Inventory

As mentioned previously, dead inventory refers to product for which there is no demand—at least under current marketing practices. Although no figures are absolute, dead inventory can represent between 20 and 40 percent of all inventory in certain industries.[12] Because dead inventory increases inventory carrying costs, reduces inven-

---

[11]Cheryl Rosen and Matthew Nelson, "The Fast Track," *Information Week,* June 18, 2001, pp. 22–24. Some reports give as low as $10.

[12]Ken Brack, "Industrial Distribution—Building a Trading Hub," *Industrial Distribution,* May 2001, pp. 55–58.

"*Something's got to go, Fenton. You, me or this inventory—and it's not going to be me.*"

FIGURE 9-5 Advertisement from a Service That Helps Firms Donate Excess Inventories to Charitable Causes

Source: Courtesy of Educational Assistance, Ltd., Glen Ellyn, IL 60137.

tory turnover, and takes up space in warehousing facilities, a structured process should be in place for managing it. One suggestion is for firms to adopt more stringent new-product development processes in that new-product failures are the largest source of dead inventory for many companies.[13]

Companies might also market their dead stock more aggressively, perhaps through drastic price reductions or bunching it with more attractive merchandise. Companies might also attempt to auction their dead inventory; several Internet sites now special-ize in auctioning off dead stock.[14] Some dead items can be donated to charitable causes, usually resulting in a partial tax write-off. Figure 9-5 is an ad from a service that helps firms find recipients for inventory donations.

Companies can also throw away dead stock, if for no other reason than to free up space in a warehousing facility. However, this "solution" should only be a last resort, because in so doing a company is, in effect, throwing away money.

---

[13]Larissa Doucette, "Making the Most of Inventory Management," *Foodservice Equipment & Supplies,* Vol. 54, No. 12, 2001, pp. 40–43.

[14]Brack, 2001.

Deals

Sometimes a manufacturer or wholesaler has an unbalanced inventory with too many slow-moving items. In order to clear its warehouses, the manufacturer or wholesaler may offer retailers a deal that involves a combination of desirable and less desirable items. The price is set so that the retailer is likely to buy in spite of the fact that some of the less desirable items may be difficult to sell, excepting at a very low price. This is offset by the fact that the deal includes some popular, fast-moving items and that its total price is relatively low. One challenge for the retailer is that the deal may increase its inventory levels of some unpopular, slow-moving items. This potential problem can be addressed in several ways, such as by selling the less desirable items to discount retailers whose competitive advantage is low-priced products (e.g., Big Lots). A number of Internet sites allow companies to sell excess or surplus inventories.

The terms *carload sale* and *truckload sale* mean that a retailer has purchased an entire railcar load or truck trailer load of a product and wishes to pass the quantity savings on to its customers. (Figure 9-6 shows the delivery of a carload of tires to a Miami retailer in the early 1920s.) Moving larger-than-usual quantities may have certain advantages from a retailing perspective, but it is almost totally dichotomous to current thinking that tends to focus on orderly on-time replenishment. Such deals occur less frequently because more buyers and sellers are entering into long-term agreements, such as VMI, whereby the seller agrees to replenish and maintain the buyer's inventory stocks.

Substitute Items

Substitute items refer to products that customers view as being able to fill the same need or want as another product. The substitutability can occur at a specific product level (e.g., one brand of cola is viewed as a substitute for another brand of cola), or it can occur across product classes (e.g., potatoes may be viewed as a substitute for rice). As pointed

FIGURE 9-6 Gearing up for a Carload Tire Sale

This photo was taken in Miami in 1921. Note that the trucks in the center and on the left of the photo have solid rubber tires.
Source: Courtesy of the Florida Photographic Collection, Florida State Archives.

out previously in this chapter, knowledge of substitutability has important implications with respect to stockout costs and the sizes of safety stocks to be maintained. Thus, if a consumer has little hesitation in making substitutions, there would appear to be minimal penalties for a stockout. However, a point may be reached where customers become sufficiently annoyed at having to make substitutions that they decide to take their business elsewhere. Because of the many possibilities for substitutability, many grocery chains target in-stock rates of 95 percent for individual stores so that sufficient substitutes exist for a customer to purchase a substitute item rather than go to a competing store.

It's also important that companies have a thorough understanding of substitution patterns. For example, in many cases, substitutions are two-way, meaning that if brand A is substitutable for brand B, then brand B is substitutable for brand A. In some situations, however, one-way relationships exist; a bolt $\frac{7}{16}$ inch in diameter could be used in place of a bolt that is $\frac{1}{2}$ inch in diameter, but the reverse may not hold.

Complementary Items

This book takes a rather narrow view of *complementary items* and defines them as inventories that are used or distributed together, such as razor blades and razors. These products may only intensify the pressures on retailers or wholesalers concerned with inventory maintenance. For example, product placement is often a key issue with complementary items. Almost any time an item requiring subsequent purchase of a refill is sold, the refills must be marketed alongside the initial item to demonstrate to buyers that they will not be impossible to find later.

Another issue associated with complementary products involves the amount of inventory to be carried. Purchasing a canister vacuum cleaner, for example, generally means that a customer will periodically need to buy replacement bags for the canister. As such, the canister bags might be slow sellers, and some might argue that the bags should be dropped in favor of faster-moving products. Others, however, would point out that the sale and display of these bags is necessary to support the sale of canister vacuums.

Two of the most common complementary relationships occur when incoming goods come from one supplier or outgoing goods go to one receiver or consignee. In such situations, the controlling factor could be the dollar value, weight, or cubic volume of the entire order. The individual items in the inventories may be of secondary consideration, except for their contribution to totals. Suppose, for instance, that a retailer schedules store deliveries for Tuesdays and Fridays. If the order for Tuesday leaves the volume and/or weight capacity of the truck underutilized, the warehousing facility may add to Tuesday's order and fill the truck with fast-moving items. This example assumes that the retailer owns the warehouse, store location(s), and inventory; as such, the systemwide costs of maintaining the inventory are the same. However, by better utilizing the truck's capacity, the retailer manages to reduce its transport costs through improved equipment utilization.

Informal Arrangements Outside the Distribution Channel

The increasing quest for customer service and customer satisfaction is leading many companies to engage in what we'll broadly refer to as *informal arrangements outside the distribution channel.* It's fairly common, for example, for all dealers of a specific brand of automobile in a particular area (e.g., northeast Ohio) to have easy access to data about the new car inventories in that area. If one dealer has a ready buyer for a specific model and color of auto that it does not have in stock, the dealer can check the inventory list to see if any other area dealers have the desired car in stock. If so, the dealers will trade cars so that the initial dealer will have the exact auto that the buyer wants. Franchised fast-food restaurants may also borrow or trade with each other, particularly among locations that are owned or controlled by the same franchisee. The transfer is often done by having an employee load the product in his or her own car for transport to where it's needed. These informal arrangements benefit all parties concerned, especially the customer—and without customers, businesses aren't going to be very successful. These examples indicate the hazards in blindly applying formal inventory analysis to certain situations and overlooking various informal relationships that can facilitate customer satisfaction.

Repair/Replacement Parts

Repair/replacement part inventories create a variety of potential challenges for logisticians. These items can be essential to customer service and satisfaction, yet it can be extremely difficult to forecast the demand for repair/replacement parts. For example, while companies might have some knowledge about the repair/replacement parts needed for routine or preventive maintenance of products, it is virtually impossible to forecast when the product might break down or fail. The difficulties in forecasting demand lead to challenges with respect to which parts to carry, as well as the stocking levels for the parts that are carried.

A second challenge involves the number of warehousing facilities that should be used for repair/replacement parts. One possibility is to locate the parts at numerous warehousing facilities in that this allows the parts to be fairly close to potential customers, and in emergency situations, where time is of the essence, this can be critical to customer satisfaction. Alternatively, the parts could be located at one centralized facility; while this would require use of premium transportation for some shipments, this cost is more than offset by the inventory cost savings that result from inventory being held in only one facility.

These and other challenges have led some organizations to outsource their repair/replacement parts business. For example, FedEx Express, an airline specializing in rapid delivery of parcels throughout the world, maintains a repair parts warehouse that is located right next to its main airline hub in Memphis, Tennessee. Various customers maintain their inventories of repair/replacement parts at this warehouse and use FedEx Express to fill and ship orders to where they are needed. Several other companies also offer so-called *parts bank* services (see Figure 9-7).

This discussion of repair/replacement parts inventories offers another opportunity to reinforce the importance of informal considerations when managing inventories and making business decisions. Several years ago, the owner of an automotive parts distributor became concerned with the amount of inventory his company was holding. A visit to the distributor's storage facility revealed that it was literally overrun with oil filters from one particular manufacturer. Indeed, it turned out that this one brand of oil filters accounted for approximately 20 percent of the facility's total inventory, a figure far higher than its actual demand.

The solution seemed pretty clear: Reduce the inventory of oil filters to a level more in line with demand. However, there was a reason for the high inventory of oil filters: The manufacturer sponsored annual contests that offered all-expenses-paid trips for two to desirable vacation locations such as Hawaii, and the trips were awarded based on the amount of oil filters purchased in a particular time frame.

FIGURE 9-7 Advertisement from a Parts Bank Service

Source: Courtesy of Associated Distribution Logistics (ADL).

Because the distributor's wife had become quite fond of these annual trips, the owner placed very large orders for oil filters, despite that fact that they weren't needed. The obvious solution to the problem—reducing the inventory of oil filters—wasn't feasible because the owner wanted to please his spouse. In this situation, personal considerations were more important than professional ones. It is important to remember that personal considerations often play a very important role in family-run businesses.

Reverse Logistics

For the most part, products flow toward the ultimate consumer in channels of distribution. As pointed out in previous chapters, an increasingly important contemporary issue in logistics management is *reverse logistics,* which involves products that flow from the ultimate consumer to other parties in a distribution channel. Examples of reverse logistics include returned items, as well as refurbished and recycled materials, and each has key inventory-related challenges.

Because return rates tend to vary across industries, returns management should be more important for some industries than for others. In fact, return rates in online commerce can approach 50 percent, compared to 20 percent in catalog retailing and about 5 percent in the auto parts industry. In addition, whereas forward distribution strives for predictability of product flow, product returns tend to be much less predictable.[15] This unpredictability of product flow can make it difficult for companies to achieve proper staffing levels at warehousing facilities.

Furthermore, forward distribution generally is characterized by relatively predictable product content in the sense that a carton labeled as "potato chips" most likely contains potato chips. There can be less predictability of product content with returned products; indeed one third-party returns specialist has discovered bricks and shirts stuffed in DVD-player boxes. The predictability of product content in forward distribution allows shipments to be monitored and recorded by computers (e.g., scanners or wands). Alternatively, the unpredictability of product content with returned goods means that every returned item needs to be physically inspected.[16] At a minimum, such physical inspections increase the processing time for returned items.

Refurbished and recycled materials present other types of inventory challenges; while both involve reverse logistics, refurbishing refers to upgrading an existing product, whereas recycling involves dismantling an existing product in order to collect component parts. Unlike return items, refurbishing and recycling are predicated on sufficient product volumes, which means that there needs to be adequate storage space. A lack of storage space can lead to products being stored outdoors, which can reduce the ability to refurbish or recycle the product.[17]

---

[15]Bob Trebilcock, "Return to Sender," *Warehousing Management,* May 2002, pp. 24–27.

[16]Ibid.

[17]A. Michael Knemeyer, Thomas G. Ponzurick, and Cyril M. Logar, "A Qualitative Examination of Factors Affecting Reverse Logistics Systems for End-of-Life Computers," *International Journal of Physical Distribution & Logistics Management,* Vol. 32, No. 6, 2002, pp. 455–479.

SUMMARY

This chapter addressed inventories and inventory management. Because many challenges are associated with holding inventories, some companies try to shift this burden to other parties in the supply chain. Many companies seek to improve their inventory turnover levels, or the number of times that inventory is sold in a 1-year period.

When deciding what levels of inventories to maintain, companies try to minimize the costs associated with both too much and too little inventory. Too much inventory leads to high inventory carrying costs; too little inventory can lead to stockouts and the associated stockout costs. The worst outcome of a stockout is to lose both a sale, and all future business, from the customer.

The chapter also addressed when to order, as well as how much to order; reorder points signify stock levels at which a new order should be placed. With respect to how much to order, the economic order quantity (EOQ) minimizes ordering costs and inventory carrying costs.

Contemporary approaches to managing inventory—ABC analysis, the JIT approach, and VMI—were discussed. The chapter concluded with a look at special concerns associated with inventory management, such as dead inventory and substitute items. This final section offered several examples of informal considerations that might affect inventory management.

QUESTIONS FOR DISCUSSION AND REVIEW

1. What is inventory turnover? How can a high inventory turnover ratio be detrimental to a firm?
2. Distinguish among cycle, safety, pipeline, and speculative stock.
3. Define what is meant by inventory carrying costs. What are some of its main components?
4. Discuss the concept of stockout costs. How can a stockout cost be calculated?
5. Distinguish between a fixed order quantity and fixed order interval system. Which one generally requires more safety stock? Why?
6. Explain the logic of the EOQ model.
7. How can inventory flow diagrams be useful to a logistics manager?
8. Discuss what is meant by ABC analysis of inventory. What are several measures that can be used to determine ABC status?
9. What are implications of the JIT approach for supply-chain management?
10. How does vendor-managed inventory differ from traditional inventory management?
11. Explain how an SKU might have different meanings depending on one's position in the supply chain.
12. Define what is meant by dead inventory. What are several ways to manage it?
13. What are substitute items and how might they impact safety stock policies?
14. Do substitute items or complementary items present the greater managerial challenge? Support your answer.
15. Why is it important for a manager to understand informal considerations with respect to inventory management?
16. Discuss some of the challenges associated with managing repair/replacement parts.
17. Which presents the greater reverse logistics challenge: (1) returned items or (2) refurbished and recycled products? Support your answer.
18. Which supply-chain participant(s) should be responsible for managing inventory levels? Why?

19. Should inventories be considered investments? Why?
20. Since the mid-1990s, many beer and soft drink cans and bottles have contained a *freshness date* stamped on them to indicate the latest date that the product should be consumed. What problems might such a system cause for the people responsible for managing such inventories? Discuss.

SUGGESTED READINGS

Beard, Luciana, and Stephen A. Butler, "Introducing JIT Manufacturing: It's Easier Than You Think." *Business Horizons,* Vol. 43, No. 5, 2000, pp. 61–65.

de Haan, Job, and Masaru Yamamoto, "Zero Inventory Management: Fact or Fiction? Lessons from Japan." *International Journal of Production Economics,* Vol. 59, 1999, pp. 65–75.

Dong, Yan, Craig R. Carter, and Martin E. Dresner, "JIT Purchasing and Performance: An Exploratory Analysis of Buyer and Seller Perspectives." *Journal of Operations Management,* Vol. 19, No. 4, 2001, pp. 471–483.

Fitzsimons, Gavin J., "Consumer Response to Stockouts." *Journal of Consumer Research,* Vol. 27, September 2000, pp. 249–266.

Norek, Christopher D., "Returns Management: Making Order Out of Chaos." *Supply Chain Management Review,* May/June 2002, pp. 34–43.

Piasecki, Dave, "Optimizing Economic Order Quantity." *IIE Transactions,* Vol. 33, No. 1, 2001, pp. 30–33, 39.

Reynolds, Dennis, "Inventory-Turnover Analysis." *The Cornell Hotel & Restaurant Administration Quarterly,* Vol. 40, No. 2, 1999, pp. 54–58.

Sabath, Robert E., Chad W. Autry, and Patricia J. Daugherty, "Automatic Replenishment Programs: The Impact of Organizational Structure." *Journal of Business Logistics,* Vol. 21, No. 1, 2001, pp. 91–105.

Stassen, Robert E., and Matthew E. Waller, "Logistics and Assortment Depth in the Retail Supply Chain: Evidence from Grocery Categories." *Journal of Business Logistics,* Vol. 23, No. 1, 2002, pp. 125–143.

Vokurka, Robert J., and Rhonda R. Lummus, "The Role of Just-in-Time in Supply Chain Management." *International Journal of Logistics Management,* Vol. 11, No. 1, 2000, pp. 89–98.

Waller, Matt, M. Eric Johnson, and Tom Davis, "Vendor-Managed Inventory in the Retail Supply Chain." *Journal of Business Logistics,* Vol. 20, No. 1, 1999, pp. 183–203.

White, Richard E., and John N. Pearson, "JIT, System Integration and Customer Service." *International Journal of Physical Distribution & Logistics Management,* Vol. 31, No. 5, 2001, pp. 313–333.

C A S E S

Case 9-1   Low Nail Company

After making some wise short-term investments at a race track, Chris Low had some additional cash to invest in a business. The most promising opportunity at the time was in building supplies, so Low bought a business that specialized in sales of one size of nail. The annual volume of nails was 2,000 kegs, and they were sold to retail customers in an even flow. Low was uncertain how many nails to order at any time. Initially, only two costs concerned him: order-processing costs, which were $60 per order without regard to size, and warehousing costs, which were $1 per year per keg space. This meant that Low had to rent a constant amount of warehouse space for the year, and it had to be large enough to accommodate an entire order when it arrived. Low was not worried about maintaining safety stocks, mainly because the outward flow of goods was so even. Low bought his nails on a delivered basis.

QUESTIONS

1. Using the EOQ methods outlined in Chapter 9, how many kegs of nails should Low order at one time?

2. Assume all conditions in question 1 hold, except that Low's supplier now offers a quantity discount in the form of absorbing all or part of Low's order-processing costs. For orders of 750 or more kegs of nails, the supplier will absorb all of the order-processing costs; for orders between 249 and 749 kegs, the supplier will absorb half. What is Low's new EOQ? (It might be useful to lay out all costs in tabular form for this and later questions.)

3. Temporarily, ignore your work on question 2. Assume that Low's warehouse offers to rent Low space on the basis of the *average* number of kegs Low will have in stock, rather than on the maximum number of kegs Low would need room for whenever a new shipment arrived. The storage charge per keg remains the same. Does this change the answer to question 1? If so, what is the new answer?

4. Take into account the answer to question 1 *and* the supplier's new policy outlined in question 2 *and* the warehouse's new policy in question 3. Then determine Low's new EOQ.

5. Temporarily, ignore your work on questions 2, 3, and 4. Low's luck at the race track is over; he now must borrow money to finance his inventory of nails. Looking at the situation outlined in question 1, assume that the wholesale cost of nails is $40 per keg and that Low must pay interest at the rate of 1.5 percent per month on unsold inventory. What is his new EOQ?

6. Taking into account all the factors listed in questions 1, 2, 3, and 5, calculate Low's EOQ for kegs of nails.

Case 9-2 Jackson's Warehouse

This case can best be assessed only by those familiar with STORM software, although other general business analysis software programs might be used. The terminology and approach are not exactly the same as used here, especially the use of Sigma lead times, which are measured in units and can be explained as measuring the "dipping" into safety stocks. Also, some of the topics will be new to readers of this text.

Located in Memphis, Tennessee, Jackson's Warehouse stores only 12 different items, which are sold to a select number of customers. Each item is known only by its stock-keeping unit (SKU) number. Table 9-A shows each SKU number, the annual demand for each, the unit cost to Jackson's warehouse, the lead time (the lapse of time between Jackson's ordering from its supplier and receiving the goods), and the standard deviation of lead time demand (sigma lead time),

expressed as the number of units by which safety stocks are drawn down in times of heavy demand.

For SKUs with a unit cost of less than $500, it costs Jackson's $30 to process an order for any number of units of that single SKU; and for SKUs with a unit cost of $500 or above, it costs Jackson's $75 to process an order for any number of units of that single SKU.

Carrying costs are calculated as 30 percent of the average inventory of each SKU. The average inventory is the safety stock plus one-half the size of each order. (It is assumed that goods move outward in a fairly even flow so, at any one time, the amount in stock is halfway between the size of a full order and zero, plus safety stock.)

Assume that the warehouse wants to stock enough of each SKU to fill orders 95 percent of the time.

TABLE 9-A Jackson's Warehouse's Needs

SKU Number	Demand (weekly)	Unit Cost to Jackson's	Lead Time (in weeks)	Standard Deviations of Demand Per Week (in units of product)
402	4	$1,500	2	40
940	20	720	1	50
660	12	500	2	60
829	30	65	1	80
301	35	250	1	90
447	48	190	1	100
799	8	200	1	30
597	12	40	2	35
27	4	210	1	50
196	20	35	1	60
258	42	250	1	115
62	180	8	1	700

QUESTIONS

1. Perform an ABC analysis. Is it of much use if the firm maintains only 12 SKUs? Why or why not?
2. Find the reorder point for each of the SKUs expressed as the point to which existing inventory must drop to trigger a replenishment order.
3. How large a safety stock should be maintained for each SKU?
4. How much money will Jackson's have as its average investment in inventory?
5. Interest rates drop, and Jackson's now assumes that its carrying costs are 20 percent, rather than 30 percent. How will this change your answers to questions 2, 3, and 4, if at all? Explain.
6. Disregard your answers to questions 4 and 5. Answer question 3, this time assuming that Jackson's wants to keep enough of each SKU to fill orders 90 percent of the time.

Warehousing Management

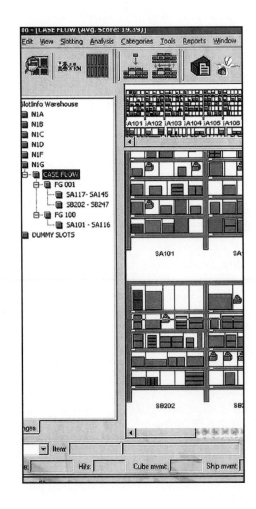

Key Terms

- Bonded storage
- Contract warehousing
- Cross-docking
- Distribution centers
- Dunnage
- Field warehousing
- Occupational Safety and Health Administration (OSHA)

- Paperless warehousing
- Private warehousing
- Public warehousing
- Regrouping function
- Throughput
- Warehousing

Learning Objectives

- To understand the role of warehouses and distribution centers in a logistics system
- To identify the various types and functions of warehouses
- To distinguish the various alternatives available in warehouse design
- To examine the different types of handling equipment available
- To analyze the issue of employee safety in warehousing

A recurring theme in previous chapters has been the changing nature of the logistics discipline and the individual functions that comprise it. In the systems approach of logistics, changes to one function impact other functions as well. Indeed, many of the changes described in previous chapters—such as electronic ordering, facility consolidation, lean inventories, and transportation deregulation—have especially impacted warehousing management. While some experts have speculated that these changes would diminish warehousing's relevance in logistics systems, warehousing has adapted by expanding offerings of value-added activities, particularly as they support mass customization programs.[1]

Warehousing has been defined as "that part of a firm's logistics system that stores products (raw materials, parts, goods-in-process, finished goods) at and between points of origin and point of consumption."[2] **Warehousing** can be provided by either warehouses or distribution centers. *Warehouses* emphasize the storage of products, and their primary purpose is to maximize usage of available storage space. In contrast, **distribution centers** emphasize the rapid movement of products through a facility, and thus attempt to maximize **throughput** (the amount of product entering and leaving a facility in a given time period).

Warehousing and transportation are substitutes for each other, with warehousing having been referred to as "transportation at zero miles per hour." Figure 10-1, which presents an example of the trade-off between warehousing and transportation, indicates that placing a warehousing facility between the producer and customers adds a new layer of costs (those associated with warehousing) into the system. Moreover, the warehousing facility generates shorter-haul transportation routes (from the producer

---

[1]James A. Cooke, "Re-inventing the Public Warehouse," *Logistics Management & Distribution Report,* May 2000, pp. 44–50.

[2]Douglas M. Lambert, James R. Stock, and Lisa M. Ellram, *Fundamentals of Logistics Management* (New York: Irwin McGraw-Hill, 1998).

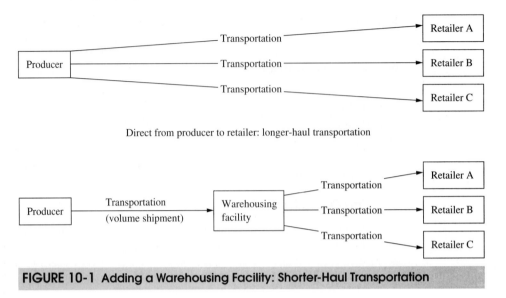

Direct from producer to retailer: longer-haul transportation

FIGURE 10-1   Adding a Warehousing Facility: Shorter-Haul Transportation

to the facility; from the facility to the customers); as a general rule, short-haul transportation tends to be more costly per mile than long-haul transportation. However, the
increased costs of short-haul transportation may be offset by lower transportation
costs per unit of weight associated with volume shipments.

If the introduction of warehousing into a supply chain appears to result in a net
increase in the total costs of conducting business, then why is warehousing desirable?
One important reason is that warehouses and distribution centers facilitate the
regrouping function in a supply chain. This function involves rearranging the quantities
and assortment of products as they move through the supply chain, and can take four
forms—*accumulating* (also referred to as *bulk-making*), *allocating* (also referred to as
bulk-breaking), *assorting,* and *sorting.* Accumulating and allocating refer to adjustments associated with the *quantity* of product, while assorting and sorting refer to
adjustments associated with product *assortment.*

Thus, accumulating involves bringing together similar stocks from different
sources, as might be done by a department store that buys large quantities of men's
suits from several different producers. Allocating, by contrast, involves breaking larger
quantities into smaller quantities; continuing with our suit example, whereas the
department store might buy 500 suits in size 42 short, an individual store might only
carry one or two suits in this size.

Assorting refers to building up a variety of different products for resale to particular
customers; our department store example might want to supply individual stores with a
number of different suit sizes and styles. Sorting out refers to "separating products into
grades and qualities desired by different target markets."[3] For example, the Dillard's

---

[3]William D. Perreault, Jr. and E. Jerome McCarthy, *Basic Marketing,* 14th edition (New York: Irwin
McGraw-Hill, 2002), Chapter 11.

department stores carry upscale suit brands in stores located in high-income areas, while some Dillard's located in less affluent areas may not carry any men's suits at all.

Warehousing is also needed because patterns of production and consumption do not coincide, and warehousing serves to match different rates of flow. Canned fruits and vegetables are examples of one extreme in which production occurs during a relatively short period, but sales are spread throughout the year. Because of changes in logistics thinking in recent years, the other extreme—sales concentrated in a relatively short time period, steady production rates throughout the year—is more likely to be addressed by having the production occur closer to the demand period.

Sometimes, larger quantities of goods are purchased than can be consumed in a short period of time, and warehousing space is needed to store the surplus product. This can occur for several reasons, such as guarding against anticipated scarcity or to benefit from a seller's advantageously priced deal.

Much of the preceding discussion could be viewed as a market-oriented approach to warehousing. However, warehousing management can also be relevant to production and raw materials considerations. For example, an automobile manufacturer might purchase extra amounts of steel in response to an anticipated steel shortage.

As previously mentioned, contemporary warehousing is characterized by a greater degree of value-adding activities than in the past. Examples include assembly, light manufacturing, product testing, and affixing state tax stamps. Some goods are repackaged and labeled prior to distribution to retail outlets. In addition, warehousing facilities are increasingly the places where retail point-of-sale displays are created and produced.[4]

Public, Private, and Contract Warehousing

Businesses must decide the proper mix of public, private, and contract warehousing to use. Because companies have different strategies, goals, and objectives, there is no correct mix of these three types of warehousing. Thus, one organization might only use public warehousing, another organization might use only private warehousing, and a third organization might use a mix of all three types. Each of these three types of warehousing has distinct characteristics that might be attractive or unattractive to potential users. These characteristics are discussed in the following sections.

Public Warehousing

Public warehouses are similar to common carriers in that they serve (are supposed to serve) all legitimate users and have certain responsibilities to those users. Public warehouses require no capital investment on the user's part, which can certainly be an important consideration when borrowing (interest) rates are high. With public warehousing, the user rents space as needed, thus avoiding the costs of unneeded space. Related to this is that users receive regularly scheduled bills for the space used, thus allowing them a fairly exact determination of their warehousing costs.

Public warehousing can also be attractive to prospective users because other parties have responsibilities for personnel decisions and regulatory knowledge.

---

[4]Cooke, 2000.

Warehousing is one of two major sources of labor in logistics (the other is transportation), and warehousing employees are often unionized, thus adding to the managerial challenges. With respect to regulatory knowledge, warehousing labor safety practices in the United States are monitored by the **Occupational Safety and Health Administration (OSHA).** From a managerial perspective, because OSHA standards are complex and lengthy, OSHA regulations can be quite costly and challenging to comply with.

Public warehouses offer more locational flexibility than do company-owned facilities, and this can be important when a company is entering new markets. For example, an organization may want to start off slowly in new markets or may be uncertain how well its products will be received in these markets, and public warehouses can provide storage services in these markets without an overwhelming capital commitment.

Public warehouses may provide a number of specialized services that aren't available from other sources. For example, public warehouses are heavily involved in such value-added services as repackaging larger shipments into retail-size quantities and then shrink-wrapping them, price marking, assisting in product recalls, product assembly, and product testing.

Two other notable public warehouse services are **bonded storage** and **field warehousing.** While there are several types of bonded storage, they all refer to situations where goods are not released until applicable fees are paid. For example, U.S. Customs-bonded warehouses hold goods until import duties are collected. Internal Revenue Service-bonded warehouses hold goods until other federal taxes and fees are collected. In addition, certain federal laws related to storing agricultural products and some state laws require warehouses to be bonded in the sense that they must carry insurance to protect their customers.

A field warehouse is a facility temporarily established at the site of an inventory of goods, often the premises of the goods' owner. The warehouser assumes custody of the goods and issues a receipt for them, which can then be used as collateral for a loan. Using one's inventory of goods as loan collateral can be helpful, although the goods are temporarily frozen in the distribution channel.

Perhaps the biggest drawback to public warehousing is the potential lack of control by the user. For example, sometimes public warehouses don't have the space availability required by a particular user. If space is available, a user may have little say in where their goods are stored—they may be placed wherever space is available, which may result in part of a user's inventory being stored in one area while the remainder is stored in another. Moreover, some public warehouses are not open 24 hours a day, meaning that prospective users may not be able to access their products as needed or that users may need to tailor their operations to fit those of the public warehouse.

Private Warehousing

Private warehouses are owned or occupied on a long-term lease by the firm using them. As such, they generate high fixed costs and thus should be considered by companies dealing with large volumes of inventory. In so doing, the high fixed costs can be spread out over more units of inventory, thus reducing the cost per unit of storage. The largest users of private warehousing are retail chain stores; they handle large volumes of merchandise on a regular basis. Manufacturing firms also utilize private warehousing. Figure 10-2 shows a distribution center built by a toy manufacturer.

FIGURE 10-2 LEGO Distribution Center

LEGO Systems, Inc. built this 225,000-square-foot distribution center about one-quarter mile from its factory in Enfield, Connecticut. There was actually an area next to the factory, but if this facility had been built on that site, natural wetlands would have been destroyed. This facility is designed to handle 66,000 cases per day. Note that its design makes the building look like it had been built with giant Legos.
Source: Permission granted by LEGO Systems, Inc.

In addition to large volumes, private warehousing tends to be feasible when demand patterns are relatively stable. Fluctuating demand patterns could at times lead to insufficient storage space for product, in which case the company might use public warehousing as a supplement, thus increasing total warehousing costs. At other times, by contrast, there could be too much space (excess capacity), which costs money, as well.

Assuming both sufficient demand volume and stability of demand, private warehousing offers potential users a great deal of control over their storage needs. For example, the storage facility can be constructed to the user's specifications, a particularly attractive feature when a company has unique storage or handling requirements, as is the case with steel beams and gasoline. Moreover, in private warehousing, companies can control product placement with a facility; some products, for instance, should not be stored on the floor. Another aspect of control is that private warehousing offers access to products when an organization needs (wants) them, as opposed to an organization having to tailor its activities to match a public facility's operating hours.

Private warehousing is also characterized by several important drawbacks, including the high fixed cost of private storage and the necessity of having high and steady demand volumes. In addition, a high-fixed-cost alternative, such as private warehousing, becomes less attractive in times of high interest rates because it is more costly to secure the necessary financing to build or lease the facility (to be fair, interest rates in some nations, such as the United States, have been relatively low in recent years).

Private warehousing may also reduce an organization's flexibility in responding to changes in the external environment. For example, companies that utilize private warehousing are susceptible to changing demand patterns, such as those experienced with the passage of multicountry trade alliances. Likewise, organizational flexibility can be impacted by mergers with, or acquisitions of, other companies, as illustrated by the case of a multibillion-dollar company that acquired a competitor's production and private warehousing facilities. While the production facilities added much-needed manufacturing capacity, the warehousing facilities were largely redundant in nature. Yet the acquiring company had little choice but to continue operating them because of substantial penalties for premature lease terminations.

Contract Warehousing

For many years, organizations had two choices with respect to warehousing—public and private—but more recently, **contract warehousing** (also referred to as *third-party warehousing*) has emerged as another viable warehousing alternative. Although contract warehousing has been defined in a number of different ways, in this text it refers to "a long term, mutually beneficial arrangement which provides unique and specially tailored warehousing and logistics services exclusively to one client, where the vendor and client share the risks associated with the operation."[5] Contract warehousing thus provides another example of supply-chain partnerships. Since contract warehousing is a relatively new alternative for logisticians, our understanding of it is not as thorough as it is for public or private warehousing.

Contract warehousing expenditures appear to be in excess of $20 billion annually and are expected to grow approximately 25 percent over the next few years. This growth in contract warehousing reflects a general acceptance of the outsourcing philosophy by many organizations; moreover, warehousing is one of the most frequently outsourced of logistics activities.[6]

Contract warehousing is becoming a preferred alternative for many organizations because it simultaneously mitigates the negative aspects and accentuates the positive aspects of public and private warehousing. With respect to the former, contract warehousing allows a company to focus on its core competencies (what it does best), with warehousing management provided by experts—experts who solely focus on the client's needs and wants.[7] Contract warehousing also tends to be more cost-effective than private warehousing, with potentially the same degree of control because key specifications can be included in the contract.

Contract warehousing tends to be less costly than private warehousing and more costly than public warehousing. With respect to changes in the external environment, contract warehousing is viewed as more flexible than private warehousing but less so than public warehousing. This flexibility depends in part on the length of the contract; as the contract length increases, the flexibility to respond to change decreases. Although a consensus has yet to develop with respect to a preferred contract length, 3-

---

[5]*Contract Warehousing: How It Works and How to Make It Work Effectively* (Oak Brook, IL: Warehousing Education and Research Council, 1993).

[6]Chris Dragan, "The Rise of the 3PW," *Transportation & Distribution,* June 2002, pp. 61–64.

[7]John R. Johnson, "Bigger and Better," *Warehousing Management,* October 2000, pp. 22–25.

to 5-year contracts appear to allow sufficient time for the warehousing provider to learn the client's business while allowing clients some flexibility in case the agreement fails to produce acceptable results.

Design Considerations in Warehousing

Figure 10-3 shows the top and end views of a distribution center. In this example, the replenishment and order-picking functions are completely separated. Order pickers work in the center aisle, while stock replenishers work in the outer aisles, moving goods from reserve to live (active) storage. As order pickers empty cartons, they place them and other wrapping materials on the trash conveyor. The trash is carried to another room, where it can be separated into different types of materials, and each type is baled and then sold to a paper-products recycling plant.

Figure 10-4 illustrates a much more complex, high-rise distribution center that receives pallet loads, breaks them down into carton lots, and then reassembles the carton lots into new, outgoing pallet loads. Pallet loads are received at point 2, where a computer-controlled stacker takes each pallet and stores it in one of the openings in the 10-aisle, 65-foot-high storage area (point 1). As goods are needed to replenish stocks on the lane loaders (point 4), they are retrieved from one of the openings in point 1 and taken by the pallet carrier to one of several depalletizing stations (point 3).

At point 3, the pallets are manually unloaded and the cartons placed aboard a conveyor system, which takes them to the lane loaders (point 4). At the lane loaders, at least one lane is assigned to each product, and cartons are loaded onto the top of each lane. The bottom of the lane feeds onto a moving conveyor belt, which is at a right angle to the lanes. The lanes slope downward toward the belt, and at the bottom of each lane (near the conveyor belt) an electrically triggered device releases one case at a time onto the conveyor belt. The lane is of sufficient slope that gravity forces the case out and onto the conveyor belt.

As orders are assembled on the conveyor belt, they move toward point 5, where they are routed to one of four loading stations and are placed aboard pallets for outgoing shipments. This is also done manually. Hence, loading and unloading pallets are the only two manual operations; the other operations are by machine, and all operations are computer controlled.

General Considerations

One of the best pieces of advice with respect to the design of warehousing facilities is to use common sense, as illustrated by the following anecdote. Several years ago, a businessperson was convinced that warehouses were visually unappealing, and thus decided to build a more aesthetically pleasing facility. To this end, he designed a warehouse with black floors, reasoning that the facility would stand out compared to other warehouses. While the black floor was certainly eye-catching, it was an unmitigated disaster: The floor showed more dirt than comparable facilities, and the floor was extremely slippery—meaning that forklifts had a harder time stopping (some actually crashed into the walls!) and warehouse workers were more prone to falling.

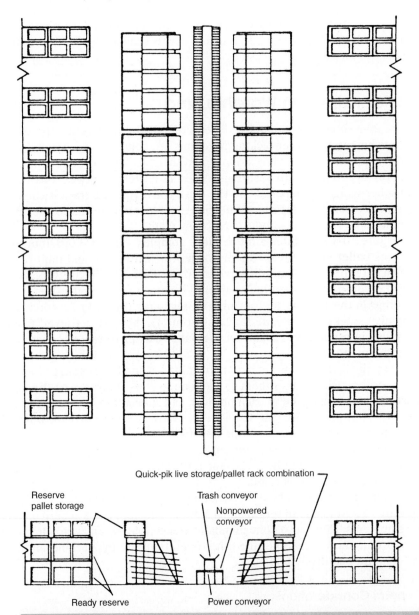

FIGURE 10-3 Top and Side Views of a Distribution Warehouse

The live storage racks slope downward toward the center so that gravity forces cartons to move toward the center.
Source: Courtesy of North American Equipment Corporation.

One common-sense piece of advice is that prior to designing a warehousing facility, the quantity and character of goods to be handled must be known. Indeed, one of the challenges of online commerce for bricks and mortar organizations has been that many of them have attempted to fulfill online orders through warehousing facilities largely designed to supply retail store locations. Online orders tend to be much smaller

FIGURE 10-4 Large Automated Distribution Center

Source: Courtesy of SI Handling Systems, Inc.

than those going to retail stores; as a consequence, picking and assembling one or two items is much different from picking and assembling a pallet load of items.[8]

A second common-sense piece of advice is that it's important for an organization to know the purpose to be served by a particular facility because the relative emphasis placed on the storage and distribution functions affects space layout. A storage facility with low rates of product turnover should be laid out in a manner that maximizes utilization of the cubic capacity of the storage facility. A distribution-oriented facility attempts to maximize throughput rather than storage.

The increased emphasis on time reduction in supply chains has led to growth of **cross-docking,** which can be defined as "a process where a product is received in a facility, occasionally married with product going to the same destination, then shipped at the earliest opportunity, without going into long-term storage."[9] While there is some disagreement as to how long a product can sit at a facility before it's no longer considered to be cross-docked (e.g., some experts argue for 1 day, others for 3 days), there is agreement that the time products are at rest in a storage facility should be as short as possible.

In order to encourage product flow (and discourage product rest), a "pure" design of a cross-dock facility would resemble a motor carrier terminal—rectangular, long, and as narrow as possible, as shown in Figure 10-5.[10] A facility designed for cross-docking would devote more space to dock operations and less space to product storage. To date, most cross-docking operations have emphasized pallet loads of product.

Trade-Offs

Trade-offs must be made among space, labor, and mechanization with respect to warehousing design. Spaciousness may not always be advantageous because the distances that an individual or machine must travel in the storing and retrieving functions are increased. Alternatively, cramped conditions can lead to such inefficiencies as the product damage that can be caused by forklift puncture and movement bottlenecks caused by insufficient aisle width, to name but two.

Before layout plans are made, each item that will be handled should be studied in terms of its specific physical handling properties, the volume and regularity of movement, the frequency with which it is picked, and whether it is fast or slow moving compared to other items. This so-called *product profiling* might suggest, for example, that fast-moving items "be placed close to where order selectors go to pick them, in an effort to reduce walking time."[11]

Many trade-offs are inevitable when designing the structure as well as the arrangement of the relevant storage and handling equipment. Several of these trade-offs are discussed in this section; the trade-offs are often more complex than they appear since they can affect one another. While there tend not to be "right" or "wrong" answers with respect to warehousing design, an understanding of the various trade-offs might help managers to make more efficient, as opposed to less efficient, decisions.

The experiences of PDI Logistics, a pharmaceutical distributor and third-party logistics provider, provide an excellent example of trade-offs among various warehous-

---

[8]James A. Cooke, "The Physical Challenges of the Virtual Sale," *Logistics Management & Distribution,* October 2000, pp. 67–73.

[9]*Making the Move to Cross-Docking* (Oak Brook, IL: Warehousing Education and Research Council, 2000).

[10]Ibid.

[11]Cooke, 2000.

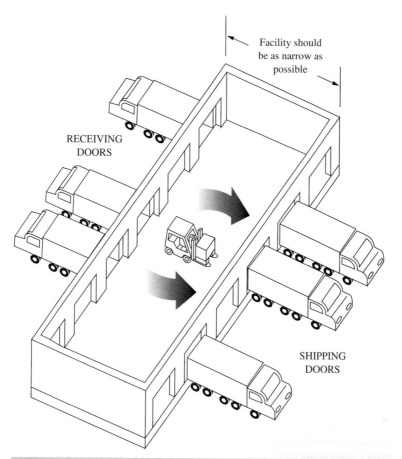

Facility should
be as narrow as
possible

RECEIVING
DOORS

SHIPPING
DOORS

FIGURE 10-5 Ideal Facility for Pure Supplier Consolidation (Full Pallet Movement)

Source: Reprinted by permission of the Warehousing Education and Research Council.

ing design factors. During the late 1990s, PDI experienced dramatic annual growth in its business—so much growth that it quickly approached the capacity of its existing storage facility. Rather than build a new facility, PDI redesigned its existing facility with very narrow aisles (less than 5 feet wide), thus permitting better storage density. PDI saved money by not having to build a new facility, but because the very narrow aisles require highly specialized lift trucks, its equipment costs increased. However, because of this new equipment, PDI uses approximately one-third the number of employees as in the past, thus decreasing its labor costs.[12]

Fixed Versus Variable Slot Locations for Merchandise

With a fixed slot location, each SKU has one or more permanent slots assigned to it. This provides stability in the sense that the company should always know where a specific

---

[12]Mary Acihlmayr, "Before Building, Cube Out with Narrow Aisles," *Transportation & Distribution,* June 2002, pp. 42–43.

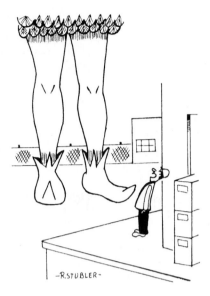

—R.STUBLER—

Sorry to let you go, but we've automated our
high-rise order picking.

FIGURE 10-6 An
Example of Labor
Displaced by Machinery

Source: Reproduced through the
courtesy of *Handling and
Shipping Management* magazine
and of Richard Stubler, the artist.

SKU is located. However, this may result in low space utilization, particularly with seasonal products. A variable slot location involves empty slots being assigned to incoming products based on space availability. While this alternative results in more efficient space utilization, it requires a near-perfect information system since there must be flawless knowledge of each product's location.

Build Out (Horizontal) Versus Build Up (Vertical)

A general rule of thumb is that it's cheaper to build up than build out; building out requires more land, which can be quite expensive, particularly in certain geographic locations. Alternatively, while building costs decline on a cubic-foot basis as one builds higher, warehousing equipment costs tends to increase. Figure 10-6 shows what might happen to labor when a company decides to build up, rather than out.

Order-Picking Versus Stock-Replenishing Functions

Organizations must decide whether workers who pick outgoing orders and those who are restocking storage facilities should work at the same time or in the same area. While the latter scenario may result in fewer managerial personnel being needed, it may also lead to congestion within the facility due to the number of workers. One suggestion to reduce congestion is for order pickers and stock replenishers to use different aisles for their respective activities—again, this requires a very good information system in order to identify where a given employee is at any time.

Two-Dock Versus Single-Dock Layout

A two-dock layout has receiving docks on one side of a facility and shipping docks on the other side, with goods moving between them. In a one-dock system, each and every dock can be used for both shipping and receiving, typically receiving product at one time of the day and shipping it at another time. Viewed from overhead, the goods move in a U-shaped rather than a straight configuration. This alternative reduces the space needed for storage docks, but it requires carriers to pick up and deliver at specific times. This alternative may also result in an occasional mix-up in that received product is sometimes reloaded into the vehicle that delivered it.

Labor-Intensive Versus Mechanization Versus Automation

As labor costs continue to increase, many organizations are actively looking for the proper mix of labor, mechanization, and automation in their warehousing facilities. True *automation,* such as automatic guided vehicles (AGVs), refers to an absence of human intervention, while *mechanization* refers to equipment that complements, rather than replaces, human contact.[13] A key trade-off among labor, mechanization, and automation involves the relevant volumes; since automation is a very high-fixed-cost option, sufficient volume is needed to make it cost-effective. One warehousing expert, for example, suggests that automation becomes economically viable only when a facility handles at least 50,000 cartons per day.[14]

Space Devoted to Aisles Versus Space Devoted to Storage

As aisle space increases, storage capacity decreases. Wider aisles make it easier to operate mechanical equipment and reduce the chances of accidents and product damage—but they increase the travel distances within a facility. Narrower aisles can increase the space utilization of a facility but often require specialized equipment, such as a narrow-aisle lift truck, to do so.

Picker-to-Part Versus Part-to-Picker Systems

Not surprisingly, in picker-to-part systems, an order picker either walks or rides a vehicle to where product is located, such as occurs with a forklift. Alternatively, in part-to-picker systems, the pick location is brought to the picker, as occurs with carousels. The two systems involve trade-offs between human (picker-to-part) and mechanized (part-to-picker) travel time, an important consideration given that travel time is "the crux of order picking."[15]

Paperless Warehousing Versus Traditional Paper-Oriented Warehousing Operations

A **paperless warehousing** facility generates and uses few or no paper documents. Monitors and wands can accomplish this; the monitor displays the instructions on what to pick, the worker scans it with a wand, indicating that the task has been accomplished, as well as the location from which the piece was picked. While wands may be hand-held, advances in technology now allow the wand to be attached to an employee's finger, thus freeing their hands.

---

[13]Mary Aichlmayr, "Making a Case for Automation," *Transportation & Distribution,* June 2001, pp. 85–90.
[14]Ibid.
[15]Mary Aichlmayr, "Last But Not Least," *Transportation & Distribution,* February 2001, pp. 33–36.

An increasingly popular paperless alternative involves *voice technology.* Initially, voice technology was used to guide workers to pick locations and the worker would record the pick on paper or via a wand. Today, by contrast, two-way voice communication is possible in that the employee can record the pick by speaking into a headset. This two-way voice communication has become extremely popular in the food industry, particularly in frozen food storage units where the low temperature poses challenges to paper-based systems because it can be difficult to write while wearing heavy gloves. The food industry has experienced numerous benefits from voice communication, including reduced training time for new employees and 80 percent increases in pick accuracy.[16]

Virtual Warehouse Versus Real Warehouse

A *virtual warehouse* occurs when a firm relies on its partners in the supply chain to perform the actual warehousing. With electronic links, its warehouses can be used to supply and ship the real goods that the firm with a virtual warehouse has sold. The buyer may or may not be aware of the goods' origin.

Other Space Needs

In addition to space for storage, throughput, and movement of merchandise, areas must be set aside for other warehousing activities. They may require detailed analysis in terms of space requirements and layout. These activities include, but are not limited to, the following:

1. Areas for vehicles waiting to be unloaded or loaded
2. Employee parking
3. Receiving and loading facilities for each mode of transport serving the facility
4. An area where transport drivers and operators can wait while their equipment is loaded or unloaded
5. Staging, or temporary storage areas, for both incoming and outgoing merchandise
6. Employee washrooms, lunchrooms, and the like
7. Pallet storage and repair facilities (Facilities that receive unpalletized materials but ship on pallets may require a pallet-assembly operation.)
8. Office space, including an area for the necessary computer systems
9. An area designed to store damaged merchandise that is awaiting inspection by claim representatives
10. An area to salvage or repair damaged merchandise
11. An area for repacking, labeling, price marking, and so on
12. An area for accumulating and baling waste and scrap
13. An area for equipment storage and maintenance (For example, battery-powered lift trucks need to be recharged on a regular basis.)

---

[16]Andrew Kaplan, "Putting Your Warehouse on Speaking Terms," *Food Logistics,* March 15, 2002, pp. 48–49.

14. Specialized storage for hazardous items, high-value items, warehousing supplies, or items needing other specialized handling (such as a freezer or refrigerated space)
15. A returned or recycled goods processing area.

Retail Storerooms

The design of warehousing facilities is not an end in itself but rather one link the distribution process. A retail store is often the next link, and some retail stores no longer have storerooms, causing products to go directly from a warehousing facility to the retailer's display shelves. In order to successfully execute such a process, retail chains often own two or three times as many truck trailers as they do tractors. Each time a tractor makes a delivery to a retail location, it leaves a trailer for the store to unload within a specified time period and picks up the previous trailer that was left to be unloaded. Hence, the parked trailer serves as a storeroom and reduces the truck-to-storeroom and storeroom-to-shelves movements to only one because the goods go directly from the parked trailer to the shelves.

Warehousing Operations

Since operating a warehousing facility has many facets, efficient and effective warehousing management can be an exacting task. Workforce motivation can be difficult because of the somewhat repetitive nature of the work. Warehouse work can be strenuous and physically demanding, and on occasion warehousing facilities can be dangerous places. Some of the more prominent operational issues are discussed in the following sections.

Storage and Handling Equipment

Although it is possible to store palletized material on top of other palletized material, this can be inconsistent with the distribution-center concept of fast throughput. The oldest pallet would always be on the bottom, and the pallet loads above it would have to be removed in order to get at the oldest pallet load (assuming a first-in, first-out philosophy). Hence, steel shelving or pallet racks are used, and each pallet sits on an individual shelf and can be stacked or removed without disturbing other pallet loads. Before installing storage equipment, companies should be familiar with applicable regulations; for example, building codes in earthquake-prone areas often limit the height of storage shelves and racks.

The use of racks may improve space utilization by allowing for narrower aisles. As previously mentioned, narrow aisles require specialized equipment capable of simultaneously moving both vertically and horizontally. Because of this, the most efficient layout of goods along any one aisle may be a path of upward and downward undulations. This would consume less time than a route that takes the equipment along a horizontal path and stops, then moves up or down and stops, then continues along the horizontal path and stops, and so on.

Goods can be moved by a combination of manual, mechanized, and automated methods, and the storage and handling equipment should be matched to the particular method. While seemingly obvious, the fact that forklifts tend be to the standard work-horse in many warehousing facilities can lead to companies purchasing (or leasing) forklifts, even though they may not be needed.

Warehouse Management Systems

Increasingly, warehousing operations are being influenced by warehouse management systems (WMS), which are software packages that "control the movement and storage of materials within an operation."[17] Activities that can be controlled by WMS include inventory management, product receiving, determination of storage locations, order selection processes, and order shipping. The least expensive WMS currently cost approximately $30,000, meaning that even relatively small facilities cannot afford some type of WMS. At the other end of the spectrum, WMS costs can run into several million dollars.

Although WMS can be somewhat expensive, payback periods generally run between one and two years. The payback can be relatively quick because WMS often lead to increased worker productivity. This, in turn, allows companies to reduce the number of warehousing employees, which translates into lower labor costs and fewer pick errors due to fewer workers. Other benefits to WMS include better utilization of a facility's capacity, improved picking procedures, and improved service to customers.[18]

Because WMS vendors are many and diverse and because software packages can vary from vendor to vendor, organizations should choose those that best fit what they're hoping to achieve. In the words of one warehousing consultant, "Don't assume all WMS are alike. They all perform the warehousing functions differently."[19] Moreover, the installation of a WMS can cause organizational upheaval in the sense that warehousing space may need to be reconfigured and current employees will need varying degrees of training to become proficient with the new system.[20]

Employee Safety

Warehouses can be dangerous places to work because goods and workers are in constant motion. Forklift drivers occasionally operate equipment in a reckless manner, which can lead to bodily injury and even death. Workers can be injured due to improper lifting procedures, trying to carry too heavy a load, failing to observe proper hand clearances, and the like. Back injuries have been especially frequent among warehouse personnel; back support belts and braces are becoming more widely used, but they are of value only if the workers also receive adequate training in how to safely lift various loads. When discussing employee safety, consider one warehousing professional's advice: "It costs more to recruit, train, and replace a worker than to provide a safe environment."[21]

Figure 10-7 depicts an emergency protective equipment supply room. It is a steel container located in close proximity to the warehousing facility and can be carried by a forklift to the appropriate site. The container holds both equipment to treat injured workers as well as equipment that can contain and potentially eradicate the particular problem.

---

[17]Dave Piasecki, "Warehouse Management Systems," www.inventoryops.com.

[18]Victoria Fraza, "More Than a Storage Facility," *Industrial Distribution,* May 2002, pp. 47–49.

[19]Steve Salkin, "Avoiding the Pitfalls of WMS," *Warehousing Management,* April 2000, pp. 36–40.

[20]Ibid.

[21]Ed Engel, "Getting a Lift from Safety," *Warehousing Management,* January–February 2001, pp. 54–57.

FIGURE 10-7 This Emergency Protective Equipment Supply Room Is Used in Warehouses and Can Be Carried by a Forklift

Source: Courtesy of Inland Star Distribution Centers, Inc., Fresno, CA.

The management of employee safety can be influenced by governmental regulations. In the United States, for example, OSHA is responsible for industrial safety practices. Standards have been set for equipment and operations, and OSHA inspectors make frequent visits to industrial workplaces to ensure regulatory compliance. In cases of noncompliance, citations can be issued and fines can be levied. An important warehousing-related OSHA initiative in recent years has involved the training of forklift drivers. This initiative mandates that forklift workers actually have to drive forklifts as part of the training process; furthermore, driver performance must be evaluated every 3 years.[22]

Warehousing facilities generate large volumes of waste materials, such as empty cartons, steel strapping, broken pallets, as well as wood and nails used for crating and dunnage. (**Dunnage** is material that is used to block and brace products inside carrier equipment to prevent the shipment from shifting in transit and becoming damaged.) The various waste materials must be properly handled because they pose threats to employee safety and may also be fire hazards.

Moreover, even with the best of practices, some goods that are received, stored, and shipped will be damaged. Special procedures must be established for handling broken or damaged items, if only from the standpoint of employee safety. A broken bottle

---

[22]Jim Truesdell, "OSHA Enacts Fork Lift Rules," *Supply House Times,* July 1999, pp. 93–94.

of household ammonia, for example, results in three hazards: noxious fumes, broken glass, and a slippery floor. Aerosol cans pose hazards that are affected by the product in the cans. For example, cans of shaving cream cause little problem in fires because if they explode, the shaving cream serves to extinguish the fire; that is not the case with aerosol cans containing paints or lacquers, and such cans are often kept in special cages because in a fire they might become burning projectiles.

Indeed, fires are a constant threat in warehousing, in part because many materials used for packaging are highly flammable. In addition, while plastic pallets last longer, are cleaner, and are less likely to splinter than wooden pallets, plastic pallets tend to be a greater fire risk.[23] High-rise facilities are more susceptible to fires because the vertical spaces between stored materials serve as flues and help fires burn.

More than 20,000 warehouse fires occur each year in the United States, most of which result only in property damage but some of which result in injury and death. The six most common causes of warehousing fires are arson, tobacco smoking, improper use of forklifts, electrical malfunctions, poor product disposal practices, and storage of incompatible materials.[24] Quite frankly, many warehousing fires can be prevented by common sense. Flammable products, for example, should not be stored near heat sources (such as space heaters).

Hazardous Materials

Hazardous materials (hazmat) must receive extra attention because of the injuries and property damage they can cause (see Figure 10-8). Government regulations often require that shipping documents indicate the hazardous nature of the materials being transported. Warehouse employees should note these warnings when receiving materi-

Yes, sir, I know freezing will not hurt your product, but what will it do to my floor when it thaws?

FIGURE 10-8 Materials Stored in a Warehouse Can Damage Other Materials or the Warehouse Structure

Source: Warehousing Review, Vol. 6, Nos. 2–7 (1977). Drawn by Art Stenholm; courtesy of International Warehouse Logistics Association.

---

[23] Andrew Kaplan, "New Fire Regulations: A Burning Issue," *Food Logistics,* June 15, 2002, pp. 42–43.

[24] Jim Whalen, "Sounding the Alarm," *Warehousing Management,* April 2001, pp. 26–30.

als and similarly should include such warnings on outbound shipping documents when materials leave warehouses.

Hazmat experts generally agree that the applicable regulations should only provide a starting point for proper storage of hazardous materials, in part because for some situations no regulations exist. These experts further suggest that hazmat storage can be managed effectively by answering four questions: *What* material is being stored? *Why* is it being stored? *Where* is it being stored? *How* is it being stored?[25] An increasingly popular hazmat storage alternative involves prefabricated hazmat buildings. Such prefabricated buildings are less costly than custom builds, they meet applicable building codes, and they can contain spills, fires, and other calamities.[26]

Warehousing Security

It is estimated that the theft and pilferage of products stored in warehousing facilities cause losses in the range of four to five times the products' value. Theft and pilferage can result in lost sales opportunities (both present and in the future), customer dissatisfaction, additional costs to prevent theft and pilferage, and the administrative time and costs associated with filing claims, and more.[27] Moreover, warehousing security has become an even more important issue for many companies since the September 11, 2001, terrorist attacks. Many cold-storage facilities, for instance, have enacted more stringent security procedures because these facilities often contain large quantities of ammonia—a key ingredient in building bombs.[28]

In general, warehousing security can be enhanced by focusing on people, facilities, and processes. In terms of people, one area of focus should be the hiring process for warehousing workers; a starting point might be determining if an individual facility even has a formal hiring process. In terms of a facilities focus, a number of different low-tech (e.g., fences) and high-tech (e.g., closed-circuit video cameras) devices can help to enhance warehousing security; an obvious trade-off is the cost of the various devices. In terms of processes to improve warehousing security, the more times a shipment is handled, the greater the opportunities for loss and/or damage. Thus, logisticians would do well to reduce the number of times an individual shipment is handled.

Sanitation Issues

Sanitation issues are an ongoing concern for warehousing managers because they can affect employee safety, morale, and the quality of products handled. In addition, unsanitary warehousing facilities aren't likely to attract many new customers and could cause existing customers to take their business elsewhere. Fortunately, warehouse sanitation is not predicated on complex theories and/or costly technology, but rather on common sense and diligence. For example, bird and rodent infestations can be kept to

---

[25]Todd Nighswonger, "Are You Storing Hazardous Materials Safely?" *Occupational Hazards,* June 2000, pp. 45–47.

[26]Paul Graham, "Taking the Hazards Out of Hazmat Storage," *Occupational Hazards,* July 2002, pp. 43–46.

[27]Roger Morton, "Keep Product from Wandering Off," *Transportation & Distribution,* June 1999, pp. 84–87.

[28]Kristi Labetti, "Designing for Security," *Frozen Food Age,* June 2002, pp. 38–39.

"SO THAT'S WHERE THE PAPAYAS ARE.
MAYBE YOU'D BETTER CALL LOGISTICON."

FIGURE 10-9 Stock Controls Are Necessary

If papayas (a tropical fruit) are kept too long they attract insects. This cartoon accompanied the text of an advertisement for a computerized warehouse inventory control system.
Source: Courtesy of Logisticon Inc., Flexible Material Management Systems, Santa Clara, CA.

a minimum by placing trash receptacles at some distance from a storage facility and by regularly picking up garbage that might accumulate around the receptacles.[29]

Stock Controls

A continuing challenge for warehousing managers is to keep an accurate count of merchandise moving through their storage facilities. If the count is off—either too high or too low—sophisticated handling procedures will be undermined. Initial errors can occur when a worker at a receiving dock assumes that the assortment and quantities listed on the shipment manifest are, in fact, accurate. A second type of error can occur when the receiving clerk assumes responsibility for on-the-spot adjustments of overages and shortages. He or she may note that there is one carton too many of brown shoe polish and one too few of black shoe polish. Because the price is the same, the clerk may accept the shipment without recording the discrepancy. The receiving clerk's single error is multiplied because counts for both colors of shoe polish are now incorrect.

Accurate counts of merchandise leaving storage facilities are important, although whoever is next to receive the goods will, if properly doing his or her job, report discrepancies. Most methods of control involve establishing systems in which a second individual must verify any one person's count, perhaps on a sampling basis, or in which manual accounts may be compared with computerized records. If perishable products are handled, stock controls are needed to move out older stocks (see Figure 10-9).

SUMMARY

This chapter focused on warehousing—the sites where inventories are stored for varying periods of time. Warehousing facilitates the regrouping function, which involves rearranging the quantities and assortment of products as they move through the supply chain. Warehousing is also needed because production and consumption may not coincide, and warehousing can help smooth out imbalances between them.

This chapter also discussed public, private, and contract warehousing. Public warehousing has a number of established duties regarding the care of goods, and customers pay only for the space that is actually used to store their products. Private warehousing is owned or occupied on a long-term basis by the firm using such facilities, and it is best used when an organization has large and steady demand patterns. Contract warehousing involves specially tailored warehousing services that are provided to one client on a long-term basis. Contract storage, a relatively new warehousing alternative, has grown rapidly in recent years and should continue this growth into the near future.

Various design considerations are relevant to warehousing, with trade-offs among them. For example, a decision to build up or out can affect a facility's utilization of labor, mechanization, and automation. Similarly, organizations that prefer a fixed slot location for merchandise may have to build larger facilities in order to have a sufficient number of storage slots.

The chapter concluded with an examination of some of the more prominent issues in warehousing operations. The discussion of warehouse management systems

---

[29]Jim Whalen, "Cleanliness Matters," *Warehousing Management,* April 2001, p. 48.

illustrated how technology can be used to improve warehousing operations. By contrast, effective management of warehousing sanitation, which involves common sense and diligence, is decidedly low-tech in nature.

QUESTIONS FOR DISCUSSION AND REVIEW

1. Distinguish between warehouses and distribution centers.
2. Explain the four ways that warehousing facilitates the regrouping function.
3. Discuss some of the value-added activities that can be performed by warehouses and distribution centers.
4. What are the advantages and disadvantages of private warehousing?
5. Distinguish between bonded storage and field warehousing.
6. Explain how common sense can be helpful in terms of warehousing design and operations.
7. What is cross-docking? How might it affect warehousing design?
8. In terms of warehousing design, give examples of trade-offs involving space, labor, and mechanization.
9. Distinguish between fixed and variable slot locations. How might they affect warehousing design?
10. Discuss the trade-offs associated with order-picking versus stock-replenishing functions.
11. Distinguish between a two-dock and a single-dock warehousing layout. Which one requires more space? Why?
12. What are some potential advantages to paperless warehousing operations?
13. Discuss how storage and handling equipment can influence warehousing operations.
14. What is a warehouse management system (WMS)? How can it benefit warehousing operations?
15. What is OSHA? What is OSHA's role in warehousing safety?
16. What are the most common causes of warehousing fires? Which do you think is the easiest for managers to control? Justify your answer.
17. What are the four questions that should be asked with respect to hazmat storage?
18. Discuss how warehousing security can be enhanced by focusing on people, facilities, and processes.
19. Do you think a distribution center where cats have been used to control bird and rodent infestations is a good idea? Why or why not?
20. Discuss why contract warehousing is becoming a preferred alternative for many organizations.

SUGGESTED READINGS

Ackerman, Kenneth B. "Designing Tomorrow's Warehouse: A Little Ahead of the Times." *Journal of Business Logistics,* Vol. 20, No. 1, 1999, pp. 1–4.

_____ *Warehousing Tips.* Columbus, OH: Kenneth B. Ackerman Publishing, 2001.

Apte, Uday M., and S. Viswanathan. "Effective Cross Docking for Improving Distribution Efficiencies." *International Journal of Logistics: Research and Applications,* Vol. 3, No. 3, 2000, pp. 291–302.

Brockman, Thompson. "21 Warehousing Trends in the 21st Century," *IIE Solutions,* January 2000, pp. 31–36.

Kuo, Chun-Ho, Kimberly D. Dunn, and Sabah U. Randhawa. "A Case Study Assessment of Performance Measurement in Distribution Centers." *Industrial Management & Data Systems,* Vol. 99, No. 2, 1999, pp. 54–63.

McKnight, Douglas. "A Practical Guide to Evaluating the Functional Utility of Warehouses." *The Appraisal Journal,* January 1999, pp. 29–36.

Making the Move to Cross Docking. Oak Brook, IL: Warehousing Education and Research Council, 2000.

Saenz, Norman. "It's In the Pick." *IIE Solutions,* July 2000, pp. 36–38.

Shamlaty, Ron. "This Is Not Your Father's Warehouse." *IIE Solutions,* January 1999, pp. 29–36.

Tompkins, James A., and Jerry D. Smith, *The Warehouse Management Handbook.* Raleigh, NC: Tompkins Press, 1998.

C A S E S

Case 10-1 Sandy's Candy

Sandy Nykerk was an operations analyst for Mannix Model Markets, a food-store chain headquartered in Omaha, Nebraska, with 55 stores in an area that extended east to Des Moines, Iowa; north to Sioux Falls, South Dakota; west to North Platte, Nebraska; and south to Emporia, Kansas. All the stores were served by daily deliveries 5 days a week from a large complex of Mannix warehouses in Omaha, with two exceptions. First, each store's produce department could buy some produce locally, which it usually did during the summer and autumn months. Second, some goods were delivered to the stores by vendors, usually operating through drivers/salespeople who would stock the goods on the shelves. Examples of these goods were dairy products, soft drinks, bakery items, name-brand snacks, beer, pantyhose, candy, and yogurt. Vendors delivered ice cream directly to the stores west of Grand Island, Nebraska, in part because Mannix was short of trucks with freezer capacity, especially during the summer months.

Mannix Model Markets was a member of a buying cooperative. The buying cooperative had forced many name-brand manufacturers to make their goods available to its members, in which case goods would be delivered first to each chain's warehouse and then via chain trucks to individual retail chain stores, where store personnel placed them on the shelves and treated them like any other product. The only good that could not be purchased through the cooperative was beer because some states had stricter regulations regarding the wholesaling of beer (and other alcoholic beverages), initially to ensure that they received all beverage tax receipts (although beer wholesalers opposed legislation to relax these regulations).

Sandy knew that most of the vendor-delivered goods were ones that Mannix Model Markets did not want to handle through its own distribution system. Milk, for example, would be very expensive to handle because it was costly to ship and had a short shelf life. Bakery products had similar characteristics, although Mannix did buy some bread from a private bakery and sold it in Omaha stores under its own label. Snack foods were also best handled by drivers/sales people working for vendors because they were handled roughly in the Mannix distribution system; by the time pretzels or potato chips reached the shelves, they were mostly broken and filled only the bottom one-third of the bag.

The buying cooperative had recently entered into an agreement with Schoenecker's Candies, a well-known regional firm that produced eight different types of candies and caramels packaged and sold in cellophane bags. Mannix's experience was that Schoenecker's candies sold much better than any competing brand, almost irrespective of price, so Schoenecker's was the only brand that Mannix would carry. Sandy had received a note from her supervisor saying that Schoenecker's candies could now be purchased directly through the buying cooperative and handled through Mannix's regular distribution system. The supervisor wanted Sandy to calculate whether Mannix should stop having Schoenecker's candies delivered by drivers/salespeople and instead purchase the candy through the buying cooperative.

If the cost comparisons were fairly close, Mannix would prefer using its own system for several reasons, including some generalities regarding drivers/salespeople and some not specifically referring to the Schoenecker drivers/salespeople.

The three objections to deliveries by drivers/sales people were the following:

1. Their deliveries could not be scheduled, and sometimes their trucks would tie up an unloading dock, which could delay a Mannix truck waiting to discharge 10 or 20 tons of groceries.
2. Some drivers/salespeople needed space in the stockroom, and this meant that unknown people were wandering in an area where pilferage was sometimes a problem.
3. When a driver/salesperson appeared, this interrupted the store manager or assistant manager, who routinely would have to approve the next order and also would have to check in the new merchandise and agree on the amount of returned merchandise the driver/salesperson was removing from the store.

Store clerks disliked some drivers/salespeople, claiming that they took shelf-stocking work away from store personnel. Store management discounted this argument because they thought that many store clerks did not like to see how quickly the drivers/salespeople worked. (The drivers/salespeople were mostly nonunion and worked on a commission basis.) Also, the shelves stocked by drivers/salespeople were always neater than those stocked by ordinary store personnel. On occasion, when store clerks disliked a particular driver/salesperson, they would sabotage him or her by rearranging the shelves after he or she had left, hiding all the products behind those of a competitor.

Sandy started working on her assignment and found that she was comparing the efficiency of Mannix's distribution system, which handled 10,000 line items, with that of the Schoenecker Candy Company, which handled only eight types of candy in several different-size packages. Soon, Sandy's project became known among her fellow workers as the "Sandy Candy Puzzle." Finally, to organize her thoughts and provide a basis for comparison, Sandy took a sheet of paper, drew a line down the middle, and listed as many comparisons as possible. Her analysis is shown in Exhibits 10-A and 10-B.

Sandy completed her tally sheets and wondered why sales per store should be higher when drivers/salespeople serviced the merchandise. She was told that this was because they did a better job of arranging the goods on the shelves, they kept abreast of changes in demand, and they sometimes placed posters and other small displays on the candy shelves.

QUESTIONS

1. Using those items of comparison for which costs can be calculated, determine the cost difference between the two delivery systems.
2. List and compare those factors to which it is difficult to assign precise costs.
3. Given the data that Sandy has, do you believe that Mannix Model Markets should get its Schoenecker candy through the buying cooperative or continue to rely on direct deliveries by Schoenecker's drivers/salespeople? Give your reasons.
4. If you were Sandy, what additional information would you like to have before being asked to make such a recommendation?
5. Candy sales increase during holiday seasons. Which of the two candy distribution systems do you think would do a better job of anticipating and supplying these seasonal increases? Why?
6. Assume you are in charge of labor relations for Mannix Model Markets. Would you like to see continued reliance on drivers/sales people to supply the chain's candy needs? Why or why not?

Present System	Alternate System
Schoenecker Candy Co. has driver/ salespeople deliver and stock shelves.	Purchase Schoenecker's Candies through buying cooperative and distribute to stores through Mannix Markets' own distribution system.

Buying Terms	
Every Friday, the d/s tallies sales for past seven days and store manager approves. Then three days later a bill comes from Schoenecker with 2% discount if paid within ten days (i.e., 13 days after the d/s makes the tally). The entire amount is due within 30 days (or 33 days of d/s tally).	Schoenecker must be paid within seven days after candy is received at Mannix warehouse. No discounts.

Wholesale and Retail Prices of Candy

Package Size	Wholesale Price Paid to Schoenecker	Retail Price	Package Size	Wholesale Price Paid to Schoenecker	Retail Price
3½ oz.	13¢	19¢	4 oz.	10¢	19¢
8 oz.	28¢	39¢	9 oz.	20¢	39¢
12 oz.	42¢	57¢	13 oz.	30¢	57¢

Average Time in Inventory	
Goods are on consignment, meaning that Schoenecker owns them and only collects for those that are sold.	Candy would be in the Mannix warehouse for an average of two weeks and on a retail store shelf for an average of one week.

Average Sales per Store per Week	
110 3½-oz. pkgs., 70 8-oz. pkgs., and 40 12-oz. pkgs.	100 4-oz. pkgs., 60 9-oz. pkgs., and 30 13-oz. pkgs. (Sales were somewhat lower because store personnel do not take as good care of merchandise on shelves.)

Shrinkage on Store Shelf	
Unaccounted-for loss: 2 percent per week, paid for by Mannix Markets.	2 percent per week, paid for by Mannix Markets.

EXHIBIT 10-A Sandy's Worksheet

Present System	Alternate System
Spoilage	
(Package torn open on shelf which cannot be sold): 1 percent a week, absorbed by Schoenecker Candy.	Same rate, paid for by Mannix Markets.
Ordering Costs	
Absorbed by Schoenecker Candy Co. However, store manager or assistant must approve order, twice a week, taking a total of 10 minutes time. Assistant manager makes $16,000 per year plus 15% fringe.	1½¢ per day, 4 days a week, for each of 24 items (8 types of candy in three sizes of package).
Shelf Stocking	
Absorbed by Schoenecker Candy Co.	20 minutes of clerk's time per week. (Clerk's hourly rate is $3.75 plus 10% fringe.) For every 10 stock clerks there is one supervisor paid $13,000 per year plus 15% fringe.
Warehousing Costs	
Absorbed by Schoenecker Candy Co.	The Mannix warehouse costs $10,000 per day to operate. Its throughput is 750 tons per day, five days a week.
Delivery to Store Costs	
Absorbed by Schoenecker Candy Co.	Only available cost figure is 3¢ per ton-mile, and the average distance from Mannix warehouse to a retail store is 50 miles.
Checking in Goods at Store	
Takes 10 minutes per of manager's or assistant manager's time.	No check-in necessary; controls are at warehouse, and truck is sealed in between warehouse and store.
Billing and Bill-Paying Costs	
Mannix Markets pays $1.00 per week to process and pay the Schoenecker Candy Co. invoice.	Believed to be less since, rather than spot-checking forms from each store, only the Mannix warehouse receipt form need be checked.

EXHIBIT 10-B Sandy's Worksheet

Case 10-2 Minnetonka Warehouse

Wayne Schuller managed a warehouse in Minnetonka, Minnesota. His major concern was the number of workers to assign to his single unloading dock. After he began contracting with motor carriers for deliveries, he found that they were assessing him stiff penalties if their trucks had to wait to be unloaded. Wayne started adding larger crews at the unloading dock, but often they seemed idle because there were no trucks to unload. Wayne recalled from college that queueing theory might be applicable to such a problem.

The theory of queueing is an analysis of the probabilities associated with waiting in line, assuming that orders, customers, and so on arrive in some pattern (often a random pattern) to stand in line. A common situation is that on the average a facility may have excess capacity, but often it is more than full, with a backlog of work to be done. Often, this backlog has costs associated with it, including penalties to be paid or customers who walk away rather than wait. If a firm expands its capacity to reduce waiting times, then its costs go up and must be paid even when the facility is idle. Queueing theory is used to find the best level of capacity, the one that minimizes the costs of providing a service and the costs of those waiting to use the service.

After some further research specific to his firm, Wayne determined the following facts:

1. Trucks arrive randomly at the average rate of four per hour, with a deviation of plus or minus one.

2. A team of two warehouse workers can unload trucks at the rate of five per hour, or one every 12 minutes.

3. A team of three warehouse workers can unload trucks at the rate of eight per hour, or one every 7.5 minutes.

4. A team of four warehouse workers can unload trucks at the rate of 10 per hour, or one every 6 minutes.

5. A team of five warehouse workers can unload trucks at the rate of 11 per hour, or one every 4.45 minutes.

6. The unloading times given in the preceding items (1–5) are average figures.

7. Each warehouse worker receives $14 per hour, must be paid for an entire shift, and—because of union work rules—cannot be assigned to other tasks within the warehouse.

8. Because of its contract with the carriers, the Minnetonka warehouse must pay the motor carriers that own idle trucks at the rate of $60 per hour while the trucks stand idle, waiting to be unloaded.

Use STORM 2.0 or other software that enables you to perform queueing operations. Note that the variable defined as number of servers (# servers) denotes number of teams of workers and accompanying equipment working as a complete server. In the situation described, the number of teams or servers is always 1, although the number varies in terms of costs and output.

QUESTIONS

1. For each of the four work team sizes, calculate the expected number of trucks waiting in the queue to be unloaded.

2. For each of the four work team sizes, calculate the expected time in the queue—that is, the expected time a truck has to wait in line to be unloaded.

3. For each of the four work team sizes, what is the probability that a truck cannot be unloaded immediately?
4. Which of the four work team sizes results in the lowest cost to Wayne?
5. Wayne is also considering rental of a forklift to use in truck unloading. A team of only two would be needed, but the hourly cost would be $38 per hour ($28 for the workers and $10 for the forklift). The two workers could unload a truck in 5 minutes. Should Wayne rent the forklift?

6. Disregard your answer to question 5. Labor negotiations are coming up, and Wayne thinks he can get the union to give way on the work rule that prohibits warehouse workers on the unloading dock from being given other assignments when they are not unloading trucks. How much would Schuller save in unloading dock costs if he could reassign warehouse workers to other tasks when they are not unloading trucks, assuming that he has picked a good team of workers and each worker works 8 hours a day?

CHAPTER

Supply Management

Key Terms

- E-procurement
- Global sourcing
- Import quotas
- ISO 9000
- Make or buy
- Procurement card

- Purchase order
- Purchasing ethics
- Request for Proposal (RFP)
- Request for Quotation (RFQ)
- Six Sigma
- Supplier development

Learning Objectives

- To understand the relationship between supply management and logistics
- To understand steps in selecting a supplier
- To recognize the potential of e-procurement
- To learn about quality programs

"No company controls all the resources they require," but supply management encompasses the acquisition of goods and services.[1] It is an important activity and closely related to logistics since the acquired goods and services must be fed into the supply chain in the exact quantities and at the precise time that they are needed. The term *supply management* means about the same as either *procurement* or *purchasing.* *Buying* is a related term but is more closely associated with acquiring materials for resale through retail outlets. The Institute of Supply Management defines supply management as "the identification, acquisition, access, positioning, and management of resources the organization needs or potentially needs in the attainment of its strategic objectives."[2]

Inbound goods can be separated into three categories. The first comprises inputs or components to be used in the manufacture of another product. The second category includes products purchased for resale, such as products purchased by a wholesaler or a retail chain or store. A third category includes products or packaging materials that are being returned as part of a recycling effort or because they are unsold. Personnel services are also acquired, and they can range from highly paid consultants to janitorial workers.

Supply management is an important activity in all firms. It has become relatively more important as firms attempt to downsize their operations and reduce staffs by going outside to buy more. Government agencies also are large purchasers. Typical tasks and objectives associated with procurement include the following:

- Maintaining optimum input quality
- Buying at the lowest possible total cost (where total cost considers all costs within the supply chain)
- Developing and maintaining reliable, competitive suppliers

---

[1]Luis Araujo, Anna Dubois, and Lars-Erik Gadde, "Managing Interfaces with Suppliers," *Industrial Marketing Management,* Vol. 28, 1999, p. 498.

[2]*Inside Supply Management* (Tempe, AZ: Institute of Supply Management, January 2002), p. 31.

- Contributing to low inventories and smooth flow of materials
- Cooperating and integrating with other functions.

In almost all supply management situations, the items purchased must be physically moved to where the buyer needs them. Assuming that one wishes to gain better control of the logistics associated with a firm's inbound movements, a number of steps should be followed, consistent with the objectives of purchasing listed above:

1. Analyze current inbound freight costs by looking at paid freight bills. For products purchased on a delivered basis, one would calculate approximate costs to the buyer if he or she were to pay the freight charges directly.
2. Convert buyers (the supply management staff) to the logistics concept, including an appreciation of the costs of maintaining inventory and the advantages of on-time deliveries. Also, buyers should insist that vendors separate transportation costs from other costs on their statements.
3. Determine the most favorable terms of purchase, taking into account risks and the time value of money. Some large firms have blanket insurance coverage, covering all of their inventories, so they could assume risks of ownership on inbound movements.
4. Review freight allowances offered by vendors. (A freight allowance is what the vendor allows the buyer if the buyer provides its own transportation.)
5. Set up rules for inbound routing and penalize vendors that do not follow them. Establish delivery windows or specify an inbound carrier.
6. Create alliances with vendors, working on matters of mutual benefit, such as bar coding for an item that can be used through the entire supply chain. Figure 11-1 shows how bar codes are used as an integrating tool within a single production facility.
7. Work with carriers and determine whether there would be advantages to designating one or a few of them to handle one's inbound movements. The possible advantages would be lower rates, advance notice of delivery, often via electronic data interchange (EDI) or e-mail, or single-time delivery of all shipments.
8. Develop an inbound monitoring system, which usually would be part of one's computerized ordering system. If the monitoring system is especially accurate, such as through use of satellites to locate trucks, it has the benefit of making the inbound goods considered as part of your inventory. (This is a subtle but important point. Goods that are merely on order are less likely to be considered as part of your stock than goods that, say, have already covered 990 miles of the 1,000-mile journey toward you.)

Purchase for Use in Manufacture

Firms choose between producing an item or making it. This choice is referred to as **make or buy.** Firms trying to reduce their workforces or engage in "lean" manufacturing rely on outside vendors to supply more of their needs. Two major determinants in the make-or-buy decision are the availability of trained labor and physical capacity. If either, or both, is lacking, the firm is more likely to outsource. The term *core competency* describes those activities that are unique to a firm and that they consider as

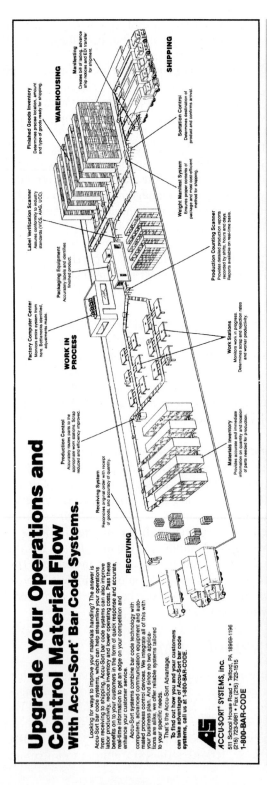

FIGURE 11-1 Use of Bar Codes Throughout a Manufacturing Process

Source: Courtesy Accu-Sort® Systems, Inc.

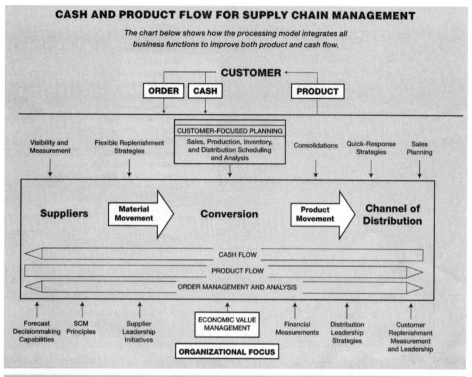

FIGURE 11-2 Flow of Information, Products, Cash, Orders, etc., Within a Manufacturing Firm

Source: David B. Watt, The Watt Group.

strengths and do not wish to assign to others. Figure 11-2 is a chart showing material and cash flow as well as inbound and outbound movements.

An important focal point is the production–purchasing interface. Within a firm, production scheduling occurs at a fairly high level. Sales forecasts determine what should be manufactured. A master production schedule (MPS) is developed, and a bill of materials (BOM) listing all of the necessary inputs is drawn up. The BOM also indicates when the inputs are needed. In addition, a sequential relationship exists. Some inputs are not needed until others arrive and are installed. Paint for a finished product is one example. **Purchase orders** (a commitment to buy) are then placed with vendors, indicating the quantities and qualities desired and the dates by which the materials must be delivered.

MRP Systems

MRP I is a computer-assisted method of managing production inventory. It takes into account a firm's master production schedule, sales forecasts, open orders, inventories, and BOMs. MRP I recognizes that the demand for all components depends upon demand for the final product. Traditionally, firms maintained large inventories of components along the assembly line because supervisors did not want the lines shut down because of a shortage on their part of the line. This practice was expensive in terms of inventory holding or carrying costs. MRP I directly challenged this concept: It maintained that very limited production inputs are required to have an efficient system that can respond to most production situations. First, the firm establishes its MPS, which is based on a sales forecast or is generated from orders that have already been received. From the MPS, a BOM—list of the specific inputs required to produce the products called for in the MPS—can be developed. When producing a number of products simultaneously, it is very likely that the same component will be utilized in a number of different products. Computers are used to track the exact number of parts required for all products to be produced during a particular time period, usually one week. The computer thus lists, or explodes, the production inputs needed for each product and then aggregates each part needed for all products to be produced during each MRP I cycle. This MRP I planning cycle takes place a number of weeks prior to actual production. At this time, the firm places orders with its vendors for production inputs, and delivery is scheduled for arrival just before the inputs are required in the production process. If the firm manufactures its own inputs, the inputs are scheduled to be produced so that they are available shortly before the assembly of the finished product.

MRP II has evolved from taking into account MRP I and adding to it the functions of marketing, finance, and purchasing.[3] One firm's use of MRP II software was described in a professional journal. The firm used 10 modules: a foundation module that established the system's framework within the firm; a resource management module that dealt with all physical inputs and outputs of the production process; a customer order management module that covered sales; a purchasing module; a warehouse management module; a resource processing module (that handled bills of materials and production routing); a planning module; a production analysis module; a financial support module; and an activity costing module.[4] Other materials flow programs also exist.

For the last 30 years, inbound logistics has received increasing attention for several reasons. First, increased fuel prices made it necessary for shippers to apply more controls to transportation costs. One way to control those costs was to increase the utilization of equipment. Firms thus began to balance inbound and outbound shipments. Second, when transportation regulatory barriers were relaxed in 1980, it was possible for more firms to use otherwise empty carrying capacity in their private fleets. Third, developments in management science have led to increased interest in inbound movements. Combine those with the ability of managers to quickly analyze and access information from desktop computers and communicate instantly worldwide, and one can see how the management of inbound logistics has become central to many firms' business strategies. It is, of course, part of supply management.

For a manufacturer, inbound logistics helps improve vendor relations and sourcing quality, cut incoming transportation time and costs, enhance materials management, and meet new production goals of quality products at competitive prices. All of this is part of supply-chain management. Vendors play a pivotal role in cost management programs. Both parties must work together carefully in developing sound alternatives for

---

[3]Norman E. Hutchinson, A*n Integrated Approach to Logistics Management* (Upper Saddle River, NJ: Prentice Hall, 1987), p. 114.

[4]G. Mirac Bayhan, "Implementation and Evaluation of an MRP II Software Package in a Sanitaryware Company," *Production and Inventory Management Journal*, Vol. 40, No. 4, 1991, pp 41–47.

cost control. These include (1) improved make-or-buy analysis; (2) redefined terms of payment; (3) realization of quantity discounts; (4) employing scientific value analysis; (5) material, part, or supply substitution; (6) changes in production, fabrication, or processing methods; (7) salvage or scrap reduction; (8) modification in tolerances or specifications; (9) mandating reasonable vendor programs related to cost reduction and control; and (10) consolidating orders.

Just-in-Time (JIT) and Kanban

Just-in-time (JIT) evolved initially to improve product quality. The logic of JIT dictates that reducing materials inventories to exactly what is required for a given run of production forces suppliers to deliver only materials that are 100 percent satisfactory in quality. Because there are no backups available in inventory, every delivered part must meet quality standards. Reducing production inventories revealed problems in component quality and in carrier service, and it forced suppliers and carriers to improve their offerings.

Customers place orders with their suppliers on basically set schedules that frequently involve daily or hourly delivery by suppliers to their customers. Ordering costs are assumed to be negligible; hence, firms order frequently to minimize inventory holding costs. "Although any manufacturer is concerned with material lead times and delivery reliability, the JIT manager must seek to minimize lead times and maximize delivery reliability."[5]

The JIT system is widely used in manufacturing products needed to fill orders. JIT is not as widely used in industries with seasonal production patterns. Canned peaches, for example, must be processed and canned during a period of a few weeks in late summer and then sold on a fairly even level over the next 52 weeks.

Kanban—literally meaning "card"—as initially used in Japan was not a computerized inventory system. Rather, the system involved two basic types of cards or placards. The first was the move card, which was utilized by assembly workers to indicate that they were getting low on an input. This card was given to the workers who brought inventory stored in the plant to the assembly-line workers. When the move card required a container of inputs to be brought to the assembly line, the production card (the second card) was taken from the container. This production card was then sent back to the manufacturer so the input could be replaced before another move card called for more parts at the assembly line. The cumbersome system of moving cards has now been replaced by electronic exchanges of information among production floor, parts supplier, and transportation provider.

Today, the terms kanban and JIT are used interchangeably, although kanban is a specific type of JIT system. Toyota uses kanban and provides a good model for contrasting its production system with the traditional methods once used in the United States.

Toyota looked at inventory as waste. In the United States, inventory was considered insurance. U.S. firms traditionally used safety stock to protect against defective parts, late deliveries, and incorrect inputs sent to the manufacturer. Because each of

---

these problems can shut down an assembly line, safety stock was considered a necessary but expensive requirement. Kanban holds that safety stock only covers up problems. The time to key in seriously on problems, identify them, and correct them quickly is when assembly lines stop.

The key to reducing inventory, the Japanese believe, is to look at suppliers as partners in the production process. In the United States, suppliers were often viewed as each other's adversaries, so the buyer constantly played one against another to get lower prices. Multiple suppliers (vendors) were frequently utilized in the United States to encourage price competition, a situation that is considered safer because if one vendor is shut down, say, by a labor dispute or a fire, the other vendor can supply the buying firm's requirements. In Japan, one supplier for each production input is the rule. Thus, at one time, Toyota had 250 vendors and General Motors had 4,000.[6] Toyota uses the following method, which is typical of kanban: Vendors are included when the firm establishes its 90-day production schedule; each vendor receives an informal order for inputs required during this time period, but only the first 30 days is an actual order from Toyota; the production schedule tells exactly what will be needed each day for the next 30 days; at the first of each month, another 90-day schedule is given to each vendor, with the first 30 days again a firm order and the next 60 days Toyota's best estimate of what production will be during this time period. Note that this system enables vendors to plan their production schedules to coincide with Toyota's.

Kanban works best in two situations, both of which are found at Toyota. First, the product should have relatively few variations so that the 90-day production schedule is accurate. This is why Toyota offers so many luxury items on its cars as standard features. It is actually cheaper to produce cars that are all about the same and then brag about the impressive list of typically extra-cost options that are standard on Japanese cars.

The second condition is that vendors be physically located close to their customers. In Japan, almost all auto production parts and the cars themselves are assembled in three city clusters. All of Toyota's vendors ship their products, often many times per day, less than 60 miles to the assembly plants. Many vendors are located in the same industrial parks as the Toyota assembly plants.

Two primary advantages accrue when the JIT inventory system is used. The first is that the level of production inputs on hand at any given time is less than without JIT. With inventory holding costs high, reduced levels of inputs can be a major cost-reduction program because less money is tied up in inventory, less storage space is required, and less physical deterioration occurs. Another effect is more inventory turns, indicating that less inventory sits around waiting to be assembled. Assume, for example, that a firm needs 9,000 units of a given input in a year. If the firm has three inventory turns, then, assuming steady production and no safety stock, the firm has an average inventory of 1,500 units. (That is, 9,000 divided by 3; half of this is 1,500. We take half because, when the 3,000 units are received, we start to use them immediately, and on the average we have half the order on hand.) However, if a firm can achieve an inventory turn of 10, the average level of inventory in stock is then reduced to 450 units (ten deliveries of 900 units divided in half). An example is Bendix Corporation's estab-

---

[6]Brian C. Kullman and Robert W. Haessler, "Kanban, American Style," *Annual Proceedings of the NCPDM* (Chicago: NCPDM, 1984), p. 105.

lishment of kanban/JIT at a production facility in Japan that supplied Toyota. Within two years after the new inventory method was established, inventory turns increased from 10 to 30 times annually.

The second advantage of kanban/JIT is quality improvement. Since there are no reserve stocks to fall back upon, the customer cannot afford to receive defective components. This improved quality also shows up in the final product, which helps increase sales.

Suppliers have learned to integrate their production with the JIT systems adopted by their customers. This has frequently meant that they also adopt JIT systems in order to turn out a much higher-quality product and deliver it in a more disciplined way. The benefits are longer relationships with customers and less dependence upon being able to continually submit the low bid. State-of-the-art manufacturers issue "evergreen contracts"—contracts with no end date—to their suppliers, which ensures the supplier's continued profitability. Current supply-chain thought advocates the development of such long-term, mutually beneficial relationships with outside firms that are part of the supply chain.

To be fully effective, JIT requires complete integration of all functions between supplier and customer. The process begins by capturing information on product movement in real-time at the actual point of sale. From there, the sales information is accumulated at convenient intervals, item by item, and can be used to reorder, forecast sales (by store, distributor, or market segment), set production schedules, route shipments, analyze the effectiveness of sales and marketing efforts, and map out future distribution requirements. In other words, the manufacturer and supplier now can operate to meet exact daily requirements. Together they can maintain ongoing sales/inventory/resupply management by customer delivery point. Shipping operations and daily routing/dispatch can be planned in a timely, cost-effective manner and in accordance with customer needs. Internal operations, including inventories, also can be planned to meet optimal needs, using all of the computer-integrated procedures that manufacturing and JIT permit.

JIT II

Sophisticated firms, such as the Bose Corporation, have developed elaborate systems that tie together the information systems and employees of their suppliers who work inside their plants in teams with their own employees. "In practice, a vendor employee sits in the purchasing office of the customer, replacing the buyer and the salesman. He is empowered to utilize the customer purchase orders and places orders on himself in effect. The vendor in-plant person is also empowered to practice 'concurrent engineering' from the in-plant location, attending any and all design engineering meetings involving his company product area."[7] Bose gives its suppliers an unprecedented level of input and control over Bose sourcing under a process known as *Total Material Control*. Total Material Control is an important component of Bose's JIT II, dealing with the acquisition of all inbound materials to Bose plants.[8] Bose is able to leverage

---

[7]Handout distributed by the Council of Logistics Management (Oak Brook, IL, September 12, 1992).

[8]Lance Dixon and Anne Millen Porter, *JIT II: Revolution in Buying and Selling* (Newton, MA: Cahners Publishing Company, 1994), p. 25.

the labor and expertise of its suppliers' "in-plant" staff to improve product quality and reduce costs. Bose Corporation manages a number of these relationships, creating value through these strategic partnerships.

A firm's logistics staff fits into the production scheduling and MRP processes in at least four ways. First, order processing often gives the firm its most accurate data regarding actual sales. This information can be read by skilled market analysts in a manner similar to that of a physician listening to a pulse or heartbeat. For example, a firm receives orders from its branches via EDI. The information on the order forms is processed so that goods will be shipped and the data on the order fed into the firm's forecast equations and then into its master production scheduling process. This then triggers raw materials purchase orders for materials needed to manufacture the precise items that the customer has just ordered or to replenish stocks that will be depleted once the customer's order is filled.

Second, the logistics staff is concerned with scheduling and managing inbound products that have unique handling or storage characteristics. The logistics staff might also have contingency plans for finding and moving critical parts in cases in which the initial source of supply proves to be inadequate or unsatisfactory.

Third, the logistics staff is responsible for all movements of materials between a firm's various plants and warehouses. Note that the production plant sees two types of inbound transportation: the inbound movements of materials purchased from various outside suppliers and the interplant movements of materials and components between plants owned by the same firm. *Materials management* often applies to movement of goods within a single facility or ownership of a single entity.

Fourth, a logistics staff works with carriers to implement the firm's goal of better management of production inventories. Transportation company GATX Logistics, Inc., manages inbound production logistics and operates a cross-docking materials management facility for Mitsubishi Motors in Normal, Illinois.

> While a high percentage of parts are cross-docked through the facility, some products shipped in truckload quantities—such as glass or large body parts—go direct to the assembly plant docks in truckload quantities because it's not economic to run them through the flow-through center. A few low-volume parts, picked up in larger-than-needed quantities to further reduce transportation costs, may be offloaded for a brief period—generally less than a shift—at the flow-through center.[9]

Deliveries of parts and components must be highly disciplined. Arrival "sometime next week, or the following Monday for sure!" is not JIT thinking. Instead, truckers might be assigned a 60-minute window on a specific day to make their deliveries. If they are early, they wait. If they are late, they pay some financial penalties; if they miss very often, they lose the contract. Just as the quality of product inputs must improve in a JIT system, so must the quality of the carriers delivering them. Also, just as the JIT system means that the manufacturer works with fewer suppliers of components, it also works with a smaller number of carriers because it expects more service from them than could be expected if a carrier is used for only one shipment.

---

[9]Leslie H. Harps, "Crossdocking for Savings," *Inbound Logistics*, May 1996, p. 32.

Supplier Product Integration

The term Supplier Product Integration (SPI) encompasses the acquisition of components, rather than individual parts. SPI transfers the responsibility for final subassemblies to a qualified supplier. "SPI is primarily centered on outsourcing the production of assemblies, whereas the supply chain management concept focuses on outsourcing parts and components along with maintenance, repair and operating supplies. A number of companies, such as Boeing Commercial Airplane Group in Seattle; Freightliner in Portland, Oregon; Mack Trucks in its Macungie, Pennsylvania plant; Mercedes Benz in Vance, Alabama; and Volkswagen in Resende, Brazil, have all successfully implemented the SPI approach for various subassemblies."[10]

Supply-chain thinking places more demands on procurement staffs. James Herman writes of the "value web," where material, information, and money flow in parallel, taking multiple separate paths through a complex network of suppliers, service providers, distributors, and customers. He describes integrating the demand function, the supply function, and the planning function. He writes, "Supply integration involves links to suppliers, contract manufacturers, and logistics service providers, as well as those upstream suppliers who feed your direct suppliers. Here the focus is on fine-tuning and adjusting forecasts and production schedules to reduce lead times, inventory, and working capital while maximizing utilization of facilities across the entire value web. An aggressive value web strategy achieves visibility beyond immediate suppliers to gain a better understanding of choke points and opportunities to eliminate unnecessary steps or movement of goods. This increased visibility also helps to prevent costly expediting of shipments or manufacturing downtime due to lack of components."[11]

Large pieces of capital equipment, even new buildings, are purchased and involve lease or buy decisions, with tax and financial concerns having a major influence. Project management becomes necessary when the item being acquired will take some time to build. In such cases, the procuring party assigns one or more members of its staff to represent its interests by overseeing that plans are followed, the project is on time, and money is released on a schedule tied to the project's percent of completion.

Purchasing for Resale

Purchasing for resale has the objective of buying merchandise that can be marked up and resold to others at a profit. This is a somewhat speculative and risky undertaking, an example being a retailer's stocking winter clothes and sports equipment and then experiencing a mild winter with little or no snow. Quality is also of continual importance because of the reseller's desire to maintain a good reputation. Coordinating purchases and inbound movements is also important because the merchant may wish to have related items on display and for sale at the same time. Actual price and value may

[10]A. Ansari, Diane Lockwood, and Batoul Modarress, "Supplier Product Integration—A New Competitive Approach," *Production and Inventory Management Journal*, Vol. 40, No. 3, 1999, p. 58.

[11]James Herman, "Global Value Webs," *Supply Chain Management Review*, July/August, 2002, p. 33.

be of less importance because the buyer is more interested in whether the good can be "marked" up and sold at a profit.

An example of a large retailer's inbound system is the apparel segment of J. C. Penney Co.'s import system, which supplies 1,300 retail department stores, six catalog distribution centers, and 470 thrift drugstores. Planning begins 12 to 15 months before the sale, with computer images of fashion designs transmitted between the home office in Plano, Texas; stores; and overseas sources. In the 10 months before the selling season, sales forecasts are prepared. Seven to 8 months before, foreign suppliers are identified and initial production and costs are negotiated. Six months before the sale, buyers conclude their plans and advertising is planned. "The buyer works with the distribution department to figure out how suppliers can pack shipments so that stores can get the variety of sizes and colors they need while ordering by the case. . . . This 'pre-packing' is important because it reduces the need for warehousing once the shipment reaches the United States."[12]

Five to 6 months out, buyers present their merchandising plans to stores, including the packing assortments that are available. Stores place orders, and Penney makes the orders firm with suppliers. The goods are manufactured, and Penney then calculates transit time. Following is an example of a shipment from Korea to Columbus, Ohio:

By sea:
- 3 days at consolidator
- 13 days port to port by ship
- 3 days at U.S. customs
- 1 day at Penney's Buena Park, California, distribution center
- 8 days in the company's transportation system (a contract trucker)

By air:
- 1 day at consolidator
- 2 days airport to airport
- 3 days at U.S. customs
- 1 day in Penney's Buena Park, California, distribution center
- 8 days in the company's transportation system

Penney uses three overseas freight consolidators; buying terms are that the manufacturer must deliver goods to the freight consolidator. The consolidator may take up to 5 days to load a container with goods from different sources. Penney gives the consolidators routing instructions and criteria for selecting carriers. These imports are purchased free on board (FOB) supplier, meaning the buyer assumes responsibility for transportation and insurance at the supplier's loading dock.

After the shipment is booked, a copy of relevant documents is sent to Penney's Salt Lake City office and entered into its import reporting system, which monitors goods through Penney's domestic distribution system. A computer directs the printing of carton labels to be applied in Buena Park. Labeled cartons go directly to outbound trucks without passing through a warehouse.

---

[12]Joseph Bonney, "Penney's System for Imports," *American Shipper*, November 1991, pp. 51–52. Penney's manager of distribution services, Byron A. Peterson, said Penney figures that warehousing adds about 6.5 percent to the cost of merchandise—3.5 percent for handling and 3 percent for inventory costs. Handling prepack costs 0.5 percent.

Goods purchased for resale may or may not continue to be manufactured. High-style clothing might be made in small quantities, and, once sold, the manufacturer will move on to new designs. The purchaser should be aware of this and should determine whether, and for how long, the producer will carry certain patterns or goods in stock. Another example of buying in a single opportunity involves Halloween pumpkins and Christmas trees, which grocery stores sell at holiday times. Often, the stores buy a single truckload that they will price and re-price so that they sell their last pumpkin or tree just before the holiday begins.

Procuring Services

Third-party logistics infers that a firm is outsourcing some of its logistics tasks. The work to be done is described in a firm's **Request for Proposal (RFP),** to which potential supplying firms or individuals will respond. The RFPs will be reviewed, and a few parties who submitted them will be invited for interviews. Eventually, applicants will be asked to demonstrate their ability to perform the requested function. A **Request for Quotation (RFQ)** may be used for either services or materials; potential suppliers are asked to quote the price they would charge to provide the specified service or material.

A purchase order (PO) is used to obtain goods and services. It is a binding document that commits the buyer to pay for certain services or goods provided that they meet the requirements specified within the purchase order. Purchase order numbers are important in the supply chain since many firms have systems that accept goods only if they are accompanied by a specific purchase order number. Also, bills will not be paid unless a specific purchase order number is cited.

Many other services, in addition to those associated with logistics and supply chains, are procured. Firms require outside legal and accounting services and computer and software consultants. Other services might include payroll service, cafeteria management, building maintenance, printing, and landscape work. Various selection methods are used, but the procedures should include some involvement of the supply management staff.

Global Sourcing

The term **global sourcing** applies to buying components and inputs anywhere in the world. It means that the manufacturer, rather than relying solely on its local suppliers, casts out a much wider net in search of sources. The Internet has facilitated global sourcing since vendors located nearly anywhere can have cataloglike product displays on the Web.

The preceding discussion about J. C. Penney showed some of the additional steps involved when one buys overseas. Chapter 12 deals with international logistics, and some of its contents also relate to sourcing in foreign countries.

A global sourcing development model would include the following components: planning, specification, evaluation, relationship management, transportation and holding costs, implementation, and monitoring and improving. Questions that must be answered include the following:

- Does our firm have the expertise to manage global sourcing in-house, or should its managers consider the use of a trading company partner?

- How important is the certainty of materials supply? How stable, politically, are the countries from which we might be importing? How good is their infrastructure?
- How will we manage the lengthened and sometimes more variable lead times that global sourcing implies?
- Will there be problems in specifying what we want?
- What about fluctuating currencies? Can barter be used?
- What terms of sale should be used?
- How does this choice impact upon landed cost?[13]
- Can our lengthened supply chain be designed and managed so that the "bullwhip" effect, caused by each party's multiplying the dimensions of some alteration, is not a problem?[14]

One trade journal described "self-importing" as "Large retailers . . . arranging a growing number of imports themselves, without going through intermediaries. The concept of 'self-importing' is simple. Instead of buying a product from a brand-name manufacturer, a retailer will go directly to a manufacturing plant in Asia, have them made to its specifications, and then market the product under its own label. And instead of waiting to take control of the shipment when it reaches a U. S. port, the retailer arranges the transportation all the way to its U. S. distribution centers."[15]

Import quotas are absolute numeric limits on the items imported from specific countries within a specific time frame. They are placed on some products brought into the United States, especially textiles and apparel. Once a nation's quota is filled, no more of that item may be imported until the next period begins. In addition, there may be absolute prohibitions on importing from certain nations. In 2002, Ikea was fined $8,000 by the U.S. Treasury's Office of Foreign Assets Control for having imported 150 rugs from a section of Afghanistan that was under Taliban control.[16]

U.S. firms also try to develop operations overseas to avoid the restrictions that developing countries place on outside firms. However, in recent years, several U.S. firms have been embarrassed by revelations that the products they sold were made by badly exploited child labor elsewhere in the world (Nike is a frequently cited example). In reaction to this, some firms adopted the 60 Minutes sourcing rule; that is, they avoided sourcing where the source might be featured on 60 Minutes for using child labor, indentured labor, or prison labor or for having squalid working conditions.

E-Procurement

E-commerce is bringing many changes to the supply management field. Indeed, the business-to-business purchase of supplies and services via the Internet is referred to as **e-procurement.** It is used in many different applications and each day more

---

[13]Donald F. Wood, Anthony Barone, Paul R. Murphy, and Daniel L. Wardlow. *International Logistics*, 2nd ed. (New York: Amacom, 2002), Chapter 14.

[14]Rachel Mason-Jones and Denis R. Towill, "Reducing 'Bullwhip' Behavior in Global Supply Chains," *Supply Chain Forum*, No. 1, 2000, pp. 40–45.

[15]*The Journal of Commerce*, December 7, 1999, p. 1.

[16]U.S. Fines 86 Firms for Business with Nations on 'Enemies' List, *The Wall Street Journal*, July 3, 2002, p. A2.

uses and more users are found. Note that it is used both within the firm and between firms.

Here's an example of an e-parts procurement operation initiated by a technician who needs a part. (1) The technician accessed the corporate Internet and goes to an electronic web-based catalog that contains information on parts from multiple vendors. The technician searches for the required item . . . and checks specification, price, stock availability, and delivery lead-time. (2) With a few clicks of the mouse, a purchase requisition is completed. (3) The purchase requisition is automatically . . . routed to the appropriate person for approval. (4) A purchase order is sent electronically to the supplier's system. The supplier's system confirms price and availability, and immediately sends a delivery confirmation back to the technician's mailbox. (5) The supplier ships the part according to the instructions on the purchase order. . . . (6) The invoice, when received from the supplier, is automatically matched with purchase order and paid.[17]

Three issues arise when establishing systems that could handle the interchange like the one described in the preceding extract. One would be whose software would be used—the buyer's or the supplier's? For many buyers the parts ordering function is one aspect of a massive production planning program that includes nearly all of their operations. Second is the issue of who will maintain the catalogs with parts, part descriptions, parts interchangeability, and prices. Will the buyer and seller be reading off of the same page? The third issue deals with security and whether one's system is secure from outside hackers. Figure 11-3 depicts a secure trading connection.

A second form of E-commerce uses the Internet as a catalog to search for potential suppliers. Once some likely suppliers are identified, they can be contacted for more

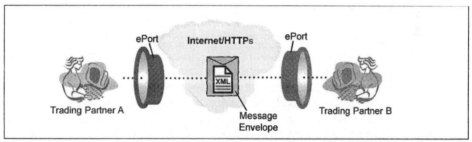

Reliable Messaging using ePort and ebXML

FIGURE 11-3 A Configuration of Internet Messaging to Provide For Secure Transmission

The message envelope can move between only the two parties and the system avoids resubmitting an order. The sender knows when the message is received. The system is designed to handle purchase orders, purchase order acknowledgments, price and availability checks, catalog updates, and file transfers. *Source:* PartNET.

[17]"Is an E-Procurement Solution Right for You? *Logistics* (Cleveland: Mercer Management Consulting, Spring/Summer, 1999), p. 32.

detailed information and, possibly, for samples. If the samples are satisfactory, one could enter into conventional purchasing negotiations.

In some trades, a third party serves as a host to buyers and sellers by setting up an auction, or online-exchange service, to which they subscribe. The third party then enters, into this marketplace with either a buying or selling offering and waits for others to bid. For a firm that is buying, a *reverse auction* is used with the first party bidding and the second party bidding a lower amount, and so on. Each exchange has its own rules as to how visible all aspects of the operation are to individual subscribers. Some of the exchanges are formed by a consortium of firms within the industry. Readers familiar with eBay or some of the airline travel e-sales have some idea how these auctions work. Subscribing to an auction service is also advantageous because one can follow current prices at which goods are moving and can use this as a benchmark to compare with prices he or she is paying through conventional markets. E-payment services and software also exist, allowing the buyer to pay for the goods purchased electronically after approving the payment.

Electronic exchanges peaked around the year 2000, and then many went out of business as the dot-com boom fizzled. The principal reasons many did not succeed was either lack of detailed knowledge about the industry they were serving or that many markets were performing adequately before they arrived and there was no extra margin left to pay a party facilitating a sale.[18] Some electronic exchanges did survive and no doubt we shall be seeing more of them.

Some ethical issues are involved with e-procurement. First, one cannot assume that information sent out electronically is secure and must assume that there is risk it will end up in general circulation. Second, ethical standards are not uniform throughout the world, and any two parties negotiating a purchase may be following two different sets of ethical standards.

Procurement cards are also called *buying cards*. Examples include the Visa and American Express cards that many people carry for personal use. Buying cards are assigned to corporations that, in turn, assign them to individual employees. Most are used for travel, although an employee may be allowed to make other purchases. Each month, the firm receives a detailed statement listing employee, details of purchases, and purchase prices. It is usually up to the card user's immediate supervisor to review her or his subordinates' monthly statement and, if necessary, to speak with the subordinate about items listed. Other vendors also issue buying cards. Office-supply chains may issue a certain number to a firm that will then distribute it to supervisors or employees authorized to make office-supply purchases. The using firm's procurement staff may have negotiated a discount with the office-supply chain that becomes greater as the total sum of all purchases increases.

Quality Programs

Today, most firms stress quality in their processes and products. In the procurement field it is necessary to match the quality levels of all buyers and sellers along the supply chain, otherwise the final product's quality will suffer. If one buys an input of lower quality, one runs the risk of lowering the quality of the final product. If one buys an

---

[18]"The State of Online Exchanges," *WERCSheet*, Vol. 24, No. 7, December 2001, pp. 8–10.

input of higher quality than one's final product, one may be paying for something one does not need. In short, in the buy–sell relationship, both parties must understand issues of quality and, usually, they should hope to raise the overall quality of their joint undertaking. Quality is very important to firms operating in the supply-chain concept since the link with the lowest quality is the likeliest one to be dropped by the others. Today, vendors are expected to have quality programs. Obviously, many have worked for years to achieve a good reputation.

One way for vendors to convince potential buyers that they, too, are capable of quality performance is through a program known as ISO 9000 certification. (ISO stands for International Standards Organization.) **ISO 9000** is a set of generic standards used to document, implement, and demonstrate quality management and assurance systems. Applicable to manufacturing and service industries, these standards are intended to help companies build quality into every core process in each department. These programs are not limited to manufacturers; a number of carriers are also engaged in ISO 9000 programs. Firms demonstrating a commitment to quality through training, reviews, and audits can receive an ISO 9000 certification.

By late 1994, each of the major U.S. auto builders had developed and put in place its own quality assurance program for its specific suppliers. At that time, the three major automakers, plus truck manufacturers Freightliner, Mack, Navistar International, Paccar (which builds Kenworth and Peterbilt), and Volvo–GM, mailed a new quality assurance document to the industry's 13,000 suppliers. The document included "word-for-word the requirements contained in ISO 9001 (one of the documents in the ISO 9000 family) plus all of the additional requirements on which the eight [auto and truck] OEM [original equipment manufacturers] could harmonize."[19] The auto and truck builders also require the 13,000 suppliers to hold their suppliers to the document's quality requirements. This is an example of the supply-chain concept at work.

ISO 14000 is another quality standard related to reduction of wastes and environmental pollution. Suppliers subscribing to this code make a commitment toward adopting environmental protection practices, although the exact wording does not appear to be very demanding. Professors Burt, Dobler, and Starling believe that ISO 14000 is rather tepid, given the dimensions of the pollution problems it supposedly addresses.[20] In the United States, many government agencies give preference to suppliers and products that have some environmentally friendly components. A common example is requiring that paper contain a certain percentage of recycled material and that copiers be able to function properly with this type of paper.

Another concept or practice is known as the **Six Sigma** approach, which emphasizes the collection and analysis of data, with the goal being to nearly eliminate errors. Those who remember the normal curve from their statistics class will recall that Sigmas are related to standard deviations from the mean. The larger the number deviations, the more area under the normal curve that is covered and the smaller area is uncovered. In the case of Six Sigmas, the area covered is 99.99966 percent, leaving a tiny area,

---

[19]*TENews*, September 1994, p. 1.

[20]David Burt, Donald Dobler, and Stephen Starling, *World Class Supply Management* (New York: McGraw Hill Irwin, 2002), p. 70.

.00034 uncovered or of error. This is obviously a high standard. Persons trained in the Six Sigma process are awarded green belts, black belts, or master belts, depending upon their level of training. "A master blackbelt is essentially an individual who has attained the highest level of understanding of Six Sigma and is capable of training others and working as an internal consultant in a corporation. Black belts become the primary drivers of Six Sigma improvements within companies by essentially managing specific projects."[21] General Electric's chairman said, "At G.E., the best Six Sigma projects begin not inside the business but outside it, focused on answering the question—how can we make the customer more competitive . . . ? One thing that we have discovered with certainty is that anything we do that makes the customer more successful inevitably results in a financial return for us."[22]

Ford is a major user of the Six Sigma approach. In North America, Ford receives materials from 5,000 vendors that move to 46 manufacturing plants, which then distributes finished products to 7,000 dealers. Ford is using the Six Sigma processes for improving the flow of all these items throughout its supply chain. In 2002 Ford had "2,400 employees—or approximately one percent of its total full-time staff—working as Black Belts."[23]

Supplier Selection and Management

The discussion in Chapter 4 about customer service dealt with how a firm kept existing customers happy. Supplier management pursues similar goals, i.e., keeping existing suppliers happy. Businesses are very dependent upon suppliers, and the upstream suppliers control, or at least influence, the quality and quantity of goods that a firm receives. At one time, a purchasing manager was expected to encourage 'cutthroat' competition among potential suppliers with a three- or six-month arm's-length contract awarded to the lowest bidder. Almost immediately, the bidding cycle would start again and another low bidder would get the contract for the next several months. More recently, as we moved into an era of partnerships, less cutthroat bidding occurred and instead negotiations and adoption of long-term evergreen contracts took place.

Selecting vendors is a procedure that involves stating one's needs and then determining how well various potential suppliers can fulfill them. Some form of weighting is used and applied to all qualified firms bidding for business. Following are the factors that most vendors consider to be important:

- Delivery
- Facilities and capacity
- Geographic location
- Performance history
- Price

---

[21]Ibid., p. 131.

[22]Ibid.

[23]Karen G. Moore, "Six Sigma: Driving Supply Chain Success at Ford," *Supply Chain Management Review*, Vol. 6, No. 4, 2002, p. 41.

- Quality
- Technical capability
- Warranties and claim policies

Weber, Current, and Desai suggest a five-stage vendor selection process.[24] Step one looks at both the internal environment and external environment within which the decision is to be made. Internally, who are the stakeholders, where is the product needed, and in what quantity and quality? The external environment would be legal and regulatory frameworks controlling the purchase and the marketplace within which the potential suppliers operate. Are there institutional impediments that will limit the buyer's ability to access the supplier's resources?

In the second step, the purchasing party lists and considers all of the available options. Because many potential suppliers can be found on the Internet, an extremely large number of possibilities exist. Certain types of computer programs might be useful here to narrow and better focus the choices.

The third step involves the actual evaluation and comparison of options. Often, so many variations are possible that one must rely on computers to perform portions of the evaluation. Humans must take the computer evaluations, give them their appropriate weight, and decide which vendors they would like to select.

Negotiations constitute step four. Face-to-face meetings are held with representatives of those potential vendors who ranked the highest in the step 3 evaluations. Part of the negotiations focus on areas where the vendor did not score highly, say, in making deliveries in a punctual manner. Tentative prices and other terms are decided, and both parties size up each other to determine how long a contractual agreement they wish to enter.

Forming a partnership is step five. Ideally, both parties see and seek the advantages of a long-term relationship. At the same time, the parties must consider their own core competencies and ponder whether to surrender any of those as they enter into contractual agreements.

Professors Krause and Scannell use the term **supplier development** as "any effort of a buying firm to increase the performance of a supplier. This definition encompasses a variety of supplier activities including supplier assessment and feedback, the use of supplier incentives, competitive pressure, and direct involvement activities that may include supplier training and investment."[25] When developing suppliers, some strategic goals are to increase the supplier's financial strength and to improve their management and technical capabilities, as well as their abilities to develop new products. Performance goals would include better-quality products, lower prices, improved delivery performance, and increased overall responsiveness. There are several ways to evaluate and provide feedback to the supplier. Lastly, it is useful to have the suppliers install and rigorously maintain quality controls in their own businesses so that it is not necessary for the buyer to inspect the product upon its receipt.

---

[24]Charles A. Weber, John R. Current, and Anand Desai, "VendOR: A Structured Approach to Vendor Selection and Negotiation," *Journal of Business Logistics*, Vol. 21, No. 1, 2000, p. 136.

[25]Daniel R. Krause and Thomas V. Scannell, "Supplier Development Practices: Product- and Service-Based Industry Comparisons," *The Journal of Supply Chain Management*, Vol. 38, No. 2, 2002, p. 13.

In recent years, Dell Computer has received considerable attention for its "build to order" programs. As part of its success, "Dell worked at length to build an effective supplier management function in order to shorten component lead-times and maintain the absolute quality standards required by the just-in-time operations," and, "the company worked with its suppliers to shorten their product life cycles, extending the Dell business model to the whole channel."[26]

In some areas of purchasing, it is necessary to continually identify new sources of supply. Anyone purchasing works from artists, musicians, or writers must always be searching for new, young talent. In Florida, California, and Hawaii, land that once grew fruit has been lost to housing, so buyers of fruit have had to find and develop new growers, often in other countries. A procurement professional might also want to do business with several sources so that they compete with each other. Commercial airline executives now have only two firms, Boeing and Airbus, to buy from. Two other major builders, Lockheed and McDonnell-Douglas, no longer compete.

Some buyers still play hardball. An article in the *Wall Street Journal* entitled "Grocery Distributor Squeezes Suppliers at Bill-Paying Time," described several disputes between grocery products suppliers and Fleming Cos., a large grocery distributor. Oil-Dri (a maker of kitty litter) complained that when Fleming paid its bill, "It arbitrarily deducted large sums for things such as product placement or early bill payment, even if it was actually paying late."[27] Oil-Dri complained that the products were never slotted in either Fleming's warehouses or Kmart's shelves. Oil-Dri was disputing several hundred thousand dollars in various charges in a breach-of-contract suit against Fleming. "In the weeks before the April 20 [2002] close of Fleming's fiscal first quarter, Fleming's suppliers received letters informing them of a slew of new deductions. Kellogg Co. found that the total amount it considered unjustified had jumped to more than $500,000, even though Kellogg had paid to become a 'preferred customer.' "[28]

Purchasing Ethics

One of the challenges in managing a purchasing/procurement operation is that it has a colorful but sad tradition of unethical behavior. Bribes, kickbacks, and acceptance of lavish gifts—the most common breaches of **purchasing ethics**—have not been uncommon. Many purchasing jobs paid low salaries but were coveted because of the opportunities to earn extra income. When one reads of financial scandals involving public agencies, more likely than not the method by which the funds were illegally diverted was through misuse of the purchasing operation.

Why is this so? Purchasing staffs spend huge amounts of money; many firms spend more than half their sales receipts on buying more materials. Selecting and procuring materials is not an exact science; there is some wiggle room for error or, perhaps, for a bribe. Salespeople are taught to do nearly anything to make a sale, and some are not

---

[26]William C. Copacino and Jonathan L. S. Byrnes, "How to Become a Supply Chain Master," *Supply Chain Yearbook 2002*, p. 39.

[27]*Wall Street Journal*, September 5, 2002, p. A1.

[28]Ibid., p. A10.

above offering a bribe or a kickback. They may be aware that the purchasing person will not accept bribes, and they will attempt to devise other methods of currying his or her favor.

Other areas of ethical concern involve handling of confidential information, family relationships, purchasing for one's own account, buying for one's employer (an example being to buy a car for one's private use while purchasing a fleet of cars for one's employer), interfering with a legitimate bidding process, and conflicts of interest.

A supply-chain conundrum occurs when another firm is both one's customer and one's supplier. Do different rules apply? Where is the profit to be made: from selling at a high price or buying at a low price? Should special enticements be used? If it stops being your supplier, will it stop being your customer?

Some corporate-level ethics deal with buying and supporting markets for materials or practices that are harmful to the environment. Volvo provides a positive example with its "program to track chemical usage. It employs a database identifying the environmental impacts of more than 5,000 chemical products. From this list, Volvo has developed two lists—a black and a gray list. The black list includes chemicals that the company has banned from use in its products. The gray list includes a similar list of chemicals for which Volvo is attempting to locate more environmentally benign substitutes."[29]

This topic is much broader than the space devoted to it here indicates. Purchasing and procurement are not the only areas of supply-chain management where bribery and kickbacks occur. However, anyone working in the purchasing and procurement field must recognize that these problems will not go away.

SUMMARY

Supply management deals with identifying needs to be met with outside sources, selecting these sources, and negotiating purchase contracts with those selected. Purchases fall into three categories: parts or components to be used in manufacture, merchandise for resale, and services.

Supply management is closely related to logistics for two reasons. First, nearly anything purchased must be moved to wherever it is needed. Second, if third-party logistics providers are used, the firm's procurement staff will be involved in their selection.

Just-in-time and kanban systems are used for parts procurement. They rely on small deliveries that result in almost no inventories. Because there are no inventory cushions, the quality of the inputs has to be high. Professionals involved in procurement practices are often involved in various quality-control programs to continually upgrade the quality of materials that they buy and, ultimately, that they sell.

When materials are purchased for resale, the buyer is concerned with the potential markup that can be applied, so that the resale price will generate a profit.

Global sourcing means looking nearly anywhere in the world for potential suppliers. This has been made easier with use of the Internet, which allows one to make contacts worldwide. This is a form of e-procurement. Auctions are also conducted via the Internet.

---

[29]*Private Sector Pioneers* (Washington, DC: The Environmental Protection Agency, ca. 2002), p. 16.

Suppliers, once selected, must be treated with care. Often they will become partners. However, a buyer must never become too dependent upon a single supplier; it is wise to keep options open.

Ethics is a matter of continual concern to those working in the supply management field.

QUESTIONS FOR DISCUSSION AND REVIEW

1. What is supply management? What is its relevance to logistics?
2. Discuss the three categories of inbound goods.
3. Discuss three steps that could be followed by firms that wish to gain better control of the logistics associated with their inbound movements.
4. Discuss the make-or-buy decision as it relates to supply management.
5. What is MRP I? What is MRP II?
6. What are JIT systems?
7. How does the Toyota (kanban) production system differ from traditional production methods?
8. What are two primary advantages that accrue when the JIT system is used?
9. Discuss the four ways that a firm's logistics staff fits into the production scheduling and MRP processes.
10. What is a value web? What does it achieve?
11. What is the difference between an RFP and an RFQ?
12. What is a purchase order? How is it used?
13. What are some questions that might be addressed by a global sourcing development model?
14. Discuss three issues that might be addressed by an e-procurement system.
15. Discuss the role of online auctions in supply management.
16. Why are buyers concerned about the quality of materials they purchase?
17. What is the role of ISO certification in quality management programs?
18. What are Six Sigma programs?
19. Describe the five-step vendor selection process presented in this chapter.
20. Discuss some of the ethical issues associated with supply management.

SUGGESTED READINGS

Ansari, A., Diane Lockwood, and Batoul Modarress, "Supplier Product Integration—A New Competitive Approach." *Production and Inventory Management Journal*, Vol. 40, No. 3, 1999, pp. 57–61.

Araujo, Luis, Anna Dubois, and Lars-Erik Gadde, "Managing Interfaces with Suppliers." *Industrial Marketing Management*, Vol. 28, 1999, pp. 497–506.

Cavinato, Joseph L. "What's Your Supply Chain Type?" *Supply Chain Management Review*, Vol. 6, No. 3, 2002, pp. 60–66.

Cooke, James A. "Should You Control Your Inbound?" *Traffic Management*, February 1993, pp. 30–33.

Dixon, Lance, and Anne Millen Porter. JIT II: *Revolution in Buying and Selling*. Newton, MA: Cahners Publishing Company, 1994.

Essig, Michael, and Ulli Arnold, "Electronic Procurement in Supply Chain Management: An Information Economics-Based Analysis of Electronic Markets." *The Journal of Supply Chain Management*, Vol. 37, No. 4, 2001, pp. 43–49.

Faes, Wouter, Paul Matthyssens, and Koen Vandenbempt. "The Pursuit of Global Purchasing Synergy." *Industrial Marketing Management*, Vol. 29, 2000, pp. 539–553.

Ferrin, Bruce. "Planning Just-in-Time Supply Operations: A Multiple-Case Analysis." *Journal of Business Logistics*, Vol. 15, No. 1, 1994, pp. 53–69.

Freeman, Blair, Steve Haasz, Stefano Lizzola, and Nicholas Seiersen, "Managing Your Cost to Serve." *Supply Chain Forum*, No. 1, 2000, pp. 18–28.

Gentry, Julie J., and Martin J. Farris, "The Increasing Importance of Purchasing in Transportation Decision Making." *Transportation Journal*, Vol. 32, No. 1, 1992, pp. 61–72.

Houghton, Tim, Bill Markham, and Bob Tevelson, "Thinking Strategically About Supply Management." *Supply Chain Management Review*, Vol. 6, No. 5, 2002, pp. 32–38.

Inman, R. Anthony, "Environmental Management: New Challenges for Production and Inventory Managers." *Production and Inventory Management Journal*, Vol. 40, No. 3, 1999, pp. 46–49.

Krause, Daniel R., and Thomas V. Scannell, "Supplier Development Practices: Product- and Service-Based Industry Comparisons." *The Journal of Supply Chain Management*, Vol. 38, No. 2, 2002, pp. 13–21.

Lancioni, Richard A., Michael F. Smith, and Terence A. Oliva, "The Role of the Internet in Supply Chain Management." *Industrial Marketing Management*, Vol. 29, 2000, pp. 45–56.

Lawrence, F. Barry, Daniel F. Jennings, and Brian E. Reynolds. *EDistribution* (Mason, OH: Thomson/Southwestern, 2003).

Maltz, Arnold, and Lisa M. Ellram, "Selling Inbound Logistics Services: Understanding the Buyer's Perspective." *Journal of Business Logistics*, Vol. 21, No. 2, 2000, pp 69–88.

Mason-Jones, Rachel, and Denis R. Towill, "Coping with Uncertainty: Reducing 'Bullwhip' Behavior in Global Supply Chains." *Supply Chain Forum*, No. 1, 2000, pp. 40–45.

Perks, Helen, and Geoff Easton, "Strategic Alliances: Partner as Customer." *Industrial Marketing Management*, Vol. 29, July 2000, pp. 327–338.

Scannell, Thomas V., Shawnee K. Vickery, and Cornelia L. Dröge. "Upstream Supply Chain Management and Competitive Performance in the Automotive Supply Industry." *Journal of Business Logistics*, Vol. 21, No. 1, 2000, pp. 23–46.

Weber, Charles A., John R. Current, and Ahand Desai, "VendOR: A Structured Approach to Vendor Selection and Negotiation." *Journal of Business Logistics*, Vol. 21, No. 1, 2000, pp. 135–167.

Wood, Donald F., Anthony Barone, Paul Murphy, and Daniel L. Wardlow. *International Logistics*, 2nd ed. (New York: Amacom, 2002).

C A S E S

Case 11-1   Easing Ira's Ire

Ira Pollack was difficult to work for. A self-made millionaire, he paid extremely high salaries but demanded much from his subordinates, including being on call 24 hours per day. In his Las Vegas penthouse, he would study and restudy each detail of his conglomerate's performance and then call some unlucky underling—at any hour—to vent his anger and demand that something or other be improved. His tantrums were legendary.

One of Pollack's underlings, Tamara Wood, was driving her new red Mercedes convertible along Rodeo Drive in Beverly Hills, looking for a parking space. Her college class from Northern Illinois University at DeKalb was holding its fifth reunion in Chicago, which she planned to attend. She wanted to buy a new outfit for the event, to show her former classmates that she had "arrived." A chauffeur-driven Rolls pulled away from the curb, leaving an empty space right in front of her favorite couturier. She swung her Mercedes expertly into the empty space, looked up, and was pleased to see that there was still nearly an hour left on the meter. "Daddy was right," she thought to herself, "Clean living does pay off."

As she turned off the ignition, Tamara's cell phone started buzzing. Wood hesitated. Would it be John, calling to thank her for that wonderful evening? Would it be Matt, seeing if she were free to spend next weekend on Catalina Island? Or maybe it was Jason, who was always wanting her to accompany him to Waikiki. She finally picked up the phone and sweetly said, "Hello."

"Dammit! Don't 'hello' me!" shouted a man's voice at the other end.

Wood's stomach churned, her muscles tightened, and she said, weakly, "Sorry, Mr. Pollack, I was expecting somebody else."

"That's obvious," he retorted. "At this hour of the day, you're on *my* time and *should* be thinking of business. How come you're not in the office?"

"I'm just making a customer-service follow-up," responded Wood, hoping that Mr. Pollack would not ask for too many details.

"Well, you *should* be worried about customer service," said Pollack. "That's why I've called. I've been studying performance records for all my operations dealing with the amount of time that elapses between our receipt of an order and when our customer receives a shipment. The performance of your distribution center in West Hollywood *stinks*! Drop what you're doing and *get back to your office* and figure out what's wrong! Then tell me what's needed to speed up your operation. Call me at any hour."

Wood heard the phone click. She forgot about DeKalb. She forgot about Chicago and the new outfit. She forgot about her night with John, about Catalina Island, and about Waikiki. She heard a faint beep to her left. She saw a maroon Jaguar, with a Beverly Hills matron motioning with one of her white-gloved hands as if to say, "If you're leaving, may I have your parking spot?"

"Dammit," thought Wood as she pulled away. "If it weren't for a hundred thou a year, I'd tell Pollack what he could do with his order-processing system."

Still muttering, she pulled into her reserved slot next to the West Hollywood distribution center. "Aloha!" chirped Ellen Scott, her assistant, as she walked in. "Jason has called three times about wanting you to fly to Hawaii. Also, you have two calls from John, one from Matt, one from your mother, who asked why you never phone her, and one from some fellow who wouldn't leave his name but said it was very personal. Tell me about the outfit you bought. I'll bet it's stunning."

"Forget about them, and hold all my calls," said Wood, crisply. "I'm not going anywhere. Pollack called me and is mad because our order-processing and delivery times are out of whack."

Two days passed. Wood had put her social life on hold and had not even phoned her mother. All her time was spent trying to figure out how to speed up her order-processing system. But she didn't know how to start. The accuracy of the system was not an issue, although additional costs could be. When Pollack paid his bonuses last year, he had told Wood that if her operation had cost one cent more to run, she would not have received a bonus. Because her bonus had paid for her new Mercedes, Wood was cost conscious, to say the least.

Wood's assistant helped her, too—at least through late Friday afternoon. Scott explained that she couldn't work on Saturday and Sunday because she'd accepted an invitation to spend the weekend at Catalina Island with an unnamed friend. Before Scott left, she and Wood had decided that there were 12 distinct operations involved in processing and shipping orders. Some could be performed at the same time, whereas others had to be performed in sequence—that is, one could not be started until the other was completed. (These tasks, the amount of time it takes to complete each, and the sequential relationships, if any, are shown in Exhibit 11-A.)

After compiling the information shown in Exhibit 11-A, Scott left. Wood was left with the task of trying to relate all those tasks to each other. She recalled a college textbook that she had never much cared for but that she had come across a few weeks earlier as she was searching for her Northern Illinois University yearbook. Wood looked at a PERT chart in that book and knew that she would have to construct something similar in order to analyze the distribution center's order-processing and shipping operations. She studied the text accompanying the chart, sighed, and thought to herself, "Where was I—or at least where was my mind—the day the professor explained all of this in class?"

EXHIBIT 11-A Order-Processing and Shipment Tasks in Approximate Order of Completion

Task	Description	Duration (in days)	Precedence Relationships (tasks on right of < cannot commence until tasks on left are completed)
A	Order received and entered into computer	0.25	A < D
B	Determine whether to fill from warehouse or ship direct from factory	0.50	B < C
C	Print picking order	0.30	C < H
D	Verify customer's credit	0.35	D < G, E
E	Check and determine buyer's eligibility for discounts	0.15	E < F
F	Prepare invoice and enter in accounts receivable file	1.00	F < K
G	Determine mode of transport and select carrier	1.65	G < J
H	Pick order at warehouse	0.75	H < I
I	Pack and label shipment	1.20	I < L
J	Notify carrier and prepare shipping documents	2.25	J < L
K	Transmit copy of invoice to shipping dock	1.20	K < L
L	Transport order to customer	3.50	

QUESTIONS

1. Arrange the tasks shown in Exhibit 11-A in a network or PERT chart.
2. Determine the critical path. What is the least amount of time it takes between receipt of an order and its delivery to a customer?
3. Considering your answers to questions 1 and 2, what areas of activity do you think Wood should look at first, assuming she wants to reduce order-processing and delivery times? Why?
4. Now that she's a Californian ready for the race down the information superhighway, Wood wants to be able to impress Pollack with her knowledge of current technology. Recently, a sales representative from a warehouse equipment company called, trying to interest her in installing a "Star Wars—Robotic" order picker for the warehouse. Controlled by lasers and powered by magnetic levitation, the device can pick orders (task H) in 15 minutes, rather than 6 hours (0.75 day), the current time needed. How valuable would such a device be to Wood? Why?
5. Another alternative is to use faster transportation. How should Wood choose between paying more for faster transportation and paying more for other improvements? Assume that her only goal is speed.
6. To offset some of the costs of speeding up the system, does the PERT chart indicate where there might be some potential savings from assigning fewer people to some tasks, thereby increasing the amount of time needed to complete these tasks? If so, which tasks are likely candidates? Why?

Case 11-2   Tempo Ltd.

Fatih Terim was in his small office in Antalya, a Mediterranean port in southwestern Turkey. He looked at the clock on the wall and realized he had spent the entire afternoon thinking about one thing and one thing only—the most recent meeting with his Romanian business "connection." Terim had just completed a trip to the Balkans and was in his office evaluating his firm's progress in the region. This was necessary since he was thinking of going to Syria for the same reasons that had taken him to the Balkans: finding goods at cheap prices and selling them with handsome markups at home in Turkey or in other neighboring countries.

Terim had established Tempo Ltd. in 1989 in Antalya. Terim, then fresh out of Akdeniz University, quickly became an entrepreneur. The focus of his business was to buy goods from nearby foreign sources and then find buyers for those products in the domestic Turkish market. The first couple of years were easy for Terim since he was working very hard and the Turkish economy was soaring. With the fall of communism, Terim saw even more opportunities. He started marketing Turkish-made goods to former communist countries around Turkey and in central Asia.

However, the Turkish economy took a major hit in April 1994. The sudden death of the country's president added to the nation's political instability. The value of Turkish lira (TL) plummeted against the U.S. dollar ($USD). In the following years, the Turkish economy took many more hits, including the financial crisis in the Asian markets, the Russian market crash, and, most recently, the Argentinean crisis. In 1999, two major earthquakes hit the northwestern part of Turkey, where one-third of the of the nation's 67 million persons reside and which is the heartland of Turkish industry. Although Turkey recovered quickly from the earthquakes, political instability continued and pushed the entire economy into a slowdown. In 1993, one U.S. dollar could buy 7,000 Turkish liras. Today, that same one U.S. dollar can buy 1,567,000 TL. In spite of these discouraging events, the Turkish economy still has opportunities for growth. One reason such a major potential still exists is the simple fact that hardworking, sharp-trading people like Fatih Terim never stood still and kept putting together the best deals they could.

Today Terim's company has some connections in almost every European country and is working very hard to maintain these connections by generating steady flows of commerce. Terim's latest trip was to the Balkan nations of Bulgaria, Romania, and Greece. Terim held meetings with key business people in all three nations. In both Bulgaria and Greece, Terim had entered into modest sales agreements that extend into the middle of next year.

In Romania, matters did not move as quickly. Terim's Romanian connection, George Hagi, was not interested in any of the small transactions that Terim was suggesting. Hagi, in an almost mysterious manner, did tell Terim that he looking for a Turkish partner willing to participate in a substantial, although not exactly legitimate, deal. The first aspect was that the customer wanted to buy Turkish chemicals to be used for fertilizers in agriculture. However, the terms of payment from the prospective customers would be in the form of barter rather than cash and the goods bartered for the chemicals would be *kereste* (lumber). Although *barter* was a term and practice with which Terim was familiar, he had no idea what to do with *kereste*. Over the years, Tempo Ltd. had concentrated its business on small consumer products. However, he wasn't going to let a detail like this get in the way of new markets. He knew he could find a market in Turkey for lumber, since little was produced

domestically and both new construction and earthquake reconstruction were underway.

What worried Terim was his new customers. He learned from Hagi that these new customers were either a large state-owned company in North Korea or the North Korean government itself, which is why Terim spent that entire afternoon thinking about just one thing. All day he tried to justify his possible decisions to himself. The problem was that North Korea was a communist regime and, beyond that, North Korea, according to NATO and the United Nations, was a country that provided support to certain terrorist activities all over the world. In early 2002, United States President George W. Bush had described Iran, Iraq, and North Korea as an "axis of evil." North Korea and those with whom it traded were under tight scrutiny from both the United Nations and the United States (which still stationed troops in South Korea).

Terim came up with the excuse that if he didn't sell to the North Koreans, someone else would eventually, so why should he give up this money? However, the solution was not that easy. Hagi said in his e-mail to Terim that if the negotiations went well a party of North Korean bureaucrats would wish to visit Antalya for "inspection" purposes and that Terim would have to cover the costs of entertainment and accommodations. Those accommodations would range from luxurious hotel rooms to young attractive companions, of both sexes, for business-related dinners and receptions. Terim knew exactly what those inspection purposes were. They were pleasure trips for certain bureaucrats in North Korea. Unfortunately, he was also aware that this was the way things worked in Third-World governments. Over the years, he had learned the tricks of the trade, and one thing he knew well was that without the *rusvet* (bribe: the grease money or large amounts of payments specifically for one-time transactions), such risky situations would end up as a "no sale." He wondered whether he should ask the Turkish agricultural chemical manufacturers to help with the entertainment costs. Also, should he and the chemical manufacturers touch base with each other with respect to the *rusvet* that would undoubtedly be expected by the North Koreans?

Terim's position regarding *rusvet* was unclear. Indeed, the chemical manufactures should be expected to give him, and/or Hagi, a kickback for facilitating the sale of chemicals.

"Talk about core competency," Terim mumbled to himself. To get his mind off these sticky issues, he looked into the logistics costs to move the bartered lumber from North Korea. He would need to know those costs before proceeding. He had a couple of options.

The first option would be to ship the lumber by sea from Wonsan, North Korea, through the Sea of Japan, across the Indian Ocean, through the Suez canal, and into the liman (port) of Antalya, Turkey. (See Exhibits 11-B and 11-C.) This would be the perfect solution, except, he suddenly realized, he would not be able to bring the lumber into Turkey legally because of trade sanctions against North Korea. Hence, this option was dropped.

His second option would be to send the lumber to a country where its entry would be legal. The country to which the kereste could be shipped legally was none other than Romania, one of Turkey's neighbors on the Black Sea. The reason was hidden in history. Since their communist years, Romania and North Korea had had strong ties that remained nearly intact after the fall of communism in Romania. So lumber could be loaded on to a *gemi* (ship) and could be shipped to Romania via the Dardanelles and the Bosphorus (the two straits that make up the gateway to the Black Sea) and finally to the port of Constantza, Romania, in the Black Sea. Once there, the lumber could be covered by new documents and eventually the origin of the goods could be stated as "Romania," not "North Korea." The lumber could then move by *tir* (truck) to Turkey. This sounded like a feasible solution, but how much would such an operation cost? Terim recalled that Hagi had said the redoing documents in situations like this cost about 16,000,000,000 TL, including *rusvets*.

Terim's mind then shifted to a third option. From Wonsan, the lumber could be shipped to a port in Syria, in this case Latakia. From there, *tirs* could haul the lumber to Iskenderun at the southeastern border of Turkey. Because the border at Iskenderun is the most laxly guarded border in Turkey, small *rusvets* to low-ranking officers at the gates would allow the *kereste* to enter Turkey without any problems. The *rusvets* would be about 10 percent of the kereste shipment's value.

The same could be done at the Liman of Antalya. However, the chances of getting caught were much higher. If Tempo Ltd. were caught red-handed, it would be fined a sum of double the total value of goods entering the country. Thus, this was a fourth, but discarded, option.

Only two options were feasible, and each came with certain risks. One was to ship the *kereste* to Romania, have new documents drawn, falsify the shipment's origin, and then send it to Turkey by *tir*. The other was to send the *kereste* by ship to Syria, truck it to Turkey, and bribe customs inspectors at the Turkish border. Terim was initially concerned with the logistics costs of getting the *kereste* inside the Turkish border. The *kereste* would be of various dimensions, bound together by metal straps into bundles measuring 1 meter by 1 meter by 5 meters, and the North Koreans would deliver and load the *kereste* aboard a break-bulk vessel in a North Korean port.

If Terim could get the *kereste* inside Turkey, it should sell for 783,500,000,000 TL. The Turkish chemical manufacturers expect to be paid 60 days after the chemicals leave the Turkish port, which will be same date as the *kereste* leaves North Korea.

Terim gazed at his notes, which were full of numbers and currency exchange rates.

Ocean transportation costs for Gemi (Shipping lines require payment in U.S. dollars):	
Wonsan to Constantza	$42,000 USD
Wonsan to Latakia	$33,000 USD
Suez Canal charges	$ 3,100 USD
Tir:	
Constantza into Turkey	$15,000 USD
Latakia into Turkey	$12,000 USD
Handling fees at the Liman (Syria or Romania)	1.25% of the total value of goods

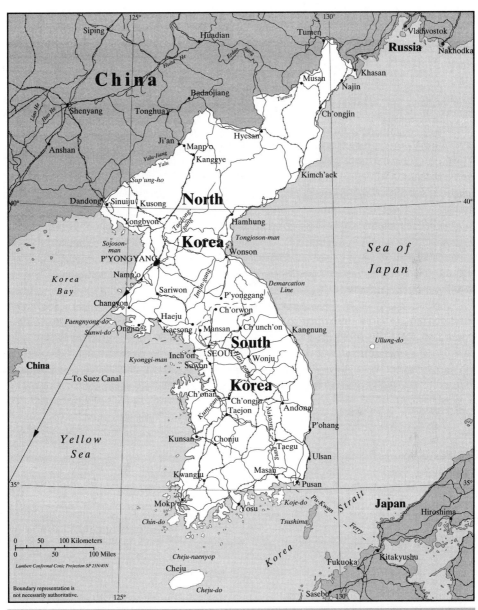

EXHIBIT 11-B Korean Peninsula

Generating false Romania-origin documents	16,000,000,000 TL	Currency exchange rates	$1 USD = 1,567,000 TL

Option 1: Wonsan/Constantza/Turkey would take 43 days

Projected amount of *rusvet* at Syrian–Turkish border	10 percent of shipment's value

Option 2: Wonsan/Latakia/Turkey would take 22 days

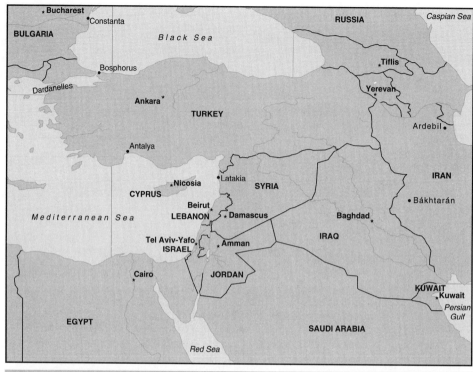

EXHIBIT 11-C Mediterranean Sea

QUESTIONS

1. Should Terim let somebody else complete the transaction because he knows that if he doesn't sell to the North Koreans someone else will?

2. What are the total costs given in the case for the option of moving via Romania?

3. What are the total costs given in the case for the option of moving via Syria?

4. Which option should Terim recommend? Why?

5. What other costs and risks are involved in these proposed transactions, including some not mentioned in the case?

6. Regarding the supply chain, how—if at all—should bribes be included? What functions do they serve?

7. If Terim puts together this transaction, is he acting ethically? Discuss.

8. What do you suggest should be done in order to bring moral values into the situation so that the developing countries are somewhat in accordance with Western standards? Keep in mind that the risks involved in such environments are much higher than the risks of conducting business in Western markets. Also note that some cultures see bribery as a way to better distribute the wealth among their citizens.

12

International Logistics

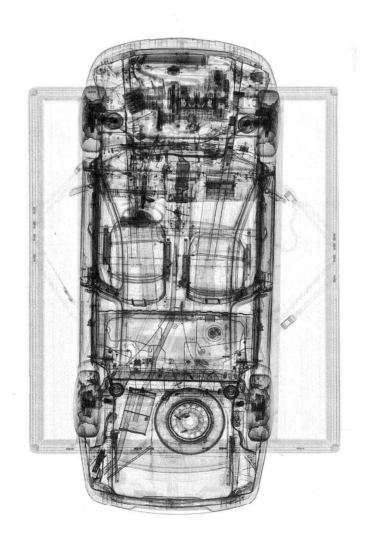

Key Terms

- Customshouse brokers
- Export management company
- Export packers
- Export trading company
- Import quotas
- Incoterms 2000
- International Air Transport Association (IATA)

- International freight forwarders
- Irrevocable letter of credit
- Land bridge
- Nontariff barrier
- Nonvessel-operating common carrier (NVOCC)
- Shippers associations
- Shipping conferences

Learning Objectives

- To identify the reasons for governmental intervention in the area of international trade
- To distinguish among the unique activities of international trade specialists
- To examine issues involved in international air transportation
- To relate activities involved in international ocean transportation

Many aspects of international logistics have been explored in earlier chapters. It is increasingly difficult to keep separate the practices of domestic and international logistics. International logistics—the movement of goods across national boundaries—occurs in the following situations:

1. A firm exports a portion of a product made or grown—for example, paper-making machinery to Sweden, wheat to Russia, or coal to Japan.
2. A firm imports raw materials—such as pulpwood from Canada—or manufactured products—such as motorcycles from Italy or Japan.
3. Goods are partially assembled in one country and then shipped to another, where they are further assembled or processed. For example, a firm stamps electronic components in the United States. It ships them to a free trade zone in the Far East, where low-cost labor assembles them, and then the assembled components are returned to the United States to become part of the finished product.
4. The firm is *global* in outlook and sees almost all nations as being markets, sources of supply, or sites for markets or for assembly operations.
5. Because of geography, a nation's domestic commerce crosses foreign borders, often in bond. For example, goods moving by truck between Detroit and Buffalo or between the Lower 48 states and Alaska, through Canada, travel in bond, which means that the carrier handling them has a special legal obligation to keep them sealed and to make certain that they are not released for sale or use within the country they are traveling through. Products shipped in bond are not subject to normal duties of the country through which they are passing.

Until World War II, concepts of international trade were simple. Industrialized powers maintained political and economic colonies that were sources of raw materials, cheap labor, and markets for manufactured products. When dealing with colonies, manufacturers in the parent country bought low and sold high. World War II brought an end to the colonial system; since then, emerging nations have attempted to develop their own political and economic systems with varying degrees of success. As emerging nations attempt to flex their political and economic muscles, they cause changes in the traditional ways of conducting international business.

Developing nations insist that an increasing proportion of assembling and manufacturing be conducted within their own borders. Because the role of these governments in their own economies is substantial, they are able to exert considerable influence over outside firms desiring to do business within their borders. They want their share of the supply chain's activity. They are becoming more insistent that much of their foreign trade be carried on vessels or planes owned by companies headquartered within their boundaries. They want their local firms to have at least their fair share of revenues from the sale of freight-forwarding services, marine insurance, and other distribution functions.

Traditionally, the United States has been a major exporter of manufactured goods and agricultural products. Because of its wealth, the United States has also imported many consumer goods. However, in the last three decades, several major changes have upset these traditional patterns. A new equilibrium has yet to be reached. The United States has been running trade deficits annually because of its large purchases of imported oil.

The fluctuating value of the U.S. dollar has an impact on the flow of both exports and imports. When the dollar is weak, it is more costly to import, but foreign customers buy U.S.-built products because to them the prices seem low. When the dollar is strong, the reverse holds true.

In the 1990s, several events changed the traditional patterns of how the United States conducts business overseas. The end of Soviet rule in Eastern Europe opened up the opportunity for engaging in much more trade with that major area of the world. In 1992, Western Europe achieved fuller economic integration, though many barriers remained (**nontariff barriers**) to the free movement of goods among all nations.[1] In addition, environmentalists in Europe are attempting to maintain restrictions on truck traffic so that more freight is forced to use rail and waterways.

> In Europe, pressure from the "Greens" (an environmental protection interest group) has caused truckers to use a ratings system, Euro I, Euro II, and Euro III, for their vehicles. Most new trucks are in the Euro II category, and soon there will be Euro III vehicles. "Austrians, who have been particularly hurt by the transport problems relative to the size of their country, allow no truck traffic across the mountains to move at night other than vehicles in the Euro II category, which are perceived as running more silently than those classified as Euro I. As a trucker in Austria, you have a choice of losing many hours or operating one of the newer, quieter, cleaner trucks."[2]

Also in the mid-1990s, the North American Free Trade Agreement (NAFTA) came into being, and efforts are being made to achieve closer economic integration

---

[1]See, for example, Spencer Henson and Rupert Loader, "Barriers to Agricultural Exports from Developing Countries: The Role of Sanitary and Phytosanitary Requirements," *World Development,* Vol. 29, No.1, January 2001, pp. 85–101.

[2]Peter Klaus, quoted in *American Shipper,* April 1997, p. 43.

among Canada, the United States, and Mexico. As this book is being revised, a major problem appears to be granting Mexican trucks and truck drivers access to the United States.

Although this text is written from the standpoint of U.S.-based firms involved in international trade, another type of firm has recently developed, one that can locate almost anywhere in the world and engage in commerce with any and all nations. The term *global logistics* is more applicable to the logistical challenges of this type of firm. Many corporations can be considered multinational.

Many degrees of involvement characterize global operations. A study of the world's auto industry presented several stages toward becoming global, with the ultimate stage being *transregional*. When "a company feels that it must integrate activities across the world in order to prioritize certain phenomenon (economies of scale, geographic convergence of markets, etc.), the configuration of a transregional company begins to take shape . . . , [and] hierarchical control is much greater, and the company's geographical organization tends toward homogeneity. Different regions are construed to be spaces of specific competencies and, from the very outset, attempts are made to coordinate these spaces through a global approach to the company's activities and to its network of alliances. A world-wide range of products is sold in various markets."[3]

Many of the preceding chapters in this book contain examples and descriptions of computer- and Internet-based applications that are revolutionizing the practices of logistics and supply-chain management. Some international settings are just as advanced, others are not. Trade involving North America, Western Europe, and parts of Asia utilizes computer and Internet applications as sophisticated as can be found anywhere. Internet usage for handling foreign logistics operations continues to increase. A survey of 77 large U.S. exporters in 2002 asked, "Which of the following export activities does your company plan to conduct online over the next three years?" Answers were export tracking, 69 percent; logistics coordination, 62 percent; transportation procurement, 47 percent; classifying products needed for calculating import duties, 39 percent; bill payment and settlement, 34 percent; and document delivery, 34 percent.[4]

As one looks at other parts of the world, the level of sophistication drops. As an extreme example, during relief efforts in Somalia during the 1990s, it was almost impossible for relief agencies to charter a ship small enough to enter into the silt-filled harbor of Mogadishu. Ships that small were no longer available in the commercial market.

Containerization is an important development in international commerce; handling at ports is faster, and door-to-door service can be provided. Containerized shipping is very important in routes between Asia and Europe, in the North Atlantic, between the United States and Europe, and in the Pacific between the United States and Asia. In the year 2000, five of the world's top six container-handling ports were in Asia: Hong Kong, Singapore, Kaoshiung, Pusan, and Shanghai.[5] In other trading regions, especially those

[3]Marie-Claude Belis-Bergouignan, Gerard Bordenave, and Yannick Lung, "Global Strategies in the Automobile Industry," *Regional Studies,* Vol. 34, No. 1, 2000, p. 43.

[4]"Where is the Payback in e-logistics?" *American Shipper,* July 2002, p. 34. An international *classification* of products is used for calculating import duties. Most ocean vessel operators use the same product description in their tariffs that determine freight charges.

[5]Donald F. Wood, Anthony P. Barone, Paul R. Murphy, and Daniel L. Wardlow, *International Logistics,* 2nd ed. (New York: Amacom, 2002), p. 91.

south of the Equator, containers are less important. The range of equipment and communication used in international supply chains varies widely. In a few areas of the world, some practices are no different from those of a half-century ago.

International Marketing

Marketing overseas is often different from marketing in the United States. Generalizations are difficult to make because each country of the world possesses unique characteristics when viewed as a market. Conventional marketing analysis is applied, although it must take into account a wide range of differences. Figure 12-1 is an ad placed by a New Jersey public utility offering to help its customers find trade leads.

In many countries, the size or scale of firms used in the distribution operation is much smaller than would be the case in the United States. Street vendors, merchants operating out of holes-in-the-wall, and small shopkeepers may be the rule. In these countries, customers shop daily and buy small amounts, and retailers are more likely to pull the requested good from a shelf behind the counter so there is less need for the type of packaging used in U.S. self-service markets. Other countries do have retail stores and shopping centers similar in scale to those in the United States.

Firms selling products under their own brand names are concerned about maintaining a reputation for quality in all markets. This can pose problems with respect to customer service. For example, how many parts depots should be located throughout the world? What kinds of guarantees can a U.S. firm make to foreign buyers? How enforceable are they? What changes must be made in a product to adapt it to export? The Internet is also creating a universal customer who may tap into the seller's system from anywhere in the world and expect to be treated as potential customers in the seller's home country.

Consumer preferences also differ. The following is an old example. LEGO, a firm headquartered in Denmark, makes children's construction toys. The product, which is sold worldwide, was once uniformly packaged in an elegant see-through carton. In the United States, LEGO lost market share to competitors that packaged a similar product in plastic buckets. Parents who purchased the toys found that the bucket was more functional and helped to encourage children to return the blocks to the bucket for storage. LEGO's U.S. management sought permission from Denmark to package LEGO toys in buckets. The head office flatly refused the request because buckets would be a radical deviation from the company's policy of standardized marketing everywhere. U.S. sales continued to drop, and it took 2 years for LEGO headquarters to reverse its decision.

In international distribution, push inventory systems are rare because the international credit system is not as well developed as the credit system within the United States or other similarly developed economic areas. In international business, if the buyer is unwilling or unable to pay, collection of the debt can prove difficult or even impossible. Furthermore, even though the buyer or borrower may be willing and able to pay, it may not be permitted to do so because of foreign exchange restrictions, expropriation, or political upheaval.

If the supplier is uncertain about receiving its payments, the supplier is unlikely to push unwanted goods onto its overseas distributors. Two ways a supplier can be assured of payment is to insist on payment in advance or to operate through an

FIGURE 12-1 Ad Placed by a New Jersey Utility Offering to Help Customers Develop Export Sales Leads, Agents, and Distributors

Source: Courtesy of TradeLink New Jersey, a program from Public Service Electric & Gas.

IRREVOCABLE COMMERCIAL LETTER OF CREDIT

Since 1852

WELLS FARGO BANK, N.A.

FORMERLY WELLS FARGO BANK AMERICAN TRUST COMPANY
HEAD OFFICE: 464 CALIFORNIA STREET, SAN FRANCISCO, CALIFORNIA 94104

INTERNATIONAL DIVISION — COMMERCIAL L/C DEPARTMENT — CABLE ADDRESS WELLS

OUR LETTER OF CREDIT NO. 27724 — AMOUNT: US$12,288.00 — DATE: April 1, 19
THIS NUMBER MUST BE MENTIONED ON ALL DRAFTS AND CORRESPONDENCE

- The Japan Co.
- Box X 25
- Tokyo, Japan

- Wells Fargo Bank N.A.
- Fuji Bldg., 2-3, 3-chome
- Marunouchi, Chiyoda-ku
- Tokyo, Japan

S P E C I M E N

GENTLEMEN:

BY ORDER OF Wards, Oakland, California

AND FOR ACCOUNT OF same

WE HEREBY AUTHORIZE YOU TO DRAW ON us

UP TO AN AGGREGATE AMOUNT OF Twelve Thousand Two Hundred Eighty Eight and No/100 U.S. Dollars

AVAILABLE BY YOUR DRAFTS AT sight

ACCOMPANIED BY
Commercial Invoice and two copies certifying merchandise is in accordance with Purchase Order No. 08142.
Signed Special Customs Invoice in duplicate.
Certificate of Origin in duplicate.
Packing List in duplicate.
Full set clean ocean bills of lading to order shipper, blank endorsed, freight collect, notify Wards, Oakland, California, dated on board not later than May 25, 19 .

Relating to: Transistor Radios from FOB vessel Japanese Port to San Francisco Bay Port.

Partial shipments permitted. Insurance to be effected by buyers
Transhipment is not permitted.

Negotiating bank is to forward all documents attached to the original draft in one airmail envelope.

Courtesy Wells Fargo Bank

DRAFTS MUST BE DRAWN AND NEGOTIATED NOT LATER THAN June 5, 19
ALL DRAFTS DRAWN UNDER THIS CREDIT MUST BEAR ITS DATE AND NUMBER AND THE AMOUNTS MUST BE ENDORSED ON THE REVERSE SIDE OF THIS LETTER OF CREDIT BY THE NEGOTIATING BANK.
WE HEREBY AGREE WITH THE DRAWERS, ENDORSERS AND BONA FIDE HOLDERS OF ALL DRAFTS DRAWN UNDER AND IN COMPLIANCE WITH THE TERMS OF THIS CREDIT, THAT SUCH DRAFTS WILL BE DULY HONORED UPON PRESENTATION TO THE DRAWEE.
THIS CREDIT IS SUBJECT TO THE UNIFORM CUSTOMS AND PRACTICE FOR DOCUMENTARY CREDITS (1962 REVISION), INTERNATIONAL CHAMBER OF COMMERCE BROCHURE NO. 222.

W/ SPECIMEN
AUTHORIZED SIGNATURE

FIGURE 12-2 Irrevocable Letter of Credit

Source: Courtesy of Wells Fargo Bank.

irrevocable letter of credit, in which a bank guarantees payment provided that the supplier meets certain conditions. (See Figure 12-2 for a sample copy. Note the terms.)

From a logistics manager's standpoint, the letter of credit controls the shipment's movement: It names vessels, specifies departure and arrival dates, dictates packaging and labeling, and so on. If changes are to be made, both the buyer and seller must agree, and the letter of credit must be amended accordingly. The risk is that the value of the product may change after the date of the original agreement, in which case one party to the agreement will also seek to renegotiate the price.

International Marketing Channels

In marketing channels, there are various arrangements of buyers and sellers in interdependent channels, depending on their function at the time. When dealing with foreign markets and sources, sometimes different channel arrangements are employed. The firm must decide how much knowledge gained from domestic transactions is applicable when dealing overseas.[6]

The five channels mentioned earlier are the *ownership channel,* the *negotiations channel,* the *financing channel,* the *promotions channel,* and the *logistics channel.* For international transactions, a sixth channel is added: the *documentation channel.* Documentation accompanying international shipments is excessive. In the 1980s, one shipment to Santiago, Chile, reportedly "required 150 separate documents."[7] Preparing these detailed documents, assembling them, and ensuring that they arrive where and when they are needed is no minor logistical operation.[8] For small items such as repair parts, the envelope with the documents will be larger than the packaged part, and the costs of documentation will be greater than the part's value. International logistics involves a system in which documentation flows are as much a part of the main logistical flow as the flow of product. In the late 1990s, an airline's magazine said, "It still takes as long to process an air cargo shipment [now] as it did 26 years ago in a process which involves up to 36 separate handling functions, generating up to 16 individual documents."[9] One recent survey of exporters reported that "Export processes add nine percent to the cost of goods sold."[10]

The following anecdote about Hyundai shows how some of the other channels relate to each other in an international setting. As Hyundai autos cross the ocean from Korea to U.S. ports, they are initially owned by Hyundai Motor America, which has purchased them from Hyundai Motor Company, and often two-thirds or more of a car carrier's capacity is sold electronically from a carrier vessel while it's at sea. At the port, "Hyundai's car preparation companies remove a protective coating from each vehicle and then accessorize every auto with 'PIOS,' port-installed options. These include mud guards, arm rests, floor mats, side moldings, sun-roof wind deflectors, as

---

[6]Rod B. McNaughton and Jim Bell, "Channel Switching Between Domestic and Foreign Markets," *Journal of International Marketing,* Vol. 9, No. 1, 2001, pp. 24–39.

[7]*Davis Database,* October 1983, p. 1.

[8]In 1997, one of this text's coauthors received a letter from a former student that said, in part, "In your classes I remember most students' eyes would glaze over when you would begin to lecture about documentation because it was perhaps the least interesting aspect in the academic world of logistics. Everybody was interested in the container vessels and planes. I cannot tell you how much I wish now that I would have paid better attention when you spoke about documentation."

[9]*KLM Cargovision,* December 1996/January 1997, p. 23.

[10]"Where is the Payback in e-logistics?" *American Shipper,* July 2002, p. 34.

well as air conditioning units slipped into prepared niches."[11] Dealers receiving cars by truck pay for them electronically the moment they're delivered to the dealership. For those arriving by train, the dealer pays when the train arrives. In both situations the money is transferred directly to Korea to pay off Hyundai Motor America's debt to Hyundai Motor Company.

Terms of Sale

Choosing the *terms of sale* involves parties working within the negotiations channel, looking at the possible logistics channels, and determining when and where to transfer the following between buyer and seller:

1. The physical goods (the logistics channel)
2. Payment for the goods, freight charges, and insurance for the in-transit goods (the financing channel)
3. Legal title to the goods (the ownership channel)
4. Required documentation (the documentation channel)
5. Responsibility for controlling or caring for the goods in transit, say, in the case of livestock (the logistics channel)

Transfer can be specified in terms of calendar time, geographic location, or completion of some task. One must think in terms of both time and location.

For many years a variety of selling terms evolved that were translated as terms of a seller's cost quotation. Each started with the product and added some additional service. The product and added services are listed in the following paragraphs, and, from the seller's viewpoint, they are the different locations, or stages, for quoting a price to an overseas buyer. They are referred to as **Incoterms 2000** because they were developed and published by the International Chamber of Commerce in the year 2000. Use of the terms is not mandatory, although one would need a very good reason to insist on some other terms.[12] For each of the terms, the respective responsibilities of the seller's and the buyer's logistics managers change.

EX-Works (EXW)

In this most basic transaction, the seller transfers all risk of loss and all responsibility for expenses to the buyer at the seller's loading dock. In an EX-Works transaction, goods are made available for pickup at the seller's factory or warehouse. *Example:* EXW Toledo Incoterms 2000.

FCA (Free Carrier)

In this type of transaction, the seller is responsible for arranging transportation to a specific carrier at a named place. For example, a shipper (seller) located in Milwaukee may sell FCA Chicago. In this transaction, the seller arranges to deliver goods to an agreed-upon carrier in Chicago. The goods are "delivered" when they are receipted by

---

[11]*American Shipper,* September 1995, p. 64.

[12]See Lauri Railas, "Incoterms for the New Millennium," *European Transport Law,* 2000, pp. 9–22.

the buyer's carrier and all risk of loss transfers to seller at that point. *Example:* FCA Chicago Incoterms 2000.

FAS (Free Alongside Ship)

In this transaction, the seller must arrange for delivery, and assume all risks, up to the ocean carrier at a port. Unofficial usage understands delivery to be "within reach of the ship's tackle." Freight costs up to alongside vessel, risk of loss, and costs of export clearance are borne by the seller. *Example:* FAS Savannah Incoterms 2000.

FOB (Free on Board)

Incoterms limit the use of FOB to carriage by water and define the point of title transfer as occurring when the goods have passed over the ship's rail. In other words, freight to a vessel, loading aboard, and export clearance are the seller's responsibilities. Once the goods are loaded, the risk of loss and costs of transport revert to the buyer. (This term is also used in domestic trade, meaning the price at a specified location.) *Example:* FOB Rotterdam Incoterms 2000.

CFR (Cost and Freight)

The "cost" portion of CFR refers to the merchandise. The "freight" portion refers to all the freight, including export clearance, up to the foreign port of unloading. What is not included is cargo insurance from the port of loading. Indeed, risks are shared in a CFR transaction. The seller must deliver over the ship's rail, so any loss up to that point is the seller's responsibility. Once loaded, the risk transfers to the buyer. This term is only used on waterborne shipments. *Example:* CFR Hong Kong Incoterms 2000.

CPT (Carriage Paid To)

This term is similar to CFR, but it can be used for any mode of transport, including air. CPT means that the seller will pay all freight costs all the way to the foreign port and that the buyer assumes all risk of loss beyond the loading port. *Example:* CPT Paris Incoterms 2000.

CIF (Cost, Insurance, and Freight)

A CIF transaction includes the costs of freight and the costs of insurance. The seller retains the risk of loss up to the foreign port of unloading. This term is used on waterborne shipments. *Example:* CIF Miami Incoterms 2000.

CIP (Carriage and Insurance Paid To)

This term is similar to CIF except that it is primarily used in multimodal transactions where the place of receipt and place of delivery may be different from the port of loading or place of unloading. *Example:* CIP Zurich Incoterms 2000.

DES (Delivered Ex Ship)

In this type of transaction, the seller must pay all the costs and bear all the risks of transport up to the foreign port of unloading, except the cost or risk of unloading the cargo from the ship. In the case of large pieces of equipment, or bulk cargoes, the costs of unloading can exceed the cost of the main freight. *Example:* DES Long Beach Incoterms 2000.

DEQ (Delivered Ex Quay)

This is the same as DES except that the terms provide for the seller to pay the costs of unloading the cargo from the vessel and the cost of import clearance. *Example:* DES New York Incoterms 2000.

DAF (Delivered at Frontier)

In DAF the seller's responsibility is to deliver goods to a named frontier, which usually means a border crossing point, and to clear the transaction for export. The buyer's responsibility is to arrange for pickup of the goods after they are cleared for export, to carry them across the border, to clear them for importation, and to pay any duties. *Example:* DAF Laredo Incoterms 2000.

DDP (Delivered Duty Paid)

This is a new term mainly used in intermodal transactions whereby the seller undertakes all the risks and costs from origin to the buyer's warehouse door, including export and import clearance and import customs duties. Essentially, the sellers pays everything in a DDP transaction and passes on all related costs in the merchandise price. *Example:* DDP Baltimore Incoterms 2000.

DDU (Delivered Duty Unpaid)

This is the same as DDP except that duty is not paid. Since the importer is generally better informed about local customs, a DDU transaction is used when the buyer wants to avoid transportation and insurance issues. *Example:* DDU Milan Incoterms 2000.

Choice of currency in which payment is to be made can also be an issue, especially if the payment is to be made in the future. Barter may also be used, rather than cash. This may result in additional duties for the logistics manager because the goods received in payment have to be moved. Alexander Ageev, marketing chief for the Moscow Aviation Production Organization, which sells the MIG fighter aircraft, said that although Russia would prefer cash from the Philippines Air Force, competitive commodities can be converted into cash and help seal the deal. "So if Manila has bananas, we will consider them. In Malaysia, where we sold 18 MIG-29s, palm oil has been supplied in part payment of the cost."[13]

Government Influences on Foreign Trade

The buying and selling parties are not always free to contract the terms to suit their needs. Often, a government pressures firms to insist on terms that will result in that nation's firms performing more of the services associated with moving products. The main goal is to conserve the nation's own currency and improve its balance-of-payments position. A nation that needs to earn Western currencies, such as China, often buys and takes title at the source; it sells on a delivered basis, using its own national shipping and marine insurance for both imports and exports.

Businesses involved in foreign trade find that government's role is more significant than in domestic transactions. In part, this is because most firms are first developed in domestic markets and take all existing governmental controls as a given factor. As a

---

[13]John Helmer, "MIGs to Manila: Yes, We'll Take Your Bananas as Payment," *The Journal of Commerce,* March 4, 1997, p. 1A.

firm expands beyond its domestic markets, it finds requirements that differ for each nation with which the firm wishes to trade. The U.S. government also places restrictions and paperwork requirements on U.S. firms that buy or sell abroad.

Government Controls on the Flow of International Trade

For several reasons, national governments play a more significant role in international transactions than in domestic transactions. The main reason is that governments tax the importation of many items. The taxes are called *customs* or *duties*. Goods, including baggage accompanying travelers, are inspected as they cross borders. If any customs are due, they must be paid before the goods can be transported farther.

Customs or duty rates are set high on many goods to protect local manufacturers, producers, or growers. Initially, local interests argue that theirs are infant industries and need protection for only a few years in order to prevent foreign-based competitors from dumping goods in the country at prices that are below cost. Once tariff barriers are built, they are not easily torn down. Rather than the infant outgrowing the crib, the walls of the crib are built high. Sometimes, the tariff the importing nation charges differs according to the nation from which the good is coming. From an international sourcing standpoint, this influences the choice of production site.

Related to tariffs are **import quotas,** which are physical limits on the amount that may be imported from any one country during a period of time. When the quota is reached, the flow of goods stops. Quotas are used for commodities for which no tariffs exist, and they serve to protect local producers in years when local prices are high but foreign prices are low.

Many nations are concerned with stopping the spread of plant and animal diseases and therefore inspect various commodities or products to make certain that they do not contain these problems. If material is found to be infested, it cannot enter the country until it is cleaned.

Entry of other products may be prohibited because they do not meet safety standards. For example, electrical appliances have different voltage requirements throughout the world. Because of the danger of earthquakes in Japan, upright refrigerators must be built so that they will remain upright even when tilted as much as 10 degrees.

Products can be modified so that they meet each nation's requirements. Conversion costs per unit are high if only small numbers of units are involved. From an inventory control standpoint, slight variations in acceptable standards mean that products become less homogeneous. Parts are less likely to be interchangeable, and stocks in one country may not be substitutes for stocks of similar products in an adjoining country.

Some nations restrict the outflow of currency, because a nation's economy will suffer if it imports more than it exports over a long term. These regulations are not concerned with specific commodities; rather, they are concerned with restricting the outflow of money. All imports require advanced approval, and goods that arrive without prior approval are not allowed to enter. When American Jeeps were first built in China, the Chinese government controlled the process by not allowing funds to be transferred outside China to bring in dies from the United States that would be needed to make a model similar to that made in the United States. This was because the Chinese government wanted Jeep to build a model more similar to an army truck already being made in China.

Firms with operations in several nations are subject to the taxes of each, and any intracompany move between two nations involves a sale for the one subsidiary and a purchase by the other. The transaction, therefore, determines the income, tax, and profit

SENEGAL

GOVERNMENT REPRESENTATION

The Republic of Senegal is represented in the United States by an Embassy at 2112 Wyoming Ave., N.W., Washington, D.C. and a United Nations Mission at 51 East 42nd St., New York. Both also act for Canadian affairs.

GENERAL INFORMATION

Customs Airports: Dakar, Saint Louis and Ziguinchor.
Collect Service acceptable to Dakar and Saint Louis only.
COD Service not acceptable.
Free House Delivery not acceptable.

DOCUMENTATION

Commercial consignments—2 commercial invoices containing the following declaration: "Nous certifions que les marchandises denommees dans cette facture sont de fabrication et d'origine (country of origin) et que les prix indiques ci-dessus s'accordent avec les prix courants sur le marche d'exportation."
Sample consignments—Without commercial value: No documents. With commercial value: same as for commercial consignments.
Gift consignments—no documentary requirements.

RESTRICTIONS

Live animals: Health certificate.
Dogs and other domestic animals: Health certificates issued not later than 3 days before shipment and stating that the animals originate from an area free from contagious diseases of the species for the preceding 6 weeks, and in case of cats and dogs, that no rabies has been detected for the same period.
PROHIBITED: Hares and rabbits.
Live plants and plant material: Health certificate.
Arms and ammunition: Special import permit.

PROHIBITIONS

All goods of Portuguese or South African origin; skins of hares and rabbits; beetroot sugar; blankets; cloth of textile fibers; cotton cloth; fibres; flower pots, stoneware, pottery, clay products, matches, ornamental bricks and other clay products for building purposes; outwear, shirts, except shirts over CFA 1700. value; shoes, except fashionable shoes over CFA 400. value; trousers under CFA 1900. value; sisal carpets and rugs; sugar cane, yarn and thread; cotton, apéritifs of alcohol or wine basis; digestives.

IMPORT AND EXCHANGE REGULATIONS

Liberalized items may be imported without quantitative restrictions on the basis of an import certificate, which is made out by the importer, endorsed by the Customs on clearance of the merchandise and delivered to an authorized bank for visa by the Exchange Control Office.
Non-liberalized goods require an import license, issued by the Director General for Economic Services and visaed by the Exchange Control Office. Validity of certificate and license is 6 months.
The currency exchange is obtained through the authorized banks on strength of import certificate or import license. No tolerance in value or quantity shown on import certificate or import license is permitted.
The importation of goods competitive with locally produced items may be prohibited from time to time.
Rate of exchange: 247 C.F.A. Francs = $1.00

SIERRA LEONE

GOVERNMENT REPRESENTATION

Sierra Leone is represented in the United States by an Embassy at 1701 19th Street, N.W., Washington, D.C. and a United Nations Mission at 30 East 42nd St., New York. Both also act for Canadian affairs.

GENERAL INFORMATION

Customs Airport: Freetown.

Collect Service acceptable.

COD Service not acceptable.

Free House Delivery not acceptable.

DOCUMENTATION

Commercial consignments—4 combined certificates of value and origin in English bearing the supplier's letterhead and his seal or stamp against his signature or that of his representative. In case of occasional shipment, when overprinting of the letterhead is prohibitive, the combined certificate must be accompanied with the supplier's own invoice duly signed against his seal or stamp, and containing the certification: "We hereby declare that this commercial invoice is in support of the attached certificate invoice No. . . . and that the particulars shown on the certified invoice are true and correct in every detail."

RESTRICTIONS

Live animals: Import authorization from Veterinary Dept.

Dogs: Additional health and rabies vaccination certificate in English.

Live plants and plant material: Import authorization from Agricultural Department.

PROHIBITED: Aniseed and Indian hemp.

Medicines and narcotics: Import license from Director of Medical services.

PROHIBITIONS

Arms and ammunition from Liberia, obscene photographs, shaving brushes from Japan, traps for night hunting.

IMPORT AND EXCHANGE REGULATIONS

Most goods may be freely imported under "Open General License." Specific import license required for a short list of specified items only . . . issued by the Import Licensing Authority of the Ministry of Commerce and Industry; the validity is generally 12 months.

Exporters should avoid overshipment of goods covered by specific import licenses. No tolerances are permitted.

The currency exchange is obtained through authorized banks. No exchange permit is required. An import license, whether specific or open, automatically entitles the importer to buy the relative foreign exchange.

Rate of exchange: 1 Leone = $1.20

FIGURE 12-3 Examples of Restrictions of Exporting to Other Nations

Source: Courtesy of Sabena Belgian World Airlines.

of both subsidiaries. Tax auditors from both countries can also be expected to ask how the price was established for this intrafirm movement and whether one of the results of the price selected was a minimization of tax liability to the country in question.

Figure 12-3 is from a guidebook prepared by an international airline that outlines, in general terms, the various restrictions that apply when shipping to two African nations. From the example of the two nations listed, it is easy to see that exporting involves complications. Note that both countries' embassy locations in the United States are listed. Consular offices are current sources of information regarding their nations' import and currency exchange regulations. Most nations maintain consular offices in major U.S. port cities, and these offices, for a fee, prepare a consular invoice, a document that contains approximately the same information as a commercial invoice. The importing nation uses it as the basis for levying applicable import duties.

Political Restrictions on Trade

For political or military reasons, nations ban certain types of shipments. The United States does not ship military equipment or certain strategic materials to certain nations. Political events often lead countries to break off economic relations. For example, U.S. trade with Cuba is restricted.

Israel and a few Arab nations do not trade with each other, and these Arab nations do not even allow vessels or planes from other nations to sail or fly directly between Israel and themselves. These few Arab nations also refuse, in varying degrees, to do business with firms that also do business with Israel. To complicate matters further, the United States has laws that discourage U.S. firms from complying with the Arab boycott.

Nontariff Barriers

All the actions of various governments described to this point tend to impede the flow of international commerce. Sometimes, a government is bound by treaty to grant another nation certain preferential (or lower) tariff charges on imports. Later, the nation wishes it had not set such low rates but feels bound by treaty to honor the specified rates. An action it then might take is to establish what is known as a nontariff barrier—a rule that has the effect of reducing the flow of imports.

Sometimes, the barriers are created by other government agencies, whose primary interests are in matters other than trade.

> Noboru Ueno, Japan representative of a Seattle-based coffee shop, tried to open a Seattle-style coffee stand in Tokyo. "Bringing paper cups from the U.S. was even difficult," he said. The health ministry required him to bring the cups to a Tokyo microscope inspection foundation run by the city government. Such inspections are expensive, troublesome, time-consuming. The cup microscope jaunt cost nearly $1,000 and several other inspections exceeded $10,000. "These officials at the ministry said to me that even though these cups are safe in the U.S., they might not be safe in Japan. . . ." Ueno continued. The inspection associations are owned by the government, Ueno said, and are staffed by former bureaucrats under Japan's so-called amakudari system. Amakudari—which literally means descent from heaven—refers to well-paid positions made available to bureaucrats before they retire, with the positions typically in areas they once regulated.[14]

---

[14]Coco Kubota, "Japan's Maze of Rules Chills 'Hot' Coffee Trend," *The Journal of Commerce,* June 14, 1995, p. 5A.

The Canadian province of Quebec requires that the French language be used on all product labels, instructions, and brochures.

Government requirements may also influence the choice of ports to be used. For example, livestock imported into the United States must arrive at designated ports that have facilities for receiving and holding the livestock until they can be inspected. They also have quarantine areas for livestock which, for various reasons, inspectors decide to deny immediate entry. In addition, inspections of the vessel or aircraft are required both before and after carrying the livestock.

Government's Role in International Transport

As in other aspects of international business, governments are more involved in international transportation than they are in domestic transportation. One reason for this is that ocean vessels and international airline aircraft operate as extensions of a nation's economy, and most of the revenue they receive flows into that nation's economy. To that nation, international carriage functions as an export with favorable effects on the nation's balance of payments. However, to the nation on the other end of the shipment, the effect is opposite because it must import the transport service, and this has an adverse impact on its balance-of-payments position. Some nations with very weak balance-of-payments positions issue an import license, or permit, on the condition that the goods move on a vessel or plane flying that nation's flag, which means it is importing only the goods, not the transportation service required to carry them.[15] Situations such as this dictate carrier choice.

In order to develop international fleets and airlines, most nations provide subsidies. Many nations train their own merchant marine officers, absorb portions of the costs of building commercial vessels, and engage in other activities to promote their own merchant fleets. Some own ocean carriers in total or in part. Many international airlines are government owned, although some are moving toward the private sector, a process called *privatization*. International air and ocean liner rates are frequently established by carrier cartels. Nations rely on carriers that they subsidize to represent national interests as they vote on international rate and service issues.

Large nations must also protect their flag carriers' interests. Japan and the United States are in a dispute regarding Japanese port practices, which allegedly are unfair to U.S. vessel lines. There are two issues of concern: "One is licensing requirements for terminal and stevedore operations. While U.S. carriers can own facilities, they have been unable to get licenses to operate them. Secondly, Japan has a system of 'prior consultation' for conducting port business. Whenever a carrier wants to make an operational change, it has to notify and get the approval of the Japanese Harbor Transportation Association. That organization is a strange mix of Japanese carrier and labor interests. American carriers believe the structure gives Japanese competitors and labor veto power over their operational moves."[16] This dispute has stretched on for years.

---

[15] As used here, flying a nation's flag is synonymous with being owned by private or public entities in that nation. Flags of convenience are issued by nations with relatively lax maritime safety and work standards to investors of other nations who want to avoid their home nations' controls and taxes.

[16] Tim Sansbury and Allen R. Wastler, "U.S.-Japan Showdown Looms in Port Row," *The Journal of Commerce,* January 10, 1997, p. 4B.

International Trade and Supply-Chain Specialists

Few companies involved in international logistics rely solely on in-house personnel to manage all shipping operations. Specialist firms have developed and are known as *international freight forwarders* (who generally handle exports) and *customshouse brokers* or *import brokers*. Sometimes, the same firm provides both services and has offices in many countries. Most companies involved in international trade eventually use one or more services that these specialists provide. All of the specialists are also intermediaries in the marketing channels and in the supply chain. All of the parties mentioned in the following sections could also be considered to be third-party logistics providers. Also, in foreign lands, other third parties would be retained to perform logistics functions mentioned previously in this text, such as managing inventory, domestic transport, or warehouses.

International Freight Forwarders

International freight forwarders specialize in handling either vessel shipments or air shipments, yet their functions are generally the same. Some of their principal functions are discussed below.

Advising on Acceptance of Letters of Credit

When a client receives a letter of credit, the document contains many conditions that the seller must meet. The forwarder determines whether the client can meet these conditions and, if it cannot, will advise the client that the letter of credit must be amended. The buyer and buyer's bank must be notified before the order can be processed further.

Booking Space on Carriers

Space is frequently more difficult to obtain on international carriers than on domestic carriers for several reasons. Vessel or aircraft departures are less frequent, and the capacities of planes or ships are strictly limited. Connections with other carriers are more difficult to arrange, and the relative bargaining strength of any one shipper with an international carrier is usually weaker than it is with respect to domestic carriers. Forwarders are experienced at keeping tabs on available carrier space, and because they represent more business to the carrier than an individual shipper does, they have more success when finding space is difficult.

Preparing an Export Declaration

An export declaration is required by the U.S. government for statistical and control purposes and must be prepared and filed for nearly every shipment.

Preparing an Air Waybill or Bill of Lading

The international air waybill is a fairly standardized document; the ocean bill of lading is not. The latter may differ between ocean lines, coastal areas through which the shipments are moving, and for a variety of other circumstances. Ocean bills of lading are frequently negotiable, which means that whoever legally holds the document may take delivery of the shipment. Because nearly every ocean vessel line has its own bill of lading, a forwarder's expertise is necessary to fill it out accurately.

Obtaining Consular Documents

Consular documents involve obtaining permission from the importing country for the goods to enter. Documents are prepared that the importing country uses to determine duties to be levied on the shipment as it passes through customs.

Arranging for Insurance

Unlike domestic shipments, international shipments must be insured. Either the individual shipment must be insured or the shipper (or forwarder) must have a blanket policy covering all shipments. International airlines offer insurance at nominal rates. Rates on vessel shipments are higher, and the entire process is complex because of certain practices that are acceptable at sea. For example, if the vessel is in peril of sinking, the captain may have some cargo jettisoned (thrown overboard) to keep the vessel afloat. The owners of the surviving cargo and the vessel owner must then share the costs of reimbursing the shippers whose cargo was thrown overboard.

Preparing and Sending Shipping Notices and Documents

The financial transaction involving the sale of goods is carefully coordinated with their physical movement, and rather elaborate customs and procedures have evolved to ensure that the seller is paid when the goods are delivered. The export forwarder handles the shipper's role in the document preparation and exchange stages. It is necessary to have certain documents available as the shipment crosses international boundaries. (The forwarder serves to coordinate the logistics, documentation, ownership, and payment channels.)

Serving as General Consultant on Export Matters

Questions continually arise when dealing with new products, terms of sale, new markets, or new regulations. The forwarder knows the answers or how to find them. A conscientious forwarder also advises a shipper as to when certain procedures, such as similar shipments to the same market, become so repetitive that the shipper can handle the procedures in its own export department at a cost lower than the fees charged by the forwarder.

Export forwarders' income comes from three sources. Similar to domestic forwarders, they buy space wholesale and sell it retail. By consolidating shipments, they benefit from a lower rate per pound. In addition, most carriers allow the forwarders a commission on shipping revenues they generate for the carriers. Also, forwarders charge fees for preparing documents, performing research, and the like. Figures 12-4 and 12-5 show forms used by forwarders. Figure 12-4 is used to prepare cost estimates for the client to use when quoting a price to a potential overseas buyer. Figure 12-5 is the form that a forwarder uses to bill a client for handling a shipment.

Nonvessel-Operating Common Carriers

In recent years, a modified form of the forwarder operation known as the **nonvessel-operating common carrier (NVOCC)** has developed. The only requirement at present is that a prospective NVOCC owner must be licensed by the Federal Maritime Commission (as must forwarders). NVOCCs can perform most, but not all, of the functions of a freight forwarder. However, they have much greater ability to enter into rate

EXPORT QUOTATION WORKSHEET

DATE_____   REF/PRO FORMA INVOICE NO._____
COMMODITY_____   EXPECTED SHIP DATE_____
CUSTOMER_____   PACKED DIMENSIONS_____
COUNTRY_____   PACKED WEIGHT_____
PAYMENT TERMS_____   PACKED CUBE_____

PRODUCTS TO BE SHIPPED FROM_____
               TO_____

SELLING PRICE OF GOODS: $_____

SPECIAL EXPORT PACKING:
   $_____   quoted by_____
   $_____   quoted by_____
   $_____   quoted by_____ $_____

INLAND FREIGHT:
   $_____   quoted by_____
   $_____   quoted by_____
   $_____   quoted by_____ $_____

   Inland freight includes the following charges:
   ☐ unloading   ☐ pier delivery   ☐ terminal   ☐ _____

OCEAN FREIGHT			AIR FREIGHT		
	quoted by	tariff item		quoted by	spec code
$_____	_____	# _____	$_____	_____	# _____
$_____	_____	# _____	$_____	_____	# _____
$_____	_____	# _____	$_____	_____	# _____

Ocean freight includes the following surcharges: Air freight includes the following surcharges:

☐ Port congestion   ☐ Heavy lift   ☐ Fuel adjustment
☐ Currency adjustment ☐ Bunker   ☐ Container stuffing
☐ Container rental   ☐ Wharfage   ☐ _____
☐ _____   ☐ _____

INSURANCE ☐ includes war risk   ☐ INSURANCE ☐ includes war risk
rate:_____ per $100 or $_____   rate:_____ per $100 or $_____

TOTAL OCEAN CHARGES $_____   **TOTAL AIR CHARGES** $_____ $_____
notes: notes:

FORWARDING FEES: $_____
Includes: ☐ Courier Fees ☐ Certification Fees ☐ Banking Fees ☐ _____

CONSULAR LEGALIZATION FEES: $_____

INSPECTION FEES: $_____

DIRECT BANK CHARGES: $_____

OTHER CHARGES: _____ $_____
             _____ $_____

TOTAL: ☐ FOB_____ ☐ C & F_____
       ☐ FAS_____ ☐ CIF_____ $_____

Form 10-020 Printed and Sold by *UNZCO* 190 Baldwin Ave., Jersey City, NJ 07306 • (800) 631-3098

FIGURE 12-4 A Forwarder's Export Quotation Sheet Showing Factors to Include When Determining the Price to Quote a Potential Buyer of a Product

Source: Reprinted with permission of Unz & Co., 190 Baldwin Ave., Jersey City, NJ.

			INVOICE NO.	
			DATE	
			YOUR REF. NO.	

CONSIGNEE:

FROM:			CARRIER:	
TO:	☐ AIR	☐ OCEAN	B/L OR AWB NO.	

INLAND FREIGHT/LOCAL CARTAGE	$
EXPORT PACKING	
AIR FREIGHT CHARGES	
OCEAN FREIGHT/TERMINAL CHARGES	
CONSULAR FEES	
INSURANCE/CERTIFICATE OF INSURANCE	
CHAMBER OF COMMERCE	
BROKERAGE FEES	
FORWARDING	
HANDLING AND EXPEDITING	
DOCUMENT PREPARATION	
MESSENGER FEES	
POSTAGE	
TELEPHONE	
CABLES	
CERTIFICATE OF ORIGIN	
BANKING: (LETTER OF CREDIT/SIGHT DRAFT)	
MISCELLANEOUS	

As amended by the United States Shipping Act of 1984.

TOTAL $

_____ has a policy against payment, solicitation, or receipt of any rebate, directly or indirectly, which would be unlawful under the United States Shipping Act, 1916, as amended

FIGURE 12-5 Invoice Form Used by a Freight Forwarder to Bill Client for Handling an Export Shipment

Source: Reprinted with permission of Unz & Co., 190 Baldwin Ave., Jersey City, NJ.

agreements with ocean and inland carriers, and they may issue single-rate quotations between inland points in one nation and inland points in another. NVOCCs frequently affiliate with forwarders so that they can offer their customers a more complete package of services. Both NVOCCs and international forwarders must file their rates with the Federal Maritime Commission. Some are meeting this obligation by posting their rates on the Internet. This places them at a competitive disadvantage with ocean carriers, whose contracts and contract rates with shippers are confidential.[17]

Figures 12-6 and 12-7 are excerpted from an NVOCC's tariff. Figure 12-6 is more than one page and serves as an index to the remainder of the document. Note all the topics covered. They establish all of the rules applicable to any shipment using that

---

[17]*Containerization International*, March 2001, p 75.

Davies Turner & Co. d/b/a Cargo Globe Tf. 001	Orig/Rev Original	Page 100,002
FROM: TARIFF ORIGIN SCOPE TO: TARIFF DESTINATION SCOPE	Cancels Original	Cancels Page 100,002
TABLE OF CONTENTS	CORR: 0	Issued: 26Jan2002

SUBJECT	RULE	PAGE
Rate Applicability Rule	3	2,000,033
Restricted Articles	2-110	2,000,029
Returned Cargo in Foreign Commerce	18	2,000,059
Scope	1	2,000,001
Seasonal Discontinuance	31	2,000,077
Shipper Furnished Containers	2-050	2,000,021
Shipper's Load And Count	2-080	2,000,025
Shippers Requests in Foreign Commerce	19	2,000,060
Surcharges and Arbitraries	10	2,000,051
Symbols	29	2,000,073
Terminal Tariffs	34	2,000,080
Time/Volume Rates in Foreign Commerce	26	2,000,069
Transshipment	13	2,000,054
U.S. Terminal Charges	23-010	2,000,065
Use of Carrier Equipment	21	2,000,062
Worldwide Ports and Points	1-A	2,000,003

FIGURE 12-6 Index for a NVOCC Tariff, Issued in Early 2002

Source: Distribution-Publications Inc. (DPI).

NVOCC. Other pages, not reproduced here, indicate that the tariff covers shipments between named points in the United States and named points in other countries.

Customshouse Brokers

A function opposite of, but similar to, that of international freight forwarders is performed by **customshouse brokers,** who oversee the efficient movement of importers' goods (and accompanying paperwork) through customs and other inspection points and stand ready to argue for a lower rate in case one or two commodity descriptions apply.

Export Management Companies

Sometimes the manufacturer seeking to export retains the services of an **export management company,** a firm that specializes in handling overseas transactions. Such companies represent U.S. manufacturers and help them find overseas firms that can be licensed to manufacture their products. They also handle sales correspondence in foreign languages, ensure that foreign labeling requirements are met, and perform other specialized functions. When handling the overseas sales for a U.S. firm, the export management firm either buys and sells on its own account or provides credit information regarding each potential buyer to the U.S. manufacturer, which can judge whether to take the risk.

    Export management companies and international freight forwarders are closely related because, together, they can offer a complete overseas sales and distribution ser-

Davies Turner & Co. d/b/a Cargo Globe Tf. 001	Orig/Rev	Page
	Original	0218-01-6855.001
FROM: TARIFF ORIGIN SCOPE	Cancels	Cancels Page
TO: TARIFF DESTINATION SCOPE	Original	0218-01-6855.001
Section 4 - COMMODITIES AND RATES	CORR: 0	Issued: 26Jan2002

Except as otherwise provided, rates apply per 1000 KGS or 1.000 CBM. Effective Dates shown below.
Items with effective dates prior to page Issue Date are brought forward without change.
Future effective items are preceded with a > symbol.

TRI	Rate	RBasis	Size & Type	Effective Thru	Expires	Publish	Amend

Commodity: 0218-01-6855 Brass, Viz: Stampings, N.O.S.

                          24Sep2002   24Sep2002 IR

From: UK PORTS (ORIG) (Group)
To: CHICAGO, IL, USA, 60601-99
Via: NEW YORK, NY, USA, 10001-99 (Port)

  0002   80.00 USD   WM   LTL PC   30Sep2002   30Sep2002 IR
      Services: SS

From: UK PORTS (ORIG) (Group)
To: NEW YORK, NY, USA, 10001-99 (Port)

  0001   55.00 USD   WM   LTL PC   30Sep2002   30Sep2002 IR
      Services: SS

FIGURE 12-7 NVOCC Tariff Page, Issued in Early 2002, Showing Rates for Brass Stampings, from Ports in the United Kingdom to Chicago and New York

Source: Distribution-Publications Inc. (DPI).

vice to the domestic manufacturer that wants to export but does not know how. Sometimes, international freight forwarders and export management firms work out of the same office, the only apparent distinction being which phone line they answer. Export management companies are also retained by large firms that have exported for many years because they can perform their very specialized service less expensively than could the client.

Export Trading Companies

Export trading companies (ETCs) attempt to combine all facets of international business: sales, finance, communications, and logistics. They are widely used by the Japanese. The Export Trading Company Act of 1982 relaxed some of the antitrust restrictions that had prevented firms that competed in domestic markets from cooperating in overseas ventures. In addition, banks were given the right (with the Federal Reserve Board's approval) to acquire up to 100 percent equity interest in export trading companies.

Shippers Associations

Widely used in foreign countries, **shippers associations** are trade groups that represent shippers of similar cargo that join together to bargain as a single entity with ocean

shipping conferences (groups of ocean-liner operators). They were not allowed in the United States prior to the Shipping Act of 1984.

The largest U.S. shippers association is Global Shippers Association and includes as members American Standard, General Electric (GE), PPG, Trane, and Xerox. The firms do not compete with each other, hence they can join. They control 25,000 TEUs (20-foot container equivalent units) per year and negotiate global contracts, one of the few entities to do so. As an example of their clout, "Through GSA's leverage, per-ton rates on resin exports from GE's Mt. Vernon, Indiana plant to Singapore, have been cut 30 percent, to $95 from $137."[18]

Export Packers

As is true for the export functions discussed previously, a specialized service of export packing is performed by firms typically located in port cities. **Export packers** custom pack shipments when the exporter lacks the equipment or the expertise to do so itself. However, when exporters have repeat business, they usually perform their own export packing.

Export packaging involves packaging for two distinct purposes, in addition to the sales function of some packaging. The first is to allow goods to move easily through customs. For a country assessing duties on the weight of both the item and its container, this means selecting lightweight packing materials. For items moving through the mail, it might mean construction of an envelope with an additional small flap that a customs inspector could open and look inside without having to open the entire envelope. For crated machinery, this might involve using open slats rather than completely closed construction (the customs inspectors would likely satisfy their curiosity by peering and probing through the openings between the slats).

The second purpose of export packing is to protect products in what almost always is a more difficult journey than they would experience if they were destined for domestic consignees. For many firms, the traditional ocean packaging method is to take the product in its domestic pack and enclose it in a wooden container. Ocean shipments are subject to more moisture damage than are domestic shipments. Variations in temperature are also more extreme. Canned goods moving through hot areas sweat, causing the cans to rust and the labels to become unglued. Campbell's Soup adds desiccants to its cartons of soup, otherwise specks of rust will appear on the cans during their sea voyage.[19]

Recent transportation equipment innovations have helped overcome the climatic problems of ocean shipping. International air freight has made it possible to reach major cities in the world within 24 to 48 hours, avoiding a long sea voyage. Packaging for international air freight is sometimes no different from packaging for domestic markets. Containerships are able to provide better care for cargo because shipments are in individual containers that come equipped with freezing, refrigerating, or air-circulating equipment in case the cargo demands it. Each container can be handled differently, and the ship's personnel are detailed to check temperature gauges outside the containers several times daily.

---

[18]Peter Tirschwell, "Huge Shipping Group Grows Even Bigger; American Standard, Trane Corp. Sign on as Members of GSA," *The Journal of Commerce*, September 18, 1996, pp. 1A, 2B.

[19]*American Shipper,* September 2001, p. 26.

In a meeting with Chinese businesspeople, one of this text's authors was queried at length as to why packaging was needed. The Chinese also could not understand why a separate packaging industry was needed; they apparently relied on scrap from their operations to serve as packaging materials. The following answer was given: Packaging is also needed for wider-scale distribution of one's product; as channels and supply chains lengthen, it is more necessary that the product be protected. Consumers also want assurance that the product they intend to buy has been well protected.

Goods sold in foreign markets require additional labels. The metric system is used in nearly every nation except the United States, so measurements of products must be expressed in metric terms.

For goods moving in foreign trade, it is not safe to assume that handlers can read English. Hence, cautionary symbols must be used (see Figure 12-8). Cargo moving aboard ocean vessels has distinct markings that identify the shipper, consignee, destination point, and piece number (in multipiece shipments). Some cartons and crates moving internationally are marked with what looks like a cattle brand. This is a shipper's mark, and a drawing of the mark also appears on the documentation. This is for use in areas in which dockworkers cannot read but need a method to keep documents and shipments together. As with domestic cargo, care must be taken so that pilferable items are not identified. This may include changing the symbols every few months. Figure 12-9 shows a package with the various markings required for movement in foreign commerce. The markings should be applied with a stencil, using waterproof ink. The bill of lading, packing list, letter of credit, and other documents pertaining to a shipment must contain similar markings. Note that markings on the box are in both inches and meters. Both weight and dimensions are given because density is a factor in determining international transportation charges.

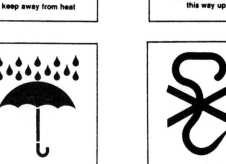

FIGURE 12-8 Some of the Symbols Used for Packing Export Shipments

The primary purpose of marking is the identification of the shipment, enabling the carrier to forward it to the ultimate consignee. Old marks, advertising, and other extraneous information only serve to confuse this primary function for cargo handlers and carriers. Follow these fundamental marking rules:

1. Unless local regulations prohibit, use coded marks, particularly where goods are susceptible to pilferage. Change them periodically to avoid familiarity by cargo handlers. Trade names should be avoided as they may indicate the nature of the contents.

2. Consignee (identification) marks and port marks showing destination and transfer points should be large, clear, and applied by stencil with waterproof ink. They should be applied on three faces of the package, preferably side, and/or ends and top.

3. If commodities require special handling or stowage, the shipping package should be so marked, and this information should also appear on the bill of lading.

4. Cautionary and handling markings must be permanent and easy to read (use the languages of both the origin and destination countries). The use of stencils is recommended for legibility—do not use crayon, tags, or cards. An example of markings on an export pack is illustrated.

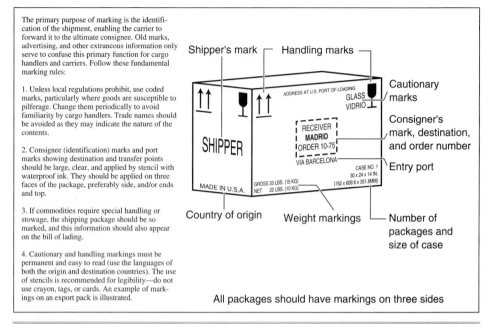

FIGURE 12-9 A Package Marked for Export

Source: From *Ports of the World,* 15th ed., a publication of CIGNA Property & Casualty.

Persons making packaging materials decisions today must be very aware of environmentalists' views as to the wastefulness of many packaging practices. Environmentalists in some areas are conducting "buy naked" campaigns that encourage shoppers to buy materials that are totally unpackaged and to leave any packaging in the retail store for disposal by the retailer. In some Western European countries, reusable packaging is stressed, and third parties assume the responsibility of collecting, re-cleaning, and returning the packaging to its original user so that it can be reused.

Logistics Channels in International Distribution

The remainder of this chapter addresses the logistics channel, which handles the physical movement of goods. Most of this section deals with transportation. The first subsection deals with the landward move to the port or airport. The second and third subsections deal with international air and ocean shipping. The last subsection deals with the landward leg in the foreign country. Although much of what is presented is from the viewpoint of the exporter, it is important to remember that the movement of goods requires cooperation and coordination among seller, buyer, and many intermediate parties.

Before moving to more visible forms of international transportation, pipelines that carry petroleum, petroleum products, and natural gas bear mentioning. In terms of tonnages and value carried, they are some of the most important forms of international transport. Their construction requires huge fixed investments.

Movement to Port or Airport

For air shipments, or for products moving by rail or truck to an adjacent country, the movement from the manufacturer's plant is similar to that for domestic sales. The only difference is that more paperwork accompanies each shipment. For a firm based in the United States, the same equipment is used for the entire haul to Canada. However, for shipments to Mexico, the product is often transferred at the border into Mexican railcars or truck trailers. Delays at the Mexican border are common.

Ports that handled foreign trade were traditionally grouped for rate-making purposes. This meant that the shipper at some inland point would pay the same rail rate and the same ocean rate, no matter which port was used. Carriers and ports competed in terms of service quality. However, because the railroads were deregulated in 1980, the concept of port equalization has been destroyed, and service contracts between railroads and shippers have disrupted traditional cargo routing patterns. We now see a few ports handling large shares of traffic.

Traffic destined to move through ports is first loaded aboard intermodal containers at an inland point and then sent forward without interruption. Vessel lines operating between U.S. Pacific Coast ports and Western Europe frequently find it cheaper to discharge and load their containerized cargo at East Coast ports and have it move by rail across the United States. The vessel line pays for the rail haul but saves the voyage through the Panama Canal. The shipper or consignee pays the same freight rate but benefits because time in transit is reduced by about 4 days. Similar service is available for East Coast firms doing business with the Orient. These services are examples of **land bridge** operations. Figure 12-10 is an ad for mini-bridge service, with trains departing from the West Coast. The vessels sail from Gulf and Atlantic ports to the Middle East. The West Coast shipper gives the cargo to the ocean shipping line in either Seattle–Tacoma, San Francisco, or Los Angeles by the specified date, and the ocean carrier moves it by rail across the United States.

International Air Freight

Air freight has had a very profound effect on international distribution because the airplane has reduced worldwide time distances. While transit times between the East and West Coasts of the United States have shrunk from 5 days to less than 1, some international transit times have shrunk from as many as 30 days to 1 or 2.

The three types of international air freight operations are chartered aircraft, scheduled air carriers, and integrated air carriers, specializing in carrying parcels. Chartering an entire aircraft is, of course, expensive, but sometimes the expense can be justified. Chartered aircraft have been used in the transport of livestock sold for breeding purposes. One charter airline carried 7,000 cattle from Texas to southern Chile. Nineteen flights were involved, each lasting 15 hours. The comparable time by sea was 20 days, and past experience showed that the sea journey was hard on the cattle, causing either lung damage or long delays before the animals could be bred. Other markets for air cargo charters include famine relief projects in Africa, buyers of textiles trying to meet quota deadlines, and owners of oil fields in Russia needing oversize equipment. The U.S. military also charters aircraft to move freight, and commercial U.S. airlines have agreed to make available portions of their fleet when requested to do so by the Department of Defense.

UNITED ARAB

SHIPPING COMPANY   The National Flag Line of the Arabian States of Saudi Arabia, U.A.E., Bahrain, Qatar, Kuwait and Iraq

USA/Middle East Express Container Service

MINI-BRIDGE DEPARTING	DARZAN V-36	JEBEL ALI V-36	ADDIRIYAH V-35	AL WATIYAH V-35
SEATTLE / PORTLAND	JUL 13	JUL 27	AUG 13	AUG 28
SAN FRANCISCO	JUL 17	JUL 31	AUG 16	AUG 30
LOS ANGELES	JUL 20	AUG 3	AUG 20	SP 3
SAILS				
HOUSTON	JUL 26	AUG 9	AUG 26	SEP 10
SAVANNAH	JUL 30	AUG 13	AUG 30	SEP 14
NORFOLK	AUG 3	AUG 15	SEP 1	SEP 16
BALTIMORE	AUG 4	AUG 16	SEP 2	SEP 17
NEW YORK	AUG 6	AUG 18	SEP 4	SEP 18
ARRIVES				
JEDDAH	AUG 22	SEP 3	SEP 20	OCT 4
DUBAI	AUG 28	SEP 9	SEP 26	OCT 10
BAHRAIN	SEP 4	SEP 16	OCT 3	OCT 17
DAMMAN	AUG 30	SEP 11	SEP 28	OCT 12
JUBAIL / ABU DHABI / DOHA	SEP 4	SEP 16	OCT 3	OCT 17
KUWAIT	SEP 1	SEP 12	SEP 29	OCT 13
BOMBAY	SEP 4	SEP 16	OCT 3	OCT 17
MUTTRAH	SEP 4	SEP 15	OCT 2	OCT 16

FCL to Iraq all vessels.
LCL accepted from EC/GULF to all ports except Iraq.
Cut off date for LCL cargo from EC/GULF ports is three (3) working days prior to ETD.
Reefer containers available from EC/Gulf ports.
Ras Al Mishab on inducement.
FCL accepted from Jacksonville, Miami, Tampa, Charleston, Philadelphia, Boston, Montreal and Toronto.

GENERAL AGENTS

KERR STEAMSHIP COMPANY, INC.

LONG BEACH	SAN FRANCISCO	PORTLAND/VANC., WA	SEATTLE	VANCOUVER	HOUSTON
4401 ATLANTIC AVE (213) 422-1132	ONE MARKET PLAZA (415) 764-0200	ONE S.W. COLUMBIA ST SUITE 450 (503) 220-2500	800 FIFTH AVE. (206) 628-6700	1135 TWO BENTAL CENTRE (604) 682-5881	2727 ALLEN PARKWAY SUITE 1500 (713) 521-9600

FIGURE 12-10 Mini-Bridge Schedule

Source: Courtesy of United Arab Shipping Company.

The schedules and routes of international air carriers are established by negotiations between the nations involved. Rates are established by the **International Air Transport Association (IATA),** a cartel consisting of nearly all the world's scheduled international airlines. The principal function of international airlines is to carry passengers. Freight is a secondary function, although some scheduled airlines use some all-freight aircraft in certain markets. Lufthansa, the German airline, was the first airline in the world to use an all-cargo Boeing 747. It was used in trans-Atlantic service and connected Germany with the Northeastern United States, replacing several smaller planes. Compared with earlier jets, the 747 has enormous capacity. Figure 12-11 shows several configurations. In addition to the planes shown in Figure 12-11, Figure 12-12 shows several container sizes used by international airlines. Figure 12-13 shows a plane with a custom body, designed to carry large aircraft wings used by Airbus Industries in Europe. As this book is being

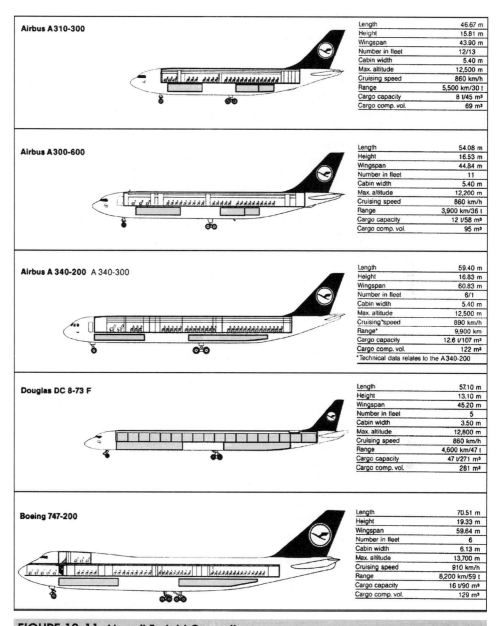

Airbus A310-300	
Length	46.67 m
Height	15.81 m
Wingspan	43.90 m
Number in fleet	12/13
Cabin width	5.40 m
Max. altitude	12,500 m
Cruising speed	860 km/h
Range	5,500 km/30 t
Cargo capacity	8 t/45 m³
Cargo comp. vol.	69 m³

Airbus A300-600	
Length	54.08 m
Height	16.53 m
Wingspan	44.84 m
Number in fleet	11
Cabin width	5.40 m
Max. altitude	12,200 m
Cruising speed	860 km/h
Range	3,900 km/36 t
Cargo capacity	12 t/58 m³
Cargo comp. vol.	95 m³

Airbus A 340-200 A 340-300	
Length	59.40 m
Height	16.83 m
Wingspan	60.83 m
Number in fleet	6/1
Cabin width	5.40 m
Max. altitude	12,500 m
Cruising speed	890 km/h
Range*	9,900 km
Cargo capacity	12.6 t/107 m³
Cargo comp. vol.	122 m³
*Technical data relates to the A340-200	

Douglas DC 8-73 F	
Length	57.10 m
Height	13.10 m
Wingspan	45.20 m
Number in fleet	5
Cabin width	3.50 m
Max. altitude	12,800 m
Cruising speed	860 km/h
Range	4,600 km/47 t
Cargo capacity	47 t/271 m³
Cargo comp. vol.	281 m³

Boeing 747-200	
Length	70.51 m
Height	19.33 m
Wingspan	59.64 m
Number in fleet	6
Cabin width	6.13 m
Max. altitude	13,700 m
Cruising speed	910 km/h
Range	8,200 km/59 t
Cargo capacity	16 t/90 m³
Cargo comp. vol.	129 m³

FIGURE 12-11 Aircraft Freight Capacity

Source: Courtesy of Lufthansa Cargo.

revised, announcements are being made of even larger aircraft, intended mainly for passengers, that will also carry some freight and, eventually, be available in all-freight configurations. The best potential market for these larger planes appears to be Asia.

One of the most significant international air cargo developments was the introduction into numerous foreign trade routes of Boeing 747s with main-deck cargo

Description Base Dims.	Prefix	Code and Illustration
Pallet/Net 2235 x 3175 mm (88 x 125 in) 2235 x 2743 mm (88 x 108 in) 2438 x 3175 mm (96 x 125 in) 2438 x 6058 mm (96 x 238½ in)	PA PB (PD) PM (PQ) PG (PS)	**P** AIRCRAFT PALLET AND NET
Igloo/Net 2235 x 3175 mm (88 x 125 in) 2235 x 2743 mm (88 x 108 in) 2438 x 3175 mm (96 x 125 in)	UA UB (UD) UM (UQ)	**U** NON-STRUCTURAL IGLOO
Structual Igloo 2235 x 3175 mm (88 x 125 in) 2235 x 2743 mm (88 x 108 in)	AA (SA) (TA) AB (AD)	**A** or **S** or **T** STRUCTURAL IGLOO
8' x 8' Maindeck Container 2438 x 2981 mm (96 x 117¾ in) 2438 x 3175 mm (96 x 125 in) 2438 x 6058 mm (96 x 238 ½ in)	AF (AR) AM (AQ) AG (S)	**A** MAIN DECK CONTAINER
Lower Deck Certified Cont. 1534 x 1562 mm (60.4 x 61.5 in) 1534 x 3175 mm (60.4 x 125 in)	AK (AV) AL (AW)	**A** LOWER DECK CONTAINER
Non-Certified Aircraft Cont. 1534 x 1562 mm (60.4 x 61.5 in) 1534 x 3175 mm (60.4 x 125 in)	DK (DV) DL (DW)	**D** NON-CERTIFIED CONTAINER (May be made from material other than metal)

FIGURE 12-12 Large Containers Used by International Airlines

Source: Courtesy of International Air Transport Association.

FIGURE 12-13 Nicknamed the "Beluga" This Custom Airbus is Used to Transport Aircraft Wings Used on Airbus Aircraft, Manufactured in Europe. The Planes Are Also Used for Other Over-Sized Cargo

Source: Courtesy of Frankfurt Airport.

configurations. Some of these 747s have a movable bulkhead that can be changed as the relative amounts of passengers and cargo vary; this model is called a *combi.* This enables the airline to adjust for seasonal changes in passenger travel. Also, the carrier has more flexibility in case of changes in the relative strength of passenger and freight movements.

For shippers of large quantities, international airlines offer a unit-load incentive in conjunction with some FAK (freight-all-kinds) rates. The airline supplies large pallets and, if necessary, igloos (a fiberglass pallet cover placed over the load to protect it and ensure that it does not exceed the allowable dimensions). To obtain the lower rates from IATA carriers, the shipper must tender the pallet loaded to airline specifications; at the other end of the journey, the entire pallet must be destined to one consignee. A special charge is made if it is necessary to unload or partially unload the pallet for customs inspection. Both the shipper and consignee may have the pallet for 48 hours each before demurrage charges are assessed.

The result of the IATA incentives to use containers and unit loads has been to increase the average size of shipments handled by the airlines. This has reduced the number of individual packages each airline terminal must handle. Air freight forwarders have benefited because they are frequently in a better position than individual shippers to take advantage of incentives offered for larger shipments or consolidated shipments.

International air freight forwarders use a document entitled the *Shipper's Letter of Instructions,* which is frequently the only document the shipper must execute. Shippers not using forwarders must have their own air waybills prepared.

International air cargo rates are published in tariffs available from the airlines. There are both general cargo rates and lower specific commodity rates. Rate breaks encourage heavier shipments. Excerpts from a tariff with freight rates from Houston to some Latin American destinations are given in Figure 12-14. Most rates today are computerized.

BULK GENERAL & SPECIFIC COMMODITY CARGO RATES FROM THE U.S. AND CANADA

2

From: HOUSTON (HOU)

Airline	Item	Commodity Description	Minimum Charge($)	1	100	220	440	660	880	1100	2200	4400	Note	Flight Days
AMERICAN AIRLINES (AA)	GEN	General Commodity	37.00											
		To: COZUMEL (CZM)		68	59	57	57	53	53	50	50	50		
EASTERN AIRLINES (EA)	GEN	General Commodity	40.00											
VIASA AIRLINES (VA)	GEN	General Commodity	50.00											
		To: CURACAO (CUR)		144	108	108	108	102	102	83	83	83		
				146	108	108	108	102	102	88	88	88		
CARICARGO (DC)	GEN	General Commodity	50.00											
		To: DOMINICA (DOM)		121	97	97	97	97	97	79	79	79		
CARICARGO (DC)	GEN	General Commodity	50.00											
EASTERN AIRLINES (EA)	GEN	General Commodity	40.00										3	
		To: FORT DE FRANCE (FDF)		115	94	94	94	94	97	79	79	79		
				155	108	108	108	108	108	97	97	97		
EASTERN AIRLINES (EA)	GEN	General Commodity	35.00											
		To: FREEPORT (FPO)		90	69	69	69	69	69	57	57	57		
CARICARGO (DC)	GEN	General Commodity	50.00										4	
		To: GEORGETOWN (GEO)		125	112	112	112	112	112	95	95	95		
CAYMAN AIRWAYS (KX)	GEN	General Commodity	39.00											
CAYMAN AIRWAYS (KX)	GEN	General Commodity	39.00											
CAYMAN AIRWAYS (KX)	0006	Foodstuffs, Spices, Beverages												
		To: GRAND CAYMAN (GCM)		80	66	66	66	66	66	55	55	55		
				80	66	66	66	66	66	55	55	55		
										35	35	35		
CARICARGO (DC)	GEN	General Commodity	50.00										1	
		To: GRENADA (GND)		116	94	94	94	94	94	78	78	78		
AMERICAN AIRLINES (AA)	GEN	General Commodity	37.00											
		To: GUADALAJARA (GDL)		44	34	34	34	34	34	31	31	31		
AVIATECA AIRLINES (GU)	GEN	General Commodity	45.00										1,3,5	
EASTERN AIRLINES (EA)	GEN	General Commodity	45.00											
TACA INTERNATIONAL (TA)	GEN	General Commodity	45.00										1,3,5,6	
AVIATECA AIRLINES (GU)	1081	Baby Poultry												
	2199	Textiles, Clothing or Footwear												
	4206	Surface Vehicle Parts												
TACA INTERNATIONAL (TA)	4742	Oil Drill Machines/Parts												
AVIATECA AIRLINES (GU)	6001	Chemicals,Drugs,Pharm.Medicine												
		To: GUATEMALA CITY (GUA)		81	81	59	59	56	56	50	50	50		
				137	104	104	104	92	92	78	78	78		
				78	78	56	56	56	56	50	50	50		
							44	44	44	44	44	44		
								45	45	38	38	38		
								45	45	38	38	38		
									50	50	45	45		
									50	50	50	50		
AECA AIRLINES (2A)	GEN	General Commodity	50.00											
AEROPERU (PL)	GEN	General Commodity	50.00											
AIR PANAMA (OP)	GEN	General Commodity	40.00											
EASTERN AIRLINES (EA)	GEN	General Commodity	50.00										2,3,5,6,7	
ECUATORIANA (EU)	GEN	General Commodity	50.00											
LADECO AIRLINES (UC)	GEN	General Commodity	50.00											
		To: GUAYAQUIL (GYE)		117	89	89	89	68	68	68	68	54	ag	
				131	98	98	98	80	80	69	69	69		
				131	98	98	98	80	80	69	69	69		
				228	171	171	171	145	145	120	120	120		
				224	168	168	168	142	142	117	117	117		
				166	125	125	125	101	101	88	88,	88		
FAST AIR (UD)	GEN	General Commodity	50.00											
LAN-CHILE (LA)	GEN	General Commodity	50.00										Daily	
		To: IQUIQUE (IQQ)		370	279	279	279	279	279	198	198	198		
				375	283	283	283	283	283	211	211	211		
FAUCETT AIRLINES (CF)	GEN	General Commodity	45.00											
LAN-CHILE (LA)	GEN	General Commodity	50.00										3,6,7	
		To: IQUITOS (IQT)		193	138	138	138	116	116	110	110	110		
				256	200	200	200	161	161	140	140	140		

Rates in Cents per Pound

FIGURE 12-14 Excerpts from an Air Freight Tariff Showing Rates from Houston to Several Latin American Points

Source: Courtesy of CRS Publishing Division, Miami, FL.

A newer development in international air freight is international parcel services offered by well-known carriers such as UPS, FedEx, BAXGlobal, Airborne Express, and DHL International. All these firms are U.S. based. Another major player is TNT Express, headquartered in Australia. All provide land pickup and delivery services for documents and small parcels and are called *integrated carriers* because they own all their vehicles and the facilities that fall in between. These courier services are of special significance to international logistics because they often provide the fastest service between many major points. They are also often employed to carry the documentation that is generated by—and is very much a part of—the international movement of materials, although many foreign trade documents can now be transferred electronically. These carriers also handle documentation services for their clients.

Ocean Shipping

The past three decades have seen two significant advances in shipping technology: larger vessels and improved shoreside cargo-handling techniques. Newly constructed tankers in use today have 30 to 40 times the capacity of World War II-vintage T-2 tankers. Methods of handling cargo are now much more efficient, especially in the handling of break-bulk general cargo. For centuries, cargo had been loaded or unloaded on a piece-by-piece basis after being lifted by a ship's boom and tackle. Today, intermodal containers are used in most major trade routes.

Types of Ocean Cargoes

Much of the world's shipping tonnage is used for carrying petroleum. The tankers are either owned by oil companies or leased (chartered) by them from individuals who invest in ships. The leased vessels are chartered for specific voyages or for large blocks of time. The charter market fluctuates widely, especially after events such as the closing and opening of the Suez Canal and the announcement of large U.S. wheat sales overseas. International commodity traders follow the vessel charter market closely because they know the differences in commodity prices in various world markets. When the charter rate between these two markets drops to the point that it is less than the spread in the commodity prices, a vessel is chartered to carry the commodity.

Dry-bulk cargoes, such as grain, ores, sulfur, sugar, scrap iron, coal, lumber, and logs, usually move in complete vessel-load lots on chartered vessels. These independent dry-cargo vessels are often referred to as *tramps*. A bulk carrier is shown in Figure 12-15.

There are also large, specialized dry cargo ships that are often owned by shippers. Nissan Motor Company of Japan, for example, owns eight auto-carrying ships, four of which can carry 1,200 autos apiece and the other four of which can carry 1,900. Most of these vessels carry autos to the United States and can then load with soybeans for the return voyages.

If a single shipper's needs do not fill the vessel completely, the vessel is topped off with compatible bulk cargo, such as grain, that can be loaded into an unused hold. This helps defray the total voyage costs for the party using the ship. Agents specialize in chartering fractional spaces (often individual holds) in vessels.

FIGURE 12-15 An Ocean Bulk Carrier Being Loaded with Export Coal Carried by a Mechanical Device at Far Left

Source: Photo courtesy of Electro-Coal Transfer Corp., Davant, LA.

Another type of vessel that combines aspects of several vessel types is the parcel tanker, which has over 50 different tanks, ranging from 350 to 2,200 cubic meters. Each can carry a different liquid and is loaded and unloaded through a separate piping system. The tanks have different types of coating; some are temperature controlled. Some of the vessels go on round-the-world voyages and carry palm oil, coconut oil, chemicals, and refined petroleum products. Stolt–Nielsen is the firm best known for this service. Some years ago, the firm's planning director, Robert F. Matthes, described its operations as "a loosely defined liner service."[20] He also noted that a significant adjustment in business planning is taking place with a move toward through transportation services. This includes not only offering through bills of lading and overland transport but also other services necessary for the transport of bulk liquids. Note that this was an early example of a carrier widening the range of services it makes available to its customers.

---

[20]*American Shipper,* May 1986, p. 78.

Shipping Conferences and Alliances

Users of ocean liner shipping have different service requirements. "Manufacturers such as Volvo, which export vehicles to customer order, require daily sailings across the Atlantic."[21] For some other cargoes, time savings are of little significance. A prime example of this is wastepaper. "Like the married couple that fights all the time but would never think of living apart, wastepaper exporters and ocean carriers represent the consummate symbiotic relationship of the transportation industry."[22] Shipping lines rely on steady volumes of wastepaper to keep their ships full. Vessel lines bump wastepaper cargoes at the last minute if they can find a load of higher-paying cargo, a practice known as *rolling.* "Carriers like wastepaper because when they overbook this cargo can be rolled, and rolled, and rolled, and rolled."[23] In turn, wastepaper exporters require stability in freight rates because they account for 60 percent to 95 percent of their landed costs. Wastepaper accounts for 18 percent of the cargo carried from the United States to Asia and, because it originates in all 50 states, it can be used to fill containers that must be repositioned in Asia.

> Wastepaper shippers may complain about how they are treated by carriers, but their industry is famous for changing destinations, letting containers sit at Asian ports for weeks until a buyer is found and paying their shipping charges late.[24]

How do carriers take into account these varying demands for service? Service contracts were permitted under the Shipping Act of 1984; they were drawn up between shipping conferences (liner companies serving the same market) and specific shippers or shippers' associations (representing related shippers). A service contract consists of a commitment by the shipper to the conference or carrier of a minimum volume of cargo, usually expressed in TEUs with rate levels indicated as intermodal, point to point, or port to port. The carrier or conference must guarantee regular service. Contracts also include clauses for damages in case the shipper does not live up to its commitment—a typical shipper's problem is loss of overseas sales. Most contracts cover containerized cargo. Discounts on service contracts are given if the carrier can operate from door to door without specifying the ports through which cargo must be routed. Discounts are also given for quicker releases of containers. Shippers using just-in-time (JIT) systems benefit from this since often they unload containers promptly. Off-peak discounts are also offered for moving traffic when business is slow.

What do shippers want in liner service contracts? *American Shipper* magazine surveyed 50 large shippers from the United States, Europe, and Asia. Following are the percentages of shippers answering "yes" to questions concerning necessary contract provisions:

- Predictable stable ocean rate, 94%
- All-inclusive freight rates (no adjustment factors), 83%

---

[21] *The Journal of Commerce,* December 11, 1996, p. 3B.

[22] Alan M. Sheps, *The Journal of Commerce,* October 21, 1996, p. 3B. Mr. Sheps is a forwarder specializing in wastepaper exports.

[23] Ibid.

[24] Ibid.

- Guarantees of ship space and container availability, 73%
- Carrier monitoring of service quality, 68%
- Prenotification of vessel arrival, 67%
- Global, multitrade contracts, 48%
- Electronic data interchange (EDI), 46%
- Carrier pays compensation for late shipments. 29%[25]

Until about a decade ago, ocean general cargo (or break-bulk) liner rates affecting U.S. ports were set by shipping conferences, which are cartels of all vessel operators operating between certain trade areas. Conferences provide stability in markets in which cargo offerings fluctuate. Recently, the number has declined, with each covering a larger geographic area. Some are now being called *rate agreements*. In the mid-1990s, another type of alliance began forming in the container trades: Carriers retain their individual identities but cooperate in the area of operations. Some of the activities that the lines do jointly are agreeing whether to join conferences, coordinating sailings and data systems, interchanging empty containers, managing container pools, operating feeder services, operating terminals, ordering new containers, purchasing new ships, and reciprocal space chartering.[26] These alliances "now dominate the world's trade routes by providing global service. They are made up of the biggest container lines in the business."[27] As of January 2000, the world's leading container service operators were Maersk Sea-Land; Evergreen/Uniglory/Lloyd Triestino; P&O/Nedlloyd; Hinjin/DSR-Senator; Mediterranean Shipping; COSCO; NOL/APL; NYK Line; CMA/CGM/ANL; and CP Ship Group. They controlled over 1,000 vessels and over half of the world's container carrying capacity.[28]

In late 2001, several of the alliances entered into negotiations with the objective of forming an even larger alliance. Why were alliances formed? Alix, Slack, and Comtois explained: "Faced with the need to provide as extensive market coverage as possible while striving to fill the ever-growing capacities of the ships, nearly all the major container lines have responded by coming together in alliances. In this way they pool resources (ships, terminal facilities, etc.), and extend market coverage (enter markets that one company alone might not be capable of serving adequately). As in other sectors of the economy, strategic alliances enable firms to confront the challenges of uncertainty, allocation of resources, and market penetration."[29] So, while alliances are not conferences, their size allows them to exercise considerable clout in their dealings with shippers, port terminal operators, and connecting land carriers.

The relationship between buyers (shippers) and sellers (carriers) and groups of sellers (conferences or alliances) has changed dramatically over the last 20 years. In

---

[25]*American Shipper,* November 1996, p. 38.

[26]*American Shipper,* October 1996, pp. 37–46.

[27]Yann Alix, Brian Slack, and Claude Comtois, "Alliance of Acquisition? Strategies for Growth in the Container Shipping Industry: The Case of CP Ships," *Journal of Transport Geography,* 1999, p. 206.

[28]United Nations Conference on Trade and Development, *Review of Maritime Transport 2000* (Geneva, 2000), p. 50. Those listed as single firms had grown be outright acquisitions of other competing and complementary operators.

[29]Yann Alix, Brian Slack, and Claude Comtois, p. 206.

Service [Refine] [Reset]	Freq.	EB / WB	Bremerhaven ☐
Norfolk VA ⌐			Bremerhaven
COSCO/"K" Line/YML/Zim - AUE (transatlantic)	Weekly	Mo / Tu	14 Mo / 15 Mo
Evergreen - NUE (transatlantic)	Weekly	Mo / We	10 Th / 12 Fr
Grand Alliance/Lykes/TMM Lines/ACL - PAX (transatlantic)	Weekly	Mo / Sa	13 Su / 12 Mo
Hanjin/Senator Lines/CSAV/Norasia - AWP (transatlantic)	Weekly	We / Mo	12 Mo / 13 Tu
Lykes/TMM Lines/Grand Alliance/Deppe/ACL/CKYHS - Gulf Atlantic Loop (transatlantic)	Weekly	Su / -	14 Su / --
Maersk Sealand/New World Alliance/CMA CGM - TA2/Atlantic South (transatlantic)	Weekly	Mo / Su	11 Fr / 22 Sa
Maersk Sealand/New World Alliance/CMA CGM - TA3 (transatlantic)	Weekly	- / Tu	-- / 11 Fr
MSC/Atlantic Container Line - North Atlantic (transatlantic)	Weekly	Mo / Mo	13 Su / 14 Mo
New World Alliance/Maersk Sealand/CMA CGM - APX (transatlantic)	Weekly	Tu / Th	11 Sa / 11 Su
Wallenius Wilhelmsen - New Ro-Ro (transatlantic)	Monthly	- / -	13 - / --
Wallenius Wilhelmsen - PCTC RTW eastbound (transatlantic)	Monthly	- / -	15 - / --

FIGURE 12-16 Excerpt from *American Shipper* Magazine's ComPair Schedules Web Site *www.americanshipper.com,* Showing the Number of Sailings Between Major Ports

Source: American Shipper magazine.

routes serving U.S. ports, this commercial relationship has moved from a tightly regulated environment to a largely unregulated environment wherein shippers and carriers are free to work out whatever commercial relationship best suits them in confidential contractual agreements. The United States policies toward liner pricing differ from those in much of the remainder of the world. A European journal said of the remainder of the world, "Liner shipping stands out in the world economy in being almost completely cartelized as far as pricing is concerned. Practically every trade route is covered by a separate coalition of liner conferences which fixes the freight rates."[30] Figure 12-16 comes from *American Shipper* magazine's Web site, which lists liner schedules in major markets. In explaining the service, the magazine reported that a number of carriers share space on the same vessel and each lists this as a separate service. There were so many multiple listings that 43 offered sailing services were, in fact, only 16 different sailings.[31] Today, major U.S. shippers use contracts with alliances for most traffic between the United States and either Asia or Europe. In other markets, shippers may deal with vessel conferences or rate agreements. Memberships in alliances, rate agreements, and conferences are very fluid.

---

[30]*European Transport Law,* XXXIV, No. 6, 1999, p. 761.

[31]E-mail from *American Shipper* editor to co-author, August 2, 2002.

Containers

Today, operators of general cargo vessels might never handle, or even see, cargo on a piece-by-piece basis. Their ships are fully containerized, which means the only way they can load or unload cargo is to have the cargo stowed inside containers. Containers dominate the traffic between Europe and the United States, Europe and Asia, and the United States and Asia.

Shippers or forwarders tender full containers, and if a shipper tenders a less-than-container lot, the vessel operator must load all the less-than-container lots into containers so that the cargo can be loaded aboard the containership. In large containerships, some of the containers are carried above the level of the deck; this increases the vessel's cubic carrying capacity.

Lighter aboard ship (LASH) vessels handle floating containers. They can be used most advantageously where the central port is connected to inland areas by shallow waterways. Similar conditions must exist on both ends of the voyage, so the applicability of the system is somewhat limited. LASH barges are approximately 60 feet long, 30 feet wide, and 13 feet deep, or about 20,000 cubic feet. They carry about 400 short tons (a short ton = 2000 pounds). The Seabee concept is similar, except that the barges are larger. A typical Seabee barge is 100 feet long, 35 feet wide, and 13 feet deep. At the present time, LASH and Seabee vessels are aging, and it is uncertain whether new ones will be built.

Roll On–Roll Off (RO–RO) vessels are somewhat like large, floating parking lots. They have large doors in their sterns or on their sides. Ramps are stretched to the shore, and cargo is moved on or off the ship in trailers. RO–RO vessels are used to carry vehicles that can move using their own power. An RO–RO vessel that operates between Florida and Puerto Rico is shown in Figure 12-17.

Although the various types of vessels have been discussed separately, many vessels carry cargo loaded by various techniques. Most LASH and RO–RO vessels, for example, also carry conventional containers.

Surface Transport in Other Countries

The quality of transport facilities in foreign nations varies. Some are as well developed as those in the United States, with two notable differences. First, few foreign nations have as wide a range of modes to choose from because the United States makes a greater effort to encourage all modes of transportation. Second, the degree of nationalization of transportation is higher in most foreign countries than in the United States.

Shipowners in the dry-cargo trades are extending their involvement along the supply chain to include land transportation and warehousing. "With margins on deep-sea shipping services 'almost nonexistent,' tramp-shipping operators see profit potential in providing landside services. . . . China, Russia, Romania and Ukraine are among the countries where dry-cargo shipowners and operators are becoming involved in inland distribution, usually with the help of a local partner."[32]

The widespread use of seaborne containers has brought about hopes of standardizing land vehicles for carrying containers on the landward legs of their journeys. The

---

[32]Janet Porter, "Tramp-Ship Operators, Following Lead of Liner Companies, Expand Inland," *The Journal of Commerce,* June 16, 1995, p. 7B.

FIGURE 12-17 An RO–RO Vessel in Jacksonville, Florida

Source: Courtesy of Jacksonville Port Authority.

European Union has been making progress in its attempt to standardize truck dimensions within its member countries. Truckborne containers are now familiar sights throughout much of the world. Trucks appear to be in universal use. However, opposition to trucks is growing in some European nations, such as Switzerland and Austria, that trucks cross while moving between other nations. They are trying to force the use of containers on rail. However, intermodal growth in Europe is not shifting to rail. "Intermodal transport enjoys solid political support across Europe, but is being undermined by market forces on the roads, and inefficiency on the tracks."[33] In January 1998, truckers were able to travel anywhere in the 15-nation European Union (EU). Opening of the EU's borders to truckers from Central and Eastern Europe has "led to an influx of low-cost truckers who are scouting for hard-currency contracts."[34]

　　Short sea shipping is ocean shipping, often along a region's coast, rather than across oceans. We think of feeder service connecting with major ports. Smaller ocean-going ships are employed. It is considered more environmentally friendly than the use

---

[33]Bruce Barnard, "EU Intermodal Growth Falls Short," *The Journal of Commerce,* February 28, 1997, p. 3B.
[34]Ibid.

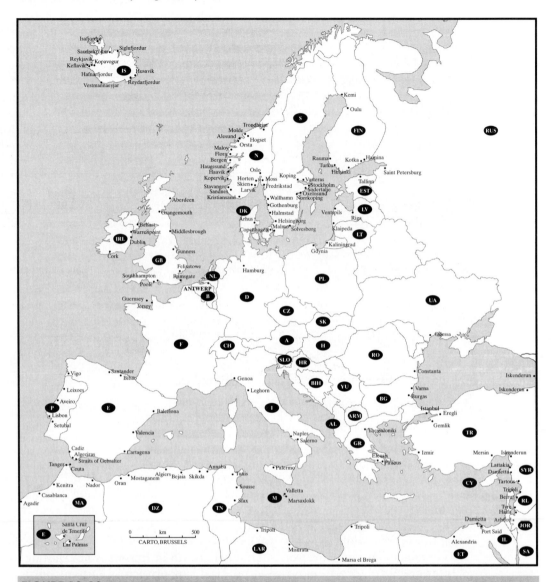

FIGURE 12-18 Ports in Europe and in the Mediterranean That Are Connected to Antwerp by "Short Sea" Water Transport

Source: Drawing copyright PUBLITRA, Belgium. Reprinted with permission.

of trucks. For example, Antwerp is connected to 141 ports in Europe and the Mediterranean by this type of service (see Figure 12-18).

Rail equipment sizes and clearances vary throughout the world, and most nations use equipment that is much smaller than that used in the United States. Containers that can be loaded two to a railcar in the United States are frequently carried on individual railcars elsewhere. A variety of rail gauges complicates the exchange of traffic between nations.

One of the difficulties in implementing international transport technological improvements is that fairly identical handling equipment must be in place at each end of the trip. In a few parts of the world, grain and sugar are still stowed or unloaded by stevedores carrying individual bags on their shoulders and walking up and down gangplanks. In handling relief cargoes in Africa, one finds that cargo-handling techniques there are primitive. Aircraft may be unloaded by workers carrying bags of grain on their shoulders.

The incidence (or burden) of costs is also significant. RO–RO shipping involves the use of trailers, rather than containers, carried aboard ships as though they were large ferry boats. Once loaded, there is considerable wasted space—essentially the height of each trailer box above the deck floor. Thus, a vessel cannot carry as much cargo within a given amount of space. Yet the required port facilities are relatively inexpensive; only a ramp for driving trailers on or off a ship is needed. The trailers can be hitched to tractors and hauled directly to or from their landward destination. So, although more is spent per ton of cargo on vessel operations, less is spent for port operations.

Vessel lines can force a port to add cargo-handling equipment by placing a surcharge against a port for all shipments until such equipment is installed. In 1995, the Inter-American Freight Conference doubled the congestion surcharge for Santos from $150 to $300 per 20-foot container. For a 40-foot container, the charges went from $250 to $500. "The carriers can't absorb the costs of ships sitting there and cargo not moving. It costs $25,000 to $35,000 a day to run these ships."[35]

International Trade Inventories

Even under the best conditions, the movement of products in an international supply chain is never as smooth as a comparable domestic movement. Because greater uncertainties, misunderstandings, and delays often arise in international movements, safety stocks must be larger.

Firms involved in international trade must modify their inventory policies or at least give them careful thought. Most nations represent smaller potential marketing areas than the United States; thus, the inventory necessary to serve any one of them will be smaller. An inventory held in one nation may not necessarily serve the needs of markets in neighboring nations because there may be minor, but significant, variations in the specifications of the product sold in each country.

Tailoring products for individual markets is also an issue. General Motors (GM) and Ford, for example, see the Asian market differently. Ford has a one-size-fits-all philosophy, turning out an Escort-like model with little tailoring for individual markets. GM builds cars tailored for each market. In Bangkok and Manila, it is hot and there are many traffic jams, so a larger cooling system is provided. In China, the roads are rough and stronger suspensions and tougher tires are provided. Air conditioning is beefed up and "even the dashboard material is made so as to withstand 12 hours of broiling sun."[36]

---

[35]Richard A. Simpson, "Ship Conference Doubles Santos Congestion Fee," *The Journal of Commerce,* June 20, 1995, p. 10A.

[36]P.T. Bangsberg, "Competing Road Maps in Asia: GM, Ford follow Different Strategies in Booming Market," *The Journal of Commerce,* December 4, 1996, p. 5A.

Also, duties may have to be paid each time a product crosses a national boundary, although a provision is common for duty drawbacks, which provide the rebate of all (or nearly all) of a duty if the imported product is exported, usually within a specified time period of its initial entry.

Return items are virtually impossible to accommodate in an international distribution operation, especially if the return involves movements of the goods across a national boundary. This has some implications for a firm trying to achieve a high level of customer service standards on an international basis, since it may be unreasonable to tell buyers to return a defective item to the factory where it was built. One U.S. retail chain tells its stores to contact domestic producers directly with questions regarding product defects. However, for imported products, no recourse is available. The stores are told to destroy the products or sell them at salvage prices.

Import and export quotas affect values of inventories. Inventory valuation on an international scale is difficult because the relative values of various currencies continually change. The value of wheat held in a nation's grain elevators will be the world market price, adjusted for transportation, unless the government places an embargo on wheat exports (or imports). The value of the wheat within the nation then becomes the domestic price. When a nation's (or the world's) currency is unstable, investments in inventories rise because they are believed to be less risky than holding cash or securities.

Computer programs have been developed that aid in managing international inventories. One such system, used by the Cummins Engine Company, is located at that firm's Brussels warehouse, which handles distribution to 18 countries in Western Europe. Some of its unique features include its multilanguage capabilities and its use of current relative values of various national currencies. The multilanguage capability allows translation into whatever languages are necessary to prepare shipping documents, invoices, and so on. The currency conversion feature enables invoices to be drawn in the buyer's home currency. Another feature is used to instruct a warehouse to fill an order in a way that minimizes the amount of duty to be paid. To accomplish this, the computer needs to know the applicable tariff rates between the goods' nation or nations of origin and the nation of sale. It must also take into account that day's relative values of world currencies, because this will have an impact on the true amount of duties that must be paid.[37]

SUMMARY

This chapter covered various aspects of international logistics, which differs from domestic logistics in many respects, such as by having a requirement for numerous documents. It is also dependent on fluctuating currency values because they cause shifts in the flows of commerce. Governments attempt to influence foreign trade, in part because export sales help their economies, balance of payments, and currency values. They also may discourage imports by imposing tariffs or other restrictions (sometimes known as nontariff barriers). Governments subsidize their international shipping and airlines.

---

[37]The system was developed by Distribution Systems Management Systems, Inc., of Lexington, Massachusetts, and is described in the firm's brochures.

Because international logistics is complex, many firms rely on specialists to help with export and import transactions. These foreign trade specialists include freight forwarders, NVOCCs, customshouse brokers, export packers, and others.

The chapter also examined the transportation elements involved in an export shipment. These include the move to a port or airport, the move aboard a plane or ship, and delivery overseas. International trade inventories were discussed briefly.

QUESTIONS FOR DISCUSSION AND REVIEW

1. Explain how developing nations ensure that an increasing proportion of supply-chain activities are conducted within their borders.
2. Discuss some of the ways in which international marketing differs from domestic marketing.
3. Discuss the role of the letter of credit with respect to international shipments.
4. Explain the purpose of Incoterms.
5. Discuss government controls on the flow of international trade.
6. Discuss the roles that a particular country's government might play in international transport.
7. Discuss four possible functions that might be performed by international freight forwarders.
8. Explain the three sources of compensation for international freight forwarders.
9. What is an NVOCC? What is its relationship with international freight forwarders?
10. What services do export management firms perform?
11. What are the two primary purposes of export packing?
12. What are some labeling issues that might be considered when selling goods in a nondomestic market?
13. Explain the land bridge concept.
14. Discuss some advantages of combi aircraft.
15. What is a parcel tanker?
16. Discuss service contracts as applied to international water transportation.
17. Discuss the role of alliances in the container trades.
18. What are RO–RO vessels?
19. Discuss some of the challenges to surface transport in other countries.
20. Discuss some of the challenges associated with inventory management in cross-border trade.

SUGGESTED READINGS

Belis-Bergouignan, Marie-Claude, Gerard Bordenave, and Yannick Lung, "Global Strategies in the Automobile Industry." *Regional Studies,* Vol. 34, No. 1, 2000, pp. 41–53.

Breyley, Mark. "Speed Bumps of the Silk Road." *Supply Chain Management Review,* Vol. 6, No. 5, 2002, pp. 10–11.

Carter, Joseph R., John Pearson, and Li Peng. "Logistics Barriers to International Operations: The Case of the People's Republic of China." *Journal of Business Logistics,* Vol. 18, No. 2, 1997, pp. 129–144.

Clarke, Richard L. "An Analysis of the International Shipping Conference System." *Transportation Journal,* Vol. 36, No. 4, 1997, pp. 17–29.

Gourevitch, Peter, Roger Bohn, and David McKendrick. "Globalization of Production: Insights from the Hard Disk Drive Industry."

World Development, Vol. 28, No. 2, 2000, pp. 301–317.

Janelle, Donald G., and Michel Beuthe. "Globalization and Research Issues in Transportation." *Journal of Transport Geography,* Vol. 5, No. 3, 1997, pp. 199–206.

Lewis, Ira, and Daniel Coulter. "The Voluntary Intermodal Sealift Agreement: Strategic Transportation for National Defense." *The Transportation Journal,* Vol. 40, No. 1, 2000, pp. 26–33.

McNaughton, Rod B., and Jim Bell. "Channel Switching Between Domestic and Foreign Markets." *Journal of International Marketing,* Vol. 9, No. 1, 2001, pp. 24–39.

Moseley, William G. "Computer Assisted Comprehension of Distant Worlds: Understanding

Hunger Dynamics in Africa." *Journal of Geography,* January/February, 2001, pp. 32–45.

Poist, Richard F., Carl Scheraga, and Janjaap Semeijn. "Assessing the Post-1992 European Experience: Perspectives of U. S. and European Logistics Executives." *Transportation Journal,* Vol. 39, No. 2, 1999, pp. 5–15.

Railas, Lauri. "Incoterms for the New Millennium," *European Transport Law,* 2000, pp. 9–22.

Roberts, Joanne. "The Internationalization of Business Service Firms: A Stages Approach." *Service Industries Journal,* Vol. 19, No. 4, October 1999, pp. 68–88.

United Nations Conference on Trade and Development, *Review of Maritime Transport 2000* (Geneva, 2000).

Vidal, Carlos, and Marc Goetschalckx. "Modeling the Effect of Uncertainties on Global Logistics Systems." *Journal of Business Logistics,* Vol. 21, No. 1, 2000, pp. 95–115.

Wijnolst, Niko, and Tor Wergeland. *Shipping* (Delft: Delft University Press, 1997).

Wood, Donald F., Anthony Barone, Paul Murphy, and Daniel L. Wardlow. *International Logistics,* 2nd ed. (New York: Amacom, 2002).

C A S E S

Case 12-1   HDT Truck Company

HDT Truck Company has been located in Crown Point, Indiana, since 1910. Its only products—large trucks—are built to individual customer specifications. The firm once produced automobiles but dropped out of the auto business in 1924. The firm nearly went out of business in the late 1930s, but by 1940 its fortunes were buoyed by receipt of several military contracts for tank retrievers—large-wheeled vehicles that can pull a disabled tank onto a low trailer and haul it to a location where it can be repaired.

Since World War II, HDT had manufactured only large off-road vehicles, including airport snowplows, airport crash trucks, oil-field drilling equipment, and the like. HDT purchased all components from small manufacturers that were still clustered in the Milwaukee–Detroit–Toledo–Cleveland area. Essentially, all HDT did was assemble components into specialized vehicles containing the combinations of frame, power plant, transmission, axles, cab, and other equipment necessary to do the job. The assembly line was relatively slow. After wheels were attached to the frame and axles, the night shift labor force would push the chassis along to its next station on the line so it would be in place for the next day's shift. By using one shift, two trucks could be assembled each day. If large orders for identical trucks were involved, it was possible to assemble three trucks per day. Quality declined whenever the pace became quicker. HDT officials had decided they could not grow and became satisfied with their niche in the very-heavy-truck market. With only two exceptions, since 1970, HDT had always had at least a 4-month backlog of orders. In the 1960s, its best market had been airports, but since 1980

its best market had been for oil-field equipment, first for the North Slope in Alaska and then for the Middle East. The U.S. military was also a regular customer.

In late 2002, HDT received an order for 50 heavy trucks to be used in the oil fields of Saudi Arabia. The terms of sale were delivery on or before July 1, 2003, at the Port of Doha, Saudi Arabia. Specifically, HDT would receive $172,000 per truck in U.S. funds FAS (free alongside ship) at the discharging vessel in Doha, which meant that HDT was responsible for all transportation costs up until the time and point the trucks were discharged from the ship's tackle at Doha. Once each truck was unloaded, HDT would be paid for it.

Chris Reynolds, production manager at HDT, estimated that production could start approximately April 1, 2003, and the order would take 18 working days to complete. Because weekends were involved, all 50 trucks would be completed by April 20 to 25. Reynolds thought that May 1, 2003, was a more realistic completion date because he had always found it difficult to restrict the assembly line to constructing trucks for only one account. The reason for this was that Vic Guillou, HDT's sales manager, liked to have trucks being built for as many accounts as possible on the assembly line at any one time. Prospective buyers frequently visited the plant and were always more impressed when they could see a diverse collection of models being built for a wide range of uses.

Norman Pon, HDT's treasurer, wanted to give priority to building trucks that were being sold on an FOB plant basis because that would improve his cash flow position. At the time the

$172,000 price had been set on the truck sale to Saudi Arabia, Pon had argued (unsuccessfully) that the price was too low. Guillou, on the other hand, argued that the sale was necessary because the Arab world represented a growth market by anyone's definition and he wanted HDT trucks there. HDT's president, Gordon Robertson, had sided with Guillou. Robertson thought that Pon was a good treasurer but too much of a worrier when it came to making important decisions. Pon, in turn, thought that Robertson had yet to shed the image he had acquired in the 1980s when his late father was president of HDT. Pon had lost count of the number of times the elder Robertson had needed cash to buy his son's way out of some embarrassing situation. Guillou was young Robertson's fraternity roommate in college, and Pon thought the two of them shared a similar love of life in the fast lane. At the time the order was signed in 2002, Guillou argued that the FAS destination port represented the best terms of sale because ocean charter rates were declining as a result of an oversupply of tonnage. Guillou predicted that by mid-2003 charter rates would be so low that the cheapest method of transport would be to load all 50 trucks on one vessel. Pon countered that HDT should try to make a profit only from the manufacture of trucks because nobody in the firm knew much about ocean shipping. Robertson, who was a gambler at heart, disagreed.

In March 2003, Reynolds had the 50-truck order scheduled to be on the line from April 2 to 29, which represented 2.5 trucks per working day. Other work was scheduled for the assembly line at the same time, so the production schedule was considered firm. Component parts for the oil-field trucks and for the other trucks were already arriving. Orders were backlogged for over 7 months, the highest figure since 1989. This was due, almost in total, to Guillou's additional sales of oil-field equipment to Arab producers. Three separate orders were involved and totaled 115 trucks.

Robertson and Guillou left Crown Point for an industry convention in San Diego. Robertson phoned from San Diego that he and Guillou had decided to vacation in Mexico for a while before returning to Crown Point. Robertson knew that HDT could function in his absence and knew that with Pon overseeing operations, the company's assets would be safe. Several days later, a Mexican postcard postmarked in Tijuana arrived, saying that both were enjoying Mexico and would stay longer than initially planned.

Pon was relieved to learn that Guillou and Robertson would be gone for a longer time and immediately began wondering what types of bills they were accumulating in Mexico and for which ones they would want company reimbursement. Both had several credit cards belonging to the company. Based on experience, Pon also expected Robertson to phone on his cell phone for a cash advance or transfer about once a week. (Robertson did not want charge records generated for some of his expenses.) As usual, Pon started wondering how paying for the Robertson and Guillou vacation venture would affect HDT's cash flow. Pon looked at his cash flow projections, which were always made up for 6 weeks in advance, in this case through the first of April, when some of the bills for components of the oil-field trucks would come due. In fact, if Reynolds's schedule were adhered to, all the components would be on hand by April 10 and, if HDT were to receive the customary discounts, all of the components would have to be paid for in the period between April 8 and April 20 (HDT received a 1 percent discount for goods paid for within 10 days of actual or requested receipt, whichever came later). For a moment, Pon thought that the worst might happen: The component bills would be due at the same time as Robertson's and Guillou's request for a hefty cash advance. He called the Crown Point Bank and Trust Company, where HDT had a line of credit, and learned that the current rate was 8 percent per annum. He then asked Bob Vanderpool, who was HDT's traffic manager, when the oil-field trucks would arrive in Saudi Arabia.

"I don't know," was Vanderpool's reply. "I assumed that Guillou had arranged for transportation at the time you decided to charge $172,000 per truck, but I'll check further." He did and phoned back to tell Pon that Guillou's secretary could find nothing in the files to indicate that Guillou had checked out charter rates. "That figures," muttered Pon. "Would you mind doing some checking?" Vanderpool said he *would* mind doing some checking. Pon then suggested to him that there were several other newer orders also destined for the Arab countries so Vanderpool should start thinking about widening his area of expertise. Vanderpool reluctantly agreed, and Pon heard nothing until Vanderpool passed him in the hall a few days later and said the assignment was much more time-consuming than he had imagined. One week later, Vanderpool said he had done as much as he could and would turn the figures over to Pon. Vanderpool also said that he did not have the authority to charter a ship and suggested that Pon determine who could do so in Robertson's absence. Later that day, Vanderpool came to Pon's office with a thick file.

"It looks like you've been doing a lot of figuring," said Pon.

"No, not me," said Vanderpool, "but two outsiders. One is Bob Guider, an international freight forwarder in Chicago whom we use for our export parts shipments. And he put me in touch with Eddie Quan, a New York ship broker who is on top of the charter market. We have two alternatives."

"What are they?" asked Pon.

"Well," answered Vanderpool, "the St. Lawrence Seaway will open in mid-April, so we could use it. The problem is that the Seaway route is circuitous, especially to reach the Arab countries. Also, there aren't many scheduled Seaway sailings to that area, and because the Seaway will just be opening again, cargo space is hard to come by. Therefore, if we're not going to charter a ship, the best bet is to use Baltimore."

"What about chartering a ship?" asked Pon. "Why not use Baltimore for that?"

"In theory, we could," answered Vanderpool. "But Quan says the size of ship we want is rather small and not likely to be sailing into Baltimore. We could arrange to share a ship with another party, but many bulk cargoes are pretty dusty and

might not be compatible with our vehicles. Quan says there is one foreign vessel entering the Great Lakes in April that is still looking for an outbound charter. Seaway vessels, you know, are smaller because of the lock size restrictions. If we want to charter that vessel, we'll have to move quickly, because if somebody else charters her, she's gone."

"What kind of vessel is it?" asked Pon.

"The vessel's name is the *Nola Pino,* the same name as a French movie actress of the 1960s. You may recall that some Greek shipping magnate named the vessel after her, but his wife made him give up both Nola Pino the actress and *Nola Pino* the ship. At present, it's scheduled to be in Chicago the last week in April with a load of cocoa beans and ready for outbound loading May 1. Quan thinks we could charter it for $2,400 per day for 30 days, which would be enough time for it to load, transit the Seaway, reach Doha, and discharge the trucks by May 29 or 30."

"Tell me about the alternative," said Pon.

"Baltimore has fairly frequent sailings to the area we want to reach," said Vanderpool. "We could load two trucks per day on railcars here and send them to Baltimore. Two ships a week are scheduled from Baltimore to Doha. It would take the trucks an average of 4 days to reach Baltimore, where they would wait an average of 3 days to be loaded aboard ship. The figure should be 3.5 days, but the railroad will hustle if it knows we're trying to connect with an outgoing sailing. Sailing time to Doha averages 15 days—a little more, a little less, depending on the amount of cargo to be handled at ports in between."

"That averages 22 days per truck," stated Pon, who had been putting the figures in his new pocket calculator. What are the charges?"

Vanderpool answered, "It costs $120 to load and block two trucks on a flatcar, which is, of course, $60 apiece as long as they move in pairs. Sticking to pairs, the rail rate for two on a flatcar totals $1,792 to Baltimore. Handling at Baltimore is $200 per truck, and ocean freight rate from Baltimore to Doha is $1,440 per truck. We also have to buy insurance, which is about $150 per truck."

EXHIBIT 12-A Map of the Northeastern United States

"That totals $2,790," said Pon, after consulting his calculator. "What are the costs if we charter the *Nola Pino?* You said it could be $72,000 for the vessel. What else is involved?"

"There are two ways of getting the trucks to port," said Vanderpool. "The loading and blocking would be only $40 per truck because we'd be doing all 50 at one time. The rail rate per truck would average out to $180 each, and it would take 1 day for them to reach Chicago and another day to be loaded. We'd be tying up a wharf for 1 day, and the wharfage charge runs $2 per foot, and the *Nola Pino* is 535 feet long. We'd be responsible for loading and stowing the cargo, and this would cost $4,000 for all 50 trucks. The Seaway tolls are $1.80 cents per ton or, in our case, $54 per truck. At Doha, the unloading costs will be $4,200 for the entire vessel. Marine insurance will be $210 per truck."

"Are there any other alternatives?" asked Pon.

"The only other one that comes close is to drive the trucks from here to Chicago," answered Vanderpool. "We would need temporary licenses and a convoy permit and pay to have the fuel tank on each truck drained before it is loaded. The problem is that the convoy would cross state lines, and we would need temporary licenses and permits in Illinois as well. We'd also need 50 drivers and have to pay for their time and for their trips back home."

"Do me one favor," said Pon. "Please call Frank Wood, our outside counsel, and ask him what steps we have to go through to charter a ship. Tell him I'm especially concerned about the liability. Give him Quan's phone number. I want to make sure there are no more costs involved. If Robertson's fooling around is on schedule, he'll be phoning me asking that I cable cash. I'd really appreciate it if you would summarize what you've told me in two columns, with the charter costs on the left and the overland Baltimore cost column on the right. Then when Robertson calls, I can ask him to decide."

"One question," asked Vanderpool.

"Shoot," responded Pon.

"Why should the charter figures be on the left?"

"Because on a map (see Exhibit 12-A), Chicago is to the left of Baltimore and that's the only way I'll keep them straight when I'm talking on the phone."

QUESTIONS

1. Assume you are Vanderpool. Draft the comparison Pon just requested.
2. Which of the two routing alternatives would you recommend? Why?
3. Assume that the buyer in Saudi Arabia has made other large purchases in the United States and is considering consolidating all its purchases and loading them onto one large ship, which the buyer will charter. The buyer contacts HDT and, although acknowledging its commitment to buy FAS Doha, asks how much HDT would subtract from the $172,000 per truck price if the selling terms were changed to FOB HDT's Crown Point plant. How much of a cost reduction do you think HDT should offer the buyer? Under what terms and conditions?
4. Answer question 3 with regard to changing the terms of sale to delivery at port in Baltimore. The buyer would unload the trucks from the railcars.
5. Is there an interest rate that would make HDT change from one routing to another? If so, what is it?
6. Assume that it is the year 2005 and the cost to HDT of borrowing money is 12 percent per year. Because the buyer will pay for trucks as they are delivered, would it be advantageous for HDT to pay overtime to speed up production, ship the trucks as they are finished via the Port of Baltimore, and collect its payment earlier? Why or why not?

Case 12-2   Belle Tzell Cell Company

Headquartered in Tucson, Arizona, the Belle Tzell Cell Company manufactured one standard-size battery for use in portable power tools and in military weapons. Nell Tzell was the company's current president. Her mother, Belle, had retired from active management 10 years earlier, although she and several of Nell's aunts still owned a controlling interest in the company. Belle and her late husband, Del, had founded the firm in 1945, and it had prospered by selling batteries and dry cells to a number of electronics firms that had sprung up in the Arizona–New Mexico area after World War II.

Toward the end of her presidency, in the late 1960s, Belle had taken one action that increased the capacity of the firm. In response to a bid by the Mexican government, she had moved part of her operations south of the bor-der into Nogales to take advantage of low-cost Mexican labor and to quell Belle's fears that both the U.S. and Arizona governments would increase their controls on pollution and require safer working conditions for employees. The Mexican government provided a low-cost loan and required Belle to enter into a partnership with a Mexican citizen, who would own 51 percent of the Belle Tzell Cell Company's Mexican operation. The operation that Belle moved to Nogales was the facility for making lead panels. This operation involved combining strong acids with lead and was considered hazardous to employee health. Noxious vapors damaged the workers' lungs, and the acidic wastes left over from the curing processes were dumped into a nearby streambed, killing aquatic life for at least 10 miles downstream.

Belle retired a few months after the Nogales plant went into production and told Nell that it would take "only a few more months to get the bugs out." That was well over 25 years ago, and, if anything, the bugs had increased. Although actual production costs remained low and the Mexican plant was still nonunion, its production was very undependable. Because it was under Mexican ownership, the Mexican who owned 51 percent of the stock insisted that most of the plant's management be Mexican also. However, neither the Mexican who owned the 51 percent of the stock nor most Mexicans capable of managing the operation cared to live in Nogales. They preferred the bright lights of Mexico City. The plant's workforce was continually changing. Despite the fact that wages were high by Mexican standards, new workers soon suffered either burns from acid splashes or lung irritation because of the fumes and would leave. Because Nogales was just south of the U.S.–Mexican border, Mexican workers preferred to cross the border illegally and work at higher-paying jobs in the United States until they were found by U.S. immigration authorities and deported. Also, maquiladoras were also developing in the area just south of the border, and they offered employment opportunities.

Although Nell would have preferred to close her Nogales lead panel plant, the cost of establishing such a facility in the United States made such a move impossible. This was because of the new worker safety requirements of the federal government, operating through the Occupational Safety and Health Administration (OSHA), and new controls on air and water pollution and toxic waste disposal administered by the U.S. Environmental Protection Agency (EPA).

Transportation costs for delivering acids to the plant would also be very high because carriers considered them to be an extremely hazardous material requiring specialized, expensive trailer tanks to avoid acid spills.

Although the Mexicans were capable of turning out high-quality products, lax supervision resulted in wide variations in the quality of the final product. Sometimes, this would not be noticed until the workers in the Tucson plant attempted to install the lead plates that had been received from Nogales.

Relatively little of the Tzell Company's operations were in Tucson. Their offices were on the second floor of a building, cramped on a narrow lot with little room for expansion. Downstairs, the lead plates from Nogales were combined with printed circuits from Taiwan and placed inside plastic cases purchased from one of several suppliers in Tucson. Each day's production filled two 35-foot trailers parked at the north end of the building. At night, the two trailer loads would be delivered to various major buyers. The Tucson plant was operating at capacity and rarely ever caught up with sales. Several times Nell had wanted to increase the number of production lines, but she was unable to expand the building at its present site. In addition, Nell's aunts, who still controlled the company, were unwilling to allow her to relocate to a new site or larger plant because the financial resources required for the move would cut into their current incomes.

The present Tucson plant was a long, narrow building set in a north–south direction between two parallel streets. The south side fronted on 17th Street and contained a receiving dock that was built to accommodate only one trailer. Street parking was not allowed on 17th Street, and neighbors would complain to the Tucson Police Department if a truck parked on the street for even a few minutes. The building stretched north, with the east and west sides within a foot of their respective lot lines. The north end of the building was on 16th Street. Here was a large parking lot used by employees and the loading dock that could accommodate three trailers. Prior to the opening of the Nogales plant, the employee parking lot filled every day, with all 32 slots occupied. Today, only about 10 slots were used because employees were using carpools and local buses. Even Nell was in a carpool, sharing rides with David Kupferman, her operations manager, who lived several homes away on the same street.

Kupferman had worked for the Tzell Company for only a few weeks, and as he and Nell were driving from work one day, she said, "Dave, you know I'm caught between two rocks and two hard places. My mother and aunts won't let me expand here in Tucson, and our Nogales plant produces more ulcers than anything else. Your predecessor left because the strain of coordinating the two plants was too great. Believe it or not, the majority of our operations take place in Nogales. You'd better visit there, soon, to see what it's like."

"I can hardly wait," responded Kupferman. "After my last argument with them over poor quality, I'm afraid they'll dunk my head in an acid vat if I ever set foot inside that plant. How come you became so dependent on Mexico for your operations?"

Nell explained the reasons, and added, "For many years the savings gave us a competitive edge. In cost or money terms, two-thirds of our operation is now down in Nogales."

"Two-thirds?" asked Kupferman. "That seems high. How do you figure it?"

"Look at it this way," said Nell. "We take in a little over $4 million per year, or about $16,000 per working day. We spend about $15,000 per working day. Of that, about $10,000 is spent at Nogales for labor, raw materials, and overhead. We spend just over $1,000 a day moving the lead plates from Nogales here, although $800 of that is import duties on the lead plates. Here in Tucson, our manufacturing operation takes only about $3,000 per day, about two-thirds for labor and one-third for the printed circuits and plastic battery cases. The remainder of the money goes for companywide overhead and for profit."

"I see," said Kupferman. "How, then, do you see the problems?"

Nell answered, "First of all, our problems are caused by our success in selling. Right now we have a backlog of orders, but I am unable to expand capacity either here or in Nogales. Mother and my aunts won't allow major capital improvements, and while I might be able to build a small addition to the north of the Tucson plant, the cost would be prohibitive, especially when one considers the small increase in capacity that would result."

"It's too bad your family won't let you expand more," offered Kupferman.

"Actually, I don't blame them," said Nell. "Our business is really volatile, and I've also

been unable to interest serious outside investors in helping me expand. Several bankers told me that I'd have to get my production act together before I should think about either expanding or borrowing much outside money. Right now, the banks will loan me any working capital I want at 12 percent, if it's secured by inventories or equipment. However, I'm unable to assemble enough funds for any type of expansion."

"I still don't understand your coordination problem," said Kupferman. "Your Nogales plant produces one trailer load of battery plates per day, which is exactly the input you need for a day's output at Tucson. The battery plates can be trucked at night, and if you can get your quality control act together at Nogales, you'd have a smooth, continuous operation."

"I hate to say this," said Nell, "but your predecessor said just about the same thing 8 months ago. And like you, he thought that quality control at Nogales was the key to solving my problem."

"So what did he do wrong?" asked Kupferman.

"He was going to use a two-pronged approach, which I'll tell you about in the office," said Nell as she wheeled her Porsche from 16th Street into the company parking lot. "Get a cup of coffee, and we'll continue this conversation in my office," she said as they climbed the stairs to the second floor offices.

Kupferman got two cups of coffee, walked into her office, and sat down. Nell was looking through her messages and exclaimed, "Damn it, it happened again! We just got penalized $3,000 because of a late delivery to Jedson Electronic Tools. They were late on delivering a government order and decided we were responsible because our delivery was late, which it was. The purchase order to us had a penalty clause in it, and now they're going to collect. This is exactly the problem we have to lick! The Nogales plant either misses making a shipment or sends a load of such poor quality that we can't use it right away. We then assign our people here to other tasks for the day, such as inserting only the printed circuits into the plastic cases. They do this until the battery plates arrive, and then they add all the battery plates. At the end of 2 days we're caught up, except that yesterday we made no deliveries and yesterday's promised output is 1 day late. That's why we lose customers. To them, we're just another tardy supplier. Right now the industry practice is to specify a delivery date, with cost penalties included for either early or late deliveries. Indeed, some of our customers are adopting JIT inventory systems and are trying to specify a 60-minute window during which they'll accept our daily deliveries. They won't accept deliveries earlier, and late ones will be penalized. Our major competitors are already dancing to this tune, and we will have no choice but to follow."

"How often do we have this kind of problem—when we can't make deliveries because of some foul-up in our quality?" asked Kupferman.

"For a long time, it was only once a month or so," responded Nell, "but as we reached our plants' capacity and there was less slack, the problem has been happening almost weekly. One week, about 2 months ago, we hit the jackpot and had 3 days in a row of bad production. That threw us out of kilter for nearly 2 weeks, even after paying overtime both here and at Nogales. That's when your predecessor's ulcer started bleeding and he left. Too bad, too, because I think he was just about ready to solve our problem."

"What changes had he intended to make?" asked Kupferman.

"Well," responded Nell, "your predecessor had studied probability in college and had computed the chances of foul-ups in Nogales occurring one right after the other. He calculated that we should close down our Tucson plant for 5 days or have the Nogales plant run 5 days of overtime so that it could produce a 5-day supply of lead battery plates. He said that if we kept the Nogales plant scheduled so that there was always 5 days' worth of plates between Nogales and Tucson, we would never have to be out of usable lead battery plates here in Tucson."

"If his calculations are accurate, why haven't you implemented his plan?" asked Kupferman.

"We couldn't figure out where to store the approximately five loads of battery plates,"

responded Nell. "It's more complicated than you think. Here, let me read to you your predecessor's memo, written while he was recovering from surgery, no less. It says, and I quote, 'There are three alternatives: warehousing in Nogales, warehousing here in Tucson, or leasing five truck trailers and parking them either outside the Nogales plant or in the 16th Street parking lot here in Tucson.'" Nell looked at Kupferman directly and continued, "David, what I want you to do is to figure out the costs of these three alternatives and get back to me with a recommendation."

Kupferman took his empty coffee cup, walked back to his office, and started gathering the cost figures Nell had asked for. He discovered that to warehouse the five loads of lead battery plates in Nogales would cost $300 per week, plus $120 per week for local drayage in Nogales (i.e., trucking the plates from the plant to the warehouse). To truck the plates directly from the Nogales plant to a Tucson warehouse rather than to the Tzell Tucson plant was the second alternative. Few Tucson warehouses wanted to touch the business for fear that the plates would contaminate other merchandise they were storing. The best quote Kupferman could get was for $350 per week plus a requirement that the Tzell Cell Company provide a bond to protect the warehouseman from damages the plates might cause. Local drayage costs within Tucson from the warehouse to Tzell's 17th Street receiving dock would be $150 per week.

The trailer idea involved leasing five trailers, loading them with battery plates, and parking them at either the Nogales plant or at the 16th Street parking lot. Trailers could be leased and licensed for use in both Mexico and Arizona for $7,000 per year each. In addition, a used truck–tractor, costing approximately $15,000, would have to be purchased and used for shifting trailers around the plants where they were stored. The truck–tractor would have a useful life of 5 years.

The advantage of storing the trailers at Nogales was to delay the payment of import duties of about $800 per trailer load of battery plates. However, a problem with the current system was that Mexican border agents, sensing the urgency in the Tzell shipments, attempted to shake down the Tzell drivers to let the trailers exit from Mexico. Trailers were subject to delays and sometimes would be searched thoroughly to make certain that they were carrying no works of art or Mexican national treasures. One Mexican agent—nicknamed "Pancho Villa"—inspected trailers ever so slowly, complaining aloud that the reason he moved slowly was that he was depressed by the fact that Christmas was coming (no matter what month it happened to be) and that he lacked sufficient money to buy gifts for all of his very extended family.

Kupferman had yet to visit the Nogales plant, but before presenting his findings to Tzell, he wanted to make certain that the parking lot at the Nogales plant was fenced. He phoned Juan Perez, the plant manager, who said very little until he realized that Kupferman was not calling to complain about something. Perez answered Kupferman's query by saying that the yard was not fenced but that it would be possible to park the loaded trailers with their closed rear doors against a solid masonry wall, making entry impossible. "Besides," he added, "this plant has such a bad reputation for causing illness and injury that no local thief would come within a mile of it."

Kupferman was trying to think of a witty response and the Nogales manager continued, "But you said 'up to five trailers.' Why so many?"

Kupferman told him of his predecessor's calculations that the Nogales plant should produce 5 days of output in advance of that needed by the Tucson plant.

"Why so many?" repeated Perez.

"To make sure that Tucson never has to shut down or be late with orders," answered Kupferman. "The only reason we have problems here is because of delayed or poor-quality shipments from you. When Tucson falls behind, we can't make deliveries, and that costs us money."

"Nonsense!" responded Perez. "You blame all your problems on us. Let me tell you two things. First, not all production delays are caused down here. It's just that we're not in the same building as the home office, and we tend to get blamed for

everything. Second, because the Tucson plant makes a single standard product, it would be cheaper to have it produce a day or two's inventory in advance, ready to use in case either the Tucson plant or my operation fouls up. You'll have to excuse me now. We've just had another acid spill."

Kupferman heard a click and then a humming sound. He hung up. He decided to walk to Nell's office and tell her what Perez had said.

She admitted that Perez was correct, "just a little bit," about some of the delays being at the Tucson plant. In fact, she conceded that Kupferman's predecessor had overlooked the problems at the Tucson assembly line when he made his calculations that the Nogales plant produce a 5-day advance supply of battery plates as a cushion. She told Kupferman to start over and assume that delays could occur by conditions in either plant or both. She felt that Kupferman would find that sales should be cut back for a few days so that either or both plants could turn out some advance production that would serve as a continual cushion of safety stock. She wanted enough inventory in reserve that the Tzell Cell Company could fill 99 percent of all orders on time. Kupferman would have 6 months to set up the system and another 6 months to test and debug it. After that, he would be expected to maintain a 99 percent performance level of filling orders on time.

During the next few days of ride sharing, Nell and Kupferman talked about everything except work. Nell commented that she missed seeing him at the community swimming pool. Kupferman responded that he had been spending his time indoors, studying probability.

After several weeks, Kupferman had finally calculated the probabilities that would allow Tzell Cell Company to maintain Nell's required 99 percent level of on-time deliveries. First of all, his predecessor had been correct, insofar as he had calculated. One solution was to have the Nogales plant produce 5 days' worth of battery cell plates in advance of the Tucson plant. This was because the Tucson plant was responsible for only two of the delivery delays in a year of 250 working days. However, Kupferman also made calculations about the sizes of completed stocks for the Tucson plant to manufacture in advance and keep as a safety stock cushion. If the Tucson plant produced and maintained as safety stock 1 day's output of completed batteries, the Nogales plant would only have to maintain a 4-day lead in production of lead battery plates ahead of their use in Tucson. If the Tucson plant produced in advance and maintained as safety stock 2 days' output of completed batteries, the Nogales plant would have to produce only 2 days' worth of battery plates in advance of their use in the Tucson plant. And if the Tucson plant made 3 days' output in advance and held it as safety stock, the Nogales plant would not have to produce a surplus of plates in advance of what was required each day in Tucson. That is, each night the truck would leave with the Nogales output and drive to Tucson, where the plates would be used the next day. Even if there were problems with the shipment from Nogales, there would be a 3-day safety stock of finished batteries in Tucson.

Kupferman intended to determine warehousing costs for the safety stocks of completed batteries in Tucson, but Nell told him to plan on using the trailer idea instead. The trailers would be parked in the 16th Street lot. At night they would be parked so that no doors were exposed. For $3,000, the lot's fence could be made more secure and a gate would be added. Nell told Kupferman to use carrying costs of 25 percent per year on both the work-in-process (plates) and finished goods (batteries).

Kupferman took a clipboard with a pad of paper and made four columns, one for each of the alternatives:

1. 5 days' worth of plates in Nogales; no extra batteries in Tucson
2. 4 days' worth of plates in Nogales; 1 day's worth of batteries in Tucson
3. 2 days' worth of plates in Nogales; 2 days' worth of batteries in Tucson
4. No extra plates in Nogales; 3 days' worth of batteries in Tucson

Each alternative would give the firm the ability to provide a 99 percent or better level of on-time order filling.

QUESTIONS

1. What are the total inventory carrying costs of alternative 1?
2. What are the total inventory carrying costs of alternative 2?
3. What are the total inventory carrying costs of alternative 3?
4. What are the total inventory carrying costs of alternative 4?
5. Which alternative do you think Kupferman should recommend? Why?
6. Tzell "wanted enough inventory in reserve that the Tzell Cell Company could fill 99 percent of all orders on time." This is, as you may recall, a customer service standard. How reasonable is a 99 percent level? Why not, say, a 95 percent level? How would Nell and Kupferman determine the relative advantages and disadvantages of the 95 percent and the 99 percent service levels? What kind of cost calculations would they have to make?
7. Jedson Electronic Tools invoked a penalty clause on a purchase order that Tzell Cell Company had accepted, and the Tzell Cell Company had to forfeit $3,000. Draft, for Nell Tzell's signature, a memo indicating when and under what conditions the Belle Tzell Cell Company should accept penalty clauses in purchase orders covering missed delivery times or "windows."
8. In your opinion, is it ethical for a U.S.-based firm to relocate some of its operations in Mexico to avoid the stricter U.S. pollution and worker-safety laws? Why or why not?
9. Should the firm be willing to pay bribes at the Mexican border in order to get its shipments cleared more promptly? Why or why not?

PART

III

Analyzing, Designing, and Implementing a Logistics System

Parts 1 and 2 presented an overview of logistics and focused on the individual components of the logistics portions of the supply chain. Part 3 examines methods of analyzing, implementing, and controlling logistics as used by a firm and those firms with which it is linked.

Chapter 13 examines the various control systems that must be implemented to ensure that the logistics system operates efficiently. Controls are also needed to minimize losses from pilferage and theft. Since September 11, 2001, concern has increased regarding the vulnerability of the logistics channel.

Chapter 14 focuses on the techniques involved in logistics systems analysis, design, and integration. These techniques are designed to isolate and reduce inefficiencies in logistics operations.

Chapter 15 looks at some of the anticipated changes that may confront logistics and supply-chain managers in the twenty-first century.

CHAPTER

Logistics Systems Controls

"Write a letter to Santa? It's easier just to
break into his computer distribution system."

Even the most traditional supply chains are vulnerable.

Source: Cartoon copyright © 1992 Harley Schwadron. Distributed by Sandhill Arts. Reprinted with permission.

Key Terms

- Batch number
- Building security
- Computer security
- Document security
- Pilferage
- Product recall

- Short-interval scheduling
- System security
- Vehicle security
- Warehouse work rules
- Worker productivity

Learning Objectives

- To understand the use of accounting techniques for logistics system control
- To examine the worker productivity issue
- To discuss problems and solutions involved in a product recall
- To learn how to reduce pilferage, organized theft, and vulnerability to terrorist activity

If logistics management entailed only establishing a system and putting it into operation, it would be a relatively simple task. However, logistics systems and supply chains do not always work the way they are expected to. The potential problems confronting supply-chain managers are numerous. This chapter introduces various logistics topics ranging from the problem of out-of-control costs to that of protecting shipments from theft. In our post–September 11 society, one must also recognize that terrorists can launch attacks against civilian targets. Supply chains could be targets or unwitting participants. Thousands of closed, sealed oceangoing containers arrive at U.S. ports every day from hundreds of origins and with no easy ways to check each of them as they are loaded or while they are at sea. Tank trucks carrying gasoline or corrosive chemicals are equivalent to moving bombs. As an example of post–September 11 developments, Figure 13-1 shows a device fitted on to a Kenworth truck that reads fingerprints. The driver's prints would need to be on file.

This chapter is of special importance to those training for an entry-level position in supply-chain management. Much of one's initial performance with a new employer is evaluated on the basis of how well one exercises control responsibilities. The inability to carry out control functions is easily spotted at the beginning levels of management.

In the process of reengineering a supply chain, the need to control the system must not be overlooked. Indeed, the control mechanisms must be built into the system, and their effectiveness must be continually monitored. This chapter focuses primarily on controlling functions that are somewhat protective in nature and must be employed to keep a firm's position from worsening. In a competitive world with small and sometimes shrinking profit margins, application of tight controls may enable a firm to maintain its position while competitors fall behind.

The word *control* is chosen deliberately. The problems discussed cannot be eliminated; they can only be controlled. A person involved in logistics management will confront the issues and problems presented in this chapter many times during the course of her or his career.

FIGURE 13-1 Device in a Kenworth Truck for Reading and Matching Fingerprints
According to a Kenworth press release dated March 20, 2002, "When the driver's fingerprint is verified . . . the vehicle can be operated at normal traffic speeds. If the fingerprint doesn't match, the vehicle can still be started but at a severely restricted horsepower, thus limiting operation to well below normal speeds." The fleet dispatcher also receives a wireless message saying that an unauthorized driver is moving the truck. The dispatcher also has the ability to use a wireless system to disable the truck.

Source: Kenworth Truck Company.

Indeed, logistics managers must have plans in anticipation of anything going wrong. Warehousing consultant Jerry D. Smith once noted that formal contingency plans can help to protect warehouses from conceivable circumstances that occur on an unpredictable basis. He suggested that warehouse managers do the following:

1. Make a list of the conceivable bad things that can happen in an operation.
2. Rank those bad things in terms of their consequences or probability of occurrence.
3. Starting with the highest-ranked problem, carefully determine, in as much detail as possible, the proper steps and actions that should be taken to resolve, eliminate, or deal with the problems when and if they occur.[1]

---

[1] *Distribution Center Management,* April 1991, p. 1.

Financial and Accounting Controls

The finance staff, which is always predicting future cash flows, depends on the logistics staff for information concerning the status of finished products that are between the end of the firm's production line and the purchaser's receiving dock. The logistics staff also has firsthand knowledge of the level of orders being received on any day. The firm's finance staff has the responsibility for allocating the firm's limited funds to projects desired by the various operating departments. For example, the staff would have to approve the commitment of major funds to purchase new materials-handling equipment. Finance personnel use several methods, such as the return on invested capital method, to determine which projects should be funded. Policies regarding investments in new inventory should also be subject to comparable financial analysis. Hence, the finance people control the levels of investments that the logistics department can make.

Budgets are a form of financial and accounting controls. Yet they also serve other functions. In the early stages, budgets are planning mechanisms and a means of fulfilling corporate goals. The logistics manager assembles a proposed budget to indicate how much money is needed to carry out the various planned logistical tasks. In drawing up the budget, all activities must not only be expressed in terms of units or financial values but also in volume, weight, pallets, boxes, and order or invoice lines. Later, after the budget for a time period has been approved, it becomes a control mechanism.

Professor Douglas Lambert has written extensively about accounting controls and their impact on logistics activities. He says costs can first be categorized by their nature or within the framework of analysis that one is working. Cost categories can be divided into the following:

Controllable versus non-controllable
Direct versus indirect
Fixed versus variable
Actual versus opportunity
Relevant versus sunk[2]

Lambert advocates the use of standard costs and flexible budgets. Standard costs involve two steps: First, one must establish standard or acceptable costs for each activity, and second, one must determine acceptable deviations from these standard costs. "The use of standard costs represents a frontal assault on the logistics costing problem because it attempts to determine what the costs should be, rather than basing future costs predictions on past cost behavior."[3] The standard costs developed should be applied to activities to determine their reasonable budget; if the standard cost of handling a pallet is $3 and 10,000 pallets are handled, then $30,000 should be budgeted for handling pallets. If the standard costs per unit change as volume handled changes, this also should be reflected in the budget. The budget is flexible in the sense that it is tied to actual activity.

Most companies have within the logistics operation an accounting section that is responsible to both the firm's chief accountant (controller) and logistics manager.

---

[2]Douglas M. Lambert, "Logistics Cost, Productivity, and Performance Analysis," *The Logistics Handbook* (New York: Free Press, 1994), pp. 264–265.

[3]Ibid., p. 281.

Logistics accounting reports provide financial and accounting consulting services to logistics management. It assists in preparing the operating and capital budgets and interim forecasts and helps establish performance standards. The logistics accounting group also prepares management reports on freight expense, fleet and warehousing operating expenses, and variance analysis. In addition, the logistics accounting group maintains and operates an internal control system for logistics and ensures adherence to corporate guidelines for the approval and payment of invoices; for handling payments that accompany orders; for expenditures for contracts, leases, and capital improvements; and for the protection of company assets. Finally, it ensures accurate reporting of all finished goods inventory.

The accountants want the logistics staff to reduce *inventory float,* which is the cash flow associated with holding inventory. In general terms, the inventory costs are for the time period from when one pays a vendor until the time one collects from the customer for the same goods. The rate of interest is the opportunity cost, that is, what the firm could have been earning on other investments during this same time. One's inventory can turn over at a rate different from cash flow, meaning that the inventory turns over, say, every four weeks but the lag between paying vendors and collecting from customers might be, say, six weeks. The accountants would prefer, if not insist, that the cash turn over more quickly than the inventory.

Accountants also insist that accurate inventory records be maintained. Inventory valuation is a matter of concern when reports are being prepared about the company's worth. In times of inflation, identical items added to the inventory at different times may each have a different cost, and it makes a difference if one uses historic cost or current value as an indicator of the total inventory's worth. One difference between the accounting staff and the logistics staff is that the accountants count inventory in dollars while the logistics staff counts numbers of stock-keeping units (SKUs). If one has an inventory of, say, grain, its value fluctuates with the commodity markets even though its quantity and quality remain unchanged, or the accountants may depreciate an inventory by a certain amount, even though the physical size of the inventory remains unchanged.

While we think of logistics as an integrating activity, so are accounting operations. Figure 13-2 shows a software company's total financial control accounting package developed for truck-body manufacturing firms. Note that the logistics functions appear in many places of the schematic drawing.

Over the years, logistics staffs have attempted to have accounting analysis performed in a way that is more useful to those managing logistics operations. This would include recognition of cost drivers and of the structural determinants of a firm's logistical activities. These cost drivers should then be measured in such a manner that their interactions can be understood, rather than merely tallying costs.[4] It is possible to establish statistical controls over logistics systems, setting tolerance ranges within which performance is considered to be satisfactory. Other functional areas within the firm are also concerned with the accounting controls and systems of the logistics operations. Logistics costs, for example, are part of the costs shared by

---

[4]Terrance L. Pohlen and Bernard J. LaLonde, "Implementing Activity-Based Costing (ABC) in Logistics," *Journal of Business Logistics,* Vol. 15, No. 2, 1994, pp. 3–4.

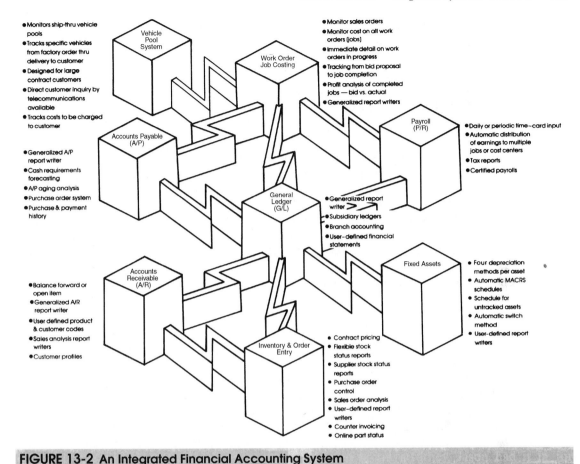

FIGURE 13-2 An Integrated Financial Accounting System

Source: Courtesy of Spokane Computer, Inc., Spokane, Washington.

or assigned to the other functions, both within the firm and along the supply chain. An example is the determination of the total costs of producing and distributing a product.

Professors Bowersox, Closs, and Stank wrote, "Asset utilization measures a supply chain's effectiveness in terms of fixed assets and working capital. Fixed assets include manufacturing and distribution facilities, transportation and material handling equipment, and information technology hardware. Working capital reflects the supply chain's inventory investment and the differential investment in accounts receivable relative to accounts payable. Overall asset utilization is a particularly important measure of firm and overall supply-chain performance as viewed by the financial market."[5]

With the advent of partnerships among different firms along the supply chain, investments, risks, and revenues are often shared. Sometimes an outside (third-party)

[5]Donald J. Bowersox, David J. Closs, and Theodore P. Stank, "Ten Mega-Trends That Will Revolutionize Supply Chain Logistics," *Journal of Business Logistics,* Vol. 21, No. 2, 2000, p. 14.

auditor or accountant is needed to look at the books of each of the supply-chain partners to ensure that costs and gains are accurately recorded and reported. Such a system should ensure "that payments are pre-audited and correctly applied to the general ledger chart of accounts, accountable cost centers, and then properly allocated to measure direct product profitability."[6]

Worker Productivity

Labor is expensive, so its efficient use is necessary for a profitable operation. The two most frequent uses of labor in logistics are in warehousing and in transport of goods. Both warehousing and trucking involve heavy investments in capital equipment (which frequently reduce the need for workers). The workers and the equipment must be used in a manner that achieves the lowest cost for a given volume of output. In many areas, warehouse workers, drivers, and helpers are unionized, and work-rule provisions influence worker productivity. In areas where warehouse workers' unions resist changes in work rules, a warehouse may become prematurely obsolete—not because of its structure or equipment, but because of high-cost work practices that the union insists on continuing.

Use of labor is usually made more efficient by scheduling work in advance. In a warehouse the time for performing each task (such as opening a truck door, stacking a pallet, or picking a case of outgoing goods) is calculated. Precise time breakdowns—to the number of seconds—are used. The location of the pallet load in the warehouse or its height above the floor makes a difference. Outgoing cases being picked require different amounts of time, again depending on their location, volume, and weight. Picking and assembling an outgoing order comprised of cases of different dimensions require more time than if the cases are of the same size. These data are used in two ways. First, they indicate that the goods within the warehouse should be arranged so that the more popular or faster-moving items are located in slots where they will require less time for storage and retrieval. Second, through the use of computer programs, an order picker's travel sequence can be arranged in a way that minimizes the time that he or she (and whatever equipment is being used) will require. According to Myron H. Nerzig, a warehouse management consultant:

> Almost every individual will work to a target, goal, or objective. We measure ourselves even if a company does not have a measurement system. That is our personal way of providing output to meet our own objectives or to satisfy our supervisors.
>
> Without good standards and a reporting system, workers will not meet a level of production that is acceptable to management. . . . Most workers want to do a fair day's work but will become disgruntled and their morale lowers when they see other employees get away doing as little as possible, and in some cases, nothing.[7]

---

[6]Cass Information Systems, cited in *WERC Sheet,* October 1997, p. 12.

[7]Comments made before the Northern California chapter meeting of the Warehousing Education and Research Council, January 28, 1988.

As might be expected, work scheduling systems become involved in labor—management controversies.

Short-Interval Scheduling

One useful method of analysis, **short-interval scheduling,** involves looking at each worker's activity in small time segments. An amount of time is assigned to each unit of work, and then the individual's work is scheduled in a manner that utilizes as much of each worker's time as possible and maximizes output for each worker.

The scheduling technique is useful to supervisory personnel. Each day's work for the operation is plotted out and is, in essence, a summation of each worker's tasks. For a warehouse, the scheduling may also be tied into departure times for delivery trucks (also controlled by computerized scheduling) and arrival of trucks with incoming freight. Large buyers frequently require suppliers' trucks to arrive within rather limited time blocks (say, 30 minutes or an hour) because this reduces congestion at the receiving dock and spreads the arrival of inbound materials throughout the working day. Because an operation's entire workday can be prescheduled, the supervisor can tell as the day progresses how the actual progress compares to the schedule. If at the end of the first hour of an 8-hour shift less than one-eighth of the work has been completed, the supervisor must take steps to catch up within the second hour (or at least to fall no further behind).

Short-interval scheduling can also be used by intermediate management to assess the effectiveness of supervision. One firm uses a Lost Time Review report that is filled out by the immediate supervisor on a daily basis. In case the immediate supervisor fails to note or explain the lost time, the information appears on an Unexplained Lost Time form, which intermediate management prepares to cover instances when more time was spent on a job than had been assigned and the immediate supervisor failed to report it.

Improving Worker Performance

Knowledge of supervisory techniques is important to students of logistics because fairly early in their career, they are likely to receive an assignment that includes supervision of others. Some workers are more obviously in need of supervision than others (see Figure 13-3); the skills of workers assigned to the same task also may vary (see Figure 13-4). The supervisor's goal should be to improve **worker productivity** and performance. Many supervisors use a three-part approach consisting of performance audit, feedback, and positive reinforcement. After a worker's performance is measured, it is important that this information be fed back to the worker so that he or she is aware of it. Once performance information is made available to workers, the next step is to reinforce their good performance with some form of reward—from an approving nod to a year-end bonus.

Computer software can measure and track labor and labor output. The cost calculations are important in two different dimensions. "The first dimension is the rate or type of pay; for example, regular pay, daily overtime, weekly overtime, as well as complex union premiums. The second dimension is what the employee did, which could be a cost center charged with the work, a work order, a task, a job, an operation."[8]

---

[8]*Material Handling Management,* February 2002, p. 28.

FIGURE 13-3 The Objective of Supervision Is to Improve Performance

Source: Reproduced by permission of the artist and the Masters Agency.

FIGURE 13-4 Employees Have Varying Degrees of Skills

Source: Reproduced by permission of the artist and the Masters Agency.

Although union work rules are often inflexible and difficult to change, sometimes, as part of the bargaining transaction, it is possible for management to get unions to agree to alter some work practices. Usually, management must demonstrate that neither the union as a group nor its members as individuals will be adversely affected by the proposed changes. Thus, when performance standards are measured, some attention should be paid to those standards that are influenced or controlled by contractual work rules. During collective bargaining sessions, management must know the savings of eliminating or altering a work rule because these calculations establish a value for each contemplated change.

Performance standards, as such, may not be included in a contract. However, provisions have to be made for giving management the right to establish and use them. Unions want protection from unreasonable standards, and mutually agreed-upon procedures are necessary for handling new or continuing employees who consistently fall below established standards.

In order to maintain and improve productivity, it is necessary to have **warehouse work rules** and to enforce them. Work rules serve many purposes, but their most important function is to keep the work force (or its individual members) from backsliding into poor performance. Figure 13-5 shows one public warehouser's set of work rules.[9]

Financial incentives may also be used to improve worker performance. Sometimes they are given as bonuses to warehouse supervisors. They can also be used carefully to encourage teamwork on the part of all employees. Some warehouses pay a bonus (beyond whatever provisions exist in the contract with workers) when certain performance elements, such as the percentage of accurately filled orders, are improved.

Another important concern in setting performance standards is safety. As performance or production increases, the potential for accidents that injure workers or damage merchandise or equipment also may increase. In warehousing, back injuries are a significant, and never-ending, problem and are the basis for many disability claims.

Driver Supervision

When discussing supervision of logistics labor, a distinction has to be made between warehousing and trucking. In warehousing, the supervisor is physically present and expected to be on top of nearly any situation. However, once on the road, truck drivers are removed from immediate supervision. In addition, they are in day-to-day contact with customers. While on the road, they and their trucks can be seen by thousands of motorists. Because of these factors, different types of supervision as well as different types of workers may be needed.

When a worker in a warehouse falls behind schedule, it is usually noticed immediately and corrective action can be taken. The work of a truck driver is more difficult to evaluate. If a truck driver falls behind schedule, it may be because of traffic conditions or a bottleneck at a loading dock. Initially, all a supervisor can do is accept the driver's

---

[9]See also Thomas W. Speh and Jennifer E. Heil, *A Model for Developing Warehouse Work Rules* (Oak Brook, IL: Warehousing Education and Research Council, 1988).

Ours is a company that has been built on service to its customers. Our business has grown both in the number of customers and in the area which we serve. We are constantly striving to improve our service, because it is only through growth and progress that a company can give to its employees the good wages, increased benefits, and job security that everyone wants.

In order to meet these aims it is necessary to adhere to a set of rules. Whenever people work together they have certain rights and privileges. Along with these rights they have certain obligations and responsibilities. So that each employee will know what is expected of him we have drawn up a list of work rules which are necessary for the orderly and efficient operation of our business. By following these rules you contribute to the progress of the company and therefore to the stability of your own job. These rules therefore benefit you rather than hinder you. They are fair rules and to keep them fair to everyone they will be enforced in every required situation.

These rules are listed in two groups, by type of violation, and are as follows:

- Violations subject to discharge on the first offense.
- Violations subject to constructive discipline.

Violations Subject to Discharge on the First Offense

(1) The possession of, drinking of, or use of any alcoholic beverages or narcotic drugs on company property; or being on company premises at any time under the influence of alcohol, or drugs, or while suffering from an alcoholic hangover which materially affects work performance.

(2) The transportation of, or failure to notify the company of, unauthorized persons on company equipment or its property.

(3) Theft or misappropriation of company property or the property of any of its customers or employees.

(4) Deliberate or malicious damage to the company's equipment and warehouse facilities or to the merchandise and property of its customers.

(5) Intentional falsification of records in any form, including ringing another employee's time card, or falsifying employment application.

(6) Fighting while on duty or on company premises or provoking others to fight.

(7) Smoking in a building or van, or any restricted area, or while loading or unloading merchandise and other items.

(8) Immoral or indecent conduct which affects work performance or makes the employee unsuited for the work required.

(9) Unauthorized possession of, or carrying of, firearms or other weapons.

(10) Insubordination — refusal to perform assigned work or to obey a supervisor's order, or encouraging others to disobey such an order.

Violations Subject to Constructive Discipline

The rules printed below are subject to constructive discipline. This means that for the first offense you will be given a constructive reprimand. For a second offense you will receive a disciplinary layoff without pay, the length of which will depend upon the seriousness of the offense; subject to the terms of the collective bargaining agreement which may exist between employee and union. For a third offense you will be discharged, subject to the collective bargaining agreement.

If you have had a violation, followed by a record of no violations for a nine (9) month period, the original violation will be withdrawn from your record.

(1) Excessive tardiness regardless of cause. (Being tardy and not ready to perform work at the designated starting time may at the company's option result in the employee being sent home without pay.)

(2) Absenteeism without just cause and excessive absenteeism regardless of cause. If you must be absent for a justifiable reason notify the company in advance. Justified absence will be

FIGURE 13-5 Sample Warehouse Work Rules

Source: Courtesy of American Warehouse Association.

excused if the company is notified as soon as possible before the beginning of the shift; however, too many justified and excused absences may be grounds for constructive discipline as well as unjustified, unexcused absence. If you are absent from work for three consecutive work days without notification followed by failure to report for work on the fourth day you will automatically be removed from the payroll with the notification "quit without notice."

(3) Failure to work reasonable overtime.

(4) Unauthorized absence from assigned work location.

(5) Failure to observe proper break periods, lunch periods, and quitting times, unless otherwise directed by your supervisor.

(6) Disregard for common rules of safety, safe practices, good housekeeping and sanitation.

(7) Unauthorized or negligent operation or use of machines, tools, vehicles, equipment and materials.

(8) Loss or damage to the property of the company or its customers which could have been reasonably avoided.

(9) Failure to complete work assignments within a reasonable length of time or loafing on such assignments.

(10) Garnishments not satisfied prior to the hearing before the court issuing same.

(11) Gambling on company premises.

(12) Use of immoral, obscene or indecent language on company premises.

(13) Trying to persuade or organize other employees to disobey any of these rules and regulations. ■

FIGURE 13-5 (Continued)

explanation. Still, it is necessary to have a control mechanism so that drivers who often encounter delays can be distinguished from those who do not. Figure 13-6 is a computer printout showing the monthly delivery performance of drivers. Shown are the number of cases and the weight handled and the amount of time spent waiting and unloading. "P" indicates that pallets are utilized and that the receiver uses a forklift truck to unload the trailer. "C" means specialized wheeled carts are used instead of pallets. Various comparisons are made including the average cost per ton and the average cost per case. "ADJ CS/HR" (Adjusted Cases Per Hour) takes into account both waiting and unloading time.

The arrangement of data shown in Figure 13-6 can be used, for example, to support a driver's contention that his or her relatively poor performance is caused by delays at the customer's receiving dock. The contention could be verified by having a different driver make deliveries to determine whether the delays still happen. If they do, the supplier would approach the customer with these printouts and indicate that improvements are needed in the receiving dock procedures.

If it is determined that the cause of the problem is an inadequacy of the customer's receiving ability, care would have to be used in informing the customer. The supplier's marketing staff would have to be made aware of the problem, and calculations would be needed of how profitable the account is at the present time, given the unloading handicaps. If it is determined that the unloading delays make servicing the account unprofitable, the supplier might threaten to discontinue service or raise prices. If it is found that servicing the account is profitable in spite of the unloading delays, a more tactful approach would be employed.

AMALGAMATED FOOD STORE SERVICES INC.   PAGE NO. 2

DELIVERY PERFORMANCE ANALYSIS
WEEK ENDING 11/01/

REPORT NO. 2 –STORE–

DRIVER	P	STORE	CASES	WEIGHT	WAIT	UNLD	CS/HR	ADJ CS/HR
B ,D.	P	AMES MARKET # 7	467	30,699	.1	.3	1,556	1,167
D ,P.	P	AMES MARKET # 7	1,055	6,000	.1	.5	2,110	1,758
F ,J.	P	AMES MARKET # 7	242		.1	.4	605	484
M ,J.	P	AMES MARKET # 7	120		.2	.3	400	240
		TOTAL	1,884	36,699	.5	1.5	1,256	942
F ,J.	C	FORD'S MARKET # 1	1,038	24,525	.1	1.1	943	865
F ,J.	C	FORD'S MARKET # 1	446	14,306	.1	.9	495	446
F ,J.	P	FORD'S MARKET # 1	50	2,000	.1	.2	250	166
		TOTAL	1,534	40,831	.3	2.2	697	613
F ,J.	C	FORD'S MARKET # 2	300	12,000	.1	.7	428	375
M	C	FORD'S MARKET # 2	729		1.2	1.5	486	270
M	C	FORD'S MARKET # 2	1,242	30,420	.1	1.8	690	653
V ,B.		FORD'S MARKET # 2	1		.1	.1	10	5
		TOTAL	2,272	42,420	1.5	4.1	554	405
G A.	C	FORD'S MARKET # 3	913	23,049	.2	1.0	913	760
M	C	FORD'S MARKET # 3	1,200	30,601	.3	1.0	1,200	923
		TOTAL	2,113	53,650	.5	2.0	1,056	845
M	C	FORD'S MARKET # 4	408	10,392	.2	.9	453	370
M J.	C	FORD'S MARKET # 4	671	15,109	.2	.9	745	610
		TOTAL	1,079	25,501	.4	1.8	599	490

FIGURE 13-6 Delivery Performance of Truck Drivers

The preceding example illustrates an important interface between marketing and logistics and within the supply chain. Care has to be used when establishing customer service standards to ensure that they do not become a drain on profits. In this example, one does not know what one's competitors would do; they are probably handicapped by the same inefficiencies at the customer's receiving dock. The buyer might respond that the problem is not at its dock, but that it runs a friendly and relaxed operation, and if delivery drivers want to have a cup of coffee and chat for a few minutes before unloading their trucks, the buyer does not mind. What the buyer does mind, however, is having this friendly atmosphere labeled as inefficient by some supplier's computer. In this situation, the customer has indicated that he or she likes the supplier's drivers but does not like the supplier's computer. The point of this example is that supervision of the driver could be related to a firm's selling efforts.

Another device used to aid in controlling truck drivers' performance is the *tachograph,* a recording instrument that is installed inside a truck and produces a continuous, timed record of the truck, its speed, and its engine speed. Figure 13-7 shows a printout of the activity recorded by a tachograph. From the information on the tacho-

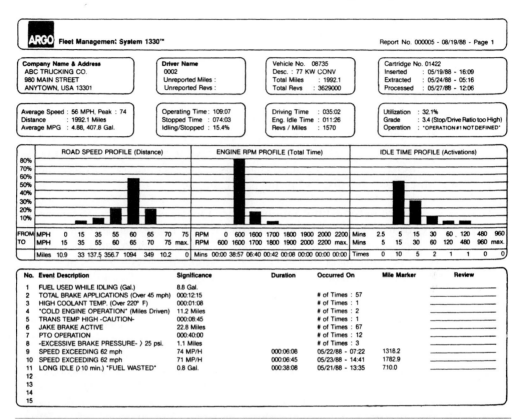

FIGURE 13-7 Printout from a Truck Tachograph

Source: Argo Instruments, Inc., Fleet Management Systems.

graph chart, one can tell how efficiently the truck and driver are being used. If the driver works on a regular route, it may be possible to rearrange the stops so that the driver can avoid areas of traffic congestion. Bad driving habits, such as high highway speeds and excessive engine idling, can also be detected. In case of an accident, the tachograph chart is invaluable in reporting and explaining what occurred just prior to impact.

The most recent development in the supervision of trucks and their drivers involves *global satellites.* In this system, the manager of the fleet and the truck drivers are connected by way of numerous satellites that circle the globe. During Operation Desert Storm, for example, U.S. soldiers were able to pinpoint their positions in the trackless desert by consulting boxes the size of paperback books that took readings from satellites. A police captain at the Port of Los Angeles, said, "Probably the biggest single advance in cargo security is technological—the use of global positioning to monitor containers. Cargo thieves don't get far when the police know exactly where a stolen container is."[10]

---

[10]*International Business,* February 1997, p. 18.

Sometimes cargo is tendered to a motor carrier for delivery. Some firms photograph or videotape drivers making pickups at their loading docks. A record is also kept of the driver's vehicle operators license number.

Product Recalls

A vexing logistics problem, and one that can cost logistics or product-line managers their jobs, involves the inability to cope with a product-recall crisis. A **product recall** occurs when a hazard or defect is discovered in a manufactured or processed item that is already in the distribution channels. It necessitates a reversal in the usual outward flow of merchandise. Following is an example:

> Washington—International Dairy Queen is recalling 150,000 water batons from kid's meals because the plastic balls inside can be released when a child sucks or chews on the end cap. . . . The Consumer Product Safety Commission said consumers should immediately take the toys away from young children and return them to their local Dairy Queen for a free kid's meal or ice cream sundae.[11]

One manufacturer that undertook a product recall instructed all of its retailers to ship the goods in question back to its plant. To its dismay, the manufacturer discovered that many of its retailers did not know how to write a bill of lading or to take any of the other steps necessary to accomplish the backward movement of goods.

In recent years, well-publicized recalls have involved soups, drugs, toys, produce with pesticide residue, autos, and mineral water. From the manufacturer's standpoint, the publicity is undesirable. This is an instance in which the saying "There's no such thing as bad publicity" does not hold. If the manufacturer plays down the amount of publicity, it runs the risk that a user will be harmed by the defective product after the defect is known to the manufacturer. In a subsequent lawsuit, the injured consumer might allege that the manufacturer failed to devote sufficient effort and publicity to the recall campaign.

For two decades, the best-known recall involved the drug Tylenol in 1982. It cost Johnson & Johnson an estimated $50 million. The firm undertook the recall action on its own after several individuals in the Chicago area died after using the product. The pain reliever had been tampered with by an individual who was believed to have removed the bottles' caps and added cyanide-laced capsules. The company already had a recall plan in place, so it could respond to the emergency effectively. The product was reintroduced with more tamperproof packaging, and within a year the firm had regained much of its one-time market share.

The most recent well-known product recall took place in the year 2000 and involved 6.5 million Firestone/Bridgestone tires, mounted mostly on Ford Explorers. The tires had been linked to a number of fatal accidents. "The recall and surrounding recriminations set off a bitter fight between Bridgestone and Ford Motor over responsibility for the crashes. The dispute destroyed the 94-year rela-

---

[11]*San Francisco Chronicle*, January 7, 1997, p. A11.

tionship of the companies."[12] The situation also showed how bad fortune can travel along a supply chain.

Once a recall campaign is completed (or underway, depending on how it is conducted), the manufacturer and its distributors must take immediate steps to refill the retailer's shelves with either defect-free batches of the same product or a substitute product. Although this step is not as important as the recall, it must be undertaken to minimize losses. Otherwise, competitors will take the opportunity to suggest that the retailer use its line of products to fill empty shelf space.

Sometimes, products are recalled through channels different from those through which they are distributed. Goods are returned to the manufacturer even though it may simply destroy them after they are received. In theory, it seems easier to authorize retailers or wholesalers to destroy recalled products. However, if the goods are hazardous, it may be desirable for the manufacturer to supervise their destruction. The risks that the defective goods will not be properly disposed of and that individuals will be injured is always present. Accounting controls are necessary to ensure that individuals returning recalled materials are reimbursed only for the goods they return. Sometimes, merchandise will be returned in addition to that which was being recalled, and a decision must be made as to how to handle those additional goods.

Product recall takes many forms, depending on the type of product. The responsible government agencies (including state and local as well as foreign governments) have their own procedures. Often, a manufacturer will initiate the recall before being forced to do so by the regulatory agency. The degree of danger posed by the defect also differs, the worst defects being those that are discovered to be directly life threatening. Less serious are the defects that are possible threats to life, such as those linked to causes of cancer if exposure is over a long period of time. An even less serious problem is posed by products that are mislabeled (such as a label that reads "contents 16 ounces" when the package contains only 12 ounces). Sometimes, the problem can be overcome by merely changing the product's label or adding a warning label. A lamp manufacturer might be required to add a sticker to each lamp, saying, "Do not use light bulbs larger than 60 watts in this lamp." In this instance, the manufacturer could have the stickers attached at some intermediate point between the place of manufacture and the retail outlet.

Federal Agencies Involved with Recalls

The Food and Drug Administration (FDA) is concerned with food, drugs, and cosmetics. In what it considers a Class I Recall (i.e., the most serious of hazards, such as botulism toxin in foods), the FDA will insist that the product be recalled at the consumer level and all intermediate levels and that 100 percent effectiveness checks be made of all distribution points. The FDA will also issue a public warning. In the week ending September 18, 2002, the FDA issued recalls for shampoo, packaged tuna sandwiches, packaged pimento cheese sandwiches, coconut cookies, pineapple/coconut-flavored lollipops, and canned soft drinks from a Florida bottler that "may be contaminated with equipment cleaning fluid."[13]

---

[12]Ken Belson, "A Return to Profitability; Big Recall Behind It, Tire Maker Regains Its Footing," *The New York Times,* August 10, 2002, p. C1.

[13]www.fda.gov/bbs/topicx/enforce/2002/ENF00761.html, September 23, 2002.

Another federal agency involved in product recalls is the Consumer Product Safety Commission (CPSC). Its main objective is to ban the sale of products deemed hazardous, thereby making it an offense for a retailer, wholesaler, or other distributor to sell a banned product. If the CPSC bans the sale of a specific item, the product becomes frozen in all distribution channels because it cannot be sold. Manufacturers and distributors may be forced to repurchase the banned items. The CPSC took over the product safety functions of several older federal agencies. It also administers some programs, such as those dealing with flammable fabrics. In mid-2001, one manufacturer recalled 650,000 childrens' strollers.

From a distribution control standpoint, the FDA has procedures for recall that result in a reverse flow of the defective products from the consumer back to the manufacturer. The CPSC merely bans the sale of the product and halts it in its place in the distribution network.

The National Highway Traffic Safety Administration is concerned with motor vehicles and their accessory parts. It does not engage in recalls; it is responsible only for causing the manufacturer to notify purchasers that a defect has been discovered. Buyers are instructed to take their vehicles to the nearest dealer to have the defect corrected at no cost. The method of notification is registered mail to the first purchaser of record. Sometimes, it is not necessary for the owner to take the vehicle back to the dealer. In one instance, the manufacturer issued a corrected sticker showing different tire pressures; the owners were instructed to place the decal over the original one (or to see a dealer if they had difficulty following the instructions).

The Food Safety and Inspection Service of the U.S. Department of Agriculture inspects meat, poultry, and eggs. It is also concerned with processed meat and poultry products and pizzas and frozen dinners containing a certain percentage of meat. It also supervises standards of state agencies that regulate the cleanliness of meat sold within that state. The agency relies on voluntary recalls and, in mid-2002, its procedures were criticized when it took 19 days to persuade ConAgra to recall ground beef that carried a virulent *E. coli* strain. Most ground beef is used within 2 or 3 days of purchase, so the 19-day delay was too long to be of much practical value. Considerable public criticism accompanied this long delay.[14] Later in the same year, the federal agency responded more quickly and more aggressively to a similar *E. coli* threat. The Department of Agriculture closed down a Cargill-owned meat-packing plant by withdrawing its inspection services, which meant that the plant's products could not be sold in interstate commerce.[15]

In addition to these federal agencies, state and municipal agencies can also inspect products and force them to be withdrawn from commerce. Individual firms may also recall products on their own, in advance of government agency involvement.

Publicity, Liability, and Fire Drills

Whatever form it takes, product recall is an extremely serious matter for the manufacturer and all parties in the distribution network. Adverse publicity and large lawsuits can be devastating. Top management must be involved in any recall activity. Other

---

[14]Scott Kilman, "Procedural Delays Undermine Recalls of Tainted Meat," *The Wall Street Journal,* August 6, 2002, p. B1.

[15]Scott Kilman, "Cargill Expands Beef Recall, Shuts Plant Amid *E. Coli* Fears," *The Wall Street Journal,* October 4, 2002, p. B4.

involved staff should include members of a firm's legal, controller, public relations, quality control, product engineering, and marketing staffs. Management, who may never have known how the firm's logistics system functioned, will be anxiously examining its effectiveness in handling a product recall. Usually, a firm designates one individual to be responsible for handling recall activity. Some firms have practice, or fire drill, recalls to determine the speed, degree of coverage, and effectiveness they can effect. All actions that a firm takes to prepare for a hypothetical recall are important, for two reasons: First, they allow better performance when the real emergency arises. Second, in case the recall is not completely successful and lawsuits result, a portion of the firm's defense might be the precautionary actions it had undertaken.

Public relations expert Deborah Lowe, in writing about crisis management associated with product tampering, notes the following:

> Media experts believe that the company must tell its side of the story in the first 24 hours for the public to perceive that the company cares. Although the company is a victim of an attack on its products and on its customers, if it does not handle the tampering crisis effectively, it can jeopardize its positive public image and this can hurt the company economically. Some suggested media guidelines for tampering incidents that have proved successful include:
>
> 1. Respond to the tampering crisis within 24 to 48 hours to the media and show concern for the victims.
> 2. With or without media inquiries, do a swift withdrawal of the threatened products from the stores or area the threat includes.
> 3. Limit the number of media spokespersons but train all top managers for crisis interviews on tampering so the same facts reach the media.
> 4. Prioritize media call backs during the crisis.
> 5. Log all phone calls and actions.
> 6. Respond to questions, but be brief.
> 7. Characterize the company as a victim, not a villain.[16]

Batch Numbers

The possibility of defective products and product recalls increases the need for positively identifying each product or batch as it leaves the assembly line with a **batch number.** If a defect is detected, it is easier to identify and locate a group or batch of items produced at about the same time (which should, at least, be inspected to ensure that they are not also defective). Items such as office machines contain serial numbers, and all their movements through a distribution system are recorded by that number. In a recall, they are relatively easy to trace. For items that do not have serial numbers, batch numbers are commonly used. For example, the batch number 33 C 3 B 2 5 would indicate the following information:

33: Day of the year (February 2)
C: Plant

---

[16]Deborah Lowe, "Crisis Management Marketing for Tampering: Strategies for International and Domestic Marketplace Terrorism," *San Francisco State University School of Business Journal,* Vol. 1, 1990, p. 87.

3: Year 2003

B: Production line B

2: Second shift

5: Fifth hour of that shift.

A computerized inventory control system can record the batch number stenciled on each carton. (This information is also used to ensure that the inventory is being turned in proper sequence.) If the batch numbers are recorded as the goods move through the distribution system, in a recall it would be possible to trace each carton to a warehouse or to a retailer. The problem, and the accompanying adverse publicity, could then be more regionalized than if the manufacturer had to undertake a nationwide search campaign.

Figure 13-8 shows one public warehouse's inventory activity report (prepared for one of its grocery customers). Every time it receives a shipment of an item, that item is

```
IRPO4                                          LEDERER TERMINAL   WAREHOUSE CO.
   ANDERSON CLAYTON FOODS          0085
   MERCHANDISE STORED AT-                      INVENTORY ACTIVITY REPORT       AS OF   1/31/80        PAGE   1
       LEE ROAD

  DATE     ITEM #           DESCRIPTION            SHP/RLS # B/L-OSD#  RCPTS    SHPPD      ADJ.        BAL

 12/31/79   01058      CS  12/8-7 SEAS HERBS & SPICES                              BEGINNING BALANCE    610

  1/03/80  LOT# 5240     TRLR 847L4OLT RIGGS       3923379  C 8611    160
  1/28/80  LOT# 6506     ACF TRK                   3925754  C 8980    160
  1/30/80  LOT# 6717     G220958 COLDWAY           3930165  C 9028    320
  1/02/80  LOT# 3508     AMERICAN SEAWAY FDS INC   3923035 3923035               60
  1/02/80  LOT# 3508     SCOT LAD FDS INC          3923465 3923465               60
  1/03/80  LOT# 3508     A & P TEA CO INC          3922970 3922970                9
  1/03/80  LOT# 3897     A & P TEA CO INC          3922970 3922970               31
  1/08/80  LOT# 3897     SCOT LAD FOODS INC        3924771 3924771              100
  1/09/80  LOT# 3897     MCLAIN GROC               3925427 3925427               13
  1/11/80  LOT# 4167     HEINENS INC               3926031 3926031               23
  1/11/80  LOT# 3897     HEINENS INC               3926031 3926031               16
  1/14/80  LOT# 4167     SEAWAY FOODS INC          3926635 3926635               60
  1/15/80  LOT# 4167     SCOT LAD FOODS INC        3926610 3926610               77
  1/15/80  LOT# 5036     SCOT LAD FOODS INC        3926610 3926610               13
  1/18/80  LOT# 5036     THOROFARE MARKETS INC     3928014 3928014               80
  1/21/80  LOT# 5036     CAHRLEY BROTHERS          3928421 3928421               52
  1/22/80  LOT# 5036     SCOT LAD FOODS INC        3928492 3928492               15
  1/22/80  LOT# 5240     SCOT LAD FOODS INC        3928492 3928492               65
  1/23/80  LOT# 5240     MCALIN GROC               3929105 3929105               26

                           ITEM WEIGHT     7,700                     640         700
                                                                          ENDING BALANCE       550

 12/31/79   01582      CS  12/8-7 SEAS GREEN GODDESS DRSG                          BEGINNING BALANCE   1,185

  1/28/80  LOT# 6621     RIGGS                     3929538  C 9008    320
  1/02/80  LOT# 9579     SCOT LAD FDS INC          3923465 3923465               20
  1/03/80  LOT# 9579     TAMARKIN CO               3923569 3923569               39
  1/04/80  LOT# 1373     GOLDEN DAWN FDS           3924195 3924195                5
  1/04/80  LOT# 9579     GOLDEN DAWN FDS           3924195 3924195                5
  1/07/80  LOT# 1373     FRANK FORTUNE GROC CO     3924551 3924551               10
  1/08/80  LOT# 1373     SCOT LAD FOODS INC        3924771 3924771               60
  1/08/80  LOT# 1373     BETSY ROSS FOODS INC      3924972 3924972               20
  1/09/80  LOT# 1373     CARDINAL FDS INC          3925085 3925085               25
  1/09/80  LOT# 1373     MCLAIN GROC               3925427 3925427               26
  1/11/80  LOT# 1373     HEINENS INC               3926031 3926031               13
  1/14/80  LOT# 1373     TAMARKIN CO               3926630 3926630               38
  1/14/80  LOT# 1373     TAMARKIN CO               3926630 3926630                1
  1/15/80  LOT# 3565     SCOT LAD FOODS INC        3926610 3926610               20
  1/17/80  LOT# 3565     ASSOCIATED GROCERS INC    3927559 3927559               10
  1/18/80  LOT# 3565     THOROFARE MARKETS INC     3928014 3928014               80
  1/21/80  LOT# 3580     CAHRLEY BROTHERS          3928421 3928421               40
  1/21/80  LOT# 3565     CAHRLEY BROTHERS          3928421 3928421               12
  1/22/80  LOT# 3767     SCOT LAD FOODS INC        3928492 3928492               38
  1/22/80  LOT# 3580     SCOT LAD FOODS INC        3928492 3928492               22
  1/22/80  LOT# 3580     THE TAMARKIN CO           3928498 3928498               78
  1/22/80  LOT# 3580     CARDINAL FOODS INC        3928736 3928736               20
```

FIGURE 13-8 Excerpt from a Warehouser's Activity Report Tracing Lot Numbers from Manufacturer to Retailer

Source: Courtesy of Lederer Terminals, Cleveland, OH.

given a new lot number; at any one time, the warehouse may have large quantities of the same product whose only difference is their lot numbers. The warehouse's computer is programmed to pick up the oldest lot for outgoing shipment. In the event of a product recall, the warehouse's records would indicate which customers received goods from the affected lot or lots.

Controlling Returned and Salvaged Goods

In addition to product recalls, goods may be returned because they are damaged or unsalable (due to their poor condition or the disappearance of a market). Returned goods must be carefully counted and the various accounting records adjusted accordingly. Unsold newspapers, magazines, and paperback books are often returned for credit. Frequently, it is necessary only to return the copyright page or the book's cover to receive credit. In the paperback book industry, some publishers were defrauded by dealers who had fake book covers printed to collect credit.

Some unsold goods are salvaged, meaning that they are saved until a decision is made concerning what to do with them. A few years ago, some Subaru autos stored at a company distribution point were damaged by a flash flood. The company decided to strip the cars of recyclable parts, which would be sold as reconditioned parts, and to have the remaining parts of the vehicles crushed. A company spokesperson said that the company did not want parts to get into their parts supply inventory or into new vehicles.

As firms increasingly become involved in recycling, they must enforce controls that will prevent them from becoming victims of fraud. The system that controls outgoing movements must also control inbound movements of materials being recycled. Many disagreements about the content and quality of materials placed into the recycling effort are likely to arise.

Pilferage and Theft

An ongoing problem facing nearly all businesses is theft, especially **pilferage**—employee theft. The materials stolen in pilferage are usually for the employee's own use, whereas what is considered theft is more likely to be conducted by outsiders, although one's employees may be involved. "The U.S. Chamber of Commerce estimates that employee theft costs companies between $20 billion and $40 billion a year."[17] Theft is conducted on an organized basis, and it is more likely that the goods are stolen for resale. Both result in *inventory shrinkage* (i.e., unaccounted-for losses of product).

Because pilferage involves a firm's own employees, controls must begin with the hiring process and continue with supervisory practices. This is an area in which double standards exist. A warehouse employee caught carrying a company-owned product out of the warehouse and placing it in his or her private auto would be subjected to disciplinary action or might even be fired. Yet the warehouse superintendent may use the company car, with company gasoline, to run personal errands.

Pilferage is widespread and cannot be completely eliminated. Employees at lower levels who engage in pilferage tend to view it as their opportunity to obtain disguised

---

[17]*San Francisco Chronicle*, April 21, 2002, p. J1.

(and nontaxable) income. Some firms find it less expensive to tolerate a small amount of pilferage than to impose a system of total control. The principal cost of total control is in employee turnover; many individuals choose not to work under such close scrutiny and supervision.

Obviously, handling pilferage is a difficult job for supervisors. Some consider that the best policy is to declare that all taking of others' property is wrong, and they proceed from that principle. Employees who are about to lose their jobs are more likely to engage in pilferage. In the early twenty-first century, articles about industrial pilferage noted that persons who were laid off or lost their pensions were likely to pilfer because they felt that the company still "owed" them something.

Organized theft involves the efforts, usually by outsiders, to steal merchandise while it is in a firm's distribution channels. "A different aspect of e-commerce is that dishonest employees no longer have to take their stolen goods to organized crime in order to have the product locally fenced (converted to cash). Today, thieves have become well-versed with the capabilities of the Internet and are finding that e-commerce provides a world of opportunities through which to sell hot merchandise. In essence, the Internet has become the ultimate high-tech 'flea market' for thieves, and business has been thriving."[18] Among the concerns about employees who use drugs is that they are vulnerable to outsiders who attempt to coerce them into aiding in thefts. For a warehouse manager, perhaps the greatest risk is an employee who steals to raise money to acquire illegal substances.

Sometimes, theft and pilferage occur while merchandise is within the custody of a common carrier or a warehouser. In this case, the common carrier or warehouser is liable. Most international shipments are insured so, if there is a loss, the insurer pays. CIGNA, a large insurance company, estimates that over 20 percent of its insured cargo losses are for theft.[19] However, even if the owner of the goods is reimbursed, the incident may still be disadvantageous to the shipper for several reasons:

1. The planned flow of the goods in the channel has been interrupted and may result in a stockout at some later stage.
2. The carrier's or warehouser's liability may not cover the entire value of the shipment.
3. Time, telephone, and paperwork costs are not covered.
4. Employees who had knowledge of the shipment's route and timing may come under suspicion.
5. The stolen products may reappear on the market at a low price to compete with goods that have moved through legitimate channels.

Building Security

In recent years, interest in providing **building security** for warehouses and other distribution facilities has increased. Figure 13-9 shows some of the security measures that can be built into a warehouse. As we become more security-conscious, we reduce access to offices, warehouses, and plants. We also insist upon positive identification of all people wanting to be "let in."

---

[18]Barry Brandon, *Security Best Practices* (Oak Brook, IL: Warehousing Education and Research Council, 2002), p. 47.

[19]*CIGNA Ports of the World* (Philadelphia: Cigna, ca. 1995), p. 55.

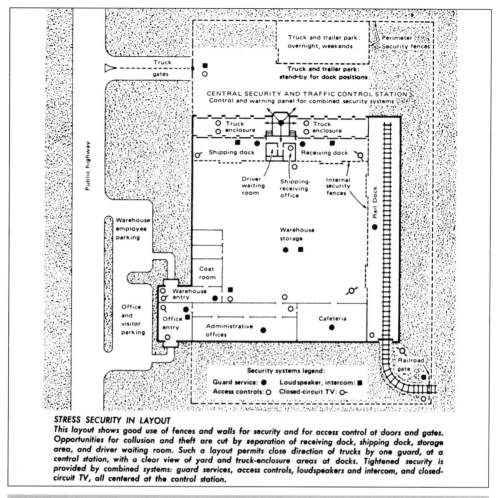

Truck and trailer park: overnight, weekends

Perimeter Security fences

Truck gates

Truck and trailer park: stand-by for dock positions

CENTRAL SECURITY AND TRAFFIC CONTROL STATION
Control and warning panel for combined security systems

Truck enclosure

Truck enclosure

Shipping dock

Receiving dock

Driver waiting room

Shipping-receiving office

Internal security fences

Rail Dock

Public highway

Warehouse employee parking

Warehouse storage

Coat room

Warehouse entry

Office and visitor parking

Office entry

Administrative offices

Cafeteria

Railroad gate

Security systems legend:

Guard service: ●   Loudspeaker, intercom: ■

Access controls: ○   Closed-circuit TV: ○⊸

STRESS SECURITY IN LAYOUT
This layout shows good use of fences and walls for security and for access control at doors and gates. Opportunities for collusion and theft are cut by separation of receiving dock, shipping dock, storage area, and driver waiting room. Such a layout permits close direction of trucks by one guard, at a central station, with a clear view of yard and truck-enclosure areas at docks. Tightened security is provided by combined systems: guard services, access controls, loudspeakers and intercom, and closed-circuit TV, all centered at the control station.

FIGURE 13-9 How to Plan a Thief-Resistant Warehouse

Source: Courtesy of Modern Materials Handling.

Electronic devices are available to perform three different functions. First, closed-circuit television cameras can be used to view different areas. The picture is shown on a monitor screen constantly observed by a guard. For areas where there should be no movements, it is possible to have monitoring devices store the image that contains no movement in digital memory and, when a change in the image occurs—such as would be caused by intruders in a freight storage area—initiate an alarm. The second type of electronic device is used for access control. An example is a magnetically encoded tag that each employee must insert into a sensing device that records the event and determines whether the door or gate should be unlocked. The third category is invisible photoelectric beams and many types of listening devices that can record unauthorized movements. Within a warehouse, heavier security may be placed around areas where higher-valued material is kept. Outside firms are sometimes retained to provide nighttime security for warehouse

FIGURE 13-10 This Curbside Camera Is at the Top of the Cab

Source: Kenworth Truck Company.

buildings. There is no limit to the sophistication or cost of the security devices that can be employed. It is, unfortunately, another cost of doing business.

Vehicle Security

Methods and equipment have been developed to discourage thefts from (or of) vehicles and to improve **vehicle security.** Numbers can be painted on top of truck trailers to make them easier to spot from the air in case they are stolen. A transponder (a small device that responds to radio signals from an outside source) can be placed aboard vehicles that are likely to be hijacked. A global positioning device would help locate a vehicle, assuming that the thieves did not disconnect the device.

Improved locking devices are helpful. Thieves have been known to climb onto the rear of a truck waiting at a traffic signal and then force their way inside the vehicle. Figure 13-10 shows a security camera on the top of a Kenworth semitractor cab, while

FIGURE 13-11 This Screen Is Inside the Cab and Allows the Driver To See Nearly 360 Degrees Around the Truck Using Five Cameras, Including Some Mounted on the Semitrailer

Source: Kenworth Truck Company.

Figure 13-11 shows the four-section screen in the driver's cab in which one can view traffic behind and on both sides. Five cameras, including some on the semitrailer, are used and provide nearly 360 degrees of coverage.

Intermodal containers can be stolen for their contents or for their own value.

> The reason that owners of open-top containers charge so much is that when the boxes go to certain Third World destinations, you never see them come back. Set on its side an open-top container makes a very nice residence if you can add a rattan wall. In Latin America, especially, stolen open-top containers are used for swimming pools.[20]

Since the North American Free Trade Agreement (NAFTA) came into being, trade journals have been filled with articles concerning thefts and security problems in Mexico. "Assault on transport operations now accounts for more than 60 percent of total losses due to theft in Mexico, according to the Mexican Association of Insurance

---

[20]Rainer Wulff, *American Shipper,* April 1997, p. 52.

Agencies." [21] To combat these thefts, trucking companies operating in Mexico are advised to remove logos from their vehicles, rotate drivers, change schedules, use only toll highways, and travel in convoys. The thieves, many of whom are ex-policemen, are so well organized that they even have their own insurance guaranteeing safe passage to shippers—for a price.

Computer and Document Security

Computer security and **document security** can be difficult to maintain when individuals (usually employees) know how a company's various computer and paperwork systems work and then use their knowledge to defraud the company. They may be able to manipulate a system so that it ships additional products, issues unauthorized refund payments, or the like. As firms adopt computerized systems to handle their logistics functions, they must take steps to ensure that the systems are safeguarded against unauthorized access and that sufficient controls are incorporated to prevent fraud. Outside hackers may penetrate a firm's computer system for fun or for profit. Some firms retain an outside consultant to periodically attempt to hack into their distribution function's computer system.

Computer records must be updated, and backup files stored at another site. One should "never allow unauthorized personnel around computer work stations. Nimble fingers can extract desired data from an untended keyboard in less than a minute."[22]

In a situation involving the security of Revlon's new computerized distribution system, the cosmetics manufacturer had its inventory control software shut down by an unexpected phone call from the software developer—a vendor with whom it was having a dispute. Revlon was unhappy with the performance of the partially installed system and balked at making further payments. The software producer "responded by using a phone link and Revlon's computer access codes to shut down its software in Revlon's computer systems."[23]

The Internet is a widely used communication device, and one must ensure that it cannot be used in a damaging manner. Especially vulnerable would be Internet-based order management systems.

International transactions and movements are especially susceptible to documentation fraud. In these instances, the owner of the goods may be thousands of miles away from the cargo and be dependent on the honesty of many different parties in different lands who prepare and verify the cargo's documents.

Product Identification Number Security

Inventory control systems based on product serial numbers or product batch numbers have certain advantages with respect to discouraging theft and pilferage. If items are discovered missing, it is possible to identify them by number. This makes it possible to reclaim the goods if they are recovered and facilitates prosecution of those in possession of the goods. These facts are also known to pilferers, thieves, and fences and tend to make the "hot" merchandise somewhat less valuable. Altering or destroying serial or batch numbers is time consuming and arouses the suspicions of legitimate buyers.

---

[21]Stephanie N. Ross, "Shutting the Door on Highway Robbery," *Business Mexico,* August 1996, p. 26.

[22]*American Shipper,* July 1998, p. 30.

[23]Ken Siegman, "Computer Firm Shuts Down Revlon; Giant Cosmetics Company Sues Small Software Maker Over Incident," *San Francisco Chronicle,* October 25, 1990, p. 1. See also "Is Your Software Holding You Hostage?" *Distribution,* April 1991, pp. 48–50. This feature is nicknamed the "drop-dead device" because buyers of the systems are often unaware that it exists.

Truck-leasing companies, in an effort to thwart truck theft, now etch vehicle identification numbers in up to 40 different locations on each vehicle—glass, frame, driveline components, various engine parts, and virtually any other part with resale value. The number is cut with a special stencil and a sandblast gun. Some autos also have their serial numbers stamped on various parts.

System Security

One of the most effective methods of protecting goods is to keep them moving through the system. Goods waiting in warehouses, in terminals, or to clear customs are more vulnerable to theft than goods that are moving. No list of methods of improving **system security** (that is, security throughout the entire supply chain) is complete; determined thieves are likely to overcome almost any hindrance or barrier placed in their way. However, a few suggestions are offered here, mainly to reflect the breadth of measures that might be taken:

- Decals are required for autos in employee parking lots.
- Forklifts in warehouses are locked at night, making it difficult to reach high items or to move heavy items.
- Seals (small wirelike devices that once closed cannot be opened without breaking) are used more and more, with dispatchers, drivers, and receiving personnel all responsible for recording the seal number and inspecting its condition. Figure 13-12

FIGURE 13-12 This Device Seals Pallets. It Has Four Clips That Fasten Together and Is Used in Conjunction with Strapping

Source: CGM Security Solutions, Inc.

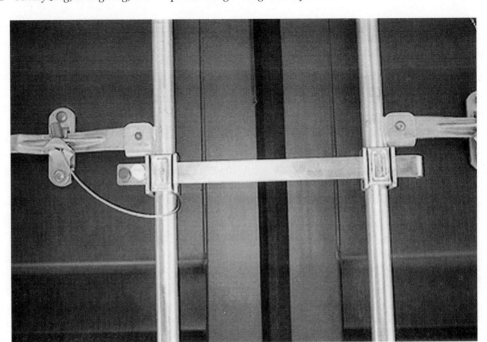

FIGURE 13-13 The Small Wire Shown on the Left Will Break if the Trailer Door Latch Is Opened. The Plug At its Upper End is Marked with a Unique Number.

Source: CGM Security Solutions, Inc.

shows a seal device used for pallet loads; and Figure 13-13 shows a seal used for truck trailer or container doors. Seals do not offer physical protection. Instead, they break easily. They have unique numbers and are difficult to replace. As a sealed product moves along the supply chain, each person assuming responsibility for it examines the seal and seal number, and will refuse to accept cargo if the seal is broken or shows signs of tampering.

- Some companies have a continuous receipt system, so that an employee is considered responsible for each item until he or she can pass the item on and have the receiver sign a receipt. Although somewhat cumbersome, this system has been helpful because it enhances the sense of personal responsibility of the employee, who tends to view any effort to steal or tamper with the goods as an assault on his or her integrity.
- Electronic tags or strips are embedded in products at the time of their manufacture, and they can activate alarms at warehouse or retail store doors.
- One retail chain requires its retail stores to report any overages received from company warehouses. On occasion, it deliberately ships too much to determine whether the overage will be acknowledged.
- Sealing tape having a pattern containing the company's logo is used for sealing all outgoing packages and cartons. Although it does not prevent theft, it does make it more difficult to cover up evidence of pilferage or theft. Figure 13-14 shows some of the distinctive tape that leaves a mark when it is removed.

FIGURE 13-14 This Tape Indicates Whether Pilfering Has Occurred Because of the design, another party could not duplicate it easily to reseal a carton. In addition the word "opened" (in this instance in both English and French because shipper is located in Canada) becomes visible. The word does not appear until about 2 hours after the thief has resealed the package.

Source: CGM Security Solutions, Inc.

This brief section has dealt only with domestic theft. When goods move in international commerce, they are much more vulnerable to theft. Entire shiploads of cargo disappear. Ships have met diverse fates. Some have vanished only to reappear under a new name and a new flag. Some are diverted to a different port, where the cargo is sold to the highest bidder while the original purchaser waits in vain. *Rust bucket fraud* involves chartering an aged ship that is loaded with goods worth more than the ship. After setting sail, it makes an unscheduled stop, sells off the cargo to the highest bidder, and exchanges its regular crew for a scuttling crew that takes it out to sea, where it runs into "bad" weather. The crew manages to escape and the hulk lies too deep for divers to examine.

Piracy is also a threat. "Unlike the sword-brandishing, eye patch-wearing pirates of seafaring lore, today's pirates typically use speedboats and handguns to ambush and then board small and medium-size ships . . . . With the number of incidents of piracy rising, maritime officials say, the South China Sea is becoming as lawless as it was when Vietnamese boat people were preyed upon 20 years ago. A critical new element in Asian piracy is that to sell their stolen goods, pirates are now choosing to go to small ports in southern China where the complicity of local officials and the eagerness of traders offer safe haven."[24] Off Ecuador, "another containership was approached by two speedboats as she neared the pilot station . . . on 30 October 2000. The ship's general alarm was sounded when the boats were spotted and the pilot station was informed by VHF. Despite these actions, one of the boats came alongside and four armed attackers boarded the ship, firing their weapons to keep the crew at bay. One container was opened and part of the contents were transferred to the attackers' boat. Eventually three attackers from the second boat boarded the vessel to assist with the removal of goods."[25]

International air freight is also vulnerable. In the mid-1990s, "Some estimates report that an average of 20 percent of all goods arriving at Moscow Airport vanish, only to appear shortly afterwards on the Russian black market."[26]

Energy-Saving Controls

With the sudden and large increases in energy costs that are taking place, logistics managers need to pay increasing attention to keeping energy costs under control.

Two areas in logistics systems are where most energy costs occur and where energy-saving measures should be focused. One is in warehouses, where both design factors (such as not placing doors on the north side of a building) and operating procedures (such as having workers turn out unneeded lights) can lower energy consumption. In some areas there are lower off-peak charges for electricity, and these times should be used for recharging the batteries on lift trucks. Solar energy can be employed to reduce purchase of the other forms of energy. One California walnut-processing and storage facility now uses shells from shelled walnuts as fuel to heat the structure.

Outside firms can be brought in to audit energy consumption. In 2002, a chemical company's 100,000-square-foot New Jersey warehouse that had 15,000 fluorescent tubes in place underwent such an audit. Timers were installed and different types of tubes and bulbs were used, some of which also produced less glare, which was easier on the order pickers' eyes. Annual electricity costs were cut by $66,000, and the new system paid for itself within 2 years.[27]

The other area of logistics where considerable amounts of fuel can be saved is transportation. Almost any changes in shipping practices and patterns that reduce transportation costs probably utilize less fuel. Indeed, part of the rationale for deregulating the domestic transportation system in the United States was to do away with some of the inefficiencies (including fuel inefficiencies) of the regulated system.

Hazardous Materials Handling

Mention has been made in several places in this text of hazardous materials and the fact that they must receive specialized and more careful handling. A firm or agency handling them would probably establish a special logistics channel to provide the addi-

---

[24]*The Argus,* April 20, 1997, p. A–7.

[25]*BIMCO Bulletin,* Vol. 95, No. 6, 2000, p. 49.

[26]*KLM Cargovision,* March 1996, p. 27.

[27]*Distribution Center Management,* Vol. 37, No. 2, May 2002, p. 3.

tional protection required by government regulations, insurance requirements, and company policy. These precautionary measures would extend through the entire supply chain. Those organizations handling hazardous materials must have in place training programs and hazmat accident investigation procedures.

Many hazardous materials travel on railroads. With our increased concerns regarding terrorism, we must recognize that the contents of some railcars, if released either accidentally or deliberately, could cause death to people nearby. Not all railcars are in motion; some chemical companies use tank cars for semipermanent storage.[28] Rail yards are not considered to be secure.

It is imperative that anybody handling or receiving hazardous materials be informed. In order to save time, some shippers have avoided labeling their shipments as hazardous and have later been subject to large fines. In one instance, a plant manager labeled a shipment of ethyl mercaptan as valves so that it would be accepted for shipment by air. The package leaked, and 41 people were hospitalized. The shipper faced up to 30 years in jail, and the company faced both fines and lawsuits from those who were hospitalized.[29] In another case, and for the first time, the Coast Guard ordered that the cargo lost overboard at sea be retrieved from the ocean floor. "We told them that 'Since you dropped it, you clean it up,'" said a Coast Guard source. "And that was done, at tremendous cost"—$23 million, by one informed reckoning. The parties at risk hired a team of divers who, after reconnoitering, found all of the drums of arsenic trioxide that had been scattered when the oceangoing containers lost overboard had broken apart on the ocean's floor. Because no human diver would agree to work near the debris, robots with picker arms were lowered to the ocean bottom and loaded the drums into positions on what looked like a giant ice cube tray, which was then raised.[30]

Maintaining Channel and Supply-Chain Integrity

As channel relationships evolve into supply chains, a continual matter of concern is maintaining the integrity of the product and the product flow. While one must trust his or her partners, one cannot assume that the partners will be able to detect everything that goes wrong. One must continually monitor the quality of materials shipped and received, as well as performance in some of the other channels.

Outside threats also occur. Product tampering is the most common, and—although it usually occurs at the retail level—the retail store, the product, and the product's name all suffer from bad publicity. Usually, several parties along the supply chain suffer.

In early 1995, a story unfolded in California regarding the alleged sale of fake Similac, a baby formula, in Safeway stores. Allegedly, an individual purchased some powdered baby formula destined for export, packaged it in cans that were nearly identical copies of the Similac can, and sold it to a food broker that regularly supplied Safeway. The broker then sold it to Safeway, and the fake Similac ended up on

---

[28]www.mapcruzin.com/chemical_catastrophe/millar3.htm, July 10, 2002.

[29]*The Journal of Commerce,* January 31, 1994, p. 12A.

[30]*American Shipper,* December 1995, p. 68.

Safeway's shelves. When the FDA moved in, over 6,000 cans of the fake Similac were recovered from wholesale and retail stocks. As might be imagined, lawsuits followed. One class-action suit alleged that Safeway "owed consumers a duty to ensure that the product it was purchasing and reselling was what it was represented to be."[31] The purpose of mentioning this incident here is to show how an existing channel can be broken into.

Sometimes, no actual tampering takes place; a person need only announce to the media that he or she has tampered with some product, and the ensuing publicity will have a similar effect.

In an effort aimed at terrorism, the Federal Aviation Administration requires airlines to have air freight forwarders and air cargo agents certify that they have either physically inspected or x-rayed all cargo that they tender to airlines. These rules took effect in early 1994, and they matched similar requirements already existing for international shipments. Note that this shifts some responsibility for security along the logistics channel of the supply chain.

Protection Against Terrorism

The terrorism associated with the events of September 11, 2001, have caused many firms to look at their supply chains and wonder whether they are immune from attack or disruption. Even, worse, they might be used by terrorists as a vehicle for carrying out another terrorist act. Consultants Joseph Martha and Sunil Subbakrishna offer several suggestions:[32]

1. Purchase "all risk" insurance, making certain that risks include acts of terrorism.
2. Cultivate alternative suppliers to reduce dependency upon single sources.
3. Have contingency plans that include the ability to shift segments of supply chain to avoid those that are suddenly disabled. (One California chain has an alternate distribution headquarters—essentially a room with several computer workstations—located in a small inland city, mainly because of the fear that a major earthquake might occur near its headquarters.)
4. Line up alternative transportation and recognize the risk that, after a terrorist attack, international borders may be closed to both people and goods.
5. Contact customers and attempt to make alternative, satisfactory arrangements.
6. Rethink or recalculate the best level of safety stocks, paying very close attention to levels maintained by other parties along the supply chain.

The U.S. Customs Service is developing a "Customs Service's Customs-Trade Partnership Against Terrorism." Companies that participate must conduct a self-assessment of their supply chains' security using guidelines developed by U.S. Customs and the trade community. A supply-chain security system must then be put into place,

---

[31]Bill Wallace, "Class-Action Suit Against Safeway over Fake Similac; Redwood City Case Charges Negligence," *San Francisco Chronicle,* February 22, 1995, p. A15.

[32]See Joseph Martha and Sunil Subbakrishna, "Targeting a Just-in-Case Supply Chain for the Inevitable Next Disaster," *Supply Chain Management Review,* Vol. 6, No. 5, 2002, pp. 18–23.

and it must be maintained. The principal advantage to the firm is that its containers are less likely to be detained by U.S. Customs for detailed inspection.[33]

SUMMARY

This chapter demonstrated the need for various types of controls. Of special importance are accounting controls and controls on worker productivity, both in warehouses and on the roads. A list of warehouse work rules is needed, including violations subject to discharge and violations subject to corrective discipline.

Supervising drivers is usually more difficult than supervising warehouse workers because drivers are on the road and out of their supervisors' immediate sight. Also, they are in contact with both customers and the public, whereas warehouse workers are not.

Product recalls are common. They involve reversing or freezing the movement of goods in the channel. Different products are subject to varying federal recall controls. Ford/Firestone tires is probably the best-known recent recall incident.

Pilferage and theft are two other important control issues. Pilferage is informal or casual thefts by employees, while thefts are committed by outsiders. Both are continuous hazards and require constant vigilance to protect against them.

Energy-saving controls are important, especially in terms of fuel costs. As the use of computers grows, precautions must be taken to prevent computers being accessed by outsiders.

QUESTIONS FOR DISCUSSION AND REVIEW

1. Discuss ways in which supply chains might be targeted by terrorist attacks.
2. Discuss some important considerations for logistics managers when drawing up their budgets.
3. What types of reports might be prepared by the logistics accounting group?
4. What is short-interval scheduling?
5. Discuss several ways in which management might persuade unions to alter some work practices.
6. Why does driver supervision tend to be more difficult than supervision of warehouse workers?
7. Describe how the tachograph functions. What bad driving habits can it detect?
8. Discuss some of the decisions that confront managers who face product recalls.
9. What U.S. federal agencies are involved in product recalls, and what are their respective jurisdictions?
10. Why is it important for companies to conduct practice, or "fire drill," product recalls?
11. How might companies become victims of fraud with respect to returned and salvaged goods?
12. What is the difference between pilferage and theft?
13. Discuss various ways that management can use to control pilferage.
14. Discuss the three security-related functions that can be performed by electronic devices.
15. What are some methods that can be used to improve vehicle security?
16. Discuss some of the challenges associated with computer security.
17. In what ways are goods moving in international commerce more vulnerable to theft than goods moving in domestic commerce?
18. What are the two areas in logistics systems where energy-saving measures should be focused? What are some suggestions for saving energy in these two areas?

---

[33]Bernard J. LaLonde, "Compliance, Collaboration, and Technology: Searching for a Pathway to Supply Chain Security," *Supply Chain Management Review,* Vol. 6, No. 5, 2002, pp. 8–9.

19. Discuss how companies might reduce supply chain disruptions that are caused by terrorist attacks.
20. Of the various issues discussed in this chapter, which do you view as most serious for effective and efficient supply chain management? Why?

SUGGESTED READINGS

Bowersox, Donald J., David J. Closs, and Theodore P. Stank. "Ten Mega-Trends That Will Revolutionize Supply Chain Logistics." *Journal of Business Logistics,* Vol. 21, No. 2, 2000, pp. 1–16.

Brandman, Barry. *Security Best Practices.* Oak Brook, IL: Warehousing Education and Research Council, 2002.

Christopher, Martin. "The Agile Supply Chain—Competing in Volatile Markets." *Industrial Marketing Management,* Vol. 29, 2000, pp. 37–44.

Helferich, Omar Keith, and Robert L. Cook. *Securing the Supply Chain.* Oak Brook, IL: Council of Logistics Management, 2002.

Holmes, Susan, Mark Power, and Clyde Kenneth Walter. "A Motor Carrier Wellness Program: Development and Testing." *Transportation Journal,* Vol. 35, No. 3, 1996, pp. 33–48.

Kerpoe, Lisa. *Using Competencies in the Warehouse.* Oak Brook, IL: Warehousing Education and Research Council, 2001.

Lambert, Douglas M. "Logistics Cost, Productivity, and Performance Analysis." *The Logistics Handbook.* New York: Free Press, 1994, pp. 260–302.

Lowe, Deborah. *Product Tampering: A Worldwide Problem.* Los Angeles: Foundation for American Communication, 1993.

Martha, Joseph, and Sunil Subbakrishna. "Targeting a Just-in-Case Supply Chain for the Inevitable Next Disaster." *Supply Chain Management Review,* Vol. 6 No. 5, 2002, pp. 18–23.

Mentzer, John T., and John Firman. "Logistics Control Systems in the 21st Century." *Journal of Business Logistics,* Vol. 15, No. 1, 1994, pp. 215–227.

Sterling, Jay U. "Measuring the Performance of Logistics Operations." *The Logistics Handbook.* New York: Free Press, 1994, pp. 199–240.

Strasser, Sandra, Jack M. Hires, and Virginia Singleton. "An Analysis of Labor Arbitration in Cases of Drug and Alcohol Abuse." *Journal of the Transportation Research Forum,* Vol. 35, No. 1, 1995, pp. 87–96.

Voss, Bristol. "Uncovering Hidden Costs." *Journal of Business Strategy,* Vol. 15, No. 3, 1994, pp. 37–47.

C A S E S

Case 13-1   Brant Freezer Company

Located in Fargo, North Dakota, the Brant Freezer Company manufactured industrial freezers. They came in one size and were distributed through public warehouses in Atlanta, Boston, Chicago, Denver, Los Angeles, Portland, and St. Louis. In addition, some space was used in the company's Fargo warehouse. Young Joaquin (J. Q.) Brant, with a fresh M.B.A. degree from the University of South Alabama, returned to the family firm, where he had once worked during summers. On his first day of work, J. Q. met with his father. His father complained that

they were being "eaten alive" by warehousing costs. The firm's controller drew up a budget each year, and each warehouse's monthly activity (units shipped) and costs were tallied.

Exhibit 13-A shows actual 2003 figures for all warehouses, plus actual figures for the first 5 months of 2004. Projected 12-month 2004 budgets and shipments are also included. If you are familiar with Excel or other spreadsheet software, you might try using it to answer the following questions.

QUESTIONS

1. When comparing performance during the first 5 months of 2004 with performance in 2003, which warehouse shows the most improvement?
2. When comparing performance during the first 5 months of 2004 with performance in 2003, which warehouse shows the poorest change in performance?
3. When comparisons are made among all eight warehouses, which one do you think does the best job for the Brant Company? What criteria did you use? Why?
4. J. Q. is aggressive and is going to recommend that his father cancel the contract with one of the warehouses and give that business to a competing warehouse in the same city. J. Q. feels that when word of this gets around, the other warehouses they use will "shape up." Which of the seven should J. Q. recommend be dropped? Why?

5. The year 2004 is nearly half over. J. Q. is told to determine how much the firm is likely to spend for warehousing at each of the eight warehouses for the last 6 months in 2004. Do his work for him.
6. When comparing the 2003 figures with the 2004 figures shown in the table, the amount budgeted for each warehouse in 2004 was greater than actual 2003 costs. How much of the increase is caused by increased volume of business (units shipped) and how much by inflation?
7. Prepare the firm's 2005 warehouse budget, showing for each warehouse the anticipated number of units to be shipped and the costs.
8. While attending classes at the university, J. Q. had learned of logistics partnerships. Should Brant Freezer Company attempt to enter into a partnership relationship with these warehouses? If so, what approach should it use?

EXHIBIT 13-A Warehouse Performance

| | 2003 Figures | | | | | | | 2004 Figures | | | | |
| | Units Shipped | | Warehouse Costs | | | Units Shipped | | Warehouse Costs | | |
	12 Months Jan.–Dec.	5 Months through May 31	12 Months Jan.–Dec.	5 Months through May 31		Projected 12 Months Jan.–Dec.	Actual 5 Months May 31		Budgeted 12 Months Jan.–Dec.	Actual Costs through May 31
Atlanta	17,431	4,080	156,830	35,890		18,000	4,035		178,000	40,228
Boston	6,920	3,061	63,417	27,915		7,200	3,119		73,000	29,416
Chicago	28,104	14,621	246,315	131,618		30,000	15,230		285,000	141,222
Denver	3,021	1,005[a]	28,019	8,600*		3,100	1,421		31,000	14,900
Fargo (company warehouse)	2,016	980	16,411	8,883		2,000	804		17,000	9,605
Los Angeles	16,491	11,431	151,975	109,690		17,000	9,444		176,000	93,280
Portland	8,333	4,028	73,015	36,021		9,000	4,600		85,000	42,616
St. Louis	5,921	2,331	51,819	23,232		8,000	2,116		56,000	19,191

[a] Denver warehouse closed by strike March 4–19, 2003.

Case 13-2   Red Spot Markets Company

The Red Spot Markets Company operates a chain of grocery stores in New England. It has a grocery distribution center in Providence, Rhode Island, from which deliveries are made to stores as far north as Lowell, Massachusetts, as far west as Waterbury, Connecticut, and as far northwest as Springfield, Massachusetts. No stores are located beyond the two northernmost points in Massachusetts. Stores to the west are supplied by a grocery warehouse located in Newburgh, New York. The Providence grocery distribution center supplies 42 Red Spot retail stores.

Robert Easter, Red Spot's distribution manager, is responsible for operations at the Newburgh and Providence distribution centers. By industry standards, both centers were fairly efficient. However, of the two, the Providence center lagged in two important areas of control: worker productivity and shrinkage. Warehouse equipment and work rules were the same for both the Newburgh and Providence centers, yet the throughput per worker hour was 4 percent higher for the Newburgh facility. Shrinkage, expressed as a percentage of the wholesale value of goods handled annually, was 3.6 percent for the Newburgh center and 5.9 percent for the Providence center. Jarvis Jason had been manager of the Providence distribution center for the past 3 years and, at great effort, managed to narrow the gap between the performance of the two Red Spot facilities. Last week he requested an immediate reassignment, and Easter arranged for him to become the marketing manager for the Boston area, which would involve supervising the operations of 11 Red Spot markets. The transfer involved no increase in pay.

Easter needed a new manager for the Providence distribution center, and he picked Fred Fosdick for the task. Fosdick graduated from a lesser Ivy League college, where he majored in business with a concentration in logistics. He had been with Red Spot for 2 years and had rearranged the entire delivery route structure so that two fewer trucks were needed. As part of this assignment, he also converted the entire system to one of unit loads, which meant everything loaded on or unloaded from a Red Spot truck was on a pallet. Fosdick was familiar with the operations of both the Providence and Newburgh centers. He has been in each facility at least 50 different times. In addition, he spent 2 weeks at the Providence center when the loading docks were redesigned to accommodate pallet loading. Fosdick was surprised that Jason had requested his reassignment to a slot that did not involve an upward promotion. That was his first question to Easter after Easter asked whether he was interested in the Providence assignment.

"I'm sorry you started with that question," said Easter to Fosdick. "Now we'll have to talk about the troublesome aspects of the assignment first, rather than the positive ones. To be frank, Fred, one of the union employees there made so much trouble for Jason, he couldn't stand it."

"Who's the troublemaker?" asked Fosdick.

"Tom Bigelow," was Easter's answer.

Fosdick remembered Bigelow from the times he had been at the Providence center. Thomas D. Bigelow was nicknamed T. D. since his days as a local Providence high school football star. Fosdick recalled that during work breaks on the loading dock, Bigelow and some of the other workers would toss around melons as though they were footballs. Only once did they drop a melon. Fosdick recalled hearing the story that Bigelow had received several offers of athletic scholarships when he graduated from high school. His best offer was from a southern school, and he accepted it. Despite the fact that the college provided a special tutor for each class, Bigelow flunked out at the end of his first semester and came back to Providence, where he got a job in the Red Spot warehouse.

In the warehouse, Bigelow was a natural leader. He would have been a supervisor except for his inability to count and his spotty attendance record on Monday mornings. On Mondays, the day that the warehouse was the busiest since it had to replenish the stores' weekend sales, Bigelow was groggy, tired, and irritable. On Mondays, he would sometimes hide by loading a forklift with three pallets, backing into any empty bay, and lowering the pallets in position (which hid the lift truck from view), and he would fall asleep. The rest of the week Bigelow was happy, enthusiastic, and hardworking. Indeed, it was he who set the pace of work in the warehouse. When he felt good, things hummed; when he was not feeling well or was absent, work dragged.

"What did Bigelow do to Jason?" Fosdick asked Easter.

"Well, as I understand it," responded Easter, "about 2 weeks ago Jason decided that he had had it with Bigelow and so he suspended him on a Monday morning after Bigelow showed up late, still badly hung over. It was nearly noon, and he told Bigelow to stay off the premises and to file a grievance with his union shop steward. He also told Bigelow that he had been documenting Bigelow's Monday performance—or nonperformance—for the past 6 months and that Red Spot had grounds enough to fire Bigelow if it so chose. He told Bigelow to go home, sober up, and come back on Tuesday when they would discuss the length of his suspension. Bigelow walked through the distribution center on his way out, and I'm sure Jason felt he had control of the matter.

"However," continued Easter, "by about one o'clock, Jason realized he had a work slowdown on his hands. Pallet loads of bottled goods were being dropped, two forklifts collided, and one lift truck pulled over the corner of a tubular steel rack. At 4:00 P.M. quitting time, there were still three trucks to be loaded; usually they would have departed by 3:30. Rather than pay overtime, Jason let the workforce go home, and he and the supervisor loaded the last three trucks.

"On Tuesday, Bigelow did not show up, and the slowdown got worse. In addition, retail stores were phoning with complaints about all the errors in their orders. To top it off, at the Roxbury store, when the trailer door was opened, the trailer contained nothing but empty pallets. Tuesday night somebody turned off the switches on the battery chargers for all the lift trucks, so on Wednesday, the lift-truck batteries were dying all day. I got involved because of all the complaints from the stores. On Wednesday, Jason got my permission to pay overtime, and the last outgoing truck did not leave until 7:00 P.M. In addition we had to pay overtime at some of our retail stores because the workers there were waiting for the trucks to arrive. While I was talking to Jason that afternoon, he indicated that he had fired Bigelow."

Easter lit his cigar and continued. "On Wednesday, I decided to go to Providence myself, mainly to talk to Jason and to determine whether we should close down the Providence center and try to serve all our stores out of Newburgh. This would have been expensive, but Providence was becoming too unreliable. In addition, we had a big weekend coming up. When I showed up in Providence, Jason and I had breakfast together in my hotel room Thursday morning, and he told me pretty much the same thing I've been telling you. He said he knew Bigelow was behind all the disruption and that today, Thursday, would be crucial. I've never seen Jason looking so nervous. Then we drove to the distribution center. Even from a distance, I could tell things were moving slowly. The first echelon of outgoing trucks, which should have been on the road, were still there. Another 20 of our trucks were waiting to be loaded. On the other end of the building, you could see a long line of arriving trucks waiting to be unloaded; usually there was no line at all. I knew that our suppliers would start complaining because we had established scheduled unloading times. However, I decided not to ask Jason whether he had begun receiving phone calls from them."

"Inside the center, the slowdown was in effect. Lift-truck operators who usually zipped by each other would now stop, turn off their engines, dismount, and carefully walk around each other's trucks to ensure there was proper clearance. Satisfied of this, they would then mount, start their engines, and spend an inordinate amount of time motioning to each other to pass. This was only one example. When we got to Jason's office, he had a message to phone Ed Meyers, our local attorney in Providence, who handles much of our labor relations work there. He called Meyers and was upset by the discussion. After he hung up, he told me that Meyers had been served papers by the union's attorney, charging that Wednesday's firing of Bigelow was unjustified, mainly because there existed no provable grounds that Bigelow was behind the slowdown. Meyers was angry because, in firing Bigelow on Wednesday, Jason may have also blown the suspension of Bigelow on Monday. Jason and I started talking, even arguing. I talked so much that my cigar went out," said Easter, "so I asked Jason, who was sitting behind his desk, for a match. He didn't carry matches but looked inside his center desk drawer for one. He gasped and I didn't know what was the matter. He got up, looking sick, and walked away from his desk. He said that a dead rat had been left in his desk drawer, and he wanted a transfer. He was in bad shape and the distribution center was in bad shape, so I had the opening in the Boston area and I let him have it. Actually, right now he and his family are vacationing somewhere in Eastern Canada. He needs the rest."

Fosdick was beginning to feel sorry that he knew all the details, but he persisted. "Then what?" he asked Easter.

"Well, I took over running the distribution center. I phoned Meyers again, and he and I had lunch. He thought that Jason had blown the case against Bigelow and that we should take him back. So on Friday, Meyers, Bigelow, the union attorney, the shop steward, Bigelow's supervisor, and I met. Jason, of course, was not there. It was a pleasant meeting. Everything got blamed on poor Jason. I did tell Bigelow that we would be documenting his performance and wanted him to know that Jason's successor, meaning you, was under my instructions to tolerate no nonsense. Bigelow was so pleasant that day that I could not imagine him in the role of a troublemaker. The amazing thing was that, when he went out into the center to resume work, a loud cheer went up and all the drivers started blowing their lift-truck horns. For a moment, I was afraid all the batteries would run down again. But I was wrong. They were plain happy to see Bigelow back. You know, the slowdown was still in effect when Bigelow walked onto the floor. I'd say it was 10:00 A.M. and they were an hour behind. Well, let me tell you what happened. They went to work! By noon we were back on schedule, and by the end of the shift we were a half-hour ahead of schedule. In fact, the last half-hour was spent straightening up many of the bins that had been deliberately disarranged during the slowdown. I tell you, Tom Bigelow does set the work pace in that warehouse!"

"So what do you suggest I do at the center?" asked Fosdick.

"Well, the key is getting along with Bigelow. Talk to Meyers about the kind of records you should keep in case you decide to move against Bigelow. Be sure to consult with Meyers before you do anything irreversible. Frankly, I don't know whether Bigelow will be a problem. We never had trouble with him that I knew about before Jason was there. According to Bigelow and the union attorney, Jason had it in for Bigelow. If I were you, I'd take it easy with Bigelow and other labor problems. See what you can do instead about the inventory shrinkage."

On the next Monday morning, Fosdick showed up at the Providence distribution center. After gingerly looking in all his desk drawers, he had a brief meeting with his supervisors and then walked out to meet the entire workforce on a one-to-one basis. Many remembered Fosdick from his earlier visits to the facility. Because it was a Monday morning, he had not expected to encounter Bigelow, who was present, clear-eyed, alert, and enthusiastic. Bigelow was happy to see Fosdick and shook his hand warmly. Bigelow then excused himself, saying he had to return to work. The truck dispatcher said that the workforce was ahead of schedule again: It was 11:00 A.M., and they were about 15 minutes ahead. Fosdick returned to his office, and there was a phone message from Ed Meyers. Meyers asked to postpone their luncheon for that day until Tuesday noon. Then Robert Easter called to ask how things were going on Fosdick's first day. Easter was pleased that things were going smoothly.

It was lunchtime. Fosdick decided to walk to a small café where he had eaten at other times. It was two blocks from the distribution center and on the side away from the office. So he walked through the center, which was quiet since it was closed down for lunch. He walked by the employees' lunchroom and heard the normal sounds of 50 people eating and talking. Just outside the lunchroom was one lift truck with an empty wooden pallet on it. As Fosdick watched, one of the stock clerks came out of the lunchroom with an opened case of sweet pickles from

which three jars had been taken. Next came another stock clerk with an opened carton of mustard from which two bottles had been removed. One of the clerks suddenly saw Fosdick and said weakly, "We take these opened cases to the damaged merchandise room." Fosdick went into the lunchroom. There, on the center table were cases of cold meat, cheese, soft drinks, mayonnaise, and bread. All had been opened and partially emptied to provide the workers' lunches.

Bigelow was making himself a large sandwich when he saw Fosdick approach. "Don't get uptight," he said to Fosdick. "You've just come across one of the noncontract fringe benefits of working at the Red Spot Providence distribution center. May I make you a sandwich?"

QUESTIONS

1. How should Fosdick respond to the immediate situation?
2. What controls, of the types discussed in this chapter, might have been used by Red Spot Markets to reduce or eliminate the problems discussed in the case?
3. What longer-range steps should Fosdick take to control the operations of the Providence distribution center?
4. What longer-range steps should Fosdick take to improve the Providence distribution center's productivity?
5. What longer-range steps can Fosdick take to reduce the distribution center's high rate of shrinkage?
6. Assume that Fosdick decides that the practice of free lunches from the opened

cases of goods must be stopped. Develop and present the arguments he should give in a meeting with the union shop steward.

7. (This is a continuation of question 6.) Assume, instead, that you are the union shop steward. Develop and present your argument that the free lunches represent a long-standing employee benefit enjoyed by the distribution center's employees and that management's attempt to stop them is a breach of an unwritten contract and will be resisted.

8. Much of the situation described in the case seems to evolve around the personality of T. D. Bigelow. How should he be treated? Why?

14

Logistics Systems: Analysis, Design, and Integration

Automatic Guided Vehicle

Key Terms

- Benchmarking
- Channels audit
- Competition audit
- Customer audit
- Direct product profitability (DPP) analysis
- Environmental sensitivity audit
- Existing facilities audit
- Integrated service providers
- Linking-pin organization
- Matrix management
- Product audit
- Simulation
- System constraints
- Systems analysis
- Third-party, or contract, logistics
- Unified department organization
- Vendor audit

Learning Objectives

- To examine the problems and opportunities involved in systems analysis
- To relate the importance of industry standards to systems analysis
- To discuss the steps involved in redesigning a logistics system
- To examine a number of organizational alternatives
- To describe a number of techniques for achieving logistics coordination and integration
- To distinguish between centralized and decentralized logistics organizations
- To distinguish between logistics within the firm and outsourcing logistics activities

Logistics concepts and practices are well in place. Sometimes, they are too well in place and might even be considered inflexible. This chapter deals with how a logistics system is analyzed with the idea in mind to redesign the system if that is found to be necessary. Part of the redesign effort also recognizes that the firm sees itself as part of a supply chain and that today's system must have closer links with both suppliers and customers than was once the case.

This chapter has three main parts. The first explores systems analysis; the second focuses on system design; and the third presents systems integration, both within the firm and within the supply chain.

What Is Systems Analysis?

Because little in the business world is static, a system that optimizes yesterday's situation may be less than optimal today and, especially, tomorrow. Logistics and supply chains, of course, are no exception. Markets shift constantly; even public utilities do not consider their demand patterns fixed. As electricity market deregulation has opened up new markets to electricity suppliers, business consumers in many locations today are being asked to choose the supplier of electricity to their places of work and negotiate prices. Relationships with partners in the supply chain also change.

As used in this text, the term **systems analysis** refers to the orderly and planned observation of one or more segments in the logistics network or supply chain in order to determine how well each segment and the entire system function. Systems analysis can be a simple operation, such as a time-and-motion study of individuals who handle incoming freight at a receiving dock, or it can be nationwide or global in scope, with the objective of completely redesigning a firm's entire logistics system, including its relationships with many longtime suppliers and customers. The observations provide data that are subjected to statistical analysis. In some situations, the next step is to incorporate the data into programmed models of the supply-chain network. A model simulates real conditions to determine how well the present system or a contemplated system would respond to various happenings. Based on the simulation and other analyses, the final procedure may involve redesigning the entire supply-chain system.

Many firms have personnel who conduct systems analysis projects throughout the firm. Other firms prefer to use outside consultants because they can be more objective. Although consultants vary in quality, they bring outside viewpoints and broader perspectives to bear on most problems. In supply-chain situations involving related firms, a consultant may appear to be more neutral than a representative of either firm.

For any type of analysis, several general questions must be asked. One set of useful questions is offered by consultant William Copacino:

Why do we perform each task?
What value is added by it?
Why are the tasks performed in the order they are?
Can we alter the sequence of the processing steps to increase efficiency?
Why are the tasks performed by a particular group or individual?
Could others perform this task?
Is there a better way for the system to operate?[1]

When we think of systems analysis in a supply-chain context, these questions become considerably more specific:

Supplier: Where to acquire materials and components?
Manufacturer: Where to produce and assemble goods? How much to produce?
Warehouse: Where to store finished goods? How to retrieve from storage?
Transportation: What fleet size? What vehicle routes? What shipment routes?
Customers: What markets to serve? What level of service? What level of cost?[2]

Answering questions such as these requires a thorough understanding of the interrelationships in the supply chain among appropriate technology use, planning, manufacturing scale versus flexibility, order fulfillment policies, life cycle management, the number of stock-keeping units (SKUs), number of vendors, lot sizes, manufacturing

---

[1]Cited in James Drogan, "The Role of Information Systems in the Preparation and Management of Transportation Service Packages," *Proceedings of Forward Motion: A Conference Sponsored by Burlington Northern* (Dallas, November 3-4, 1988), p. BNS-5.

[2]Adapted from Donald H. Ratliff and William G. Nulty, "Logistics Composite Modeling," a technical white paper from CAPS Logistics, 1996, p. 3.

capacity and expandability, service levels and stocking locations, order processing, forecasting and forecast errors, scheduling, and warehouse efficiency (among others).

Problems in Systems Analysis

How to focus a logistics systems analysis (or audit) is the first and often the most difficult part of developing a system. Should it focus on the work practices at the receiving dock, on the dock's location in the building, or on the building's location in the system? Are the products being handled properly? Are customer service standards adequate, or should the order management function be fully automated? What is the competition doing?

The types of systems analyses that might be performed are limited only by the analyst's imagination and the amount of money that the firm or client is willing to spend for the analysis. Figure 14-1 shows a checklist prepared by a consultant; it lists some of the questions that a firm should address in determining whether systems analysis is needed. Firms with high scores (more needs) are advised to "conduct a strategy study to redirect the logistics functions to more closely correlate to the business strategy of the company."

Another problem of focus deals with the time span for the implementation of new ideas. Some improvements might be only for specific adjustments within the supply chain without altering the chain member relationships. Ordering procedures or packaging may be changed, or a decision might be made to change some aspect of shared information systems. More basic changes, such as changes in the number and location of distribution centers, take more time to implement. There might be a period of overlap when the old system is being phased out as the new one is being phased in. Maintaining levels of customer service during this period would likely be difficult. Long-range changes (taking from 2 to 5 years to implement) result from decisions to redesign a firm's entire logistics system and its relationships with others in the supply chain.

Friction is inherent in any attempt to analyze and redesign a supply-chain system. Operations managers are typically performing as well as they can. Systems analysts, whether employees of the firm or outside consultants, cannot continue in business by telling every client that all aspects of the present operation are perfect. If analysts did so, they could not justify their functions. Thus, their goals and the goals of operating personnel and operating managers differ. Labor may view with suspicion any suggestion that appears to be a speed-up, that might reduce the hours or number of workers needed, or that hints that facilities might be closed.

When considering any logistics reengineering or full system analysis, consider the following five issues suggested by Professors Ratliff and Nulty:

1. Multiple business functions (beyond logistics) are impacted.
2. There are trade-offs among conflicting objectives.
3. Logistics system impacts are difficult to precisely evaluate.
4. There are business issues unique to each logistics system.
5. Quantitative analysis is essential for intelligent decisions.[3]

---

[3]Ratliff and Nulty, 1996, p. 3.

To analyze your business, answer the following Key Logistics Strategy Questions........

Circle the appropriate number next to the question.

	Significant	Moderate	Somewhat	Not Applicable

COMPANY MARKETS

1) Has your company recently opened (or closed) new market areas generating need for additional logistics and customer service capability? — 6 4 2 0

2) Has there been a shift in the shipments to the types of customers within your company? (wholesalers, distributors, retailers, etc.) — 9 6 3 0

COMPANY PRODUCTS

3) Have there been additions and/or deletions to your company's product lines? — 6 4 2 0

4) Has a recent ABC analysis produced a difference in major and minor volume products? — 4 3 2 0

CUSTOMER SERVICE

5) Has a survey of representative customers indicated service problems? — 4 3 2 0

6) Has the customer service complaint level increased recently? — 4 3 2 0

7) Have there been any changes in EDP systems or order processing which have resulted in modifications to order cycle times? — 6 4 2 0

8) Have other system changes altered inventory reporting, resulting in increased stock outs? — 6 4 2 0

LOGISTICS OPERATIONS

9) Have internal distribution center operating factors such as labor or facility costs caused changes in location and/or operations? — 6 4 2 0

10) Has purchasing, engineering, or marketing made changes to type, quality, pack, unit, or size of product packaging? — 6 4 2 0

11) Has marketing or sales altered the characteristics (size, cycle, timing, etc.) of product promotions? — 6 4 2 0

12) Have you reached capacity in terms of volume or inventory of existing distribution facilities? — 9 6 3 0

13) Do you shuttle amounts of product between distribution locations? — 6 4 2 0

TRANSPORTATION OPERATIONS

14) Has the profile of product shipments changed in terms of TL, LTL, UPS, etc.? — 6 4 2 0

15) Does the company move inbound and outbound products across common shipping lanes? — 6 4 2 0

PRODUCT OPERATIONS

16) Has the company changed or introduced new production source points for products? — 9 6 3 0

17) Has product capacity been changed at existing production locations? — 6 4 2 0

18) Do frequent changes occur in production schedules and between product source points? — 4 3 2 0

OTHER

19) Have distribution and transportation costs increased as a percent of sales? — 9 6 3 0

20) Have there been internal structural changes within the company resulting in integration or segregation of primary business operating units? — 9 6 3 0

TOTAL POINTS

If your total points are:

* **Less than 40** - you have outlined minor issues which should be addressed as a part of your overall planning process

* **Between 40 and 70** - you should prioritize these issues and structure an analysis effort to resolve them as a part of a specific plan

* **Over 70** - you should conduct a strategy study to redirect the logistics functions to more closely correlate to the business strategy of the company.

FIGURE 14-1 A Scoring Checklist Used to Determine Logistics Planning or Strategy Study

Source: Courtesy of Robert E. Murray of REM Associates.

453

Partial Systems Analysis

It is often not feasible to examine all functioning aspects of a system. What follows are examples of analysis focused on a single aspect of logistics. Sometimes, for the purposes intended, partial analysis is sufficient. However, its confined focus is also a limitation because whatever findings are developed are also narrow. They cannot be used to improve an entire system, nor do partial systems analyses work well within the context of an overall reengineering effort.

Figure 14-2 shows the dockside operations of the Beaver Island Boat Company ferry *Emerald Isle* in Charlevoix, Michigan (*www.bibco.com*). The forklift is handling a large metal basket container with sides folded down to accommodate loose construction material. Similar basket containers, folded up, are also shown on the dock. These containers provide the advantages of unit-load handling while allowing a wide variation in the size and shape of the individual cartons (or smaller building blocks). The use of such specialized equipment would probably be justified after analysis of practices by shippers to the island, as well as at the businesses on the island where they are received and unloaded. The combined transportation and handling savings for both the shippers and receivers must be sufficient to justify the investment in the equipment. If the savings are not evenly divided between the shippers and receivers, the party enjoying the greater share of savings may have to compensate the other, in order for the other party to agree to make whatever changes

FIGURE 14-2 Operations of the Beaver Island Boat Company

are needed to accommodate the new equipment. Such decisions would be the result of partial systems analysis.

The only danger posed by making decisions based on partial analysis of a system is that one might inadvertently commit the entire system without having tested whether the entire system would benefit. An example is a commitment to use only railroads for outbound shipments of oversized machines while the firm's marketing planners might be deciding that the best potential for sales growth is, for various reasons, customers who are not located on railroad sidings.

Partial analysis is one of the building blocks of total systems analysis. It is difficult to measure a system's overall performance without measuring and understanding the performance of the various components that make up the entire system. Partial analysis contributes toward an understanding of how an entire system functions. Several examples are cited on the following pages. An explanation of why partial analysis was performed in each case is also offered.

Customer Profitability Analysis

The following example is an old one but a very useful teaching tool. It deals with a route-analysis system that a large dairy chain used to help its delivery personnel analyze the profitability of each stop on their routes. The accompanying forms are filled out by hand. Although both the forms and the procedures appear unsophisticated by today's standards, they force the individual involved to focus directly on the question of what makes a customer profitable or unprofitable. Figure 14-3 is a time tally sheet completed by the driver/salesperson's supervisor on a day he or she travels along, carrying—and using—a stopwatch.[4]

The data collected on the form shown in Figure 14-3 and from the driver/salesperson's monthly records were transferred to several other forms so that they could be analyzed more critically. Figure 14-4 is a tally sheet showing each customer's dollar volume across the top and the number of deliveries the customer receives along the vertical axis. It uses the same data and points out which customers are to be considered over-serviced. A high dollar volume combined with a low number of deliveries per month is the goal. Thus, entries toward the upper right-hand corner of the chart show more desirable stops. Entries in the lower left-hand corner of the chart represent less desirable stops. A step downward, a diagonal line is drawn between the upper left-hand and lower right-hand corners. The inference drawn is that entries below the diagonal should be shifted either upward or to the right or both (or eliminated).

The reason these forms are relatively unsophisticated is that the driver/salesperson is an independent or semi-independent operator. He or she sells, delivers, and decides who should and should not receive various types of service. Because the driver/salesperson is paid a salary plus commission, the commission portion of his or her pay is an incentive not to waste time. However, the dairy is interested in time utilization because it pays the salary part of the wages. Rather than tell the driver/salesperson whom he or she can and cannot serve, the dairy has to use this approach to demonstrate how time can be reallocated in a more productive manner.

---

[4]The dairy supplying these forms asked not to be identified.

```
AM Starting Time, Load a/o Unload_____  Time_4:10_  Salesman_Gary H_
Starting Mileage (at plant)_____568_____  Time_4:15_  Route #_9_
Mileage at First Stop_____569_____  Time_4:18_  Super._Alan B_
Mileage at Last Stop_____590_____  Time_11:45_
Ending Mileage (at plant)_____573_____  Time_11:54_
PM Ending Time, Load a/o Unload_45 min_  Time_12:41
Check In (Finish Day)_____12 min_____  Time_12:56_
                    Total Time:  Hours_8_   Minutes_46_
```

	Front Porch			Back Porch	Inside or Ask		Solicitations		
Time 1st hour: 5:18	45	35	30	85			Hour_6 xL_ Time_:51_		
	55	30	35	75			Hour_6 xL_ Time_5:03_		
Miles 1st hour: 574	90	110	120	85			Hour_6 xL_ Time_1:01_		
	63	55	34	103	NONE		Hour___ Time___		
Dollars Sold: 30.31 ave 1.13	88	35		50			Hour___ Time___		
	50	55					Hour___ Time___		
Accounts Served: 20 5 10	45	51					Hour___ Time___		
	45	30							
Time 2nd hour: 6:18	20	35	42	30	75		Collections from Customers		
	23	87	38	30	120		not receiving delivery:		
Miles 2nd hour: 577	35	60	28	50	60		Hour_2 AD_ Time_3_ _0_		
	30	30	25	70	61		Hour_7 TH_ Time___ _33_		
Dollars Sold: 25 ave 111	182	38	48	60	60	NONE	Hour___ Time___		
	30	108	70				Hour___ Time___		
	23	64	82				Hour___ Time___		
Accounts Served: 22 5 10	45	44	37				Hour___ Time___		
Time 3rd hour: 7:18	20	30	40		120		Hour___ Time___		
	25	38	23				Hour___ Time___		
Miles 3rd hour: 580	42	41					Hour___ Time___		
	55	41					Hour___ Time___		
Dollars Sold: 33 ¼ ave 193	70	28		NONE			TOTAL → 3 33 ½		
	92	65							
Accounts Served: 18 5 9	22	45		53	85	195	Rest/Eating Stops:		
				56	128	240	Hour_3 RD_ Time_30:0_		
Time 4:__	44			120	95		Hour_4 TH_ Time_11:8_		
Dollars Sold: 31 ¼ ave 100	30			55	98		Hour_7 TH_ Time_31:4_		
	17			50	97		Hour___ Time___		
	20			60	120		Hour___ Time___		
Accounts Served: 10 7 9	27			35	20		Hour___ Time___		
							TOTAL → 58 min 12 sec		
Time 6th hour: 10:18	20			73	170		REMARKS:		
	31			73	110		MARK UP Book 1 ST. 7.00		
Miles 6th hour: 586	10			90	85		" " " 2 ND 5.20		
	75			45	60		" " " 3 RD 3:00		
	55			75	180		" " " 4 TH 4:00		
Dollars Sold: 3401 ave 148	58			75	120		STRAIGHTEN TRUCK OUT 6.00		
	30			126	120		MARK UP Book 6 TH 3:50		
Accounts Served: 7 8 18				117	126		TOTAL → 28 min 50 sec		
c 7th hour: 11:18	30			65	77		BROKE UP 2 TIMES BECAUSE OF		
	48			60	290		DEAD END STREET TOOK ≈ 30 sec		
Miles 7th hour: 589	23			63	77				
	47			40	85				
	42				90		DELIVERIES	170	
Dollars Sold: 14.49 ave 104							DOLLAR SALES	191.53	
Accounts Served: 5 4 15							COMMISSION	32.92	
							SALES PER STOP	1.13	

FIGURE 14-3 Home Delivery Route Management Growth Program Tally Sheet

Warehousing Productivity Analysis

In determining the productivity of warehousing, many variables must be considered, not all of which will be relevant to all kinds of distribution facilities. Typical measures of *warehouse productivity* may include costs of storage, packing, marking, and shipping; vehicle, dock, or facility throughput; losses and damage; demurrage charges incurred or

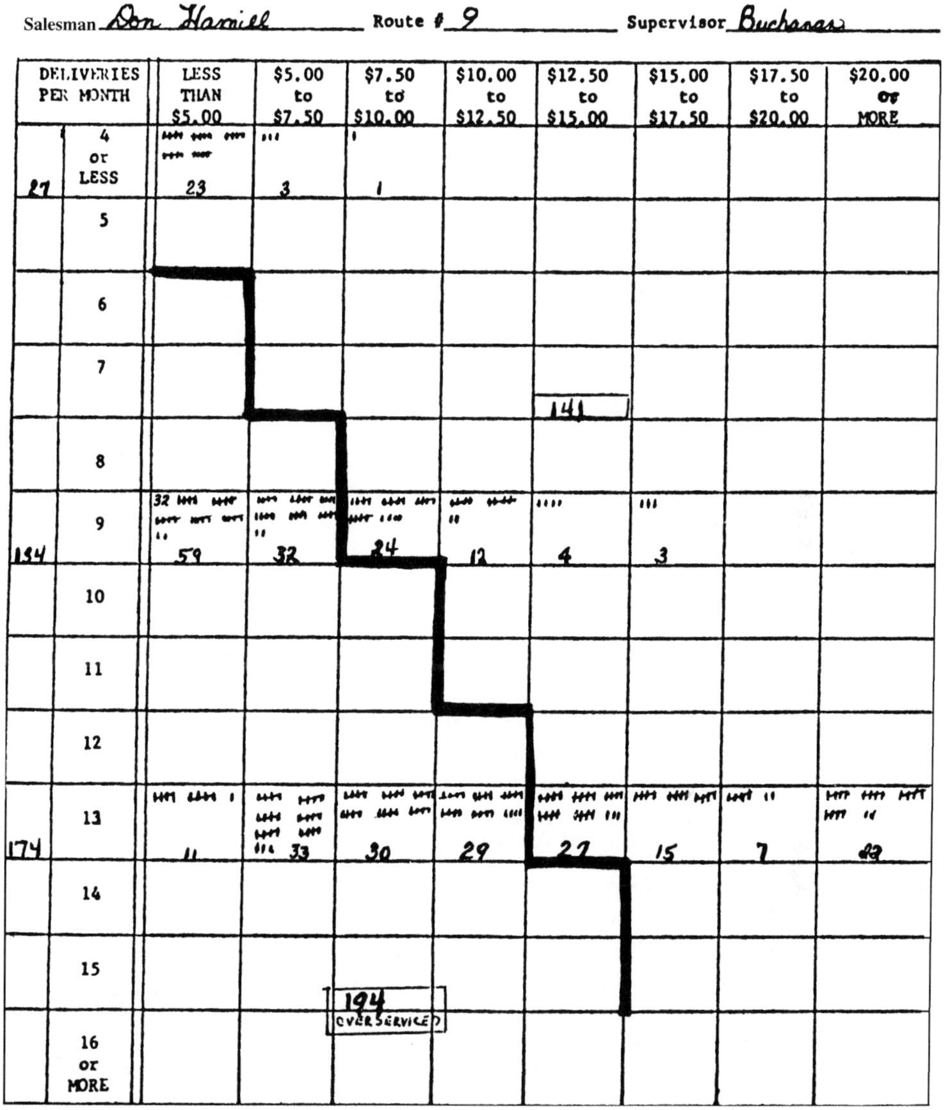

Salesman _Don Hamill_ _____ Route # _9_ _____ Supervisor _Buchanan_ _____

DELIVERIES PER MONTH		LESS THAN $5.00	$5.00 to $7.50	$7.50 to $10.00	$10.00 to $12.50	$12.50 to $15.00	$15.00 to $17.50	$17.50 to $20.00	$20.00 or MORE
27	4 or LESS	23	3	1					
	5								
	6								
	7					141			
	8								
154	9	59	32	24	12	4	3		
	10								
	11								
	12								
174	13	11	33	30	29	27	15	7	22
	14								
	15		194 OVERSERVICED						
	16 or MORE								

FIGURE 14-4 Home Delivery Route Management Growth Program Graphic Analysis

avoided; labor costs and efficiencies; customer satisfaction; and taxation and investment issues. One could make various comparisons for each warehouse activity (such as packing and marking) or for all specific activities combined (in the category of overall output or throughput). Benchmarking comparisons could then be made with other facilities or with measures for other time periods in order to determine the relative performance of each activity.

In the early 1990s, the Warehousing Education and Research Council (WERC) released a software package developed by Professor Thomas W. Speh for determining warehousing costs. The spreadsheet model allows costs to be analyzed by several variables, such as handling expense per labor hour, storage expense per gross foot, and handling and storage costs per unit.[5] During the late 1990s, many warehouse operators found themselves facing downsizing as a means to control costs. WERC recommended warehouse operators to first reengineer their businesses and then consider appropriate downsizing. They identified five key steps in warehouse engineering:

1. Develop critical success factors and performance measurement systems. In general, this involves asking the question "What do we have to do to become successful?" Once critical success factors are identified, managers must develop ways to measure progress toward success.
2. Assess the current environment. This assessment must include a frank evaluation of the organization and jobs, along with flowcharting the activities required to distribute products.
3. Identify profit improvement opportunities. This step requires identifying which processes add value for customers and which do not. The presumption is that customers are willing to pay for value added.
4. Design target environment and change plan. The organization examines its goals and current situation and begins to design a process for change. Managerial ideas for profit improvement must be specified in ways that can be implemented.
5. Implement target environment and follow up. As implementation is rolled out, performance measurement systems developed in step 1 must be used to monitor progress and success.[6]

Transportation Cost Analysis

With the widespread use of computers, it is now much easier to analyze transportation costs. UPS offers a service to shippers of small packages that examines inbound or outbound deliveries for a representative period of time using data gathered from the company's actual paid freight bills. The service also includes an analysis of what costs would be if varying combinations of UPS's three priority systems—UPS Next Day Air, UPS 2nd Day Air, and UPS Ground—are used.[7] UPS's competitor FedEx has a similar service that allows its customers to analyze transportation costs, using FedEx-supplied software running on the customer's computers and accessing an online FedEx data base.[8] Most freight carriers will work with shippers to determine whether individual shipments or shipment patterns can be improved.

Transportation cost analysis often focuses on outbound freight; not to be overlooked are potential savings on inbound freight costs. With the emphasis on supply-chain management, optimal performance also requires that a firm examine inbound

---

[5]*A Model for Determining Total Warehousing Costs for Private, Public, and Contract Warehouses* (Oak Brook, IL: Warehousing and Education Research Council, 1991).

[6]Adapted from Brian Peregoff, "Reengineer Before You Downsize," *WERC Sheet,* October 1995, p. 5.

[7]www.ups.com.

[8]www.fedex.com.

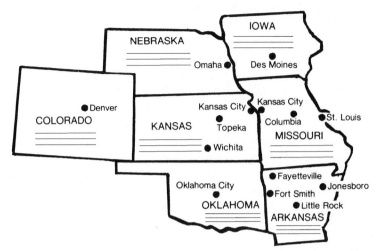

The user is instructed to list on the lines within each state the cities to which shipments from a common point are made, and their weights. The circles indicate cities where the carrier who supplies this form has terminals.

FIGURE 14-5 Excerpt of 48-state Worksheet for Preliminary Freight Consolidation Analysis

Source: Interstate System, Marketing Department, Physical Distribution Audit Map (Grand Rapids, MI). Reproduced with permission.

freight costs as aggressively as it does outbound. In the past, many managers preferred to simply include inbound freight in the cost of goods, thus ceding control of an important cost center to the expertise of the firm's suppliers. Because inbound freight is more related to internal operations with a firm (as opposed to outbound freight being more connected with customer satisfaction), it should be viewed in transportation cost analysis from the perspective of planning and control.[9]

Consolidation Analysis

Transportation costs are lower per unit of weight for larger shipments. Because of this, there is always a motivation to consolidate small shipments into larger ones. Figure 14-5 is from a worksheet once used for *consolidation analysis.* One would write the shipments going to each state on the sheet. Today, computer programs that handle shipping documentation generate similar analysis using zip codes.

U.S. retailer Dress Barn, specializing in women's apparel, uses the consolidation expertise of a freight forwarder to consolidate shipments from its suppliers in India, Pakistan, Sri Lanka, and Bangladesh to ensure that its goods move in 40-foot containers rather than in 20-foot containers. "If we moved freight in twenty foot containers, we would be paying 75 percent of the cost for a forty foot container," said Henry Snell, the traffic manager for Dress Barn.[10]

---

[9]Jack Ampuja and Ray Pucci, "Inbound Freight: Often a Missed Opportunity," *Supply Chain Management Review,* Vol. 6, No. 2, pp. 50–57.

[10]Chris Gillis, "Cents-able Shipping," *American Shipper,* June 1996, p. 28.

Direct Product Profitability Analysis

Often used in the grocery industry, **direct product profitability (DPP) analysis** involves calculations of the "real costs and profitability of distributing each individual product item for the manufacturer, through all the distribution activities (transportation, handling, storage, order processing, etc.) to the final customer."[11] Custom software is written and used for DPP—although a spreadsheet can be used—and some simplifying assumptions have to be made regarding cost allocation (for example, how does one determine and allocate the costs of shelf space in a retail store or of slots in a warehouse?). Even determining the precise costs of the goods may be difficult because some discounts and allowances are based on the dollar size of the entire order, whereas transportation costs or savings are often based on the order's total weight (or cubic volume). The DPP system is most useful to manufacturers looking to analyze alternative packaging and product densities, different routes, different handling systems, and the like.

Benchmarking

Benchmarking of logistics operations, as practiced today by firms in the United States, involves having four to six noncompeting firms get together to analyze and measure how they compare with each other when performing various tasks and/or processes. For benchmarking, one tries to find other firms that are logistically similar enough that something can be learned from studying their operations. A firm would be concerned when costs of its operation seem high compared with those of other participants in the same category. For example, five firms that all warehouse pallet loads could compare warehouse operations and costs in terms of costs as percentage of sales, costs per units handled, and units per worker hour. Costs could be broken down into labor, space, and equipment.

Benchmarking is also used to compare a firm's service measures to noncompeting firms or to some theoretical ideal system. For example, a firm may wish to consider its operations in terms of orders shipped complete, timeliness with which an order is received, order accuracy, customer satisfaction, or any other characteristic related to service operations. By benchmarking both costs and service measures, a firm is better able to understand the trade-offs that necessarily exist in its own system. Firms may also use internal benchmarking to study changes in their own operations over time.

Benchmarking consultants Debra Hofman and Larry Lapide offer five suggestions for improving benchmarking:

- [Measures] should evaluate progress in implementing the best-practice and technology enablers that affect operational performance.
- Benchmarking needs to occur routinely to accommodate rapid changes in technological capabilities.
- Ownership needs to move beyond the functions to a strategic level that . . . focuses more on the overall strategic goals of the business.

---

[11]Donald Firth, et al. *Profitable Logistics Management,* rev. ed. (Toronto: McGraw-Hill Ryerson, 1989), p. 316.

- A balanced set of customer-focused [measures] linked to the business strategy and benchmarking results must be consistently managed.

They rightly point out that a firm need not be number one in each activity and that some activities performed may actually have trade-offs from a customer service standpoint (e.g., transportation costs versus delivery times). And finally,

- Benchmarking must be conducted beyond a company's immediate group of competitors—and beyond even its industry. The latest innovations in technology and business practices may not reside within your industry.[12]

Industry Standards Analysis

Industry standards analysis is performed by a trade association (rather than an individual firm) on an industrywide basis. Individual firms cooperate by supplying data about their operations to a centralized research body. The researcher then compiles data for the entire industry and reports the data in a manner that maintains each firm's anonymity. The participating firms then use the tabulations to determine how their performances compare to that of the industry as a whole.

One example of such a study involved periodic tabulations regarding operations of grocery chain distribution centers. Respondents responsible for operating 50 different distribution centers supplied the data. The researchers then compiled and analyzed the data and found five key measures: tons per worker-hour of direct labor, cases per worker-hour of direct labor, tons per hour of total labor, cases per hour of total labor, and cases selected, or picked, per worker-hour. Data were also given for rates of unloading trucks, picking orders by use of various types of equipment (tow trains, chain tows, hand trucks, and pallet jacks), and loading outgoing trucks with cargo that is unitized or in baskets or cages. Good performance by some criteria must sometimes be paid for by poorer performance by other criteria.

Industry standards are also sometimes used by industry groups to bring about industrywide changes that will result in the smoother, lower-cost flow of materials. One example is the grocery industry, which has achieved standardized pallet and unit-load dimensions, minimum standards for load stability, maximum weight per carton, and uniform markings. A firm may try to get the industry to move in a more efficient direction. Apple Computer, for example, tried to get the computer industry to move from the use of pallets to slipsheets. One reason for this is that many of the industry's inputs originate in Japan, where the cost of wooden pallets is about five times their cost in the United States.

Logistics System Design

Logistics encompasses a wide range of activities. Because the various functional areas of logistics interact, logistics system design is a complex undertaking that requires sophisticated analytical techniques. One commonly used procedure—simulation—is examined briefly later in this chapter.

---

[12]Debra Hofman and Larry Lapide, "The New Benchmarking," *Supply Chain Management Review,* Vol. 6, No. 1, 2002, pp. 15–16.

Unlike partial systems analysis, in which a part of the system is examined, logistics system design looks at the entire logistics system to determine how well all of its components function together.

Establishing Objectives and Constraints

Before a logistics system can be designed or redesigned, it is imperative that the system goals and the system objectives of the analysis be delineated. Is cost cutting the objective? Are profits and return on investment the goals? Must customer service standards be improved? How would improved control over the flow of inbound materials influence the performance of the assembly line? Are the goals long- or short-term in nature? Following is an example of a clearly stated objective:

> **Eighteen months from the start of this study, the objectives stated here will be achieved at the lowest possible cost.**

1. Order transmittal time for our customers will be less than 24 hours.
2. Orders will be processed within 16 working hours of receipt.
3. Eighty percent of orders will be completely assembled within 16 working hours. All orders will be assembled within 24 working hours.
4. Order delivery time from our dock will be no longer than 96 hours for 85 percent of all customers. All domestic orders must be delivered within 6 days of tendering to the carrier.
5. Stockouts will not be accepted for greater than 7 percent of units requested. Customers experiencing a stockout will be immediately advised by phone. The out-of-stock product will be replaced within 10 days, and expedited transportation will be used to reach the customer.

Note that the example presents measurable objectives. This is important because when the study is completed and the new system implemented, it will be possible to determine whether the objectives are being met. Objectives that can be measured also serve as a psychological stimulus to managers, who can use them to determine whether their efforts are successful. Each objective presented above is also specific in terms of task and timing. Objectives must also be achievable within the context of a firm's operational scope.

Goals tend to be somewhat broader than objectives; examples are increased market share, cost minimization, and profit maximization. Two frequently mentioned goals today are developing and adhering to quality programs, and being a leading-edge or world-class logistics partner.

Quality Programs

Quality is often defined, in terms of goods or services, as those which meet or exceed customer expectations. Quality and *quality programs* have always been important to logistics operations, and today nearly all firms pursue so-called quality objectives for several reasons. One is the just-in-time (JIT) inventory system approach, which leaves no spare inventory to fall back on in case a defect is found. A second is dramatic improvement in logistics operations technology. An example of this would be the use of radio-dispatched warehouse forklifts with on-board computers, which help to improve order pick accuracy and orders shipped complete. A third reason is that as possibilities for partnership arrangements present themselves, a company is wary of being linked to a supplier that does not share similar ideas or beliefs about quality measures or concepts. There are a number of independent sources of quality standards. The International Organization for Standards (ISO) (*www.iso.org*) offers engineering-based standards for developing, sustaining, and managing quality. (Some quality programs were discussed in Chapter 11.)

World-Class Logistics Programs

Some firms have already achieved such outstanding competence in their practice of logistics that it sets them apart from their competitors. For some, this is slightly different from a quality program, in that its focus is on activities in the logistics chain. For a firm that already has a world-class logistics operation, those attempting to design or reengineer the system should realize that this is a competitive advantage that should be maintained. Efforts should be made to get other functions of the firm and its supply-chain partners to function at equally high levels. A firm that is already in a world-class position might not be engaged in reengineering its processes. However, it would keep reorganization and restructuring options open. Planning—whether it involves structural change or not—is important.

> It is also important to realize that logistical change typically requires the alignment of many aspects of a company's operation that are outside the direct control of the logistics executive. One executive stressed the fundamental importance of leadership by estimating that only 20 percent of the typical logistical change initiative involves the direct work of logistics and the remaining 80 percent involves the responsibilities of other managers impacted by the logistical process. Thus, logistical change leaders must sell ideas and serve as cross-functional catalysts. Managing change through others is a difficult task that logistics leaders need to master.[13]

Before system design or redesign can be initiated, there must be agreement on the goals and the measurable objectives. System constraints must also be considered.

System Constraints

System constraints, if any, must also be specified; these involve factors in the system that cannot be changed for various reasons. The following are some examples of system constraints:

1. The distribution center at Detroit will not be closed nor its employment decreased because the firm has publicly pledged to support the downtown area of this city.
2. Order transmittal will continue to be based on an Internet-based system because the software and equipment were purchased just 6 months ago at a cost of $2.5 million.
3. Ron's Trucking Company will be utilized whenever it has competitive trucking rates.

---

[13]The Global Logistics Research Team at Michigan State University, *World Class Logistics: The Challenge of Managing Continuous Change* (Oak Brook, IL: Council of Logistics Management, 1995), p. 296.

4. No operational unit of the company may have more than 50 employees in a single location.[14]

In one sense, each system constraint simplifies the situation because it tends to reduce the number of alternatives to be analyzed. However, it is usually fair for the study team to question some of the constraints, especially if their impact may run counter to the stated goals and objectives.

An example of a real constraint from a fantasy situation involves Disneyland in Anaheim, California. Only nighttime (11:15 P.M. to 7:15 A.M.) deliveries are allowed from a central warehouse to 110 vending locations throughout the theme park. When Disney World in Florida was built, this constraint was overcome by constructing a network of tunnels and distribution, storage, and preparation facilities beneath the new park so that shops and restaurants are serviced, invisibly to park guests, at any time. Vendors in Disney World, freed from the physical constraints of Disneyland, operate with lower inventory and warehousing costs.

Another system constraint is shown in Figure 14-6. Here, the bridge opening limits the width of what can pass through.

Organization of the Study Team

Once the measurable objectives are established and the system constraints outlined, the next step is to organize the firm's personnel for the analysis. It is preferable to have two separate groups working on the analysis. One group, the working analysis team, includes the managers of the functional areas involved and other staff and quantitative specialists. The customer service director, transportation manager, warehousing manager, director of purchasing, production scheduler, and other relevant managers are members of this team. Any outside management consultants that are used work with the working analysis team on a daily basis. The team is responsible for the actual analysis performed and for the testing, design, and implementation of the new system.

The other group, the management supervisory committee, works with the working analysis team. Its members represent a broader perspective or the overall viewpoint of the firm. Marketing, law, finance, and production personnel, as well as accounting executives, are represented on the committee. The group is on call to clarify and amplify system objectives. It also occasionally probes the working analysis team about why certain actions are being taken.

Data Collection

Another important stage in designing a logistics system involves data collection. Obviously, the validity of the study can be no stronger than the accuracy of the database. Seven comprehensive audits must be performed. They are the product, existing facilities, vendor, customer, channels, competitor, and environmental sensitivity audits.

---

[14]A consultant actually encountered exactly this constraint in building a simulation model for a company's distribution system. The rationale for the constraint was that more than 50 employees at a single location might lead to the formation of a union in this currently nonunion company.

FIGURE 14-6 A Floating Dry Dock Passing Through a Bridge in Portland, Oregon

Source: Courtesy of Port of Portland, and Ackroyd Photography, Inc.

Product Audit

The **product audit** is a comprehensive analysis of both the existing product line and new product trends. The specific information that must be determined for each product includes (1) annual sales volume; (2) seasonality; (3) packaging (including size, weight, and special handling needs); (4) transportation and warehouse information; (5) present manufacturing or assembly facilities; (6) ease with which manufacturing of product can be scheduled; (7) warehouse stocking locations; (8) present transport modes utilized; (9) sales by regions; (10) complementary products that are often sold at the same time as the product under consideration; (11) relationship to other products in the firm's total product line; and (12) product profitability. This list is not exhaustive; it simply indicates the type of product information needed. Most of the information needed to perform a product audit is available in a firm's existing records.

Existing Facilities Audit

The **existing facilities audit** is performed next. Since each logistics system is unique, the working analysis team must have a comprehensive audit of its facilities. This includes (1) the location and capacity of production plants; (2) the location and capacity of storage warehouses and distribution centers; (3) the location of the order-processing function; and (4) the transport modes utilized (especially when the firm is somewhat locked into use of a particular mode). When constraints are present, they typically involve aspects of existing facilities that are not to be changed. The existing facilities audit, which tells where a firm is utilizing facilities, provides essential data for determining (or limiting) changes in the system.

Sometimes, currency fluctuations cause unusual logistics facilities usage patterns. U.S. exports of frozen food to Japan are sometimes stored in the United States, rather than in Japan. Considering the high costs of real estate and warehouse storage in Japan, when the Japanese yen has a higher value than the U.S. dollar, it can be considerably less expensive to store frozen foods on the West Coast of the United States than it is to store them in Japan.

Facilities audits often include evaluations of work crews, job descriptions, and performance ratings of managers or supervisors. Constraints can exist for personnel as well as for physical facilities.

Vendor Audit

The **vendor audit** looks at sources of supply for raw materials and components. This includes (1) their location, (2) their dependability, (3) the quality of their work, (4) their reputation for innovation, (5) the costs and performance of inbound transportation, and (6) their compatibility with the firm's information and order-processing systems.

In all these audits of existing conditions, it is also permissible to include other options, in this case, say, potential vendors. In fact, before the audits begin, those establishing the study objectives should give some indication of the direction in which they want some studies to go. For example, Pfizer specifies "an evaluation of e-marketplaces, portals, and exchanges in order to identify possible opportunities for enhancing the value that our division provides."[15] It will be helpful to those auditing the existing vendor situation to know in advance that the company is contemplating—or has as a goal—a change in its manufacturing philosophy.

Customer Audit

The **customer audit** focuses on determining the characteristics of current customers. Potential new customers are also analyzed. Typical information might include (1) the location of present and potential customers; (2) the products that each customer orders; (3) the seasonality of customers' orders; (4) whether customers buy FOB-origin or destination; (5) the importance of customer service; (6) special services customers require; and (7) the volume and profitability of sales for each customer. The customer

---

[15]Lisa Martin, "Charting Pfizer's Path to e-Procurement," *Supply Chain Management Review,* Vol. 6, No. 3, 2002, pp. 20–26.

audit provides a key input for system analysis because, in the end, the system is designed to satisfy the needs and requirements of a firm's customers.

The Ford Motor Company uses Six Sigma quality processes based on customer research to deliver on its Customer Satisfaction Bill of Rights. These rights include the right product, the right quality, the right place, the right time, the right value, the right service, and the right information. Customer feedback and the use of Six Sigma allow Ford to focus on customer needs, and "anything that does not positively relate to delivering on those rights is waste, and waste must be ruthlessly and continuously attacked."[16]

Channels Audit

Since current logistics thought includes the development of long-term, supply-chain relationships with other firms in one's distribution and supply channels, a logistics system design study should include some contact with these parties in the logistics channel to determine whether mutually beneficial agreements might be negotiated or, if in place, continued. This is the **channels audit.** At the very least, one wants to keep these options open and remain flexible in terms of being available for future partnerships (see Figure 14-7). When looking at suppliers and customers, one should also examine

They're a heck of a nice outfit to do business with!

FIGURE 14-7 Flexibility Makes It Easier to Work Together

Source: Copyright © Seaway Review, *Harbor House Publishers,* Boyne City, MI 49712. Reproduced with permission.

---

[16]Karen Moore, "Six Sigma: Driving Supply Chain Success at Ford," *Supply Chain Management Review,* Vol. 6, No. 4, 2002, pp. 38–43.

the possibilities of leveraging the assets of both. While leveraging is often thought of in monetary terms, it could be in other terms also, say, customer service.

Channels audits are also used today to determine whether some channels can be shortened. With the advent of electronic data interchange (EDI) between buyers and sellers, the services of some agents are no longer needed. Wal-Mart, for example, has eliminated the role of a number of middlemen because their functions have been absorbed either by Wal-Mart or its suppliers. This is consistent with the logic that a channel intermediary must add value or it should not exist. *Disintermediation* refers to the removal of channel layers.

Channel or supply-chain rearrangement is always a possibility. Currently, music companies are scrambling to deal with the implications of digital distribution of their artists' recordings through the Internet. The music piracy enabled by products such as Napster and KaZaA has reduced sales revenues to the music companies, forcing them to embrace new paid distribution to consumers via the Internet.

Competition Audit

The **competition audit** outlines the competitive environment within which a firm is selling. The following information should be ascertained: (1) the order-transmittal methods of competitors; (2) the accuracy and speed of competitors' order processing; (3) the speed and consistency of carrier movements used by competitors; (4) the ratio of orders given to competitors that could not be filled because of a product stockout; (5) competitors' experience with loss and damage claims; and (6) a narrative statement regarding customers' perceptions of the customer service strengths and weaknesses of the firm and its competitors.

Unlike the other audits, the information required for the competition audit is generally not available within a company's own records, although salespeople can often provide some of it. Outside marketing research firms are used to survey competitors to gather the required data. Outside research firms can usually design questionnaires to disguise the ultimate recipient of the information.

Environmental Sensitivity Audit

Many firms operate in markets or in political areas where there is a growing public awareness of environmental protection issues. The **environmental sensitivity audit** should look at current practices along the supply chain regarding packaging materials used and the recyclability of both packaging and product. A related study would be of the potential markets for the materials being recycled; they must be strong enough to yield prices that will support recycling.

> Avoiding stock-outs and late shipments, going the extra mile to meet your customer's emergency needs, and shortening your customer's order-to-delivery cycles may seem like sure-fire ways to win and retain customers across the [European] continent. But new environmental legislation, as well as environmentally conscious customers, are demanding more. . . . Increasingly legal requirements and consumer preferences are making a supplier or manufacturer responsible for a product beyond its sale and delivery. In parts of Europe, the manufacturer is now responsible for taking back and disposing of packaging, rejects and excess, as well as curing any environmentally unfriendly

aspect of the end product. . . . Traditional approaches to logistics management are giving way to "green logistics."[17]

Analysis of the Data

Once the information from the various audits is assembled, the next step is to examine and analyze it. This can be accomplished using relatively unsophisticated techniques or complex methods. The sophistication of methods has improved greatly with the widespread use of computers, which both generate data in a form that can be easily analyzed and can analyze it. The scale of problems addressed is also greater. Not long ago, the pin-and-string method of routing trucks was frequently used. It involved a wall map with a thumbtack stuck at each place a delivery had to be made. One end of the string would be tied to the thumbtack at the distribution warehouse and then an effort would be made to loop the string in a manner that touched all thumbtacks, and returned to the origin, using the minimum length of string. Contrast this with the following abstract of a paper entitled "Consolidating and Dispatching Truck Shipments of Heavy Petroleum Products," published in 1995:

> Mobil Oil Corporation consolidates and dispatches truck shipments of heavy petroleum products—lubricants in packages and in bulk—from ten lubricant plants nationwide. They dispatch hundreds of orders daily either individually, or as consolidated truckloads, using a very non-homogeneous fleet of Mobil-controlled and contract vehicles, and common carriers. Shipment schedules may span several days, and include stops to pick up returned drums or entire trailers. Shipping costs depend upon the vehicle used, the shipment size, the locations of all required stops, and the route distance and time. Candidate consolidations are generated automatically, or with dispatcher assistance. Then, an optimal, minimal-cost set of schedules is selected. Mobil has been using this system for three years, reducing annual transportation costs by about $1 million (US).[18]

Many computer and operations management courses taught in business schools today contain some assignments associated with logistics operations. Many operations research techniques are appropriate to studying logistics operations; this book touches on only one method: simulation. Simulation assumes that the relationships among the studied variables are known; it is used to determine how well an actual or proposed system will perform under varying stresses.

Simulation

The computer technique that is most widely used for logistics system planning is **simulation.** It usually involves a computer model that is a series of mathematical relationships, often expressed as a series of linear equations. Simulation reliability is achieved by making the model as much like a real-world situation as possible. Such factors as transport mode availability, transportation costs, location of vendors, warehouse

---

[17]Jack Berry, Greg Girard, and Cynthia Perras, "Logistics Planning Shifts into Reverse," *Journal of European Business,* September–October 1993, p. 35.

[18]Dan O. Bausch, Gerald G. Brown, and David Ronen, "Consolidating and Dispatching Truck Shipments of Heavy Petroleum Products," *Interfaces,* Vol. 25, No. 2, 1995, pp. 1–17.

locations, customer locations, customer service requirements, and plant locations must all be accurately reflected in the model. Although logistics simulation models may require many programmers working together for long periods, they enable the firm to answer questions such as the following:

- If we reduce the average order cycle time for our customers from 12 days to 7 days, what will be the additional cost involved? Will sales increase?
- If we presently use our trucks for outbound movements only and are debating whether to use them to pick up some of our inputs on their return trips, how will this affect our current schedules of outbound deliveries?
- If we reduce the number of distribution warehouses from 32 to 19, what will be the effect on customer service standards? What about costs?
- If our vendors improve the accuracy of their delivery times, by how much can we safely reduce our stocks of components?
- If the minimum order accepted is increased from $20 to $100, what will be the effect on total sales?
- If private carriage is substituted for motor common carriage, what will be the changes in total logistics costs, and what effect will this have on customer service standards?
- What will happen if we shift the order penetration point nearer to or farther from the customer? (The order penetration point is when and where a specific item in an inventory or production process is earmarked for a particular customer.)

The primary advantage of simulation is that it enables the firm to test the feasibility of a proposed change at relatively little expense. In addition, it prevents firms from experiencing the public embarrassment of making a major change in their logistics system that might result in a deterioration of customer service levels or an increase in total operating expense.

Career logistics people should familiarize themselves with computer simulations because they are important to logistics planning and will become even more important in the future. Many consultants have developed expertise in simulation techniques and have devised computer-based models that can be used by their various clients.

A typical simulation consulting project involved a major U.S. fast-food company as the client with a need for a simulation model of its distribution commissary system for the eastern half of the United States. The company was concerned with the inefficiency of the bread-baking equipment located at each of its 45 existing distribution centers. Specifically, the company wanted to know if it could establish fewer regional baking centers and improve the cost efficiency of its existing network by baking bread in fewer locations. This type of analysis is ideal for simulation study.

The research team gathered data on costs, customer orders, delivery locations, warehouse throughput, fleet capacity and deployment efficiency, bread-baking capacity, and distribution constraints (bread has a relatively short shelf life, and this company's quality standards mandated daily bread deliveries to its franchisees and company-owned shops). A system of equations was specified that defined the relationships among the variables. Once input into the simulation model, the model was validated. Validating the model involved inputting current operational data and examining the model output to determine whether or not the model adequately captured the current working distribution network's performance.

When the model was adjusted following validation, it was then capable of providing the company with the answer to a number of what-if questions. The firm discovered that an optimal cost and efficiency solution involved the building of nine regional bread-baking centers to provide bread to the existing 45 distribution centers. The bread would then be cross-docked into local delivery trucks for shipment to the retail shops. Bread baking was taken out of the commissaries' distribution requirements, saving the firm about $10 million annually.

Simulation models may include, for example, statistical analyses, rules-based (heuristic) decision making, nonlinear modeling, minimization, maximization, and optimization routines. Almost as many analytic tool combinations are available to the simulation modeler as there are problems to study. The problems studied range from partial systems analysis involving perhaps a dozen variables and constraints through building a supply-chain–wide model of operations involving hundreds of thousands of constraints and millions of variables (and a good many expensive consultant hours!).

Simulation is a powerful analytic tool, but a poorly constructed simulation involving bad data or inaccurate assumptions about the relationships among variables can deliver suboptimal or unworkable solutions to logistics problems. For example, one General Motors manager using a simulation model to study changes in a materials handling system found that "No matter how we changed the design of a power-and-free conveyor delivering empty carriers to an automated storage and retrieval system, throughput kept dropping off." He later identified the fundamental problem: The conveyor equipment could not be operated at a speed high enough to meet the system requirements.[19] In this case, an accurate simulation model pinpointed a system constraint that could be redesigned or re-specified. Had the simulation model been developed with bad data or inaccurate assumptions, the manager would likely have never discovered that his problem had a simple solution.

Design Implementation

The final activity in logistics system design is design implementation. However, only rarely is an operating logistics system completely revised at one time. A one-time, across-the-board revision is typically too traumatic for most firms to tolerate because it inevitably results in a breakdown of customer service functions. Orders are lost, incorrect quantities are shipped, stockouts are frequent—these are the typical problems that occur when a system is changed too radically in a short period of time. In addition, personnel may resist the changes.

Most firms prefer to use simulation analysis or other study techniques to find those areas that should be changed first, because these functions are the greatest bottlenecks to efficiency. Also, the payoffs may be greater.

Design implementation may also involve the design, construction, and placing into operation of very large and specialized facilities. Figure 14-8 is a drawing of automated warehouse equipment. For a facility of this size, considerable analysis would be needed to determine the amounts of materials flowing into and out of the facility and to select the site. A facility such as this is but part of a total system.

---

[19]Karen A. Field, "Data Quality Can Make or Break a Simulation," *Modern Materials Handling,* January 1997, p. 57.

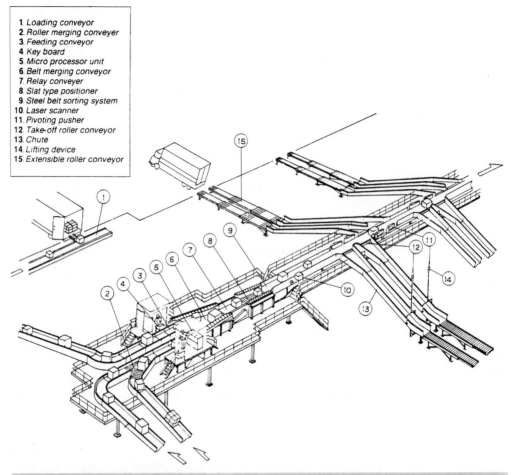

1. Loading conveyor
2. Roller merging conveyer
3. Feeding conveyor
4. Key board
5. Micro processor unit
6. Belt merging conveyor
7. Relay conveyer
8. Slat type positioner
9. Steel belt sorting system
10. Laser scanner
11. Pivoting pusher
12. Take-off roller conveyor
13. Chute
14. Lifting device
15. Extensible roller conveyor

FIGURE 14-8 Schematic Drawing of Automated Sorting System

Source: Sandvik Process Systems.

Systems Integration: Logistics Within the Firm

The question of how many of the different functions should be under the control of the firm's logistics director gives us some perspective on the span of supply-chain integration. Common logistics activities under such control include warehousing, transportation management, facility location, global logistics, order processing, inventory control, purchasing, packaging, order entry, product planning, and sales forecasting. Recently, logistics managers have significantly increased the span of their control in these areas. The logistics staff often shares responsibility with other groups in areas such as packaging, strategic planning, sales forecasting, and so on.

Although this chapter deals mainly with domestic corporations, brief mention is made of several other forms of organization in which the principles mentioned here may also be applicable. International corporations with operations in many countries, for example, must organize whatever structure suits best their multinational interests. The international logistics manager must be familiar with domestic logistics operations in many nations and with the physical and legal complexities involved in transferring materials between nations.

Dispersion of Logistics Activities

The size of a firm also influences the placement of logistics functions. In small firms, definite limitations impact how thinly managerial talent can be spread. In such situations, one consideration in organization may be to even out the workloads of supervisors. The current focus on integration of inbound and outbound movements is not surprising. Managing inventory in all forms, from raw materials transformed through manufacturing to finished goods, is a key concept in supply-chain management.

Achieving Coordination

Effective logistics operations cannot exist without a high level of coordination among the various functional areas. At minimum, such coordination requires efficient and accurate communications among the different logistics functions. To achieve a high level of coordination within the firm, one can choose one of the three organizational strategies: optimizing the present system, experimenting with unique ways of coordination with the existing system, or reorganizing the functional areas of logistics into a logistics department. Other alternatives are available, but they are only variations of these three strategies. Which strategy to choose may depend on a firm's strategic plans, including those formulated to cover its logistical activities. Considerable thought must go into organizing or reorganizing the firm—and its vendors and buyers—to achieve a more desirable flow of goods and services.

The Status Quo

For some companies, it is feasible to obtain the required coordination among the logistics functional areas without any formal change in the organizational structure. This is accomplished by both formal and informal operating procedures that guarantee that the various areas will coordinate and discuss their various problems and proposals. This concept of coordination is generally most feasible when the overall size of the firm and the number of employees trying to coordinate across departmental lines are not large. For many firms, this is a viable alternative, and it avoids the problems associated with actually transferring and reassigning functional areas.

One problem of maintaining the status quo organizational structure is that the influence of logistics thinking never gets an opportunity to express itself. Because logistics activities are scattered throughout the firm, they always remain subservient to the objectives of the senior department (i.e., marketing, manufacturing, finance) in which they are housed.

The Linking-Pin Concept

Another organizational structure, similar to the status quo option, is the **linking-pin organization,** in which certain individuals are assigned the responsibility of ensuring coordination among logistics activities. The individuals are known as *linking pins,* and are assigned to work in two or three functional areas. An individual may simultaneously be assigned to the traffic department (which can be a part of production) and to the warehousing department (which can be a part of marketing). The advantage of this system is that the linking pins of each work group are able to coordinate and express the problems and concerns of each decision as it relates to the respective department within which the linking pin operates.

However, some serious problems come with the linking-pin structure. The most basic is that it violates the classic organizational principle of unity of command. Linking pins in effect belong to two or more departments, so who is their boss? Who evaluates job performance? Who decides about promotions? Linking pins may find themselves in the position of having no home. It is possible for linking-pin members to alienate all the departments for which they work, especially in situations where department managers may have conflicting objectives. The departments may feel that the linking-pin members are too global in outlook and no longer members of the home department's team. Also, under the linking-pin arrangement, logistics is close to being considered a staff rather than a line function, with the accompanying inference that staff activities are never quite as important as line activities.

A Unified Department

The **unified department organization** combines all functional areas of logistics into one department. This approach is intuitively the best because coordination among inbound and outbound traffic, warehousing, inventory control, production, and other functional areas is facilitated when they are combined into one operating department. This alternative has worked well for many companies and appears to be the preferred solution to overcoming the coordination problems in a logistics department. Under the unified department strategy, logistics is a line activity.

One consultant reported that the "new" logistics manager (titled chief logistics officer) was in the middle of the organization and concerned with five major areas: corporate strategies, information systems and flows, procurement, manufacturing, and sales. The consultant believed that this new chief logistics officer dealt more with general management than with specific logistics issues. The consultant used the categories of old logistics and new logistics: The old logistics included managing the logistics pipeline, managing and collaborating with logistics personnel, partnering with logistics suppliers, and integrating the elements of the physical distribution function. The new logistics includes creation of breakthroughs in customer delivery practices; partnering with other functional heads, customers, and suppliers; and selecting and developing the best system to get the job done, often changing elements inside and outside the company. "The old system emphasizes costs. The new system emphasizes profits. The old contained limits (a system could only become so efficient). The new is limitless (as it helps grow the company). The old rewarded creative rearrangement of familiar elements. The new takes its creative practitioners into unfamiliar ground."[20]

---

[20]Jim Stone, "The New Logistics," *Logistics Resource,* No. 2, 1993, p. 2.

Centralization Versus Decentralization

An important issue in logistics organization strategy is whether the logistics department should be centralized or decentralized. A *centralized logistics organization* implies that the corporation maintains a single logistics department that administers the related activities for the entire company from the home office. A *decentralized logistics organization,* in contrast, means that logistics-related decisions are made separately at the divisional or product group level and often in different geographic regions.

The size of a firm, its products, and the geographic area in which its sales are made and its inputs are purchased are what determine whether centralized or decentralized decisions should be made. Several arguments favor the centralized logistics organization, and two are given here. One is related to information systems, which are revolutionizing many aspects of business and changing many traditional ways of interacting both inside and outside the firm. Logistics managers control some of a firm's most important, timely, and sensitive data, since so many of their activities deal with sales and orders. Today, more than a thousand different software programs are available for use in logistics functions. The various programs are divided fairly evenly among personal and mainframe computers. The important point is this: As firms and markets restructure themselves around the functions of information handling, processing, transmittal, exchange, and control, logistics should end up doing well. In situations in which closer communication is needed with customers, the logistics function will be in an enviable position. Computers and communications are likely to lead firms in the direction of centralized management (even if only through linked computers).

The second observation has to do with relations within the firm. Here, we continue to see an increasing interest in combining the outbound product flow functions with inbound product and input flows, in part because of our improved ability to manage information across organizations. It is now possible to link via computer the incoming orders for a firm's output to its own orders of replenishment stocks. When negotiating a contract with a carrier, one can press for a lower rate by offering a greater total tonnage or more balanced (inbound–outbound) hauls. Thus, load balancing (or any form of freight consolidation) appears to work best in a centralized system.

The arguments in favor of the decentralized logistics organization stress the unmanageability of a centralized system in large, multidivisional firms. In highly decentralized firms it is often preferable for the line distribution functions to remain in each autonomous division. The decentralized organizational system appears to function best when the various product lines of each division have very little in common.

Advocates of decentralization question the ability of a centralized logistics department to provide required levels of customer service. Customers willing to wait 30 to 60 days to receive orders may be adequately served by a centralized logistics department of a multidivisional firm. However, for customers requiring 24-hour service, the centralized logistics function may not be responsive enough. In order to meet such customers' needs, an in-house department (i.e., one within the division) is needed, one that is attuned to the specific requirements of the division. In this case, too, geography can be a factor. Many global firms need to decentralize operations because centralized management may be impossible to achieve. Figure 14-9 shows a firm that sells medical supplies having sources spread throughout the world.

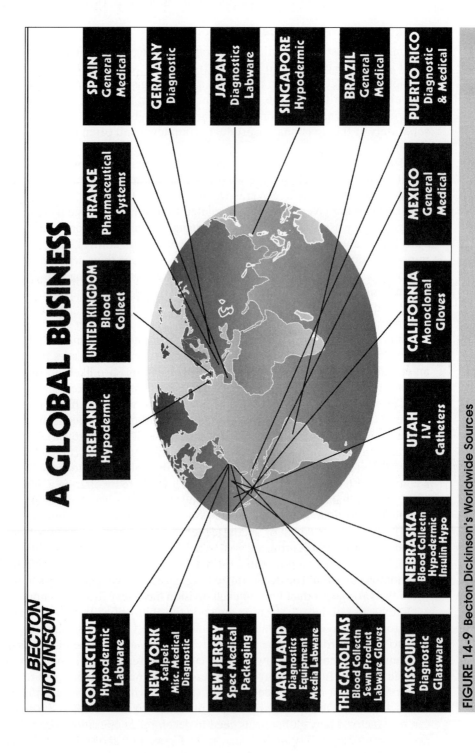

FIGURE 14-9 Becton Dickinson's Worldwide Sources

Source: Courtesy of Becton Dickinson and Company.

Matrix Management

Another useful form of management organization is referred to as **matrix management.** In this approach, a manager may have responsibilities under two functional areas. For example, the manager of small appliances for a diversified manufacturer may report to both the vice president of marketing and the vice president of logistics. In this example, the manager of small appliances has responsibilities for small appliance marketing and logistics. The advantage to such an organizational structure is the integration of two or more functional areas within the span of control of a single manager. When so organized, these dual-function managers can be quite powerful and, thus, very responsive to their customers' needs. The disadvantage to this organizational structure is its cost (usually more managerial-level employees are required than in other structures) and the complexity of the information systems necessary to support the matrixed managers.

Often, a firm will maintain a conventional management structure for handling most routine matters. However, certain employees are periodically assigned on a short-term basis to cross-functional, matrixed teams established to deal with specific, unique problems. The employees assigned to these short-term projects are chosen because they possess special skills. An example of a one-time assignment would be to deal with the closure of a plant and the relocation of some of its operations.

Systems Integration: Logistics Activities Outside the Firm

Very few firms conduct absolutely all of their own logistics activities. Some are outsourced to be performed by others. One West Coast–based U.S. retailer of high-fashion women's apparel operates its own distribution center but partners with FedEx to provide second-day delivery of all clothing shipped to its 165 North American stores. The contract with FedEx specifies movement in 100-pound lots to help minimize transportation costs. While use of FedEx for such routine shipping may seem excessively costly, this firm has been able to reduce its inventory-in-transit and improve its inventory turnover rate and has actually reduced overall costs. A side benefit to this strategy is that the merchandise in its retail stores is always fresh. This partnership is just one example of what is often known as **third-party, or contract, logistics.** Public warehouse personnel perform many assembly and distribution functions, and in some states they also perform deliveries. These channel members act as intermediaries between the manufacturer and the ultimate customer. Some intermediaries perform more logistics functions for the manufacturer than others. Of course, for doing this they expect to be additionally compensated.

Sometimes, operations are given to others in order to reduce exposure to risk. Since the Exxon *Valdez* disaster, U.S. oil companies have been cutting back on their ownership of tankers in order to reduce their exposure to lawsuits (and bad publicity). They now buy tanker transportation services from fleet operators. In some cases, the oil companies have sold their tankers and operations to fleet operators only to immediately buy back transportation on the very same ships they formerly owned. For similar reasons, many chemical companies have replaced their own truck delivery fleets with fleets provided by outsiders.

What are key success indicators for integrated supply chains today? Professor Larry Smeltzer suggests five new "realities" for successful integration in the Internet-enabled age:[21]

1. *Supply chain rules based on electronic commerce between large companies are already in place.* EDI has now been in place for a number of years between the largest firms in most supply chains. This has provided increased accuracy and shortened transaction times. The remaining challenge is to extend the power of EDI to all members in the chain through wider use of Internet-based technologies.

2. *Large companies are fundamentally different from smaller companies—a fact that hinders e-commerce adoption.* These differences are in three areas: (a) large and mature firms have coordination and control systems, while small firms seldom have the time and resources to devote to supply-chain integration; (b) large firms can allocate costs of new systems over more units of production than can small firms, thus lessening the financial impact; and (c) small firms rarely have the internal development and maintenance capabilities of large firms.

3. *Inertia and the status quo are hindering full supply-chain connectivity.* To encourage small firms toward supply-chain integration, they must face low and predictable costs, require minimal changes in their behavior, and receive some compelling benefit to induce the behavioral change.

4. *Targeted technology, a proven process, and dedicated resources are needed to connect and support the thousands of members that make up the supply chain.* Professor Smeltzer points out that true supply-chain integration deals with thousands of back-office processes, some as mundane as fax and e-mail, and some as challenging as business rules dealing with normal and exceptional procedures for order quantity variances and delivery dates. Thus, a simple switch to EDI for the majority of a supply chain's partners is insufficient.

5. *Technical advances are needed to maximize the value of connections across the supply chain.* Complex transactions within the supply chain require investment in the development of complex technical tools and systems.

Total Logistics Firms: Integrated Service Providers

Firms known as **integrated service providers** contract to perform the entire range of logistics services for others. One such firm is Martin–Brower, which handles all distribution functions in certain parts of the country for fast-food chain McDonald's. Martin–Brower operates thousands of tractors and trailers and controls the inventory levels for its customers. The firm also handles purchasing, pricing, sales analysis, and planning functions for its clients. It delivers food, napkins, plastic containers, and so on in quantities that both make good use of the truck trailer's capacity and take into account the limited storage space in the franchise restaurants. Each restaurant receives one delivery of all it needs. Many similar large integrated service provider firms have assumed responsibility for supplying a number of restaurant chains and are among the nation's largest purchasers of food and restaurant products.

---

[21]This discussion based on Larry R. Smeltzer, "Integration Means Everybody: Big and Small," *Supply Chain Management Review,* Vol. 5, No. 5, 2001, pp. 36–44.

Monitoring Third-Party Performance

It is necessary to monitor the performance of third-party logistics providers. Methods of monitoring are often specified within the agreement. Two examples of monitoring measures follow. One company that supplies materials to the health care industry uses the following measures to evaluate its third-party provider: number of orders shipped on time; number of outbound orders confirmed on time; number of orders picked and loaded accurately; number of transfers of goods confirmed within 24 hours. The company penalizes for billing errors and damage to product noted by its customers.

A second company is an automobile importer and distributor. Its evaluation form lists 19 different items with accompanying scores. The points, which are merits or demerits, total 104. Items worth up to 10 points are equipment condition, tie-down procedures, truck loader training, vehicle clearances, and vehicle handling. Items worth up to 5 points are height measurement of truck, lighting, pavement surfaces, seat and floor protectors, skid and ramp angle settings, and supervision. Items worth up to 3 points are handling of keys, housekeeping, loaded vehicle condition, loaded vehicle in park/neutral, security, storage of excess tie-down chains and hooks, striped bay markings, and vehicle inspection prior to loading.

Typically, performance measures are specific to the supply-chain arrangement and responsibilities retained by the parties to the agreement. Since most of these third-party arrangements are strategically important and usually specified by contract, the parties have mutual benefit in ensuring high levels of performance. When performance becomes substandard, great effort is usually exerted to facilitate improvements before either party will consider ending their outsourcing agreement due to the logistics disruptions that would follow in the wake of such a termination of services.

SUMMARY

This chapter covered three main topics: the analysis of logistics systems, their design, and their integration. Most systems analysis undertaken is considered partial in nature; that is, it looks at how well some specific activity is performed or is functioning. Total system analysis involves looking at the overall picture. It is often performed by an outside consultant with specialized skills because it is usually a massive undertaking. In addition, outside consultants may be more objective. Several examples of partial analysis were given, including customer profitability, vendor quality control, warehouse productivity, and transportation costs.

One approach to total system design involves establishing objectives and constraints, organizing the study team, collecting data, analyzing the data, and so on. One analytical technique, simulation, is performed through the use of mathematical modeling, including statistical and operations research techniques. Assuming that changes are called for, the new system must be implemented.

This chapter also covered various approaches to organizing a firm's logistics system. An initial concern is the relative importance of logistics (usually expressed in terms of cost) to a firm's overall operations. The centralized versus decentralized organization issue was discussed, as well as the various organizational means of achieving coordination: the linking-pin concept; unified department organization; matrix management; and third-party, or contract, logistics. Relying on outside parties to perform logistics functions is becoming more common.

QUESTIONS FOR DISCUSSION AND REVIEW

1. Define logistics systems analysis, and give an example.
2. What are some problems associated with logistics systems analysis?
3. What is partial systems analysis? Why is it used?
4. What are some possible measures of warehouse productivity? Should they be uniformly applied? Why or why not?
5. What opportunities might be ignored if companies fail to consider their inbound freight costs?
6. What is direct product profitability (DPP) analysis? How might it be used?
7. Should benchmarking be conducted beyond a company's immediate group of competitors? Why or why not?
8. When designing logistics systems, why is it important for there to be measurable objectives?
9. How do system constraints increase the difficulty of decision making? How do system constraints simplify decision making?
10. What are five types of information that could be useful when doing a product audit?
11. What are the main components of an existing facilities audit?
12. Name four possible components of a customer audit. Why is a customer audit important to logistics systems analysis?
13. What are some ways to collect relevant information for a competition audit?
14. Name the seven types of comprehensive logistics systems audits that should be performed. Which do you view as the most important? The least important? Why?
15. With respect to logistics systems design, what is simulation? What are its strengths and weaknesses?
16. "Design implementation is often accomplished in stages rather than all at once." Is this logical? What are the strengths and weaknesses of a gradual approach to design implementation?
17. Describe the status quo approach to logistical coordination. What are its advantages and disadvantages?
18. How is a "new" logistics manager different from an "old" logistics manager?
19. What is the difference between a centralized and decentralized logistics department? Which is more desirable? Why?
20. Which "new reality" for supply chain integration do you view as most important? Why?

SUGGESTED READINGS

Bhatnagar, Rohit, and S. Viswanathan. "Re-engineering Global Supply Chains." *International Journal of Physical Distribution & Logistics Management,* Vol. 30, No. 1, 2000, pp. 13–34.

Elmuti, Dean. "The Perceived Impact of Supply Chain Management on Organizational Effectiveness." *Journal of Supply Chain Management,* Vol. 38, No. 3, 2002, pp. 49–57.

Ellram, Lisa M., and Baohong Liu. "The Financial Impact of Supply Management." *Supply Chain Management Review,* Vol. 6, No. 2, 2002, pp. 30–37.

Fawcett, Stanley E., and Gregory M. Mandan. "The Rhetoric and Reality of Supply Chain Integration." *International Journal of Physical Distribution & Logistics Management,* Vol. 32, No. 5, 2002, pp. 339–362.

Garcia-Dastague, Sebastian J., and Douglas M. Lambert. "Internet-Enabled Coordination in the Supply Chain." *Industrial Marketing Management,* Vol. 32, No. 3, 2003, pp. 251–263.

Handfield, Robert B., and Ernest L. Nichols. *Supply Chain Redesign: Transforming Supply Chains into Integrated Value Systems,* Upper Saddle River, NJ: Financial Times-Prentice Hall, 2002.

Haughton, Michael A., William L. Grenoble, Evelyn A. Thomchick, and Richard R. Young. "The Role of

Benchmarking in the Performance of the Import Process." *International Journal of Physical Distribution & Logistics Management,* Vol. 29, No. 9, 1999, pp. 551–568.

Lowson, Robert. "The Implementation and Impact of Operations Strategies in Fast-Moving Supply Systems." *Supply Chain Management: An International Journal,* Vol. 7, No. 3, 2002, pp. 146–163.

McGinnis, Michael A., and Jonathan W. Kohn. "Logistics Strategy Revisited." *Journal of Business Logistics,* Vol. 23, No. 2, 2002, pp. 1–17.

Poirer, Charles C. "Achieving Supply Chain Connectivity." *Supply Chain Management Review,* Vol. 6, No. 6, 2002, pp. 16–22.

Smeltzer, Larry R. "Integration Means Everybody: Big and Small." *Supply Chain Management Review,* Vol. 5, No. 5, 2001, pp. 36–44.

Stank, Theodore, Michael Crum, and Miren Arango. "Benefits of Interfirm Coordination in Food Industry Supply Chains." *Journal of Business Logistics,* Vol. 20, No. 2, 1999, pp. 21–41.

Towill, Denis, and Martin Christopher. "The Supply Chain Strategy Conundrum: To be Lean or Agile or To be Lean and Agile?" *International Journal of Logistics: Research & Applications,* Vol. 5, No. 3, 2002, pp. 299–310.

van der Vorst, Jack J.A.G., Stephen J. van Dijk, and Adrie J.M. Beulens. "Supply Chain Design in the Food Industry." *International Journal of Logistics Management,* Vol. 12, No. 2, 2001, pp. 73–85.

C A S E S

Case 14-1 Columbia Lumber Products Company

The Columbia Lumber Products Company (CLPC) was headquartered in Portland, Oregon, where it had been founded in 1899. For many years, its principal product had been only lumber; in the 1940s it began producing plywood, and in 1960, particle board. The first two products, lumber and plywood, were produced at various sites in Oregon and marketed on the West Coast and as far east as Chicago.

Particle board was produced in Duluth, Minnesota, at a plant built in 1962 with a U.S. Area Redevelopment Administration Loan. Initially, the input to the plant was trimmings and other scrap from CLPC's Oregon operations. Particle board sales increased so quickly that the Duluth operation consumed not only all of the former waste from CLPC's Oregon plant but also waste purchased from various lumber and wood products operations in Minnesota and northern Wisconsin.

In terms of product volume, CLPC's sales doubled between 1960 and 1990. However, nearly all the growth had been in particle board; lumber and plywood sales remained relatively constant (although varying with changes in the home construction industry). In 1996, exports accounted for 9 percent of CLPC's sales. Nearly all of this was plywood sold to Japan. Fifteen percent of CLPC's 1996 purchases was from foreign sources, 5 percent was mahogany from the Philippines used for plywood veneer, and 10 percent was wood scrap purchased from Ontario, Canada, for use in CLPC's Duluth plant. Particle board produced in Duluth was marketed in all states east of the Rocky Mountains, although

sales in the southern United States were somewhat less than spectacular.

The slowdown in home production, which started in the late 1970s and, in the Midwest, really never ended, resulted in many years of little or no growth in CLPC's sales. Common stock dividends had been cut several times. In 1996, they were 37 cents per share, down considerably from their peak—in 1976—of $2.21.

Stockholders, the outside directors, and various lending institutions were becoming increasingly unhappy. After a long, tense board of directors meeting, agreement was reached only with respect to what some of the organizational problems were. A partial list follows:

1. The corporation headquarters was in Portland, although any growth occurred in the Midwest. Possibly the headquarters, or at least more functions, should be shifted to an office in Duluth, where the plant was, or to Chicago, where the largest sales office was. A major relocation away from Portland would be difficult. Many employees would choose to remain on the West Coast. Even for those willing to relocate, there was a split between those willing to relocate to Duluth and those willing to relocate to Chicago.

2. There were too many vice presidents (see Exhibit 14-A). Because four vice presidents (engineering, finance, human resources, and purchasing) would reach mandatory retirement age by 1997, the number of vice presidents should be

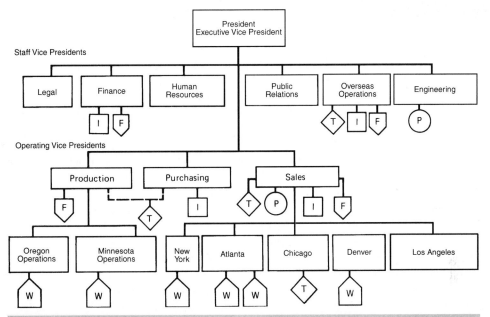

EXHIBIT 14-A Columbia Lumber Products Company's Organizational Chart (as of January 31, 1996)

reduced from nine to no more than six (plus one executive vice president).

3. Logistics and distribution costs were higher than industry averages. The majority of customer complaints dealt with poor deliveries. In Exhibit 14-A, a T shows where a traffic management function was located. Geographically, the traffic manager for overseas operations was located in Seattle, which was a foreign trade center for the Pacific Northwest. The Chicago sales office had a traffic manager who handled all fiberboard distribution, and lumber and plywood distribution east of the Rockies. Production and purchasing shared a traffic manager who was head-quartered in Portland and whose principal duty was overseeing shipments of waste products from Oregon to Minnesota. Another traffic manager (in Portland), who reported to the sales vice president, was acknowledged to be the firm's senior

traffic manager and more or less coordinated the efforts of the other three. Recently Irwin Buchanan III had been promoted to that post. He was the only one authorized to initiate action before regulatory bodies, and he also handled the negotiations with carrier rate-making bodies and with carriers. (CLPC used contract truckers and rail for most of its shipping.)

4. The purchasing department handled the details of fleet management, which included about a hundred autos on long-term lease for use by management and by the sales force. Several light trucks were leased for use around the plants.

5. CLPC also owned two small aircraft, which often were the target of questions during stockholders' meetings. One plane was based at Portland, the other at Duluth. Each was used in its respective region for trips to sites without scheduled airline service. Both planes were under

control of the production department. Other departments, especially sales, complained that the planes were being used for the benefit of the production department, rather than for the benefit of the entire firm.

6. P in the exhibit shows two packaging engineering functions. The one under engineering was located in Portland and dealt with plywood products. The one under sales was located in Chicago and handled particle board products. The two packaging engineering functions saw their roles differently. The one in Portland was concerned mainly with safe packing and packaging of products moving between CLPC plants or from CLPC plants to customers. The Chicago packaging engineers were interested in finding new markets for particle board and lumber as packaging materials to be sold to others. w in the exhibit shows where there are company-owned warehouses. Numerous public warehouses were also used, although not continually. I shows locations of individuals concerned with inventory levels. All four individuals were located in Portland. F indicates where sales forecasting took place. Only sales and production devoted much staff to forecasting. Each quarter, however, the financial vice president's office coordinated all forecasts to ensure comparability. Computer operations were under control of the engineering division. CLPC's executive vice president determined priorities for computer access and use.

7. The human resources department handled employee moves, although only a few had taken place since 1980. An outside director, who was familiar with current federal legislation, suggested that CLPC negotiate a contract with a household goods carrier to handle all CLPC employee moves. This action would be especially significant if a major reorganization resulted in numerous employee transfers.

QUESTIONS

1. Draw a new organization chart for Columbia Lumber Products Company that you feel overcomes best the directors' criticisms of CLPC's present (January 31, 1996) organization. Indicate the geographic location of all operations shown on the new chart. Explain why you established the organization chart the way you did.

2. Assume that the firm should be reorganized in a manner that emphasizes sales and marketing. This would include a physical distribution system, which would support the marketing effort. Draw an organization chart that you think would accomplish this aim. Indicate the geographic location of all operations on the new chart and explain why you drew the chart as you did.

3. Assume that a major reorganization appears unlikely but that you are told to draw up a plan for implementing the linking-pin concept. Describe how you would accomplish this. Between which functions or geographic sites would you establish linking pins? Why?

4. Assume that the firm wants to reorganize into a highly centralized form, closely managed from a single home office. Draw a new chart that takes this into account. Indicate the geographic location of all operations on the chart and explain why you organized it as you did.

5. Assume, instead, that the firm wants to reorganize into a highly decentralized form, where many important decisions can be made out in the field. Draw up a new chart, including the geographic location of all activities. Explain why you drew it up as you did.

6. Young Irwin Buchanan III, the firm's senior traffic manager, heard rumors that the

number of vice presidents was to be reduced. He felt that this would reduce his chances of ever achieving vice presidential—or presidential—status. Luckily, he had access to some money in a family trust fund. He wondered whether he should propose to form a separate, third-party firm to contract with CLPC to perform CLPC's

logistical operations. What functions should it offer to perform?

7. (This is a continuation of the situation in question 6.) Assume that young Buchanan does decide to form an outside firm to handle CLPC's logistics operations. Draft his letter to CLPC's management containing such a proposal.

Case 14-2   Trigo Export Co., Ltd.

The Trigo Export Company, Ltd., of Montreal, was appointed to be the manufacturer's export agent for the Ziola Tractor Company, Ltd., of Winnipeg. The tractor company was best known for its snow blowers, but the same 4½-horsepower engine and frame were modified to become a garden tractor. The Trigo Company specialized in agricultural implements sold in Central and South America, and its agreement with Ziola covered only sales to that area.

Trigo's sales force was aggressive and, after only two weeks, got the chance to bid on a large shipment of garden tractors to be delivered to Belem (a Brazilian port near the mouth of the Amazon). The customer was a charitable organization, and the only quantities mentioned were "somewhere between 40 and 100 units" of the Ziola Speedwagon model. After the shipment arrived in Belem, the tractors would be distributed by the charity to various settlements in the Amazon basin. Trigo's sales representative advised his home office that he thought price per unit would be an important criterion that the buyer would use in evaluating bids. He also said that two U.S. firms and a Korean firm were submitting bids. All bids would be FAS (free alongside) vessel in Belem.

He said that Trigo should quote prices for (a) 40 units; (b) 100 units; and (c) whatever

quantity between 40 and 100 that had the lowest cost per tractor. In case either 40 units or 100 units happened to have the lowest cost per unit, quotes would be needed for only (a) and (b).

Trigo's staff, with some help from people working for Ziola, began gathering facts. Following are some of them:

1. No import duties, permits, or licenses are required.

2. Documentation costs would be CAN$250 per shipment.

3. Ziola would sell to Trigo any quantity of tractors up to 500 at CAN$700 each, FOB (free on board) plant (at Winnipeg). This price would include packaging for export and a separate, related bar code for each carton in the shipment. The packaging materials consisted of at least 40 percent recycled contents. Ziola would load the packaged tractors into 20-foot intermodal containers and deliver the loaded containers to the railroad's Winnipeg container station.

4. Trigo had to select a port. Canada has two major East Coast ports, Montreal and Halifax. Montreal is positioned better to handle traffic to and from Europe, while Halifax is the northerly stop used

by vessel lines calling along the Atlantic Coast. Trigo decided to use the port of Halifax. Combined rail/ocean costs through this port were the lowest. Sailing services were less frequent than at some U.S. North Atlantic ports, but time saving did not appear to be an issue. Three scheduled liner operators—Frota Amazonica, S.A.; Ivaran Lines; and Hanjin Shipping Co.—all quoted similar rates. Their rates included port charges in Halifax and unloading in Belem. Port charges in Belem would be separate (but would be assumed by the buyer of the tractors).

5. Rail charges from Winnipeg to the container terminal at Halifax were CAN$400 per 20-foot container. This was cheaper than using a truck.

6. The exterior dimensions of each packaged tractor was 1 meter by 1 meter by 1 meter. The weight of each tractor was 200 kilos, and the package weighed 20 kilos for a total of 220 kilos per tractor. (Shipping charges by weight include both the tractor and its package.)

7. The interior dimensions of the 20-foot containers are 2.35 meters wide, 6.12 meters long, and 2.50 meters high.

8. Ocean rates from Halifax to Belem for loaded containers carrying cargo of this type are CAN$110 per ton (of 2,200 pounds). However, the ocean lines also use the rule of the measurement ton, which means that if a cubic meter weighs less than 1,000 kilograms, the cubic meter shall be considered as weighing 1,000 kilograms. Freight charges would have to be paid just before the cargo was loaded aboard ship. Rail transit time from Winnipeg to Halifax was 5 days.

9. Insurance charges were 1 percent of the shipment's value while the goods were in Canada and 2 percent while they were at sea.

10. Ziola expected to be paid the day the loaded containers were delivered to the railroad in Winnipeg. The Brazilian buyer would pay for the tractors as they were unloaded from the ship in Belem. Trigo would own the tractors for an estimated 25 days: 5 from Winnipeg to Halifax, 2 in Halifax, 17 at sea, and 1 in Belem. Trigo's line of credit at the Bank of Montreal was currently costing 12 percent interest annually.

11. Trigo wanted to mark up all costs by 10 percent to cover its overhead and profit.

QUESTIONS

1. Ziola's export packaging materials consisted of at least 40 percent recycled contents. Should this be mentioned in the quotation given to the potential Brazilian buyer?

2. Each package in this shipment will be bar coded. Is this an example of supply-chain integration? Why or why not?

3. What price should be quoted for 40 tractors?

4. What price should be quoted for 100 tractors?

5. Is there another quantity between 40 and 100 where the costs per tractor are lower? If so, what is it? What are its costs per tractor?

6. For how long into the future should the price quote be made (i.e., for how long should Trigo agree to deliver at a certain price)? Why?

7. In what currency should Trigo ask to be paid? Why?

8. After preparing the bid, Ziola calls Trigo and says that they are thinking of redesigning the tractor frame so that it can be disassembled, taking up half the space. A Ziola Speedwagon could fit into an export package measuring 1 meter by 1 meter by 0.5 meter. The weight of the packaged tractor would continue to be 220 kilos. By how much, if at all, would this new package size reduce the answers for questions 3 and 4?

15

Supply Chains: Future Directions

Key Terms

- Collaborative Planning, Forecasting, and Replenishment
- Customer relationship management
- Environmentalism
- Extended producer responsibility programs
- Logistics service providers
- Private trading exchanges
- Production sharing
- Recycling
- Relationship management
- Resiliency
- Service economy
- Supplier relationship management
- Vendor-managed inventory

Learning Objectives

- To understand how increased international trade will affect logistics and supply-chain management
- To learn more about the impacts of the service economy on logistics and supply-chain management
- To understand how information technology will influence logistics and supply-chain management
- To appreciate the natural environment's role in contemporary logistics and supply-chain management
- To learn more about relationship management
- To understand why collaboration is at the heart of successful supply-chain management

The preceding chapters of this book examined the fundamentals of logistics and supply-chain management as they are practiced today. This final chapter looks at future directions for logistics and supply-chain management. More specifically, the first part of the chapter presents several key macro-environmental issues, along with how logistics and supply-chain management might be impacted by these issues. The remainder of the chapter addresses several key issues that are more specific to logistics and supply-chain management. The chosen topics are likely to have strong impacts on those readers who are in the process of preparing for careers in logistics and supply-chain management.

Macro-Environmental Issues

Macro-environmental issues are those issues that are largely uncontrollable by individual organizations but that nonetheless influence their strategies, tactics, and activities; these can include business, economic, sociocultural, technological, and regulatory issues. Four key macro-environmental issues are examined in this chapter: international trade, the service economy, information technology, and attempting to preserve the natural environment.

International Trade

The field of international logistics, which was discussed at length in Chapter 12, is expected to assume increased importance in the future; quite simply, international logistics is necessary to facilitate the growth of international trade. International logistics is inherently complex, with one example involving export documentation. An export shipment can typically require between 10 and 20 separate documents, with most of the paperwork being required by the receiving country. Missing, incomplete, and/or erroneous documentation means that shipments cannot clear customs, thus potentially disrupting supply chains.

Moreover, international logistics is an expensive undertaking. Whereas the logistics costs of domestic operations are estimated at 5 percent to 6 percent of the total cost of each order received, for international shipments the figure jumps to between 10 percent and 25 percent. One reason for these increased costs is the often lengthy transit times associated with cross-border shipments. Another is that nondomestic sales typically involve larger ratios of inventory to sales because of longer lead times between when orders are placed and when they arrive.

There is little question that international trade—and by extension, international logistics—will continue to grow into the foreseeable future. Indeed, Alan Greenspan, Chairman of the United States Federal Reserve Board, has suggested that cross-border trade has generally resulted in higher standards of living for those countries engaged in such trade—and these countries, for the most part, are eager for their living standards to increase even more.[1]

One powerful factor propelling world trade activity is the concept of **production sharing**—for example, a high percentage of the baseball gloves sold in the United States are manufactured in Japan. However, the leather used to make the gloves is typically U.S. cowhide, shipped to Brazil for tanning before traveling elsewhere for manufacturing. Many of the products that state "Made in Japan" are actually assembled in Singapore, Indonesia, or Nigeria, where wage rates are considerably lower than in Japan. This trend is likely not only to continue but to accelerate.

Several key international trade issues should be closely monitored during the early years of the twenty-first century. One involves the growing worldwide economic clout of China. Without question, China's economy has exhibited impressive growth during the past 30 years and appears to offer tremendous opportunity in the coming years, due in part to its entrance into the World Trade Organization. In addition, China's status as the most populous nation in the world might increase its attractiveness to many companies, particularly those that focus on consumer goods.

This attractiveness notwithstanding, Chinese logistics can be quite challenging. For example, although the logistics infrastructure—in the form of highways, railways, airports, seaports—is improving, it is still lacking by Western standards and the improvements are most pronounced in urban areas, meaning that distribution outside of these areas can be quite problematic. Infrastructure issues aside, moving shipments across different provinces often necessitates valid operational licenses for each province; it's not uncommon for truck drivers to stop in one city and give the delivery to another carrier because the first truck driver doesn't have a valid license to continue further.[2] At a minimum, such behavior adds to transit time and increases the chances of shipment loss or damage.

---

[1]Alan Greenspan, "Globalization Vs. Protectionism," *Vital Speeches of the Day,* April 15, 2001, pp. 386–388.
[2]Jennifer B. Shah, "Logistics Networks Difficult to Establish in China," *EBN,* October 7, 2002, pp. 2, 52.

A second key trade issue during the early part of the twenty-first century involves multicountry free trade agreements. The main thrust of these agreements is the facilitation of trade through reduced trade barriers (generally in the form of lower tariffs) among the signatories to the trade agreement. Impressive economic gains can be made through participation in such agreements; through its participation in the North American Free Trade Agreement (NAFTA), Mexico is now the number-two trading partner of the United States. Moreover, Mexico's participation in NAFTA and other trade agreements has resulted in it becoming one of the world's ten-largest trade nations, as measured by combined exports and imports.

The future for additional multicountry trade alliances appears to be favorable through the first decade of the twenty-first century. For example, the European Union (EU) is scheduled to add 10 new countries, primarily Central European countries such as Hungary, Poland, and Slovakia, in 2004. Several other countries (e.g., Bulgaria and Romania) may also be admitted to the EU sometime between 2005 and 2010.

Moreover, in 2002, the U.S. Congress gave President George W. Bush fast-track trade authority, meaning that the Congress could approve or deny—but not modify— new trade agreements. With this in mind, President Bush has signaled his interest in negotiating a NAFTA-like trade agreement with numerous Central and South American nations by 2005, a Free Trade Area of the Americas.

While other free trade agreements have recently been agreed to and are currently being negotiated (e.g., between the Association of South-East Asian Nations and China), it's important to recognize their potential logistical impacts. For instance, both the EU expansion and the Free Trade Area of the Americas would involve a number of economically poorer countries with less developed logistical infrastructures and limited knowledge about contemporary logistical and supply-chain practices. Limited knowledge about contemporary logistics and supply-chain practices might be manifested in long-standing activities and practices that are both ineffective and inefficient—but extremely difficult to modify or eliminate.

Chapter 8 indicated that both the EU and NAFTA influenced trade patterns among the participating nations, with these trade patterns, in turn, influencing the design of distribution networks. Thus, the EU expansion in 2004 would appear to facilitate east–west trade patterns. Will this result in EU distribution hubs, such as those currently located in the Benelux (Belgium, the Netherlands, Luxembourg) region, being pulled toward the east?

The Service Economy

One macro-environmental issue that is likely to continue, particularly in the United States and other economically well-developed nations, is the shift towards a **service economy.** This means that an increasing percentage of a country's economic activity will be devoted to providing services rather than physical goods. Economically well-developed nations—such as the United States, the United Kingdom, and Germany— tend to devote a greater portion of their Gross Domestic Product (GDP) to services rather than to goods.

The implications of this trend for logistics are significant. For instance, inventories are a key component of many logistics systems, and inventories need some place to be stored, such as a warehouse or distribution center. Services, by contrast, are difficult or impossible to store; service providers cannot store repair calls, shoeshines, or consultants' visits. Likewise, empty airline seats for a particular flight cannot be stored to meet demand for another flight. Thus, service organizations have to become masters at matching the supply of, and demand for, their particular offerings.

Logistics also deals with transportation, and we can look at services in terms of which party, or parties, has to travel in order for service to be performed. In some instances, the service provider must travel (e.g., plumbers who make home repairs, workers who travel to a construction site). In other instances, however, the user must travel to where services will be provided (e.g., visits to a hospital). At other times, both the user and provider may be able to travel, but the user prefers to pay an additional amount to have the provider do the traveling (e.g., a veterinarian who makes home visits).

The proximity between provider and user is often a key issue in the logistics of service industries. Certain services can be provided by the telephone or some other means of electronic communication. For example, sounds from a patient's heartbeat can be transmitted via telephone and diagnosed by a physician listening many miles away. In addition, cable and satellite television provide home shopping channels that enable buyers to place orders through the use of toll-free telephone numbers or the channels' Web sites. Likewise, online shopping via corporate Web sites has grown in popularity and should continue to do so in the future. Note that the home shopping television channels and Internet shopping have brought important changes to distribution channels in the sense that no retail stores stock the various products.

Travel and tourism are service sectors that are important sources of global trade. Figure 15-1 shows a travel trailer being loaded aboard a RO/RO vessel. Airplanes, which have revolutionized the inventory, warehousing, and customer service strategies of many firms, are doing the same in the travel and tourism industry by reducing the time and money it takes to reach all parts of the world. In this area, there will be continued growth and more situations to which logistics and supply-chain principles can be applied. Teleconferencing, for example, is now a substitute for business travel, and emerging Internet-based conferencing and group-work software will likely supplant some business travel in the years to come.

A discussion of the logistical implications of the service economy would not be complete without mention of **logistics service providers** (LSP), or those companies that specialize in providing various types of logistics service such as transportation, warehousing, and freight forwarding, to name but a few. In recent years, some LSPs have acquired various companies in an effort to allow current and potential customers to purchase multiple logistics services from one source (the one-stop shopping concept). We expect that more LSPs will choose to pursue the one-stop shopping concept into the near future.

For example, in the late 1990s FedEx Corporation acquired an international freight forwarder (Tower International) and a regional less-than-truckload carrier (American Freightways). These acquisitions now allow FedEx to offer express delivery (FedEx Express), small-package ground service (FedEx Ground), regional less-than-truckload service (FedEx Freight), dedicated service for time-critical shipments (FedEx Custom Critical), and customs brokerage and international freight forwarding (FedEx Trade Networks), as well as information technology and supply-chain solutions

FIGURE 15-1 Loading a Travel Trailer Aboard a RO/RO (Roll On/Roll Off) Vessel in the Port of Seattle

Source: Don Wilson, Port of Seattle

(FedEx Services).[3] In a similar fashion, the German-based Deutsche Post has acquired an express carrier (DHL) and two international freight forwarders (Danzas, AEI) in recent years and will rebrand them under the DHL moniker. In early 2003, Deutsche Post's DHL announced plans to buy the ground operations of Airborne Express.

Information Technology

Chapter 3 explored the important role of information technology (IT) in contemporary logistics and supply-chain management. Clearly, advances in information and information exchange will continue to bring significant changes to logistics and supply-chain management in the early years of the twenty-first century. For instance, application-specific software programs, such as warehouse management systems (WMS), will increasingly include newer capabilities, such as labor planning, kitting, and manufacturing. At the same time, some of the more prominent enterprise resource

---

[3]More in-depth discussion of these companies can be found at www.fedex.com/us.

planning (ERP) providers will offer application-specific software such as WMS, although its effectiveness is likely to be inferior to best-of-breed WMS packages.[4]

Special mention must be made of how the September 11, 2001, terrorist attacks have influenced, and will continue to influence, logistics and supply-chain technologies in the twenty-first century. According to one expert, in the future these technologies must provide **resiliency,** which can be defined as the "ability to bring back a company and its supply chains to normal operations after catastrophic disruptions" whether these disruptions be natural or human-made in origin. Possible ways to facilitate resiliency include the use of application service providers (see Chapter 3) and mobile devices, to name but two.[5]

Moreover, two likely IT trends during the first decade of the twenty-first century— *intelligent voice recognition everywhere* and *pervasive wireless*[6]—appear to have important implications for logistics and supply-chain management. As noted in Chapter 3, voice recognition has tremendous potential with respect to warehousing operations, particularly in terms of order picking. Likewise, wireless technology can streamline warehousing and order picking operations. For example, wireless technology can transmit and record orders, print invoices, locate products for shipment, and automatically restock warehouses. Wireless technology can also be used to schedule vehicle loading and unloading, as well as to keep track of transportation vehicles.[7]

Yet another logistics-related application of wireless technology was announced in late 2002. Specifically, Motorola and FedEx Corporation have developed a pocket personal computer that will allow FedEx couriers to "wirelessly send and receive near real-time information and updates from any location." From a customer service perspective, this new technology should give customers more speedy access to package information and will no longer require FedEx couriers to return to their delivery vans to upload package information, thus cutting the transaction time per service call.[8]

Any discussion of IT's role in logistics and supply-chain management in the coming years would not be complete without mention of the Internet. As emphasized throughout this text, the Internet emerged as a global business medium during the late 1990s, and has revolutionized logistics and supply-chain management in many different ways. The Internet's fast, easy, low-cost, and reliable exchange of information has facilitated relationships among suppliers and producers, as well as among producers and customers.

There's little question that the Internet will continue to have profound impacts on logistics and supply-chain management in the coming years. For example, e-mail is rapidly becoming an acceptable—indeed, a preferred—method of communication between various supply-chain parties. E-mail has become so pervasive that some experts suggest that 40 percent to 60 percent of a company's intellectual property is

[4]Amanda Loudin, "Software for the Future," *Warehousing Management,* Vol. 8, No. 7, 2001, pp. 35–37.

[5]Ram Reddy, "The Evolution of Supply Chain Technologies—Part 2," *IntelligentEnterprise.com,* February 21, 2002, pp. 50, 52.

[6]Tim Kraskey, "Ten Predictions for the Decade," *Network World,* Vol. 19, No. 27, 2002, p. 35.

[7]Len Lewis, "Fat Pipe Syndrome," *Progressive Grocer,* Vol. 80, No. 7, 2001, pp. 47–48.

[8]"Motorola, FedEx Develop Wireless, Pocket PC for Couriers to Enhance Customer Service," press release of FedEx Corporation, November 26, 2002, retrieved from www.businesswire.com /fdx.

stored in e-mail addresses at any given time. Because of this, the so-called "revenge of the techies"—the deletion of e-mail inboxes—can have potentially devastating consequences for companies by disrupting customer relationships and/or deleting customer orders.[9]

Moreover, many companies have barely scratched the surface in terms of utilizing the Internet for more effective and efficient supply-chain management. This is likely to change as companies increasingly focus on what can be achieved by technology as opposed to focusing on technology itself. Some experts believe that a myriad of excellent opportunities still exists to substitute information for inventory in supply chains, and that the Internet provides low-cost, or no-cost, access to relevant information. To this end, world-class companies such as Wal-Mart and General Electric are using the Internet to develop **private trading exchanges** to coordinate the flow of information across supply-chain participants.[10]

Private trading exchanges (PTX) are "owned or controlled by a single company, but are accessible by external customers, suppliers, and partners as well as internal users."[11] In addition, a PTX is more advanced than Web-based applications or extranets; PTXs "facilitate both external interactions with customers, suppliers, and contractors, and internal interactions among corporate departments."[12] If properly implemented, private trading exchanges offer the potential to facilitate connectivity among various supply-chain participants—with this connectivity resulting in increased effectiveness and efficiency across the supply chain.

The Natural Environment

The preservation or improvement of the natural environment, sometimes referred to as **environmentalism,** emerged as a powerful issue in the latter decades of the twentieth century.[13] The Green party was one way the movement expressed itself politically. This emphasis on preserving or improving the natural environment, which is now worldwide, is forcing individual nations to adopt more environmentally sound laws, as well as to place greater expectations upon businesses to follow more environmentally friendly practices. Moreover, the International Standards Organization (ISO), perhaps most famous for its quality standards (e.g., ISO 9000), has also formulated an international environmental standard known as ISO 14000.

Previous research indicates that key environmental issues that influence logistics include hazardous and solid waste disposal, as well as water pollution, with salvage and scrap disposal, packaging, and transportation viewed as the logistics functions most likely to be impacted by environmental issues. In addition, the recycling of materials

---

[9]"The E-mail Overload," *Country Monitor,* Vol. 9, No. 41 October 22, 2001, pg. 5.

[10]Q & A with AMR Research Analyst John Bermudez, "Why the Internet Is Still the 'Next Big Thing'," *Supply Chain Management Review,* Vol. 6, No. 3, 2002, pp. 54–58.

[11]Marc McCluskey, "PTXs Bid to Be the Glue of Extended Utility Enterprises," *Energy IT,* Vol. 7, No. 2, 2002, pp. 52–54.

[12]Ibid, 2002.

[13]Some of the material in this section is drawn from a series of articles by Paul R. Murphy, Richard F. Poist, and Charles D. Braunschweig.

FIGURE 15-2 The Recycling of Aluminum Cans

Source: Courtesy of Aluminum Company of America.

and reduced consumption are suggested to be the most frequent strategies for managing and responding to environmental issues in logistics.

Many areas in the United States and other developed countries are running out of space to dispose of garbage and waste, and there is increasing scrutiny of waste-disposal practices. One response to these concerns has been greater emphasis on product recycling, and Figure 15-2 shows an example of how aluminum cans might be recycled. For the logistics professional, **recycling** means many things, such as understanding how a product's ability to be recycled adds to its value; recognizing how recycling establishes new channels in the supply, distribution, and return movement networks; and appreciation of how recycling influences the choice of materials for packaging a product.

A product's ability to be recycled adds to its value because at some point in time the item, or selected component parts, can be resold to other parties. The various markets that currently handle recycled products differ in sophistication and coverage. The used car market has been in existence since the early years of the automobile industry, and automobile manufacturers have learned the nuances of increasing or decreasing the supply of used cars.

On the other hand, a relatively new market for recyclables is the personal computer and its various component parts; at the present time, this market is much more fragmented and poorly organized compared, say, to the used car market. However, as the personal computer industry becomes more mature, we expect the market for recycled computers and computer parts to become better defined and organized.

With respect to channel design, one concern involves whether recycled goods should be handled by an existing channel that is merely reversed or by a newly established channel. Returnable beer bottles, for example, might be best served by a system that uses the existing channel in reverse. Alternatively, recyclable products that create environmental problems (e.g., automobile batteries contain acid and lead) might be best served by newly established channels.

Although packaging materials that can be reused are often desirable, some materials are so stable that they may not decompose for long periods of time. While Styrofoam packaging peanuts, for example, are relatively inexpensive and widely used, Styrofoam takes a long time to decompose. This is not a recycling issue per se, but it does demonstrate the difficulty in selecting packaging methods and materials.

Many firms and government agencies use *affirmative procurement* policies, which mandate the recyclability of packaging or finished goods or which specify the portion of content of a product that must be made from recycled materials. In addition, **extended producer responsibility programs** have become more popular, particularly in Western Europe. These programs shift responsibility to the manufacturer for the end-of-life of products and have led to packaging improvements that use fewer resources, require less transportation, and generate less waste disposal.[14]

Specific Logistics and Supply-Chain Issues

Unlike the macro-environmental issues, which are largely uncontrollable by individual organizations, specific logistics and supply-chain issues refer to issues over which individual organizations can exert some degree of control. For example, in tracing the history of strategic logistics concepts, John Kent and Daniel Flint describe the decades of the 1980s and 1990s as ones in which logistics became a strategic differentiator, mainly through early efforts at supply-chain integration and superior management of information. Seeing a convergence of intellectual thought in marketing, engineering, operations management, and logistics, they believe that the early decades of the twenty-first century will be the time when logistics will focus on the understanding of consumers' perceptions of a firm's logistics system and on boundary-spanning activities, as supply chains continue to consolidate and integrate operationally.[15]

Professors Donald Bowersox, David Closs, and Theodore Stank have offered insights into 10 megatrends, or paradigm shifts, that they believe will revolutionize supply-chain logistics in the first decade of the twenty-first century. The 10 megatrends are these:

1. *Customer service to relationship management:* Movement away from internal standards towards a focus on customer success.
2. *Adversarial to collaborative:* Less emphasis on maximizing individual corporate goals and more on the benefits of firms collaborating to achieve common goals.
3. *Forecast to endcast:* Movement toward developing supply-chain plans to best serve end customers.

---

[14]Cheryl A. McMullen, "Who's Responsible for This?" *Waste News,* October 30, 2000, pp. 3–4.

[15]John L. Kent and Daniel J. Flint, "Perspectives on the Evolution of Logistics Thought," *Journal of Business Logistics,* Vol. 18, No. 2, 1997, pp. 15–29.

4. *Experience to transition strategy:* Less emphasis on an experience curve and more on adaptation to new competitive patterns.
5. *Absolute to relative value:* Less emphasis on absolute market share in terms of sales revenues and more on growth of profitable revenue streams.
6. *Functional to process integration:* Increasing recognition that functional excellence is relevant only in the context of the processes they serve.
7. *Vertical to virtual integration:* A shift from owning various levels in a channel to utilizing the expertise and synergy of external parties.
8. *Information hoarding to sharing:* Hoarding allows companies to exploit information, while sharing allows companies to leverage it.
9. *Training to knowledge-based learning:* Less emphasis on job-related skills and more on enhancing each employee's value-creating ability.
10. *Managerial accounting to value-based management:* Less emphasis on cost figures and more emphasis on stakeholder value.[16]

Some of the megatrends are more developed in practice than others. For example, Bowersox, Closs, and Stank indicate that "functional to process integration" has experienced greater implementation than "training to knowledge-based learning."[17] Space limitations here preclude an in-depth discussion of each megatrend but allow examination of the first two—**relationship management** and **collaboration**—in part because they have been some of the most prominent manifestations of the supply-chain concept.

Relationship Management

The discussion in Chapter 2 indicated that a long-term orientation was one of the hallmarks of supply-chain management and that such an orientation tends to be predicated on relational exchanges. Some key attributes of relational exchanges are trust, commitment, dependence, and shared benefits. Importantly, relational exchanges signify that supply-chain management cannot be successful without relationship management, which can be defined as creating, maintaining, and enhancing strong relationships with customers and other stakeholders.

Indeed, **customer relationship management** (CRM) has become one of the hottest topics in the contemporary business world. Significantly, CRM attempts to facilitate customer loyalty, as opposed to customer satisfaction; satisfied customers do not always translate into loyal customers, whereas loyal customers tend to be highly satisfied. Moreover, loyal customers are repeat purchasers—the lifeblood of businesses.

While a detailed explanation is beyond the scope of this book, CRM—at least conceptually—offers the opportunity for a company to learn a great deal about the behaviors, activities, and attributes of individual customers. This knowledge, in turn, offers the opportunity for companies to tailor their marketing tactics and practices to the needs and wants of individual customers. The end result, ideally, is loyal customers who become customers for life.

Unfortunately, a number of actual experiences with CRM have yet to live up to the potential promises. For example, recent estimates have suggested that upward of

---

[16]Donald J. Bowersox, David J. Closs, and Theodore P. Stank, "Ten Mega-Trends That Will Revolutionize Supply Chain Logistics," *Journal of Business Logistics,* Vol. 21, No. 2, 2000, pp. 1–15.
[17]Ibid.

50 percent of CRM implementations have not succeeded among United States and European organizations.[18] One reason is that CRM requires a massive database, as well as specific software packages, both of which can be quite costly and time consuming to implement. Moreover, CRM requires that companies become customer-centric (that is, truly focused on the customer) rather than product-centric—and that is difficult, if not impossible, for many organizations to accomplish.[19]

Nonetheless, a cadre of supporters believes that CRM is still a viable concept and that organizations simply need to be smarter in their approaches to managing it. For example, although senior managers often lend lip-service support for CRM, they may not always understand the implications of a customer-centric focus. In an effort to remedy this shortcoming, one company requires its top managers to meet—in person—with disgruntled customers and to listen to the reasons for their dissatisfaction. Alternatively, organizations can encourage customers to participate in certain activities relevant to the customer experience.[20] Southwest Airlines, for example, has recruited its frequent flyers to participate in the selection process for new flight attendants, in part because frequent flyers are most likely to interact with the flight attendants on a regular basis.

Furthermore, CRM implementations should focus greater attention on increasing the value of individual customer relationships, rather than on specific tools and technologies. Importantly, an effective and efficient supply chain can be integral to increasing the value of individual customer relationships. For instance, we've previously mentioned the concept of *tailored logistics,* which refers to providing different types and levels of logistics service to different customers. In this vein, CRM data can be utilized to learn about the logistical requirements of individual customers, and thus permit different logistical service to be provided to different customers.[21] As such, individual customers are less likely to be either overserved or underserved when it comes to their specific logistical and supply chain needs.

Whereas CRM involves the relationships between an organization and its customers, an evolving concept known as **supplier relationship management** (SRM) involves the relationships between an organization and its suppliers. Similar to CRM, SRM requires a massive database, as well as specific software packages. The starting point with SRM tends to be supplier rationalization or a reduction in the number of vendors used by a particular organization. Unlike CRM's focus on customer loyalty, SRM attempts to "synchronize the flow of incoming parts with their production schedules."[22]

Proponents suggest that SRM implementation offers several potential benefits to an organization, including shorter sourcing cycles, reduced time-to-market cycles, lower material costs, and markedly lower inventory costs.[23] However, because SRM is

---

[18]Arthur M. Hughes, "Editorial: The Mirage of CRM," *Journal of Database Marketing,* Vol. 9, No. 2, 2002, pp. 102–104.

[19]Ibid.

[20]Ruth Le Pla, "Seven Breakthrough CRM Strategies," *NZ Marketing Magazine,* October 2002, pp. 8–14.

[21]Jennifer Reed, "For Success, Building a Customer-Centric Strategy Is Key," *Electronic News,* October 16, 2000, pp. 54–55.

[22]Sidney Hill, Jr. "True Supply Chain Management," February 2002, p. 48–49.

[23]Katherine Jones, "Source Smart: The Need for Supplier Management," *Manufacturing Systems,* August 2002, pp. 56–57.

still a developing concept, particularly when compared to CRM, anecdotal evidence from companies that have adopted SRM is relatively sparse. As a result, it will be interesting to see if some of the mistakes made with CRM adoptions, such as an overemphasis on technology, are repeated in SRM implementations.

Collaboration

Chapter 2 also pointed out that optimal supply-chain performance will be elusive without coordination across organizations. Moreover, the likelihood of successful coordination can be increased when these organizations are working toward a common goal (or common goals)—in other words, collaboration. Indeed, collaboration appears to be lacking in many underperforming supply chains and may be the critical success factor that distinguishes successful from unsuccessful supply chains.[24]

One of the most prominent collaboration techniques is **Collaborative Planning, Forecasting, and Replenishment** (CPFR), which can be defined as "a retail industry initiative in which trading partners share all sorts of critical planning and forecasting data."[25] Although CPFR has been in existence only since the late 1990s, CPFR adoptions appear to have met with more success than some other recent logistics and supply-chain initiatives.

For instance, Ace Hardware, which does business in over 60 countries, has expanded its initial CPFR program from 1 supplier to approximately 15. Ace's benefits from CPFR include improved forecasting accuracy, lower freight costs due to higher order weight, higher inventory turns, and higher order fill rates. According to Ace's management, CPFR benefits can only be achieved when the various participants are committed to achieving common goals.[26]

Another widely used collaboration technique is **vendor-managed inventory** (VMI), which refers to a situation in which the size and timing of replenishment orders are the responsibility of the manufacturer (as opposed to the retailer). (VMI was discussed in Chapter 9, Inventory Management, but the emphasis in that discussion was on VMI as a contemporary approach to managing inventory.)

VMI can be complementary to CPFR in the sense that VMI can take time (such as faster order cycles) and money (reduced inventory levels) out of the supply chain. Like CPFR, a number of VMI implementations appear to have been successful; on average, VMI pays for itself within 6 to 12 weeks, and inventory reductions of over 30 percent are not uncommon. VMI's benefits emanate from automating select processes, such as placing orders and paying invoices, that previously involved primarily manual or semi-mechanized systems. As is the case with CPFR, VMI is most effective when suppliers are committed to constantly working with customers.[27]

In terms of the future, Professor John Langley suggests that "there is not a whole lot that you can do *to improve the supply chain that doesn't involve collaborating with*

[24]Gary Forger, "Collaboration—The Supply Chain's Defining Factor?" *Supply Chain Management Review,* Vol. 4, No. 3, 2000, pp. 97–98.

[25]Lisa H. Harrington, "Planning for Profit," *Transportation & Distribution,* Vol. 43, No. 5, 2002, pp. 58–62.

[26]James Aaron Cooke, "Why Ace Is Becoming the Place," *Logistics Management,* Vol. 41, No. 3, 2002, pp. 32–36.

[27]Jim Fulcher, "Supply-Side Smoothness," *Manufacturing Systems,* Vol. 20, No. 8, 2002, pp. 44–47.

each other (our emphasis)."[28] As a result, collaboration should be an essential aspect of logistics and supply-chain management in the coming years. Future logistics and supply-chain collaborations should begin to move away from data sharing and toward more strategic applications, such as one company stationing its employees at key supplier and/or customer locations. According to most experts, this strategic collaboration is likely to first be implemented among several key business partners before becoming more widely applied.[29]

Although logistics and supply-chain collaboration appear to have a bright future, successful collaborative techniques such as CPFR and VMI require expensive technology—and some companies are hesitant to commit the necessary resources, particularly when faced with the uncertain economic situation of the early twenty-first century. Some may feel that too many managerial initiatives are floating about. (See Figure 15-3.) In addition, successful collaboration is predicated on trust among various supply-chain parties—and some companies are still hesitant to share sensitive data with other companies.[30]

FIGURE 15-3 Some May Feel That There Is An Overabundance of Systems Options

Source: Used with the permission of Material Handling Management, copyright Penton Media, Inc.

---

[28]Mike Verespej, "Supply Chain Collaboration," *Frontline Solutions,* September 2002, pp. 20–24.
[29]Ibid.
[30]Ibid.

SUMMARY

This chapter looked at future directions for logistics and supply-chain management. The first part of the chapter discussed several key macro-environmental issues that are likely to impact logistics and supply-chain management in the years to come. International trade, the service economy, information technology, and the natural environment were discussed.

The second part of the chapter looked at relationship management and collaboration, which are considered to be key megatrends affecting logistics and supply-chain management in the twenty-first century. While customer relationship management appears to have a great deal of potential, actual experiences with CRM programs have been less than favorable for many companies. Alternatively, actual experiences with collaboration techniques appear to have been generally favorable.

QUESTIONS FOR DISCUSSION AND REVIEW

1. Why is international logistics so expensive?
2. Discuss some of the potential challenges to conducting logistics in China.
3. Are multicountry trade alliances, such as NAFTA, helpful or harmful to the world's economy? Support your position.
4. Discuss some of the ways in which multicountry trade alliances can influence logistics and supply-chain management.
5. What are some logistical implications of the shift toward a service economy?
6. Do you think that one-stop shopping—purchasing multiple logistics services from one company—is a good or bad idea? Why?
7. Discuss how you think the September 11, 2001, terrorist attacks will influence logistics and supply-chain technologies.
8. Which IT trend—intelligent voice recognition or pervasive wireless—do you think will be more important to logistics and supply-chain management in the coming years? Why?
9. In what ways can the so-called "revenge of the techies" be detrimental to logistics and supply-chain management?
10. Do you agree, or disagree, that many companies have barely scratched the surface in terms of utilizing the Internet for effective and efficient supply-chain management? Why?
11. What is a private trading exchange?
12. What is environmentalism? Will it increase or decrease in importance during the early years of the twenty-first century? Why?
13. Discuss some implications of recycling for the logistics professional.
14. What recycling activities do you engage in? Should recycling activities be mandatory or voluntary for individual consumers? Support your position.
15. The chapter discussed four macro-environmental issues that might impact logistics and supply-chain management in the early years of the twenty-first century. Identify another macro-environmental issue, and explain how it might impact logistics and supply-chain management.
16. Which of the 10 megatrends outlined by Professors Bowersox, Closs, and Stank do you believe is the most important? Why?
17. Discuss potential advantages and disadvantages associated with customer relationship management.
18. Do you believe that customer relationship management has the potential to positively impact logistics and supply-chain management? Why or why not?

19. Do you believe that customer relationship management or supplier relationship management has more potential to positively impact the supply chain? Why?
20. Do you agree or disagree with Professor Langley's assessment that there's not a lot that can be done to improve supply chains that doesn't involve collaboration? Why?

SUGGESTED READINGS

Bowersox, Donald J., David J. Closs, and Theodore P. Stank. "Ten Mega-Trends That Will Revolutionize Supply Chain Logistics." *Journal of Business Logistics,* Vol. 21, No. 2, 2000, pp. 1–15.

Daly, Shawn P., and Lindsay X. Cvi. "E-Logistics in China: Basic Problems, Manageable Concerns and Intractable Solutions." *Industrial Marketing Management,* Vol. 32, No. 3, 2003, pp. 235–242.

Hingley, Martin. "Relationship Management in the Supply Chain." *International Journal of Logistics Management,* Vol. 12, No. 2, 2001, pp. 57–71.

Jiang, Bin, and Edmund Prater. "Distribution and Logistics Development in China: The Revolution Has Begun." *International Journal of Physical Distribution & Logistics Management,* Vol. 32, No. 9, 2002, pp. 783–798.

Kehoe, Dennis, and Nick Boughton. "Internet Based Supply Chain Management." *International Journal of Operations & Production Management,* Vol. 21, No. 4, 2001, pp. 516–525.

Kent, John L., and Daniel J. Flint. "Perspectives on the Evolution of Logistics Thought." *Journal of Business Logistics,* Vol. 18, No. 2, 1997, pp. 15–29.

Kurnia, Sherah, and Robert B. Johnston. "Adoption of Efficient Consumer Response: The Issue of Mutuality." *Supply Chain Management: An International Journal,* Vol. 6, No. 5, 2001, pp. 230–241.

Lancioni, Richard A., Michael F. Smith, and Hope Jensen Schau. "Strategic Internet Application Trends in Supply Chain Management." *Industrial Marketing Management,* Vol. 32, No. 3, 2003, pp. 211–217.

McCarthy, Teresa M., and Susan L. Golicic. "Implementing Collaborative Forecasting to Improve Supply Chain Performance." *International Journal of Physical Distribution & Logistics Management,* Vol. 32, No. 6, 2002, pp. 431–454.

Montabon, Frank, and Steven A. Melnyk. "ISO 14000: Assessing Its Perceived Impact on Corporate Performance." *Journal of Supply Chain Management,* Vol. 36, No. 2, 2000, pp. 4–16.

Nairn, Agnes. "CRM: Helpful or Full of Hype?" *Journal of Database Marketing,* Vol. 9, No. 4, 2002, pp. 376–382.

Poist, Richard F., Carl A. Scheraga, and Janjaap Semejin. "Preparation of Logistics Managers for the Contemporary Environment of the European Union." *International Journal of Physical Distribution & Logistics Management,* Vol. 31, No. 7/8, 2001, pp. 487–504.

Sheffi, Yossi. "Supply Chain Management Under the Threat of Terrorism." *International Journal of Logistics Management,* Vol. 12, No. 2, 2001, pp. 1–11.

Whipple, Judith M., Robert Frankel, and Patricia J. Daugherty. "Information Support for Alliances: Performance Implications." *Journal of Business Logistics,* Vol. 23, No. 2, 2002, pp. 67–82.

C A S E S

Case 15-1 Shimamoto Toy Company

The Shimamoto Toy Company was headquartered in Kobe, Japan. The firm had built toys for the U.S. market since the mid-1930s. After World War II, it specialized in metal toy cars, trucks, and construction equipment. In the 1970s and 1980s, it shifted to building remote-controlled, battery-powered toy vehicles and also began developing electronic games. Two-thirds of Shimamoto's entire market was the United States. Toy sales are associated with Christmas in the United States, and 60 percent of the toys Shimamoto sold in the United States would be shipped during August or early September. Other toy markets were in Western Europe, Australia, and several of the increasingly prosperous Asian nations.

Because of the current high Japanese wage rates, Shimamoto had almost no production facilities operating in Japan. Its first plant outside Japan was in Pusan, Korea. Plant operations in Korea were satisfactory, but older Koreans recalled the harsh Japanese occupation of Korea during the first half of the century, and Shimamoto's officials never felt especially welcome there. Many firms were locating facilities in Taiwan, but Shimamoto decided not to since it realized that eventually it might want to expand into mainland China and was uncertain whether the People's Republic of China (PRC) would look kindly on its operations in Taiwan. In 1987, Shimamoto located a new plant in Thailand and, in 1991, a new plant in Vietnam. As of 2001, it had its production divided approximately as follows: Korea, 32 percent; Thailand, 30 percent; Vietnam, 25 percent; and Japan, 13 percent. Shimamoto's Japanese plant was old, and its wage costs high. Shimamoto management intended to close it and shift its production to an existing facility or to a new facility in mainland China.

Locating in China was a long-time goal, or dream, of many manufacturers. China boasted a large workforce in a disciplined setting. Several of Shimamoto's major competitors were already establishing manufacturing operations in China. Firms with operations in China tolerated considerable interference from the Chinese government and apparently were willing to do so because of the great potential for long-term gains. Also, once established, Shimamoto would probably try to persuade the Chinese government not to let in more competitors.

Until a few years ago, Shimamoto had consolidated all of its U.S.-bound shipments in Osaka, Japan, where they were containerized and shipped east to U.S. West Coast ports. In 1988, Hong Kong became the consolidation point. In 1997, Hong Kong reverted to Chinese control, and Shimamoto's management was uncertain whether, or how, this might impact Hong Kong's performance as a consolidation center. Hong Kong was one of the world's busiest container ports. Critics of the PRC predicted that Hong Kong's port would fall from eminence now that the Chinese had taken over. The opposite point of view was that China's exports were growing so rapidly and that, since Hong Kong was the country's main port of exportation, the Hong Kong port would choke on such an expanded flow of traffic. Either way, Shimamoto's management had some questions on their minds concerning the long-term prospects of Hong Kong as the company's principal consolidation point.

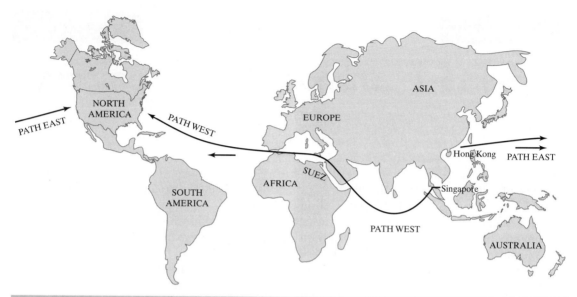

EXHIBIT 15-A Shimamoto's Toys Could Go Either West or East

An alternative consolidation point was Singapore, far to the south, nearly at the Equator. Singapore was the historic gateway between Asia and Europe and had port facilities comparable to those in Hong Kong. Singapore had a stable, if not rigid, government.

Both Hong Kong and Singapore had excellent container-line service. Most of Hong Kong's routes stretched eastward, across the Pacific. Singapore's liner routes went east and west. Most of those routes went west through the Suez Canal and then either to Europe or to North America (see Exhibit 15-A). Within Asia itself, many smaller container vessels shuttled containers between either Hong Kong or Singapore and 10 to 20 other smaller Asian ports. Nearly all Asian container traffic moving into or out of Asia was funneled through either Hong Kong or Singapore. Both were giant hubs where traffic was consolidated.

Carrier alliances (or rate agreements) across the Pacific were enjoying very busy and prosperous times. As evidence of this, they raised their rates and various surcharges more than did conferences serving other world markets. Shimamoto's management was always conscious of transportation rates because its product was bulky and transport costs constituted 15 to 20 percent of its wholesale, delivered cost.

U.S. West Coast ports, especially Los Angeles/Long Beach, were also becoming increasingly congested, resulting in containers being delayed and sometimes misplaced for weeks. Toy traffic was often subject to delays because those handling it would say, "It's just a load of toys," and give preference to some other cargo.

Shimamoto's distribution manager received a sales call from two men, one representing a large Singapore freight consolidator and the other a major container line serving Singapore and points west (including Western Europe and the East Coast of North America). The men said they were trying to divert Asia-to-North America traffic that been moving across the Pacific. They said that the time that the cargo would be in transit longer using their route, but to a toy manufacturer who produces at a steady rate all year and sells over half its product in a 2-month season, longer transit times should be of little consequence.

QUESTIONS

1. How should Shimamoto go about deciding where to expand its toy production? List and discuss the steps.
2. What are some of the concerns (possibly in addition to those appearing in the case) about doing business in mainland China?
3. How stable do you think Hong Kong will be as a port and consolidation point now that the Chinese have taken it over?
4. The case includes this statement: "Time that the cargo would be in transit would be longer using their route, but to a toy manufacturer who produces at a steady rate all year and sells over half its product in a 2-month season, longer transit times should be of little consequence." Do you agree with it? Why or why not?
5. How would Shimamoto go about studying whether it would be more advantageous to have its goods destined to the United States be imported through a U.S. East Coast or West Coast port?
6. Assume that Shimamoto wants to choose between Hong Kong and Singapore as its major consolidation point. List all the factors that it must consider.
7. Which of the two consolidation points do you think Shimamoto should choose? Why?

Case 15-2   Donelly Metal Stampings Company

Donelly Metal Stampings Company is located in East St. Louis, Illinois, where it has been since its founding in 1887. In its old and relatively small plant, it operates 20 punch presses of varying sizes. Punch presses cut and shape metal pieces and parts, such as bases for scaffolding and the metal boxes used to contain electrical outlets. Donelly's principal customers are in the St. Louis area, though a number are scattered as far west as Kansas City, to the northeast as far as Chicago/Hammond, and to Kentucky in the southeast, where some new auto assembly plants are located.

The outgoing product is usually shipped by truck. If the stamped item can be nested, the shipment is very heavy. When the product cannot be nested, the loads are bulky. An ideal outgoing load is a mixture of dense, nested items below and bulky items above. Donelly operates its own fleet of eight trucks for making deliveries. Production and delivery are closely coordi-

nated, and Donelly offers a high level of customer service (measured in terms of on-time delivery). Richard Ritter of the marketing department is in charge of scheduling the outgoing deliveries and dispatching the fleet of trucks carrying goods to customers.

The principal input is sheet steel, usually purchased from mills in the Chicago/Hammond/Gary area. Steel producers usually charge uniform amounts for their product but compete in terms of absorbing the freight costs of making the deliveries. Obtaining these concessions requires astute bargaining. Herb Wiggins is the assistant director of purchasing, specializing in transportation.

There is little coordination between those responsible for outbound and inbound shipments at Donelly. Consider the Following:

1. Ritter and Wiggins do not get along personally, and neither has been inside the

other's office for as long as most employees can remember. Mail or phone calls directed to "the transportation manager" cause problems since either is offended when the other gets the letter or call.

2. Attempts to use Donelly's private fleet of trucks for carrying inbound sheet steel as a backhaul have not worked out, in part because steel is better suited for carriage by rail and in part because neither Wiggins nor Ritter has tried to make the backhaul system work. Ritter has developed occasional backhaul business carrying for other firms, but the depressed economy in the East St. Louis area has resulted in few inbound loads.

3. During a wildcat rail strike in the Chicago area, Donelly attempted to get some motor carriers to carry steel from Hammond to East St. Louis. It was unable to contract with any truckers because regular carriers know that Donelly usually uses rail and has its own trucks, and so the shipments of Donelly steel represented temporary business. In addition, these truckers had all the work they could handle, hauling for regular accounts during the rail strike. Harold Donelly III, the firm's president, had to personally tell Ritter to release some trucks from making deliveries and to go to Hammond to pick up steel. By the time the trucks arrived in Hammond, the rail strike was over. However, the Donelly plant was without steel and had to shut down for 2 days. Its competitors, however, relying solely on contract truckers, were able to receive sheet steel and remain open.

The wildcat strike experience brought matters at Donelly to a head. Withdrawing trucks from making deliveries and being shut down for 2 days caused the loss of several key accounts to competitors.

At this point, Wiggins's boss sent a memo to Harold Donelly outlining the problem. He laid heavy blame on Ritter, recommending that a new post—director of transportation—be established and suggesting that Herb Wiggins was qualified to fill the post.

Ritter and his boss believed that Ritter had been unjustly blamed since he was not responsible for inbound movements. They countered with an even longer memo, recommending that Ritter be named director of transportation and that Wiggins serve as his assistant. They both knew that Wiggins would resign rather than be Ritter's assistant, but they considered this one advantage of their plan.

Within a week, Donelly's management was split into two camps: one favoring Wiggins as the new director of transportation and the other favoring Ritter. Harold Donelly realized that he had to make a controversial decision. If he named either Ritter or Wiggins, he would alienate the other individual as well as about half of his management team. He could bring in an outsider, but the firm could not afford a three-person transportation department. In addition, neither Ritter nor Wiggins was considered flexible or easy to work with, so it was unlikely that either could be reassigned elsewhere within the firm.

On Thursday afternoons, Harold Donelly has a long-standing golf date with some friends. He, Sid Burroughs, and Louis Milsted are sitting in the clubhouse waiting for a fourth member to arrive. Donelly tells the others about the problem.

Burroughs says, "I'd fire both Wiggins and Ritter and start from there."

Milsted comments, "Do you need a transportation department at all? Why not buy on a delivered basis and make your vendors agree to deliver sheet steel as you need it. Sell on an FOB-dock basis, and your buyers will have to pick up their purchases. The buzz words these days are 'forming partnerships' with your vendors and customers. You'll save the cost of transportation people as well as that of your eight trucks."

QUESTIONS

1. If either Ritter or Wiggins is named director of transportation, what assignments should be given to the other?
2. Comment on Burroughs's suggestion. Should both Wiggins and Ritter be fired? Why or why not?
3. Wiggins and Ritter do not get along, and their feud has management divided. Who is responsible for the problem? Discuss.
4. Assume that both Ritter and Wiggins are no longer part of the transportation operation. You are asked to prepare a job description for a new transportation manager. Prepare the draft of such a job announcement.
5. Instead of a transportation department, should Donelly create a logistics department? How about a supply-chain management department? Discuss.
6. Comment on Milsted's suggestion. Should Donelly follow his advice? Why or why not?
7. Are there situations, industries, or firms for which Milsted's suggestion might be more applicable? What are they?
8. In what types of situations, industries, or firms is it more important to closely control inbound shipments but not outbound ones? Give examples.
9. In what types of situations, industries, or firms is it more important to control closely outbound shipments but not inbound ones? Give examples.

Glossary

ABC analysis In inventory management, the placing of items into categories A, B, and C with respect to monitoring stock levels.

Adjustment function Selecting a point in the exchange channel to concentrate goods, make a new selection from that concentration, and form a new selection of goods to move forward in the channel.

Application service provider (ASP) ASPs allow individuals or enterprises to rent/lease particular software applications for a particular period of time.

Artificial intelligence (AI) Sophisticated use of the computer in which it is programmed to "think" as a trained, skilled human in specific situations.

Backhaul A return trip or movement in a direction of secondary importance or purpose.

Back order Materials requested by a customer that are unavailable for shipment at the same time as the remainder of the order. They are usually shipped when available.

BAF (bunker adjustment factor) Additional charges by ocean liners to take into account that the price of fuel (bunkers) has increased.

Bank payment plan A service provided by banks for shippers. Carriers send freight bills to the bank to be paid. The bank pays the carrier and subtracts the payment from the shipper's account. Also called freight payment service.

Bar-code scanners Electronic devices that read bar codes and can be used to keep track of inventory, reorder inventory, and analyze inventory patterns.

Barter Paying for goods with other goods, rather than cash.

Base stock Inventory needed to satisfy demand during an order cycle.

Batch numbers Numbers put on products when they are manufactured for identifying when they were made and at what factory.

Belly freight Cargo that is transported in the lower freight compartments of airplanes.

Benchmarking Using measures of another's performance to judge one's own performance.

Bill of lading A contract stating that a carrier has received certain freight and is responsible for its delivery.

Bonded storage The most common type involves the collection of excise taxes, such as those on cigarettes. Excise taxes do not have to be paid until the product leaves the bonded warehouse.

Break-bulk cargo In ocean shipping, cargo handled piece by piece by stevedores, rather than in bulk or in intermodal containers.

Break-bulk distribution center A warehouse where large shipments are sent by a shipper. Shipments are broken down by customer, and each consignee receives what was ordered.

Brokers Companies that help both shipper and carrier achieve lower freight rates and more efficient utilization of carrier equipment. They also help match carriers to loads.

Building-block concept Combining smaller packages into larger units that can be more efficiently handled at one time.

Bulk cargo In shipping, cargo stowed loose, without specific packing, and generally handled with a pump, scoop, or shovel.

CAF (currency adjustment factor) Additional charges by ocean liners to take into account that the foreign currency that they must buy to pay port costs in foreign nations requires an increasing number of U.S. dollars to purchase.

Carload sale An old retail advertising term, meaning that the retailer purchased an entire carload of product at a reduced cost and is presumably passing these savings on. Today, the term truckload sale is sometimes used.

Carrier An individual or firm in the business of carrying cargo and/or passengers.

Cartage Local hauling of freight.

Center-of-gravity location An approach for locating a single facility that minimizes the distance to existing facilities.

Charter In international transportation, the leasing or renting of a vessel or aircraft for a specific trip or time limit.

Classification Numbers assigned to various types of freight, based mainly on the carrier's costs of handling that type of product, and, along with weight and distance, used as a basis for determining the costs of shipment.

Co-branding One location where customers can purchase products from two or more name-brand retailers.

COFC (container on flatcar) Piggyback traffic, or the shipping of containers on rail flatcars.

Collaboration When several organizations work towards common goals.

Collaborative Planning, Forecasting, and Replenishment (CPFR) Retail industry initiative where trading partners share planning and forecasting data.

Common carrier obligations Over time, common carriers assumed four legal obligations to their customers: service, delivery, reasonable rates, and avoidance of discrimination.

Complementary goods Inventories that are used or distributed together (e.g., razor blades and razors).

Concealed damage Damage not initially apparent but discovered after a package is opened.

Consignee The receiver of a shipment.

Consignor The shipper of goods.

Consolidate Assemble small shipments into a single, larger shipment.

Containers Large boxes, about 8 feet high, 8 feet wide, and from 20 to 55 feet long that can be transported by rail, truck, air, or water carrier (though air containers are often smaller).

Contract carrier Found in the trucking industry; recently, railroads have also offered contracts to their customers. A contract carrier provides specialized service to each customer based on a contractual arrangement.

Contract logistics A long-term arrangement between a shipper and another party to provide logistics services.

Contract warehousing A type of contract logistics that focuses on providing unique and specially tailored warehousing services to particular clients.

Co-opetition Recognizes that companies can be competitors in some situations, while working together in other situations.

Cost tradeoffs Changes to one logistics activity cause some costs to increase and others to decrease.

Cross-docking Immediately moving cargo as it is being received at a warehouse to a loading dock where it is loaded aboard outbound trucks.

Cross-traders Ships that transport cargo between two countries, neither of which is the nationality of the vessel. A U.S.-registered ship carrying products from Mexico to Spain would be engaged in cross-trading.

Cube out Occurs when a bulky cargo takes up a vehicle's or a container's cubic capacity but not its weight capacity.

Customer service Assisting an existing customer.

Customer service standards A service level that a selling firm wants to achieve, such as the ability to fill 95 percent of all orders completely within 48 hours.

Customs collection Tax payments collected by a government when foreign products enter its country.

Customshouse brokers Companies that help buyers bring imports into a country by preparing customs reports, arranging for transportation, and the like.

CWT 100 pounds.

Data mining Utilizes sophisticated quantitative techniques to find hidden patterns in large volumes of data.

Deadhead A concept associated with the trucking industry that is characterized by driving an empty front haul in order to pick up a load on the back haul.

Dead stock Product for which there is no demand.

Decision support system (DSS) Help managers make decisions by providing information, models, or analysis tools.

Dedicated equipment In railroading, cars assigned for use by a specific customer.

Delivered-pricing systems A price that includes delivery to the buyer.

Delivery window The time span within which a scheduled delivery must be made.

Demurrage A charge assessed by rail carriers to users that fail to unload and return vehicles or containers promptly.

Detention A payment from a shipper or consignee to a truck carrier for having kept the carrier's equipment too long.

Dim weight Dimensional weight, when the shipment's dimensions (length, height, etc.) are sufficiently extreme that they determine the rate charged by the carrier.

Distribution center A warehouse with an emphasis on quick throughput, such as is needed in supporting marketing efforts.

Distribution requirements planning (DRP) Inventory management of finished products that is linked to sophisticated sales forecasting.

Door-to-door Through carriage of a container from shipper to customer.

Dovetailing When vendors (suppliers) locate their plants in close proximity to customers. The idea is growing rapidly because of JIT inventory systems.

Draft The depth in the water to which a vessel can be loaded.

Drayage Local trucking, and used today to describe the truck movement of containers and trailers to and from railyards and port areas.

Drop shipments Shipments delivered to a handful of designated sites.

Dunnage Wood and other packing materials used to wedge and otherwise keep cargo in place.

E-fulfillment Coordinated inbound and outbound logistics functions that facilitate the management and delivery of customer orders placed online.

Economic order quantity (EOQ) An order size that minimizes the combined storage and processing costs.

Electronic commerce Economic activity that can be conducted via electronic connections such as EDI and the Internet.

Electronic data interchange (EDI) Buyers and sellers are linked by computers and use computers to exchange orders and other routine information.

Embargo A carrier's temporary refusal to accept certain shipments, usually because it is unable to deliver them (such as during a strike or a flood).

Enterprise resource planning (ERP) Systems that attempt enterprise-wide coordination of relevant business processes by allowing (conceptually, at least) all functional areas within a firm to access and analyze a common database.

Enterprise zone A deteriorated area designated to receive some tax relief in order to encourage new commercial developments.

Expatriate workers Employees who are sent to work in other countries for extended periods of time.

Expedited shipment A shipment that a carrier moves more quickly than usual.

Export declaration A form filled out by a U.S. exporter for governmental statistical and export-control purposes.

Export management companies Firms that help a domestic company become involved in foreign sales. They often locate foreign firms that can be licensed to manufacture the product in the foreign country. They also take care of the details involved in exporting.

Export packers Companies that prepare the protective packing for shipments transported overseas.

Export trading companies Companies that provide total help to exporters. They often involve a number of firms that may be domestic competitors and that are allowed to combine forces to be more effective in foreign sales.

Extended producer responsibility A program that shifts responsibility for the end-of-life products to the manufacturer.

FAK (freight-all-kinds) rate A rate applicable to a mixture of products.

FIFO (first in–first out) An inventory management procedure whereby the oldest item in stock gets shipped first.

Fixed order interval system Inventory is replenished on a constant, set schedule and is always ordered at a specific time; the quantity ordered varies depending on forecasted sales before the next order date.

Fixed order quantity system Inventory is replenished with a set quantity every time it is ordered; the time interval between orders may vary.

Fixed warehouse slot location Each product is assigned a specific location and is always stored there.

Flags of convenience Flags of nations that have lax maritime registration rules. Many ships are registered in these countries because of their lenient safety requirements.

Flying a nation's flag A ship that is registered in a particular country (e.g., a ship registered in France flies the French flag).

FOB destination (delivered) pricing Price that includes both the price of the product and the transportation cost of the product to the purchaser's receiving dock.

FOB (free on board) pricing Price at seller's place of business. Buyer must carry away.

Foreign trade zone An area, usually near a port or an airport, where goods can be stored or processed before entering through the importing nation's customs inspections.

Fourth-party logistics (lead logistics provider) General contractor that insures that third-party logistics companies are working towards relevant supply chain goals and objectives.

Freight absorption Buyer pays a lower freight charge than the shipper incurs in shipping the product.

Freight payment services See Bank payment plan.

Full-cost pricing The carrier prices the transportation service to each customer so that the full cost of providing the service is charged to each customer.

Global sourcing Willingness to buy anywhere in the world.

Goods in transit Goods moving between two points, often accompanied by a live bill of lading.

Green movement Individuals and groups trying to save our environment.

Grid systems A location technique utilizing a map or grid, with specific locations marked on the north–south and east–west axes. Its purpose is to find a location that minimizes transportation costs.

Hazmat (hazardous materials) Goods that pose hazards to those handling them, to other cargo, or to the public and for that reason require special handling.

Hijacking Theft that typically involves stealing both the transport vehicle and the cargo inside it.

Hub and spoke A carrier's route system with many routes (spokes) radiating out from a single center (hub).

Import quotas Absolute limits to the quantity of a product that can be imported into a country during a particular time period.

In bond Cargo on which taxes or duties have yet to be paid. The owner must post a bond or use a bonded carrier or warehouse to guarantee that the materials will not be sold until the taxes or duties are paid.

Inbound logistics Movement and storage of materials into a firm.

Incentive rates Charging less per unit of weight for heavier shipments.

Intermodal Using a container that can be transferred from the vehicle of one mode to a vehicle of another, and with the movement covered under a single bill of lading.

International Air Transport Association (IATA) A cartel, or group, that sets rates for international air transport.

Inventory carrying costs The costs of holding an inventory, such as interest on investment, insurance, deterioration, and so on.

Inventory flow Depicts the demand for, and replenishment of, inventory.

Inventory "turns" The number of times an inventory is used or replace each year.

KD Knocked down; when goods are packaged and shipped in an unassembled state, so that their bulk is reduced by about 67 percent, they receive a lower classification number and a lower rate per pound is paid.

Knot 6,082 feet per hour.

Landed costs Price of the product at its source plus transportation costs to its destination.

Landed price Total cost of goods delivered to one's door.

LIFO (last in-first out) Last in, first out inventory procedure.

Liner conference An organization of ocean-liner operators that sets rates. Also called rate agreement.

Load center A major port where thousands of containers arrive and depart per week. These ports specialize in the efficient handling of containers.

Load factor Percentage of capacity utilized.

Loading dock A warehouse or factory door where trucks are loaded or unloaded.

Logistics The flow of materials and services and the communications necessary to manage that flow.

Logistics exchanges Online portals that offer logistics services in several different categories.

Logistics information system (LIS) People, equipment, and procedures to gather, sort, analyze, evaluate, and distribute needed, timely, and accurate information to logistics decision makers.

Logistics service provider (LSP) Companies that specialize in providing various types of logistics services.

Loss and damage Loss or damage of shipments while in transit or in a warehouse.

LTL (less-than-truckload) A load that is too small to qualify as a "truckload" under motor freight classification rules. As such, it pays a higher rate per pound.

Macro-environmental issues Issues that are largely uncontrollable by individual organizations but that influence their strategies, tactics, and activities. Examples include interest rates, economic growth, and technology change, among others.

Make-bulk distribution center Frequently utilized for the shipment of production inputs. Vendors ship their relatively small shipments to a nearby warehouse. At the make-bulk distribution center a number of small shipments are combined to take advantage of the lower freight rates per pound available when large shipments are given to the carrier.

Maquiladora Manufacturing plants that exist just south of the U.S.–Mexican border.

Marginal analysis Analyzing the impacts of small changes, such as adding or subtracting one unit of input.

Marshaling Accumulating products or materials needed for a project.

Materials handling The efficient movement of products into and out of warehouses. The term also applies to bulk materials and to the handling of components on an assembly line.

Materials management Movement and storage of raw materials, parts, and components within a firm.

Materials requirements planning (MRP I) Using computers to manage production inventory.

Matrix management A logistics alternative that utilizes task forces established to solve specific problems. Members are drawn from various functional areas that impact on the problem. Once the problem is solved, the task force is disbanded.

Measurement ton In ocean shipping, the use of forty cubic feet (or some similar cubic measure) as the equivalent of one ton for calculating transportation charges.

Metric conversion Adopting the metric system of weights and measures.

Metric ton 2,204.6 pounds.

Nesting Packaging tapered articles inside each other to reduce the cubic volume of the entire shipment.

Nontariff barriers Governmental barriers that restrict trade but do not involve tariffs or quotas. An example is a government that requires all imports of a specific product to enter the country through one small port.

Nonvessel-operating common carrier (NVOCC) In international trade, a firm that provides carrier services to shippers but owns no vessels itself.

Occupational Safety and Health Act (OSHA) A 1970 federal law regulating workplaces to ensure the safety of workers.

Ocean liners Ships in regularly scheduled operations that specialize in less-than-shipload quantity shipments.

Opportunity costs The cost of giving up an alternative opportunity.

Order cycle Elapsed time between when a customer places an order and when the goods are received.

Order-dedicated inventory Inventory pledged to a customer that will soon be shipped to the customer involved.

Order picking and assembly In a warehouse, the selection of specific items to fill or assemble a complete order.

Order transmittal The time from when the customer places or sends the order to when the seller receives it.

Overnight delivery Goods shipped on one day and delivered the next morning.

Package testing Simulation of the types of problems that the package will be exposed to in warehouses and in transit.

Packaging Materials used to protect a shipment physically when it is in a warehouse or in transit.

Pallet A small platform, usually 40 by 48 inches, on which goods are placed for handling in a warehouse.

Palletization See Unitization.

Parcel In transportation, a small quantity or small package.

Perishables Cargo that spoils quickly and requires special attention.

PERT (program evaluation and review technique) A form of network analysis that places all component parts in the sequence in which they must be performed.

Phantom freight Occurs in delivered pricing when a buyer pays an excessive freight charge calculated into the price of the goods.

Physical distribution Storage of finished product and movement to the customers.

Piggyback Truck trailers on flatcars, also referred to as TOFC.

Pilferage The stealing of cargo on a casual basis, usually by one's employees.

Pipeline (in-transit) stock Inventory that is in route between various nodes in a logistics system.

Place utility Having products available **where** they are needed by customers.

PO Purchase order, a commitment to buy.

Postponement The delay of value-added activities such as assembly, production, and packaging to the latest possible time.

Private carrier Carrying one's own goods in one's own vehicles.

Private trading exchange (PTX) Exchanges that are owned or controlled by a single company, but that are accessible by external customers, suppliers, and partners as well as internal users.

Private warehousing Owning or leasing storage space for one's exclusive use.

Procurement Raw materials, component parts, and supplies brought from outside organizations to support a company's operations.

Product recalls A company asks customers to return certain products that are found to be defective.

Program evaluation and review technique See PERT.

Project cargo Cargo destined for one project, say, a dam being built in Africa.

Public warehouse A warehouse whose owner leases space and provides services to a variety of customers.

Pull inventory system An inventory system that responds to actual (rather than forecasted) customer demand.

Pull materials Materials that lose no weight in processing.

Push inventory system An inventory system that responds to forecasted (rather than actual) customer demand.

Rail siding A short rail track leading from a main line to a customer's plant or warehouse.

Rate bureau (conference) An organization of carriers that sets rates.

Rate negotiation Negotiation between the shipper and the carrier on the rate to be charged by the carrier.

Relationship management Creating, maintaining, and enhancing strong relationships with customers and other stakeholders.

Released value The limits to a carrier's liability for a certain shipment, in the sense that the carrier may agree to charge a lower overall rate if the shipment's stated value is lessened.

Reorder point A stock is consumed, and the balance remaining drops to this point, at which time a replenishment order is placed.

Reparations Payment from a carrier to a shipper for having charged the shipper excessive rates in the past.

Requisition A request that a procurement office supply or acquire some good.

Reverse logistics Goods that flow from the consumer to the manufacturer (e.g., product recalls and product recycling).

RFID Radio-frequency identification.

Right-to-work laws State laws that specify that a worker at a unionized plant does not have to join the union to work permanently at the facility.

RO–RO (roll on–roll off) Ships similar to floating parking lots that are loaded by driving tractors and trailers on ramps.

Safety stock A reserve inventory, in addition to that needed to meet anticipated requirements.

Seamless distribution A logistics organization strategy that removes impediments to the flow of information and goods.

Shipment consolidation Freight rates are less expensive per pound shipped when large shipments are given to the carrier at one time. Therefore, shippers try to group shipments bound for the same general area.

Shippers' associations Shippers that join together to negotiate more favorable ocean shipping rates.

Shippers' cooperatives Nonprofit groups of shippers that join to consolidate shipments.

Shipper's load and count On a transport document, the term means that the carrier did not independently count the items said to be shipped.

Shipping "wind" Declaring that a shipment weighs more than it actually does in order to pay a lower total transport charge, when the rate per pound is less for larger shipments.

Short-interval scheduling An analysis of workers' productivity over short periods of time. Each worker is assigned specific duties that he or she should be able to complete during the time period provided.

Shrinkage Losses in inventory that are difficult to account for.

Simulation A technique used to model the systems under study, typically using mathematical equations to represent relationships among components of a logistics system.

Skid See Pallet.

SKU (stock-keeping unit) Each separate type of item that is accounted for in an inventory.

Slipsheet Thick sheet of cardboard placed under a unit load, instead of a conventional pallet.

Slurry pipeline system Transports products that are ground into a powder, mixed with water, and then shipped in slurry form through a pipeline. The concept has been successfully used for transporting coal.

Stacker/retriever (S/R) system Used in automated warehouses to store goods and remove them when needed.

Staging Accumulating or assembling goods before sending them.

Stockout Being out of an item at the same time there is a willing buyer for it.

Stockout costs Costs to seller when it is unable to supply an item to a customer ready to buy.

Strategic logistics Using logistical competency and channelwide partnerships to gain competitive advantage by developing long-term logistical alliances with customers and suppliers of materials and services.

Stuffing Loading a container.

Supplier parks Component suppliers locate in industrial complexes adjacent to assembly plants.

Supply chain All activities associated with the flow and transformation of goods from the raw material stage, through to the end user, as well as the associated information flows.[1]

Supply-chain management The systematic, strategic coordination of the traditional business functions and the tactics across these business functions within a particular company and across businesses in the supply chain, for the purposes of improving the long-term performance of the individual companies and the supply chain as a whole.[2]

System constraints Restrictions that cannot be violated in the logistics operation being planned.

System goals Broader than objectives and more general, such as the goal of increasing market share slowly over time.

System objectives Measurable factors that enable management to know if it is meeting its goals, such as whether 98 percent of orders are being shipped within 6 hours of receipt.

Tachograph An electronic device that records the road speed and the engine RPMs (revolutions per minute) on a truck and tells a lot about the vehicle that has been driven.

Tapering rates Transportation charges that increase as distance increases, but at a slower rate; that is, the average cost per mile drops.

Tare weight Weight of the empty container or vehicle.

Tariff A book containing a carrier's charges for transportation services or the charges assessed on items imported into a country.

Tax-free bonds Issued by local and state governments, the bonds carry lower interest rates than corporate bonds because the interest on corporate securities is fully taxable.

Terminal A carrier or public facility where freight (or passengers) is shifted between vehicles or modes.

Third-party logistics "Farming out" some logistics functions to others to perform.

Throughput A term expressing output in warehousing and in pipelines; it is expressed as the number of units moving through a specified system in a given period of time.

Time utility Having products available **when** they are needed by customers.

TOFC (trailer on flatcar) Piggyback traffic, or loading truck trailers onto rail flatcars.

TQM (total quality management) Programs dedicated to maintaining and improving quality.

Tracing A carrier's attempt to find a misplaced or delayed shipment.

Traffic lane Traffic between two points, being subjected to consolidation analysis.

Uniform order bill of lading This form is considered negotiable, and whoever holds it may claim the goods.

Uniform straight bill of lading The most widely used bill of lading. The carrier may deliver the goods without requiring the original copy.

Unitization The placing of goods on pallets, or designing a materials handling system to accommodate pallet loads of goods.

Unit load A pallet load, or a similar-sized load on a slipsheet.

Unit train A train with cars permanently linked, used for repetitive hauls, usually of coal.

Value-added Measure of benefits from using a certain product or service.

Variable warehouse slot location A warehouse where incoming products are stored wherever there is empty space available.

Vendor audit An analysis of a firm's vendors (suppliers) in terms of their locations, dependability, quality of work, and so on. Part of the data-collection phase of logistics analysis.

Vendor-managed inventory Refers to a system where the size and timing of replenishment orders into a retailer's system are the manufacturer's responsibility.

Warehouse Storage facility where products stay for extended periods of time.

Warehouse work rules A set of rules that specify correct procedures at a specific warehouse. Each worker should be required to know them thoroughly.

---

[1]Robert B. Handfield and Ernest L. Nichols, Jr., *Introduction to Supply Chain Management,* Upper Saddle River, NJ: Prentice Hall, 1999.

[2]John T. Mentzer and colleagues, "Defining Supply Chain Management," *Journal of Business Logistics,* Vol. 22, No. 2, 2001, pp. 1–25.

Warehousing Places where products are stored.

Weighted center-of-gravity approach Similar to the center-of-gravity locational approach, excepting that shipping volumes are also taken into account.

Weight-losing product characteristics A product that loses weight during the production process must therefore be processed as near to its origin as possible. The finished product, which weighs less, is transported.

Wind, shipping Declaring that a shipment weighs more than it actually does in order to qualify for a lower per-pound rate, which results in a lower total shipping cost.

Work rules Often established by contracts with unions, these rules specify exactly the duties of each worker. They sometimes restrict workers from doing more than one type of function.

Subject Index

Name Index